Mongolia

THE BRADT TRAVEL GUIDE

Jane Blunden

Bradt Travel Guides Ltd, UK
The Globe Pequot Press Inc, USA

Published 2004
Reprinted July 2004 and December 2005

Bradt Travel Guides Ltd
23 High Street, Chalfont St Peter, Bucks SL9 9QE, England
www.bradtguides.com
Published in the USA by The Globe Pequot Press Inc, 246 Goose Lane,
PO Box 480, Guilford, Connecticut 06475-0480

Text copyright © 2004 Jane Blunden
Maps copyright © 2004 Bradt Travel Guides Ltd
based on sources provided by Jane Blunden and Alan Sanders
Photographs © 2004 individual photographers (see below)

The author and publisher have made every effort to ensure the accuracy of the
information in this book at the time of going to press. However, they cannot accept any
responsibility for any loss, injury or inconvenience resulting from the use of information
contained in this guide.

All rights reserved. No part of this publication may be reproduced, stored in a retrieval
system, or transmitted in any form or by any means, electronic, mechanical, photocopying,
recording or otherwise without the prior consent of the publishers.
Requests for permission should be addressed to Bradt Travel Guides Ltd,
23 High Street, Chalfont St Peter, Bucks SL9 9QE in the UK;
or to The Globe Pequot Press Inc,
246 Goose Lane, PO Box 480, Guilford, Connecticut 06475-0480
in North and South America.

ISBN 1 898323 94 1
ISBN 9 781841 621784

British Library Cataloguing in Publication Data
A catalogue record for this book is available from the British Library

Photographs
Front cover B Moser/Hutchison Picture Library
Text Pete Oxford (PO)

Illustrations Carole Vincer (fauna); Liz Chaddick (flora);
paper-cut prints courtesy of Off the Map and Sarah Fox-Pitt
Maps Alan Whitaker

Typeset from the author's disc by Wakewing
Printed and bound in Italy by Legoprint SpA, Trento

Author and Contributors

Jane Blunden, one of six daughters of Anglo-Irish parents, both of whom served in the Royal Navy, spent her childhood with her five sisters at their family home in Co Kilkenny. She was educated at Glengara Park near Dublin and later travelled the world for five years with her twin sister, Caroline, and a cousin, Robin Kenyon. As a writer and journalist she has worked for *The Irish Times*, *The Times* and many other national newspapers and magazines; she ran her own film production company and also worked for ABC News, the American national television network. Her first visit to Mongolia was in 1978 and she has returned many times to explore and write about her fascination for this country, which began with her search for Przewalski's horse, the *takhi*, the famous Mongolian wild horse. When not travelling, Jane lives in the Cotswolds with her partner, Robin Kindersley.

CONTRIBUTORS
Belinda Ryan, Alan Saffery, Sue Carpenter, Jim Edwards, the late Nicholas Gardner, Michael Senior, Antonia Tozer, Paul and Pinkie Wakefield, the late John Colvin, Anthony Wynn, Nicolas Maclean, Jeremy Halford, Anthony and Fiona Greenwood, Marianne Heredge, Bob Lee, Ian MacKenzie, Alan Craghill, Christopher Johnston, Bill Shaw, Kirsty Fergusson, Zahava Hanan, Dr Natalie Teich, Benedict Allen, John Hare, Prof George Archibald, Dr Josh Ginsburg, Priscilla Allen, Dr Tom McCarthy, Prof Malcolm McKenna, Sir Christian Bonington, Sir Reginald and Lady Hibbert, Baroness Trumpington, Iain Orr, Dr David Sneath, Nicolle Webb, Karen Skjott, Christine Sapieta Fremantle, Deidre Livingstone, Susie Penny, Austin Wheeler, Dr Mark Elvin, Prof Urgunge Onon, Barrie Evans, D. Baatar, Ed Brown, George Fitzherbert, Serena Fass, Kevin Richards, Lucy Ainsley, Lucy Helm, Hetti Jackson-Stops, Sorrel Shepherd-Cross, Kate White, David Bernasconi, Alice Walters, Amy Gordon, Aza Ulzii, Tom Morton, Elizabeth Haynes, Alice Seferiades, Fred Yaeger, Felix Pezold, Nikolaus Steinbeis, Graham Taylor, Neil Taylor, Neil McGowan, Dr Felicity Richardson, Prof Guy de Thé, Lucia Scalisi, Michael Wisburg, Liz Jones, Shona Stewart, Elly Morgan, and Antoni and Caroline Daszewski.

See *Acknowledgements*, page VII.

FEEDBACK REQUEST
I would appreciate hearing from any readers if they have some interesting stories to tell about adventures in Mongolia, or if they find errors in the current text. Please write to me c/o Bradt Travel Guides Ltd, 23 High Street, Chalfont St Peter, Bucks SL9 9QE, UK, or at info@bradtguides.com, and I shall do my best to incorporate them in subsequent editions.

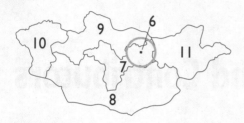

Contents

LIST OF MAPS

Foreword

Mongolia – remote, mysterious, homeland of the greatest conqueror of all time, Genghis Khan; a country of rugged mountains, rolling steppes and the awesome Gobi Desert. Who wouldn't want to go there and see it for themselves? My wife and I were lucky. In 1997 we were given the opportunity of a posting to Ulaanbaatar and jumped at it – a decision we never regretted.

During our two-and-a-half years in Mongolia we managed to visit all 21 provinces. Travelling such long distances, sometimes by air, sometimes overland, in summer and in winter, was not always easy but it was always rewarding; breathtaking scenery, fascinating wildlife and wonderfully hospitable people made every journey worthwhile and memorable. Imagine being in the Gobi Desert after a freak thunderstorm and seeing a raging river where there is normally an arid valley. Imagine taking off from a provincial airport and flying over a herd of antelope with a large wolf pack hard on its heels. And imagine watching the unsurpassed skills of the Mongolian nomads as they round up semi-wild horses on the open steppes. These are only a few examples of what Mongolia can offer to the adventurous traveller. You really should go there and, like us, you will fall in love with this unique country.

Whether you plan to visit Mongolia as a tourist or on business, Jane Blunden's well-researched, comprehensive and up-to-date guide is essential reading, both for first-time visitors and those who have been before. We will certainly have a copy with us when we next return to Mongolia in 2004.

John Durham, former British Ambassador to Mongolia

PUBLISHER'S FOREWORD
Hilary Bradt
What adventurous traveller hasn't longed to go to Mongolia, the symbol of untouched remoteness? I've never achieved it, but became acquainted with Mongolia when publishing the *Trans-Siberian Rail Guide* (no longer in print) in 1987. The history and possibilities for exploration fascinated me, and I was enormously jealous when my parents took the train a year later and spent a few days in Ulaanbataar. Jane Blunden has now made Mongolia accessible to everyone, whether on an organised tour to savour the wilderness or passing through on the Trans-Siberian Express. This is a welcome addition to the Bradt list of unusual destinations.

Acknowledgements

This guide has been put together from original sources by those who have experienced Mongolia firsthand and those who have read, listened and learned and been generous enough with their time and efforts to contribute to this guide. These are the true authors. Inevitably, the writing of any book is a team effort. I am happy with the result of our combined efforts and the values – generosity, giving and sharing – that the work has been based upon. I acknowledge with respect those who, having put a hand to the plough, did not turn back.

Errors will continue to crop up, despite all our efforts, and I take full responsibility for them. While no guidebook is up-to-the-minute – since information on a country is always new and forever changing – there are some things in this book which will change little over time: the general overview, for instance, which incorporates many different experiences of life in Mongolia. The things that change – hotels, restaurants, addresses and so forth – will need updating in subsequent editions.

I have tried to let people and circumstances speak for themselves. I am in no position to judge what may appeal to you; some details may bore one reader and thrill another. My sincere thanks to all those who have helped me so willingly (listed below). My thanks, too, to Hilary Bradt and Tricia Hayne of Bradt Travel Guides Ltd for commissioning this guide and my special thanks to Dr Adrian Phillips and Tricia Hayne who painstakingly edited the text. Without them, the guide would not have made it to publication. My only sadness is that some of the key people acknowledged below, who helped me enormously before and during the writing period, did not live to see the guide completed.

Particular thanks to Alan Sanders for his valuable linguistic expertise and scholarly support throughout the entire production of the book; also to Sir Alan Goodison, Nicholas Haydon, Alan Copps, Joanna Switalska and Julian Shuckburgh, who contributed, unstintingly, their valuable insights, corrections and advice. My thanks to Dervla Murphy and John Durham for kindly reading the manuscript. Special thanks to Allan Stokes for computer help; Gunjimaa Ganbat, Marie von Karaisl, Susan Ellis and Mary McKenzie, a formidable research team; Maurice Temple Smith and John Clark for editing advice; Mongolian ambassador Tsedenjavyn Suhbaatar; British ambassadors John Durham and Kay Coombs and Mongolian desk officers at the Foreign and Commonwealth Office, Sue Curtis, Eric Taylor, Claire Allbless, Naomi Kyriacopoulos and Karen Maddocks; Chuluun Ganbold for his generosity and assistance in Ulaanbaatar and for providing the Mongolian Email Daily News Service; Dr Ian Jeffries (Cardiff University), and Dr Alicia Campi (US-Mongolia Advisory Group) for information on the Mongolian economy; Prof J. Bat-Ireedui (National University of Mongolia), the Mongolian National Tourism Centre, Kh. Ankhbayar of 'Juulchin', Prof S Shagdar, Catherine and Enkbold Darjaa of Off the Map Tours for valuable information on Mongolia; Dr Liz Chaddick for her drawings of Mongolian flora; Catherine Darjaa and Sarah Fox-Pitt for

Mongolian paper cuts, Julian Matthews and his company Discovery Initiatives for his support and information on the Khövsgöl area; Pemmy and Clay Frick, Paul and Cecily Pennoyer for financial and personal support; the late Dr Guido Pontecorvo, the late Roland ('Bee') Beamont and Charles Lysaght for wisdom and inspiration during the writing period; the late James Teacher, the late Sydney Watson, John Watson, Bob and Chrystal (Ibsen) Loverd and Anthony Athaide for sponsoring my early journeys to Mongolia; Ch. Sharavrentsen, my first guide in Mongolia (1978); the late Professor Owen Lattimore for the greatest conversations on Mongolia; Dr Gerry Piel for excellent Bombay gin lunches to help me face my publisher; academician Vladimir Sokolov, for inviting me on the Joint Mongol/Soviet Gobi Expedition to look for wild horses in 1979; Dr Richard Teng (acupuncturist), and Bikram yoga (instructors Ian and Debbie, Salisbury Yoga Trail) for treatments and exercises to help counteract long hours at my computer. A big, special thanks to the many representatives of Mongolian tour companies at home and abroad – especially drivers, guides and ger hosts in Mongolia – unfortunately too numerous to mention by name. Finally, thanks to my mother and twin sister Caroline, and to Robin Kindersley, my long-suffering partner, for both being there for me and for his great cooking! Apologies to all my friends and family for neglecting them for far too long. All I can say is a journey to Mongolia is worth the distance.

At the end of his travelling days, when asked, 'Is there anywhere else you wished you had travelled to?', Wilfred Thesiger, one of the greatest explorers of our times, replied, 'Mongolia is the place I am always sorry not to have visited.'

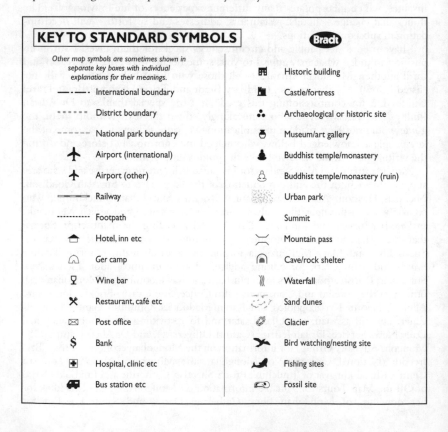

KEY TO STANDARD SYMBOLS — Bradt

Other map symbols are sometimes shown in separate key boxes with individual explanations for their meanings.

—·—·— International boundary	Historic building
······ District boundary	Castle/fortress
- - - - - National park boundary	Archaeological or historic site
✈ Airport (international)	Museum/art gallery
✈ Airport (other)	Buddhist temple/monastery
▬▬▬ Railway	Buddhist temple/monastery (ruin)
············ Footpath	Urban park
⌂ Hotel, inn etc	▲ Summit
⌂ Ger camp	‿ Mountain pass
♇ Wine bar	Cave/rock shelter
✕ Restaurant, café etc	Waterfall
✉ Post office	Sand dunes
$ Bank	Glacier
✚ Hospital, clinic etc	Bird watching/nesting site
Bus station etc	Fishing sites
	Fossil site

Introduction

There are few places left where there is still a sense of adventure and where you feel you are treading on undiscovered ground. Most of the blank places on world maps have been filled in. But not so Mongolia. My own experiences in Mongolia began when, aged 29, I fought my way around the then impenetrable system, designed to keep Western tourists out, and entered Mongolia by the Eastern Gateway through China – also virtually closed to foreigners in those days. In October 1978, I picked up one of the 400 telephones in Beijing and asked for the tourist office in Ulaanbaatar. I spoke to whoever answered my call in rudimentary Mongolian and politely asked for my visa to be sent immediately. The next thing I knew I was on the international Trans Siberian Railway en route to Ulaanbaatar; the first leg of my journey had begun.

A long love affair followed, as I helped to return the *takhi* – the famous Mongolian wild horses known to the equine world as *Equus przewalskii* – from world zoos to Mongolia. It took time and patience. I might add I was not alone in this effort; there were many hundreds of dedicated individuals who helped to unlock doors, open gates and break down visible and invisible barriers. The country itself had come through the communist period (1921–90), including the Cold War (1947–89), to begin building democracy in 1991. The following year a small band of *takhi* returned to the freedom of their native land, flown from zoos and semi-reserves in Holland and elsewhere, much to the joy of the Mongolian people still celebrating their newly found political freedom.

My own reaction when I first reached the South Gobi Altai, in autumn 1990, was to fall on my knees in awe at the magnificence of the empty desert at dawn. For a short instant I felt I had arrived, and yet in the next instant I realised there was still a long, long way to go. Wearily, I recognised I had barely scratched the surface. Such travel to a distant country both brings us home and teaches us about ourselves – revealing, perhaps, our true identities and, maybe, our deepest desires and greatest fears.

For a journey to Mongolia you will need stamina and lots of courage. Travels to a far-off place like Mongolia involve personal commitment and purpose, friendship and, not least, a sense of style. In this guide I have asked the question, 'How do we Westerners – tourists and others – approach the frontiers of Mongolian culture and step into a land so vastly different from our own?' The first thing, of course, is to leave all preconceptions aside. You could just turn up with a rucksack and good walking boots, although not everyone wants to travel that way, and helicopters and horses are available, both equally dangerous at times. Mongolia offers amazing opportunities to travel throughout the country since it opened its doors to the Western world in 1990. But there are some constraints – for one thing, Mongolia is a huge country, twice the size of Turkey, four times that of Japan and more than six times the size of Great Britain. Thus some sort of planned approach is essential, especially if you travel independently.

Mongolia is not a country to visit in a hurry. It is a fabulous wide-open land of extreme climate and extraordinary natural environment. People call it a 'mythical land' or the 'Land of Blue Sky' because of its shimmering, clear air and cloudless skies for most of the year. It is a land of horses and herdsmen and one of the last great undisturbed wilderness areas on earth. Among its 2.4 million people are some of the last truly nomadic pastoralists in the world, and visitors can experience the unique pleasures of staying with nomads and living a lifestyle of centuries ago.

New ground

This guide breaks new ground by including much information on responsible tourism and 'giving something back', which encourages local self-help and volunteer-tourists to participate in local wildlife and cultural projects. Embedded in these plans is the ethos of sustainable development – which means protecting ecosystems, obeying environmental laws and travelling in such a way as helps to build a healthy future for Mongolia. Through tourism (and in other ways) the outside world can help to support Mongolia's nomadic people so that they become part of the modern world while, at the same time, preserving the cultural traditions of their unique lifestyle which has served them so well over the millennia.

Theme, purpose and layout

The underlying theme of the guide is to trace the development of the Mongolian identity from times past to the present day, taking into account the recent changes and their repercussions, together with the impact of such changes on the culture and the natural environment. At times these changes bring about extraordinary juxtapositions and culture clashes, such as the experience of sitting with herdsmen sipping tea in the timeless steppe to the noisy background of strident TV advertisements. These juxtapositions may surprise (and even dismay) visitors but not the Mongolians, fully aware of their role as an emerging Asian nation.

The first part of the guide aims to equip the traveller with a thorough background to Mongolia. This, I believe, is best absorbed slowly before you begin your travels (or if you run out of time, the same can be done on your return). The guide as a whole is principally written for tourists, but it is also an up-to-date reference book for development agency staff and for those with business interests. Compiling the information has been made possible by the fact that email communications came into existence in Mongolia at just the right time. An army of volunteer information-gatherers of all ages and nationalities – friends and friends-of-friends, academics, tour-group leaders, field biologists, tourists and Mongolians themselves – helped me to put together the guide. I could not have done it alone.

As a result, the guide's flavour comes from the contributors' boxes, which 'salt and pepper' each chapter with specialist information. To me, the boxes are pearls of wisdom, which range from the effervescent stories of excited first-time travellers to specific background knowledge from seasoned academics, diplomats, adventurers and on-the-spot volunteers from various organisations. These volunteers are the people who know the country well, having experienced Mongolia by working alongside young Mongolians as park rangers, fire fighters and pit-latrine builders ... to help prepare the way for you.

To those who have yet to live and experience the thrill of travelling in Mongolia, may I wish you great enjoyment and happy travels!

Part One

General Information

Kazakh hunter

2

MONGOLIA AT A GLANCE

Location Central Asia, bordering Russia and China
Area 1,564,116km^2 – the size of most of western Europe
Relief Mountains to the north, centre and southwest comprise 40% of the land, the remainder, rolling plateau with great expanses of steppe, semi-desert, and desert plains.
Highest point Khüiten Peak (4,374m) in the Tavan Bogd range in the Altai mountains
Climate Continental, marked by four seasons, with sharp variations
Average temperatures 20°C in summer and –24°C in winter
Government Parliamentary democracy with a president elected every four years
Regions 21 aimags (provinces) or administrative regions
Population 2.4 million of which 81.5% are Khalkha Mongols, 12% Mongol minorities and 4.3% Kazakhs
Capital Ulaanbaatar (Ulan Bator) formerly known as Urga; abbreviated to UB
Language Mongolian (an Altaic language); Russian and English widely spoken
Religion Predominately Tibetan Buddhism; Christianity; Islam among the Muslim minorities in the west; traces of ancient Shamanism
National flag Red/blue/red (vertical), with golden *soyombo* symbol in the hoist segment
National anthem *Khairt Mongol Oronoo Manduulyaa* ('Let us Make our Beloved Country Flourish')
Public holidays New Year's Day (December 31/January 1), *Tsaagan Sar* (three-day New Year holiday, celebrated late January or early February), Mother and Child Day (June1), *Naadam*/National Holiday (July 11–13), Republic Day (November 26)
Tourist season Mid-May to mid-September (peak season July–August)
Entry regulations Full valid passport with an entry and exit visa
Health No special vaccination requirements
Air and rail access Via the international airport in Ulaanbaatar, or by rail via China or Russia
Road links Ulaanbaatar to Ulaan-Ude in Russia and Erlian (Erenhot) in China
Currency Tögrög (abbreviated to T, Tg or MTG). US$1 = T1,157 (September 2003).
Hotels Available at reasonable prices in the capital with few hotels outside UB
'Ger' camps The normal accommodation in the countryside
TV system PAL, SECAM
Weights and measures Metric system
Electricity 220 volts/50 Hz with two-pin sockets (straight-sided)
Time Three time zones. Three westernmost provinces of Bayan-Ölgii, Uvs and Khovd are one hour behind the capital; Dornod, Sükhbaatar and Khentii are one hour ahead. Rest of the country follows Ulaanbaatar time: GMT +7 or +8 hours (depending on summer or winter).

Background Information

GEOGRAPHY

Mongolia is a fabulous wide-open land of extreme climate and extraordinary natural environment. It's tough at times and even bitterly cold, with surprise snow showers in summer and unusual breakdowns in the middle of nowhere which add to other challenges, like fording rivers in full flood. Mongolia lies northeast of the Pamirs, above the Tien Shan Mountains and comprises the great mountain ranges of the Altai, Khentii and Khangai, towering above grasslands and deserts. Like the whole of Central Asia, it is cut off by its outer mountains from the monsoons of oceanic Asia. The land, sharply contrasted to the skies, stretches from horizon to horizon in bands of colour, which, on the whole, denote the major vegetation zones: in the south are the grey-gold, gravelly grounds of the Gobi, merging into green-brown steppe lands or grasslands with barren rocky hills, while further north and west are high mountains, perennially snow capped, with their lower reaches covered by fir, pine and spruce.

The huge landmass of Mongolia is situated on the Central Asian plateau at the headwaters of the river systems of Siberia and the Arctic, China and the Pacific, and the closed systems of Central Asia. Like the rest of the Central Asian plateau it has a highly distinct set of geographical features. Essentially these spring from the fact that it is an ancient dry land (once, over 200 million years ago, an inland sea), with an average elevation of 1,580m. The whole area was lifted to very high levels by successive geological upheavals and as a result it is a deeply eroded mountainous country, with snow-capped mountain ranges, forested slopes, open high-plateau steppe land, rolling into semi-desert Gobi and cold, sandy desert in the extreme south.

Central Asia is cut off by its outer mountain walls from the monsoons of oceanic Asia. The prevailing winds blow mostly from the northwest but they are dry winds. This has resulted over millions of years in making China the beneficiary of Mongolia's soil erosion.

The country lies between latitude 42° and 52°N and longitude 87° and 119°E, and extends for 2,392km from west to east and 1,259km from north to south. The total area is 1,564,116km², over six times the land area of the UK and nearly three times that of France. It is the fifth-largest country in Asia.

Mongolia's political borders are with the Russian Federation to the north (3,543km) and with the People's Republic of China to the west, south, and east (4,677km). Mongolia is thus a landlocked state, and its nearest access to the sea is at the Chinese port of Tianjin.

Topography

Western Mongolia is dominated by the Mongol Altai Mountains. This major mountain chain is a continuation of the Altai Mountains of Siberia. It extends southeastwards within Mongolia from the Tavan Bogd peaks, at the western

3

junction of the borders of Mongolia, Russia and China. The Mongol Altai is bounded by the Züüngar Basin (in China) to the southwest, and by the low-lying area of the Great Lakes to the northeast. There is marked glaciation in the Tavan Bogd area, where the Potanin glacier stretches 19km. The Gobi dominates southern Mongolia and, although it is known as a desert, this is not strictly true since the Gobi provides grazing for herds of camels, sheep and goats. Rolling steppe covers one-third of the country, where pastoral nomadism has been the way of life for centuries. The grasslands of the eastern plains are home to hundreds of thousands of migrating gazelle. Mongolia's many lakes contain curative minerals and medicinal mud. The numerous hot springs around the country make one wonder if they will become a future tourist attraction. (See *Appendix 3, Springs and spas,* page 381.)

Some 63% of Mongolia's territory is within the permafrost zone, and 30% is sporadically covered by rocks and soils frozen down to a depth of 5m or more. The western half of the country is a region of intensive mountain building and high seismic activity, and small tremors are relatively frequent. There were powerful tremors in 1957 (Gobi Altai) and 1967 (Mogod), but because of the nomadic life-

style and the scattered population, damage to buildings or injury to people from earthquakes have been very rare. Dariganga on the country's southeastern border with Chinese Inner Mongolia is a volcanic plateau with the cones of extinct volcanoes.

Geology

The geological record shows that Palaeozoic marine flora and fauna developed extensively across the territory of Mongolia. In the Mesozoic the Gobi was covered by lakes, and the warm climate and plentiful vegetation encouraged the development of molluscs and crustaceans. The Mongolian Cretaceous period was rich in dinosaurs, including herbivores like protoceratops and hadrosaurus and predators like velociraptor and oviraptor. The world's first nest of fossilised dinosaur eggs was discovered in the South Gobi by American palaeontologist Roy Chapman Andrews in the 1920s. The Chapman Andrews expeditions were followed by Mongolian, Soviet and Polish ones in the communist period and, since 1990, American teams are again making new discoveries.

Mountain chains (Nuruu)

Some two-thirds of Mongolia is covered by mountains. The main ranges are the Altai and the Khangai mountains which run from northwest to south, across the northern-central part of the country. These forest and mountain zones are relatively well watered and surrounded by mountain-meadow and flat grassland. From the western mountain chains open steppe stretches to the southeast and merges into semi-desert in the south. The Sayan Mountains mark the boundary between Siberia and Mongolia north of Lake Khövsgöl, while the Khentii range is located north of Ulaanbaatar in the central northeastern part of the country. The southern Gobi contains the famous 'Three Beauties', or Gurvansaikhan, mountains, one valley of which shelters a tiny 'glacier', in its surprising alpine/desert setting. This accumulated frozen snow along the sheltered riverbed of the Yolyn Am valley canyon survives (most years) throughout the hot summer months.

Mongolia's highest mountain, Khüiten (4,374m), is found in the Tavan Bogd area of the Altai mountains. Mönkhkhairkhan (4,204m), Mongolia's second-highest mountain, rises on the border of Bayan-Ölgii and Khovd aimags, or provinces. Due to their isolation, they represent a challenge to the most skilful mountaineers. The Gobi Altai Mountains are a continuation of the Mongol Altai chain. They extend southeastwards 700km to descend into the Gobi. There are no big glaciers or snowfields. The highest peak, Ikh Bogd peak (3,957m), is in Bayankhongor Aimag.

The Khangai Mountains give rise to Mongolia's major rivers which flow in a northern direction. Spurs extending north and northeast form the watershed between the Arctic Ocean and Central Asian basin. Slopes forested by birch and larch drop down from snow-covered crests to fine pastureland. Sheer, rugged peaks include Otgontenger (4,021m), the range's highest summit, in Zavkhan Aimag at the western end, with a glacier and eternal snow.

The third range of importance is the smooth and rounded Khentii range, which stretches 200km from the Mongolian capital to the northern border and forms part of the watershed between the Arctic and Pacific oceans. The highest point is Asralt Khairkhan (2,800m), some 60km north of Ulaanbaatar.

Lakes (Nuur)

Water is distributed unevenly in Mongolia, predominately in lakes and rivers to the northwest. The low-lying area between the Mongol Altai and Khangai mountains is often called the 'Depression of the Great Lakes', although it is technically not a depression (ie: below sea level). The area is 600km long and up to 250km wide. At its lowest, northernmost point is Lake Uvs, Mongolia's largest saltwater lake (3,350km²). Lake Uvs is relatively shallow, 20m at its greatest depth; it lies 759m above sea level. The northeastern corner of the lake lies on Russian territory. Gobi-type soils and sands fill this low-lying area where smaller lakes and the world's northernmost sand dunes are found.

Lake Khövsgöl, the deepest lake (282m), is the country's largest freshwater resource. Over 90 rivers enter it, and one flows out, the Egiin gol (475km), a tributary of the River Selenge which flows into Lake Baikal, in Siberia. Baikal is the world's biggest body of fresh water and is linked by the rivers Angara and Yenisey to the Arctic Ocean. Lake Khövsgöl is the second-largest lake in Mongolia (2,760km² and 136km long).

The lowest point in the country is a small lake, Khökh Nuur (560m above sea level), in Dornod (eastern) Aimag, not far from the border with China. Another lake, Buir, measures 615km² and averages 10m in depth on Mongolia's southeastern border with China. Although its commercial fish and water resources are within Mongolia, that does not put a stop to Chinese poaching. All Mongolian lakes freeze in winter.

Rivers (Gol)

In the mountainous northwest, large rivers originate draining into either the Arctic or the Pacific. A continental watershed divides the country and the smaller rivers of the south tend to be lost to the dry ground. There are 3,800 rivers in Mongolia, and were one to add their combined length it would total 67,000km. The largest rivers entering the closed Central Asian basin are the River Khovd (593km), running from Tavan Bogd into Khar Nuur, and the River Zavkhan (808km) in western Mongolia, which flows from the Khangai westwards through the desert into Airag Nuur and Khyargas Nuur.

The River Delgermörön (445km) rises in the mountains near Khövsgöl and joins the Selenge (1,024km in total, 615km in Mongolia) to flow via Lake Baikal to the Arctic Ocean. Other tributaries of the Selenge include the Orkhon, which flows near the former capital of Mongolia, Karakorum, and the Tuul, on which Ulaanbaatar stands. The Orkhon (1,124km) rises in the Khangai mountains and the Tuul (704km) rises in the Khentii range.

The largest rivers reaching the Pacific Ocean are the Onon (298km in Mongolia), rising in the Khentii range and flowing across the border with Russia into the Shilka and the Heilongjiang (Amur) River and the Kherlen (1,090km), which also rises in the Khentii and drains into Dalai Nuur (Lake Hulun) in China. The Khalkhyn Gol (233km) flows via Lake Buir into Dalai Nuur, which is linked (except in dry years) to the Heilongjiang (Amur) by the River Ergun.

All Mongolia's rivers freeze in winter for five or six months, the ice averaging 1m thick. Rivers in the mountains remain ice-bound until mid-May, while those in the plains usually become free of ice a month earlier. Spring floods from mountain snow melt occur in April–May, and rain storms may cause more floods in July and August.

Steppe

Steppe (grassland) covers much of the country and predominates in central and eastern areas. The Eastern Plain, averaging 1,100m above sea level, extends for several hundred kilometres. It is gently undulating grassland with hills of 50–100m.

Deserts and the Gobi

Sand and sand dunes occupy about 10% of Mongolia's territory, but much of the Gobi is a plain of scrub and gravel rather than sand, with scattered salt and soda lakes. Summer flash-floods spread widely across the impermeable surface to create raging torrents which cut channels a metre or more deep as the water drains off to find its level and then soaks away. These dried-up channels represent a hazard to cross-country vehicles.

The Trans-Altai Gobi, between the Gobi Altai and the border with Chinese Xinjiang, is the last known habitat of the *takhi*, the Mongolian wild horse or Przewalski horse, which was returned from captive-bred foreign stock (in international zoos, reserves and private collections) after the pure native variety became extinct (see box, page 113). Also to be found in this region are *khulan*, or wild asses, and saiga antelope – found only in southwest Mongolia.

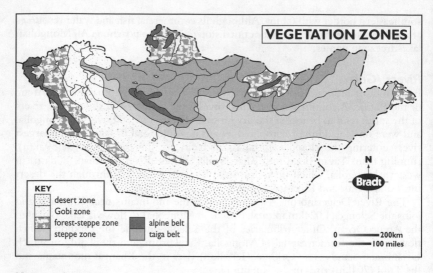

Vegetation zones

Mongolian scientists divide the country into the following natural zones:

• The high-mountain zone, roughly 4.5% of the whole territory, largely consisting of alpine meadow
• Mountain taiga (4%), particularly the Khövsgöl area and parts of the Khentii Mountains, with dense cedar and cedar-larch forest
• The mountain forest-steppe zone (23%) including most of the Khangai, Khentii and Mongol Altai mountains, where there is alternation of forest and steppe, the forest growing on the upper parts of the northern slopes, with strips of larch and birch
• Steppe (grassland) occupies some 26% of Mongolia's territory, in particular the plains of eastern Mongolia, with various feather grasses and pea-shrubs (Caragana)
• The transitional desert-steppe zone (21.5%), especially the Gobi Altai region, with low grasses and semi-shrubs
• Desert accounts for some 10%, especially in the southern border zone, where any vegetation is extremely sparse but includes zag (saxaul or *haloxylon*) bushes, whose wood the Mongols burn for fuel; the Trans-Altai Gobi oases have poplar trees fed by ground water.

Desertification

Recent drought conditions are causing waves of sand to menace desert dwellers. Pastures that used to exist are now barren land. The grasses have all but disappeared. Rising sands and barren ground are part of a new desert and are the result, scientists say, of severe overgrazing that has destroyed the thin topsoil. A decade of hotter, drier weather means the menace is here to stay, threatening exposed, rural settlements and the nomadic herders' only means of livelihood – their flocks of camels, horses, sheep, and goats and hence, in time, their way of life. The significant factor is that once the desertification process gets started it tends to expand very fast.

Nomadic pastoralists have to roam further afield to find edible grass and some are forced to pay for winter fodder, a thing they never had to do during socialist times. Although some winter fodder has been stockpiled around the country it remains a huge logistical process to deliver it to the hardest-hit areas in time, and it is usually not enough. Emergency shipments of grain and relief food supplies were flown in from Russia and elsewhere to help the nomads to cope with *zud* disasters of recent winters. (The expression *zud* describes the conditions that prevent livestock from grazing, including drought, or deep snow or overcrowding. See page 10.)

CLIMATE

Mongolia has an extreme continental climate: that is, hot summers and very cold winters. The country lies at the heart of continental Asia, far from seas and oceans, in the lee of surrounding high mountains – all factors that contribute to its dry climate. There is a marked decrease in cloudiness from north to south, where average annual sunshine reaches 3,200 hours. As a result, Mongolia is known as the 'Land of Blue Skies'. In winter, the weather is dominated by a stable high-pressure region over northwestern Mongolia; there is little cloud and little snow cover, but intense cold. In spring, warm winds from the south meet cold winds from the Arctic Ocean, and wind and dust storms are typical of this season.

Wind is more forceful in the southern regions and violent dust storms whip the ground at speeds that could knock over a *ger*, although these regions are virtually uninhabited. Weather changes can be abrupt and storms can strike with little or no warning.

Precipitation exceeds 500mm a year in the mountains, 200–300mm in the steppe and less than 150mm in the Gobi; 65–75% of annual precipitation falls as rain in the three warm summer months, while autumn is cool and dry. The Khentii and Khövsgöl regions are the wettest parts of Mongolia. Marshes in mountainous areas are sometimes a barrier to summer travel, and drought is not uncommon elsewhere because of low average soil water levels. High mountains are snow-covered from October to April, but elsewhere snowfall is usually not significant and does not accumulate but melts, evaporates or is dispersed by the wind. The most serious condition for animals is '*zud*', which causes massive losses to livestock over severe winter weather.

January is the coldest month of the year, with the average temperature at –35°C in the valleys and –20°C in the Gobi. The lowest recorded temperature was –55°C at Lake Uvs in northwestern Mongolia. July is the warmest month, with the average temperature between 15 and 20°C in the mountains and 20–25°C in the south. A temperature of 40°C has been recorded at Sainshand in the Gobi.

An important consequence of the Mongolian climate, with its hard winters, late spring and early autumn frosts, is the short period of plant growth, which is limited to about 100 days – from late May to the end of August. If you travel in Mongolia during summer time you will have an illusion of richness – knee-deep grass as far as the eye can see and meadows garlanded with millions of wild flowers. But in fact the flora is not as diverse as the flora of neighbouring China, Siberia or eastern Kazakhstan. In Mongolia, due to the altitude, relief and wind, there is considerable diurnal variation in temperature which may fluctuate by up to 30°C. You may experience blistering hot days and chilly or freezing nights – days that warm up and cool down equally dramatically as the sun rises and sets.

Although the Mongolian winter is the longest season, lasting from about November to March, it is also the sunniest. Throughout the year the skies are blue and the sun shines for over 250 days. There are four distinct seasons, each with its own special attraction. In winter, because of the dry air, there is a crisp atmosphere, even when the sun is out and the daytime temperatures rise; without the damp chill factor even the cold seems less biting. Beware, when the sun goes down, the temperatures plummet, so you have to wrap up well at night. Spring can be cool, windy, dusty and changeable. Summer is short, hot and rainy – but not too rainy. The warm October days in autumn are the finest, with ideal temperatures, when the lowering sun casts long amber shadows across the craggy boulders that tower above the burned, summer grasslands. Overall, Mongolia is a very dry country, and the almost continuous blue skies help you feel on top of the world. However, bring warm clothes even in summer. These are, of course, essential in winter when temperatures drop to –30°C (see *Chapter 5, What to take*, page 173).

Climate change

Climate change is associated with unrestrained increases in emissions of greenhouse gases (GHG) particularly CO_2. The United Nations predicts that global average temperatures could rise between 1.4°C and 5.8°C over the next century. This would mean more droughts, the melting of glaciers and the extinction of species. Mongolia, being far removed from industry, might seem unlikely to be much affected by global warming, but this is not the case because change comes to the most marginal lands. The whole of Mongolia's fragile landscape, and herding and agriculture based upon it, is therefore directly involved (see box *Climate care – responsible tourism and sustainable development*, pages 132–43).

NATURAL DISASTERS

Zud literally means 'lack of grazing' but is also translated as 'starvation due to fodder shortage'. *Zud* occurs when there is a thaw followed again by freezing conditions. The grass becomes sheathed in a film of ice and the animals cannot graze and subsequently they die, by the thousands. There is either too much snow for stock to get to the fodder, or not enough snow to serve as a substitute for water. The different types of *zud* are:

- *Gan zud* The ground is covered with a layer of ice after a warm spell in winter.
- *Khar zud* ('black zud') A lack of snow in a waterless region.
- *Tsagaan zud* ('white zud') Heavy snowfall prevents livestock from grazing.
- *Tuurain zud* ('hoof zud') Pasture is trampled down as a result of overcrowding, predominately a man-made situation. It is considered to be the most catastrophic.

Zud disasters of the winters of 1999/2000 and 2000/2001 will go down in history for claiming around six million heads of Mongolian livestock. Eighty-five per cent were sheep and goats, the remainder being horses, cattle and camels. Long-term loans from the World Bank and other aid organisations helped to restock sheep and goat herds. Since then the Mongolian government has taken pre-emptive measures to ensure better-organised distribution of sufficient fodder to formerly badly hit regions during excessively cold weather – something which was sorely lacking in recent *zud* winters. There has also been help from the international community (for details of aid programmes, see pages 39–43; and ways in which individuals have helped Mongolian families see box *Blue Heaven Project*, page 42).

THE PROVINCES (AIMAGS)

The territory of Mongolia is currently divided into 21 provinces (aimags) and the capital territory (Ulaanbaatar city). Each province is further divided into rural districts (sum), usually around 15 to 20. In this guide the provinces are grouped into

THE PROVINCES (AIMAGS)

Central aimags	Provincial centres
Töv (Central) Aimag	Zuunmod
Övörkhangai Aimag	Arvaikheer
Arkhangai Aimag	Tsetserleg

Southern 'Gobi' aimags, 'arid aimags'

Ömnögobi Aimag (South Gobi)	Dalanzadgad
Dornogobi Aimag (East Gobi)	Sainshand
Gobi-Sümber Aimag	Choir
Dundgobi Aimag (Central Gobi)	Mandalgobi
Bayankhongor Aimag	Bayankhongor
Gobi-Altai Aimag	Altai

Northern aimags, 'forest aimags'

Khövsgöl Aimag	Mörön
Zavkhan Aimag	Uliastai
Bulgan Aimag	Bulgan
Orkhon Aimag	Erdenet
Selenge Aimag	Sükhbaatar
Darkhan-Uul Aimag	Darkhan

Western aimags, 'mountain aimags'

Khovd Aimag	Khovd
Bayan-Ölgii Aimag	Ölgii
Uvs Aimag	Ulaangom

Eastern aimags, 'grassland aimags'

Khentii Aimag	Öndörkhaan
Sükhbaatar Aimag	Baruun-Urt
Dornod Aimag	Choibalsan

Also:

The territory of Ulaanbaatar	Ulaanbaatar

If you are travelling around the provinces, a highly recommended book is *Fifty Routes Through Mongolia* and a new edition *A Hundred Routes through Mongolia* (in production) by Professor S Shagdar, available in Mongolia.

five regions: central, southern, northern, western and eastern. Some national parks and protected areas cross provincial boundaries, and are noted in more than one province. A complete summary of these areas, accompanied by a map, can be found in *Chapter 4* (pages 122–32). The major parks are covered more fully under the relevant aimags.

The guide concentrates on the most-visited provinces relating to Mongolia's 'Golden Circuit'. The classical routes which make up the 'Golden Circuit' take you to the Orkhon Valley via the central provinces of Töv, Övörkhangai and Arkhangai, to Lake Khövsgöl in Khövsgöl Province, and to the South Gobi, Ömnögobi Aimag – usually via Ulaanbaatar, where road and flight connections are more easily managed.

HISTORY
Chronology
Early history: partial chronology of North China

475–221BC	Warring States period: expansion of the Xiongnu (Huns)
221–207BC	Qin dynasty
206BC–AD5	Western or Former Han dynasty (the western Han was overthrown in AD5 and restored in AD25 as the Eastern Han
AD6–24	Xi dynasty
AD25–220	Eastern or Later Han dynasty; drove Xiongnu back to the Altai mountains
AD266–316	Western Jin dynasty
AD386–528	Northern Wei dynasty of the Xianbei (Toba)
AD317–420	Eastern Jin dynasty
AD581–618	Chinese Sui dynasty supports western Turks against eastern Turks
AD618–907	Tang dynasty controls northern China
AD744–840	Uighurs, allies of the Tang, displace Turks from Mongolia
AD840–920	Mongolia controlled by the Yenisey Kirghiz
AD947–1125	Sinicised Mongol Qidan drive away Kirghiz and establish the Liao dynasty in North China
AD960–1127	Northern Song dynasty
AD1034–1227	Xia (Tangut) dynasty
AD1115–1234	Jin (Jürchen) dynasty

From the birth of Genghis Khan to the end of the 19th century

We possess minimal records of the Mongols during the period of their greatness in the 12th and 13th centuries at the time of the Mongol empire, despite the Uighur script being introduced in 1204 by Genghis Khan for keeping records. Among the few surviving records is the 13th-century *Secret History of the Mongols*. Their character and habits at the time are only slightly known to us, because, like other nomads, they left little in writing. There is some archaeological evidence of early tribal history, but on the whole Mongolian history cannot be compared to English or European histories. One reason there are so many unfilled gaps is that original sources were compiled by historians of other cultures, so great linguistic skills and cultural understanding are required to piece together the Mongol past from languages that include Mongolian, Persian, Arabic, Chinese, Japanese, Russian, Latin and others.

1162	Birth of Temüchin, the future Genghis Khan
1189	Proclaimed Genghis Khan after rallying the Mongol tribes
1206	Proclaimed Great Khan of all Mongolia
1227	Died after defeating the Tanguts
1229	Ögödei Khan (Genghis's third son) proclaimed second Great Khan
1235	Ögödei Khan builds the Mongol capital Karakorum
1236	Invasion of Russia, and establishment by Batu Khan (Genghis's grandson) of the Russian khanate known as the Golden Horde
1246	Guyuk (Ögödei's son) proclaimed the third Great Khan. Visit to Mongolia by the Pope's envoy, John of Plano Carpini
1251	Mongke Khan (son of Genghis Khan's youngest son) proclaimed fourth Great Khan
1260	Mongke's brother Kublai proclaimed fifth Great Khan
1275	Marco Polo at the Mongol's summer capital Shangdu (Cambaluc) – so it is alleged!

1294   Death of Kublai Khan, followed by several short reigns
1368   Ming dynasty founded in China
1380   Mongol capital destroyed by Ming army
1414   War between the Oriads (western Mongols) and the eastern Mongols
1450   A time of peace between the Mongols and the Ming boosts trade links
1578   Altan Khan of the eastern Mongols converted to Buddhism
1586   Founding of Erdene Zuu, Mongolia's first Buddhist monastery
1639   Zanabazar proclaimed Öndör Gegeen, leader of Mongol Buddhists
1642   Manchu forces cross the Great Wall
1644   Qing (Manchu) dynasty established in China
1691   Mongols swear allegiance to the Manchu emperor
1728   Russia and Qing China sign the Kyakhta border treaty
1832   First 'tsam' religious dances performed in Ulaanbaatar (at that time called Urga or Khüree)
1838   Founding of Gandan monastery in the capital
1869   Birth of the eighth, the last Öndör Gegeen

The 20th and 21st centuries
1904   13th Dalai Lama flees to Mongolia from British troops in Lhasa
1911   Declaration of Mongol independence: eighth Öndör Gegeen proclaimed Bogd Khan
1915   Russian-Chinese-Mongolian Treaty awards Mongolia autonomy
1917   Bolshevik Revolution in Russia brings political change
1919   Chinese troops invade Mongolia
1921   Revolutionaries of the Mongolian People's Party (MPP) install 'People's Government' with Soviet help
1924   Former religious and political leader Bogd Khan dies
        Mongolia proclaimed the Mongolian People's Republic
        Capital renamed 'Ulaanbaatar' (previously Niislel Khüree)
        MPP renamed Mongolian People's Revolutionary Party (MPRP)
1937   Choibalsan becomes minister of war; campaign against Buddhism launched
1940   Tsedenbal becomes secretary general of the MPRP
1946   Mongolia recognised by Republic of China
1961   Mongolia joins the United Nations
1962   Mongolia joins the Council for Mutual Economic Assistance (CMEA, also known as Comecon)
1974   Tsedenbal becomes head of state
1974   Jambyn Batmönkh becomes prime minister
1984   Jambyn Batmönkh becomes president
        Tsedenbal removed from post.
        Batmönkh becomes MPRP general secretary and head of state
1990   Demonstrations for democracy
        MPRP Politburo resigns; Gombojavyn Ochirbat becomes general secretary
        Punsalmaagiin Ochirbat becomes head of state
1991   Gombojavyn Ochirbat replaced by Dash-Yondon as MPRP leader
        Privatisation vouchers issued
1992   New constitution
        Country's name changed to Mongolia
        Puntsagiin Jasrai appointed prime minister
        Democratic parties unite to form the National Democratic Party
        Last Russian troops leave Mongolia

1993   Country's first presidential elections won by Punsalmaagiin Ochirbat
1996   MPRP loses the election and for first time in 72 years Mongolia no longer
        ruled by communist ideology; a coalition of the Mongolian Social
        Democratic Party and Mongolian National Democratic Party (MNDP)
        now in power
1997   Natsagiin Bagabandi elected president
2000   MPRP returns to government
2001   Nastsagiin Bagabandi re-elected president
2004   June elections result in tie between MPRP and Democrats; final outcome
        and formation of new government delayed

Pre-Mongol history: the steppes through the ages

The life of the Mongolian nomad has remained virtually unchanged for centuries.
Like contemporary nomads, the early inhabitants of the Central Asian steppes were
tent dwellers moving from pasture to pasture with their herds of horses, camels,
sheep and goats.

The Scythians

Between 750 and 700BC, according to Greek historians, the Scythians, who were
also known as the Saka (an Indo-Iranian nation), lived as nomads on the steppes of
southern Russia, moving into Turkestan and the Tien Shan (a mountain range in
northeast China). They are famous for their decorative animal-style art in gold and
bronze. The Scythians invaded the Caucasus and were allies of the Assyrians.
Darius launched a campaign against them around 514BC, but the Scythian nomads
joined forces with Finno-Ugrian tribes from northeast Russia and the Persians
were unable to conquer them.

The Sarmatians

Around 179BC, another nomadic nation related to the Scythians, known as the
Sarmatians and from the Aral Sea area, crossed the Volga and pushed the Scythians
southwards. The motifs of their animal art were similar and were developed by the
Siberian craftsmen of the upper Yenisey and Sayan foothills, who made bronze
daggers and other iron tools and weapons from around 200BC.

The Huns

The eastern steppes were dominated by the nomadic people known to the Chinese
from the 3rd century BC as Xiongnu – the Huns. Archaeological discoveries
indicate that Hun territory covered a vast area from Lake Baikal to Chita in the
north, the whole of present-day Mongolia, and as far south as the Yellow River and
Ordos in China (which was then a much smaller state than it is today). The various
kingdoms of northern China organised defences against the marauding nomads,
developing their cavalry and building fortifications. These were linked together to
form the first stage of the Great Wall of China by the first emperor of the Qin
dynasty (221–207BC). Our knowledge of this early period comes from Chinese
annals, whose authors naturally gave Chinese names to the various ruling
dynasties, although they were not all Chinese. Their descriptions of the physical
appearance and dress of the Xiongnu, and their titles and military organisation,
suggest that they were similar to the later Turks and Mongols.

Under their ruler, the shanyü, the Huns devastated what is now North China,
besieging the Han dynasty capital of Taiyuan and driving the Yüehchih (Tokharians)
westwards out of Gansu, a region in North China. Divisions amongst the Huns
(AD25–220) and their eventual defeat by Han China put an end to this threat. China

was then able to gain control of Turfan and the Silk Road through what is today called Xinjiang. The northern Huns in the Orkhon valley were subjugated around AD155 by Mongol Xienbei tribes. The southern Huns established a dynasty called the Northern Han, proclaimed in AD308 by Hun chief, Liu Yuan, at Taiyuan; they captured the Chinese Han dynasty capital Loyang. This was a period of great instability, with much of northern China overrun by nomadic tribes.

Their leaders' feuding led to the Huns' decline, division and eventual dispersal. The western Huns reached the Carpathians and Hungary in the 5th century AD. In AD441, Attila crossed the Danube but, in AD451, his advance across France was halted by the Roman and Visigoth armies at Troyes. Attila's empire disintegrated after his death in AD453.

The Jujuan

In the 4th century, northern China was dominated by the Northern Wei dynasty of the Toba Turks, who fought with the Mongolian Jujuan (Juan-Juan) tribes for control. The Jujuan forced the Xiongnu to the northwest, their ruler Shelün assumed the title 'khagan' (khan) in 402. His capital was in Arkhangai Province in central Mongolia. His state was eventually weakened by division, and the Jujuan khanate was absorbed by the Altai Turks.

The Turks

The Turks, known to the Mongols as T'u-chüeh, or Tujue, formed an alliance in 546AD under their chief, Bumin (T'u-men), with the now sinicised Toba to defeat the Jujuan. The Turkic khanate under Bumin established its capital in the Orkhon valley – often called the cradle of Mongolian civilisation. Known as the Orkhon Turks, they were excellent craftsmen in iron and stone, besides being herdsmen, hunters and warriors. Monuments to their leaders are inscribed in Turkish runic script on stelae, standing stone slabs that still survive today in the Mongolian countryside. In AD553, Bumin's son became khan of the eastern khanate (Mongolia), while his brother received the western khanate (Djungaria and Issyk Kul). After 50 years of rule by Tang dynasty China, the Turks re-established their khanate, but violent revolt and infighting broke out among the tribes, which led to the destruction of the Turkish khanate in AD745 and the supremacy of their former Uighur subjects.

The Uighurs

The Uighur khanate which followed reached its peak under Moyunchur Khan (AD745–59). The Uighurs made their capital at Khar Balgas on the Orkhon River (see Arkhangai Aimag, pages 265–70). They were primarily Shamanists but religions such as Buddhism, Manichacism and Nestorian Christianity were permitted. They adopted the Sogdian script (derived from Aramaic), a script that the Mongols later utilised for their language. Attacked by the Kirghiz from the north, the Uighur khanate declined in AD840. The Kirghiz themselves were threatened and eventually driven away by the Qidan (Khitan), a tribe related to the Mongols.

The Qidan

At its greatest strength, the Qidan state (947–1125) controlled central Mongolia and much of northeastern China and established a hereditary monarchy known as the Liao. The Qidan had their own literature in a script based on Chinese characters. It was a settled period when the arts and sciences flourished, but in 1125, under the combined attacks of Song dynasty China and the Jin state of the Jürchen, the Qidan state collapsed.

The Mongol Empire to Manchu control
The Mongols

The Jürchen, a Tungusic people, fought several unsuccessful battles against the Borjigin Mongols, a clan that emerged in central Mongolia in the 12th century. In 1161, however, the Jin defeated them by joining forces with the Tatars, their former enemies, who lived on the River Kherlen. Yesügei, a descendant of the Mongol Qabul Khan had a son, born in 1162, whom he named Temüchin, after a Tatar captive. This child was later to becme the greatest of all Mongolians, know to the world as Genghis Khan. Temüchin's father was murdered by the Tatars soon afterwards and he, his mother and brothers were forced to scavenge on the steppe for their survival. To nourish her children, Lady Ho'elun, their mother, used a pointed juniper stick to dig up wild leeks, onions, and garlic which they ate with freshwater fish. It was a hard struggle for the family to survive and during his youth Temüchin learned the value of building strong friendships. As a young man he made alliances and rallied tribal leaders. Charismatic and with a strong personality he had natural qualities of leadership and from obscurity he shot to the rank of a world leader. In 1189 the Mongol tribes proclaimed him Genghis Khan of the Mongols. In 1198 and 1202 he twice defeated the Tatars, and after the submission of the Naiman, the Mongol tribes were eventually united. In 1206 Genghis Khan was proclaimed the Great Khan of All Mongols. He then began a series of campaigns against neighbouring states – the Tangut (1207), the Uighurs of Turfan (1209), the Jin (1215), the Qidan (1218), and Samarkand (1221) – and died in 1227, having finally destroyed the Tangut. Genghis Khan achieved his vision of forging a Mongol world empire, a legacy which he passed to his sons and grandsons, who further enlarged it to form different khanates extending from Mongolia and China: the Golden Horde in Russia, the Chaghatai Khanate in Central Asia, the Ilkhanate in Persia.

Genghis Khan's successors

Genghis Khan's third son Ögödei was proclaimed the second Great Khan (1229–41). His forces stormed into Europe to Poland and Hungary and were poised to attack Vienna in 1241 when Ogödei Khan died and the Mongols turned and rode back home; the succession then passed to Ögödei's son Güyük (1246–48). Jochi's son Batu was enraged by this decision to bypass the eldest son Jochi's line, and with his support Möngke, son of Genghis Khan's youngest son Tolui, was proclaimed the fourth Great Khan (1251–58). The Mongol forces continued their rampage through China and western Asia to deal a deathblow to the Abbasaid caliphate, taking Baghdad in 1258. Möngke's brother Kublai succeeded in 1260, but was challenged by another brother, Arigbökh. In 1264 Kublai's victory over Arigbökh confirmed him as the fifth Great Khan. Kublai moved the Mongol capital to Beijing and proclaimed his Yuan dynasty in 1271.

Batu Khan had invaded the weak Russian principalities in 1236 and Kiev fell to the Mongols in 1240. From 1243 Batu's khanate became known as the 'Golden Horde'. Batu died in 1255, but Mongol rule over the Russians continued – the 'Tatar yoke' as they called it. The Russian princes were required to offer submission and pay tribute to the Great Khan. In 1380, the year the old Mongol capital at Karakorum was destroyed by Chinese Ming dynasty troops, the Golden Horde suffered a heavy defeat at the hands of Grand Duke Dmitrii Donskoi at the Battle of Kulikovo. However, the 'Tatar yoke' was not cast off until 1480, when Grand Duke Ivan III forced the Golden Horde out of Russian territory.

By the end of the 13th century the Mongol empire was the largest land empire in history, stretching at its greatest extent from central Europe to China and

THE OLDEST SON?

Jochi, Genghis Khan's eldest son, died just before his father, thereby resolving any dispute about his right to the succession – he may have been conceived while his mother Borte, Genghis Khan's first wife, was briefly a captive of the Merkits. Shortly after their marriage, Borte was abducted by the khan of the neighbouring Merik tribe. Her warrior husband rode to her rescue during a night raid, and when Borte recognised Temüchin's call, she struggled from her captors and the two escaped in the darkness of night. Although Genghis Khan had many wives, Borte, who was a year older, remained his favourite. Their marriage was arranged by his father when they were children of just nine and ten years old (see box *Genghis Khan*, page 19).

Korea, and from Russia to Iran and Vietnam. The Mongols learned naval warefare on the Yangtze River and attempted to invade Japan in 1274 and again in 1281, but storms scuttled Kublai's fleet. In 1293 there was an unsuccessful attack on the island of Java in Indonesia, where the tropical climate proved to be the Mongols' undoing. However, during the reign of Kublai Khan, Genghis's grandson, there were periods of peace and prosperity in the territory of present-day Mongolia and mainland China, when the arts and culture flourished. After Kublai, the Yuan dynasty in China was weakened by internal struggles and the Mongol empire in China faded and declined. In 1368 a peasant uprising spawned the Chinese Ming dynasty which replaced the Mongol Yuan dynasty. The power of the Mongol empire declined as suddenly as it began, and most of the Mongols returned to the steppes.

The Manchus

As the Mongol empire broke up into its component parts under the new dynasties inaugurated by Genghis Khan's successors, there was a long period of civil war in Mongolia itself, as Mongol chiefs fought for control of the tribes. The Oirat, or western Mongols, became a new power, threatening the Khalkha Mongols of central Mongolia. To the northeast, a great expansionist power was on the move – the Manchus. In 1624 the Manchus advanced from what is now northeast China into the border area of southern Mongolia and subjugated the Gorlos and Khorchin tribes. In 1636 the Manchus proclaimed their Qing dynasty, and in 1644 they took Beijing as the Ming emperor committed suicide. In 1673 the Khalkha came under renewed Oirat attack and sought refuge beyond the Great Wall. In 1691 the Khalkha princes joined the southern Mongol chieftains in swearing allegiance to the Qing emperor, Kang Xi, at Dolonnor.

Lamaism

Kublai Khan had established a special relationship of patron and priest with the Tibetan Phagspa Lama, but in 1578 Altan Khan of the Tümet, a southern Mongol tribe, recognised the Tibetan religious leader Sonam Gyatso as the 'Dalai Lama'. It was his Gelugpa, or 'yellow hat', school that was promoted under Qing rule. The influence and power of Tibetan Buddhism (Lamaism) was greatly enhanced, with the building of many monasteries and temples and the translation from Sanskrit and Tibetan, and later the xylographic printing, of many Buddhist works. Mongolia meanwhile had produced its own Buddhist leader, Zanabazar, the son of a Khalkha prince. He was proclaimed the incarnation of the Tibetan Javzandamba Khutukhtu in 1639 and accorded the title Öndör Gegeen, or 'High Enlightened One'. Ranking third in the Lamaist hierarchy after the Dalai Lamas and Panchen Lamas, the Mongolian Khutukhtus were the Mongols' spiritual leaders. The eighth Javzandamba Khutukhtu, who was also head of state (Bogd Khan) from 1911, died in 1924.

The Russians

Russian expansion into Siberia (with the founding of Tobolsk in 1587 and Irkutsk in 1661) eventually led to a series of clashes with the Manchus. Qing troops destroyed the Russian fort at Albazin in the Amur (Heilongjiang) valley in 1685. Manchu and Russian envoys met at Nerchinsk in 1689 to negotiate and sign a treaty partitioning the disputed territory east of the Argun (Ergun) river. In 1728 representatives of the two empires concluded the Treaty of Kyakhta, which determined the border between Imperial Russia and Qing China from the Argun to Shabin Dabaga, a mountain pass on the northern border with Krasnoyarsk region. Russia thereby acknowledged Manchu control of the whole of Mongolia, including Uriankhai (Tuva).

At the start of the 19th century, both British and Russian empires were embroiled in an ever-increasing rivalry for power and influence in the area, known as 'The Great Game', whereby Imperial Russia pushed across central Asia to meet British India. New knowledge was urgently required of the great wildernesses in between, so far uncharted and unexplained to Western science. The journeys of Colonel Nikolai Przewalski to western China and Tibet date from this period. In 1904 the British Younghusband expedition to Lhasa forced the 13th Dalai Lama to flee Tibet and take refuge in Urga (Ulaanbaatar) with the Javzandamba Khutukhtu. Completion of the Trans-Siberian Railway in 1905 coincided with Russia's increased interest in Mongolia at a time when Qing power was in decline.

Selected history

This section is based on the life and times of Genghis Khan, and the great Mongol empire which he and his family created and which dominated the known world from 1206 to 1368.

Genghis Khan and the Mongol Empire

Mongol history really begins with Genghis Khan. Most reliable reports prior to the 12th century were written down by others, since the Mongols remained illiterate until then. *The Secret History of the Mongols* (usually abbreviated to *The Secret History*), the first Mongol account of their world, is a curious mixture of myth and reality. It describes the life of Genghis Khan and his unification of the Mongol tribes and begins with the following verse:

> There was a blue wolf which was born
> Having [his] destiny from heaven above,
> His spouse was a fallow doe.

In the legend, the offspring of the wolf and the fallow doe (or of two people with these names) represents the birth of the Mongol nation. *The Secret History* contains many passages of fine poetry that recall the Scandinavian sagas and paints a picture of the young hero Temüchin, who later becomes Genghis Khan. By 1206, he had unified the disparate tribes into a formidable army. The account of his epic rise to power describes numerous alliances and betrayals.

GENGHIS KHAN (1162–1227)

Genghis Khan: 'World Conqueror', 'Emperor of All Men', 'Scourge of God' or 'Savage Genius'. Whatever the title used, most people have heard of him. Admired as the unifier of the Mongols and founder of the Mongol empire, Genghis Khan has always had a special place in the hearts of all Mongols. In the last decade a fast-growing personality cult has restored him to centre stage, where he is now a national obsession. To Mongols, he represents the unshakeable symbol of a glorious past.

At birth, following an ancient custom, Genghis was given the name Temüchin, after one of his father's defeated enemies. The virtue, strength and courage of the enemy was supposed to pass to the newborn baby. His early years were dogged by family difficulties and great hardship; he murdered his half-brother in a teenage dispute, yet grew up to unite the disparate Mongol tribes, who proclaimed him Khan of all the Mongols. He married Borte, an early arranged marriage, and had several other wives.

The only substantial Mongol work about Genghis Khan and the early Mongol empire is recorded in the partly legendary *The Secret History of the Mongols*. The 'Conqueror of the Steppe' was no simple, savage warrior. On his way to victory, Temüchin was not totally blinded by either greed or lust, and although subjugation came first, policy followed. He organised the nomad world; he then used engineers from defeated armies to build mangonels and siege works before launching his light cavalry against the citadels of civilisation. All his moves were politically calculated. Until his death in 1227, Genghis Khan strongly believed he conquered with the authority of the Ruler of Heaven. By 1280 the Mongol empire established by Genghis, his sons and grandsons stretched from the Yellow Sea to the Mediterranean. As a military genius, Genghis Khan stands above Alexander the Great, Hannibal, Caesar, Attila and Napoleon.

It is difficult to separate Genghis Khan the statesman and lawgiver from Genghis Khan the warrior. Had it not been for his incredible ability to cross the boundaries of his native steppe and to conquer and claim for himself and his country the world's largest land empire, he might have lived as an unknown local chieftain. The genius of Genghis Khan lay in his military leadership, his knowledge of men and his organisational ability. He was a charismatic personality, astute, intelligent and cunning. No one around him challenged his authority and his orders were carried out immediately. Genghis was also a reformer and he had a profound effect on the morality of the Mongol people. His laws and disciplines gave the Mongol tribes an identity, which they are proud of to this day. Outside Mongolia, however, in contradiction to his countrymen's hero worship, Genghis Khan is regarded as one of the world's arch villains.

Genghis Khan died in August 1227, during a campaign against the Tanguts. The popular belief is that his body was taken back to his birthplace in Khentii Province, northeast of Ulaanbaatar. Huge mystery also surrounds his burial: herds of horses were said to have galloped over the ground; trees were planted and guards posted until the trees grew; accounts say that the Mongol guards who completed the burial were killed to a man. At Delüün Boldog, in Khentii Province, a monument was built in 1962 to mark the 800th anniversary of his birth.

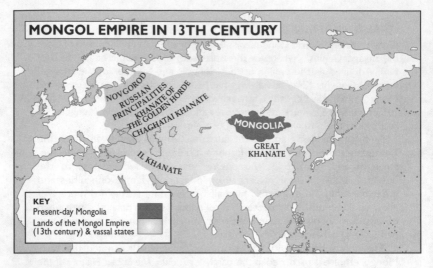

Genghis Khan – the Law Giver

Genghis gave instructions that his laws (*yasa*) should be written down – as far as we know he, like many nomads of his time, did not write, but his powerful intelligence more than compensated for his lack of literacy. When the princes assembled to discuss affairs of state, they produced the *yasa* and lived by the rule of law. The *yasa* prescribed the death penalty for desertion, theft, adultery and false testimony, and lesser punishments for taboos like urinating in rivers, or polluting running water by returning water used for washing to the river. Beheading was the usual form of execution, although, because it was decreed that noble blood should not be spilled, nobles were strangled with bowstrings, had their backs broken or were rolled in carpets and trampled by horses.

The Mongol Army

Genghis Khan learned the value of a personal following, which included his keenest generals (or his 'four hounds', as they were known) – Jebe, Jelme and his brother Sübatai, and Kublai of the Barulas clan. They formed the core of his conquering army in the early period. Genghis structured the way in which his soldiers led their lives. From the age of 14 men were expected to join the army corps. Warriors' wives and children followed behind the troops with herds of sheep and horses, including several re-mounts per man. Warrior units were organised in multiples of ten, an *arban* (10) being a unit of ten men; ten *arban* made up a *jagun* (100), that is, a unit of 100 men; ten *jagun* formed a *minggan* (1,000 men); and ten *minggan* formed a *tümen* (10,000 men). Speedy communication by mounted couriers was later developed (see opposite).

Training was based on the hunt, a favourite Mongol sport, with the quarry representing the enemy. Various manoeuvres were practised, such as 'ringing' or driving the hunted animals in an arc. Mongol hunters/warriors were experts in signalling to each other using banners, whistling arrows and drums. Every battle was carefully planned and prepared with the help of spies. The soldiers learned the importance of discipline and co-ordination and became the finest army of their time.

All of this is remarkable considering the lowly origins of the Mongol people – obscure nomadic tribes from Asia's remotest uplands. The key to their dominion over those they conquered was the horse. Since its domestication during the second millennium BC, the horse's speed and stamina was exploited by the Mongol nomads. Their principal weapon was the compound bow, made from willow wood and bound by a mixture of silk and resin. They developed the first stirrups on the northern Steppe, which allowed warriors to turn in the saddle and shoot arrows back at their pursuing enemies while galloping ahead at full pace, a military tactic known as the 'Parthian shot' and invented by the ancient Parthians (250BC–AD230). These skills contributed to the emergence of their military might.

Genghis Khan had left his generals to complete this task as his military dream 'to rule the world' led him west, where Samarkand and Bukhara, the great cities of Islam, were destroyed in 1221. Meanwhile, his military commanders defeated the Russian-Kipchak alliance in the Don valley and the Volga Bulgars were dispersed. From Mongolia Genghis attacked and destroyed the neighbouring Tangut (Xixia) capital in 1227, the year he died.

The mounted couriers

The mounted courier service, known as *yam*, was key to the maintenance of the Mongol empire and dispatch riders on horseback travelled enormous distances at breakneck speed to deliver messages, protected by Genghis Khan's *yasa* (laws). Military units were responsible for the protection of the service and caravan traders also benefited from it. Trade flourished along the protected routes within such a framework of discipline and security. At each post, horses were saddled and waiting for the khan's couriers and news could be relayed at terrific speed, with the riders putting the service ahead of their own lives. Passes called *paiza* were issued to official users of the system but finally traders were obliged to pay for using the *yam* posts.

The Mongol Dynasty following the death of Genghis Khan
The 'Golden Family'

Genghis's four sons – Jochi, Chaghatai, Ögödei and Tolui, by his first wife Börte – formed the Mongol Khanate dynastic inheritance. Ögödei was chosen to succeed as the Great Khan and his brother Tolui promised their ageing father to support him, as *The Secret History* states:

> I shall be at his side
> His faithful companion,
> Reminding him of things he has forgotten,
> Waking him when he has slept his fill.

By nominating his third son Ögödei, Genghis Khan broke with tradition. Ögödei was proclaimed the second Great Khan in 1229. This caused acute rivalry and led to fighting among members of the 'golden family' – family tensions not explained in *The Secret History*. The Mongol empire continued to grow in the third generation, but Genghis Khan's sons and grandsons fought among themselves and lost sight of the 'big idea' of one empire under one ruler, preferring to build their own personal empires on the territories they had conquered, and adopting the customs and religions of their new subjects. Nonetheless the achievements were enormous: Genghis Khan and his successors created the largest land empire the world has ever known.

Mongols attack Europe

During Ögödei's reign, Mongol troops invaded their eastern neighbour Korea while at the same time mounted warriors rode west. The horsemen from the east

GENGHIS KHAN'S GENETIC LEGACY

The astounding statistic that one in 200 men alive on the planet today are related to Genghis Khan was recently discovered by an Oxford University scientist, Dr Cris Tyler Smith, and colleagues in China. Over a period of ten years they collected blood from 16 populations that live in and around the Mongol empire. The analysis of DNA studies of the Y chromosome, used to establish human lineage, shows a genetic signature which passes from father to son. The blood of none of the people outside the Mongol empire carries this particular genetic signature, except the Hazara people of Afghanistan and Pakistan, former Mongol soldiers who claimed to be descended from Genghis Khan. The genetic chromosome signature belongs to the Mongol ruling house and Dr Tyler Smith believes that the Mongol khans had access to large numbers of women in the lands they conquered and ruled for two centuries. The evidence is incomplete because the tomb of Genghis Khan has never been found, although it is now established that one-fifth of present-day Mongolian men carry the khan's genes and it is possible that they shared a common ancestor – the Great Khan himself.

made Europe's knights look like laggards when they swept across the northern steppe towards Europe from Central Asia's frozen heights. First when they subjugated southern Siberia and then moved on to ravage Transcaucasia and destroy the Kievan army on the Kelka River; and later, when one of Genghis Khan's grandsons, Batu, took Moscow (from the southwest by crossing the River Volga) in 1237. Ögödei's son Godan staged the invasion of Tibet but was converted to Buddhism by Sakya Pandita, whose pupil Phagspa later became Kublai Khan's teacher. In 1241 Mongol troops defeated the Polish and other armies at Legnica (Liegnitz). As proof of their victory the Mongols were reported to have collected nine sacks full of right ears from the bodies of the slain. A famous account of the capture of Kraków is commemorated to this day by a trumpet call known as Hejnal (see box opposite), which sounded the approach of the enemy. After the battle of Kraków, another branch of the Mongol army raided Hungary, resulting in a great slaughter of the Magyar princes under Bela IV beside the River Tisza. Hungarians described the invaders as 'dog-faced Tartars'. Europeans had no knowledge of the lands beyond the Ural mountains until the marauding Mongol hordes arrived, leaving a trail of destruction in their wake. Had it not been for the death of Ogödei Khan in 1241, European history might have taken a very different course, because the Mongol forces turned and rode home to elect his successor.

The Golden Horde: conquest and colonisation

However, the Mongols remained in Russia and set up camp between the Don and the Volga rivers, where they created the 'Golden Horde', named, it is thought, after the colour of the first khan's tent. The Mongols destroyed the Volga Bulgars and changed the political frontiers of Asia and Europe for several centuries. The Mongol empire transformed the character of the many regions they conquered and opened up the East to the West and vice versa.

The Mongols were able to defeat the disunited and jealous Russian princes one by one. Furthermore, the princes of Rus were obliged to pay heavy tributes to the khan and were put through rituals they considered humiliating, such as

HEJNAL

Hejnal derives from the Hungarian word for the dawn and by extension for *reveille*. The word passed into the Polish language (the 'l' at the end of *Hejnal* is pronounced 'w') and became one of the most noted trumpet calls in the history of Europe, from the time when it first sounded the alarm of the Mongol invasion of Poland in 1241 (see opposite). As the story goes, the trumpet call rang out from the tower of the ancient church of St Mary's in Kraków, which overlooks the city square. It was normally sounded every hour, day and night, and repeated four times to the north, south, east and west, and consisted of a simple melody. Today the melody is always stopped short in the final cadence. It commemorates the trumpeter who, while raising the alarm, was shot through the throat by a Mongol arrow; nevertheless, his call allowed the citizens of Kraków to flee the city. The survivors endowed a trumpeter to continue this call in perpetuity, and this tradition has been maintained for some 700 years! The melody has been adopted as the signature tune of Polish radio. It is a living memory of the irruption of the Mongol hordes into the heart of Europe.

being obliged to walk between blazing bonfires and made to prostrate themselves before the khan. Marco Polo's father described the Russian province of the khans as a region of darkness, where tall, fair-haired, Christian men of a light complexion pay tribute to the kings of the western Tartars. He also noted it was an exceedingly cold region. It took the Russian princes several centuries to unite against the Mongols.

FROM THE MONGOL EMPIRE TO THE 20TH CENTURY

There is a gap in Mongol history between the colonising of the great land empire of the Mongol khans, from its establishment in the late 12th century until its general collapse in the mid-14th century (although the Golden Horde survived in Russia into the 15th century) and the early 20th-century revolution. The curious reader wonders what happened between then and now. The answer is nothing much. The Mongols retired to their upland homeland and continued to herd as nomads in the manner of their forebears, which a small nomadic population do to this day. Against this background were inter-tribal conflicts, and during this period Buddhism spread throughout Mongolia.

The Mongol empire imploded after the collapse of the Yuan dynasty (1368) and the Ming dynasty was established in China. Many of the scholar-bureaucrats who found favour during Yuan (Mongol) rule suffered under the Ming rulers. Thousands of people were put to death, and once high-ranking officials became clerks. Meanwhile the famous Chinese civil service examination system got into its stride. Members of the Mongol royal family were kept in the capital, Beijing, and indoctrinated. In 1374 a member of the Mongol royal family was sent back to Mongolia in the hope that he would succeed as khan and eventually bring the whole of Mongolia under Chinese suzerainty. This did not happen.

After 1368, Mongolia was in a state of disorder for many years, so it was natural that some lesser nobles looked to the south to secure a better deal for themselves. The Chinese did their best to encourage this and tried to sinicise them, as their authority surged further north. Guerilla warfare was waged by the Mongol princes

MARCO POLO
Frances Wood

Marco Polo (c1254–1324) is widely assumed to have been the first 'foreigner' to reach the Mongol heartlands, to converse with Kublai Khan and to travel throughout China on the khan's orders. Though the original manuscript no longer exists, several early-15th-century copies of *Description of the World*, said to have been written by Marco Polo and the romance-writer Rustichello of Pisa, survive. The first versions of the text were written in medieval French but it was soon translated into most of the major European languages and many dialects. The fact that it first circulated in manuscript has led to problems, for errors crept in as copies were made, and manuscript versions varied quite widely before the first printed versions appeared later in the 15th century.

A prologue which survives in some manuscripts describes how Marco Polo's father and uncle, traders who normally travelled between Venice, Constantinople and the Black Sea, were driven eastwards by Mongol wars and found themselves at the court of Kublai Khan. When they left, they promised to return with holy oil from Jerusalem, and travelled back overland, bringing young Marco with them. Legend has it that he was chosen by Kublai to travel all over southern China and report back on the area that was still being conquered by the Mongols. This he did for 20 years before returning by sea, with his father and uncle, to Venice.

There are several interesting aspects to the Polo legend. The first is that, despite his self-proclaimed closeness to Kublai and his twenty years' service, there is no mention of him in any of the innumerable Chinese annals, nor in Mongol sources. Some have also questioned the fact that he makes no mention of the Great Wall, tea-drinking, foot-binding or the use of chopsticks, but perhaps even more problematic are the passages where he describes the impossible. For example, he claimed to have ended the Mongols' five-year siege

along the Chinese-Mongol border. The 15th and 16th centuries were dominated by internal struggles to decide between the various claimants to the Mongol throne, although few of these struggles lasted for very long. The 17th century was marked by the rise of Manchu and Russian power in Asia, culminating in the absorption of Mongolia into the Manchu Qing empire (1644–1912). From 1644, for the next two hundred years Buddhism spread amongst the Mongols. The early 20th century saw Mongolia's unsuccesful bid for its independence and its absorbtion into the Soviet empire and, at this period, Mongolia's modern history begins.

The modern period
Autonomous 'Outer' Mongolia

The Mongols and Tibetans believed that the Manchus ruled Mongolia and Tibet not as Chinese provinces, but under separate treaties. When the Manchu throne fell, Mongolia, Tibet and China were automatically separated. As the Qing dynasty collapsed in 1911, 'Outer' (Khalkha) Mongolia proclaimed its independence. The 'Living Buddha', head of Buddhism in Mongolia, was acknowledged as head of state with the title *Bogd Khan* and enthroned on December 16 1911. One of the first acts of the *Bogd Khan* was to order the confiscation of the Manchu emperor's livestock, which was shared out among the Mongol nobility and high lamas. During this turbulent period, the Republic of China was proclaimed in 1912.

of Xiangyang by constructing mangonels to fling stones into the Chinese city; however, Xiangyang fell in 1273, a year before the Polos could possibly have entered China. He 'describes' Japan and Russia, but no experts think he went to either place. Some have suggested that Marco Polo's *Description of the World* may be a second-hand compilation, based perhaps on Near Eastern sources, in which context it is worth noting that most of the nouns and proper names are Persian or Turkish in origin and not Mongol or Chinese as might be expected.

The Polos' reputation as the first Westerners in Mongolia is also a myth. The first eyewitness account of Mongolia was made in 1246 by Friar John of Plano Carpini, a disciple of St Francis of Assisi, and much detail of the cosmopolitan community in Karakorum, which included a Parisian silversmith (captured by the Mongols in Belgrade in 1254), a Greek doctor and a man called Basil, son of an Englishman and nephew of a Norman bishop, was given by Friar William of Rubruck, a papal envoy who reached the city in 1254.

Arguments over the veracity of Marco Polo's account have raged for over 300 years; the fact remains, however, that *Description of the World*, attributed to him, contained a wealth of information about Mongolia and the Far East in the 15th century. The fact that the manuscript was widely copied and translated, and that printed versions in all the major European languages have been produced from the 15th century up until the present day, testifies to European interest in Mongolia and China throughout the centuries.

If you wish to read further on this subject, you might try one or more of the following:

Yule, Colonel Sir Henry *The Travels of Marco Polo* London 1920; New York, 1993
Franke, Herbert *China Under Mongol Rule* Aldershot, 1994
Wood, Frances *Did Marco Polo Go To China?* Westview Press, USA, 1998

An agreement with Russia in November 1912 seemed to accord Russian recognition to Mongolia's independence, but Russia promised only to help protect its autonomy. China remained in charge of foreign relations. Autonomous 'Outer' Mongolia had appealed to all Mongols to join together in one independent Mongol state, but China retained its hold on Inner Mongolia, and 'Outer' Mongolia's 'independence' proved short-lived, as Chinese troops occupied the capital of Autonomous Mongolia, Urga (Niislel Khüree), in 1919. The 20th century saw Mongolia free itself from two centuries of Manchu rule, but there was an unsuccessful struggle for independence, a brief occupation by China, followed by a national revolution that succeeded with the support of the Soviets.

Mongolia's revolution

A group of Mongolian nationalist revolutionaries took shelter in Siberia in 1920 and were helped by the Soviet authorities to rebel against the Chinese occupation forces in Mongolia. The Mongolian People's Party was set up at a meeting of 26 revolutionaries. They adopted what are called the 'Ten Aspirations', promising to resolve matters of external and internal policy in the long-term interests of the nation, but warned of harsh measures to eliminate things which were backward or did not benefit 'the people'.

In May 1921, Urga was captured by a force of Tsarist Siberian Cossacks and Mongol mercenaries under the command of a Baltic baron, Roman von Ungern-

'OUTER' AND 'INNER' MONGOLIA

Not all Mongols live in Mongolia proper – or Outer Mongolia, as it is historically referred to – nor are they the majority of Mongols. Most Mongolians live in Inner Mongolia and Xinjiang Autonomous Region of China, bordering the area south of the Gobi Desert along the eastern Silk Route.

Inner Mongolia (Övör Mongol or 'Front/Breast' Mongolia) is part of China and largely settled by Chinese people, who outnumber Mongols by 14 to 1. Outer Mongolia (Ar Mongol or 'Back' Mongolia) – the Mongolia of this guide – is a country in the process of democracy, located in the heartland of the Central Asian plateau, formerly a communist country for 70 years, and during that time closely linked to the Soviet Union.

Internal conflict and tribal disunity continued to blight Mongolian unity from the 16th century until the modern period. Chinese annals are full of accounts of 'barbarian raids' from the north (Outer Mongolia) on the people living around the Great Wall, which extended in an east–west direction across northern China. Below it was the famous Silk Road, where Turkic-speaking oasis people traded silks and spices from the East to the Mediterranean Sea. This international highway was at its height in the 14th, 15th and 16th centuries. The ascendancy of the western (Oirat) and southern Mongols passed to the Ordos Mongols, located in the great loop of the Yellow River, under Altan Khan (1543–83). From them the supremacy passed to the southern tribes living near the Great Wall. At this period Manchu power from China flooded north and their rule encompassed the Mongol tribes. By 1644 the Chinese Qing or Manchu dynasty was established, with profound effects on the fate of the Mongol tribes. Over the next century the northern Mongols of Outer Mongolia were added to their empire. Fighting between the Mongol tribes persisted and the western and southern Mongols revolted against the Manchus in the 1750s. The rebellion was quelled and the Mongol tribes again were dispersed and redistributed. Chinese colonisation encroached on the pasturelands of Inner Mongolia and this uneasy situation was compounded by economic distress. Inner Mongolia was declared an Autonomous Region of China while 'Outer' Mongolia became a separate state.

Sternberg, later know as the 'Mad Baron' (see box opposite). The Mongolian Bogd Khan, the political and religious leader, who had been taken hostage by the Chinese, was released by von Ungern-Sternberg, who set up a new government. But in July that year, the baron's forces were overcome by the Soviet Russian Red Army and Mongolian revolutionaries, who installed a 'people's government'.

The revolutionaries, encouraged by the Soviets, adopted a communist, rather than nationalist, approach and there was a limited monarchy until the Bogd Khan's death in May 1924, after which new incarnations and 'Living Buddhas' were forbidden. Mongolia's ties with Soviet Russia were strengthened and the Mongolian People's Party was renamed the Mongolian People's Revolutionary Party (MPRP).

At the end of 1924, a national assembly, or Great Khural, approved the country's first constitution and a second chamber of 30 members, the Little Khural, was elected. It then elected a five-man Presidium and chose the government. The Mongolian People's Republic (MPR) was proclaimed and the capital renamed Ulaanbaatar ('Red Hero'). The Great Khural resolved that Soviet Russia was

THE MAD BARON

Freiherr Roman von Ungern-Sternberg came from the landed nobility of the Baltic German barons whose ancestors had served the tsars. He was commissioned at the age of 24, in 1908, in the Transbaikal Cossacks. With his liking for adventure and hard riding, he much preferred this to life in one of the fashionable guards regiments. The following year, the collapse of the Manchu dynasty in China and the proclamation of Sun Yat-Sen's republic led to events which were to change von Ungern-Sternberg's life.

He is described as red-haired, with a sabre scar to his head. This scar was inflicted after an officers' brawl resulted in a duel, and gave him spells of madness from time to time. He would wear a fur hat, a short Chinese jacket of cherry-red silk, blue cavalry breeches, and high Mongol boots, with a bunch of twinkling charms hanging from a bright yellow cord fastened around his waist.

In 1914 he won the order of St George while serving on the German front during World War I. In 1916 he was sent to the Persian border, and in 1917, at 33, he was promoted to major-general. In 1917/18, during the civil war that broke out after the Russian Revolution, he joined Kolchak's 'white' army in Siberia, but with them he was driven back towards the east by Trotsky's new Red Army. Learning that the 'Reds' had killed his wife and child, von Ungern-Sternberg vowed to kill anyone who looked remotely like a Bolshevik.

The baron assembled a force of Russian Cossacks and moved south into Mongolia. He believed himself destined to create a vast Asiatic empire like that of Genghis Khan, or that he was the reincarnation of the Mongol god of war. At any rate, he won a reputation for appalling atrocities. On October 31 1920, his force attacked Urga (Ulaanbaatar), but was repulsed by the larger and better-armed Chinese garrison, and had to withdraw. Trying again six days later, the baron's men nearly forced the Chinese out, but the attack failed again.

This reverse encouraged the Chinese to seize and imprison the 'Living Buddha' (Bogd Khan) to the fury of the Mongols, with the result that many of them joined the baron's force. The baron invited the Chinese to surrender and join his army before he launched the attack. Instead they called for reinforcements from Peking. He planned to make the Chinese believe he had more men that he really did by lighting fires on the hills above Urga. One of his men accidentally let off a rocket, and the Chinese retaliated with all they had. The baron advanced, inflicting heavy losses and destroyed the Chinese quarter.

The people of Urga saw the baron as their liberator and the 'Living Buddha' bestowed the title of khan on him. In spite of this, he continued his atrocities. Meanwhile, the Mongolian leader Sükhbaatar and his followers set up their revolutionary base at Kyakhta on the Russian frontier with Mongolia. The baron left Urga to attack the 'Reds' as they advanced, but he was beaten off; Sükhbaatar and his revolutionaries captured Urga on July 6 1921. After several more engagements, the baron was captured by the 'reds' in northern Mongolia, when he was betrayed by his Mongol escort. He was executed by the Bolsheviks in Novosibirsk on September 15 1921, although a German source says he was shot three days later in Irkutsk.

DAMDINY SÜKHBAATAR

Damdiny Sükhbaatar was a young, gallant people's warrior of the 1921 revolution. Born in 1893, he came from a poor family; he had great ability as a military leader and in 1921 was appointed Commander in Chief of the Mongolian People's Revolutionary Army. A brave fighter and an inspirational leader Sukhbaatar became 'Hero of the Revolution', but died two years later (1923) in mysterious circumstances at the age of 30. He set the course of the Mongol revolution towards loyalty to the Russian alliance. In his honour Urga, the capital, was renamed Ulaanbaatar (meaning Red Hero) and the main square in Ulaanbaatar bears his name.

Mongolia's 'only friend and ally' and that, 'in alliance with the Soviet working class', the MPR would 'bypass capitalism and enter socialism'.

The aristocracy and religious leaders still held most of the country's wealth. A swing in the MPRP leadership from moderate 'rightists' to extreme 'leftists' set in motion the confiscation of 'feudal' property, forced collectivisation of stock breeding, the expulsion of Chinese traders and the imposition of a Soviet trade monopoly in Mongolia. The MPRP ordered seizure of religious property, expelled the lamas from the monasteries and imprisoned or killed their leaders in purges

THE BATTLE OF NOMONHAN (KHALKHYN GOL)
John Colvin

The Battle of Nomonhan (or Battle of Khalkhyn Gol), fought in 1939 on the Manchurian-Mongol border, ended Japanese ambitions to control Siberia. Japan's real objectives, it would seem, were to create a buffer state between the port of Vladivostok and Lake Baikal and to integrate the Siberian economy with Japan's. It is one of the most important battles of modern history, taking place only weeks before the outbreak of World War II. The Japanese desire to enlarge their territory by conquering Russia was an appalling dream, if the voices of the Japanese casualties (20,000 men) of the Battle of Nomonhan could be heard. The shattering defeat of the numerically superior Imperial Kwantung Japanese army by Russian/Mongol forces marked the end of Japan's search for raw materials and their hopes of expansion in the north. Russia and Japan signed a non-aggression pact. Instead of 'planting the flag in the Urals and watering their horses on the Volga', the outcome of this little-known but decisive battle meant that, from 1940, the Japanese army concentrated its expansion plans on nations to the south. Thus Burma, Malaya, Singapore, Indochina, the East Indies and the Philippines were invaded and the flags of colonial powers like the British and Dutch were lowered. The Mongols have always regarded their geopolitical position as central to Soviet requirements and this battle proved it. Had they sided against the Russians, history would have been dramatically different. All this Japanese history prefers to forget and nowadays refers only to the Battle of Nomonhan as a border incident. The victory for the Russians allowed them to move their Far Eastern forces west, and to inflict defeat upon Germany.

For further details of this extraordinary battle, see John Colvin, *Nomonhan* (Quartet Books, 1999).

that all but destroyed Buddhism. Herdsmen, urged to join the government-run collectives, took fright and slaughtered their livestock and, by 1932, terror and food shortages brought the people to the brink of civil war, prevented only by Soviet intervention. This halted political and economic extremism for a while, but purges of party and government officials continued, taking the lives of prime ministers Genden and Amar, who were both arrested and executed in the USSR. Supreme power was then concentrated in the hands of the prime minister, Marshal Choibalsan – later known as 'Mongolia's Stalin'.

These events coincided with the establishment of Japanese control in neighbouring Manchuria and the threat of further expansion. In 1939 Manchukuo (Manchurian) forces with Japanese military support invaded Mongolia across the eastern border at the Khalkhyn Gol (see box opposite). Some historians consider that Japan's defeat at Khalkhyn Gol persuaded its leaders to give up plans for the invasion of the USSR in favour of the invasion of Southeast Asia, again changing the course of history.

Mongolia's Great Khural met once every three years to draw up basic policy, revise the constitution and elect the Little Khural, where power was concentrated in the hands of a small group of leaders who ran the country for long periods free from the need to explain their actions.

Meanwhile, at the Yalta conference in early 1945, Churchill, Roosevelt and Stalin agreed terms for the Soviet declaration of war on Japan. These included Western recognition of the status quo in Mongolia (ie: quasi-independence under Soviet control). In October 1945, the United Nations held a plebiscite in Mongolia, organised by the Mongolian authorities to satisfy China, in which there was an overwhelming vote for independence. China was required to give up its claim on Mongolia following the Yalta Conference held under UN auspices; in January 1946 China accepted this and finally recognised the MPR. Ironically it took Mongolia 16 years to join the United Nations. In 1949, on the founding of the People's Republic of China (PRC), Mongolia transferred its recognition to the People's Republic. Marshal Choibalsan died in 1952 and Stalin died in 1953. After Choibalsan's death Mongolia was ruled by Tsedenbal, the MPRP secretary general (first secretary) from 1940 to 1954 and 1959 to 1984, and concurrently prime minister (1952–74) and president (1974–84) of Mongolia.

Building socialism

In 1940 Mongolia had predominantly a nomadic livestock-raising economy, but in the post-war years herding was collectivised, arable farming was expanded and mining and light industry developed considerably. The Trans-Mongolian Railway linking the USSR and PRC was put into operation in 1955. Nearly a quarter of the deputies of the People's Great Khural elected in 1960 were classed as workers. The Mongolian coat-of-arms, showing the heads of the 'five animals' and mounted herdsman, was re-designed to show a cog-wheel and wheatsheaf, symbols of industry, agriculture and progress. The goal was to transform Mongolia into an 'industrial-agricultural' nation. By the mid-1950s, collectivisation began to work. Although Mongolia was nominally an independent socialist state, the country depended heavily on financial help from the Soviet Union, and Soviet influence in many ways modernised the country. However, the socialist dream was ultimately to evaporate.

International status

Mongolia became a member of the United Nations in 1961; a member of the CMEA (Comecon) in 1962; opened diplomatic relations with the United

Kingdom in 1963; agreed a new Mutual Assistance Treaty with the USSR in 1966. Mongolia's relationship with China, which had been restored after the proclamation of the PRC, went into sharp decline during the Chinese 'Cultural Revolution' and the Sino-Soviet ideological and territorial dispute. Tsedenbal developed a close friendship with Brezhnev, the Soviet Party general secretary and president (1964–82), and Soviet influences in Mongolia grew enormously. Mongolians benefited from this relationship in terms of the standard of living, even if the price was continued political obedience to the Kremlin.

The end of the Cold War, together with the disintegration of the Soviet Union, has fundamentally changed Mongolia's geopolitical environment. Mongolia is now a nuclear-free country with a foreign policy based on political realism, non-alignment and the pursuit of the national interest, at the same time keeping and developing good neighbourly relations.

The 1970s and 1980s

Milestones of the 1970s and 1980s were diplomatic relations with Japan in 1972; new confrontations with China over territory and the role of Chinese residents; the first visit to Mongolia by the Dalai Lama in 1979; the completion of the 'Erdenet' copper combine and the first space flight by a Mongolian in 1981; and Tsedenbal's unexpected dismissal from office on grounds of ill health in 1984. In the 1980s the Soviet leader Mikhail Gorbachev's plans for *perestroika* and *glasnost* sounded the end of socialism. Most Mongols were ignorant of the new realities of the Western world. Tsedenbal's successor, President Batmönkh, sensed the need for change but could not deliver. The Berlin Wall collapsed.

The 1990s

Mongolia set up legal and constitutional institutions to become a democracy in a peaceful process which brought Mongols into contact with the modern world. The 1990s may be called the decade of change in Mongolia. For details of the

---

'THE DECADE OF CHANGE': A TRANSITION PERIOD, 1990–2000

Huge changes happened in Mongolia during the 1990s – the transition period after the fall of the Soviet empire and Mongolia's decision to become a democracy. For most of the 20th century, under the domination of Soviet Russia, Mongolia was virtually closed to Westerners. 1990 was the turning point in its modern history, when the country sought economic independence, political and economic reforms and an independent foreign policy. Two years later a new democratic constitution was adopted. In June 1992, voters in remote areas rode or drove to polling stations throughout the land to return brimming ballot boxes in a turnout of 85%.

During the decade of change, social security systems fell to pieces, unable to keep pace with the rapid political changes that reduced many people to unemployment and poverty in the towns, while natural catastrophes, such as the severe summer droughts and freezing winters of recent years, caused great livestock losses that have brought severe hardship to the rural population. New measures to cope more satisfactorily with the distribution of fodder in times of need have been authorised by the Mongolian government, which should help alleviate some of the stress which the herders have had to shoulder over extra severe winters.

democratic revolution in Mongolia, see *Politics* section below. The present-day situation is best reflected through the many changes of government and radical changes in society during the period of the 1990s' 'Decade of Change'. (See box, *The decade of change*, opposite.)

POLITICS

December 10 2000 marked the tenth anniversary of Mongolia's democratic reform and the people assessed the achievements of the 'decade of change', looking back, without regret, on the communist system they had abandoned. Democracy is still new and fragile but on the whole the reforms have succeeded and have gone deeper and proceeded faster than many former socialist countries, although Mongolia's transition to a market economy is far from complete.

Hemmed in between China and Russia, Mongolia's geographical location has always been a decisive factor in shaping the country's destiny. After the collapse of the Mongol empire, the region known as Outer Mongolia grew progressively weaker over the centuries. Indeed, Mongolia remained subdued and isolated for most of the 20th century during its socialist period, and despite improvements in healthcare and education, there was little contact with the Western world until it accepted Western ideas and democracy in 1990.

20th-century background

Mongolian autonomy was achieved with Russian support in 1911. China attempted to reassert its rule following the Russian Revolution of 1917, but was overcome by combined Russian/Mongol troops in 1921. A short-lived restoration of the traditional feudal Buddhist monarchy was followed in 1924 by the declaration of a People's Republic under the Mongolian People's Revolutionary Party (MPRP). (For details of this, see *History*, page 26.)

In the lead up to World War II, Mongolia followed Soviet ideology and accepted the ideas of communism. China finally recognised Mongolian independence in 1946. When the People's Republic of China was created in 1949, Mongolia found herself surrounded by two giant communist states, China and Russia. The Sino-Soviet split at the end of the 1950s temporarily dashed hopes of a good relationship between the three countries.

During the Cold War, Mongolia fell victim to two long, costly periods of isolation. Moscow stationed 75,000 troops in Mongolian territory and had there been a war between China and Russia, Mongolia would have indeed become a battlefield. As it was, Mongolia remained a buffer zone. Mongolia joined the United Nations in 1961. At the end of the Cold War in 1989, after *perestroika*, *glasnost* and the fall of the Berlin Wall, Mongolia was quick to move forward towards democracy.

Politics of the 1990s: the decade of change

The winter of 1989/1990 was marked by (illegal) student associations calling for democracy, spurred on by events in eastern Europe following Gorbachev's political reforms. Among the young idealists were Sanjaasürengiin Zorig (see page 33), Erdeniin Bat-Üül and Davaadorjiin Ganbold.

The removal of Stalin's statue from central Ulaanbaatar in February 1990 was a potent symbol of the changing times. It focused people's attention on Mongolian victims of the 1930 purges, many of whom were murdered or died in Siberian camps of the Gulag.

Mongolia's leaders, seeing the wind of reform was blowing hard across the Soviet empire, decided to adopt a policy of gradual change and promised multiparty elections within months. General Secretary Batmönkh, who had assumed the office of president in 1984 (taking over from Yumjaagiyn Tsedenbal, leader for 30 years), resigned – along with the entire politburo. He was replaced by Gombojavyn Ochirbat. A general election held in July was won by the MPRP, although it led to some power sharing with the new political reformers in the Little Khural (standing legislature). By the end of the year the principles of transition from a command economy to a market economy were agreed upon.

Among the countries of Asia and eastern Europe, Mongolia is considered by experts to be one of the most successful of the eastern post-communist countries to emerge in the 21st century, although it does not compare with Hungary or the Baltic states. Yet it is worth stating that to speak of a direct transfer from communism to capitalism is too direct. Mongolia and other states are in transition. One might say that communism was not fully achieved, therefore in this guide, it is referred to as the communist period – an accepted shorthand.

From the beginning of 1991, all Mongolia's external trade settlements had to be in hard currency and Soviet credit and long-term aid from Comecon (CMEA) came to a halt. Everything was thrown further into confusion during the August coup against Gorbachev. Japan granted Mongolia financial aid to help it over its economic difficulties.

The new constitution of 1992 changed the country's name to Mongolia and abolished the former assemblies. The five-pointed star was removed from the Mongolian flag and the country adopted a new coat-of-arms. The constitution also established a single chamber of 76 members and a directly elected president approved by the Great Khural (parliament). In June that year the MPRP won 71 of 76 seats in the new Mongolian Great Khural and formed a new government. Several opposition parties amalgamated to become the Mongolian National Democratic Party (MNDP). During the next two years many new laws were passed.

The country's first direct presidential election was won in 1993 by the opposition democrat's candidate, Punsalmagiin Ochirbat. Democracy and liberalisation together with a free press were opening up the country. Inflation began to fall in 1994, but transport was affected by fuel shortages. Mongolia was entirely dependent on Russia for petrol and diesel. Supplies and the payment for them were irregular due to economic disruption all around. Meanwhile the EU helped to fund the TACIS programme, the European Union's special tourist development aid programme.

In June 1996 general elections swept the MPRP from power and a new government was formed by a coalition of National Democrats and Social Democrats with 50 seats. For the first time the MPRP was no longer the ruling party, but the winning Democratic Alliance (DA) was to be dogged by misfortune:

PARLIAMENT OR IKH KHURAL

The government, elected for four years, comprises the prime minister and cabinet members. The prime minister is nominated by the president in consultation with the majority party. The Ikh Khural discusses individually each of the ministerial candidates proposed by the prime minister and votes on the appointments. Members of parliament appoint, replace and remove the prime minister and members of the cabinet.

The president: Political parties with seats in the Ikh Khural nominate presidential candidates. He or she is elected for a four-year term and can be re-elected just once.

SANJAASÜRENGIIN ZORIG

In 1992, at the age of 30, Sanjaasürengiin Zorig was murdered in his home – which was a political disaster for Mongolia. He was the nation's father of democracy, and was referred to as 'Mr Democracy'. Born in 1962, he graduated from Moscow State University and became a lecturer at the Mongolian State University. He abandoned Marxism/Leninism to found the Mongolian Democratic Association in December 1989 and later founded the Mongolian Republican Party in 1991. Finally, the Mongolian National Democratic Party and other parties merged in October 1992 to form the Mongolian National Democratic Party of which Zorig was a member of the general council. He became the Minister of Infrastructure and Development and was tipped to become Mongolia's next prime minister. Zorig's death was a sad loss to the country's political life. A statue to commemorate him stands opposite the Central Post Office in Ulaanbaatar.

the quorum of the Great Khural is 51 and they were one seat short. The MPRP's defeat led the party to appoint a younger, more dynamic, general secretary, Nambaryn Enkhbayar, and the second presidential election in 1997 was won by the MPRP candidate, Natsangiin Bagabandi.

In spring 1998 the DA began to look as though it was coming unstitched due to internal bickering. The new MNDP leader Tsakhiagiin Elbegdorj announced that in future the leader of the majority party in the Great Hural would become the leader of the DA coalition and prime minister. The government resigned, Elbegdorj was appointed prime minister, and in May he formed a new government. At this stage the country was in political turmoil. The coalition formed two more governments between 1998 and 1999, so that Mongolia was dubbed a country of 'revolving-door governments'.

The most prominent political event at the end of the 20th century centred upon the brutal murder of Sanjaasürengiin Zorig on October 2 1998 by persons unknown (see box above). Zorig was one of the founding members of the 1989 Democracy Movement. At the time of his murder he was Minister of Infrastructure and Development and possibly in line for DA nomination for prime minister. After Zorig's funeral a constitutional debate took place on the right of ministers to be members of parliament. (As in the USA, government ministers did not have seats in the parliament.) After a five-month hiatus on this issue the government settled back to work.

21st-century politics

The elections of June 2000 saw the fall of the Democratic Alliance and the re-election of the Mongolian People's Revolutionary Party (MPRP), the former communist party, by a decisive majority taking 72 of the 76 seats. Thus the political pendulum had swung from the MPRP to the Democratic Alliance in 1996 and back to the MPRP in 2000. Up to this point, things were described (by political observer Sheldon Severinghaus) as political sandstorms befitting the Gobi Desert. When the dust settled and the new government got down to work, they prioritised a policy of poverty reduction following the *zud* disasters (see box, *Difficulties facing the Mongolian government*, page 34). The major foreign policy event of that year was the visit of President Vladimir Putin.

There have been some very confusing months and years, which have caused pain and hardship to many people. But there has also been a willingness to press

DIFFICULTIES FACING THE MONGOLIAN GOVERNMENT

Recent difficulties facing the Mongolian government have been the extremely severe winters that resulted in an environmental disaster, known as zud, when a freeze/thaw/freeze occurs and snow conditions make it impossible for animals to graze. Herders' animals die by the hundreds, adding up to the loss of millions of head of livestock, which has major economic and social ramifications. Blizzards and fierce winds struck in the winter of 1999/2000 and again in winter 2000/2001 when zud conditions in the successive bad winters claimed around six million domestic stock and unknown numbers of wild animals. To compound the situation summer drought leads to poor plant growth on lands where animals cannot fatten up sufficiently to survive the cold winters on the steppe. It also means that herders are unable to put aside natural fodder to feed their animals during the winter and, with unusually deep snow and temperatures plummeting to -40°C, and at times to -50°C, it has been difficult for them to cope.

Winter losses are a frequent occurrence in Mongolia, but the extreme temperatures experienced recently usually happen only every 50 years or so, when millions of animals die under such conditions. Many families lost their livelihood entirely and were left with nothing. International media coverage resulted in promises of significant disaster relief assistance.

On the other hand in recent years the numbers of livestock had increased, with the privatisation of livestock in the early 1990s, leading to a ten million increase in livestock. To nomads, wealth is on the hoof. However, the land cannot sustain this impact – its capacity was exceeded in many places and overgrazing resulted, especially around towns and settlements. Since 2002 the government has redressed this situation by being better prepared and better planned although there is nothing anyone can do about the weather. Winter reserves of (mainly) hay are stockpiled around the country, but in the recent past they have been too small and often too remote to be much help. There are also enormous logistical problems of transporting and delivering additional food in times of shortage.

Mongolia has also been hit by the disaster of foot-and-mouth disease, which affects animals with cloven hooves, including the vast population of Mongolian deer on the Eastern Plains.

During the communist period, agriculture was divided between state farms with waged employees and collectives, where members had shares. There were government-regulated quota systems, which held things in check and also calculated for livestock losses – providing extra food during heavy winters. Today's farmers are unable to take out enough loans to cover their costs. Crop production (wheat), which began in the 1950–60s, is much reduced and has fallen by more than half, from 700,000 tonnes produced annually a decade ago to 300,000 now. Deliveries of winter fodder arrived too late to alleviate the zud problems of the past winters. The total bilateral aid figure was around five million dollars, but it did not nearly cover the losses. Consequently the government is considering the system of concentrating the most productive livestock on farmsteads, where they can be fed and sheltered in winter.

forward despite all this and the market-orientated democracy brought about through the election process seems to have taken root, assuring the country of a constitutional democracy. Many Mongolians have fought hard to achieve this despite the swing of voter support for old-school politicians of the MPRP in the 2000 elections. It is worth stating that in the wake of a peaceful democratic revolution, Mongolia, along with 15 independent states in Asia, emerged from the fall of the former Soviet Union. To speak of a direct transfer from communism to capitalism is too direct: Mongolia and other states are in a period of transition.

The 21st century opened with the usual concerns about corruption, poverty, unemployment, crime, alcoholism, domestic violence, street children, health, education and other pressing issues. However, looking on the bright side, the transition to a market economy appears to be going well. Communication with the outside world has greatly improved in recent years, due, in part, to Mongolia's internet explosion which provides broader access to world markets and is a source of information for everyone when they keep the websites up to date. There is also greater mobility abroad for government officials and businessmen and women. Another encouraging factor is the government's co-operation with NGOs to carry out a range of social programmes. Regarding social issues, the government intends to triple the minimum wage and double the salaries of civil servants, and reduce the tax burden on businesses by 30%. It pledges to increase the annual growth rate to 6% by 2004.

International donors agreed a 320-million-dollar loan package for 18 months in June 1999 and 330 million for one year in 2001 as a sign of confidence in Mongolia's ability to deal with the economic, political and social issues now facing the country. Seventy per cent of the economy is in the private sector and privatisations of large enterprises like the Gobi Cashmere Company have just been postponed again because 'market conditions' are not right.

SOCIAL CHANGE, SOCIAL PROBLEMS AND DEVELOPMENT AID

The Mongols of the 20th century have either to modernise their society
… or perish

Owen Lattimore, American Mongol scholar (1900–89)

The political swings and roundabouts of rapidly changing governance in the 1990s showed how the transition from a command-style economy to a market-orientated one placed additional pressure on the rural economy leading to economic difficulties and widespread poverty. People moved away from the cities to the countryside in the early '90s when, with the political upheavals and the collapse of the formerly subsidised industries, they could no longer find jobs. This situation appears to have been reversed at the start of the 21st century, due to the severe winters of 2000–01 and people are heading back to the settlements and towns. Alongside the population drift there were major human-development concerns, such as food security and the improvement of women's health, childcare and education.

A middle ground has developed, whereby some women of herding families have set up a shop or a restaurant which they supply from their own produce. This is a welcome change as women are coming into their own in business. However, it is a situation which also means that many less-educated Mongolian men are being left behind (especially in the countryside because they work with livestock). Both in the city and in the countryside, educated women are beginning to advance in the modern world and although schools are co-educational, women have been quicker to pick up on the more subtle modernising values of the entrepreneurial world in which they are now placed.

STUDENT LIFE IN THE COLD WAR DAYS
Jeremy Halford

I arrived in Ulaanbaatar on a mid-winter's day in the middle of the Cold War to study Mongol history. But my steepest learning curve, I soon found, lay in how to deal with the elements. I learnt that −40°C is the point where degrees centigrade equal degrees fahrenheit. However, it was ten degrees colder than even that; if you took alcohol with you to warm you on forays into the countryside, you had about 90 seconds to drink it once poured, before it froze over. Shortly before, a Western ambassador who shall remain nameless had sought to remove the ice from his embassy's car park by spraying steaming hot water on it – within two minutes he had created a perfectly smooth iceskating rink which kept his vehicles grounded for two months!

The People's Republic of All Peaceable Mongols, as it was then known, formed the strategic fence between Beijing and Siberia. But the Mongols did not have the luxury of sitting on it and had fallen firmly within the Soviet camp. Theirs was the first state to which the adjective satellite has been applied by foreign commentators. In Ulaanbaatar, in scenes which would have been familiar to anyone who had seen colonialism in action, Russians had their own housing blocks, their own stores (replete with goods Mongols could only dream of) and their own buses. Non-Russians were not admitted.

Outside the Academy of Sciences, where I was to work, stood one of the few remaining statues of Stalin in the world. It set the political tone of the state. The communist party ruled and was seen to rule. Its flagship newspaper, Unen (meaning 'truth' as does the Russian word pravda), brooked no dissent and few foreign journalists received visas, so alternative views did not receive an airing. My Mongol-language teacher at the university once made an engaging attempt to justify this rigidity: 'Imagine that the only people from your country that foreigners had heard of were Attila the Hun and Genghis Khan. Wouldn't you be cautious about what image you let be projected?'

To return from the academy to the student hostel that was my home involved traversing the huge expanse of Sükhbaatar Square. To do so after midnight could be enervating. The only sounds were your footsteps and the barking of packs of wild dogs or wolves which could be heard and sometimes glimpsed through the ice fog, circling lone pedestrians as they hurried on their way. An additional hazard was that these animals had become such a menace that the police had been armed with rifles and offered a bounty for each one shot. Sometimes pot-shots from the corners of the square punctuated the night air. Fortunately, standards of Mongol marksmanship had not suffered in the transition from bows to carbines.

Sadly, in the city, contact between Mongols and Western foreigners was

Change and the people

Recently Mongolian women have organised themselves into a new women's movement called the Liberal Women's Brain Pool (LWBP), also referred to as the Liberal Women's Intellectual Foundation. It is a women's movement which arose like a phoenix from the ashes of the communist period. From the 1990s, independent citizens' groups began to take charge and become instruments of change with more success than many government initiatives.

The LWBP was established in 1992 and has branches throughout the country. One surprising fact is that a high percentage of Mongolia's graduates are women.

restricted from the Mongol side as a matter of policy. Those that there were were often monitored and many that might have been were no doubt nipped in the bud by the understandable reluctance of Mongols to draw unwanted attention upon themselves from the authorities. So the handful of Westerners mingled with other nationalities in a cosmopolitan melting pot: it was not unknown for parties to include ten people speaking variously in seven or eight languages. On special occasions, a visit to one of the two discos in the main hotels might take place. But woe betide those who did not take their own tapes as the discos usually only had one each of their own. Little did Boney M know that they had made it to the top of the unofficial Mongol charts. 'Ra-Ra-Rasputin' never sounded so good.

Getting food was a major concern unless you were as avid a meat eater as the Mongols. Even if you were, you could still have problems. Meat was specified by the name of the beast and a quality grade between one and three (the latter the lowest grade). Horse Grade 3, I soon discovered, was so tough that my Western teeth couldn't even rip pieces off the hunk provided with a view to trying extended chewing later on. At weekends you could visit the *zalch* market to the north of the city, where members of the city's small Chinese community sold home-grown vegetables. Every few months, deliveries occurred of exotica such as Vietnamese pineapples and we feasted for weeks afterwards. On one occasion, I was invited to the opening of Mongolia's first supermarket. Along with the worthies, I marvelled at the long aisles stacked with cans of food. Only when I walked all the way round did I discover that they were only selling three different products in the whole shop.

As winter passed into summer, a three-week trip by truck was offered and seized upon by those wishing to see something of the steppe and Gobi. Many memorable evenings ensued under the felt roofing of Mongol *gers* as we drank the evenings away, experimented with fermented goat's milk and listened to the haunting melodies of 'khöömii' two-tone singing. Even the presence of official minders could not keep the warmth and hospitality of the Mongol herders from breaking through. A message to the wise traveller, however. In a country with virtually no roads, take thick-soled (preferably parachuting) boots. One of my fellow travellers was thrown fully out of the back of the truck when we hit a particularly big bump. He sailed through the air and landed upright and looking very bemused in the middle of the road about 20 feet behind us.

All too soon it was over. I returned to Britain, a small-scale Rip van Winkle who had heard nothing of the outside world for six months. My ignorance soon showed. A passing acquaintance on the bus back from the airport asked if I had seen *Saturday Night Fever*, then all the rage. 'What's *Saturday Night Fever*?', I asked. She looked appalled: 'Where have you been? In Outer Mongolia?' 'Ah,' I replied.

It is difficult to verify the exact figures, but the underlying reason seems to be that women were usually housebound and, although they were often looking after young children, many of them also had more opportunity to study than men, who did office or manual work in the towns and outdoor work like herding in the countryside. Despite this, men predominately govern the country and are involved in most of the decision making. Fewer than ten per cent of the 76 members of parliament are women.

The feminisation of society is a hotly debated issue amongst the student population and in the Mongolian press. While the numbers of women who do well at university continues to rise, male student numbers have fallen dramatically. In 2000 the faculty of journalism enrolled 1,150 students of which 900 were girls, while medical students are over 80% female.

One imagines Mongolian men to be the warrior type, bold and fierce and macho. This is true, but there has been a recent identity crisis because many men found themselves out of work due to the recent changes. As a consequence, many Mongolian men have lost their self-esteem and some have turned to alcohol and gambling (although they also drank plenty in the former socialist days). Everyone had a job during the former communist period, which kept people occupied (albeit often with unproductive shift work); in the 21st century it is everyone for himself/herself.

The transition to a market economy was very abrupt and did not give people enough time to adjust. Although small enterprises are starting, it is mainly the women who run them. In general, Mongolian women have more experience in dealing with the family's financial affairs, leaving the men feeling inadequate. As one woman said, 'Men are sitting on our shoulders. I wouldn't mind if they would sit steady and not kick so much.'

The economic transition has brought with it some more difficult changes in Mongolian society, which have given rise to street children – perhaps the last thing a tourist might expect to see in a country of just 2.4 million people. Social workers put the causes down to social upheaval in the new economy. Under the former command economy there was a safety net to take care of people's education and medical needs and to provide jobs. In spite of government subsidies, the burden of the changes has fallen on the weakest members of society – children, the abandoned housewife, the sick, the elderly and the unemployed. Mongolian street children in Ulaanbaatar have caused a stir worldwide. Foreign television crews have given huge publicity to the plight of these children, living in appalling conditions. Save the Children and other charities are working hard to help to alleviate this situation (see opposite).

Problems with health and education systems

Twenty years ago literacy was not a problem in Mongolia – nearly everyone aged eight to 80 could read and write. However, new figures show a drop in literacy. Again, the transfer from a command to a free-market economy has meant that more than 40,000 children between the ages of 11 and 16 have dropped out of school. Often children skip school because their parents need their labour; other reasons are that they are either too remote or cannot afford the costs of books and courses.

Health services and welfare systems, which practically disappeared when the Russians walked out, are in need of improvement. Before 1921 there was no modern medicine and Mongolians relied on traditional healers, but during the former communist period (1921–90) the improvements in health and education were remarkable and included the rural population. Then, during the transition to democracy, people were rushed into a new situation with little training and few skills to cope with running their country after seven decades when the state was in total control.

Ten years have seen many changes and huge improvements at management level. The main health services are still state-run, even if there are a few private doctors and hospitals, but there is still a long way to go to develop Mongolia's health and education services and, in general, its infrastructure.

Both the health and education services were severely hit by the budgetary restrictions of recent years with cuts of 24% and 53% respectively in real terms since 1990. There was a decline in the number of clinics, primary schools and kindergartens, a cut back of staff, a shortage of teachers and basic teaching materials. However, infant mortality has decreased since 1990.

A particular source of concern in the countryside is a lack of safe drinking water, as well-water in Mongolia contains a high concentration of mineral salts, and basic sanitation. The average life expectancy is 64 years (2000). Regarding nutrition, while protein levels remain high there is a lack of vitamins and minerals – especially vitamin D, and iron deficiency is high among mothers and children. Throughout the country, berries have traditionally provided a much-needed source of vitamin C. Although nutrition has improved in the city, it is still a problem in rural areas where it undermines health.

Poverty alleviation

Government poverty programmes have suffered from financial constraints facing the country in general. At the turn of the 21st century, people living below the poverty line constituted almost a third of Mongolia's population, over half of them in urban areas. Street children have appeared and begging is now commonplace – it is worth being wary of pickpockets in public places such as markets, buses and shops.

A Poverty Alleviation Programme, run by the World Bank between 1996 and 2000, enabled 30,000 families to improve their standard of living. A budget of US$15.6 million helped 13,000 small projects to start up locally, designed to generate income and also to make improvements in rural health and education. Herding families most threatened by poverty as a consequence of livestock losses due to severe winter conditions were also helped financially to restock. It is reported in the Mongolian press that the government's aim is to reduce poverty by 70% by the year 2006.

Charities and aid organisations

Ulaanbaatar Rotary Club For further information and donations, contact the British Embassy in Ulaanbaatar (see page 235). Individual cases are vetted by the Rotary Club, which supports vocational work, awards educational grants to music students and helps street children. The Rotary Club also raised funds to help emergency relief work during the national *zud* disasters of recent winters. Another example of small project funding allowed the distribution of a hundred smoke-free stoves to hardship families in *ger* compounds on the outskirts of Ulaanbaatar.

Raleigh International 27 Parsons Green Lane, London SW6 4HZ; tel: 020 7371 8585; email: sonia@raleigh.org.uk; web: www.raleigh.org.uk. Projects undertaken include: *Straw Bale Clinic project* Straw bale technology was recently introduced to Mongolia. The bales provide effective but lightweight insulation for extremes of temperature. Straw is readily available in many areas, where timber to provide building material is in short supply. A clinic of 16m x 9m was constructed in summer 1999 in Khentii Aimag (province) in eastern Mongolia, with the help of a team of UK Raleigh venturers.

Wash 21 programme The Wash 21 programme in Mongolia aims to develop a national water, sanitation and hygiene education programme for the 21st century. This gave Raleigh's venturers an opportunity to interact with local people, and to visit schools in remote rural areas. The latrines are known as VIPs – ventilated improved pit latrines.

Save the Children Fund 17 Grove Lane, London SE5 8RD; tel: 020 7703 5400; web: www.savethechildren.org.uk and www.savethechildrenmongolia.mn (a more interesting site!). Save the Children Fund (SCF), a non-government organisation supported by charitable donations, and the UK's leading international children's charity, has been involved in helping social work programmes operate in Mongolia since 1994. SCF has

SMALL PROJECTS INVOLVING SOCIAL DEVELOPMENT

International aid agencies and overseas organisations have initiated many small projects in agriculture, environment, engineering, childcare, health, education and other fields. Without going into too much detail, here are some examples of typical projects:

Shuttle Vet Project In a nation with 14 head of livestock for every person, vets play a key role. One organisation, in partnership with the Mongolian Private Herders Association, developed a new model of providing veterinary care for animal health in response to the breakdown of state-provided animal health services. The project provides practical information and training. The Vet Net Project is an expansion of the Shuttle Vet project, where the focus is on research and development of a vaccine against brucellosis, a very important public health problem in Mongolia.

Blind School The Mongolian Association for the Blind has identified that one of the challenges facing blind people living in Mongolia are the kerbs and sidewalks which are not at all reliable. Paving stones are broken, there are holes in the road and the kerbs are ill defined. These problems are gradually being dealt with.

***Ger* kindergarten project** This project has met a variety of needs of disadvantaged children and their families living in the *ger* compounds around Ulaanbaatar. The project employs a holistic approach and includes education, social care, nutrition, healthcare and a community approach to problem-solving.

Zavkhan Timber Project This project is located in Uliastai, the provincial capital of Zavhan Province in western Mongolia. With overseas help, Zavhan Province has built a drying kiln and work began on the timber products project.

developed sustainable and appropriate models of training to make positive changes in the lives of vulnerable children and their communities. Training-needs assessment was completed in 1996 and by mid-1997 programmes were put into practice. These included working with children and families and with street children. Welfare centres and children's camps have been successfully established.

SCF supports Mongolia's National Poverty Alleviation Programme (NPAP) and provided funds for a Targeted Assistance Fund (TAF), designed to provide aid to the

SAVE THE CHILDREN FUND AND STREET CHILDREN

Save the Children Fund began its work with these very vulnerable children in 1994. The Philippines SCF produced a documentary entitled 'Forgotten Future'. In late 1996 SCF opened five self-managed shelters for 125 street children supported by volunteers. By 2001 the numbers increased to 250 children in ten shelters. SCF works closely with the children's police to rehabilitate street children and to design preventative strategies to help overcome this crisis. It is estimated that there are 4,000–8,000 street children in this transitional state. There is only one institution for street children where they stay under police supervision during winter; for the most part they otherwise live in underground heating ducts during the cold weather.

The project involves a Mongolian furniture factory that produces the wooden lattice framework for gers, as well as furniture used in them. The change-over to a market economy meant the large saw mill that previously provided lumber for most of western Mongolia was closed, resulting in a shortage of lumber in the region. The furniture factory was handicapped by lack of raw materials. Foreign finance supplied a portable saw mill and two types of solar-powered drying kiln. The factory uses the kiln-dried lumber to produce essential housing materials. Buying and selling timber, hauling logs and running the saw mill are part of the project.

Goat project There are around 8.5 million goats in Mongolia, mostly kept for cashmere production. Little attention has been given to goat milk production. However, in the suburbs of UB, families keep goats for milk purposes; the goat is known as the poor people's cow. There are big problems with overgrazing as the number of goats is too great for the amount of pasture. The aim of the project is to develop better dairy goat products to help poor families have better nutrition and to generate income. The project is carried out in co-operation with the Agricultural University of Ulanbaatar. By using cross-breeding with artificial insemination treatment, it is hoped that the new goats will produce better milk yields.

Agricultural Development in the Gobi Altai Traditional agriculture consists of herding animals and selling unprocessed skins, wool and meat, while new development projects focus on arable farming, livestock/ dairy management and the setting up of small-scale family businesses. Cheese-making and other food processing techniques are being developed and women are being encouraged to produce knitted items and handcrafted jewellery and other small souvenirs for sale to tourists.

poorest families in the community and their children. SCF works in close collaboration with the British Embassy, which it assists with the British Small Grants Scheme. The latest schemes include one to reduce the number of pupils dropping out of school, and another to integrate disabled children into ordinary kindergartens. For details of the charity's work with street children, see box opposite.
Christina Noble Children's Foundation (CNCF) PO Box 74, Post Office 48, Ulaanbaatar; tel: 976 11 315611; email: mongolia@cncf.org. UK office: 11–15 Lillie Road, West Brompton, London SW6 1TX; tel: +44 (0)20 7381 8550; email: uk@cncf.org; web: www.cncf.org. Mongolian street children in Ulaanbaatar have caused a stir worldwide. Foreign television crews have given huge publicity to the plight of these children, living in appalling conditions. Founded by Christina Noble, OBE, the CNCF funds a ger shelter project for street children and orphans and also prison education and healthcare projects. CNCF's sponsorship programme also seeks to prevent children ending up on the streets by providing financial assistance to destitute families, enabling a child to remain living at home and in full-time education. A US$24 monthly contribution can change the life of a child and provide them with the security to complete their education and therefore bring them a step nearer to breaking the cycle of poverty.
Voluntary Service Overseas (VSO) 317 Putney Bridge Rd, London SW15 2PN; tel: 020 8780 7500; email: enquiry@vso.org.uk; web: www.vso.org.uk. VSO's programme in Mongolia aims to equip disadvantaged Mongolians with needed skills to manage the transition to democracy and a free-market economy. It targets specific regions where people

BLUE HEAVEN PROJECT
Liz, Shona, Elly, Batbayer and a camel called Blue Heaven
In July 2000 a group of 24 left Britain to take part in a charity challenge, organised by The Guide Dogs for the Blind Association, to ride across the Mongolian steppe accompanied by the world's greatest horsemen, the nomads of the steppes. The experience was to change the lives of three of the group, Shona Stewart from Scotland, Elly Morgan from Wales and Liz Jones from England.

Over the two weeks the group were to see the skills of the horsemen first hand, dealing with runaways, making bridles from sheep hide, milking mares and breaking in youngsters. The six horsemen who accompanied the group would often sing to their horses and calmness would spread over the whole herd. What also struck the group about the nomads was their kindness and generosity; sharing everything they had, not only with each other but also with them.

On returning home word filtered back to the women that the Mongolians were suffering the effects of a terrible winter (2000/2001), followed by a very hot, dry summer. The results in the countryside were catastrophic: millions of head of livestock on which the nomads were dependent for their survival had died. On hearing this news the three women resolved to return to see the horsemen and their families, taking whatever aid they could. Over the next few months they raised enough money to buy new stock, and also acquired wind-up torches to help the herders locate their horses during the dark winter nights.

For two weeks the British women, Batbayer and other Mongol horsemen travelled on horseback across the steppe to the Mongol's homeland near Kharkhorin. On the way they bought horses from other nomadic families, building up a herd of over 20 animals. The horsemen have since formed a co-operative with the herd, which included a stallion and mares, with the aim to build up enough breeding and riding animals to take tourists on trail rides in the future. The next stage in The Blue Heaven Project (named after British explorer Benedict Allen, whose book is titled *Edge of Blue Heaven*) has been to organise challenge trips to Mongolia. These expeditions will give others an opportunity to experience life with the nomads as well as providing funding to help secure the future for the herdsmen. If you would like to ride with these nomads and support the Blue Heaven Project for further details see: www.blueheaven project.org.uk.

need help. The organisation is aware of the importance of the responsible use of natural resources and volunteers are placed in education and training which focuses on the environment. English-language teaching is needed and VSO teachers work in schools and colleges around the country. Fire-fighting is a programme which illustrates the sort of job VSO does (see box, page 139). At present the organisation has 35 members in Mongolia, in the areas of education, health, business and social development, and the environment. It costs VSO £25 per month to support each volunteer in his or her work overseas. To make a donation, call the credit-card hotline on 020 8780 7234.

Deutsche Gesellschaft fuer Technische Zusammenarbeit (GTZ) Sky Centre 14, PO Box 1264, Ulaanbaatar 21; email: gtznaturecon@magnicnet.mn; or the Mongolian Ministry of Nature and Environment, Hydromat Building, Room 119, Khudaldaany

GIVING BACK – COMMUNITY PROJECTS

As a visitor how do you 'give back' to a country like Mongolia where people in general are so kind and hospitable, so eager to go forward and at the same time so desperately poor and backward in many ways? One Japanese woman noticed that Mongolia's nomads lacked a simple thing like soap. She returned to Japan, raised awareness among Japanese women wanting to help Mongolian women and, in this way, one million bars of soap were distributed to the nomadic community. There are a couple of important questions to ask. First, do local people want it? And, second, does it suit the practical and cultural conditions? There are numerous small projects in need of funding and one good way to do so is through existing organisations like the Save the Children Fund or the UB Rotary Club (see page 39 for details).

Gudamj 5, Ulaanbaatar– 210646; tel: 976 11 329323; fax: 976 11 312282. Literally translated as the German Association for Technical Co-operation, GTZ helps to monitor work in the national parks of Mongolia.

United States Peace Corps Contact Peace Corps Mongolia on tel: 976 11 311518/311580; web: www.peacecorps.gov. The US Peace Corps is the largest volunteer organisation in the world and operates in Mongolia, where its goals are to provide technical assistance, and programmes which allow US citizens to learn about Mongolia. Since 1991, Peace Corps volunteers have taught English, helped with environmental work and organised computer projects.

Gap year travel

Those who wish to become involved in charitable projects in Mongolia during a gap year should contact Raleigh International or Voluntary Service Overseas (see pages 39 and 41), Discoveries Initiatives (web: www.discoveryinitiatives.com) or Earthwatch Institute (web: www.earthwatch.org/europe).

ECONOMY

The three most important sectors of the Mongolian economy are mining, agro-industry and the more recently established tourism sector (see below, pages 44–9). Mongolia still remains a mix of the modern and the ancient. While it is a youthful country, where almost 57% of the population are under 25, it was very difficult for everyone, Mongolians and foreigners alike, to keep pace with the changes in Mongolia's economy during the transition period of the 1990s. This was the 'decade of change', when the country transferred from a centrally planned, directed economy under communism to a democratic, free-market system. Socio-economic changes have forced new systems of administration and vice versa. Mongolia is still coming to terms with all its new systems, including plans for the privatisation of the larger state enterprises – the Erdenet Copper Mining Corporation, the Gobi Cashmere Company and MIAT, Mongolia's international airline.

The Mongolian economy is based primarily on livestock and minerals. Mongolia's main imports are machinery and equipment, minerals, and oil and its products. The country exports copper concentrate, animal products and textiles, most of which go to China, the USA, Russia, Britain, Italy and Japan. Foreign aid promised at the 2002 Donor's Conference came to US$330 million. The annual total from all sources is much greater.

Mongols are a people who live for the moment, celebrating their folklore and their wonderful countryside. Any idea of foresight and saving seems to have been abandoned, even in the government's thinking, and almost entirely by ordinary people (with the exception of a few experienced herdsmen). Getting a feel for the new economy means that Mongolians are learning to do things differently. The summer season is short and 'hay making' (in every sense of the term) must be done or else not only will the animals perish, but the country as a whole will suffer financial hardship. But the fact that inflation has been relatively low since the late '90s, and that Mongolia has weathered both the Asian and Russian 'economic flu' is highly thought of, despite the pressures that this has put on the domestic governmental services.

The Mongolian people have previous experience of weathering the toughest storms, so despite some economic difficulties, the general impression of the 'informal' domestic economy (perhaps not reflected in the overall statistics on recorded output) is that the country is thriving. People own their own houses and new enterprises and shops are opening up and doing well. With modern equipment, printing and publishing are forging ahead while the previously neglected service industries have developed enormously, including new hotels and restaurants catering for Mongolians as well as foreign visitors.

The three mainstays of Mongolia's economy
Agro-industry
Animal husbandry is the mainstay of Mongolia's economy and represents about 33% (figures for 2000) of the gross domestic product (GDP), though only 5% of exports. The herd remains vital to the Mongolian economy. In 1975 the national herd stood at 24 million head and according to expert opinion a population of 27 million head of stock is sustainable. However, overgrazing is now widespread and is posing new difficulties for the herders. In the past decade herd size has dramatically increased in Mongolia to around 33 million – far above the proposed land-carrying capacity – and yet meat exports have not risen nor expanded into new markets.

Opportunities abound for renovating and creating animal by-product processing plants and introducing Mongolia's totally naturally grown meat, skins, and casings to the world markets. Mongolia is the world's second-largest producer of cashmere after China. Yet net earnings from the export of all cashmere products have barely grown since 1992 because of the collapse of market prices and the failure of Mongolia to attract investment in higher value-added processing plants. Chinese itinerant pedlars are roaming the southern Gobi provinces and buying directly from the nomads as they did in the 19th century, and the central government is losing considerable taxable revenue because of extensive cross-border smuggling.

The herding economy was hit with a series of environmental disasters such as *zud* – a combination of drought and intense cold, particularly the cold conditions of recent winters (1999/2000 and 2000/2001). It is estimated that over two million livestock died each winter, leaving many of the smaller herders facing ruin. In a livestock census in December 2001, 26.1 million animals were counted. International relief has been flowing to Mongolia and this disaster may be a turning point for the country. Problems such as overgrazing and poor productivity of herds are now being studied. The government realises that sustainability of the rural areas, where almost half the population lives, depends on modernising the livestock sector and encouraging the growth of food processing and improving land management.

In one area agricultural crop production is improving: the growing and marketing of vegetables is increasing from year to year and in the summer

Ulaanbaatar's vegetable markets supply root and green vegetables, tomatoes, and lettuce. In this respect the diet of townspeople is becoming distinctly different from that of their country cousins. However, figures show that between 1990 and 2000 potato production was down by half.

Mongolia never had private land ownership. Nomads were concerned about land usage and migratory rotation rights. This explains why Mongolia has been slow to create a land ownership law for crop (1.5% of territory) and steppe (90%) land. Novel solutions such as long-term land leasing are being debated by the parliament to solve land tenure disputes.

Traditional processing industries, manufacturing foodstuffs, leather goods and woollen textiles, have had a difficult transition from state to private ownership.

Cashmere

The story of cashmere is market economy with a vengeance. In recent years new factories, especially in China, have sprung up because of a boom in overseas and domestic demands since 1992. The best cashmere comes from goats living in cold, mountainous areas, with specific climatic conditions, so output cannot be easily increased, but what has happened in recent years in the Gobi is a cause for grave concern. Intensification of animal grazing, especially goats, has threatened the fragile ecosystem and a combination of necessity, greed and demand has despoiled the traditional animal-production ratios. Under socialism a series of quotas kept strict guard on production but free enterprise is now showing that freedom to produce what sells is accompanied by new responsibilities. In addition, global warming and desertification in the Gobi area have added to the dilemma.

The world cashmere output is between 9,000 and 10,000 tonnes a year. China

CASHMERE PRODUCTION

The cashmere goat originated in the Himalayan region of Kashmir. Cashmere, or *nooluur* in Mongolian, comes from one of the many different types of goats that produce wool, meat and milk. Each cashmere goat produces on average 141 grams, or five ounces, of cashmere each year; this amounts to just a quarter of a jumper! Unlike sheep, which are sheared, cashmere is combed from the goat each spring. Cashmere is the rich, downy undercoat, the inner layer that keeps the goat warm. Good cashmere is both warm and lightweight. It is the queen of animal products – delicate and beautiful – and it is also referred to as 'golden fleece'.

'De-hairing' is a complex process of separating the goat's coarse 'guard-hair' from the soft undercoat of cashmere. Buying cashmere can be as tricky as purchasing a diamond. It is precious and fashionable mainly because it is not available in abundance. The higher the altitude the finer the raw material the goat will produce. It takes up to four years, depending on the size of the goat and the quality of the cashmere, for one goat to make enough cashmere for one cardigan! Over time it will become evident whether one has chosen a high-quality cardigan or not. Poor-quality items have a greater tendency to 'pill' – a deterioration whereby tiny balls of lint form on the surface of the garment. A tightly woven garment made up of single ply, or twisted strand, of the finest cashmere outranks a two-ply item of inferior-grade cashmere. Again, the proof is in the touch.

is the premier source, producing 5,000, Mongolia produces around 3,300 tonnes, with the rest from Iran, Turkey and other countries. The combined effect of Chinese competition and free-market capitalism has left Mongolia's cashmere industry in disarray. The world's finest cashmere comes from Mongolia and it is unmixed with lower-quality produce. Unfortunately, a world cashmere glut, on top of a booming cashmere industry in Inner Mongolia, has not given Mongolia much economic benefit.

Good cashmere fibres are between 13 and 16.5 microns thick – in other words, the finer the fibre, the warmer the garment. Chinese manufacturers blend short and long fibres while, in general terms, Mongolian cashmere has longer fibres than cashmere produced in China. Much of Mongolia's exports of raw cashmere and wool pass into China through official crossing points on the southern border but there are concerns about illegal trade in cross-border smuggling. In recent years Mongolia has produced roughly 3,300 tonnes of cashmere per annum. Western consumers and buyers are beginning to discriminate and recognise the higher quality of its fibres and particularly of its white cashmere. (For further details, see box *Cashmere production*, page 45.

Mining and oil

Mongolia is one of the world's major copper producers. Its copper joint venture with Russia in the northern city of Erdenet increased its copper concentrate output (ie: which has to be exported in bulk and smelted abroad) in the 1990s, but falling international copper prices have resulted in declining government revenues (see box *Mining*, opposite). Mongolia has large deposits of coal which meet most of its energy requirements. American and Canadian companies are particularly active in developing the mining and oil sectors. There have been proposals for gas pipelines from Russia to China through Mongolian territory. Fluorspar, an industrial mineral, is an important export too.

The mountains of Mongolia, especially the Khangai and Khentii ranges, are treasure-troves of untapped gems and mineral resources. It was an old Mongolian custom not to dig the ground or disturb the rocks so little prospecting was done in the past. Gems include white rock crystal, sky-blue turquoise, yellow and various other types of topaz, blood-red garnets, tourmaline and fluorite. Silver, copper, iron and manganese are found in the Palaeozoic layers in the mountains, while coal, marble, granite, quartz and graphite are found in the Mesozoic layers.

Gold is mined in Ömnögobi Province and in the river valleys of northern Mongolia. Past gold taxes have rendered some mines unprofitable but, despite a depression in the global gold markets, this industry has seen an increase in production. Mongolia's low labour costs have helped to absorb some of these disadvantages. Mongolia has a predicted 3,400 tonnes of gold reserves and around 7,500 people are currently employed in the gold-mining industry. The income tax gained on gold mining makes up between 7 and 9% of the total income of the state budget.

All the big power stations burn lignite (soft coal), which contributes to serious urban air pollution caused largely by the urban poor who burn the poorer-quality coal on inefficient stoves, especially in winter. About five million tonnes of this coal is mined each year. In outlying areas, unconnected to the country's electricity grid, power supplies come from diesel generators. Many of these have broken down, and some are being replaced, but they remain dependent on regular supplies of diesel oil being trucked in.

Although exploratory extraction of oil has been restarted by Western companies in Dornogobi Province and the Tamtsag Basin in eastern Mongolia (Dornod

MINING
Austin Wheeler, Mining consultant

Mongolia is a major mining nation. Almost 40.5% (2000) of its foreign earnings comes from the mining sector. The major mining products are copper, gold, molybdenum and fluorspar. Mongolia also mines coal, tin and phosphate and has deposits of uranium and oil, which are not currently being fully exploited, although plans are in place to increase production if world prices rise sufficiently.

The Erdenet Mining Corporation is Mongolia's biggest producer of copper and molybdenum. It is the largest company in Mongolia, jointly owned by the Mongolian government (51%) and Russian government (49%). Erdenet exports over 400,000 tonnes per year of copper concentrate (to smelters in China and Russia) and 3,000 tonnes per year of molybdenum concentrate. In order to keep these levels of export, the Erdenet mine extracts over 20 million tonnes of ore each year. This makes it one of the largest copper mines in the world. It is due to be privatised but both governments are slow to decide how to go about it.

The city of Erdenet was built in 1973 and is the third-largest town in Mongolia, housing over 70,000 people, mostly employed in mining and its service industries. The support industries are owned and run by subsidiaries of Erdenet Mining and include a cement and lime industrial complex, a construction company and a number of farms.

Besides Erdenet, there are over 200 other mining operations in Mongolia, with heavy investment from foreign-owned companies. Exploration licences have been granted for around 25% of the national territory. The world's mining industry considers Mongolia an exciting prospect for new deposits and more than 30 international mining and trading companies have branch offices in Mongolia.

In 2000, Mongolian gold production exceeded 11 tonnes per year for the first time and if the growth of production continues, Mongolia may become a world player in the gold market. In order to ensure this status Mongolia has recently built a gold refinery. Until now it has exported dore (a semi-refined mix of gold and silver) to Japan for final refining. However, continued increases in gold production for Mongolia will be heavily reliant upon a marked increase in the price of gold, which has seen a reduction from US$400 per ounce to US$280 per ounce over the past two years, making marginal gold mines worldwide uneconomic to operate. Whether mining is economic depends on extraction costs relative to the world price, which has recently (January 2002) risen above $300 per ounce.

For further information, see *Mining Journal*, based at 60 Worship St, London EC2A 2HD; tel: 020 7216 6060; fax: 020 7216 6050; email: editorial@mining-journal.com; web: www.mining-journal.com.

Province), where it was first found by Soviet geologists, output from the wells is low. It is stored in barrels and trucked across the border into China, where it is piped to a refinery. However, Mongolia has an estimated six billion barrels of oil reserves. No natural gas deposits have been found in Mongolia so far, but in the 21st century a giant pipeline from Kovykta in Siberia to China may or may not be built across Mongolia. The latest information (released in January 2002) is that this plan is on hold.

Tourism

> Man's joy is in wide open empty spaces.
>
> Mongol saying

The third major economic sector for Mongolia is tourism. There was little reliable data on tourism before 1998. Although the country has many attractions connected with its ancient culture to interest foreign visitors, the government has been slow to initiate a national effort to promote tourism. In 2000 there were 33,232 tourists and there has been considerable improvement in the industry since then. Mongolian airline MIAT, Russia's Aeroflot, as well as Japanese, Korean and Chinese airlines fly into the country (see *Airlines*, page 155). Manufacturing and handicrafts are small and local in character but they form an important part of an industry that is growing due to tourism. Woollen and leather products, furs, wood items and wooden toys and sculptures, traditional items of clothing, watercolours and jewellery are increasingly needed as gift items for the tourist trade. The food and drinks industry is included in this growth. The raw product is available – the whole country is a natural paradise – but there is a strong need for improvement in basic services, which the industry will require if it is to survive. There are few high-quality hotels around the country and air and rail seats for travellers are limited. This does not only demand financial resources but the will to re-train and re-think. Tourism is a fragile and fluctuating industry, vulnerable to change, often without warning, therefore it is as unpredictable as the weather or the stock market, but reliant on both. Tourism is a naturally interdependent industry and its roots go deeply into the rural economy (as we in Britain have learned). Mongolia, like other nations, is learning to balance these interests.

The focus of Mongolia's tourism is nature and the environment, the nomadic way of life and places linked with Genghis Khan. It is now possible to visit this 'last place on earth'. In the final decade of the 20th century Mongolia opened its doors to the world and with air travel and the advantages of the internet, Mongolia is, virtually, a step away. For centuries Genghis Khan and the Mongol empire have held a fascination for the Western reader and many people have dreamed of going there.

The country is of enormous size and magnificent proportions – with sights to fill the imagination for a lifetime. It is a land that invites exploration and when you get there you will see for yourself the undisturbed beauty and freshness of its wilderness areas – a vast land sparsely inhabited by some of the last nomadic people on earth. Mongolia's herdsmen are still living the life of semi-nomadic pastoralists, just as their forefathers did for centuries, unchanged by the passage of time. But this may not last, since television brings the latest world news and along with it the intrusion of modern civilisation.

Ulaanbaatar is the only city of note in the entire country. Other towns are either mining settlements or simply service centres for the country's isolated hinterland, small rural settlements with one-storey buildings and a number of *ger* compounds heavily guarded by fierce, barking dogs, the worry of many a traveller who has received a nip at the heels, or been made to run and jump on to a horse or spring into a jeep at top speed.

Tourism is linked to the principles of sustainable development and may be seen in action in distinctively different branches of tourism as noted below. (See also *Responsible tourism*, pages 138–43.)

Different branches of tourism

Eco-tourism involves tourists with wildlife conservation work and environmental programmes – as volunteers or clients. People have a choice to participate in wildlife projects or simply to book into specially designed eco-*gers*, often sited in a national park visitor zone, which help the local community financially and otherwise. Eco-tourism comes in many different shades (dark to lighter green) depending on how intensely eco-conscious you are.

Cultural Tourism involves participants in restoration work on temple buildings and craft-based projects and businesses. A growing number of volunteer tourists choose to spend their holidays this way. Cultural tourism is a two-way stream, whereby the host country signposts people to major sites of cultural heritage and offers traditional entertainment which attracts tourists for example to travel to Mongolia for a festival like *Naadam*. It invites them to participate not only as audiences, but to become involved and to help develop local projects (hands on!).

Winter Travel is the youngest branch of Mongolian tourism, and is very new. For details, see page 152.

Adventure Tourism – the strongest branch of tourism – involves both individuals and groups who decide to travel on expeditions and specialised tours, which involve horseriding, biking, climbing or whatever their particular interest happens to be. Mongolia offers world-class adventure tours. See the sections *Riding, hiking and biking* (pages 190–7) and *Sport and adventure* (pages 197–205), as well as *Tour operators* (pages 148–52).

Transport and trade

Mongolia's 1,000km railway line from the Russian border to the Chinese border passes through Ulaanbaatar and several other towns. It is of great economic importance, since it handles most of Mongolia's export and import goods and it is a transit route for goods traded between Russia and China. Moreover, the main line and its various branch lines carry significant quantities of internal freight, especially coal.

The red lines marked on many maps of Mongolia suggest that there is an established network of main roads, but only about 1,500km of Mongolian roads have a hard surface, and most of those are in or between the main towns. Some roads may have 'improved' (levelled-gravel) surfaces, but most are simply sets of wheel ruts across the countryside. Driving anywhere outside the towns takes a long time and is often rough and uncomfortable.

Lake Khövsgöl and some of Mongolia's northern rivers are navigable during the summer but hardly used as transport routes. MIAT flies at least once a week to most aimag (provincial) centres, but these are essentially passenger services, and very little freight is carried. Currently there are no scheduled cargo services to district centres other than Bulgan in Khovd Aimag, which is near a crossing point on the western border with China.

Imports and exports

Mongolia's chief export, in terms of bulk, is copper ore concentrate (see box *Mining*, page 000). Minerals account for 40.5% of Mongolia's export earnings, while textiles and textile products (including cashmere knitwear and woollen goods) account for nearly 41.3% per cent. Exports of livestock and hides and hair make up another 14% of the total. Mongolia hopes that exports of live animals to Russia can be resumed soon. The recent foot-and-mouth outbreak (2002), and the fact that Russia stopped buying meat from Mongolia as a consequence, has contributed to financial problems in the agricultural sector.

The bulk of Mongolian imports are listed as oil, machinery and equipment, including in particular some 300,000–400,000 tonnes a year of petrol, diesel and aviation fuel from Russia. However, Mongolia also imports a wide range of goods, including medicines, buses, paper and newsprint, and consumer goods like television sets, refrigerators, cars, tobacco and cigarettes, beer and soft drinks.

Finance, aid and investment

Mongolia joined the IMF (International Monetary Fund) and the World Bank in 1991. It is also a member of the Asian Development Bank and receives aid from the EU's Technical Assistance Programme. During the period 1991–2000, foreign countries and international organisations pledged US$2.6 billion of assistance, including loans at non-commercial interest rates, technical assistance and grants. Much of this money has been spent on the country's new infrastructure – on banking and financial restructuring, energy and communications, municipal and other services. The government is now concentrating its efforts on developing the social infrastructure and agriculture, which badly need help.

Addressing local needs, training programmes and the creation of small businesses are part of the donor-supported restructuring programmes underway in health and education. These programmes are supplemented by direct government assistance to the most vulnerable groups under a National Poverty Alleviation Programme.

In recent years Mongolia has been able to build GDP growth achieving 3.5% growth in 1998, with a target of 6% per annum by 2002. The rate of inflation has been falling and the decline in value of the Mongolian currency, the tögrög, has slowed to hold at around T1,139 to the US dollar (March 2003). The IMF allocated its 'second annual arrangement' of about US$20 million for banking reform in 1999; this had previously been withheld because of bank privatisation problems, and since then further loans have been secured.

During the years of Soviet domination, Mongolia's economy was heavily subsidised, but since these subsidies evaporated Mongolia has won the support of the IMF and other international financial bodies as well as of generous individual donor countries. Mongolia's total aid for 1991–98 was US$1.5 billion, of which loans amounted to US$714.7 million and grants US$813.9 million. The eighth Mongolia Assistance Group Meeting, held in Paris in June 2000, provided Mongolia with a record US$330 million in aid for one year. Some 62% of aid to Mongolia until 1994 was emergency aid for the transition to a market economy, but it declined to 27% of the total between 1995 and 1998, as capital assistance and project financing increased. The shift towards long-term project funding is evidence of Mongolia's economic stability and growth. Some 60% of GDP is already generated by the private sector. Mongolia's long-term aim is to replace foreign aid with foreign investment, especially in gold, rare and non-ferrous metals, crude oil, and tourism.

Background to privatisation

In the past the Mongolian economy was developed under a series of five-year plans, with large-scale assistance from the Soviet Union. Communist Mongolia actively promoted light industry and urbanisation at the expense of the traditional herding economy. After the collapse of this system of factory subsidies and a closed domestic market, many small-animal-by-product processing plants went bankrupt and their empty factory shells dot the urban centres. The manufacture of textiles, leather goods, and foodstuffs has declined, but sharp increases in private gold production, textiles, and small retailing outlets have led the economy to grow 3–6% annually since 1995. The thorniest problem to date is the disposal of the remaining large state enterprises including MIAT (Mongolia's national airline), the Erdenet copper mine, the Gobi cashmere company, several banks, and the stock exchange.

It is expected that within the next five years most of these will be privatised. Privatisation of the animal herds and small- and medium-sized industries was completed by 1998, as was the privatisation of most of the smaller mining operations.

Hard times ahead

The record size of livestock herds (previously restricted by consumption) indicates a natural herd increase, because raw-hide production and other businesses relating to animal hides and other products have dropped below the former communist-period levels; in addition, the Russian market for Mongolian goods collapsed. However, milk and butter production has declined to the point that it cannot satisfy urban demands. Transport costs have risen and it has become more difficult to get the meat to market. At the same time townspeople have turned increasingly to cheaper imported foodstuffs. In the countryside, the paradox is that while the herders and their families are 'rich' in livestock, they subsist, having virtually no market for their produce and therefore no cash. They can only barter for the necessities of rural life such as canvas, clothing, footwear, flour, sugar, tea, tobacco, batteries and so forth.

There have been other difficulties, too. The state veterinary service, which met the needs of the poorest herdsmen in the remotest settlements has been privatised and few herdsmen can afford the new veterinary costs their animals might incur. Membership of co-operatives cushioned them against livestock losses in times of severe weather, but privatisation has broken up most co-operatives and individual herdsmen cannot afford the insurance premiums, let alone the costs of new services.

In the 1980s the Mongolian government encouraged the Soviet 'industrial' approach to agriculture, which was to raise dairy cattle, pigs and poultry in specially built enclosed farmsteads. These depended on centralised heat and electricity supplies and on deliveries of fodder and concentrates from other specialised enterprises. When the command economy of the communist period collapsed in the 1990s, these farms also broke down. They were left without money to pay their bills for wages, electricity and foodstuffs when the wholesale purchasers ran out of money to buy their butter, pork, eggs and broilers. Problems of ownership and payment have still not been fully resolved.

The giant state-owned grain farms have suffered a similar fate. Few private companies are able to operate on the same scale, with similar massive investment in tractors, ploughs and harvesters, irrigation, fertiliser and herbicides and, moreover, to obtain bank credit to cover their costs and investments between harvests. Mongolia had grain surpluses ten years ago, but now it produces less grain than it needs for its own consumption and has to import flour. For the same reasons the herding co-operatives have had to give up 'industrial' production of fodder crops, so that the ever-larger herds of animals are completely dependent on natural pasture.

The dire prospect of bankruptcy for many small-to-medium businesses in the countryside has been further increased by the hard winters of recent years. For herdsmen it has been a disaster, with millions of domestic livestock lost in the *zud* of the winters of 2000 and 2001. The changeover from a command economy to a market economy seems to have struck a heavier blow to men in particular and their ability to cope as breadwinners. Women with children, whose husbands are out of work or who have abandoned them, are trying to educate their children on a herder's income which is not sufficient, while their capital is tied up in their livestock but not available to spend.

MONGOLIAN LAND OWNERSHIP
The Mongolian Constitution of 1992 (Article 6) says: 'the land, its subsoil, forests, waters ... belong to the people alone and are under state protection.' Most of the land belongs to the state. Under the law (effective from January 1 2003) only 0.9% of the entire Mongolian territory is being privatised while 99.1% remains state-owned. Mongolian nationals are entitled to own 0.07ha per family in Ulaanbaatar city, 0.35ha in aimag centres or 0.5ha in district centres, for household use and to help improve family welfare by creating plots for vegetables, fruits and berries. Foreign nationals are not permitted to own land.

BUSINESS

At the beginning of the 21st century, both small- and large-scale business opportunities abound in Mongolia. The country offers favourable opportunities for foreign investors, with little inflation, a literate workforce, extensive untapped natural resources and a strategic location between the large markets of Russia and China. Mongolia would like to become a bridge between Asia and Europe. The Mongolian government considers the infrastructure surrounding mining, agriculture and tourism as a high-priority area for investment. A One-Stop Service Centre was opened by the Foreign Investment and Foreign Trade Agency in January 2000, to attract new investors and improve transparency in registration and monitoring activities. Free-trade zones are planned in the towns of Sükhbaatar, near the Russian border, and Zamyn-Üüd, on the Chinese border.

More than 1,000 companies from 70 countries have active investments in Mongolia, which encourages further investment. The GNP growth is forecast to remain steady at 4–6%. The private sector contributes two-thirds of the GDP. According to the national press, the transition to a market economy would appear to have been achieved despite its many setbacks, including a lack of skilled people such as doctors and technicians, but in reality there is still some way to go.

Banking and insurance

Before 1924 Mongolia had no banks or currency of its own (foreign silver coins or silver ingots were used for payments). Commodities were bartered, so that, for example, livestock was exchanged for tea. The new socialist government transformed this chaotic monetary situation. In 1925 the tögrög became the official national currency. Only in 1933 did enterprises start to keep accounts and use banks – detailed paperwork was not the strong point of a previously nomadic, religious, general population. The first bank, the Mongol Bank, was government-controlled. It handled all international trade and operated locally through its 400 branches around the country. In the late 1980s, the State Bank granted short-term credits to co-operatives and state enterprises and long-term credits to the country's industrial sector. It worked closely with the Ministry of Finance, which also controlled a national-insurance and welfare system. All this changed with the new institutions of democracy when people had to take charge of their own lives and begin to operate private businesses. There are now a number of major private banks in Ulaanbaatar, including the Golomt Bank of Mongolia. (See pages 233–4 for banks in Ulaanbaatar.)

Laws and taxes

Mongolia has passed an impressive array of administrative, regulatory, and fiscal laws to improve the attractiveness of its business climate. Among them are two

TIPS WHEN DOING BUSINESS IN MONGOLIA

Mongols tend not to respond promptly to business communications. Traditionally, communication was in person, and the former communist period's 70 years of isolation only reinforced tolerance of a slow work style. If asked several questions in one letter, Mongols often do not answer until they have all the information, which can take months. Such practices are misinterpreted by foreigners as signifying a lack of interest in a particular project, which may not be the case. Another delaying factor is that many Mongolians are unsure how to phrase or lay out a business letter. It is not the English that troubles them but the polite form – for example, whether to use 'yours sincerely', 'yours truly' or 'warmest regards' in signing off. Mongolians battle with this and find it difficult as they don't wish to offend. Taking nuances into account is very Mongolian. So it is a good idea to have a Mongolian associate in the country to visit the person with whom one is doing business, to encourage prompt replies and even write letters or send messages.

foreign investment laws, a mining law and a banking law. The minerals law of Mongolia, approved by parliament in 2001, is said to be one of the ten best laws in the mining sector in the world (for further information see web: www.mram.mn). The effectiveness of the new taxation systems required by the market economy has been reduced by delays in payment of business tax by large enterprises and firms and the avoidance of personal income tax. In order to attract foreign investors, corporate taxes will be frozen until 2005.

With the intensive development of tourism in the country, a new bill imposing an official tax on hotels and on citizens travelling abroad is aimed at improving the budget. Foreigners pay US$65 for an average hotel, while it is T6,500 for Mongols. According to the new law, a 2% tax will be imposed on the total hotel bill. Travellers will pay US$3–10 tax depending on the means of transport by which they cross the border. Unfortunately, since changes filter from the capital to the countryside rather slowly and information is not up to date, the new regulations are rarely properly understood, which tends to be confusing for both local officials and travellers.

Future plans

Future plans include the division of Mongolia into five development zones: western, Khangai, central, eastern and Ulaanbaatar; and the construction of a new millennium road (a 2,400km east–west highway). The Millennium Road Project, 2001–2010, will lead to the development of eight to ten large towns. In Ulaanbaatar a new Commercial Street 2005 project is being developed. The city will pay for the engineering and infrastructure for the construction of a US$100 million supermarket, trade and service complex, and international trade, banking and business centre. Assistance for interested businessmen is available from the Mongolian Chamber of Commerce, Sambuu Str-11, Ulaanbaatar 21; tel: 976 11 327176/312501/312371; fax: 976 11 324620; email: mnchamb@magicnet.mn; web: www.mol.mn/mcci.

The UN is working to create the Tumen River Area Development Programme (in North Korea) which, if it goes ahead, would include eastern Mongolia. The Tumen River project aims to create a transit centre linking North Asia to Europe, on the Tumen River, taking advantage of the Trans-Siberian Railway. At the moment cargo from the Pacific coast takes around 40 sea-days to reach Europe; by using the railway, this could be cut to ten days. It is a long-term vision for the

CHALLENGES FACING MONGOLIA

Until the turn of the 20th century there was a tendency to 'live for the moment' and not to bother unduly about the future, apart from the usual traditions of storing household food for the winter. During 70 years of socialist reforms (1920s–1990s), herders got out of the habit of thinking for themselves because Soviet Russia guaranteed a safety net which a market-orientated economy cannot be relied upon to provide.

Due to the economic upheaval since 1990, the Mongolian government has not been financially able to provide sufficient disaster relief and has had to appeal to the international community for aid. Relief agencies prefer to develop more market-orientated projects and they have become involved with both the herders and the government at national and local levels, so that the rural community will not become completely dependent on government subsidies as it was in the past.

However, with little guaranteed security the herders are at risk, 'waiting for the next disaster to happen'. They are, nonetheless, beginning to come to terms with new ways of working. In some ways the communist system evened things out but as a result of a series of new (and inexperienced) governments in the last ten years the country has had a bumpy ride. It was not surprising that the MPRP, the Mongolian People's Revolutionary Party – old-school, former communist politicians, stormed back to power in the July 2000 election.

21st-century Mongolia is adapting with difficulty to tumultuous events. Mongolians are dealing with multiple challenges simultaneously, as they juggle between the 'old' and 'new' systems, and experience the impact of political upheaval upon their lives. They have acquired new social political, artistic and other freedoms while they battle with economic hardship – for example, the nomad doesn't understand share certificates and still has to barter wool and hides for a living, while the modern Mongolian artist has no experience in selling his/her paintings. Mongolian nomads are wondering if they have a future in the modern world.

Future challenges for the whole nation include:

- achieving sustainable development and managing the interaction between people in rural and city life;
- overcoming isolation with new technologies, accepting that worldwide opportunities exist and taking responsibility for the country's development;
- working out ways to transfer from the 'old' Soviet political system to 'new' democratic systems, which means changing from receiving government handouts to negotiating first-time contracts and monetary loans;
- tough consumer choices and difficulties in balancing regional budgets, while keeping a firm grip on the economy;
- the need to provide a totally new system for social services and education and to develop tourism.

development of this area, which includes building towns across Mongolia's vast land and urbanising 90% of the population over the next 30 years. In the immediate future it is planned to link the Mongolian railway's eastern branch line to Choibalsan with the Chinese railway system.

The People

'There are more animals than men, so they still have the world as God made it, and the men are the noble synthesis of Genghis Khan, the warrior, and the Dalai Lama, the gentle religious leader.'

Zahava Hanan, Canadian writer and poet

Mongolia is a land of horses and herdsmen and one of the last great, undisturbed wilderness areas on earth. Among its 2.4 million people are some of the last truly nomadic pastoralists in the world – but how long they will survive is questionable. About one-third of the scant population are concentrated in the capital, Ulaanbaatar, whereas the dwindling population of nomads, herdsmen with their millions of head of livestock, are spread throughout the country. The people are well matched to the land they inhabit, they are tough, resilient, stoical by dint of necessity, but genuinely fun-loving, easy going and kind.

Since earliest times, tribes have moved across the great Central Asian plains and mountain ranges that cover present-day Mongolia, but little is known of the ethnic origins of the proto-Mongol people. The mystery lies tangled in the fact that we are dealing with a fluid and changeable nomadic society. The division between Inner and Outer Mongolia (the latter being the area covered by this guide) was effected by the Qing dynasty Manchus of China (1644–1912), who conquered southern (Inner) Mongolia before northern (Outer) Mongolia. This has resulted in differences between the two areas.

On the whole, within the city, the nomadic culture of the countryside mixes easily with the modern urban culture of Ulaanbaatar and the two often combine without fuss. This is best seen in Ulaanbaatar, where a Mongol teenager wearing a silk tunic, fur hat and long leather boots might jump off his horse (which is quickly ridden away by a friend since, according to recent law, animals are not allowed in the town centre), contact his mother by mobile phone to say he will be home late, and then spend the evening with his girlfriend, either shopping in a modern supermarket, or dancing in one of the city's new bars or discos.

Mongolia is connected to the fashion houses of the world through its marketing of cashmere. In Ulaanbaatar it is not surprising to see the latest Asian or European up-to-the-minute designs in clothing and trendy footwear. Young city Mongols are very style-conscious; chart music in UB discos is as modern as it is in London or Tokyo. Internet café culture is well established and the capital can boast many new restaurants serving international cuisine.

What is clear is that the life of the Mongolian nomad is changing drastically. Prime Minister Nambaryn Enkbayar said, 'In order to survive, we may have to stop being nomads.' On the steppes, a few satellite phones (if not more numerous trucks) have taken the place of horseriding couriers, who in the days of the Mongol empire covered vast distances at a gallop, bringing news to and from outlying regions. As more modern machinery enters a Mongolia that is beginning to abandon its ancient disciplines, one wonders what it will do to the countryside and its people. The slow and fast tracks of the ancient as well as the modern world have their individual and separate consequences. The nomad is slowed down by lack of machinery and his workload increased, whereas machines only present more problems in isolated places when it comes to replacing broken parts. Extreme concerns are that although Mongolia is open to the world of trade and tourism, the natural environmental and traditional livelihood of the nomads is likely to suffer, unless financial assistance for rural development, with stricter laws on planning, and other controls are put in place. This is particularly the case following the hard winters that in recent years have brought about overwhelming livestock losses alongside other socio-economic difficulties. Should this situation last, it could threaten the original identity of all Mongolians, particularly the truly pastoral nomads who embody Mongolia's cultural heritage. The thought that they might face extinction is an irony because it was their heritage, with its openness and toughness, which helped to make the successful switch from a command economy to a market-orientated one.

MONGOLIAN NATIONAL GROUPS

The Mongols constitute one of the principle ethnographic divisions of Oriental, or Asian, peoples. Over time the once great corridor of migration across the northern grasslands between Hungary in the west, and Manchuria in the east, became blocked by man-made divisions in the name of civilisation. The geographic origin of the Mongols themselves is from the Tungus people (the modern Evenki) in the northeast corner of present-day Mongolia, and in the west from the Huns, or Xiongnu and their Turkic-speaking successors.

Although the total population of Mongolia is just 2,373,500 (2000 census), it has consisted of many different nomadic tribes from ancient times until the present day. On the surface, visitors may only notice that in the countryside some tribal minorities wear slightly different dress, but there are differences between minorities, especially Oirat and western Mongols, and the Khalkha majority who predominate. Generally, the further west of Ulaanbaatar you go, the more different the people are, until you reach the Uriankhai and Kazakh minorities. Population figures are given for the various national groups described below (2000 census).

Khalkha Mongols

The Khalkha (Halh) Mongols number over 1.9 million and account for some 81.5% of the total population. They live all over Mongolia and their language is the state language.

The 50,800 Bayat (2.1 %), mostly now inhabiting the far western Uvs Aimag, but who may have come originally from the Selenge valley in central Mongolia, and the 31,900 Dariganga (1.3%), who live in Dariganga district of Sükhbaatar Aimag in southeastern Mongolia, also speak dialects of Khalkha.

Northern Mongols

The 40,600 Buryat (1.7%) inhabiting the northern border areas of Dornod, Khentii, Selenge and Khövsgöl Aimag are related to the 300,000 or so Buryats of the Buryat Republic and adjacent regions of the Russian Federation. Mongolia's Buryats arrived from Russia in the 20th century, mostly as political refugees from tsarism or communism. Their northern Mongol dialect has its own strong literary tradition in the Buryat Republic.

Some 2,500 Barga (1.05%), a tribe related to the Buryat, live in Dornod Aimag; on the border with China. There are over 70,000 Barga living in Hulun Buir league of Inner Mongolia Autonomous Region in China, where their territory was once also called Barga.

Southern Mongols
Small groups of Mongols like the Chakhar (Qahar) and Kharachin (about 123 and 266 persons respectively) live near the border with China in the south and are related to tribes of the same name in Inner Mongolia Autonomous Region, where they are much more numerous.

Altai Mongols
The 25,180 Altai Uriankhai Mongols (1.1%) inhabit upland areas of Khovd and Bayan-Ölgii aimags.

Oirat Mongols
The Oirats of western Mongolia are descendants of the tribes of the Jungarian khanate who survived slaughter by the army of the Manchu Qing dynasty in the 18th century. The 66,700 Derbet (2.8%) found in Uvs and Bayan-Ölgii Aimag in far western Mongolia constitute the largest Oirat tribe. The 29,800 Zakhchin (1.3%), another Oirat tribe, live in Khovd Aimag, southwestern Mongolia. Other minorities are the 12,600 Torgut (0.5%), concentrated in Bulgan district of Khovd Aimag and on the border with China's Xinjiang region. The 14,600 Ööld or Eleuth (0.6%) live in Khovd and Bayan-Ölgii aimags, and the 6,000 Mingat (0.25%) live in Myangad district of Khovd Aimag.

Mongolia's Turks
Mongolia's 102,900 Kazakh (4.3%) form the largest minority nation and live mostly in western Mongolia's Bayan-Ölgii and Khovd aimags, with concentrations in industrial towns elsewhere. There have been several migrations, including the arrival of Kazakhs from Xinjiang in the 1880s, and in recent years the departure of Kazakhs from Bayan-Ölgii in large numbers to work in Kazakhstan. The Kazakhs are herdsmen who hunt with eagles and live in *ger* similar to Mongolian *ger*. The crops grown by settled communities include melons. The Kazakhs are traditionally Sunnis, and mosques that were destroyed during Mongolia's anti-religious campaigns have been rebuilt.

The 9,000 Khoton (0.4%) who live in the far western Uvs Aimag speak Oirat (western Mongol) dialect, while the 29,700 Darkhad (1.2%) who live in northern Mongolia' s Khövsgöl Aimag, are also Mongolised Turks but speak Khalkha.

Other nationalities
There are officially 8,100 residents of other nationalities (0.3%), predominantly Russian and Chinese, although in reality there are many more than this, particularly Chinese traders and other visitors. Among the tribes of very limited numbers are 565 Khamnigan, Evenki people who are members of a Tungusic tribe in Khentii and Dornod aimags, and most of whom speak Buryat, the language of neighbouring southern Siberian Buryats. There are also some 300 Tsaatan, the reindeer people who live near Lake Khövsgöl.

Mongolians outside Mongolia
Not all Mongols live in Mongolia proper, nor are they the majority of Mongols. Most numerous are the Mongolians who live in Inner Mongolia and Xinjiang

Autonomous Regions of China, south of the Gobi desert, above and along the Silk Route.

The Hazara of Afghanistan

There are three types of Mongols living in Afghanistan, collectively known as Hazara or Hasarajar. These tribal people, living in the high mountainous central plateau of Afghanistan, are said to be the descendants of Genghis Khan's grandsons, whose armies crossed through this country, in bands of a thousand horsemen, known as *hazara* (*hezār*: 'one thousand' in Persian). The Mongols withdrew leaving a remnant trapped in this inhospitable terrain, where they have remained ever since. The Hazara resemble Mongols and are distinguished from other Afghans by their facial features – high cheekbones, broad, flat faces and almond eyes. They are also a nomadic people. The western Hazara in Afghanistan are Sunni and they speak Dari (an Afghan/Persian language). The eastern Hazara who live in Iran are Shi'i (Shi'ite) and their language contains a sprinkling of old Turkic and Mongol words. Fascinating recent genetic studies show that the Hazara people are indeed related to Genghis Khan and carry evidence in their genes to prove it.

MONGOL CHARACTERISTICS

Nomadic people are by nature self-assured and proud; they are survivors in an extremely difficult climate and harsh land. At times one wonders whether they can be the descendants of the highly trained mounted warriors of the 12th- and 13th-century Mongol khans, with their discipline and obedience. History has shown that the Mongols were indeed wild and bloodthirsty, murderous and uncouth, but it must be remembered that the early historic Mongol character has changed radically with the passage of time under the influence of Buddhism and Soviet 'nannying'.

There is an apparent split in the Mongol personality. On the one hand they are vivacious, open and carefree, with a tendency to live for the moment, yet on the other they are prudent, cautious and disciplined. Perhaps this is a direct result of their extreme climate and inhospitable environment – the same environment that nurtures in them a great sense of hospitality and giving.

The lack of a permanent home, the portability of possessions, the fact that wealth is calculated in the amount of livestock, and a reckless sense of self-sufficiency surrounds the Mongol nomads and cultivates in them endurance, hardiness, hospitality and a spirit of freedom. Each person of the household, isolated in his tented home, is both dependent on the others and in turn his own master.

Waiting for an auspicious moment is a distinctive Mongol characteristic and, in general, is part of Mongolian lifestyle. Tourists need to understand this at the start of their holiday. In many cases auspicious signs and omens help Mongols reach a decision and can lead to baffling delays, which leaves the visitor distraught, especially when little or no explanation is given. Perhaps it is that some Mongols prefer to think back on their glorious past than to move forward with the anxieties and expense of modern technology? One could say it is how Mongolians choose to conduct themselves in a charming, relaxed and flexible way. Mongolian time-keeping is slack. So take a break, switch to holiday mode, wind down and try not to get upset. Mongolians are enormously laid back.

Mongolians, like all Asians, do not like to say a direct 'no'; they would rather remain quiet or change the subject ... and naturally, of course there are unavoidable delays. Mongolians also hate to 'lose face'. They often choose to ignore difficult behaviour such as drunkenness, a personal embarrassment or a public showdown.

MONGOLIAN PROVERBS

He who has read the book of proverbs requires no effort to speak well.

While your father is alive, get to know people.

A man with acquaintances is the size of the steppe.

When the ibex antlers reach the sky, the camel's tail touches the ground (ie: don't try to reach for the moon).

The greatest treasure is knowledge.

Material wealth is of least importance.

If a man fails seven times, he succeeds on the eighth.

Something worth mentioning is the Mongol temper, infrequently displayed, because for the most part it lies dormant, placated by centuries of Buddhism. It appears that the cruelty of 'the armies of Genghis Khan' has been transformed and mellowed into human tolerance and kindness. Perhaps this is the result of being subjugated for so many generations (as well, of course, as the influence of Buddhism), so that no unkind thoughts, no shouting, no killing and so on are the principles that, by and large, govern the lives of the majority today.

Good humour must be the essential Mongolian characteristic that goes hand in hand with hospitality and entertainment. Mongolians are not just good to foreigners, they are extremely good-natured to each other. Respect for older people is common practice and strict forms of etiquette are observed, especially in the countryside. Hours are spent chatting with friends. Most Mongols enjoy a good joke and have a great sense of humour. Conversation is a national pastime in towns, whereas country folk may be shy and are more likely to smile and say little.

In business Mongols are adept and agile traders, using Asian customs and manners, although they are, on the whole, unaccustomed as yet to many forms of Western business etiquette. For years the northern nomads have had to deal with Chinese traders, and experience has warned them not to allow themselves to be tricked. As a result, today's Mongol businessman or businesswoman is a careful deal maker. Unfortunately, by contrast, herdsmen may be 'taken for a ride' because there is little else they can do in remote circumstances when 'needs must' and they have to barter wool for everyday necessities.

Mongolian nomads have survived in a predominately 'barter society'. Once money was introduced in the 1920s they used it. One shudders to see green dollar signs appear in the eyes of Mongolia's youth and even in the eyes of remote tribes like the Tsaatan or 'reindeer people', around Lake Khövsgöl, when the helicopters land and the tourists arrive. But such are the opportunities of the 21st century and this generation must take them or they will not survive.

APPEARANCE

In physical appearance Mongolians are black-haired and golden-skinned. Some have ruddy cheeks and round faces, while others have more angular features with high cheek bones and fine beaked noses (like the Afghans). Some of the most beautiful women in Asia are Mongolian and one can well imagine that they are the descendants of the ancient khans, who chose, or were given, wives from the people and ruling nobility whose lands they conquered.

RESPECT FOR THE ELDERS

Respect for the elders is deeply rooted in the Mongol character. According to tradition, the man of the family was highly respected. Wives addressed their husbands by their names with the addition of the word 'ta', which signified respect. The head of the family always sat at the north end of the ger. This 'place of honour' (also for important guests) is called the khoimor in Mongolian. His hat and belt were treated with special care and placed on a chest near the altar. He was first to be offered tea and food in a separate bowl. He never performed household chores.

His job was to entertain guests and to make all the important decisions – when to move camp, where to move and which pastures to select. Some more traditional rules forbade family members from carrying out business deals such as buying and selling animals without his permission. All important matters needed his approval and it was his duty before his death to ensure his authority continued by nominating his successor.

This might suggest a male-dominated world amongst the nomads, which in many ways is true. Nevertheless, Mongolian women, unlike other Asian women, have always played an important role and shared many responsibilities besides household duties. Although the old family traditions still survive, things have changed dramatically in the past decade. Mongolian women have taken on the role of breadwinners and since they have had more time to study they have ended up better educated than the menfolk, who have stuck to herding and the outdoors. Mongol women are wondering when to take future leadership roles. In politics, for example, they are amply qualified but lack experience.

Dress
Mongolian deel

The *deel*, the colourful national dress, is worn by men and women. It is an elegant three-quarter-length gown that buttons at the right shoulder to a high round-necked collar. That worn in winter is made of cotton lined with sheepskin and, in summer, of silk with traditional patterns and designs, in shining bright colours – red, orange, blue and green. The winter colours are darker – deep purple and dark blue – and are brightened up by a colourful sash of a contrasting colour. The sleeves are so long that they cover the hands so Mongols never need wear gloves. Heads are covered by exotic fur hats and scarves.

In towns, people dress for work in conventional European clothing, and in the capital it is not surprising to see pinstriped suits for gentlemen and chic, well-tailored couture suits for ladies, although the usual scruffy duffle coat and beret or bobble hat are more commonplace. However, everyone has a best *deel* for special occasions. In the countryside the *deel* is the practical everyday working garment and may be quite dirty and shabby from wear and tear. A *deel* has multipurpose uses, acting as a blanket at night, as a mini tent when getting dressed or undressed, and as a private canopy when there is no cover (for miles!) and you need to relieve yourself with a little dignity.

Mongolian boots

Mongolian knee-length boots, *gutal*, have exotic upturned toes and are made of brightly coloured leather, stencilled and incised with patterns. The leather is also stained in different colours and decorated by scoring the surface or stamping with a hot iron. Nowadays, *gutal* are almost exclusively the footwear of wrestlers. They are worn with thick felt socks embroidered round the top. Today country people don long Russian leather boots, or felt boots that are both comfortable and warm in winter.

Mongolian hats

The unusual spiked hats worn by Mongol men in the past have sadly gone out of fashion for everyday use, but may still be seen in museums or stage productions. Fur hats, or padded hats with ear-flaps, are worn in winter, and in summer trilby hats are popular with the men while the women wear shawls or scarves. However, traditional Mongolian hats, especially those for men, are used mainly during wrestling competitions to honour the winner. They are uniquely designed and sculpted, complete with their raised top knots and cause a real stir when worn in the West.

Traditional costume

In former times, Mongol women wore traditional silver and coral jewellery – rings, necklaces, earrings and pins. Head and hair decorations (for married women) divided the hair into extraordinary looking 'wings' on each side of the head. The hair was clipped back with silver pins, plaited and passed through two silver tubes that dropped to the waist on both sides. Mongolian men still carry embroidered pouches for their drinking bowls and tobacco, which are tucked into their sashes, along with a modern cigarette lighter instead of the ancient flint and steel! Examples of all these items may be seen at the National Museum of Mongolian History in Ulaanbaatar (see page 239).

GREETINGS

Mongolia has a unique tradition of greetings; some are only understood by Mongols, as there are many puns and hidden meanings. For example, to greet someone by asking 'Are you wintering well?' has the connotation of asking if they are happy and well. The word 'peace' means 'good wishes' and is part of many Mongolian greetings. It is a good thing as a visitor to memorise a Mongolian greeting as it will create an immediate bond with the people you meet. For some examples, see the language section in *Appendix 1*, page 373.

COLOUR AND SYMBOLIC MEANING

The symbolic meaning of colours plays an important role in Mongolian life. Three colours – red, black and white – are associated with an early culture pre-dating the introduction of Lamaism. White signifies truth, honesty and kindness. Black is representative of misfortune and disaster, and is associated with poverty or loneliness. Red is the colour of joy. Mongols also love the colour blue, which symbolises eternity and loyalty. They even called themselves the 'blue people' in the past. Gold or yellow are respected colours and the word gold, *altan*, was often added to descriptions of the steppe. Primary colours are mainly used when painting buildings. Red is the special colour for nearly all household utensils and furniture. The dying of fabrics or felt was not known in Mongolia, except by the Kazakh people in the far west. Most brocade, silk and other material was purchased from Chinese itinerant merchants. Mongolians attach specific colours to the points of the compass – black for north and red for south. Dairy foods are called 'white foods'.

When saying goodbye to guests, the Mongolian tradition is to wish them a happy journey and then to invite them to visit again and again. If you offend in some way, Mongolians are fairly relaxed because they believe that where there is ignorance, there should be no embarrassment or punishment. Mongols are very tolerant, especially regarding drunkenness.

Traditional pipe smoking

From ancient times, the pipe and tobacco pouch have been the sign of peace and manhood, and smoking (as with the indigenous tribes of North America) has specific symbolic meaning. When nomads meet on the steppe, they light a pipe. This in itself is a form of greeting, showing mutual respect. Smoking ceremonies have rituals. Before entering a *ger*, a herdsman would leave his whip outside and arrange his clothes. Inside, he would greet his host, inquire about the health of the elders, and listen intently to the replies. When all were seated, and silent, then was the moment to light a pipe.

A man's smoking set consists of a pipe, a cleaning stick, flints, a pouch and a fastener with a cord for tying it to the nomad's belt. By tradition, the pipe is carried at the top of the right boot, and the pouch (with its effects), is tied to the left side of the belt. Pipes vary in design from province to province. They are usually made from willow wood and many are ornately carved and inlaid with semi-precious materials. The mouthpiece might be crafted from silver, copper, amber or wood.

Snuff

When men greet one another, snuff bottles (with the lid slightly opened) are passed around in the upturned palm of the right hand. The recipient takes a pinch of snuff with a tiny spoon-like scoop which is attached to the lid, and places it on the back of his hand before inhaling it, or he may hold the bottle to his nose and pass it on. Snuff bottles are traditional items and, after his horse, one of the most valued possessions of a Mongolian man. Snuff bottles are carved from semi-precious stones or wood and also made of porcelain. These valuables are carried in carefully embroidered pouches and indicate the wealth and status of their owners. The demand for unusual and costly snuff bottles was an indirect, but important, sign of the wellbeing of the rural population.

CUSTOMS AND CEREMONIES
Sitting customs

There are several traditions on how to sit in a Mongolian *ger*. These apply to different age groups and to different types of people (but not to foreigners, who are not obliged to sit in any special way). For example, it is considered offensive for teenagers to sit cross-legged in the lotus position, since lamas usually sit this way. The following are some of the customs that apply:

- **Sitting on bent legs** For young women.
- **Sitting with legs extended** Natural for children.
- **Squatting** The position of a herdsman.
- **Sitting with knees crossed** Considered a sign of disrespect.
- **Sitting in a position with fingers of the hand spread out** Expresses profound sadness.

Ovoo (mountain/rock shrine) ceremony

Ovoos are cairn-like piles of rocks, branches and other natural materials. They belong to ancient Mongolian beliefs and folk religion and are considered by

Mongols to be sacred places where people come to pay their respects to the spirits of nature. *Ovoo* ceremonies take place traditionally at the end of winter and are mainly private occasions, not easily intruded upon. Local people gather on certain dates to leave offerings of money, milk, cheese and curds by the stones. Monks who attend chant prayers to the mountain gods (each mountain has its own), asking the spirit of the mountain to bless the region, to grant good weather and to increase the livestock herds. Those present – usually men only – walk around the *ovoo* three times. This is a regular ritual, especially when going on journeys, to ensure safety en route. The driver will stop by an *ovoo*, and he and the passengers will silently walk around the stones. Where and when the *ovoo* tradition originated is unknown.

Milk-sprinkling ceremony

Milk sprinkling is done to honour the gods of fertility and protection. To perform a traditional 'finger-dipping' ritual, the middle finger is dipped in milk, or vodka, and a few drops flicked in the air. A small amount of milk poured over an object is a method of asking for a blessing. It is performed to wish 'bon voyage' to travellers when milk is sprinkled on the horse's head and rump and in the direction the traveller is taking, while everyone present prays or, as the Mongols say, thinks good thoughts.

Felt-making ceremony

Country people make felt at the end of summer. They usually celebrate the occasion with a party or ceremony. The order is as follows: a date is announced, family members gather and some of their neighbours join them. First tea is served and then food before the work begins. Wool is cleaned and pounded with short sticks to loosen and fluff up the fibres. At this stage it is laid out evenly in layers on a piece of start-up felt or 'mother roll' and moistened with water. Layer upon layer is added to the 'mother roll', which is finally bound by leather straps and attached to a camel or a horse who pulls it for several kilometres, allowing it to roll along the ground. Milk or *airag* is ceremoniously sprinkled on top to ensure the felt turns out well. Riders keep the roll turning for 15–20km until the wet fibres bind into a thick mat. When unrolled and thoroughly dried the result is a blanket of felt, which is ready to wrap around the *ger*.

Hair-cutting ceremony

Traditional hair-cutting ceremonies take place when a child reaches four years old. This is a big family affair and cause for celebration with food, drink and music. There are also times for cutting animal hair and auspicious days are set for catching foals and trimming horses' manes.

Wedding ceremony

During the communist period, traditional Buddhist weddings were stopped. Instead couples married Western style – in white dresses and dark suits, at the 'Wedding Palace' in Ulaanbaatar. After the recent political changes, statues of Buddha reappeared. Small braziers (*tulga*) are lit to represent the eternal bond between the bride and groom as 'two flames becoming one'. Monasteries have become involved again in the marriage ceremony, which is nowadays blessed by a local lama.

Although young Mongols are getting married later than they used to, marriage remains an important tradition in the countryside, where weddings take place in the family home. A new *ger* is usually provided for the young couple. The groom's

OUR MONGOLIAN WEDDING
Karen Skjott

Erik and Karen Skjott, a young Danish couple, decided to marry in Mongolia in 1992. After months of planning and preparation they boarded the Trans-Siberian Express in Moscow and headed for Ulaanbaatar. This is their story:

> We decided to go by train to ensure that our spirits travelled with us all the way, which the Mongolians said was a good idea. The ceremony was co-ordinated with the help of friends at the University of Mongolia. My husband-to-be, Erik, kept everything a secret so it was with some suspense that I arrived for the fitting of my wedding dress – a beautiful silk *deel*. I knew that much, but nothing else about the arrangements, which turned out to be the best surprise of my life.
>
> The ceremony was extremely serious and everyone who took part wanted it to be both meaningful and typically Buddhist. We met with our lama in the afternoon of the first day and were immediately given a bowl of *airag*, fermented horse's milk, which I learned to like. The lama said the Tibetan calendar confirmed that the best date for us would be September 2, the sign of the snake, at a certain time of day which corresponded to the signs of the sheep and the horse. We found no reason not to accept. Incense was offered and rituals symbolising fertility and prosperity were performed at the altar along with prayers said by the lama.
>
> Next we found ourselves 60 miles outside UB, sitting in a Mongolian family *ger* – for the occasion we were both adopted by different Mongolian families – where we were welcomed by more bowls of *airag* and the traditional exchange of snuff. The next two days took us through a labyrinth of traditions and rituals. An English-speaking professor from the University of Mongolia acted as our translator.
>
> At the very beginning Erik had to set up our own *ger* where we would spend our wedding night. All the male members of 'his family' helped. The women did not participate and my task was to help them milk the horses which turned out to be quite a challenge, and later to find and capture a fat-tailed sheep for the wedding breakfast. My Mongolian father, a famous Mongolian folk singer, slaughtered the animal, which is not a procedure to be seen by squeamish people. That evening young and old gathered to celebrate the first day of our wedding. Erik was not allowed to drink vodka as he was not yet a married man.
>
> The wedding itself passed like a dream. We spent the whole day at the Buddhist temple where dancing and other celebrations took place, following a solemn ceremony. The fun part came when Erik had to raid 'my family' *ger* at night and carry me off on horseback to our new home. I shall never forget the surprise and delight of being married in Mongolia!

relatives visit the bride's family to ask her hand on an auspicious day, and are often refused several times in a show of feigned but respectful denial. Eventually, when the bride's parents agree, she receives presents and both sides settle the marriage date. The mother gives her daughter a present of some milk before she leaves the parental home. In the groom's family prayers are said and then the wedding party begins. After a few days the wife's relatives visit the young couple to see if they have settled down and the celebrations begin again.

The traditional Mongolian calendar, like the Chinese and Tibetan calendars, is based on 12 years named after 12 animals. The years are divided alternately into male and female, or hard and soft, years. It was traditionally important, in the case of marriage, that a bride and bridegroom were compatible according to the various animal signs. For instance, the bridegroom born in the year of the mouse would be unwise to choose a wife born in the year of the tiger in case he lost his authority as head of the household. Animal names are linked to the five elements – wood, fire, earth, iron and water – which match an auspicious colour system of blue, red, yellow, white and black.

For herding and other customs specific to Mongolian nomads, see below.

'ON THE MOVE': THE WORLD OF THE MONGOLIAN NOMAD

Most Mongolians now live in urban centres and visit relatives in the country. Of Mongolia's 2.4 million people only 35-40% live as nomads or semi-nomads away from towns and they are almost totally dependent on animal herding for their livelihood. But of the total population only 15% are fully nomadic, that is to say, constantly on the move. However, at heart, every Mongolian is a nomad.

Several conditions define Mongol life and culture. The principal one is that the people are pastoral nomads and, therefore, unable to possess many precious things, except the absolute essentials. In fact, they live and travel with little heavy baggage and few personal belongings. So from the earliest times they tended to ornament objects of daily use, such as knives and saddles, and to carve and decorate the posts and doors of their tented homes – the *ger* – along with small items of furniture like stools and tables, which traditionally were, and still are, painted an orange/red colour.

Mongolian national identity is grounded in their nomadic culture. Animal husbandry and herding are part of the country's agro-industry, but at the same time they are an integral and important part of Mongolian heritage. Over the centuries Mongolian nomads have not always been free to roam where they pleased. In other words, there were strings attached: ancient tribal loyalties and family ties and other limiting factors, like walls (eg: the Great Wall of China) and state boundaries imposed by history and politics. During the 17th and 18th centuries Mongol herders were subjects of local khans, under the thumb of the Manchu (Chinese Qing dynasty) authorities, when their freedoms and mobility were further restricted and transhumance practices – seasonal migration to pasture animals – were curtailed. Old herding patterns were broken. They were again fragmented in the 20th century by communist ideology and agricultural reforms.

State farms and collectives

State farms, which came and went in the 20th century, were state-run enterprises that had paid employees. Mongolia's state farms, like those in the USSR, mainly grew wheat and other crops, but had some livestock. Collectives, on the other hand, which owned most of the livestock, were a type of co-operative (*negdel*), run by a committee of members, in which herders had shares and payments usually took the form of barter. After several false starts, collectivisation was completed in 1957 as part of the socialist restructuring and development of agriculture. They were disbanded in the early1990s. At first they were resisted and herders preferred to kill their stock rather than give them to the state, but gradually they were drawn into the system.

Collectivised herders, state farm workers and other citizens were permitted to keep some animals of their own. Model farms were on display and workers were rewarded by being given medals for excellent performances or high productivity. These systems were swept away by the recent political changes.

Age-old traditions meet modern realities

For centuries Mongolian nomads have eked out an existence on the desolate, isolated Central Asian steppes, but, whatever the circumstances, they have lived in their own smaller world, happy to mix among themselves and free, to a greater or lesser extent, to do what they wanted. The nomads have fought hard to retain this measure of freedom. But recently, having thrown out a command economy and the restrictions it imposed, they are about to be reined in once more by the harsh reality of their lack of finance, which is required for modernisation and a market economy. As the late Professor Owen Lattimore, foremost authority on Mongolia in the 20th century, once remarked, 'the poor nomad is the pure nomad'. But who wants to be kept poor and pure these days? Not Mongolian nomads.

The nomadic population is not only under threat from economic hardship, but also under pressure from urbanisation and climate change.

The day-to-day life of nomads

To see nomads moving camp is an age-old sight: a dismantled *ger* and other possessions are loaded aboard home-made carts when they move from exhausted pastures to new grazing. Depending on the time of year and the size of its herds, a family may have to 'move house' every two months or so. Until the 21st century, relatively small populations and open grassland made such mobility possible without undue competition. But there are recent concerns: the newly introduced market economy and larger herds, together with the possibility that land may at some time in the future be privatised, could destroy the traditional patterns of nomadic life.

Agriculture is not large-scale in Mongolia. Potato and cereal crops are grown in the northern and western regions, where you see cultivated areas of barley and wheat. Long-distance food distribution is extremely difficult. The centralised transport system no longer exists. Nomads live on meat and dairy products from their own herds, supplemented with game and other wild foodstuffs. They sell or barter wool, sheepskins and meat to obtain manufactured materials and other necessities.

Obtaining and transporting food is easier than it was in the past, when it took a camel ride to stock up on provisions – if there were any. These days a trip by truck or a hitchhike to the local shop, which is fairly well stocked, can easily be achieved on a weekly basis. The greatest change in recent years to the herders' lives is political, although their basic living conditions and herding routines remain unaltered. Under communism, nomads were salaried and collectives provided unlimited veterinary care and winter fodder in times of shortage. Today this is not the case and the nomads must fend for themselves.

In the past, pack animals, like yaks, usually transported the household goods. More recently, however, there had been increasing reliance on motorised transport. However, when it breaks down, Mongol herders have to return to animal transport and the age-old method of cutting hay by hand, which slows them down and increases their workload. But Mongols are very philosophical and as one wise old nomad said, 'machines sometimes only bring us more trouble'.

Herding

Transhumance is an age-old practice of herding livestock in accordance with the seasons. Herding families move with their cattle, sheep or horses to higher ground when the first fresh grass appears – a lifestyle that occurs in many areas of the world. In Mongolia, the journeys to fresh 'spring' pastures are across country (covering long treks) as well as shorter journeys up and down the mountain valleys. Some herding families make all their seasonal moves in one area, generally moving from the lower ground where they winter to high spring and summer pastures as they do in the Swiss Alps. Others undertake much longer treks. Herding households around Lake Khövsgöl, in the north, use the lakeshore pastures to winter their cattle, because the snow is sometimes deeper in the valleys, and when spring arrives they migrate to higher ground and remain there until the weather turns cold again.

Agronomists say that eco-efficiency is the key to sustainable development. In simple terms this means continuing to follow age-old practices that have been carefully tried and tested over generations. Mongolian herders are now seeking the

AGE-OLD MONGOL HERDING SYSTEMS AND LIFESTYLE

The following account of the herding systems and the lifestyle of Mongolian herders was related to me by the late Professor Owen Lattimore, American Mongol scholar:

The Chinese describe nomads as people who follow grass and water, implying that any type of grass and water would be suitable, which is not the case. Nomads practise a system of interlocking rotation of pasture and animals geared to the changing seasons, and they herd more than one kind of animal. Each animal type grazes differently on the same kind of pasture and some do better than others on different pastures.

Altitude, temperature and rain have a great deal to do with the conditions under which nomads live and pasture their animals. In the semi-arid steppe, grasses which contain salt and soda deposits are good for the animals, whereas in the Gobi, low bush-type foliage provides fodder for camels only and is unsuitable for other animals. Sheep dislike burrs or grass heads but horses can graze this type of pasture, eating the top of the grass, whereas cows graze the foliage lower down the stem and sheep crop plants closest to the ground. Therefore, you can follow horses or cows with sheep but not the other way around.

A diversity of animals is the nomads' 'insurance policy'. Sheep and goats are their main 'money-earning' flocks, supplying all the basic needs: food (mutton), clothing (wool), housing material (felt), fuel (dung) and milk and cheese. The yearly cycle involves bringing livestock through the severest winters. Horses survive best as they can uncover the grass through snow by using their hooves, whereas cattle and sheep must be kept at lower levels or where the wind blows snow into drifts exposing pasture. In the past, cattle were kept in corrals with covered sheds and let out to graze every few days. Special breeds of Mongolian sheep have adapted to various pastures from high cold pasture to low and sandy grazing grounds.

From time immemorial nomads have shared herding responsibilities with neighbours. One family will take the camel herds and keep them watered, while others will see that the sheep and goats are well pastured. In fact travellers seeing animals waiting by a well looking thirsty will often water them using hand-hauled buckets of water, which they spill into long, wooden troughs. Such traditions will continue to dominate in the countryside because people and their livestock must rely on each other to survive. In the past as now, pastoral nomads and their livestock have survived and will continue to do so, not by rules, but by good practices.

HERDING RULES AND CUSTOMS
- Treat nature with respect.
- Do not stay too long in one place.
- Recognise the quality of pasture and find suitable pasture for your herds.
- Follow restrictions on killing or frightening animals.
- Do not shout at your horse – it is man's best friend.
- Choose your campsite wisely according to the season.
- Do not cut flowers or spoil plants needlessly.
- Do not kill animals for pleasure.
- Take care of the environment and it will take care of you.

There are different rules regarding the herding of cattle, horses and other animals:

- It was forbidden for a Mongol herder to ride on a saddled animal into pasturing cattle in case it disturbed the cattle who would then lose condition.
- Superstition did not allow Mongol herdsmen to count cattle by pointing with a finger in case it resulted in the decline of numbers.
- Mongols do not put a sweating horse on a hitching post on an overcast day. This common-sense rule is meant to avoid the horse getting cold, should it rain.
- Mongols do not bridle a horse that is hobbled. This avoids difficulties in catching an animal and shows mutual respect and trust between man and animal.
- Mongols always mount a horse from the left (near) side. Choose the right day for trimming a horse's mane.

advice of their elders on how to deal with the *zud* disaster of recent winters and with herding ecology.

The ger – the nomad's tent
The *ger* (pronounced 'gair') is the focus of the herdsman's world and its circular shape is repeated for him in a concentric outside world. Nomadic lifestyle over the centuries has principally depended on this classic, collapsible, round tent. The *ger's* durability, lightness and low cost are all points of tremendous advantage to the nomad.

The *ger* is more than a tent, it is a 'home', since Mongols live in their *ger* throughout the year and tend to prefer them to other forms of housing. The Russian name for *ger* is *yurta*, from which we get yurt. The *ger* is a unique model of engineering – an ingenious prefabricated home. The design of this compact tent is ideally suited to nomadic lifestyle. It combines coolness in summer and warmth in winter. Made mostly of wood and other locally available materials, it can be quickly assembled or taken to pieces, and is easily transported from place to place on camelback or, more often than not these days, by truck.

Construction details
The lower portion of the *ger* consists of sections of trellis-like wall made of willow wood, incorporating the door within its circular framework. The upper part consists of two long upright poles supporting a central wooden roof ring, or 'window', on to which numerous thinner poles are placed, like the fan of an

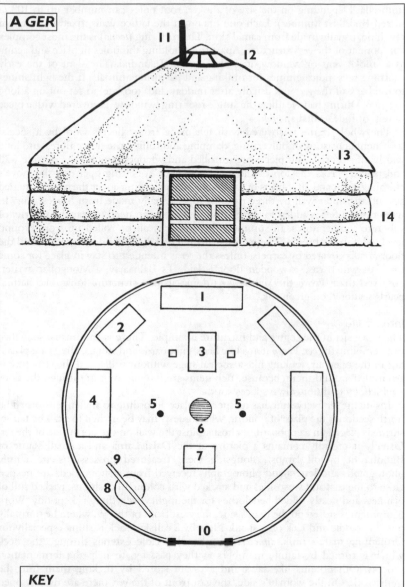

A GER

KEY

1	cupboard	8	koumiss bag
2	chests	9	shelves
3	low table and stools	10	door
4	beds	11	stove pipe
5	roof posts	12	roof rings
6	stove	13	canvas cover
7	fuel box	14	horsehair ties

umbrella. Depending on the size of the *ger*, roof poles can number up to 108 (a sacred Buddhist number). Each one fits on to the lattice walls, fixed by straps of raw hide, usually made from camel skin. The roof ring (*toono*) is the most complex component of the *ger's* structure. Apart from holding the poles in place and acting as a smoke vent or window, it is also a natural sundial. The slant of the early morning rays indicate times for milking and pasturing animals. If the light shines to the back of the *ger*, it is usually after midday and 'too late' to set out on a long journey. During bad weather, the single roof ring 'window' is covered with a piece of felt, or hide, called an *örkh*.

The whole frame is covered with felt made from sheep's wool by a special treatment consisting of pulverising, damping and rolling the fleece fibres into long widths of material. Felt pieces are unrolled and wrapped around the outside wall and placed across the top of the *ger*, leaving the roof ring open for the stove's chimney, light and air. Sheets of canvas for waterproofing cover the *ger* and are tied around the outer wall by three rows of rope, usually made from horses' hair. In winter, extra felt is added for insulation so there is no need to fear the severity of sub-zero temperatures. In summer, the wall felt can be rolled up from ground level to let in the breeze. The *ger* is usually pitched directly on the ground, and the floor area is covered by carpets, unless the *ger* is intended to stay in place for some time, in which case a wooden floor is laid. Ts Balhaajav, a Mongolian writer, observed that, 'From the air the *ger's* dome-shaped structure looks like natural pearls scattered on green silk.'

Interior life

The stove sits in the centre and furniture is simple. There is an unusual sequence in assembling the *ger*. Large items like beds, cupboards and storage chests are placed out in the open air, looking like a surreal stage without walls, and the structure is assembled around them, because such items are too big to fit in through the door – which, by tradition, always faces south.

Inside the *ger* everything has its specific place according to ancient custom. The north section is the place of honour, where guests may be invited to sit. The family shrine is placed on a cupboard or chest against the wall on the north side of the *ger*. Usually it proudly contains a picture of the Dalai Lama and a small statue of Buddha lit by oil lamps. Alongside these treasured possessions are family photographs and letters and photographs received from visitors. Beds are nestled close to the east and west sides and stacked with colourful cushions, packed full of blankets and neatly folded bedclothes for the night. Everything is kept tidy. Work equipment is stored on the man's side, the west front of the *ger*, where he normally puts his saddle and tack on a stand. Near by a calfskin sack is slung especially for fermenting mare's milk, *airag*. A long-handled ladle extends through the neck which is turned by family members as they pass by, to help the fermentation process. Other items like saws and axes are stored by tucking them into the trelliswork. On the woman's side, the east front of the *ger*, there are usually open shelves for jugs, pans and bowls with space beneath for milk churns and a cupboard for other cooking and eating utensils.

At dawn, the woman of the house rises first to light the stove. She sprinkles a little incense on the flames, which gives a lovely aromatic smell. The fuel box is usually placed next to the stove on the door side. Fuel may be wood or even coal briquettes if the *ger* is situated in one of the big-fenced *ger* encampments in towns. In the countryside, animal dung (which is odourless and burns like coke) is used. It dries out naturally in the low humidity and is collected in a special basket.

Exterior life

The area surrounding the *ger* has to be kept clean and tidy, so that the rubbish tip and latrine pit are some distance away. Some families have a second *ger* that is used for storage. The outer ring is where the horses are tied and domestic work is done, and outside that is a much larger area where sheep and goats are tended by the woman or older children. The man's herding area is bigger still, and as the concentric world of the herder expands he may take his cattle and horses to pastures and water many kilometres away only to return home at nightfall.

Herdsmen and their families live between 12 and 20 miles, or sometimes further, from their nearest neighbours. As members of herding co-operatives during most of the 20th century, nomadic families were visited regularly by co-operative officials to enquire if their quotas were being met and to check out their political duties (eg: voting in elections). Now that they live independently the arrival of an unexpected visitor is something of an event. In the past, Mongol herdsmen were always hospitable to casual visitors, and offered food and drink and even a bed for the night and it was unheard of for travellers to steal from rural families; changing times, however, have made them more cautious. They are curious and sharp-sighted, and quickly aware of the dust of an approaching jeep.

Food and drink

Mongolian women and girls usually do the milking, while the men and boys look after the animals and ensure that the herds have enough fodder and water. You will see lines of horses tethered to a long rope pegged to the ground, or suspended in the air like a washing line, between two posts. The animals are tied to this line by ropes attached to their rough, leather halters. During the summer months, weathered boots and tack are repaired or replaced; hides are tanned in a salt and whey solution to fashion into strips of leather, while horses' hair is cut and twisted into ropes. Bags are cut and stitched from cow hide to hold *airag* (mares' milk) their favourite drink. On the whole, Mongol herders are closely bonded to their animals – particularly their horses (see section on the *Mongol horse*, page 75). They are experts in the treatment and handling of their livestock.

Over the years, Mongolian nomads have developed a number of unique dairy products, which include different types of yoghurt, cottage cheese, dried curds and *koumiss*. To make *airag*, fresh mares' milk is poured into large, wooden churns or hide containers that are traditionally slung on the trelliswork or stand to the left side of the *ger* door. A long-handled ladle protrudes from the churn or sack, which churns the milky contents a thousand times or more – pummelled to aid fermentation by everyone coming in or going out about their daily business. The choicest *airag* is made in autumn after the animals have eaten their fill of summer grasses. It has a tangy fizzy taste. It may be further distilled to produce a more intoxicating drink called *shimiin airag*. During the cold winter months, cows' milk is also distilled to produce *shimiin arkhi* – best consumed when warm and fresh. When and how to consume milk products was bound by strictly observed rules among nomads, who only used dairy products from mid-spring to mid-autumn, a habit which has almost died out. Some milk is boiled in large pans to make *tarag* (a sour drink). During the summer months, cheese is squeezed between rocks to remove the moisture and dried to form protein-rich nuggets, which are preserved to last during the long winter months.

Meat, usually mutton, is eaten in the cold season and is dried during summer. Mongolian nomads slaughter their sheep by blocking the main heart artery by hand, through a neat cut in the animals chest. This is done as quickly as possible to avoid the animal pain or suffering. Because Mongolians hate to waste any animal products they use a sheep's stomach for storing butter. After slaughtering a sheep, the blood is collected in a bowl and added to mincemeat, along with some fresh herbs, onions and salt, and used to make sausages by stuffing this mixture into the sheep's intestines. The result is delicious when barbecued. Nomads also collect and store animal dung for fuel for cooking, which saves cutting down brush wood, like saxaul, in the Gobi.

Visiting nomads

Happy is he whom guests frequent. Joyful is he at whose door guests' horses are always tethered

Mongolian proverb

Few places in the world provide an opportunity to experience a lifestyle that has changed so little over hundreds of years. Mongolian cultural traditions are so different that it is possible you might unknowingly offend your hosts in some small way, so it is probably best to observe quietly what goes on around you when you enter a family *ger* for the first time. The language barrier does not seem to get in the way as Julia Roberts, the film star, discovered on her visit there. Mongolians are very warm and friendly and soon make you feel one of the family. The most humbling thing is when your Mongolian hosts (sometimes an elderly couple) insist on giving you their bed and then proceed to sleep on the floor beside you. This is not considered at all unusual – it is never too much trouble to prepare food and to share with you whatever they have.

Most nomadic families have not been exposed to the full blast of Western lifestyle and its modern conveniences – which we so often take for granted. The majority of nomads live a simple life of natural survival, miles from any services. They slaughter animals for their food; draw water from wells and carry or truck river water home in buckets – in winter bringing home large blocks of ice from the frozen rivers to melt down for drinks and other purposes. But times are changing and modern living is reaching even the remotest corners of the country. Some people have introduced technology to their camps in the form of wind and solar power and it is not unusual to find a group of nomads huddled together in front of a blurred and often badly tuned television set watching the CNN News. Itinerant outdoor shows are brought to *ger* encampments in remote places where word goes around for every one to turn up and see the show.

Tourists need to be conscious that although it is the custom to show hospitality to guests, there is work to be done. Although the lifestyle appears to be easy and attractive during the summer days, it is quite the opposite for most of the year. Try to help out in any way you can and be aware not to overstay your welcome. It is a balance which you must weigh up for yourself, since visits mean a great deal to isolated nomads and often they will press you to stay on.

The unwritten law of hospitality

The hard conditions of Mongolian life have given them a tradition of friendliness and there is an unwritten law of hospitality that has evolved from experience over centuries. Traditionally, complete strangers could enter a *ger* without knocking. There was an understanding in the countryside that should a traveller come to an unoccupied *ger*, the door would not be locked, travellers could enter, brew tea and eat there, before continuing on their way. Herdsmen shared their food and drink freely and usually provided travellers with a small bundle of provisions for the onward journey. A word of caution though; however friendly the nomads may be, watch out for their dogs – they can bite. If you approach an unknown *ger*, it is advisable to shout *'nokhoi khor!'* – 'hold the dog!'. Shout loudly in any language (the dogs seem to understand) and they will get out of the way! They will certainly sense it if you hesitate and are afraid of them; the main thing is not to catch their fleas, so don't even try to pat them and always carry a stick!

Between nomads there is no payment because they know they will also ask for hospitality many times during the year, perhaps when beaten off track by bad weather, or just broken down on the road, which often happens, judging from the number of truck and jeep carcasses one sees dotted along the Mongolian country tracks. Local *gers* automatically provide an emergency 'rescue service' which has worked well over time, like the bush telegraph.

Payment to nomads

The situation is changing with regard to receiving day visits from foreign tourists. Some form of payment is usually pre-arranged by tour companies. If not, perhaps you might consider other ways to compensate the nomads for their help and hospitality. One of the best ways is to buy their merchandise or souvenirs, if they produce any, or offer to pay for the musical entertainment, if they will accept. Bring a few small presents to give away, such as non-spicy packet foods or simple household items, books and pens for children. For other suggestions, see *What to take*, page 175.

First-time visit to a Mongolian family ger

Visitors usually sit around the stove on small stools at a low table, where various dried cheeses and fried pastries are available. First the host offers tea, to which the hostess adds butter, salt and sometimes roasted millet for taste, before adding milk. Vodka, or local drinks, *airag* (fermented mare's milk) or *shimiin arkhi* (cow's-milk vodka) may also be offered. In summer, the nomads tend to eat less meat and more 'white food' – the dairy produce of their own animals. In winter, especially during family celebrations, dried-milk products are arranged in spectacular tiers on a large dish and offered to guests.

Meals mostly consist of mutton (with surprise delicacies such as goat meat or marmot). The table is spread with great care and bowls of steaming stew are handed round to each guest by the host, who holds the bowl with both hands when he offers food in a traditional Mongolian manner to each person in turn, starting with the eldest or most important person. To show his or her appreciation, the guest receives the bowl, likewise, with both hands, or by taking it with the right hand supported at the elbow by the left. Silence means that one accepts the dish with thanks. Another way to honour the guest is to offer him or her a special portion of meat. The best piece of mutton is considered to be the massive rump, which is usually placed in the centre of the dish. The host cuts a slice and offers it first to the guests, then everyone begins to eat. Mongolians are always delighted if visitors enjoy their food.

After the meal Mongolians have a tendency to burst into song – even the most timid-looking nomad is persuaded to sing. A small cup of vodka is passed around and if it stops in front of you then it is your turn, so come prepared. Nomads enjoy this sort of entertainment. Sitting in a *ger* in the middle of nowhere, singing or just listening is a magical experience.

Most tour operators offer special programmes and visits to nomads can easily be arranged (see *Tour operators*, pages 148–52). During the day guests may accompany their hosts on the steppe, riding out to water their herds of camels and horses. You may experience some of their routine tasks closer to home, where the women and girls milk the goats and horses while the men go herding, or even help them to move camp and set up a *ger*. Then you can really appreciate and understand their natural lifestyle and lack of personal possessions.

Washing facilities at family gers

Further from Ulaanbaatar conditions are very basic. In the remote Gobi Altai, for example, there is usually no running water and washing is done by dampening a cloth and giving your face and hands a wipe. A simple water urn with an open top and a small tap attached to the base is sometimes found, hung on the left front wall by the door. A stand with a tin wash basin allows adequate provision for washing and doing teeth (rinse outside). If the *ger* is newly sited on summer pasture, it may have no pit latrine; if this is the case just walk away from the residence to urinate. If the *ger* is semi-nomadic or pitched in a settlement or compound, there are usually pit latrines in a shed behind the *ger*. Your host will point the way. It is wise to bring a flashlight with you at night.

Future concerns
Survival – a fragile balance

The Mongolian climate is so extreme that winter storms, droughts and desertification all threaten the nomads' existence, affecting the livelihood of Mongolian nomads. Summer drought and stunted forage have resulted in animals not gaining sufficient weight to withstand the ferocity of the super-cold winters of late. Nomadic pastoralists have had to roam further afield to find edible grass for their animals and some have been forced to buy winter fodder where available. Emergency shipments of grain and food supplies have been supplied by Russia and other countries, to help the nomads cope with the fodder shortages, due also to a preceding drought in the winter of 1999 – the worst conditions in living memory. The following winters, 2000 and 2001 have been almost as bad.

Recent droughts are causing problems, especially in the Gobi where water is so scarce. In steppe areas, pastures that used to exist are now arid and useless because the grasses have all but disappeared. Desertification is a gradual process when the grass is uprooted leaving the soil bare and prone to erosion. A decade of hotter drier weather means that this situation will not go away and directly threatens the herders' only means of livelihood – their flocks of camels, horses, sheep and goats – and over time will erode their way of life. The trouble is that once the desertification process starts it tends to expand very quickly.

Mongol nomads have a deep respect for nature, based on an extensive knowledge of pasture, plants and vegetation. They have managed their natural resources very economically and effectively over hundreds of years to meet the requirements of their livestock under difficult and extreme climatic conditions. But there is a precarious balance between respecting the ecosystem and the new demands placed upon it by human activity. Unfortunately, scrap metal, old tyres and other rubbish are dumped along the main routes of travel.

Large-scale overgrazing is presenting the rural economy with a new problem: it is not just the number of animals that is important but the ratio of one type of animal to another. Many ancient herding rules have been broken by the 'gold rush' to farm cashmere with the result that in South Gobi Province, for example, the herds of goats outnumber the sheep herds in many cases. Experts currently calculate 1.4 hectares per animal are needed, ideally, to avoid this problem. At present less is available.

Although the herding community was badly hit and the country as a whole suffered greatly from recent severe winters, the *zud* disaster has highlighted the urgent problems of overgrazing and animal ratios, which are now being studied.

The government has realised that sustainability in rural areas, where almost half the population lives, depends on modernising the livestock sector, encouraging the growth of food processing, improving land management, improving breeds and yields and building more winter shelters.

It is thought that the transition from a strict quota system (under communism) to a free-market economy (from 1990) prompted herders to increase the numbers of their livestock far beyond the carrying capacity of the fragile steppe land. This was particularly true of the sharp growth in goats as the cashmere industry took off. Also the rural population rose slightly and became better off as a result of the increased stock holdings, while unemployment hit settled communities. The trend had been of a population shift back to the land but it is now the reverse as nomads crowd into the towns.

MONGOLIANS AND THEIR DOMESTIC ANIMALS

Tavan hoshuu mal in Mongolian means 'five kinds of animals'. The word *hoshuu* translates as 'muzzle'. It is interesting to note that Mongolians devide their animals into warm-muzzled and cold-muzzled types: horses and sheep are warm muzzled, while cows, camels and goats are cold muzzled. Mongolia's herding economy depends on the horse, cattle, Bactrian camel, sheep and goat. These provide the herdsmen with food and drink, transport, and raw materials, such as felt to cover their *ger*, leather for harness, boots and household items, and wool and cashmere for sale.

Mongolian horses

These were the key instruments of war and conquest and notable proof of a nomad's status and success. Mongol horses are really pony size – around 14 hands high. For generations, these tough little horses have provided the herder with transport and entertainment, such as racing. The range-bred horse has great strength and stamina and can withstand all types of weather without additional feeding as it can kick back the snow and ice in winter, to uncover the grass beneath. Coat colours vary from deep brown to dapple grey. Horses are bred throughout the country and almost outnumber the human population (the ratio is 2.2 million to 2.4 million). The famous Mongolian wild horse (*Equus przewalskii*), the *takhi*, an ancestral horse type, survived in Mongolia only up to the 1960s when it became extinct in the wild. A number of *takhi* were returned to Mongolia in 1993 (see *Natural history*, page 113).

The horse
The cult of the Mongol horse

Man and the horse have been intimately linked through the ages. The cult of the horse has grown from ancient times and it was even stronger than the cult of the Great Khan himself. Horses were status symbols belonging to princes and warriors. As the contents of steppe tombs have revealed in different regions across the Eurasian steppe, horses have been worshipped – and also sacrificed, so that chieftains can ride into the next world – for thousands of years. Bones, bridles and bits tell the story of their supreme value to the nomads.

Mongolian nomads and their horses are inseparable. In fact, one without the other is unthinkable. In terms of identity, the Mongol horse symbolises the free spirit and independence of all Mongols. It is relevant in many ways to nomadic culture and to the steppe economy. Not only is the horse the chief means of transport on which the nomads have most relied over centuries, but it is also a comrade and friend. Much of a nomad's enjoyment in life is derived from his horse, as Mongolian folk songs testify.

Small, muscular and swift, the Mongol pony provided the ideal mount for the many tasks a soldier had to perform in battle. They could wheel around quickly and their size meant the nomad/warrior could dismount easily and jump back quickly on to his horse. Mongolians have so many ways to identify a horse (the language is rich in horse descriptions) that they have no need to give them individual names. One way to describe a good horse is to say his eyes are full of fire. Genghis Khan himself was described as having fire in his eyes – recorded in *The Secret History of the Mongols*. In many respects his success was due to the lifestyle of the nomads and above all to the stocky, range-bred Mongol pony which gave his army the mobility it needed.

The horse and the pace of life

Riding, I soon found, wasn't much fun.

Beatrice Buxtrode, 19th-century traveller

The herder's pace of life is governed by the speed of a horse. The Mongolian horse has eight different paces, one of which is ambling. Some Mongol ponies will automatically break into this pace over long distances as it is much more comfortable for the rider. The range horses give a thoroughly uncomfortable ride. The solution is to do what the Mongolian herdsmen do, and rise at the trot and stay standing in the stirrups, balancing with the legs and letting the ankle, knee and thigh joints take the strain. That is all very well if you have cast-iron leg muscles, but if you haven't, as travellers have discovered, it is agony. On other occasions the herdsman's technique is to allow his body to relax, and here *airag* or vodka serves its purpose, helping him to sit (or slump) in the saddle, relaxing every limb.

Riding equipment
Saddles

Saddles are decorative as well as functional. Often the more ornate saddles belonged to women and were a part of their dowry. Decorative saddles are prized possessions in Central Asia both as items of daily use and as examples of material wealth. The pommel, or front part of the saddle, is high and the back part curves. The seat is hard and uncomfortable. Felt or fleece padding enables the rider to sit astride with more comfort. Although it is customary for Westerners to rise to the trot on every second stride, Mongol horsemen usually stand in their stirrups avoiding the bumpy, seated position. On expedition or riding tours there is no need to bring a Western riding saddle as a Russian or leather Mongol riding saddle is adequate.

Ironwork and the bit

According to the 13th-century Persian historian Rashid-ad-Din, the Mongol tribes of 2,000 years ago were so fierce that they destroyed one another until just four couples remained. They settled in a remote valley and begat a new nation. These pioneers discovered how to forge iron by making a huge bellows from the skins of bulls and horses that they used to smelt iron ore at high temperatures by burning surface coal and wood. The trade of the blacksmith began. Iron bits, found in Altai tombs, date back to the 5th century BC.

Cattle (including yak)

Concentrated in the central and northern provinces and raised for meat and milk. Cattle graze close to nomadic settlements and often take themselves to pasture and return in the evening with little attention from the herder. Yaks and *haynags* (cow/yak cross) account for a fifth of the country's cattle. Yaks (Tibetan oxen) number 500,000.

They are shaggy beasts but agile and well adapted to high mountain pastures, because their long, thick hairy coats can withstand the cold. Yak hair is collected by plucking after the winter is over. They are used to transport *gers* in the northern regions. Clotted cream (*öröm*), is partially dried to turn into soft round cakes – a high-cholesterol treat! Yak milk is particularly rich and makes delicious yoghurt.

Sheep

Raised for wool and meat. Mutton is the staple food of Mongolia and sheep's milk is made into cheese and curds, which are dried in summer for winter use. Selection and cross breeding have developed different varieties of sheep in different regions: in the east the black-headed fat-tailed sheep predominate; the Orkhon Valley sheep are known for their semi-fine fleece; and the long large-tailed sheep have coarse but very white wool. Argali (*Ovis ammon*), the rare Mongolian wild sheep variety, are also known as 'blue sheep' or 'Marco Polo sheep'. They are found in the Gobi Altai mountains and hunted by trophy hunters.

Goats

Famous for their hair (cashmere), not for their meat. They are herded with sheep and are concentrated in the central and southwestern provinces. The national herd numbers around 9.7 million. Cashmere is the rich, downy undercoat, the inner layer that keeps the goats warm. In spring, cashmere is combed (not sheared, like wool from sheep) from the goats' underbelly and back. The fibres of Mongolian cashmere are top quality, long and very fine. Mongolia accounts for about 30% of the world's raw cashmere exports.

Bactrian camels

The two-humped variety. Used for riding and as draught animals. They can carry up to 200kg. Their meat is not usually eaten, but their milk is made into curds and cheese. Camels are concentrated in southern and western provinces and numbered about 285,000 in 2001. Some people comb out, others shear, the hair in June. Camel wool (for blankets and other garments) provides a good source of income for the herders. In recent times the camel population has been in gradual decline. But there is grave concern among conservationists about the plight of the wild camels (*khavtgai*) found in the Gobi regions, because they are becoming dangerously few in number (see box *Wild camels*, pages 302–3).

HOW THE MIGHTY CAMEL LOST HIS ANTLERS

The following is a folk tale explaining how the camel came to lose its antlers:

> One day the camel went down to the spring for a drink. There he met a deer, which had been looking longingly at his magnificent set of antlers. Finally the deer plucked up courage and asked if he could borrow the camel's antlers for just one day. The camel, being a generous beast, said, 'Yes, of course you may borrow my fine antlers.' The following day he went to the spring to retrieve his precious headgear, but there was no sign of the deer. To this day the camel will raise his head when drinking and look out across the country in search of the deer and his missing antlers.

Mongolians describe the camel's trait as being one who is over-generous to his own cost.

Camel milk and riding habits

The two-humped Bactrian camel, unlike the one-humped dromedary, can survive exceedingly cold temperatures. Newly born camels (*botgo*) arrive at the end of the long, hard winter when there is hope of fresh grazing in March or April. Yearlings (*torom*) are tied to a rope on the ground while their mothers are milked. Milking is a special skill and females have to be coaxed by whistles and songs to let down milk. Camels' milk tastes slightly tangy and rather salty. It is not everyone's favourite drink.

Bactrian camels live to be 14 or 15 years old and can be ridden from the age of five or six. A camel saddle is made without any wood and fits snugly between the two humps. The camel's gait is unlike a horse's but one soon gets used to its sway and horseriders will easily adapt. The camel saddle is more comfortable than the traditional horses' saddle with its thick under-saddle carpet and thicker top-saddle carpet.

The foot area of the camel stirrup is almost round in shape and made of a much heavier metal than a Western riding stirrup. The camel drops to its knees to enable you to mount. This may not always be easy, depending on the temperament of your camel – and they are temperamental creatures. Camel halters are made from rope attached to a peg in the nose. Reining is 'cowboy-style' neck reining – rein to the right to go right, rein to the left to go left. Stopping is more difficult for beginners and the word 'whoa!' (which is the same in Mongolian) is accompanied by a tug on the rein. If for any reason your camel bolts, take a good hold, hang on and relax as it will eventually run out of steam.

LANGUAGE

When the Mongol empire collapsed, the majority of Mongols returned to their beloved uplands. They settled back to their usual herding occupations and fought among themselves – forgetting about military conquests. Despite such isolation, the Mongol language was greatly enriched by its international past.

Mongolian (Mongol) is an Altaic language, related to the Turkish spoken in modern Turkey and other Turkic languages of Central Asia like Kazakh and Tuvan. It is the language of the majority Khalkha Mongols. Together with its various dialects, it is spoken by some six million people in Mongolia, Russia and China. There are four main dialects:

- **Oirat** Spoken in the western regions.
- **Buryat** Spoken on the northern borders near Lake Baikal.
- **Khalkha** The main dialect of Mongolia.
- **Inner Mongolian dialects** Found among people living near Mongolia's southern borders; corresponding to the dialects of similar adjacent tribes in Inner Mongolia.

The Mongol-Turkic vocabulary of the ancient nomads has expanded over the centuries to embrace Tibetan and Sanskrit expressions from Buddhism, Chinese and Manchu words introduced during the rule of the Qing dynasty rule, Russian technical and political terms from the period of Soviet influence, and, during the 1990s, English words that are part of the international language of commerce, science and computers.

Transcription, spelling and pronunciation

Mongolian has many sounds that are unfamiliar and difficult for English speakers. It is not an easy language to learn and its transcription is complex. Mongol words consist of stems to which suffixes may be attached consecutively (ie: agglutinated).

Altaic languages feature vowel harmony which means that 'back' and 'front' vowels (produced at the back and the front of the mouth) do not mix together in the same word, so the vowels of the suffixes harmonise with those of the stems.

New Mongolian spelling doubles its vowels to indicate a stressed vowel length. Thus 'Ulan Bator' becomes 'Ulaanbaatar'. The choice of h or kh in transliteration is a difficult one, as there is currently no standard transcription system for translators to follow. The letter x in Cyrillic is rendered as either h or kh; I have opted in this guide for the most used system of kh, which sounds like the ch in 'loch', as pronounced with a raspy Scottish accent. The use of i and y also varies. The endings g or k, and to a lesser extent d and t, are practically impossible to distinguish by ear. There is little consistency and until very recently practically no guidance for the beginner wishing to study Mongolian. Words run together. Often the first syllables are the accented ones, while the rest of the word tails off in a 'shwoosh' of descending tones. There is no agreement about the spelling of Mongol names in foreign languages – some books use one system, and some another; what one has to watch out for is a random mixture.

In this guide the most common Mongolian words like *khan* and *aimag* are not printed in italics, but other Mongolian words like *airag* (vodka), *deel* (Mongol tunic/dress*)* and *ovoo* (cairn) are printed in italics. For further information, see *Appendix 1, Language*, page 373.

Script

Mongol was put into writing 800 years ago on Genghis Khan's orders, according to *The Secret History of the Mongols*. Mongolia has used a number of scripts throughout its history but the most used has been the Uighur Mongolian script. The Mongol script is based on the 14-letter Uighur alphabet, derived in turn from Sogdian. Uighur and Sogdian were both written horizontally and vertically, but Mongolian script is written in vertical columns from left to right. Its letters vary slightly in shape depending on whether they are at the beginning, the middle or the end of a word, as in Arabic. Over the centuries some new letters were introduced into the Mongol script, initially to reduce ambiguity, and later in order to incorporate certain Tibetan and Russian words. Attempts to reintroduce the Uighur Mongolian script in recent years have failed because Mongolian cursive script had been abandoned in favour of Russian Cyrillic – children were not taught to write it, books were not printed in the 'old' Mongolian writing, and during the 20th century only grandfathers and grandmothers kept it alive. Schools and other institutions thought it would prove too disruptive to introduce, and there was also a shortage of suitable typesetting equipment. Most people tended to prefer a modified Cyrillic for everyday use.

Khalkha Mongolian is written in the Russian Cyrillic alphabet with two extra letters. Following a political decision in the 1940s to abandon the experimental romanisation of Mongol and minority languages in the USSR, this modified Cyrillic alphabet was brought into general use in Mongolia in 1946. It is much closer to modern spoken Mongolian than the classical language of the Mongol script, whose use was discouraged.

RELIGION

> Mongolian herders have a reverence for the land, although many will tell
> you they don't know why they feel this way.

> Anonymous

Shamanism and folk religion have ancient roots. But as the Mongol empire expanded, the Mongols came into contact with Nestorian Christianity, Buddhism and Islam. Each established some influence at the Mongol court. Genghis Khan seems to have been interested in Tibetan Buddhism and Christianity, although this bred rivalry among the shamans. It is said that Genghis Khan was interested in all religions and in none. Mongolia was converted to Tibetan-style Buddhism twice, first by the example of Kublai Khan, Genghis Khan's grandson, who adopted it as the state religion in the 13th century, and again in the 16th century, when Altan Khan took Buddhist vows.

As of mid-1999, there were some 136 registered monasteries, temples, mosques and churches in Mongolia. About 120 of these were active Buddhist monasteries and temples with some 5,000 lamas (monks) holding regular religious services. The numbers are imprecise because there are many small Buddhist temples in the Mongolian countryside that are opened only for festivals. Others are *ger süm*, or felt 'temple-tents', for religious services at the sites of monasteries and temples destroyed during the anti-religious campaigns of the 1930s.

Communist ideology persecuted all religions, and both monks and shamans were killed by the thousands during political purges. Since 1990 there has been more freedom to practise religion. Buddhism, the main belief, has experienced a strong resurgence. While it would be true to say that Mongolians respect, even revere, religious rituals and practices, communist ideology shattered their beliefs. Although some say that in the past Lamaism burdened the ordinary people with an impossible degree of servitude, when the ideals of communism were snuffed out, a vacuum was created for both spiritual and political 'belief'.

Mongolians in the 21st century are reviving their grandparents' religious beliefs and many are open to the acceptance of other faiths. Christianity is an alternative religion and appeals to young people, who are keen to trust more and learn new values following the collapse of communism. Shamanism has also been revived and has an interest for cultural reasons.

Shamanism

This religion, the oldest religion practised in Mongolia, centres on beliefs and rituals associated with a shaman, a man or woman regarded as having access to the 'spirit world'. Mongolian shamans enter an ecstatic trance state in which the shaman is empowered to engage with the spirits in order to protect and heal members of the community, to guide souls and cure illnesses. Shamanism is found in many primitive cultures like those of the Siberian Tungus, from whose language the word shaman (*samán*) derives. Under Genghis Khan's rule, the 'eternal blue

OVOOS – SACRED STONES

These cairns of stones and rocks occur on mountain passes and at crossroads. They are sacred, ceremonial places. Most people are unaware of why they walk around an *ovoo* and will admit to not knowing why with a shrug of their shoulders. They do it to make sure the truck doesn't break down or that things go well on a journey. According to an ancient rite it is proper to walk around the *ovoo* three times in a clockwise direction. *Ovoo* ceremonies led by a lama are meant to banish demons and plagues, stop wolves from attacking flocks, and thieves and brigands from attacking travellers. Another explanation is that in the days of Genghis Khan, each warrior accompanying him on a campaign had to place a stone on a pile. On return, each warrior removed a stone and the number left on the pile indicated the number killed in action.

sky' was idolised as the source of his power. A shaman at his court named Kököchü was appointed *Teb Tenggeri* ('great heaven'), and would select favourable days for moving camp, getting married, declaring war, or choosing a successor. He tried to stir up trouble between Genghis Khan and his brother Qasar, and had his back broken as a punishment by order of the khan. Shamanism is a faith without books. All teaching and instruction has been given orally, passed from shaman to shaman over the centuries, and its traditions learned by heart.

Shamanism went underground and almost died out during the former communist period. Becoming a shaman involves the gift of divination, such as psychic power, and further involves initiation rites. His or her dress also has symbolic significance; in some cases it is decorated with gleaming plates, bells and strips of cloth, all attached to the costume. The shaman might wear a headdress to resemble a bird, with the tail of a pheasant and the body costume of a fish. Drums are used to help the shaman enter the trance-like state, as chanting begins and the shaman 'transcends' into another world while the body dances, swirls or totters with jerky movements. Post trance, the shaman sometimes tells those present about the experience to help cure the sick, or just collapses with exhaustion on the floor. People are very secretive about the whole subject and it is not something they like to discuss.

Folk religion

Folk religion is concerned with individuals and families and, like shamanism, has ancient roots and traditions. It is based upon superstitious beliefs and involves the worship of sky, fire and ancestors. Incense is burned and blessings chanted. In contrast to shamanism, these prayers were written down. Many of the ancient rituals and ceremonies, such as the *ovoo* ceremonies (see box opposite), are steeped in a mixture of folk and other religions. The 'white old man' appears in many folk prayers. He is portrayed dressed in white, leaning on a stick and has a long white beard. His title is 'lord of the earth and the waters'. Mythological figures include Geser Khan, son of Hurmast Khan, ruler of the heavens. Equestrian deities bestow good fortune on hunting and protect flocks and herds, allowing the 'windhorse flag' to fly, which guards domestic stock from predators such as wolves. Mounted deities are said to have military prowess.

Buddhism

Buddhism is a world religion with a historical founder, Prince Siddhartha Gautama. He is thought to have lived between 563 and 483BC. Buddhism, like Hinduism, teaches that reincarnation (a cycle of death and rebirth) is based on karma (acts or deeds). When Buddha became 'enlightened', he achieved a blissful state known as nirvana. In so doing he eliminated the causes and cycle of rebirth. The Buddhist doctrine contains 'Four Noble Truths' and the 'Noble Eightfold Path'. The Four Noble Truths state the following:

- To exist is to suffer
- Suffering is caused by attachment
- Suffering ceases once attachment ceases
- There is a 'way' to end suffering

The Noble Eightfold Path involves:

- Right speech
- Right livelihood
- Right action

SKY BURIAL

Until the 20th century, the Mongols practised Lamaist 'sky burial' (like the Tibetans). The dead were laid on the ground in designated places and after a simple lama ceremony, abandoned for nature to take its course. This practice was stopped after the communists took over and burial became the custom. If you visit graveyards in the Ulaanbaatar area, you may see graves with motorcar engine fans spinning in the wind – the modern equivalent of the temple prayer wheel.

- Right effort
- Right mindfulness
- Right concentration
- Right opinion
- Right intention

The aim is to achieve wisdom beyond mere faith and instruction. Subsequent stages, called 'attainments', bring awareness and joy and finally there is a cessation of perception and feeling. A monk's duties are his spiritual exercises and the instruction of novices and lay people. Esoteric Buddhism (Vajrayana) was practised in Mongolia. It shortens this process, but for this you need a teacher or 'guru'. Tantric Buddhism is symbolised by the union of male compassion with female insight – often depicted in art form by an embrace, known in Tibetan as yab-yum. The 16th century saw the massive conversion of Mongols to Tantric Buddhism, as practised in Tibet.

History of Mongolian Buddhism

Kublai Khan appointed a Tibetan lama, Phagspa Lama, to be the spiritual leader of his Yuan dynasty. Phagspa Lama interpreted Mahayana Buddhism so as to make Kublai Khan a Buddhist 'universal king' – an important agreement giving Kublai the temporal power and Phagspa the religious power. This form of Tibetan Buddhism combined the scholarly Sakyapa doctrine with tantric mysticism and ritual; it is sometimes called 'Red Hat' lamaism, after the red hats worn by its followers. In Mongolia monasteries were built and texts translated, but Buddhism took firm root only among the Mongol aristocracy. When the Yuan dynasty fell in 1368 the Mongols reverted to Shamanism.

A school of reformed Buddhism called Gelugpa was founded in Tibet at the end of the 14th century, and because the lamas wore yellow hats during ceremonies it became known as 'Yellow Hat' lamaism. It began to spread in Mongolia in the second half of the 16th century. Altan Khan, who considered himself the successor of Kublai Khan, met the Tibetan leader Sonam Gyatso and awarded him the title of 'Dalai Lama' – dalai means 'ocean' or 'all-encompassing' in Mongolian and lama means 'spiritual master' in Tibetan. Buddhism was adopted as the official religion in Mongolia and the first Buddhist centre was developed at the monastery of Erdene Zuu in the Orhon Valley.

Tibetan lamas came to Mongolia in large numbers to organise the systematic translation of religious literature into Mongolian, and this in turn greatly encouraged the growth of literacy amongst Mongols and the flourishing of Mongol culture. Altan Khan banned ancient rites of sacrifice at funerals but, while opposing Shamanism, the new religion absorbed some Shamanist rituals, in particular the mountain-top *ovoo* ceremonies (see box *Ovoos – sacred stones*, page 80).

In 1639 Tüsheet Khan, who claimed descent from Genghis Khan, proclaimed his five-year-old son Zanabazar as the highest incarnate lama in Mongolia, and bestowed on him the title Öndör Gegeen. After his monastic studies in Tibet, Zanabazar was recognised by the Dalai Lama and became the head of Mongolian Buddhism. In the course of his long life, Zanabazar did much to cultivate Buddhism in Mongolia, establishing monasteries and temples. He devised a new alphabet and was also a great artist and sculptor (see page 98). He is also credited with the founding of the Mongolian capital of Urga, now called Ulaanbaatar.

The Bogd Khan ('Holy Khan')

Mongolia has had a succession of eight High Lamas, or Öndör Gegeens, who rank after the Dalai Lamas and Panchen Lamas. The eighth Öndör Gegeen had a marathon-length name, not often referred to for obvious reasons: Javzandamba Agvaanluvsanchoijindanzanvaanchigbalsambuu. He was born in Tibet in 1869, enthroned in Urga in 1874, and made the Mongolian head of state in 1911, when the Manchu rule over Mongolia finally collapsed. As head of the church and state he became the 'Holy Khan' or Bogd Khan, monarch of a theocracy.

The Bogd Khan was ill and weak, and most accounts say that he was manipulated by the Mongol princes who took advantage of his authority. The Bogd Khan was briefly held prisoner at Manzshir monastery by the Chinese. After the victory of the nationalist revolution in Mongolia in July 1921, the Bogd Khan remained head of state, although over the next few years his powers were greatly restricted. The Bogd Khan died in May 1924, and the then increasingly communist ruling party in Mongolia decreed that the search for his incarnation was forbidden. In 1927 all new incarnations were banned. His Russian-style two-storey winter palace has become a museum (see *The Bogd Khan's Green Palace, Ulaanbaatar*, page 236).

Buddhism under communism

The Buddhist Church in Mongolia remained very powerful and wealthy in the 1920s. It controlled perhaps 700 monasteries and temples with large estates and thousands of lamas and monastery serfs. As the young communists consolidated their political position and promoted their reforms, the aristocracy and high lamas

VISITING A BUDDHIST MONASTERY

- Visitors should speak in low voices and watch how Mongolians act.
- Mongols worship by turning prayer wheels and by chanting prayers. Prayer wheels are supposed to be filled with prayers on the inside and are decorated with prayerful inscriptions on the outside. The idea for the devout believers who turn the wheel is that by so doing they acquire as much merit as if they were repeating the prayers themselves. Setting prayer drums in motion has the same effect.
- Visitors who wish to offer money may do so, but should not give torn or crumpled notes.
- Do not take photographs or videos inside a temple without the written or oral permission of the head lama.
- Gifts may be purchased. You may also commission paintings of a Buddhist nature. Prayers for specific people may be said and offerings given. Do not buy consecrated items unless you are a believer.

THE DALAI LAMA VISITS MONGOLIAN BUDDHISTS

His Holiness the 15th Dalai Lama first visited Mongolia in 1979. His fairly frequent visits are always a source of inspiration and a cause for celebration among Mongolia's Buddhists. Across the open steppe, conch shells and long horns announce his arrival. During his visit in 1997 he spoke to an audience of thousands, urging the people to drink less vodka and suggesting they stick to mares' milk (which is less intoxicating). He appealed for help for street children. Throughout his visit people hung on his every word. The Dalai Lama always draws enormous, enthusiastic crowds. But his status in Mongolia is anomalous. Because of sensitivities about the Chinese control of Tibet, the Mongolian government cannot host the Dalai Lama, who visits as a private individual. Even more anomalous is the position of the Tibetan lama, recognised to be the eighth Öndör Gegeen, leader of Mongolian Buddhism by the Dalai Lama. He lives at the Dalai Lama's headquarters in Dharamsala and visited Mongolia for the first time in the summer of 1999. He was taken to Erdene Zuu and enthroned, but the Mongolian government was nervous because of a visit by the Chinese president.

(the 'black and yellow feudalists') became their chief targets. Following the enactment of a law to limit the powers of religion, in 1926 an uprising of lamas in eastern Mongolia was suppressed. In 1929/30 the country's political rulers set about expropriating feudal property, and in March 1930 there were new uprisings by lamas from western Mongolia. Further counter-revolutions were fiercely suppressed.

In 1935 a new law was published requiring lamas to leave their monasteries and go to work in society, by which the political leaders meant get proper jobs. As the political purges gained momentum, monasteries were closed by the army. Monasteries were looted and precious paintings and religious sculptures were destroyed. Lamas were forced to work on the land, to join the army and even to marry, all of which were contrary to their beliefs. To resist meant to be shot, and many were.

Nearly all the capital's many monasteries and temples were destroyed. The Gandantegchinlen monastery (known as Gandan for short) was closed for many years but somehow survived, to become a showpiece for religious freedom, with a few practising lamas. Folk religion and Shamanism were practised in secret. Otherwise the country was devoid of religious activity.

Buddhism today

In the summer of 1990 everything changed. Russian advisors withdrew from Mongolia and the country was freed from the anti-religious sentiment of communism. Monks, under the guise of ordinary citizens, returned to practise their faith openly. Family shrines were unveiled and monasteries began to accept new young monks for training. Mongolian abbots are committed to preserving and promoting the teachings of Buddhism in Mongolia. Prior to this there had been some concessional changes, like the visits of the Dalai Lama and the opening of monastery schools in the 1980s. Following the Buddhist religious renaissance of 1990, there have been numerous changes, including people of all ages requesting prayers or a blessing, which they were forbidden to do during the communist period; the opening of more than 200 monasteries – mostly ger-temples and converted wooden buildings since the rebuilding of permanent monasteries takes time and money; the return of 2,000 monks to monasteries to teach and learn; hidden treasures silently reappearing in monasteries and temples; small communities of elderly monks emerging from hiding; and women setting up religious communities to become nuns. Despite this, however, perhaps only around 50% of Mongols are Buddhist believers, the rest seeing Lamaism as part of Mongol heritage.

There are four main monasteries outside Ulaanbaatar, located in the cardinal directions: Baldan Bereeven to the east, Manzushri monastery to the south, Erdene Zuu to the west, and Amarbayasgalant monastery to the north. Erdene Zuu monastery (the oldest, built in 1585) in Arkhangai Aimag and Amarbayasgalant monastery (founded in 1722 as a resting place for Zanabazar) near Darkhan, have been returned to the Buddhist authorities for religious use, although they are better known as museums and architectural monuments. Baldan Bereeven monastery (built in the 1770s) and Manzushri monastery (built in 1733), near Zuunmod on the far side of the Bogd Uul, near Ulaanbaatar, are slowly being restored, as are many of the provincial monasteries. Further information on all these appears in the relevant sections of Part Two.

At Amarbayasgalant, the magnificent walled monastery, lively young monks in training rely on four elderly abbots, the only survivors of 300 monks who once trained together and practised there. To them it is essential that the teachings are passed on. Charles Bell, a British diplomat and friend of the 13th Dalai Lama, noted that in Lhasa some of the most learned monks came from Mongolia. The sadness is that so much of this learning has disappeared. Manzushri monastery was destroyed in the purges of the 1930s, and while craftsmen are busy at work repairing the temple buildings, the sound of chanting monks resonates once again within the monastery confines. Seemingly the people of Mongolia want Buddhism revived as a living religion.

However, some Mongolian lamas do not want to reconstruct monasteries on original sites that today have become abandoned. They are not interested in 'preservation' in the usual sense of the word, but rather in the preservation of a community, known as a sangha (body of monks), which becomes part of the lay community. The yearning for what has disappeared is enormous and the grief is still being borne by the few who remember.

The income of monasteries comes from Mongolian Buddhists in the form of offerings and donations, including those from overseas Buddhist organisations. Small donations go a very long way in helping to publish books and to meet other modest needs.

After many years of repression, the collective memory of great religious occasions is dim and people are more than curious to learn about religion. For example, the Kalachakra ('wheel of time') initiation is a mysterious ritual believed to have a profound effect on the area where it takes place. However, the modern threats to Mongolian Buddhism no longer come from the authoritarian leaders but from the pressures of modern life and the insecurity and instability of a society caught up in the whirlwind of changing times. Perhaps the most important enemy is time itself as the now ancient lamas take on the new generation's educational needs.

Islam

Islam is an Arabic word meaning 'submission'. Muslims submit to Allah – God. The word of God was revealed to the prophet Muhammad (born in AD540) and written down in the sacred book the Koran (Qur'an). The Koran contains some material from the Jewish and Christian traditions. Islam is a very simple religion with a fivefold path (see below) and consists of belief in the oneness of God.

Mecca is the city where the prophet Muhammad died in AD632 and is a place of pilgrimage for all Muslims. The religion of Islam has neither a clergy nor a liturgy and early Islam did not require a holy place in which to worship. Wherever a Muslim is found there is 'masjid' (literally a place where one can prostrate to worship God), from which we get the Westernised word 'mosque'. The mosque is the place where prayers are led by an imam. It also has an educational role, and teachings there range from advanced theology to the teaching of children.

The 'five pillars of Islam' are:

• **Profession of the faith** There is no God but Allah and Muhammad is Allah's messenger.
• **Prayer** The act of worship is performed five times a day. Muslims face the direction of Mecca and bow in a special series of movements.
• **Alms giving** An offering known as a 'zakat', or poor tax, is given annually by all pious Muslims.
• **Fasting** Muslims fast from before sunrise until sunset every day for one month a year. This period is known as Ramadan. People do not eat, drink or smoke during the daylight hours at that time, although the elderly, the sick, children, and travellers are exempt.
• **Pilgrimage to Mecca (the *hajj*)** Should be undertaken at least once in a lifetime by those who can afford it. Pilgrims walk seven times around a building called the Kaaba. There are great ceremonies and feasts and animals – goats, sheep or camels – are sacrificed.

Islamic law is called the Sharia, in which religious rules, duties and punishments are specified.

History of Islam in Mongolia
The religious life of Mongolia's Sunni Muslim community, being a small national minority, proceeds largely out of the public eye. It is uncertain how many Kazakhs and other Muslims suffered at the time of the anti-religious campaigns of the 1930s, when their mosques were destroyed. It is known that there were several mosques in what is now called Bayan-Ölgii Aimag, where most of Mongolia's Kazakhs live, two more in the neighbouring Khovd Aimag and at least one in the suburbs of Ulaanbaatar. Kazakh Muslims are increasingly influenced by contacts with the outside Muslim world.

During the period of industrialisation, many Kazakhs gave up pastoral life in western Mongolia to work in the new factories and mines of the central region. Since 1990 some mosques have been rebuilt (not the one in Ulaanbaatar) and Muslim rites and customs are now practised again to some extent. Mongolia's Kazakhs may make the *hajj*. It is less clear whether there are now medressehs, or teaching establishments, as well as mullahs.

As in the case of Mongolian Buddhism, the number of people preserving national customs but no longer practising the religion of their parents and grandparents is quite large. The official leader of Mongolia's Muslim community is Mr Sairann, president of the Mongolian Muslim Society.

Christianity
Christians believe there is one Godhead with three persons, known as the Holy Trinity. God the Father, the creator of the universe; God the Son (Jesus), and God the Holy Spirit. Those who believe become Christians by being baptised – that is, they receive the Holy Spirit. Jesus taught, 'Love the Lord your God with all your

heart, with all your soul and with all your mind.' This is the greatest and most important commandment. The second commandment is like it: 'Love your neighbour as you love yourself.' Christians remember Jesus's last supper with his disciples on the eve of his crucifixion by celebrating the Eucharist, in which prayers are said and bread and wine (representing the body and blood of Jesus) are consecrated and distributed to those present.

History of Christianity in Mongolia

The Mongols have had various encounters with Christianity over the centuries. Christianity was first brought to Central Asia in AD635 by Alopen, an ambassador of the eastern Church. Little happened in Mongolia until the time of the Great Khans, when papal envoys shuttled between Rome and Mongol Asia, usually with political as well as religious agendas. Kublai Khan was sympathetic to Christianity (possibly because his mother, Lady Soyo, was a Christian). He asked Rome to send a hundred Christian men skilled in its religion – an invitation that was not answered for many centuries.

However, during the reign of Kublai Khan, two Nestorian Christian monks from Central Asia, Rabban Sauma and his young Mongol disciple called Mark, set out on a pilgrimage to Jerusalem, travelling west along the Silk Road. They carried Kublai's *paiza* or passport of 'free travel' – an engraved gold or silver plate, which hung around their necks. Mark was ordained at Seleucia, near Baghdad, and subsequently became head of the Nestorian Asian Church.

Between the 7th and the 12th centuries, Nestorian Christianity was established in most trading towns along the Silk Road and influenced at least four pre-Mongol tribes. From the 17th to the 19th centuries, when the Silk Road was no longer travelled, cultural and religious life collapsed. In the latter part of the 19th century, Protestant missionaries focused mainly on Inner Mongolia. In the early part of the 20th century, Mildred Cable and Francesca French spent 25 years in the Gobi working as missionaries and published their famous book *The Gobi Desert*. Outer Mongolia was just too far away, although in the far northwest frontiers some Tuvan communities were converted by missionaries working in Siberia.

Christianity today

The Christian Church is newly arrived and recently established in Mongolia. In 1991 there were few Christians; ten years on there are thought to be around 10,000 Mongolian Christians. Christianity appeals to the younger generation because it is new and something quite different from the old beliefs. For the over-50s, it is a foreign religion and something they have difficulty in accepting. Young Mongolians who recently received theological training are now the leaders of their local churches.

A translation of the New Testament into Mongolian has helped the Church to grow. Work on the Old Testament continues. Various overseas organisations have helped to fund this emerging Church and there are now many small congregations in the countryside.

In the early 1990s, the government, in response to Church growth, introduced a law on religion to try to regulate the relationship between Church and state, which created uncertainty as to the status of the Christian Church. The Law on State–Church Relations (1993) sought to restrict the dissemination of religions other than Buddhism, Islam and Shamanism, but it was amended after challenges by human rights campaigners as being unconstitutional. In Mongolia, 'the state respects religion and religion honours the state' according to the constitution of 1992. The state may not carry out religious activity, and temples and monasteries may not carry out political activity.

By the 21st century there were over 70 Christian congregations in the country, mainly in Ulaanbaatar. Christian agencies joined together to form Joint Community Services International (JCS). JCS helps Mongolian people to run projects that include agricultural development, teaching English as a foreign language, a shuttle vet service, a textile project, a *ger* kindergarten and other relief work.

The Russian Orthodox Church was established in Mongolia in the early 20th century but it did not survive the revolutionary period of the 1920s. Holy Trinity Church, which stood in Ulaanbaatar, was closed in 1928 and later demolished. The Russian Orthodox community has taken its name again and is led by Father Anatolii Fesechko; he takes care of the long-term Russian resident community, about 100 members, and other members of the congregation that number 150 people (2002). Holy Trinity Church community is to be found at 55 Jukovyn Gudamj, Ulaanbaatar.

The Roman Catholic mission in Ulaanbaatar is headed by Bishop Fr Wens Padilla. The Vatican maintains a diplomatic mission in Beijing. The Association of Mongolian Protestants is led by a Mongol pastor, Boldbaatar. Outreach work includes helping street children and the poor.

Authentic Adventures in the Real Mongolia

RunWild ®

- ❂ **Adventure Tours**
- ❂ **Trekking**
- ❂ **Horse & Camel Riding**
- ❂ **Fishing**

40 Miangat Street, Building 68,
Sukhbaatar District, Ulaan Baatar
Mongolia

Phone/Fax: (976-11) 315374
info@outer-mongolia.com
www.outer-mongolia.com

MEMBERS OF THE MONGOLIAN TOURISM ASSOCIATION

Culture

If you drink the water from a place, then also follow the customs of that place.

Mongolian saying

Culture is born of history, language and ideas, and many other invisible strands that make up and characterise a distinct group of people like the Mongols. The Mongolian national identity and culture is best seen in practice in the life and traditions surrounding the *ger*, the nomad's home (see pages 68–71), and to a lesser extent in urban life through social customs and business practices. It is clearly present in religious celebrations, national festivals, sport, music, theatre and film. Deeply rooted in the natural environment, Mongolian culture has been moulded under the harshest of climates; the identity of these ancient tribal peoples has survived for hundreds of years within traditional nomadic practices. This is reinforced in a statement, attributed to Genghis Khan, that when the Mongol people lose contact with their nomadic lifestyle, they will lose their true identity.

During their greatest period of expansion at the time of the Mongol empire in the 13th century, the mobility of the equestrian culture of the Mongols brought them into contact with other cultures and allowed them to absorb many different ideas and influences. Diverse cultures, like those of Persia and countries further afield, reached Central Asia along the trade routes of the Silk Road, which, at that time, stretched from the Sea of Japan in the east to the shores of the Mediterranean Sea in the west. Silk, spices and ideas travelled overland from east to west and vice versa; and to some extent on a north/south axis. Buddhism, for example, was introduced to Mongolia from Tibet and India. The Mongols, however, did not bring home many comforts from the civilised countries they conquered; nor, it seems, were they particularly interested in doing so.

Although the Mongols conquered vast territories from the saddle, it was impossible to rule these lands from the back of a horse. Instead Kublai Khan moved the Mongol capital from Karakorum in the heartland of the Mongolian steppes, to Beijing, in northeast China, from where he and his successors ruled the Mongol empire during the Yuan dynasty (1271–1368), absorbing Chinese civilisation. In recent times, Mongolia has absorbed political and cultural influences from both of her big neighbours and has been ruled and further influenced by them with many consequences. A 270-year Manchu rule by the Chinese Qing dynasty (1644–1911) was followed by a revolutionary period in the 1920s and then 70 years of socialist reform under a communist party was backed by the Soviet Union. Some simple examples of dress and eating customs makes clear the ways in which these countries have left their distinctive marks. For example, the everyday use of the knife and fork over chopsticks, is typically

TRAVEL IN STYLE
Antoni and Caroline Daszewski

Travelling in Mongolia means travelling in style and putting the clock back at least a hundred years. The size of our entourage for just the two of us was amazing: we travelled by jeep accompanied by our interpreter and our trek leader, who also happened to be a lecturer at the Mongolian State University in Ulaanbaatar, while the cook and assistant cook joined us travelling in an ex-Russian army cook truck. At camp, besides our sleeping tent, we enjoyed the luxury of a dining tent, complete with a super-efficient, wood-burning (or yak-dung) stove, pine chairs and tables, but ironically it was the loo tent that regularly boasted some of the best views in the world. The food was unfailingly excellent and really fresh, as our truck driver proved to be an ardent and successful fisherman, so many meals consisted of delicious and unusual Mongolian freshwater fish; meat was sometimes bought from local families, who also provided wonderful homemade yoghurt. Every dietary whim was catered for and the only problem seemed to be the super-abundance of food. Each meal became a party, often accompanied by beautiful folk songs sung by our Mongolian staff. On one such evening we were camped on the beach at Khoton Lake, in Bayan-Ölgii Province: after dinner an enormous bonfire was lit and we taught the home team how to dance the tango in the snow, by the light of the flames. In contrast, another night, we dined by candlelight – a romantic twosome – in great style, under the star-encrusted Gobi sky.

Riding in Mongolia is to discover another dimension to life. Three Mongol horseman and ourselves left the vehicles, having made a rendezvous to meet them ten days later. We unpacked the handmade Western saddles, which had come with us from the city so that we could ride in comfort, and watched, amazed, as the horsemen expertly loaded the pack ponies with all the gear, including a more compact dining tent, as well as the smaller travelling stove, complete with collapsible chimney. We set out and were quite free to ride at whatever pace we felt like. Mongolian horses are small and wonderfully behaved, so sometimes we would amble along beside the horsemen, entranced by their singing and at others we galloped like the wind over the vast, empty, endless steppe. Another day the two of us accompanied the 12-camel caravan of a family on the move; we splashed through rivers, and at one point had to gallop after them through the brilliant autumn woods when we had loitered too long enjoying the scenery. We don't believe there is anywhere else in the world which offers such a style of travel – and travel in such style.

Antoni and Caroline's tailormade six-week itinerary was planned by email over a six-month period with a Mongolian travel agent, Genghis Expeditions (see page 225). Excluding international fares, but including everything else (internal flights, hotels, food, staff, transport) it cost around £3,000 each.

Russian, whereas the *deel*, the traditional Mongolian gown, has similarities to the Chinese tunic. The northern Mongols, who were not absorbed by the Chinese (unlike the Mongols of Inner Mongolia), have put aside most things Chinese. The irony is that Mongol culture and folklore today – lineages, family history, folk stories and so on – are in some places remembered in Inner Mongolia more than in Mongolia proper, which was subject to sweeping reforms that destroyed much of the local culture.

What has allowed Mongolian culture to survive is the people's adaptability to change and their philosophical readiness to move with the times. During the Soviet period new opportunities were opened up to them through education in European history and culture. The Mongols are resourceful and resilient. Despite the financial difficulties of the present and the purges and revolutions of the past, Mongolians believe that their cultural heritage is something to be cherished and kept alive. The isolation of Mongolia during the 20th century – geopolitically, culturally and in other ways – is now over, and Mongolian arts, sciences and religion are free to bloom as an exotic combination of an ancient culture in a modern world, without being influenced and restricted by the former Soviet regime. The future looks less culturally isolated for Mongolia's nomadic population, as it becomes linked to the towns and settlements via new roads and communication services, which will bring all Mongolians, both city and country dwellers, in line with the realities of global survival. This may take time and until then the nomadic population will remain in physical isolation.

ARCHITECTURE

Nomadic architecture is not carved in stone for posterity, but best represented in the transient materials of wood and cloth, in the form of the circular tent, or *ger*, the main Mongolian home.(For further details of the construction of the *ger*, see pages 68–71.) Ancient tribes pitched camp in enclosures or *khürees* for protection. The custom to line up the *gers* in order of social importance, with the top people in the westernmost *ger*, was reported by Friar William of Rubrouck, who described Möngke Khan's camp in the mid-13th century.

Images of *ger* camps are carved on rocks from the late Bronze Age and early Iron Age. The Mongolian *ger* has retained its original form and its structure is a unique feat of design for ease of construction, movement and survival. It represents a large part of the culture and traditions of Mongolian nomadic life. Patterns made by dark horsehair ropes across the white felt tent are carefully arranged according to tradition and are considered an ornamentation.

The description and architecture of temple and monastery buildings is dealt with in Part Two. It is significant that early Mongolian building styles used no nails in the construction of the buildings. Before the monasteries (16th century) there weren't cities or towns and villages throughout the country, other than a few scattered ruins of feudal warfare and disunity which lasted for a long period of time. Contemporary city architecture includes the Ardyn Bank building in Ulaanbaatar, listed as one of the best thousand buildings in the world. It is better known as the blue glass building, designed by the Mongolian architect G Batsükh.

LITERATURE AND LEGEND

Oral traditions have remained at the root of Mongolian culture and are among the most precious of their arts. Songs and legends travelled widely with the nomads, transmitted by bards, and thus preserved through the centuries. As an unlettered people the nomads left no written accounts, and a Gobi-like void existed concerning written work until the 13th century. The earliest form of nomadic literature begins with *The Secret History of the Mongols,* often abbreviated to *The Secret History.* The exact title and origin of this important document is unknown. Several authors of translations suggest that the title may be taken from the first line of the text. Professor Urgunge Onon takes as the title of his translation *Chinngis Khan, the Golden History of the Mongols.* It is known to the Mongols as the *Tobchi'an* or *History;*

other names include *The Secret History of the Mongols, The Life of Genghis Khan, The Real Record of Chinggis Khan* and *The Secret History of the Yuan Dynasty*. The explanation of the 'secret' is that it was kept by the Chinese as a dynastic record and not available to the public - therefore 'secret'. A copy of the text only came to light at the end of the 19th century and, since then, scholars have been working on this uniquely important early manuscript, the only near-contemporary account of the life of Genghis Khan and the accomplishments of his son Ögödei Khan (see box opposite). Next to this is the *Altan Tobchi, or Golden Chronicle*, supposedly written in the early 17th century. The third Mongolian classic is a work called *Erdeniin Tobchi, or The Precious Chronicle*. All three combine legend and history.

The earliest family histories preserved by herdsmen date back to the 18th century. More recent family records were lost or destroyed in the political purges of the 20th century, along with numerous Buddhist manuscripts. These manuscripts comprised single, long-leafed, unbound sheets, kept between similar-sized wooden slabs or decorated tablets and then wrapped in silk, cotton or leather for protection. European-style books appeared in Mongolia shortly before the revolution of 1921.

Descriptions of the Mongols during the reign of Genghis Khan's grandson, Kublai, are exotic and tinged with a dream-like quality. Some lines have lodged in the minds and imagination of the English-speaking (Western) world through Samuel Taylor Coleridge's poem *Kubla Khan* (first published in 1816, inspired by reading Marco Polo and smoking opium). It conjures up evocative images. Coleridge may not have described the scene correctly, but he alludes to the extravagant nature of Kublai's court at his summer capital Shangdu (Kaiping), near Dulon.

> In Xanadu did Kubla Khan
> A stately pleasure-dome decree:
> Where Alph, the sacred river, ran
> Through caverns measureless to man
> Down to a sunless sea.
> So thrice five miles of fertile ground
> With walls and towers were girded round
> And there were gardens bright with sinuous rills
> Where blossomed many an incense bearing tree;
> And here were forests ancient as the hills,
> Enfolding sunny spots of greenery.

Buddhist religious literature from the 16th century onwards provides many poems, plays and stories written as teaching material. By the end of the 20th century, although the state had suppressed religious teaching ruthlessly, the country achieved 95% literacy, in part due to educational reforms under socialism but at the expense of much oral tradition. *Ülgeriin Dalai* (*The Sea of Parables*) is a collection of short stories, similar to Aesop's fables. These stories are commonly told by the older generation in order to teach children good behaviour and better manners. Other popular tales are of Geser Khan, a mythical character of Tibetan origin and Jangar Khan, a legendary hero of the Oirat Mongols.

One popular fable from *The Sea of Parables* is that of the frog and the geese. A long time ago, there lived two geese and a frog by a small, isolated mountain lake in the Gobi Altai mountains. As time went by the water in the lake began to disappear causing grave concern. The two geese decided to move elsewhere but the frog, knowing he would be left behind beseeched his friends, 'Be merciful please and take me to a place where there is water.' The geese replied: 'Tell us how to transport you and we shall do so.' The frog then produced a small stick and

THE SECRET HISTORY OF THE MONGOLS (MONGOLYN NUUTS TOVCHOO)

The Secret History of the Mongols, a fusion of history, folklore and poetry, is a unique document in Central Asian literature as it is the earliest surviving Mongolian source about the life of Genghis Khan and his son Ögödei Khan. Scholars believe it was written in the 13th century – the presumed date is sometime during the 1240s after the death of Ögödei Khan in 1241. Its author is unknown. The history has an epic quality similar to the Scandinavian sagas.

The early part of The Secret History deals with the origins of the Mongol nation, said to descend from the union of a wolf and a doe. The story then enters the real world to provide an historic account of Genghis Khan's childhood and his rise to power and describes the accomplishments of his son Ögödei. It portrays the lifestyle, thoughts and beliefs of the 13th century and ends with the instructions given by Ögödei Khan after his accession in 1228 on the death of Genghis Khan.

The earliest known version is in Mongolian, transcribed phonetically into Chinese characters. It demanded something of a code-breaking effort to decipher. It was first translated by a Russian Orthodox priest at the end of the 19th century. Translations by eminent scholars include those of Igor de Rachewiltz, Francis Woodham Cleaves, Urgunge Onon and a modern adaptation by Paul Kahn.

explained: 'I shall grasp the middle of the stick in my mouth if you two would kindly hold the ends in your beaks and fly off with me.' When the two geese flew through the air as instructed by the frog, people looking up exclaimed, 'How wise and skilful these geese are to carry the little frog with them.' This was repeated over and over again, until, at length, the frog could stand it no longer and as he opened his mouth to say 'It was my idea!', he let go of the stick and fell to his death. The moral of the story is that people must overcome the temptation to take vain pride in themselves without allowing credit to be given to others.

Artistic expression is best captured in the legend of the horse-head fiddle or *morin khuur*, a traditional two-string musical instrument which traces its origin back to the time of Hunnu tribes (otherwise known as Xiongnu or Huns), who inhabited the present territory of Mongolia, circa 400BC. The instrument is an integral part of Mongolian culture (see page 94). There are many folk stories on the origin of the *morin khuur* – here is one:

Once upon a time, a horseman rode through the night sky and spotted the tent of a beautiful herdswoman. He stayed with her for one night and at dawn he rode away. The second night he returned to the woman's delight, but at dawn again he disappeared. After several nights the woman determined to keep the horseman by her side. While he slept she crept out to untie his horse and noticed that the animal had little wings above its hooves. In a drastic moment she cut off the horse's wings. When her lover left the following morning his mount fell to the earth and died.

Despairing over the loss of his horse the man grieved night and day. To sooth his sorrow he carved the horse's head from a piece of wood and transformed it into a two-string instrument, using the bone and hide of the dead horse.

Contemporary literature

Modern Mongolian literature was born in the revolutionary period of the 1920s and until then the Oriental trend dominated. Oriental and Western literature developed alongside one another and Mongolian readers gradually became familiar with the world classics. The writings and poetry of the 'national poet' Dashdorjiin Natsagdorj (1906–37) promoted a revival of traditional culture. His lyrics are distinguished by a chiselled rhythm of perfect harmony, and he is famous for his poetry about the beauties of the Mongolian countryside. Most Mongolians know by heart his poem 'My Homeland', of which one verse is quoted below:

> Mongolia's name resounds through all the world.
> My love for her lies deep within my heart.
> Her tongue, her ways, will hold me till I die –
> Eternal home, my Motherland, Mongolia!

Natsagdorj was also a brilliant prose and short-story writer; among his stories are *The Winged Dun Horse* and *Tears of a Lama*. His only opera, *Three Sad Hills*, is about the 1921 revolution.

Another founder of Mongolia's new literature was the poet and writer S Buyannemekh, along with Ts Damdinsüren who wrote about nature, man, revolution and society.

Much-loved 20th-century Mongolian writers like B Rinchen did their best to preserve what they could of the traditional Mongolian culture in the new age of 'socialist internationalism' (in which the Soviet lead was followed and in many ways traditional art suffered).

By the mid-20th century, many Mongolians had exchanged the nomadic life for sedentary, urban living. Students began to travel to the former Soviet Union for further education and became familiar with both Asian and European art and literature. Since 1990, many young people are being educated in colleges and universities in Europe, America and elsewhere. One can be certain, however, that whether at home or abroad, the nomadic life and its ancient folklore and culture is the inspiration for the expression of their creativity.

MUSIC

There is nothing Mongolians love more than music and the urge to burst into song happens spontaneously. Hour upon hour when travelling across country a Mongol *arat* (herder) will hum or sing and, when happy, he will gallop at full speed in top voice. Singers and musicians are greatly valued in Mongol communities. Nowadays every country town has a pop group, but the Mongols, like the Irish, on the whole prefer traditional music, which is usually played at weddings and other family festivals, when the local horse-head-fiddle players (*morin khuur*) and benediction singers (*yeröölch*) are called in.

The Mongol khans of the 13th century all kept large troupes of dancers and musicians at their courts accompanied by *morin khuur* and drums. The Western traveller, Friar Johannes de Plano Carpini, mentions 'saddle songs' of the Mongol warriors, and both Marco Polo and Friar William of Rubruck noted the strange musical instruments they saw at the court of the khans.

The horse-head fiddle is an ancient two-stringed instrument and is thought by some musicologists to be the father of European bowed string instruments. *Morin khuur* was very much a part of everyday life of nomads, who worship the fiddle. It is still a custom to keep the instrument in the most sacred part of the home, at the back by the household altar. There was a time when every man could play the *morin khuur*. Its music drifted across the steppes and shepherds would listen to it at

KHÖÖMII – OVERTONE OR THROAT SINGING

Throat singing (khöömii) involves changing the shape of the mouth and creating overtones in the throat, chest or abdomen to imitate the sounds of nature – bird and animal noises as well as the sounds of storms and rivers. Khöömii is a truly unusual Mongolian vocal technique where one singer produces two voices simultaneously. The sound of the two voices, steely bass combined with a whistle-like tone, produces an overtone that can only be described as otherworldly, although the predominant bass tone sounds more like the hum of a poorly maintained refrigerator than a human voice.

Khöömii is produced by making a drone and an overtone, simultaneously. The technique is not difficult to learn. Say the letter I and reinforce your breath on the I sound. Then pronounce two vowels e and ou by modifying your mouth cavity and you will find you can change the pitch. To achieve the whole range you move your tongue backwards and forwards with surprising musical results. One famous Mongolian overtone singer can produce this effect without the drone by using his open mouth only, which defies all explanation.

the end of the day to forget their weariness. In the early 1940s, the Music College in Ulaanbaatar trained professional musicians to master the *morin khuur*. The famous 'Melody of Mongolia', composed by Jantsannorov, was performed by 108 players at the National Festival of *Morin Khuur* in Ulaanbaatar in 1989. The National *Morin Khuur* Ensemble, founded in 1992, has toured internationally and has released a number of CDs.

Other instruments include the *yatga* or zither, which looks like the Chinese *guquin*, a seven-stringed plucked instrument. Strings are made from silk, horse hair or goose gut and the instrument is played either holding it upright or placing it flat on a table or on the player's knees. The *khuuchir*, a bowed string instrument, uses a small round soundboard covered with sheep or snake's skin, while its long neck is made from copper or wood. Another bowed string instrument is the *shudraga*, a three-stringed instrument. Similar instruments were noted in 14th-century Persian literature from where it spread from Persia into China and Japan. Other instruments include the *yoochin*, a dulcimer and cymbals, which produce a light, clashing sound, commonly heard in much Asian music and in many countries from Asia to the Baltic. The flute or *limbe* accompanies the other instruments. It is often played by lone herders to while away the time and its haunting notes may be heard drifting across the grasslands.

The Mongols have always had several singing styles, the most important being *tuuli*, or 'epic songs' – the tales of heroes and great warriors. *Tuuli* performances can be spread over several days. The length of the songs vary – stages of travel can be marked out by songs which take a long time, although this is also a genre, known as 'long songs' (*urtyn duu*). The themes are largely pastoral and celebrate the way of life and magnificence of the steppes, mountains and rivers, lakes and deserts. Great Mongol singers are known to have amazing vocal range and a voice quality that billows and gusts like the wind across the wide-open plains. 'Short songs' (*bogino duu*) are sung at informal occasions (but may be quite long!), with improvised or satirical texts. The tempo of a song depends on the occasion and the mood of the singer. Galloping tunes and songs in praise of horses are well-known favourites. There is a traditional practice of soothing domestic animals with music, especially to induce them to nurse abandoned lambs and young camels. Specific repetitive encouragements of no specific meaning are said to different animals – '*toig, toig*' to lambs, for example, and '*khöös khöös*' to young camels!

The unique sound of Mongolian 'overtone' or *khöömii* ('throat singing') has given Mongol singers a worldwide musical identity. This is a sound produced mainly in the throat (see box, page 95) and, because of the muscular strength it demands, is mainly the preserve of male singers whose voice range spans five octaves.

For details of modern music, see *Chapter 6, Ulaanbaatar*, pages 231–2.

DANCE
Folk dancing
Folk dancing originated in ancient times in connection with the rituals of daily life and nature. Simple circular dances evolved imitating the way birds flew and the way in which animals were trapped by a circle of hunters. A traditional form of this type of dance is accompanied by a tune on the horse-head fiddle. The dancer uses the fluid movements of her arms and upper body to sway to the music. Wrestlers also move in this style between bouts with their arms held high, imitating the flight of the Garuda bird, to celebrate victory over an opponent.

Tsam dance
In the past, religious festivals included temple dances called *tsam* dances, in which lamas wearing elaborate costumes and brightly painted papier mâché masks acted the roles of various Buddhist gods – the red-faced Begze and the blue-faced Makhakala, each with three eyes and a tiara of skulls. Garuda, king of the birds, was originally a Hindu deity, but he took on a Buddhist role, first in Tibet and then in Mongolia, becoming a leading character in *tsam* dance dramas. *Tsagaan Övgön*, or the 'white old man', is also an important legendary figure. The masks are works of art, and are displayed in Mongolian temples and museums.

Tsam dance is being revived after an interruption of more than 60 years. The training of many young people has been a success and leading craftsmen have created new costumes and masks for this special ritual dance, which nowadays serves tourism rather than religion.

ART
There are several distinct periods in Mongolian art, which stretches from prehistoric ancient rock art of Palaeolithic and Neolithic times to present-day literature, sculpture and painting:

- Bronze Age art (4th–2nd century BC) consists of depictions of deer, wolves and horses and other hidden treasures in gold and wood, found as artefacts in the frozen tombs of the Altai area and preserved by permafrost.
- Steppe art of the Turkic/Uighur empires (3rd century AD) produced standing stones and burial monuments built at different periods up to the 11th century.
- A gradual blending of foreign influences took place following the establishment of the great Mongol empire in the 13th century.
- Mongol traders made direct contact with Chinese and Persian traders on the Silk Road which flourished between the 13th and 16th centuries.
- The emergence of Buddhism as a religious power in Mongolia in the 16th century brought Mongolia in contact with Tibetan and Indian cultures.

- The monk Zanabazar (born in 1635) was recognised to be an important incarnation of a Tibetan scholar and proclaimed the leader of Mongolian Buddhists. As an artist, he created many fine sculptures in bronze.
- 20th-century Soviet Russia transformed Mongol art and architecture along the lines of 'socialist realism', as it did the lifestyle of the religious and herding populations, when political reforms closed monasteries and many monks became artisans and took to sedentary, urban living, while *arats* (herders) were collectivised.
- In the 21st century, contemporary Mongol artists are experimenting with new art forms and are free to travel and attend international art colleges and to exhibit and sell their work worldwide.

Rock art of the first millennium

Mongolia's heritage begins with Stone Age rock carvings, showing animal life. The impact of these animalistic drawings on bare rock remains as strong and fresh today as the day they were created. It is as if the artist froze where he stood, to observe and capture the spirit of the animals he sighted. Pre-Hun culture may be glimpsed through the artefacts of the Bronze Age tribal chieftains whose *kurgans*, or burial mounds, have been excavated. Megaliths and monuments to dead chieftains stand silently on the steppe, as a reminder of the past. Ruined walled towns may be seen in the Orkhon Valley and on the eastern steppe.

Early art of the steppes

The culture of the Central Asian steppes expresses itself vividly in the lifestyle of the nomads who produced 'animal-style art', particularly in the region of the Altai mountains where gold and silver were mined. Early sites associated with nomadic tribes date back to the 7th century BC, but unfortunately many of the big kurgans have been plundered. Archaeological discoveries shed light on the nomads of the time, whose material culture reflected their lifestyle. We may only surmise that felt rugs, animal skins and carpets adorned the walls and floors of their simple dwellings.

The arts and crafts of Mongolia developed over the centuries from the early 'animal-style' bronzes of the so-called 'Karasuk style' of the second millennium BC. Karasuk is on the River Yenisey in Siberia, across the northwest border of Mongolia.

Objects excavated from the kurgans

The woollen rug found at the Pazyryk burial mound in the Russian Altai represents one of the most ancient rug-weaving techniques in the world. From a later period low furniture (with removable legs) and horse trappings were found decorated with fantastic zoomorphic images. Creatures like deer and elk were carved with precise detail, which showed not only the powers of observation of the artist, but an understanding of the animals themselves. Such ornamental pieces were laid alongside the body of a dead chieftain to accompany him to the 'other world' – a place where fantasy replaces reality. They included delicate antelopes with oversized antlers, gargoyle-type griffins with large, bulging eyes and fantastic creatures with sharp teeth or fearsome beaks. Sometimes the heads combined the features of several animals, and can only be described as creatures of the imagination.

Representations of deer, horses, bears and birds were carved in wood, decorated in a unique style and then covered by a thin sheet of beaten gold – fit, one assumes, for that journey to the 'other world'. Examples from the Altai tombs were first excavated in the early 20th century and represent the most important finds of nomadic art, dating from the 5th–2nd century BC. Surprisingly, some wool and felt objects also survived. The tombs were situated in the high mountains in cold, dry conditions all the year round. They were covered by large heaps of loose stones, which created a patch of permafrost underneath, and cold air sank into the tomb freezing everything inside. Thanks to these conditions, the contents of the tombs were preserved for centuries.

The early discoveries were made by Soviet archaeologist M P Griaznov in 1929 and further researched by S I Rudenko in the late 1940s. Recent excavations of burial mounds on the Russian-Mongolian western border were made by N V Polos'mak in 1996. Among examples of steppe art are the felt swans of Pazyryk, now in the Hermitage Museum in St Petersburg.

Religious art

Buddhism has had an enormous impact on the culture of the Mongols in many spheres of life. Theatre, dance, music, painting and other artistic skills were developed in the monasteries. *Tankas* (sacred paintings) are portable icons of the Buddha and various deities, painted or embroidered and mounted on silk or cotton. They are rolled and stored in scroll form. These religious paintings were introduced to Mongolia from Tibet, following the introduction of Buddhism in the 16th century, and used to hang in many temples, such as Erdene Zuu, along with masks, used in ritual *tsam* dances. The paintings are venerated and act both as teaching aids and for meditation purposes. Many Buddhist objects were destroyed during the 1930s' purges, along with most Mongolian monasteries. Precious items, however, like *tankas*, were hidden and, since 1990, some have reappeared to hang on the walls of newly opened monasteries.

Zanabazar

Zanabazar (1635–1723) was a remarkable man, both as a monk and an artist. At the age of 15 he travelled to Tibet where he was recognised as the incarnation of the lama Tarantha. He was known popularly as 'the great saint' and became the religious ruler of Mongolia, the first to hold the title of Öndör Gegeen ('High Enlightened One'). During his long life he greatly influenced religious, social and political affairs and contributed to the country's development in the arts. Best known for his sculptures of deities, cast in bronze, copper and brass, often covered in gold, he was also a painter. Museums in the capital, Ulaanbaatar, and at Erdene Zuu monastery in Övörkhangai Province, have some fine examples of his work. The Mongolian goddess of mercy, Tara Ekh, sculpted in bronze, shows a profoundly human expression of beauty. He was guided by his desire to save people from wrath, ignorance, lust, contempt and ill will. His meditative Buddha figures have a serenity that transmit peace and harmony in a troubled world. It is said Zanabazar entered the soul of the Mongol people and expressed it in his art.

Traditional Mongol *zurag* painting

The country's most striking art form is the unique traditional Mongol *zurag* painting, a type of story-telling art without words that may be described as a developed form of naive painting. Mongol *zurag* portrays everyday country life with images of people, horses and *gers*, combined with folk motifs and legends. Fine line drawings were coloured with natural mineral pigments, such as red ochre and charcoal, until lacquer paints became available in Mongolia.

The best-known master of Mongol *zurag*, Marzan 'Joker' Sharav, painted in the early 20th century. His ethnographic works on monumental backgrounds gave an insight into Mongolian nomadic culture. Sharav's *Day in the Life of Mongolia* depicts dozens of small scenes with men herding livestock, hunting, making felt, putting up a *ger* and slaughtering animals, while women and girls milk animals and prepare food. In the different scenes, people are living and dying, engaged in archery and wrestling, attending religious ceremonies, fighting and making love.

Contemporary art

Modern Mongolian painting is colourful, interesting, and represented in a variety of styles. It can be seen in a number of modern galleries in Ulaanbaatar. An exhibition that travelled to the USA in 2000 included the works of the artists Tsultemin Enkhjin, Monkhorin Erdenbayar and Batbayar Gansukh. Subject matter usually includes nomadic life, the landscape of the windswept steppes, animals and abstract themes. Works are in oil on canvas and in watercolour on paper. Many country museums sell watercolour paintings, which make excellent presents.

Baatar, a contemporary artist, follows the ancient Mongol *zurag* tradition, using a visual vocabulary of ancient Mongolian references, such as interlocking triangles, which refer to married women. Her colours are bright and clear although her perspective is quite flat. Stylised clouds hang in the sky. Baatar's works are highly sought after in Germany, France and Japan.

The modern sculptor, Gankhuyag, recently exhibited his *Mirage of the Dream*, an abstract work in copper, in New York. In 1996, the internationally acclaimed British sculptor Richard Long drew inspiration from his visit to the Gobi, and produced works in sand and stone called *Gobi Desert Circles*. Circles, he claims, are timeless, understandable and easy to make. These works were photographed and then left to disintegrate naturally in the desert. Long's idea was to pioneer new ways of thinking about art and environment.

ARTS AND CRAFTS

With the introduction of Buddhism in the 16th century, arts and crafts absorbed elements of Indian, Tibetan and Nepalese art. This is reflected in the Buddhist ritual vessels, incense burners and musical instruments for wind and percussion. Objects of everyday life, dress design and jewellery illustrate the development of crafts, such as leatherwork, appliqué and embroidery.

Through the ages, Mongolian women have occupied themselves with artistic needlework, skills that they may now convert into entrepreneurial activities for the gift industry, as tourism develops. In the past, special garments were decorated with small river gems, corals and turquoise, stitched with fine gold thread by women. The same is done today using modern designs. The complex embroidery and appliqué of coloured leather for saddles, harnesses and leather boots was traditionally achieved by the stronger masculine hand.

The Mongolian *ger* was richly ornamented in times past and decorated both inside and out. A song by an unknown writer describes the ornamentation:

> Sculpted on the upper beams are
> Peacocks and pheasants,
> With outstretched necks.
> Hewn on lower beams by doors are
> Kites and tumblers,
> Swooping in the clouds.
> The *ger* is a rich and happy abode,
> On firm birch props,
> Clustered with animals.

Folk art contains many deeply symbolic meanings hidden in the designs that may decorate the door of the *ger* or other household utensils. Many of these swirling or geometric designs symbolise prosperity and protection; over time they have been combined and intertwined to express feelings of reverence for the beauty of nature. The most popular motif is the 'endless knot', one of the eight sacred symbols of Lamaist iconography. Others include linked circles known as the 'bracelet of the khan'. Mongols are people whose minds are tuned through centuries of Buddhist tradition to seek an inner meaning in abstract forms. So Mongolian decorative art is mostly abstract and manages to create in itself another language.

Embroidery, appliqué work and carving

Embroidery in colourful Chinese silk threads is still widely practised. Its chief purpose is to decorate the much-prized tobacco pouches. One technique employs a series of coloured threads, intricately knotted, with the help of wooden cross pieces. Among the most intricate of modern Mongolian craftsmanship are the chess sets of delicately carved pieces. Besides wood, carvers use amber and bone. In the past, camel bones were boiled to become snow white and then used in craft and jewellery making. Drinking bowls were hollowed from birch-tree roots and rimmed with beaten silver. Hide and wood have been the main materials in the herders' homes. Metal, once used for weaponry and food cauldrons, is still used to produce the central iron stove. The making of musical instruments is considered an art and the carving, joinery and carpentry work that goes into them is of the highest quality. A special paste called *zümber* is made from crushed porcelain, birch sugar and glue. It is used to create an embossment – a technique known as *tesso duro* in Europe, and probably introduced from Italy by the Dominican monks who visited the court of Genghis Khan.

CRAFTSMEN

It is only in recent times that craftsmen have become settled. During the last 200–300 years it was normal for journeymen or itinerant craftsmen to travel the country much as they did in medieval times in Europe. In the 1930s the closure of the monasteries, which had fostered arts and crafts, created a flood of Mongolian artisans, whose role had previously been filled by Chinese immigrants.

Herdsmen practising semi-skilled crafts like woodwork did not make a living from craftwork. Children were trained in a form of apprenticeship with a master craftsman. No money passed hands but the pupil was expected in turn to offer training. The smith was regarded with great superstition and, like a shaman, was respected for his knowledge of the supernatural. The practice of metalwork had certain rituals attached to it. The supernatural world was revered by the nomads, who consulted the deities before moving camp, branding horses, casting an ornament and so forth. The spirits represented by inanimate and natural objects were all-powerful and certain simple rituals, such as flicking milk in the air before drinking or burning juniper twigs in the fire before branding, ensured they were respected.

The manner in which the craftsman worked was meaningful in Mongolia. The calm and concentrated way that Mongol craftsmen and craftswomen worked was associated with the belief that creating is a religious act.

Banners and flag-making continue to employ appliqué skills, although the manufacture of the rich silks and brocades that lined the *gers* of the khans has become a memory of the past. There has been, however, a recent revival in modern tent-making, including interior and exterior decoration.

Socialist realism

Under communism, 'socialist realism' was adopted in literature and art, which became filled with communist leaders and labour heros adopting striking poses against 'politically correct' backgrounds and slogans. The genre is best seen in municipal sculpture created by artists during the 20th century, such as S Choimbal's equine monument on Sükhbaatar Square in Ulaanbaatar of the revolutionary hero Sükhbaatar, sitting astride a giant horse. Many political statues of that time, for example those of Lenin and Stalin, were torn down or removed by young radicals during the 1990s democracy movement.

Certain crafts were adapted to 'socialist realism' by adding a red star; the star shape was an unknown motive in Mongol ornamentation until then. The genre is also manifest in the municipal Soviet-style tower-block buildings, which make up the main residential and government buildings in the capital and, in general, in every provincial centre, although in the provinces the buildings rarely exceed two floors. The painting style of socialist realism, mainly in oils, may be seen in the art galleries of museums in Ulaanbaatar; this style is considered old-fashioned and out-of-date by present-day artists.

In the 20th century the Mongols have managed to preserve some traditional art forms while acquiring new ones from Russian and other European sources, like opera, ballet, theatre and circus. The numerous 'houses of culture' and libraries set up in the communist period no longer receive any government money to operate, and the arts in Mongolia must fundraise in order to survive. Mongolian artists – musicians, actors and painters – now travel the world.

SPORT

The most important sports in Mongolia are horse racing, wrestling and archery, known as the 'three manly sports'. They are the focus of the national Naadam, the Games, held annually in Ulaanbaatar on July 11, to celebrate National Day (see *Festivals*, pages 186–8).

Mongolia's 'three manly sports'
Horse racing

Two things set Mongol horse racing apart – the length of the race and the age of the jockeys. The Mongols, once the world's greatest riders and cavalrymen, are interested in stamina; horses therefore race in different categories over distances between 15km and 30km. Since it is considered that it is the horse and not the jockey that wins the race, children aged six to 12, girls as well as boys, take part as jockeys, being far lighter than adults. They are supposed not to force the horse but only to guide it to the winning post. In the big races, jockeys over nine years old are barred. The reason is that the Mongols want to bring out the horses' willingness as well as their speed.

The youngest horses (two-year-olds) race over a distance of 15km; three- to five-year-olds race 20–25km, and separate races are held for stallions. The big race for mature horses is over 30km, and many of the young jockeys ride bareback, which is a feat in itself. The winning horse is garlanded with blue ribbons and sprinkled with *airag* (fermented mares' milk), while its jockey is given a pat on the head and a prize and disappears into the crowds. Most prize money goes to the

WINTER HORSE RACE

Travelling back to Ulaanbaatar from the South Gobi one winter by jeep, motoring carefully across the snowy plains, my eye spotted a dark speck in the distance, larger than the size of a yak. It transformed into a colourful herd of horses and riders about to start a race, unusual for the time of year as racing normally takes place in summer. The warm breath of shaggy ponies clouded the clear air. They were ridden by children aged between five and 12, some of whom were being led to the start by anxious-looking parents. The youngest laughed and joked while their older brothers and sisters appeared to be more serious. An announcement from a nearby van called them into order. Finally, around 100 children mounted their winter-coated ponies, assembled and dutifully trotted out of sight behind a hill to the start.

They then turned to gallop back at full pace through the snow fields, cutting a path over the frozen surface and churning up a plume of shimmering snow particles that were carried on the wind as the ponies swept into sight. Sheepskins were bound to the legs of some jockeys to prevent chafing, while others rode bare back. Their riding skills and energy were extraordinary to witness. There was huge excitement among the racing crowd, who were brilliantly attired in silk fleece-lined deel – the traditional knee-length Mongolian tunic, worn by men and women. The colours contrasted brilliantly against the white snow – tunics of green, purple and deep red, tied at the waist by saffron sashes. Since it was mid-February, most nomads wore fox-fur hats. Many had ridden for miles to attend the meeting. I was surprised to see several herders pull out binoculars to scan the distant hillside for the first sign of the oncoming riders. When they did appear, the crowds roared and cheered. Many parents ran on to the course to encourage the young riders but were held back by race officials. The trainer of the winning horse, ridden by a child of seven, is now the happy owner of a motorbike. The atmosphere differed little from the excitement experienced by enthusiastic race goers anywhere in the world.

owner and racehorse trainer. A song called *Bayan Khodood*, meaning 'full stomach', is chanted when the last horse comes in – no disgrace for the horse or rider but the trainer is teased for not doing a proper job.

Around 100 horses, from all 21 aimags, compete in each of the five or six separate races at the national Naadam in Ulaanbaatar. The winning five horses are given the title *Airagiin Tav*. In other words, they are 'placed', as in English horse races, when the first three, not more, are 'placed', or the first four in handicap races. The most coveted prize in the rural Naadams is a motorbike. At the national games the prize money is good. For the jockeys, mud, dirt, tears and sweat characterise a horse race, while the roaring crowds and anxious faces fixed on the winning post resemble horse-racegoers the world over.

Wrestling

Wrestling has always been a favourite sport of Mongolians, as the new wrestling palace in Ulaanbaatar testifies. Radio and TV broadcasts from the arena keep its audiences transfixed throughout the year – not only during the Naadam festival. Balance and agility are more important than brute strength. No agonising holds are used and wrestlers try to out-kick or throw their opponents. Bouts can be over in seconds.

A match is won when any part of the loser's body, except the soles of his feet, touches the ground. (New rules do not allow fingers or palms to touch the ground.) When this happens, the loser passes under the arm of the winner who then imitates a Garuda, raising his arms above his head, before meeting his next opponent. The final winner at the Naadam games becomes a national hero.

The wrestling costume consists of long boots with up-turned toes (*gutal*), a short jacket with long sleeves (*zodog*), tightly fitted across the back and open-chested, and short trunks (*shuudag*), like swimming briefs. The material used is top-quality silk, usually in red or light blue colours for the trunks, and incised and ornamented leather for the *gutals*. The reason that Mongolians wear an open-fronted jacket is that long ago a lady wrestler, disguised as a man, took part in the games, and only when she had won did she reveal herself to be a woman.

Each contestant must have a second (*zasuul*), as in duels, who stands close by to advise him during the contest, to hold his hat and to announce his titles at the beginning of the third, fifth and seventh rounds. This announcement is made to encourage the wrestler and his fans.

Mongolian national wrestling has unique features: bouts are not limited by time, there are no weight categories, and many pairs of wrestlers meet simultaneously. This allows large numbers of competitors to take part in contests within a short period of time. Wrestlers are listed according to their title and rank: Falcon (*Nachin*) is awarded to a wrestler who wins five rounds in a nationwide competition; Elephant (*Zaan*) is given after six wins, three times in the state Naadam; Lion (*Arslan*) after nine wins. The title Titan (*Avraga*) is awarded to the Lion who has won a tournament in the past. There are several categories of Titan: Oceanic Titan, Worldly Titan and the highest, Invincible Titan, granted to the Worldly Titan who wins a tournament for the second time. Mongolia's greatest wrestler, Invincible Titan Bat-Erdene, carried the Mongolian flag at the Sydney Olympic Games (2000).

Archery

What distinguishes Mongolian archery is that the archer does not aim at an upright bull's-eye target, but at targets made up of cork wrapped with leather straps, positioned flat on the ground. The arrow has to rise into the air and descend (like a javelin) to hit the ground targets without overshooting or undershooting. While this is happening, a wail goes up from the crowds and the cries '*mergen*' ('good shot') and '*uukhai*' ('hit') are followed by thunderous applause.

In the countryside there is less emphasis on archery and even in the city it doesn't draw as many crowds as the wrestling and horse events. Spectators stand near by to cheer on the contestants. Judges stand near the targets to signal results by a sign language of hand movements and shouts of '*uukhai*'. Prize money for the winner amounts to T300,000.

Archery has as ancient a history as wrestling and both are mentioned in *The Secret History of the Mongols*, the 13th-century Mongolian chronicle that describes the life of Genghis Khan. An ancient rock inscription records an arrow shot of 335 spans – estimated at about 500m. The Mongols used a compound bow built of layers of horn, sinew, bark and wood. Bows were also made of horn and strung with bulls' tendons; the result was as powerful as the English longbow.

The Mongols handled their bows on horseback and used what is known as the 'Parthian shot' – an arrow shot made by turning in the saddle to shoot arrows over their shoulders at the enemy while galloping away.

REGENT HOLIDAYS

The tailor-made specialists to

Mongolia

- Tailor-made individual and group itineraries
- Stop-overs en route to China or Russia on Trans-Siberian Railway
- Trekking and hiking, camel and horse riding, climbing
- Jeep safaris, cultural tours and eco-tours

Tel: 0117 921 1711
Fax: 0117 925 4866
E-mail: regent@regent-holidays.co.uk
www.regent-holidays.co.uk
15 John Street, Bristol BS1 2HR

"Contact our Specialist to start planning your Mongolian experience today!"

Natural History and Conservation

NATURAL HISTORY

The real problem is not to preserve the species, it is to preserve a living
animal and plant community.

William Conway, conservationist

What impressed me were the different sizes of the plant species as we
moved from the taiga (forests) to the steppe (grasslands). I saw orange
sedum, which I'd never seen before. I was really excited and wanted to
know more about it all.

Visitor to Mongolia, 2000

People travel to Mongolia to discover another world. Many people visit Mongolia
to see the wonders of nature and find themselves overwhelmed by examples of its
rare animal life and unusual plant species. Fly-fishing and wildflower walks are
hugely enjoyable. Remember to bring a rod and a plant identification book and
prepare to be amazed. This chapter aims to stress the extent to which natural
history and conservation are closely interconnected.

Part of the country's allure lies in its wildness and undisturbed natural beauty.
The play of light and shade upon this wild landscape has a magnetic charm that
pulls the traveller back. Mongolia's geological assets, the bedrock of the country,
are as varied as they are beautiful. Fragments of life millennia ago are found in
fossil and skeletal remains – particularly dinosaurs, for which Mongolia is famous.
Gems and rich mineral deposits are another legacy of pre-historic times found
underground. Geologically, Mongolia comes under the Ural-Mongolian fold belt
and flying over Mongolia on a clear day is the best way to see the land formation.
You will see numerous mountain folds descending south in smooth, curved arcs.

Mongolia's ecosystems are of global importance because of their diversity, size
and continuity. The climate, topography and natural formations divide the country
into six zones which comprise desert, Gobi and steppe (grassland) zones, and
forest, Alpine, and taiga (northern mountain/forest) zones. Mongolia is part of the
Central Asian plateau. It is a land of contrast and great biodiversity, teeming with
rare and exotic species.

The fauna and flora of Mongolia are as distinctive as the vegetation zones they
occupy. This is mainly due to the country's unique location between the Siberian
taiga and the desert steppe. Mongolia has over 4,000 plant species, 136 species of
mammals, 436 species of birds, 75 fish species and more than 15,000 insect species.
Conifer forests cover around 11.5% of the territory, some 18 million hectares of
land. These forests, principally of Siberian larch, form the southern edge of the vast
taiga zone, the largest continuous forest system on earth. Less numerous deciduous
species, like aspen, white birch and black poplar populate the forests of the forest-
steppe zone. The forests are home to most wild animals and birds, which live

undisturbed, since the majority of the area is uninhabited and inaccessible to human settlement. The rivers are literally full of unusually large fish, like the taimen species, belonging to the salmon family. It is no fisherman's tale that they measure over six feet in length. Numerous insect and tiny rodent species abound. They need specialist classification because of their multiple variations.

Lagoons, lakes and rivers, streams, marshes, oases and other wetlands in each of the six zones support their own distinctive flora and fauna. Wetlands provide crucial habitat for the waterfowl and water-frequenting birds that form the majority of Mongolia's migratory bird species. For keen ornithologists, the reed marshes surrounding the lakes of the western Great Lakes' basin and the floodplains of larger rivers provide excellent bird-watching possibilities, and, in the far west, in rivers you can spot beaver (*Castor fiber*), muskrat (*Ondatra zibethica*) and otter (*Lutra lutra*).

Two excellent booklets dealing with the flora and fauna of specific areas in Mongolia are *Lake Khövsgöl National Park – A Visitor's Guide* and *The Gobi Gurvansaikhan National Park*. (For details, see *Further reading*, pages 385–7.)

Wildlife habitats of Mongolia's different vegetation zones
Taiga/forest zone
Mongolia's taiga zone is part of the vast forested region of southern Siberia. It is found in the Khentii Mountains in the mountainous areas near Lake Khövsgöl, and on the north and east slopes of the Khangai Mountains. These Mongolian coniferous taiga forests are comprised of mainly Siberian larch (70%) and, at higher elevations, Siberian pine, mosses and lichens are abundant. The taiga forests of Mongolia cover around five per cent of the country and these areas remain largely undisturbed. In the forests mosses and lichens are abundant and wildlife includes: musk deer, moose, reindeer, sable and brown squirrel. Among the bird species found in the taiga forests are cuckoos and great grey owls. These wilderness zones are a reminder of the once numerous primaeval forests of Europe – which survive today in isolated pockets in the Carpathian mountains, in Transylvania, and in a few other parts of Central Europe.

Mountain forest steppe zone
The mountain forest steppe zone is found on the lower slopes of the Khentii and Khangai mountain ranges, in the Mongolian Altai Mountains, in the Orkhon and Selenge river basins, and in the mountains in eastern Mongolia. Steppe species dominate the mountain forest steppe of the Altai whereas taiga species tend to dominate the northern ranges of the Khangai and Khentii. There is a high degree of biological diversity and wide river valleys separate the territory of the mountain / steppe zone which covers about 25% of Mongolia. Mixed coniferous forest is found on cooler, moister northern slopes, while steppe vegetation predominates on other slopes. Species include elk, wolf, roe deer and Eurasian badger, while the bird life of the forest/steppe regions includes: Daurian partridge, black kites and great bustards. Wild boar and marmot are hunted for the pot (their meat tastes delicious when steamed in earth ovens or roasted on open fires). Herbs and wild grasses add to the natural profusion of meadow flowers.

Steppe zone
Extensive grasslands, or steppe, make up the heart of Mongolia both geographically and economically. The entire far eastern part of the country falls into this area, extending west below the Khangai range to the Great Lake basin of Uvs Province. This sea of grass covers rolling undulating land for as far as the eye can see

encompasing 20% of Mongolia's territory. It provides most important grazing lands for Mongolian livestock herds. Some of the southeastern steppe is largely uninhabited and underdeveloped where hundreds of thousands of migrating gazelles live undisturbed. Distinctive flora and fauna include: various steppe grasses; gazelles and small rodents such as voles and pika; rare species of cranes and birds of prey. Flocks of migratory birds make the eastern plains their feeding grounds for a season and, in the same region, thousands of free-roaming white-tailed gazelle reside, migrating south into China when winter comes.

Desert steppe (semi-desert)
Desert steppe occupies 20% of Mongolian territory between the grasslands and the deserts. It includes the Great Lakes basin and most of the lands between the Altai and the Khangai ranges, as well as the eastern Gobi. Low-lying salt plains predominate and rainfall is sparse (100–125mm per annum), and winds and dust storms ravage the countryside; but despite these harsh conditions many pastoral nomads find a livelihood with their flocks of camels, sheep and goats in these semi-desert regions. Desert grasses and shrubs provide grazing including feather grasses and various types of pea shrub. The wild animals that survive here, like the wild camel and the saiga antelope, are some of the rarest in the world. Hundreds of interesting rodents, lizards and snakes inhabit the stony dry ground, and other species like the long-eared hedgehog and a variety of different types of pika (small rodents) live in these regions of sparse vegetation. Kozlov's pygmy jerboa is found in the Transaltai Gobi along with the thick-tailed pygmy jerboa also found in the semi-deserts of the southwest.

Gobi Desert
Once an ancient inland sea, the Gobi Desert occupies much of southern Mongolia and northeastern China. It is a place that attracts many fossil collectors. The landscape is rugged and inhospitable, with little vegetation, but it varies enormously, from mountain massifs with barren rocky outcrops to the flat plains where you find poplar-fringed oases and sand dunes. It is the habitat of threatened species, such as wild camel, Gobi bear, and *khulan* or wild ass. The Dzungarian Gobi, in the west, presents a unique combination of animal and plant life. The extreme climate averages less than 100mm rainfall annually. Temperatures fluctuate from 40°C in summer to –40°C in winter. During the spring and autumn strong winds of speeds up to 140km per hour scour the land.

Fauna
Mongolia is rich in fauna and is home to some of the world's rarest wildlife. The more exotic rare species include the snow leopard (*Uncia uncia*), the Gobi bear (*Ursus arctos*) and the wild ancestors of three of mankind's most important domesticated animals – the wild camel (*Camelus bactrianus ferus*), the Asiatic wild ass (*Equus hemionus luteus*) and Przewalski's horse (*Equus przewalskii*). Many international wildlife conservation projects are helping Mongolian organisations to safeguard these rare wild animals. Nine species of bird and 38 plant species are on the verge of extinction and there are mounting concerns about the fate of the Gobi bear, the wild camel and the saiga antelope (*Saiga tartarica mongolica*), among other large mammals.

Threatened species
Below are some of the most threatened of Mongolia's rare species, together with details of the conservation measures that are aimed at helping to preserve them.

Snow leopard (Uncia uncia)

Irves in Mongolian (sometimes spelled 'irbis'). Snow leopards are among the most beautiful of the great cats. They are so well camouflaged that the big black rosettes of their tawny spotted coats, which resemble rocks and shade, make them almost impossible to see in their mountain habitat. Males weigh up to 54kg and females slightly less. They breed in winter

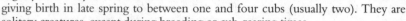

giving birth in late spring to between one and four cubs (usually two). They are solitary creatures, except during breeding or cub-rearing times.

Worldwide, the range of the snow leopard is restricted to the Himalayan ranges and the high mountains of Central Asia, which include the Mongolian Altai range. Snow leopards are extremely elusive creatures. When they are spotted, it is usually in areas of steep, broken, rocky slopes at elevations up to 5,500m. The world population is estimated, perhaps optimistically, at 7,000, although 4,000 is more likely.

The snow leopard is listed in the Mongolian *Red Book* as very rare and in the IUCN *Red Data Book* as endangered. The Convention on International Trade in Endangered Species of Fauna and Flora (CITES) prohibits its trade, and hunting these animals is considered illegal by conservationists, although a ban is difficult to enforce in Mongolia. These shy felines are distributed over a wide area of western Mongolia, in Kharkhiraa Uul in the Altai, and Khankhökhii Nuruu in the Khangai mountain ranges, as well as in some isolated mountainous sections of the Trans-Altai Gobi. Their total range in Mongolia is some 100,000km². The Mongolian population estimates vary from 800 to 1,500 animals. Highest densities are thought to be in the South Gobi, Central Trans-Altai Gobi, and northern Altai. Remnant populations occur in the Khangai and possibly in Khövsgöl Aimag, although no leopards have been sighted in Khövsgöl Aimag since the 1960s.

Competition with domestic stock and poaching are causes for their declining numbers, which is a similar case for their principal wild prey, ibex and *argali*. Because their wild prey has also declined, in some areas the leopards are becoming increasingly dependent on domestic livestock kills, which leads to more and more human/leopard conflicts.

Despite legal protection, hunting of the spotted irves in Mongolia is legal. Legislation adopted by the government, in December 2001, taxes the snow leopard at 100,000 tögrög per head when hunted for 'cultural or scientific purposes'. However it is not listed among the animals that foreigners can hunt. Since the leopards often kill domestic horses, yaks and camels, which roam freely in areas where they hunt for their survival, the economic impact to herders can be substantial.

Snow leopards exhibit extremely patchy distribution which, in time, will reduce genetic interchange, making them even more vulnerable. In Mongolia this is already happening to the isolated populations in the Khangai, Great Gobi, South Gobi and other sites. The potential for further fragmentation of the snow leopard's habitats is increased as herding in remote areas intensifies.

Conservation measures Since the early 1990s research efforts to preserve the snow leopard have been carried out by the Mongolian government, the Mongolian

Association for Conservation of Nature and Environment (MACNE) and foreign scientists. A long-term study using satellite-radio collars on snow leopards in the Gobi-Altai has led to many interesting discoveries, including information about their home ranges, which may be as great as 1,000km² – more than 20 times the size of reported home ranges elsewhere. Snow leopards in Mongolia were found to be capable of crossing up to 56km of open desert to reach a neighbouring mountain habitat. Clearly, leopards in Mongolia are on the ecological fringe of their range and must travel farther to gain food.

Given the obvious need to involve and include Mongolia's semi-nomad herders in conservation measures, a unique community-based programme was launched in 1998 called Irbis Enterprises, which seeks to foster tolerance and appreciation of the cat among herders who live in the leopard's habitats. Herders agree not to kill either leopards or their prey and to abide by grazing regulations in protected areas. In exchange, Irbis Enterprises provides much-needed access to local and foreign markets for herder-made handicrafts such as felts, mats and goods knitted from camel wool and raw cashmere. To learn more about snow-leopard conservation or to participate in active research studies in Mongolia, visit the websites www.irbis-enterprises.com or www.discoveryinitiatives.com.

Gobi bear (Ursus arctos)
Mazaalai in Mongolian. The first exciting reports of an unknown bear living in an isolated haunt, deep in the Gobi Desert, were recorded in 1900 by V Ladygin, who found bear tracks and diggings near several oases. The first confirmed sightings did not come until 1943. The range of the Gobi bear is currently thought to be restricted to Sector A of the Great Gobi Strictly Protected Area (GGSPA), encompassing 15,000–16,000km². Areas of bear activity centre around the Atas Bogd, Shar Khulst and Tsagaan Bogd mountains. Little investigation of this secretive species has been conducted and information suggests that as few as 40 animals remain, although some people put the figure at 25. Living in such a harsh desert environment, which has been subject to climate change in recent years, it is feared that the bears' continued existence is precarious. The Gobi bear is listed in the Mongolian *Red Book* as very rare, and in the IUCN *Red Data Book* as endangered. No hunting is allowed.

Worldwide, the distribution of the brown bear includes Europe, Asia, and North America. However, the Gobi bear, or *mazaalai*, is unique among brown bears in its use of a barren desert habitat. In contrast to other brown bears, Gobi bears are relatively small. Adults weigh between 100kg and 120kg. The Gobi bear has a light-brown coat, with darker colouring on its head, belly and legs. Light stripes, or a collar of colour, are often discernible around its neck. DNA studies based on hairs taken from empty bear beds, or found on trees against which the animals rub, will help biologists to establish how closely Gobi bears are related to other brown bears – for example, to the far-away Tibetan brown bear, and other brown bears from the nearby Altai mountains or the neighbouring Tien Shan range in China. It is important to determine the uniqueness of the Gobi bear in order to set appropriate conservation programmes for the animals.

Although humans pose few threats because the Gobi bear's range falls almost entirely within the core area of the GGSPA, where human activity is highly restricted, the bears are being affected by recent climate change – drought and the general drying up of oases and more limited food resources.

Conservation measures Currently management includes leaving supplemental food near key oases each spring when the bears emerge from their winter dens. Additional conservation measures include moving bears between activity centres to improve the genetic interchange. To determine if such measures are needed, recent studies have used non-invasive techniques (genetic fingerprinting using shed hairs) to study the bears. At least 15 individuals are now 'known' and natural movement between oases is being studied.

Recent work on Gobi bears and other unique animals of the Great Gobi has been sponsored by the David Shepherd Conservation Foundation, UK (web: www.dscf.demon.co.uk), the Wildlife Conservation Society, USA (web: www.wcs.org, and Discovery Initiatives, UK (web: www.discoveryinitiatives.com).

Wild Bactrian camel (Camelus bactrianus ferus)

Khavtgai in Mongolian. Despite the occurrence of domestic Bactrian camels across much of Central Asia, the continued survival of their wild forebears was not revealed to science until the late 1870s, when the explorer Przewalski visited the Lop Nor region of China and reported their existence. Hunted for its meat and exceedingly shy of human contact, the wild camel's range has been dramatically reduced since its discovery. The world's remaining wild Bactrian camels struggle to survive today as a fragmented, remnant population with half their numbers (perhaps 350) occurring in Sector A of the GGSPA in southwestern Mongolia. The Gobi National Park 'A' was established in 1976 to reflect the then known range of the wild camel. It encompasses 44,190 km^2 and is the largest protected area in Mongolia. By Mongolian law, all human activity, except research, is precluded in the core areas and only limited uses, such as national border patrols, are allowed elsewhere in the reserve. The wild camel is listed in the Mongolian *Red Book* as very rare and in the IUCN *Red Data Book* as endangered. No hunting is allowed.

Although well protected legally in Mongolia, camels are threatened by illegal hunters. Poaching is rare but it does occur. Detection of illegal activity in the reserve is difficult because the reserve is one of the largest in the world, but has a staff of less than ten rangers, few of whom have vehicles (so they rely on their own camels for transport).

Concerns are that domestic camels are allowed to graze in close proximity to the wild camels' range and there is probably some crossbreeding with unknown effects on the wild gene pool. One of the most serious concerns today is the lack of young in the herd. Recent studies have not been able to determine if this is due to poor reproduction or poor survival of calves. Wolves are the natural predators of camels and may be responsible for the loss of young, contributing to their population decline.

Conservation measures A semi-captive herd of wild camels is held at the GGSPA headquarters in Bayantooroi, Gobi-Altai Aimag. Several calves have been produced by the herd, but it has not yet been proved if transplanting captive-raised young into the wild is viable. Research into the causes and effects of low calf numbers is planned.

Recent work on wild camels and other animals of the Great Gobi has been sponsored by the David Shepherd Conservation Foundation, UK (web: www.dscf.demon.co.uk), the Wildlife Conservation Society, USA (web: www.wcs.org), and Discovery Initiatives, UK (web: www.discoveryinitiatives.com). To join a research team in the Gobi, visit the Discovery Initiatives website. (See also the box on *Wild camels*, pages 302–3.)

Gazelle

During the migration seasons over a million gazelles cross the eastern Mongolian grasslands, unhampered by fences, to both China and Russia. During the migration seasons, herds of up to 50,000 gazelle or antelope are seen at a time.

They migrate south to China when the weather gets colder and move north in the hot season. New conservation measures are now in effect to protect them – not only the animals but the land they move across. The goal is to protect both the wild creatures and their ecosystems. Two types of Mongolian gazelles are described below, the white-tailed gazelle and the black-tailed gazelle.

White-tailed gazelle (Procapra gutturosa)

Tsagaan zeer in Mongolian. The herds of white-tailed gazelles on Mongolia's eastern plains are one of Asia's great wildlife spectacles. The eastern grasslands themselves are unique and represent one of the few remaining steppe regions where undisturbed animal migration is possible in large groups of between 30,000–50,000 animals. Mongolian gazelles were once widespread in the Central and Khentii provinces, where they are now rarely found because of hunting, although small groups have been found in the Tuul River valley and in areas of the northern Altai. There are around 3,000 white-tailed gazelles in the Gobi Gurvansaikan National Park in the South Gobi region that are isolated from the eastern herds and do not migrate with them.

The white-tailed gazelle is also known by three other names: Mongolian gazelle or *tsagaan zeer* in Mongolian, *dzeren* in Russian, and Persian gazelle. The gazelles graze on different varieties of grasses, such as allium, artemisa, stipa and festuca. In the hot and hostile conditions of the semi-desert, surface pools provide drinking water after heavy summer rains.

Unfortunately the migratory herds have an uncertain future due to proposed plans for large-scale development of their habitat, which could eventually threaten their steppe-land paradise. Oil drilling and mining ventures are opening up the area by introducing improved roads and pipelines, along with future plans to build a railroad. The poorly understood, yet wide-ranging movements of the gazelles make it impossible to contain them in reserves. This means that sustainable development must be balanced with land management and wildlife conservation to ensure the preservation of the gazelles' migratory patterns across the vast eastern steppe, without impeding its natural development. The gazelles themselves constitute an important natural economic resource. Hunters shoot a certain number of antelopes each year for commercial purposes. The gazelle hunt, which has taken place annually for over 60 years, took around 50,000 head, averaging 726 tonnes of meat per year from 1951 to 1961. In recent years, the numbers have fluctuated from 10,000 to 40,000, taken during the short shooting season from mid-November to December. The meat is sold abroad.

Conservation measures Wildlife conservation and management programmes are actively helping to preserve the entire ecosystem, with participation by a number of organisations, among them the Wildlife Conservation Society (WCS) and UNEP, who have established an Eastern Steppe Biodiversity Project (ESBP). Conservation projects include helping in the training and education of local hunters. Foreign experts are working alongside the hunters in an integrated programme with local companies to ensure that veterinary care and international standards of meat processing are met. Mongolian veterinarians are trained to monitor the gazelles, since domestic animals and wild gazelles co-exist. Health and safety checks are done to help to prevent the spread of any potentially serious diseases, like foot and mouth. Furthermore, the ESBP has also established a project to monitor a number of radio-collared gazelle calves, tracking them over 10,000km^2 of the eastern plains. Further research concentrates on their spring and autumn migration patterns, the distribution and size of the herds and their population dynamics within a larger study area of 75,000km^2.

To join a research team working with animals on Mongolia's eastern plains, contact Discovery Initiatives for their latest information on eco-tours (email: enquiries@discoveryinitiatives.com).

Black-tailed gazelle (Gazella subgutturosa)

Khar süült zeer in Mongolian. Black-tailed gazelles are not as numerous as the white-tailed (Mongolian) gazelles, and are found in the South Gobi area where they number around 1,800 head. They form mixed herds with Mongolian gazelles but never with other livestock. In summer the herds are seen in unisex groups of between two and ten animals. In winter they form larger herds of 200–300 animals for protection against wolves. Fawns are born in late June and the young may be left to sleep on the ground where they are perfectly camouflaged by their russet-brown coats, while their mothers feed on saxaul, a desert shrub, and search for water. Black-tailed gazelles were hunted for their meat and horns, but, since the species is becoming endangered, hunting is now restricted. Their most important predator (besides man) is the wolf.

Conservation measures Environmental protection is similar to that for the white-tailed gazelle. Hunting of these gazelles is restricted.

Saiga antelope (Saiga tatarica mongolica)

Bökhön in Mongolian. There is mounting concern for the safety of the Mongolian antelope. This species numbered three million in the 1940s, but since then herds have plummeted in number. These snub-nosed antelopes are now confined to one small area of western Mongolia and are thought to number between 1,000 and 2,000 in total. They are a sub-species and differ from the saiga antelope of Russia and neighbouring Kazakhstan.

Conservation measures There is an attempt to re-establish a second population of Mongolian saiga, which would require the hand-rearing of young antelopes.

Przewalski's horse (Equus przewalskii)

Takhi in Mongolian. Przewalski's horse are the only wild horses to survive in modern times. They were once common throughout Mongolia and neighbouring territories, but in time, because of the effects of hunting and the competition of domestic stock at waterholes, they became extinct in the wild in the late 1960s. The species was returned to Mongolia from world zoos and reserves to two sites (Takhiin Tal and Khustain Nuruu). The wild horses interbreed easily with domestic horses; therefore, the two populations must be kept separate. They may be distinguished from domestics by their appearance and also, scientifically, by a difference in their chromosome numbers: 66 chromosomes for the Przewalski and 64 for the domestic. Wild horses are stocky creatures with mealy mouths, zebroid stripes on the hocks and a dorsal stripe that runs along the backbone from the shoulder to the tail. They have thick hairy tails, short brushy manes and dun-

MONGOLIAN WILD HORSES RETURN TO MONGOLIA

This rare horse species became extinct in the wild in the late 1960s. In 1993, 16 *takhi* reached the Khustain Nuruu reserve area (now a national park) sponsored by a Dutch Foundation in co-operation with the Mongolian Association for the Conservation of Nature and the Environment (MACNE). The same year, a German businessman, Christian Oswald, funded the transport of 12 *takhi* to Takhiin Tal, a remote site in western Mongolia, bordering Great Gobi National Park (Area B).

It took over 90 years of breeding, planning, patience and diplomacy for this to happen. The wild horses were first discovered by the explorer Colonel Nikolai Przewalski, an officer in the Russian Imperial Army, on one of his journeys through Central Asia in 1878 and made known to Western science. The capture and transportation of wild horses to the zoo parks of Europe and America is an adventure story in itself, instigated by the Duke of Bedford, of Woburn Abbey in England, and Baron Edward von Falz-Fein, of Askania Nova, in the Ukraine. But of the 54 Przewalski's horses taken into captivity in 1900 only a few produced foals. The world population descends from 12 of these animals and another wild horse caught at a later period and shipped to the Ukraine.

For almost a century the wild horses survived in international zoo parks and private collections, while in Mongolia their numbers declined. The last recorded sightings were in 1968, in the Takhiin Tal area of the southwest Gobi Altai, after which it became evident that the *takhi* had become extinct in the wild. Little knowledge of the *takhi* reached the West during the Cold War period and the area of Takhiin Tal was impossible for Westerners to visit. The Species Survival Commission (SSC), a branch of the World Wildlife Fund for Nature (WWF), helped to raise awareness of the wild horses' plight and zoo breeders took serious steps to initiate stallion exchanges between America and Europe to increase the gene pool and prevent inbreeding. Interest groups were established, like the Foundation for the Preservation and Protection of the Przewalski's Horse, who provided semi-reserves and organised breeding groups which helped to pave the way for future introductions of wild horses to Mongolia.

While breeding plans got underway, zoologists and other experts made site surveys and funds were raised by the general public with some government help, to return the wild horses to Mongolia. The Przewalski stud book records are kept at Prague Zoo, one of the oldest pedigree studbooks in the zoo world. *Takhi* are extremely popular in the minds of Mongolian people, who equated their newfound political freedom of the 1990s with the return of this last-known wild horse species, in 1992.

coloured coats, which turn a lighter colour, especially on the underbelly, during spring and summer when they lose their shaggy winter coats. This heavy-boned ancient horse type survived the extreme winter conditions of the Eurasian steppe by scraping the icy ground with their front hooves in winter to reveal the scant vegetation beneath. Foals are born in spring and usually have a light yellow coat that darkens with age.

Conservation measures These include a continued captive management programme and breeding control based on genetic knowledge. Breeders had an initial objective to return Przewlaski's horses to their natural habitat in Mongolia, which has happened, and additionally to set up a long-term sustainable population of *takhi* in free-ranging conditions. The first objective was achieved in 1992 when 21 wild horses were transported from Western zoos and reserves to release sites at Khustain Nuruu (16) and Takhiin Tal (five). The ultimate goal at the Khustain Nuruu site is to see up to 500 free-ranging Przewalski's horses in the park. This is a secure wild habitat where sufficient numbers of wild horses should ensure their continued survival. Besides the Mongolian groups and the captive population in European and American zoos, Mongolian wild horses are found in Canada (in Alberta), France (Cévènnes National Park), Holland (semi-reserves of the Dutch Foundation), in the Ukraine (at Askania Nova) and on the Hungarian steppes (Hortobagy Puszta National Park). The world herd numbers over 2,000 Przewalskis (2002). A once-endangered species in the 1970s is now a notable conservation success story.

Mongolian wild ass (Equus hemionus luteus)

Khulan in Mongolian. The total population of the Asiatic wild ass is estimated at around 10,000, surviving in the southern semi-desert regions. They possess many horse-like features and their vocalisations sound like something between the neigh of a horse and the bray of an ass. The sub-species of Asian wild ass include the *khulan*, the onager, the kiang and the Indian wild ass. The largest animals of this group are the kiang, found in the highlands of Tibet and Qinghai Province, in China. The greatest number of *khulan* occur in the Gobi, mostly in the area of the Great Gobi National Park. *Khulan* are considered globally threatened. Locally they are classified as rare animals and protected under Mongolian law. The *khulan* may be hunted for 'cultural and scientific purposes' (but not by foreigners) at T20,000 per head.

Recently, the population in the southern Gobi has been extending its range. *Khulan* now regularly occupy areas near the southeastern boundaries of the Gobi Gurvansaikhan National Park, with the highest population density south of the Zöölön Mountains. When cold weather comes they form winter herds of more than 1,000 animals. In summer, these groups break down into smaller grazing units. Large groups have a higher breeding success because their foals are better protected against wolves. The *khulan* prefer to graze on the desert steppe grasses since the alpine meadows are inaccessible to them and they rarely graze the mountain steppe. *Khulan* seem to be able to sense water below the surface and will dig in riverbeds to reach it; therefore, they can take advantage of pastures not accessible to domestic herds. Some waterholes are known by the local herdsmen as 'khulan waters'. Wild *khulan* wait their turn at waterholes and seepages frequented by domestic animals but, unfortunately, they are considered pests by the locals and are hunted or scared away. Their meat is rarely eaten but is considered sweeter than horse meat.

Conservation measures Hunting is banned for foreigners, although because of its practise in the recent past, *khulan* are very timid and flee at the slightest sound of danger. They can only be observed from a considerable distance.

To join a research team working with *khulan* and other species, contact Discovery Initiatives for their latest information on eco-tours (email: enquiries@discoveryinitiatives.com).

Other species
Manchurian red deer (Cervus elaphus)
Bor göröös in Mongolian. Live in the Mongolian Gobi Altai mountains, which range across nearly two-thirds of the country. A large species with a reddish-brown summer coat, which becomes thick brown-grey in winter. Some of the time they live among the inhospitable craggy peaks, along with snow leopard and ibex, where the harsh climate keeps man at bay, but are usually found on the lower reaches where they scrape their antlers on trees leaving behind distinctive traces. They are browsing animals but also live on nuts and fruit. Wolves are their principle predators, although hunters also kill them for meat and their antlers are used in traditional medicines.

Ibex (Capra sibirica)
Ibex, *yangir* in Mongolian, occur in the mountain regions of Mongolia and according to a recent survey there are approximately 19,000 Asiatic ibex in the Gobi Gurvansaikhan National Park. In general, ibex congregate during the breeding season in autumn and they gather in herds during winter when up to 70 animals at a time can be observed. The best time for observations is the rutting season, starting late September or early October before the herds disperse in spring. Females give birth in June. Ibex share their pasture with domestic goats and other species, which they follow on to the lower slopes in winter. As the number of domesticated goats has grown over the last few years, the wild species must move to higher altitudes for summer grazing. Natural enemies of the ibex are the snow leopard and wolf. Herders hunt ibex, especially in the beginning of winter, but their meat is not as popular as the meat of wild sheep.

Mongolian wild sheep (Ovis ammon)
Argali in Mongolian. Listed in the Mongolian *Red Book* and as a species they are considered threatened. There are 12 *argali* species in the world. A male Altai *argali* weighs 200kg and moves at a speed of 60km per hour. *Argali* occur throughout the mountainous areas of Mongolia and the overall number is estimated at 13,000. They can be observed most frequently in the Gobi Gurvansaikhan National Park where some 3,000 argali live within the park borders, one of the most densely populated areas for this species in the country. The total population in Mongolia is estimated at 12,000–15,000 head. The *argali* graze in the mornings and evenings, and prefer to spend the day in the shade of rocks. Often they graze together with domestic animals such as goats, sheep, horses and camels when they come down from the hills to graze in the surrounding steppe areas. They join up in herds at the beginning of the breeding season at the end of September. Their worst natural enemy is the wolf, which attacks them on the lower ground, especially in winter. Local people hunt them frequently, mainly in autumn and winter. (Foreigners are allowed to hunt them at a price but the numbers are strictly limited.)

Marmot (Marmota siberica)
Tarvaga in Mongolian. Two of the world's 14 species of marmot inhabit the Mongolian countryside: black Altai marmot and yellow steppe marmot. The most numerous is the steppe marmot or Siberian marmot, *Marmota siberica*, known as

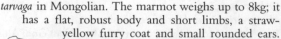

tarvaga in Mongolian. The marmot weighs up to 8kg; it has a flat, robust body and short limbs, a straw-yellow furry coat and small rounded ears. The fur on its head is dark brown to black. Its strong tiny claws dig the hard earth, as it hibernates underground during the long Mongolian winters. It has two lairs, one for winter and another shallower lair for summer. Since it never digs in sand its lairs are on higher ground in clay and gravel soils, which also provide good grazing. They are social animals and enjoy living in colonies. Mating takes place in the open when the males are seen to fight over the females, who later give birth to a single litter of up to six young per year. *Möndöl* is a marmot cub. When frightened marmots warn each other by a series of loud shrieks, whereupon they all dart back to their holes. They can harbour a flea species known as *Oropsylia silantevi*, which carries bubonic plague. (See also *Hunting marmot*, page 119.)

The steppe wolf (Canis lupus)

Chon in Mongolian. The steppe wolf is a sub-species of the grey wolf, which is found in Central Asia. The wolf is a particularly important animal in Mongolian life, since it is both revered and feared. In ancient folklore, it was said that the Mongol people derived from the union of a doe and a wolf (or people with these names), but they are also a threat and have become man's enemies because wolf packs attack the herders' sheep and other animals. Overall the numbers in Mongolia are decreasing, but in some pockets of the northwest their density is high. The national wolf hunts of the recent past, held biannually, are no longer held, but individuals continue to hunt. The tradition for the hunters was to spread out in a large circle, climbing to the higher ground and then begin to shout in order to drive the wolves from their hiding places. In this way the hunt would comb through an area and when the wolves appeared, wild chases on horseback hunted them down, until the exhausted animals were lassooed and laid out (Mongolian euphemism for killed). Wolves usually live and hunt in packs in a known territory. However, lone wolves that move on without territories are called trekking wolves. Increasing numbers of these solitary creatures do more damage than the better-integrated packs, which hunt more efficiently. In winter wolf packs mainly feed on red deer and to a lesser extent on wild boar, roe deer and smaller animals such as steppe marmot, hares and rodents. Cubs are born in May and June, and since the wolves hunt far from home, they communicate to one another by howling, especially at night, which the young cubs imitate. This orientates them and defines the different packs and their territories.

Mongolian birdlife

Mongolia lies on the migratory routes of a large variety of geese, duck and cranes. There are 30 game-bird species, including capercailie and grouse. Some species produce edible eggs, but Mongolians tend not to make much use of them. Swans and other rare birds are identified and protected, among them the golden pheasant and snow partridge. Larger birds of prey like eagles can be seen throughout the country, and several species of buzzard are protected. Owls are also protected because they prey on the millions of small rodents that swarm over the pastures and ruin them.

Lakeshores, lagoons, lowland fens, meadows, and woods provide habitats for many different birds. Indigenous game birds are found in the following regions:

- **Great Bustard** Scattered widely over the steppes and along the open river valleys.
- **Grey partridge** or **Daurian partridge** Very widely distributed, except in the Gobi areas and parts of the eastern steppe.
- **Hazel hen** Found in the coniferous forests of the Khentii, Khangai and Altai ranges, and in the mountains around Khövsgöl.
- **Black grouse** Found in the mountains around Khövsgöl, river basins and forests of Selenge and Khentii provinces, and along the Khalkh River in the far eastern tip of the country.
- **Capercailie** Found in the Khangai and Khentii mountains, the mountains of Khövsgöl, and the Selenge Valley.
- **Willow ptarmigan** Found in the Mongolian Altai, Khangai and Khentii mountains, and the mountains of Khövsgöl.
- **Pallas's sand grouse** Found in the Gobi and semi-Gobi areas.
- **Chukar partridge** Found in the Mongolian Altai, Gobi Altai and the southwest Khangai mountains.
- **Hawks** Abundant on the steppe, where they prey mainly on voles. Since there are few trees to nest in, hawks settle on the ground and nest at the bases of structures like telegraph poles.
- **Eagles** Trained by the Kazakh people of western Mongolia and used in hunting foxes and smaller steppe creatures for the pot.

Hunting

Every year the Ministry of Nature and Environment release quotas and licences on certain numbers of animals and birds that can be hunted by foreign tourists. Tourists keen on hunting have a great opportunity to hunt deer, game birds and *argali* (wild sheep). (The cost to trophy hunters of one *argali* is US$20,900, bear US$4,750 and lynx US$3,800.)

In general, hunting is widespread and one Mongolian family in four owns a gun. It is seen as a natural right and some local people don't understand why hunting should be forbidden inside the national parks and protected areas. They feel threatened (in some instances justifiably) because a no-hunting policy prevents them from hunting wolves that attack their flocks of sheep and goats, but gradually people are beginning to understand that the new conservation laws make long-term sense, although poaching continues. Wild sheep are hunted because of their tasty meat and big horns, and snow leopards because they are regarded as a threat to the livestock. Nowadays this is less likely to happen due to the great efforts of national park staff and conservation education.

Hunting traditions

One ancient conservation law states that it is forbidden to hunt black-tailed gazelles in autumn when the ground is frost-covered. Hunting was also forbidden if the winter was very severe. Mongolians were careful not to touch animals' dens and would not let a human shadow fall on a bird's nest. In 1640, the fine for destroying a nest was a two-year-old cow. It was an unwritten rule to shoot at close range. No Mongolian hunter ever uses the word 'kill'; instead, he 'lays out' an animal.

TO COOK A MARMOT

Heat some large, round stones on the fire. While they are heating, scoop out the marmot's innards through the throat cavity, using your hands. Place the hot stones inside the carcass, tie the neck and roast on an open low fire, or steam in an earth oven until done (usually after two hours or so). The meat, although fatty, is very tender and delicious and falls away from the bone when well done. The remains are made into soup and the 'cooking stones' make excellent comforters and, like a hot water bottle, help to relieve aches and pains.

Game hunting and fishing

Although better known for its big-game hunting, Mongolia's vast grasslands are also home to a variety of upland birds such as the hazel grouse, Hungarian partridge, common quail, blackcock and other species. Sand grouse and black grouse hunted for private purposes cost T2,000–5,000 per permit. The Great Lakes regions of western Mongolia offer tourists some shooting and fishing, strictly under licence. Fishing licences vary from US$1 to US$80, depending on the fish. Sturgeon longer than one metre cost T20,000 and under a metre T15,000; taimen cost T10,000 (See section on *Fishing* in *Sport and adventure*, pages 197–203.) Please note that the above costs are subject to change. Tourists are offered some upland shooting by the rivers and lakes of the northern forest-steppe in autumn and spring. However, the birds are so unused to danger that they present themselves to the guns as easy targets. Over 200,000 game birds are reportedly shot each year by Mongolian and other hunters, who must first obtain licences.

THE RICHNESS OF MONGOLIAN FLORA DURING THE SUMMER SEASON
Ann Hibbert

The Mongolian spring begins in early February, in the 'white month', when the lambing season starts and milk is flowing again. Spring, as we know it, begins much later when the ice has broken on the rivers. By the middle of April there is still no sign of a single flowering plant, only the brilliant lichens on the rocks to give colour to the landscape. Towards the end of the month the early anemone, a mauve *pulsatilla*, appears sheltering among rocks quite high in the hills. It is soon followed by yellow and white varieties that grow on the uplands in clearings among the larches.

Gradually the flowers begin to appear. Among the first are wild pansies, bigger than English heartsease and bright yellow. Large violets grow in the woodlands and in the open meadows, single, tiny iris, both yellow and mauve. The earliest flowers seem to prefer the higher ground on the northern slopes, which is where the heaviest precipitation falls and where the trees are thickest. At the beginning of June, climbing a hill, we found a carpet of minute flowers, although in the valleys they were still sparse. We came across alyssum, saxifrage and vetches of all kinds, fennels, minute asters and primulas and in general a wide range of alpine varieties. As the rainy season developed we noted a brilliant crimson lily, whole hillsides of them, whose root is regarded in Mongolia as a sort of wild potato.

Hunting marmot

It is common to see one or two hunters with ancient rifles slung over their shoulders, riding in search of marmots. Marmots are easily mesmerised. An old hunting trick is to distract them by waving a dried yak's tail on a stick in the air. This trick surprises the marmot and makes him sit bolt upright to watch what is going on. He becomes a stationary target, which makes the shot easier. The idea is to make a clean shot in the head so as not to damage the skin. Hunters take some 150,000 marmot skins per annum.

Mongolians are uneasy about offering marmot meat to foreign tourists as it sometimes makes people ill. Some marmots may carry fleas, and therefore bubonic plague, which is the most likely reason for their caution.

Flora

Mongolian flora has remained undisturbed for centuries, in areas of pristine vegetation, often the last of its kind in the world. The Mongolian steppe is unsurpassed as an open pastureland and various types of grasses thrive on different ground and landscape conditions – from mountain to meadow steppe. There are many different types of steppe – generally named after the geographical terrain or a predominant plant species – just as there are many different types of Gobi. Formations and colonies of plants live in harmony with the soil and climate, where the only danger apart from the severe climate is from natural forest fires or desertification. But things may change, and the dangers grow as

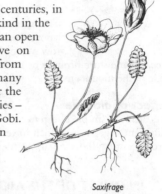

Saxifrage

As the summer advances, the variety of vegetation becomes overwhelming. In the dryness and cold of Mongolia even the most common plants have extraordinarily deep roots. On open rocky hillsides we found stonecrops and great patches of sweet-smelling wild thyme. In places near streams, where in England there would be buttercups and daisies, crowds of golden globe flowers grow and a kind of white anemone, which we gathered in armfuls. Gentians and edelweiss grow like weeds in the open steppe. Meadows filled with delphiniums and larkspur thrilled me and in the broad open valleys the blue iris stretched like wide, shallow lakes reflecting the sky. There are acres of scabious and yellow mustard and fields of asphodel. In the woods, pink roses grow close together and the pale flowers of the Siberian clematis twining among the silver birch trees have a ghostly look. Blue azaleas are to be found in the cool shade of mountain copses, and lovely waxen Solomon's seal hide in the dark crannies and rocks. Some plants grow to an immense size by English standards – wild rhubarb, whose creamy, feathery blossoms reached above our heads, and thistles that grow so big that a true Scot might turn pale with envy.

As August turns into September, the number of varieties begin to dwindle and our attention turned to collecting mushrooms. Some are exceedingly poisonous, besides smelling very unpleasant when drying. By mid-September everything was brown again, and in October the hard frost clamped down once more. It is difficult to convey an adequate idea of the richness of the Mongolian flora during the summer months.

Clematis

roads develop and tourism opens up the country. Certain plants like peonies thrive in shady or cool places (see box below), while others, like saxifrage, can live on dry slopes exposed to the parching wind and powerful sun. Mongolia's diverse and distinctive vegetation includes an important part of Asia's plant life. Over 150 Mongolian plants are listed as endemic species; 133 plants are considered very rare and are registered in the *Red Book* of Mongolia (see *Further reading*, pages 385–7).

Due to Mongolia's severe continental climate and its altitude, the flora of Mongolia is not as rich as the flora of neighbouring southern Siberia. Where the plateau descends into southern Siberia, summer temperatures become warmer. In northern Mongolia, another point of interest which you might observe is that trees grow well on the flanks of the northern-facing mountain slopes because moisture brought by the wind from the northern ocean falls as rain on that side of the mountains.

Effect of altitude

Vertically, a simple climb from the valley to the snow line reveals some distinctly different vegetation, which in terms of sheer variety is effectively equivalent to a cross-country (horizontal) journey of 1,000km or more.

IN QUEST OF THE MONGOLIAN PEONY

Kirsty Fergusson

I must confess to an initial apprehension about the wisdom of committing myself to riding a 200km stretch of the Orkhon Valley on Mongolian ponies, with 18 people I had never met before, in order to raise money for charity, but I also had a dream: to find the elusive Mongolian peony.

However, ten days later, although our little group had been drenched, frozen, burnt, whipped by winds blowing from Siberia or the Gobi, we were a happy – if rather dirty – crew as we rode the last leg of the journey that had taken us through barren steppe and rushing rivers, high mountain passes and dense forest, towards the great waterfall in a rocky gorge near the source of the Orkhon River. So far, no peonies. On the way we'd been sung to by trained throat singers in the capital, and by boys on their horses in the wilderness. We'd passed herds of yaks and horses and galloped through meadows of sweet thyme and pungent artemisia, dodging marmot burrows and outcrops of volcanic rock. We'd been haunted by vultures and kites, keen-eyed followers of the chuck wagon and mess tent. By luck we had come upon a local horse race, where barefoot children raced their beribboned ponies, whooping and screaming, the length of a ten-mile valley, and witnessed the heroic comedy of a Mongolian wrestling match. We'd been offered *airag* (fermented mare's milk) and salty tea in a nomad family's *ger* and seen poverty matched and outdistanced by resourcefulness and freedom. At night, our horses, hobbled in pairs, grazed freely amongst the flocks and herds of local families on the open steppe.

So, there we were, on the last day, approaching the Orkhon waterfall. I'd

In the northern and central mountains, beyond the tree line, you will find alpine turf with clumps of flowers – often tiny, bright cushions of startling pink heads and multicoloured lichens that tinge the rocks many different shades of green, yellow and deep orange. The Mongolian timber line is found at around 2,400m. There is no universal pattern, but it is interesting to note the differences in tree-line vegetation in Mongolia compared to other countries. More than 90% of high-mountain species are adapted to a short growth period. Look out for saxifrages, rock jasmines and gentians. The flat expanses of the Mongolian steppe – averaging 1,580m – are at the altitude of a high mountain village in the Swiss Alps, and you will have no trouble recognising familiar alpine plant species. The forests bordering on meadows are places where Martigan lilies and wild clematis are found, while orchids, like the delicate pink-slipper variety, appear close to the ground. Lowland fens and meadows are the ideal habitat for delphiniums, primulas, anemones and different kinds of grasses. Meadow flowers are profuse; large white gentians and hardy species of edelweiss give the impression that Mongolian soil is richer than it is.

Pedicularis

Herbs and grasses thrive on the thinner soil of the steppeland. Pasture land covers 1.22 million km², of which 20,000km² were used for hay, but since the

seen drifts of *Iris sibirica* in the damp valleys dotted with purple orchids, mountain sides swathed in tiny alpine flowers humming with bees and other insects, and woods choked with wild roses, veronicas, delphiniums and anemones. It was enough, I'd told myself, as I'd waited to follow the example of our horsemen, who had prayed as they pressed forehead and palms against the trunk of a sacred pine at the mountain-top Buddhist monastery of Tüvkhiin Khiid, the day before. The elusive Mongolian peony would have to live in my imagination for a while yet.

But a brief reconnoitre revealed a steep and rocky path to the foot of the gorge by the waterfall. Wild gooseberries, potentilla and berberis sprang from the rocks: precarious and prickly handholds in the sharp descent. Last down, I could hear the laughter of my companions echoing through the gorge as they made their way through the larches and pines, hunting for a suitable place to bathe in the tumbling, icy river. And suddenly there, under a canopy of wild cherry trees, amongst a tide of wild roses and strawberries, Himalayan geraniums and thalictrums, clusters of peonies revealed themselves. Huge, established clumps and little self-sown seedlings: the more I looked, the more there were. True, they had finished flowering and only a few faded, dark pink petals still clung to the calcyces, but the fat, shiny seed pods clustered over the elegant, finely toothed leaves like pudgy green fists clutching treasure.

That night, while horsemen sang, I lay in my tent looking up at the bunches of pods suspended above, drying in the chill, moistureless air. I closed my eyes and saw again the smiling hermit priest of Tüvkhiin Khiid and the sacred pine, and breathed once more the dark aroma of the twisted bark as I pressed my face and hands against it, trying not to ask for too much.

HERBAL CURES FOR AILMENTS
Edelweiss Good for the blood
Potentilla fruticosa (one of the numerous varieties of cinquefoils) Boiled in salt water and used to cure toothache
Yellow poppies Used to help heal wounds
White gentians Collected for lung and chest complaints

'Unknown treatments' for wobbly stomachs or hangovers consist of potent herbal measures, which you should treat with caution – and remember to ask your guide to note down the contents for future reference!

dissolution of the state collectives fodder production has declined.

Certain plants are known to have curative properties, and many wild flowers are used in folk remedies. If you have an interest in wild flowers it is advisable to take

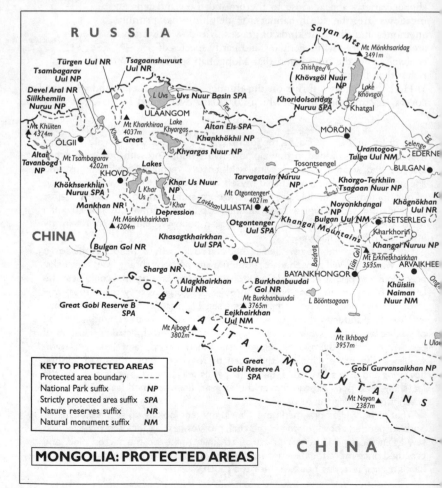

MONGOLIA: PROTECTED AREAS

KEY TO PROTECTED AREAS
Protected area boundary	----
National Park suffix	**NP**
Strictly protected area suffix	**SPA**
Nature reserves suffix	**NR**
Natural monument suffix	**NM**

a good plant dictionary with you such as *The Flora of Britain and Northern Europe* or Grubov's *Mongolian Flora* (which is difficult to find).

NATIONAL PARKS

Large tracts of Mongolia's territory have been turned into national parks, and the aim is to place 30% of its territory under Nature Protection. Currently over 12% of the territory is designated for special protection. Areas are designated for protection in four different categories:

* **Protected Monuments** To protect historical and cultural monuments and natural formations (both inside and outside national parks and reserve areas)
* **National Reserves** To protect natural features and natural resources
* **National Conservation Parks** To include natural and less-threatened zone areas, some in a position to be developed for tourism
* **Strictly Protected Areas** To protect unique features and areas of cultural and scientific interest

The national parks system is a wonderful way of safeguarding the countryside and habitats of millions of species. Mongolia has led the world in establishing one of the first protected areas, the Bogdkhan Uul Reserve beside Ulaanbaatar. Very often hunting reserves were turned into nature reserves, and it is clear from conservation history that hunters were the ones who became the world's leading conservationists. An excellent book, *The Penitent Butchers*, traces this process over 75 years of wildlife conservation. The authors' observation was that besides keeping track of the biodiversity in our world, we need beautiful places in order to face the future with confidence. The recent international award-winning project to preserve the crane, *Grus vipio* (see box in *Dornod Aimag*, pages 370–1), shows how seriously integrated conservation measures are taken in Mongolia.

The first step in preserving wild species and their habitats in general was to set up reserves and national parks. There were few examples that could, in the modern sense, be regarded as wildlife sanctuaries before the mid-19th century. Bogdkhan Uul Reserve, established 200 years ago, would rank as one of the world's earliest reserves. Over the centuries Mongolians have passed laws to patrol and protect special areas. The first environmental laws date from the *Ikh Zasag* (Great Code) which recognised a number of mountains and hunting grounds as specially protected places in the 12th/13th centuries.

For further information, contact the Protected Areas Bureau, Ministry of Nature and the Environment, Baga Toiruu 44, Ulaanbaatar 11; tel: 976 11 326617; fax: 976 11 328620. A book on the subject, available at bookshops in Mongolia, is *Special Protected Areas of Mongolia*.

Visiting national parks

The following rules apply when visiting national parks:

- Visitors must pay the appropriate park-entry fees and be in possession of a valid permit at all times. The fees are payable at the park office or directly to rangers. Permits are available through the few existing parks offices, but it is best to plan in advance and obtain them at the head office in Ulaanbaatar. Park-entry fees currently stand at T1,000 (roughly US$1) per person and an additional charge of T3,000 (around US$3) per vehicle, although in the future these modest charges may be increased.
- Keep your entrance receipt in case of spot checks.
- Take all solid waste to a disposal site outside the park.
- Stay on designated routes and travel at reasonable speeds. Do not make new tracks.
- Camp outside core areas (maps to some parks eg: Gobigurvansaikhan National Park in the South Gobi are provided with your permit) and away from water courses and livestock.
- Report any unorthodox activity to park rangers.
- Be efficient with your use of water, and where possible avoid using soap. Water in the park is relied upon by local people and livestock, and is very limited. Do not build fires; liquid-fuel or gas stoves should be used.

Special protected areas

Establishing protected areas is a means of protecting and preserving Mongolia's rich cultural heritage for future generations, including numerous threatened and endangered animal and plant species, different ecosystems and monuments or sites of cultural importance. It also serves to develop tourism in specifically allocated zones, with eco-*ger* accommodation and special adventure and nature activities, such as climbing or birdwatching, allowed.

The following information was compiled by Mikkel Wisborg, Tourism Consultant, from material provided in the booklet *Special Protected Areas of Mongolia* (2000). This booklet is available from the Environmental Protection Agency. For further details, contact the Bureau of Special Protected Areas Environmental Protection Agency, Government Building No 3, Baga Toiruu 44, Ulaanbaatar 11; tel: 976 11 326 617; fax: 976 11 328 620; email: epa@magicnet.mn.

Natural monuments of Mongolia
These include areas of unique natural formation such as volcanic mountains.

> **BARE FACTS**
> Areas of unique natural formations

Bulgan Uul
1,800 hectares
This area is situated near Tsetserleg, in Arkhangai Aimag (central Mongolia). It forms part of the watershed between rivers of the internal and Amur river basins and enjoys a special local microclimate. This area is suitable for re-introducing sable antelope.

Uran-Togoo-Tulga Uul
5,800 hectares
Situated in the territory of Bulgan Aimag (northern Mongolia). An inactive volcano with a unique natural landscape formation.

Khüisiin Naiman Nuur (8 lakes)
11,500 hectares
The area is in Övörkhangai Aimag (central Mongolia). Khüisiin Naiman Nuur, with its exceptional configuration, is surrounded by landscape representing the middle part of the Khangai mountain range. These freshwater lakes include the eight lakes known as Khüisiin Naiman Nuur: Shireet, Khaliun, Bugat, Khayaa, Khüis, Shanaa, Döröö and Baga.

Eejkhairkhan Uul
22,475 hectares
Eej Khairkhan Uul is located in Gobi-Altai Aimag between Tsogt and Altai sums (southwest Mongolia). The rocky strip near Khairkhhan Mountain divides the Middle Gobi Mountains on the western side of Eej Khairkhan Mountain. A cave in the region is a major tourist attraction.

Ganga Nuur
32,860 hectares
This lake is located in southeastern Mongolia in Sükhbaatar Aimag close to the border with China. The area surrounding the lake grew as a result of a sand block formed by wind movement. It is a beautiful freshwater lake located between the mountain steppe and Gobi with its own special microclimate.

Süikhent
4,830 hectares
This area is located in Dornogobi Aimag (southern Mongolia). The site is protected because of its unusual petrified trees, rarely found in Mongolia.

Mongolian nature reserves

> ### BARE FACTS
> Areas designated to create conditions for protecting, preserving and restoring certain natural features as well as natural resources.

Batkhan Uul
58,800 hectares
This area is located in Övörkhangai Aimag and Töv Aimag (central Mongolia). Batkhan mountain area is part of the Khangai and Khentii mountain ranges; visitors driving west from Ulaanbaatar often stop here to camp and enjoy the scenery, as the area is conveniently near the main road from Ulaanbaatar to Arvaikheer.

Nagalkhan Uul
3,076 hectares
This nature reserve is located in Töv Aimag (central Mongolia). The nature reserve was designated as a reserve to protect the southernmost part of Khentii mountain range and the surrounding forest steppe.

Bulgan Gol (river)
1,840 hectares
This reserve is located in Khovd Aimag (northern Mongolia). It was initially designated as a wildlife reserve to protect species such as the beaver, silver-tipped black sable, stone marten and others.

Lkhachinvandad Uul
58,500 hectares
The reserve is located in Sükhbaatar Aimag (southern Mongolia). The purpose of the reserve is to preserve and protect the elk habitat in the mountain steppe.

Ugtam Uul
46,160 hectares
The area is in Dornod Aimag (northeastern Mongolia). It includes two holy mountains, Ugtam and Khairkhan, and the ruins of a Buddhist monastery. It is a particularly beautiful place located in the transition area between forest steppe and steppe zones.

Sharga-Mankhan (two areas)
390,071 hectares
This reserve consists of two parts located in Khovd and Gobi-Altai aimags – the distance between the two is about 200km. It is home to some of the last Mongolian antelope. The reserve is designated to protect the antelope's breeding grounds.

Alagkhairkhan
36,400 hectares
This area is situated in Gobi-Altai Aimag (southwest Mongolia). It is one of the highest mountains of the middle part of the Mongol Altai mountain range, and supports a habitat of rare and very rare plants and wildlife species (*argali*, ibex, snow leopard, and snowcock).

Burkhanbuudai Uul
52,110 hectares
This nature reserve is in the Gobi-Altai Aimag (southwest Mongolia). Many small rivers have their beginning here, and many unique natural rock formations are found. Local people worship a brown stone located at the top of Bogd Mountain that looks like a sheaf of wheat.

Ikh Nart
43,740 hectares
This area is situated in Dornogobi Aimag (southern Mongolia). The northeastern limit of *argali* (wild sheep) habitat. It was designated to extend *argali* territory, and to protect the natural environment.

Zagiin Us
273,606 hectares
Zagiin Us extends into Dundgobi and Ömnögobi aimags (southern Mongolia). The Zagiin Us Valley is composed of saline soil with dry, circular salt marshes and sand dunes. It is a mixed landscape of special ecological interest. It also has areas of saxaul, a bush that grows in the semi-desert; it is the northern limit of the black-tailed gazelle's distribution range and the western extention of the white-tailed gazelle's range.

Ergeliin Zoo
60,910 hectares
This area is situated in Dornogobi Aimag (southern Mongolia) where many famous dinosaur-fossil finds have been discovered. People refer to this region as 'Altan Uul' (Golden Mountain).

Khögnökhan Uul
46,990 hectares
Situated in Bulgan Aimag (northern Mongolia). The reserve represents taiga (forest) and steppe plants in an area that comprises several different natural vegetation and climatic zones.

Toson-Khulstai
469,928 hectares
This area covers parts of the Khentii Aimag and the Dornod Aimag (eastern Mongolia). Toson, Khulstai Nuur and Salbariin valleys are the main habitats of the white-tailed gazelle. It was designated to extend its distribution from the Kherlen River northwards.

Khar Yamaat
50,594 hectares
This area covers parts of Khentii Aimag and parts of Sükhbaatar Aimag (eastern Mongolia). The special formation of Khar Yamaat and Turuu Öndör Mountain is a continuation of the Khankhentii mountain range. Natural vegetation includes pine and aspen groves, berries and medicinal plants rarely found in steppe areas.

Yakhi Lake
251,388 hectares
Yakhi Lake is situated in Dornod Aimag (eastern Mongolia). It is part of the white-tailed gazelle distribution, and is one of the main habitats for migrating birds.

Devel Aral (island)
10,300 hectares
The island is situated in the Usankhooloi and Khovd rivers that feed from Achit Lake located between Bayan-Ölgii and Uvs aimags (northwest Mongolia). This area is home to ring-necked pheasant, wild boar and beaver, which are becoming increasingly rare in Mongolia. It is a main distribution area of sea buckthorn. The area is designated to protect the wild boar and beaver habitats.

Tsagan Shuvuut Uul and **Türgen Uul** reserves in Uvs Aimag are also marked on the Protected Areas map in this guide.

National parks
The 14 national parks listed below are designated for future tourist development but in many cases this has not yet happened. Very few of the areas listed are equipped with tourist facilities, such as offices and entrance gates, information, and on-the-spot services. Among the better-known national parks open to tourists are Gorkhi-Terelj, Lake Khövsgöl, Gobi Gurvansaikhan and Khustain Nuruu. In the remoter areas of western and eastern Mongolia there are no services and visitors must take in everything: transport, tent and food supplies. Be warned, too, that there are no proper roads or route directions; signposting is totally absent.

> ### BARE FACTS
> Areas containing natural original conditions that are relatively preserved and which have historical, cultural, scientific, educational and ecological importance. They are designated for tourism development.

Khorgo-Terkhiin Tsagaan Nuur (lake)
77,267 hectares
This area is located in Arkhangai Aimag (central Mongolia). It contains spectacular mountain scenery and rock formations formed by volcanic eruptions. Accommodation is available locally in tourist *ger* camps.

Khövsgöl Nuur (lake)
838,070 hectares
The lake is situated in Khövsgöl Aimag, which is named after it (northern Mongolia). Known as the 'dark-blue pearl of Mongolia', the lake is one of the largest and most scenic protected areas in the country. Bordering the Sayan Mountains to the north and the Khoridalsaridag range to the west, it is 136km long and 3km wide, and is part of the protected area. Tourist accommodation is available in *ger* camps in the vicinity.

Gobi Gurvansaikhan
2,171,737 hectares
The Gobi Gurvansaikhan is situated in Ömnögobi and Bayankhongor aimags (southern Mongolia). The park protects the main natural characteristics of the Gobi-Altai mountain range. Its landscape includes high mountains, mountain valleys, arid steppe and desert. It is also designated for ecotourism, and ecotourists, for example, participate in the park's conservation projects. There are tourist *ger* camps in the vicinity.

Gorkhi-Terelj
293,168 hectares
The Gorkhi-Terelj National Park is situated in Töv Aimag (central Mongolia). It is one of the most visited national parks in Mongolia because it is so close to Ulaanbaatar. It offers beautiful scenery and the region is well suited for tourism with its *ger* camps around the Terelj resort.

Khustain Nuruu
50,620 hectares
This national park is in the Töv Aimag (central Mongolia). It is an example of the steppe landscape of the southwestern part of the Khentii mountain range. It is home to the *takhi* (wild horses), recently re-introduced to Mongolia from European captive-bred zoo stock by a Dutch Foundation. There is a *ger* camp in the vicinity.

Altai Tavanbogd
636,161 hectares
Situated in Bayan-Ölgii Aimag (western Mongolia). The landscape of this national park represents special characteristics of high mountains, crystal-clear rivers, mountain valleys, and steppe landscape. It is the habitat of *argali*, ibex, elk and other mammals, and bird species like snowcock, eagle and lammergeyer. This area is ideal for mountain sports and tourism, yet to be developed.

Khangai Nuruu
888,455 hectares
This national park is comprised of the central part of the Khangai mountain range, which borders on Arkhangai Aimag, Övörhangai Aimag and Bayankhongor Aimag (in central and southern Mongolia). The area includes high mountains, lakes, forests and meadows. The mountains are of ancient formation producing a variety of landscapes. The rivers flow to either the Pacific or Arctic oceans. Currently undeveloped for tourism.

Khar Us Nuur
850,272 hectares
This area is situated in Khovd Aimag (northern Mongolia), located near the Great Lakes basin covering a large area of desert steppe and arid semi-desert with its unique climate and environment: fresh water resources, Gobi desert, and steppe valleys alongside the Mongolian Altai Mountains. It is home to rare wildlife and marsh-bird species. Currently undeveloped for tourism.

Noyonkhangai
59,088 hectares
This mountain area is situated in Arkhangai Aimag (central Mongolia). It is an area of mineral water springs, and rare flora and fauna. It is also an area of age-old traditional worship, as Mongols worship certain mountains. Springs and good camping areas at the base of the mountain attract tourists.

Tarvagatain mountain range
525,440 hectares
This national park is located in both Arkhangai and Zavkhan aimags (central and western Mongolia). The area is the source of the River Selenge, the largest river in Mongolia. The national park comprises areas of historical, cultural and natural

heritage. It has great potential to develop its mineral water springs as health spas for tourism, but these areas are not yet developed.

Siilkhemiin Uul (mountain range)
140,080 hectares (in total)
The national park consists of two parts, A and B; both are situated in the Bayan-Ölgii Aimag (western Mongolia). The park is designated to protect the area's resources and the habitat of the mountain sheep (*argali*).

Khankhökhii-Khyargas Lake
553,350 hectares
Situated in Uvs Aimag (western Mongoia). Khankhökhii Nuruu (mountain) is located on the boundary of Uvs and Khyargas lake basins. The area plays an important role in maintaining the ecological balance by limiting the increase of desert-steppe areas. The area provides a home to numerous endangered migratory bird species. The region is an area of international scientific research, visited by tourists, but there are limited facilities available.

Tsambagarav Mountain
110,960 hectares
This mountain is located between Khovd Aimag and Bayan-Ölgii Aimag (western Monglia). The area is of significance for the study of glaciers and is home to the rare snow leopard. No tourist facilities.

Onon-Balj basin
414,752 hectares
This area is situated in both Khentii Aimag and Dornod Aimag in northeastern Mongolia, and consists of two parts, A and B. The area forms a unique geographical zone of northern taiga forest surrounded by arid-desert steppe valleys. A border area not frequented by tourists

Strictly protected areas

BARE FACTS
Areas that represent unique features and characteristics of natural zones, preserving the original conditions that are of special scientific and cultural significance.

Khasagtkhairkhan
27,651 hectares
This mountain is located in the Gobi-Altai Aimag (southern Mongolia). It is a forested part of the Mongol Altai mountain range and a homeland for various plant and wildlife species of mountainous steppe and Gobi regions.

Bogdkhan Uul
41,651 hectares
Located at the southern edge of the Mongolian capital (central Mongolia), Bogdkhan Uul marks the borderline between the forest steppe and steppe (grassland) regions, as well as the southern limit of larch-forest growth. Visited by

tourists; you need a permit to go hiking; *ger* camps and hotels nearby at Zuunmod; a day trip from Ulaanbaatar.

Great Gobi
5,311,730 hectares
It consists of two parts. Gobi A and Gobi B: Gobi A is in Gobi-Altai and Bayankhongor aimags; Gobi B is located in Khovd and Gobi-Altai aimags (in southern Mongolia). It protects a large undisturbed part of the vast Gobi desert and provides a refuge for very rare species like the wild camels and Gobi bears. In 1991 the United Nations designated the Great Gobi an International Biosphere Reserve, the fourth-largest biosphere reserve in the world, and the largest in Asia.

Khökhserkhiin Nuruu
65,920 hectares
This crest of the Altai Mountains is situated in Khövd and Bayan-Ölgii aimags (western Mongolia). This area is the main habitat for ibex and *argali* herds. It also helps maintain the original features of the Altai Mountains and the ecological balance of the territory.

Mongol Daguur
103,016 hectares
This protected area is divided into two parts, both in the Dornod Aimag (eastern Mongolia). The larger northern part is contiguous to Russia's Daurski Reserve, and comprises rolling steppe and wetlands, on the southern shore of Lake Torey. The southern part of the protected area encompasses part of the Ulz River and its pristine wetlands, classified as a protected area to conserve the white-necked crane's breeding grounds, and those of other rare crane species.

Eastern Steppe
570,374 hectares
This area is located in the Dornod and Sükhbaatar aimags (eastern Mongolia). It represents the only steppe land region where there are no economic activities. The eastern Mongolian steppe is home to 25 species of mammal, dominated by herds of gazelle (over 70% of the white-tailed gazelle population of Mongolia inhabits this area). The protected area is only a small part of the eastern steppe.

Nömrög
311,205 hectares
This area is situated in the Dornod Aimag, and covers the remote and uninhabited far-eastern tip of Mongolia (eastern Mongolia). Ecologically distinct from the rest of Mongolia, this reserve includes the westernmost end of the Hinggan mountain range, which extends into Mongolia from China. One-fifth is forested by small groves of Scotch pine, white birch and willow. Manchurian flora and fauna, which occur nowhere else in Mongolia, are found here. Species include Ussurian moose, black-necked oriole, white-breasted rock thrush and the great black water snake.

Otgontenger Uul
95,510 hectares
It is situated in Zavkhan Aimag and is the highest peak in the Khangai mountain range (central Mongolia). This area represents the biodiversity of the Khangai mountain range and is home to rare and very rare wildlife.

Khankhentii Nuruu
1,227,074 hectares
This mountain range is part of the Khentii Mountains situated in the Töv, Khentii and Selenge aimags (central and northern Mongolia). These mountains have preserved their original features and are located between the Eurasian forest taiga and the Central Asian steppe. Three major river systems spring from the protected area: the Tuul, which flows into the Orkhon and then the Selenge, to Russia's Lake Baikal and on to the Arctic Ocean; the Onon and Kherelen rivers flow east to join the Amur which flows into the Pacific Ocean. The area represents basic characteristics of five different types of *taiga* landscape. It is the home of Genghis Khan.

Uvs Lake basin
712,545 hectares
The Uvs Lake basin is located in the Uvs Aimag (western Mongolia), and named after it. The immediate change of ecological zones in this relatively small area of the Uvs Lake basin is matched by few places in the world, with its perpetual snowfields and permafrost in the Türgen Mountains extending to the sand dunes of Altan Els.

Small Gobi
See *Great Gobi* above for the total area under protection.
The area represents the main characteristics of the southeastern Gobi region and has preserved most of its original natural features and conditions. It is the main habitat for rare and very rare wildlife, such as *khulan* (wild ass), black-tailed gazelle, *argali* (mountain sheep), and ibex. About 50% of the *khulan* population of Mongolia inhabits this area.

Khoridolsaridag Nuruu
18,8634 hectares
This area is situated in the Khövsgöl Aimag (northern Mongolia). Khoridolsaridag is a steep-sided mountain range that combines various landscapes – tundra, taiga, forested steppe and mountains – all at close proximity. Wildlife species such as *argali*, ibex, Siberian moose, snowcock and sable roam these areas.

CONSERVATION

> We must work with the grain of Nature ....it is all too easy for us to forget
> that mankind is a part of Nature and not apart from it.

HRH the Prince of Wales, Reith Lecture 2000

Modern conservation history began in the 1970s with the Club of Rome meeting in Stockholm (see box opposite). Wildlife conservation is an involved and complicated task. People who respect nature will try, in their own way, to do something positive to hand over its resources to the next generation without destruction and damage. In the face of many difficulties, governments are tightening the legal frameworks, and imposing conditions that will continue to allow us to enjoy the world's truly wild places – like Mongolia.

Vehicle tracks in the semi-desert cannot be rubbed out and the impacted damage done to the ecology – increasingly by tourist vehicles – stays for generations. The problem of overgrazing stock on the fragile Gobi environment is easy to see, but very difficult to deal with in human and environmental terms. Likewise, the damage caused by climate change may be irreversible. Some of

FOUNDATIONAL BACKGROUND TO RED/GREEN THINKING: CONSERVATIONISTS SPEAK OUT

Club of Rome, 1972 At this international meeting, conservationists and other experts examined limits to growth in the light of long-term trends in world population, resource availability, food production and industrialisation. In the same year the United Nations held a conference on the human environment in Stockholm, which led to the establishment of the UN Environmental Programme (UNEP).

World Conservation Strategy (WCS), 1980 The initiatives at the Club of Rome were followed by a programme called the World Conservation Strategy. The WCS retained the traditional concept of development with an additional objective: to improve the quality of human life. The WCS's approach concluded that sustainable development was needed that incorporated social and ecological considerations in long- and short-term planning. Thus conservation was linked to development.

Brundtland Commission, 1987 The WCS was followed by the Brundtland Commission, which redefined development as 'that which seeks to meet the aspirations of the present without compromising the ability to meet those of the future' – similar to WCS's definition of conservation.

In the process of improving the quality of life and in caring for the earth, we must look at what we are doing so that we do not unwittingly decrease biological diversity.

these issues are beyond our control. We cannot reverse the effects of global warming but we can put a brake on it provided there is the will to do so. We can steer in a direction that helps to solve parts of the problem – for example, by grazing a sensible ratio of sheep to goats and understanding that the Mongolian cashmere industry (presently going through privatisation difficulties) is reliant on the primary resources of the pastures on which the production chain of cashmere is based.

A key element of sustainable development and Agenda 21 (see section on *Responsible tourism*, page 138) is that the well-intended effort to protect the environment is not just about conservation or even local development, but about people owning these concepts and living them. The Earth Summit in Rio de Janeiro in 1992 made it clear that to develop a sustainable way of life on our planet, we must learn to understand, and if necessary to rethink, the directions in which we are heading. Subsequent world environmental summits must voice this message with more urgency as we enter 'injury' time in terms of environmental resources.

In Mongolia, conservation efforts are focusing on the destruction caused by the use of natural resources for fuel – the deforestation of saxaul in the desert regions, and the loss of timber in the northern mountain areas due to forest fires and the cutting of wood without licence. Other concerns include the destruction of ecosystems through development, overgrazing of pastureland by domestic herds, poaching and illegal hunting of rare Mongolian wildlife, and the unauthorised collection of herbs for medical use.

The Mongolian government is committed to protecting its biodiversity and has passed a number of environmental laws to safeguard its natural resources. It is vitally important that Mongolian wildlife, forests, vegetation, water and air pollution are properly monitored and managed, although the scale of the task is a daunting one.

Mongolia has signed a number of international agreements, including the Convention on International Trade in Endangered Species (CITES) and the international conventions on biological diversity, and participates in a number of other international environmental programmes, including UNESCO's 'Man and the Biosphere' programme. It has several World Heritage sites: the Uvs Lake basin, the ancient desert of Gobi Gurvansaikhan, and Part A of the Great Gobi Strictly Protected Area.

Vast steppes still cover Mongolia – the largest tracts of undamaged grasslands anywhere in the world. An awareness of the importance of unspoiled landscape is needed in order to preserve this environment for future generations as part of Mongolia's heritage. The grasslands stretch from horizon to horizon, at times, when stirred by the wind, looking like a giant ocean wave of swaying seed heads. The steppe itself reflects a vision of the past; it is both treeless and fenceless. It is also vulnerable to impact, especially human impact, like mining and tourism. Wild and endangered species are among the important attractions of Mongolia to the outside world, which has lost much of its own wildlife heritage. For information on some of the endangered species to be found, and on the conservation measures being taken to protect them, see the section *Fauna*, pages 107–17.

Sustainable development

> Research is easy. Conservation most definitely is not. It cannot be imposed from above. It must ultimately be based on local interests, skills and traditions.
>
> Dr George Schaller, conservation biologist

One of conservation's goals is to build a sustainable society. The word 'sustainability' has been popularised in such a way these days that people have begun to question its use and meaning. An overall definition of sustainable development translates as improving the quality of human life while living within the carrying capacity of supporting systems. In theory it sounds easy, but it is difficult to put into practice, especially in poorer countries where extra finance for essential social well-being is not available.

Incentives are being offered to investors to create innovative sustainable livelihood projects (currently being identified by the World Bank in Mongolia) to provide longer-term security, especially in depressed rural areas, so that in addition to government support and aid agency efforts, environmentally integrated private capital will be used for sustainable development. It is an illusion to think that a transfer to sustainable development will happen otherwise. For further information on responsible tourism, see pages 138–43.

Conservation biology

Conservation biology is conservation through science, carried out by field biologists, universities and institutes. The American conservation biologist, George Schaller, put it simply: 'The goal is not to tie up neat little packages of data but to spend time revealing the possibilities of new knowledge about a species in order to pass it on to the next generation.' The single most important conservation

Abore The 20m gold-and-bronze statue of Megjid
Janraiseg, Gandantegchinlen Monastery, Ulaanbaatar

Above right Temple of Buddha, Erdene Zuu Monastery,
Övörkhangai

Below Bronze Age 'Deer Stones' at Uushiin Övör,
sacred site of reindeer hunters

Above Constructing a Kazakh *ger* in western Mongolia

Right Interior of a *ger* restaurant in Bogdkhan Strictly Protected Area

Below Gers with livestock, Bogdkhan Strictly Protected Area, near Ulaanbaatar

measure to focus on is the preservation of ecosystems with interlocking habitats, which will give wildlife conservation the opportunity to work.

As Mongolia transfers from one political system to another, the process of conserving such a truly pristine environment, it seems, is becoming more and more complicated.

Future outlook

The rounded project takes on board observations of landscape and an awareness of human culture. What begins by being a simple conservation programme ends by gathering momentum and finally by touching and involving many branches of life. Apart from collecting crucial data and devising conservation strategies, local biologists need to be trained to cope with the aspirations and demands of nomadic people. There is the need to inter-relate and co-operate with a number of different agencies, both government and NGOs, which is not an easy job, but one where we cannot afford to become complacent.

Biodiversity

All life on earth is part of one great interdependent system, which began to evolve four billion years ago, and our world, as far as we know, grew from simple organisms. Biodiversity includes domesticated as well as wild species of plants and animals and is a new term for nature's extraordinary wealth.

Ecology

The word 'ecology' is derived from the Greek *oikos*, meaning 'house' or 'place to be', literally the study of organisms 'at home'. The shortest and best definition perhaps is 'the science of the living environment' or simply 'environmental biology'. To understand its scope, it must be considered in relation to other branches of biology and other '-ologies'. Biologists estimate that species are being lost at an increasingly faster rate due to man's industrial development. The frightening thing is that the loss will not be replaced by evolution in a time-scale that means anything to us.

Conservation Mongolian style

Mongolian people have an honoured and cultural tradition of taking a
caring approach towards nature and behaving in accordance with the
natural cycles.

Natsagiin Bagabandi (President of Mongolia)

Mongolian culture is permeated by the traditions of nomadic life, the use of land and nature protection. Nomads in times past had their own rules, norms and values, determined by religion, social practice and land use. They realised that their land was fragile and that disturbing the soil or water sources would be dangerous to the future survival of viable pasture. In order to stress these principles, folk legends and cautionary tales were created to preserve and pass them on and at the same time safeguard the pasturelands for the future. Methods of animal husbandry unchanged for centuries are still in use today, and it is important for the young herders to learn them.

For many Mongolians nature conservation and concern for the environment is part of rediscovering their culture, having experienced limitations within the structures of communism. Mongolians have a long history of nature protection. As long ago as the 1st century AD, the Huns, thought to be the ancestors of the Mongols, respected nature – the blue skies and the towering mountains were sacred. Mongolian Shamanism, derived from worshipping nature, has determined

STEPPE AND FOREST FIRES: A HISTORIC OVERVIEW
Bill Shaw

A heavily forested landscape with brown bears and moose roaming through it is not an image that springs to mind when one thinks of Mongolia; but trees it has, and in abundance! About 8% of the land surface is forested (this doesn't sound much, but remember Mongolia is the 14th-largest country in the world). Forests are located in the north of the country and form the southern edge of the vast taiga zone.

The trees are largely coniferous, and most of the area is uninhabited and inaccessible. Unfortunately these rich forests are now being damaged by raging wildfires. Reasonably accurate records of both forest and grassland (steppe) fires exist only from 1981. From 1981 to 1995, an average of 1.74 million hectares of forest and steppe burned annually. In 1996 and 1997 the burning increased dramatically to 10.7 and 12.4 million hectares. In these two years alone more forest was burnt than had been harvested for timber over the previous 65 years. Most fires occurred in the grasslands that lie in the east of the country, but the areas hardest hit by the increases were the forested regions. In 1998 and 1999, the area burnt decreased to 3 million hectares per year – an area the size of Wales. In 2000, another 5.1 million hectares were reduced to ashes.

In spring and autumn, 97% of fires are started by careless human activities, such as throwing away a still-burning cigarette end, not putting out a campfire

the nomads' behaviour towards nature and set rules for its protection. To Mongolians, the earth is the mother of all things and the sky the father. Hunting was based on elaborate rituals and on the concept that animal spirits gave fertility and prosperity to man who was responsible for the soil and animal herds.

Genghis Khan adopted one of Asia's first decrees to protect the environment, prohibiting, for example, damaging rivers by waste pollutants. Although Mongolians have a deep respect for nature, more recently Soviet communism allowed the Mongols to become careless. Like the Russians, they thought about 'conquering nature', and thereby spoiled it. Look at the massive coal and copper mines and gold mines with the use of poisonous chemicals, and the old car tyres, scrap iron and other unorthodox rubbish in the countryside.

Conservation in national parks

Mongolia has a number of recently introduced laws relating to the environment, some of which are concerned with tourist activities. Hundreds of years of nomadic culture has in its own way preserved and conserved environment and many species of wildlife and vegetation have survived, whereas in other parts of Asia they are dying out or have already disappeared. The worry is that more ruthless commercialisation may disturb these ancient practices. The Khustain Nuruu National Park, home of the free-ranging *takhi* (Mongolian wild horses or Przewalski horses) has become an example for Mongolian parks and reserves. National parks are divided into specific zones and tourism activity is accordingly limited to particular areas within the protected area boundaries. Visitors are asked to respect these limits. Park maps will indicate the zoning.

Khustain Nuruu National Park is considered as an oasis in an otherwise overgrazed part of the steppe. A Dutch Foundation together with the non-governmental and self-financing Mongolian Association for the Conservation of Nature and the Environment (MACNE) has helped to develop a variety of

properly, or by not maintaining a vehicle or chain which might then throw out sparks. Only a small number of fires are started by lightning – an additional cause during the summer months. The most recent information on outbreaks of forest fires is reported nowadays by satellite.

Forest fires have an extremely negative effect on the local economy, as millions of dollars of potential timber revenue are destroyed by fire. Many countryside families in the burned areas previously supplemented their low incomes by collecting secondary forest products, such as pine nuts, berries, mushrooms and red-deer antlers (used in Chinese medicine and by European markets for knife handles, buttons and other articles). Ecologically, repeated fires lead to an irreversible transformation of highly diverse forest to grassland through the loss of all the native seed trees. This badly affects the land's water-retention capacity, leading to faster run-off and flooding in some areas and, in others, to the drying up of streams and springs. Recent studies show that soils newly exposed to direct sunlight (due to the removal of the tree-cover by fire), are experiencing increases in temperature that are causing the permafrost to melt. Additionally, in these areas the ground becomes saturated and no longer suitable for tree growth. National statistics revealed that 29 people died and 79 were badly injured due to fires between 1995 and 2000.

The Mongolian government, in its desperate need for money, has approved the cutting of trees in vast numbers for export to China.

projects which help both the wildlife and the local people. For further details of national parks, and their part in conservation, see pages 123–32.

Fire-fighting: local conservation initiatives

The economic and political changes in Mongolia led to a decrease in fire-fighting efforts. The single most important factor was the grounding of the aerial patrol service, a Soviet-backed programme. The financial support stopped abruptly and Mongolia could not afford to maintain and operate the needed fleet. Mostly the fire-fighting service parachuted fire-fighters from Antonov An-2 biplanes, but these are old and many are unserviceable. The German Government Development Agency (GTZ), and British VSO volunteers stepped in to focus on a project in the Khankhentii and Gorkhi-Terelj Protected Area – a heavily forested and mountainous region lying northeast of the capital Ulaanbaatar.

Cross-border (transfrontier) conservation

Cross-border conservation efforts are concentrated in the northwest and northeast of Mongolia, and are part of a joint Mongolian-Russian system of strictly protected areas on both sides of the frontiers in eastern Mongolia. The World Wildlife Fund for Nature (WWF) has designated '200 eco-regions' for protection and Mongolia's Altai Mountains in the west and the Sayan Mountains in the north are included in this worldwide programme. For further information, see Dornog Aimag (the conservation of cranes and gazelles; pages 369–71) and Gobi Altai Aimag (the conservation of wild camels, snow leopard and Gobi bear; pages 300–4) in *Part Two*.

International conservation efforts

The National Service for Protected Areas and Ecotourism (NSPAE) was established in 1993 to manage Mongolia's protected areas and to encourage and develop tourism. With the preservation of biodiversity as its goal, the Mongolian government is implementing the Mongolia Biodiversity Project, associated with the United Nations Development Programme (UNDP).

The Mongolian Ministry for Nature and the Environment (MNE) – the government organisation responsible for developing and implementing conservation policy – has been working together with the World Wildlife Fund for Nature (WWF) to research and assess potential additions to the protected area system and to foster sustainable development around existing protected areas. A 'nature conservation and buffer zone development' was created by GTZ, the German government's technical co-operation programme to improve the management of the national parks in the Gobi and other areas. Other governments have also set up environmental projects, supported by the UNDP, Asian Development Bank, World Bank, and the Commission for the Protection of Endangered Species.

Useful addresses

Mongolian Association for the Conservation of Nature and the Environment (MACNE) CPO Box 1160, Ulaanbaatar 11; tel: 976 11 324836; email: macne@magicnet.mn. Manages many different conservation programmes.

Institute for Mongolian Biodiversity and Ecological Studies (IMBES) Contact via Mongolian Academy of Science, Ulaanbaatar, or IMBES, c/o Philadelphia Academy of Natural Sciences, 1900 Benjamin Franklin Parkway, Philadelphia, PA 19103, USA; tel: +1 215 299 1000; email: webmaster@acnatsci.org. Works with the Mongolian Academy of Sciences (MAS) to encourage environmental protection as part of Mongolia's economic development.

RESPONSIBLE TOURISM

> The primordial layer may not be open to many of us today, but it is still there in Mongolia.
>
> Zahava Hanan, Canadian writer and poet

Responsible, or sustainable, tourism, may be defined as tourism that puts the principles of sustainable development into practice. This type of tourism is carried out by promoting interaction based on mutual respect and an understanding of different cultures. In Mongolia, responsible tourism seeks to maintain a delicate balance between the modernisation of the nomads' lifestyle and suppressing change. It claims to 'tread lightly' and will not take the blame for large-scale environmental impact from social and economic development.

A 'green' approach to tourism addresses a growing awareness of the responsibilities that tourism carries. There is a huge expectation of what the industry can do – from identification and data gathering, involving volunteer tourists or eco-tourists, to running hotels that are sympathetic to the natural environment in their recycling and staff education programmes. This is beginning to happen in Mongolia, and ultimately benefits the tourist industry and helps it to prosper.

Around the world there are tour companies and tour operators working together to establish a number of core principles. The hard work has been done and Mongolia is in a fortunate position to put into practice much of this received wisdom so that it will have a positive effect and help to preserve the country's tourist sites, wilderness areas and rare, wild species.

Part of tourism today is to educate travellers on how they can play a part in responsible tourism. It is vital to modern tourism that some benefits are retained

FIRE-FIGHTER IN MONGOLIA
Bill Shaw

I went out to Mongolia with Voluntary Service Overseas (VSO) for a job placement with the Khankhentii Protected Area, and soon got stuck into working on the prevention side of things.

The key element was to work closely with the local people, so we quickly formed a fire-prevention team, consisting of local schoolteachers and two officers who ran the environmental information centres set up by the German government. The aim was to educate both adults and children on how to behave carefully when in the countryside. The message was communicated in a number of different ways. A fire-prevention curriculum was prepared for schools, which has become a compulsory module, accepted by the Mongolian Ministry of Education. To front the campaign we devised a mascot (along the lines of 'Smoky the Bear' in the USA). A much-loved forest animal, the squirrel, was chosen and named Sonorkhon, which means alert or watchful in Mongolian. Sonorkhon appears in different promotional material and if you ever reach the communities of Batschireet, Erdene Sum, Möngönmorit, Tünkhel or Züünkharaa you will see children wearing a Sonorkhon badge. If not, please ask them where their badge is!

Countryside fire-education excursions taught the children and their parents environmental games, and everyone learned how to build, light and then extinguish a campfire safely. A fire-prevention song was composed and sung, dramas, and physical contests were held and poster displays were put up in the information centres, which grew in number. All in all we had a great time and received a wonderful response from the local people. We also achieved our aim in the communities where we were active, as the number of fires began to decrease! Was it the prevention work, or the sterling efforts of the trained fire-fighters, or just luck? Hopefully a mix of the first two.

for the local people. Tourism is the largest industry in the world, yet seldom is it used in a constructive manner. According to the World Tourism Organisation, less than ten per cent of all tourist dollars make it into the hands of local communities. UK's Voluntary Service Overseas (VSO) has launched a worldwide tourist campaign to increase awareness of these problems.

Good information about the customs and culture of the country is crucial to the tourists who travel abroad each year. Tour operators have much to gain in goodwill from both their customers and the host country. Although there is great awareness of the importance of travel information, a VSO report confirms that all it requires is a little effort and imagination on the part of every tour operator to provide the advice already offered by some. For example, you might ask:

- Can we see some local handicrafts and where can we buy them?
- Can we meet local people?
- Do local people own and manage the tourism in their area?

Building a sustainable society

One of Mongolia's goals is to build a sustainable society. Sustainable development means ensuring that the economy and society of Mongolia reach their fullest

DON'T LET YOUR TRIP COST THE EARTH!

On an overseas holiday your flight will cause more environmental damage than all other activities combined. This is because aeroplane engines produce a cocktail of exhaust gases that contribute to global warming. During an eight-hour flight each passenger contributes as much to global warming as the average Indian citizen per annum. On a return flight from the UK to Ulaanbaatar every passenger will be responsible for about 2.6 tonnes of the global-warming gas carbon dioxide (CO_2). Despite the debate nowadays as to whether or not global warming is actually happening, huge CO_2 emissions are still harmful.

Climate Care is a company based in Oxford that lets you 'repair' the damage by providing funding for projects that reduce the amount of carbon dioxide in the atmosphere. Examples are renewable energy, energy efficiency and rainforest restoration. The first two mean that less CO_2 is released and the third absorbs CO_2 from the atmosphere.

Climate Care's projects remove as much CO_2 from the atmosphere as your share of the flight, meaning that your travel is climate neutral. The cost of offsetting the emissions is just 95 pence per person per hour of air travel.

Climate Care is scrutinised by an independent Environmental Steering Committee to ensure projects meet the highest standards. To find out more about Climate Care, and how to offset your emissions, tel: +44 01865 777770; fax: +44 01865 777771; web: www.co2.org.

potential within a well-protected environment, without compromising the quality of that environment for the enjoyment of future generations and the wider international community.

Ideally, sustainable agriculture provides high-quality food from a high-quality, well-managed environment, while securing an acceptable quality of life for the rural community – which in practice is difficult to evaluate and sustain. The move to sustainable development is a long-term and evolutionary process. Mongolian agricultural issues are currently affected by political changes which have led to overgrazing – there have been significant increases in the number of sheep and goats in the last ten years, especially around towns – and this is causing soil erosion in many regions. Other issues include waste management and the effects of modern litter, such as plastic and tin cans. An important question for tourists is whether the drinking water is safe. Since this is not the case everywhere tourists may wish to buy bottled water, or purify their drinking supplies.

Mongolia is very new to any type of eco-auditing (as are most countries) and has few means to measure progress towards sustainability.

The guiding principles of sustainable development and tourism

Certain guiding principles underlie sustainability and it is best to understand them as an underlying philosophy rather than an immediate, practical solution. The signposts might read: take out, give back, maintain, and balance. Tourism has adopted some of these principles in order to market its products but the economic return is often a long way down the road.

Guiding principles of sustainable tourism are:

- The environment has an intrinsic value that far outweighs its value as a tourism asset for long-term enjoyment and survival

- Tourism contributes to the benefit of the local community as well as to the visitor
- Tourism and the environment must be maintained and managed jointly, where possible, for long-term sustainability
- Development should respect the scale, nature and character of the site to be developed, and do so in the best interests of protecting this site
- Change should not operate independently of other factors like the environment and the well-being of the local community
- Local industry, as well as tourism and environmental agencies, have a duty to respect these principles and to work together to achieve a practical realisation of them

The question of how to put sustainable development into practice has been surveyed by the United Nations Environmental Programme (UNEP) and a full report may be found on their website at www.uneptie.org/tourism/new.html.

Responsible organisations

The **Centre for Environmentally Responsible Travel (CERT)** is a membership organisation for tour companies based in the UK that involves the traveller and the travel industry in aiming to develop a sustainable future for holiday destinations. Those who sign up commit themselves to an environmental policy. For information, contact CERT, Indaba House, 1 Hydeway, Thundersley, Essex SS7 3BE; tel: 01268 795772; fax: 01268 759834; email: certdesk@aol.com.

Greenstop.net is an environmental website that promotes the use of eco-friendly practices, particularly within the tourism industry, helping companies to combine environmental action with additional marketing and promotion, without spending large sums of money. The main aim is to set up a co-operative body of genuinely eco-friendly companies and market them to the general public with the simple three-point classification, so that the public can understand the product offered and in so doing create a demand for, and raise awareness about, environmentally responsible tourism. For further information contact Greenstop.net; tel: 01663 744606; fax: 01663 744696; email: patricia@greenstop.net; web: www.greenstop.net.

EARTH SUMMITS

The Earth Summit at Rio de Janeiro in Brazil in 1992 was the product of global environmental worries. In 1972, 70 governments convened in Stockholm for a conference which created the United Nations Environmental Programme (UNEP). The aim was for UNEP to encourage governments to take care of the environment, while a sister organisation UNESCO aimed to improve environmental education. The Rio conference on the environment brought together 179 states, who debated the needs of the present in the light of the future, and the ability of the future to meet these needs. The result was a document called Agenda 21, which was adopted at the Rio Earth Summit. It states some critical agendas that act as guidelines – not fixed by law or carved in stone, but which outline some desirable goals and solutions, to help protect our globe and life as we know it. A decade later, in 2002, the second Earth Summit, held in Johannesburg in South Africa, made clear that escalating environmental destruction can only be curbed bit by bit and that the process will be one long, uphill battle.

Green Globe 21 Any travel or tourist company can apply to belong to this international organisation, as long as it wants to be recognised and involved in sustainable development and eco-tourism. Through partnership with Green Globe 21, companies aim to signpost the route to responsible tourism. Green Globe 21 provides information and advice on the ways that operators and companies can improve the environmental quality of their operations. The Green Globe 21 logo is a way to show the membership qualification of participants. It involves establishing environmental management systems and paying a membership fee, the amount of which depends on the size of the business. The verification of Green Globe 21's standards is undertaken by an international, independent team of experts. For more details, visit Green Globe's website at www.greenglobe21.com. Alternatively, contact: Green Globe Asia Pacific (tel: 00 61 2 62302931; fax: 00 61 2 62302930; email: customer.services@ggasiapascific.com.au).

Eco-tourism

Eco-tourism is a convenient label for a number of related concepts including low-impact tourism and anything 'green' in the way of tourism. Broadly based, it is particularly related to wildlife and species conservation. The good thing about this type of tourism is the fact that eco-tourists are willing to pay premium rates to visit 'unspoiled' nature, the sort that Mongolia provides in abundance. As yet there are no quotas or restrictions on tourist numbers, but small parties of nature watchers are encouraged rather than mass tourism. Due to its poor infrastructure, lack of major tourist facilities and its extreme climate, Mongolia is unsuited to mass tourism.

When it comes to eco-tourism, Westerners have little to teach Mongolian nomads and they on the other hand have a lot to offer us. Nomadic family *gers* are genuinely eco-friendly. They use natural building materials – felt, wooden trellis and ropes made of horse hair – to construct their homes, and in daily living they use or recycle practically everything. When killing a sheep for example, every bit is used and the dogs are thrown only the well-picked bones.

Eco-gers

One of the main goals in developing the tourists' interest in the environment is to invite them to book accommodation in an eco-*ger*. This gives the local people the opportunity to welcome guests and to increase their living standards, as the visitors pay them directly. A small percentage of the booking costs goes to the local national park organisation who helped to establish the eco-*gers*. For example, there are three eco-*gers* located on the Tuul and Bayan rivers in the Gorkhi-Terelj National Park and adjoining Khankhentii Strictly Protected Area. This national park is a short distance from Ulaanbaatar and it is an ideal place to go for a weekend visit. Horses and ox carts are available for hire, local guides accompany visitors and food provisions may be bought from families in the neighbourhood.

Conservation work using volunteers or eco-tourists

Discovery Initiatives is one of the tour companies which support eco-tourism linked to conservation programmes and project work, which allows their groups to join wildlife experts to enter national parks, like the Great Gobi National Park, an area which otherwise requires special permission. Volunteer tourists are actively involved under the expert guidance of field biologists – helping to gather data on rare wild animals such as the snow leopard, the wild camel and Gobi bear – as part of established conservation programmes. For details of how to contact Discovery Initiatives, see *Tour operators*, page 148, or visit their website at www.discoveryinitiatives.com.

Gobi Biodiversity Project

This programme is funded by a number of conservation organisations: the Mongolian Ministry of Nature and Environment and MACNE (Mongolian Association for Conservation of Nature and the Environment) and the American Wildlife Conservation Society (WCS). It involves conducting surveys in critical oases, such as establishing the patterns of wild camel feeding habits. The thinking is that the more information gathered the greater the possibility of helping to protect valuable, rare creatures like the wild camel.

After a day's hard work climbing rocky mountains looking for spoor marks and gathering other data, those involved develop huge appetites. Volunteers soon discover that boiled mutton, sheep intestines and rock-hard cheese-curds never tasted so good! Mongolians are enthusiastic and happy to welcome the researchers into their homes. Part of the repayment for their hospitality is to simply sit and share in conversation and meals. Any Mongolian tour company will provide *ger* visits and arrange for you to meet nomadic families.

Cultural tourism

The preservation of culture and artefacts is important to maintain diversity and cultural identity on an ever-shrinking planet. The destruction of cultural heritage and cultural landmarks, and the emergence of tourism as the largest industry in the world, highlight the need to address the possible negative effects of both. There is growing concern in Mongolia over the destruction of cultural heritage and also about the adverse affects of tourism. An innovative approach is to involve tourist volunteers in helping to save cultural heritage sites currently under threat. Alongside many components of Mongolia's cultural heritage, such as temple buildings, museums and cultural artefacts, that have been neglected as a result of political turmoil or economic stress, some people predict Mongolia's nomads themselves are at the point of extinction.

The Cultural Restoration Tourism Project (CRTP)

CRTP aims to help communities in Mongolia to restore artefacts of cultural importance, to promote responsible tourism to help the local people, and to provide a model of alternative funding for other non-profit organisations.

CRTP's programme currently involves the restoration of Baldan Bereevan Monastery, a Buddhist temple that was destroyed in the 1930s (see pages 360–1). Baldan Bereevan is about 300km east of Ulaanbaatar in Khentii Aimag. The restoration began in 1999, with the approval of the abbot and community members. Labour and funds are donated by volunteer tourists. Participants are given the unique opportunity to become part of a community-based effort to develop Baldan Bereevan as an international Buddhist retreat centre. For further details, contact Mark A Hintzke, The Cultural Restoration Tourism Project – Baldan Bereevan Monastery, 410 Paloma Avenue, Pacifica, CA 94044, USA; tel: +1 415 563 7221; email: crtp@earthlink.net; web: www.crtp.net.

MONGOLIAN culture thrives in this unspoilt and beautiful country. Discover it for yourself in small group or tailor-made trips. We have our own comfortable accommodation, extensive facilities, and experienced guides. Our trips are expertly organised to suit local customs and the environment. A unique and enriching experience. Phone or email us for a brochure.

4th **W**ORLD
ADVENTURE

www.4thworldadventure.com
Telephone 0845 1300 448

MONGOLIA

Khangai – Hosvgol – Altai Mountains
Small group adventure trekking,
with a European guide (fluent in Mongolian)

www.**Himalayan Kingdoms**.com
Tel: **0845 330 8579**
E-mail: info@himalayankingdoms.com

AiTO
THE ASSOCIATION
OF INDEPENDENT
TOUR OPERATORS

www.tourismconcern.org.uk

TOURISM CONCERNED

There is a need to be...

We have nearly all travelled and seen the negative effects of tourism. For many people who live in tourist destinations around the globe their culture and homes are being destroyed through a lack of consideration of their interests and rights.

Tourism Concern campaigns to raise awareness of the many abuses that take place and encourage change to eradicate these negative effects on the indigenous population. Through our educational work, campaigning and challenging the tourism industry we aim improve the quality of life in the host locations.

You can help by becoming a Tourism Concern supporter, member or donor and help us change tourism for the better.

For more info, visit our website or call or E-mail us below.

E-mail: info@tourismconcern.org.uk
Call: 020 7753 3330

TourismConcern
Transforming the negatives into positives

Practical Information

WHEN TO VISIT AND WHY

The focus of Mongolia's tourism is nature and the environment, the nomadic way of life and places linked with Genghis Khan. In the final decade of the 20th century this 'last place on earth' opened her doors to the world and with air travel and the advantages of the internet Mongolia is, virtually, a step away.

Summer (including the short spring and early autumn) is the main Mongolian tourist season, starting in May and ending in September (sometimes until mid-October if the weather holds).

However, Mongolia now offers a winter holiday season, which includes cross-country skiing. Most people would not choose to visit in the depths of winter, but it is an interesting season to travel there, bearing in mind that it is it an unusual choice for individual travellers and small groups, and arrangements are equally limited by the weather. Tourists visiting Mongolia in winter must be prepared to wrap up warmly as the temperatures drop to below -35°C. Central heating is turned up so high in the major hotels and offices that it reaches tropical temperatures indoors. The solution is to dress in light layers (silk, cotton and wool) and to keep furs, gloves and hats handy when nipping outside. There are a number of things to do in winter which make it worth considering as a time to visit Mongolia. There are so few tourists that you will get wonderful individual attention, especially if you are invited around *Tsaagan Sar*, the New Year festival. These journeys need special planning. There is the possibility of skating on frozen rivers. If skiing overland, warm clothes and appropriate boots are

ANNUAL CHART

	Av temp °C	Humidity %	Precipitation mm
January	−26.1	75	1.5
February	−21.7	73	1.9
March	−10.8	66	2.2
April	0.5	50	7.2
May	8.3	47	15.3
June	14.9	56	48.8
July	17.0	65	72.6
August	15.0	65	47.8
September	7.6	64	24.4
October	−1.7	65	6.0
November	−13.7	72	3.7
December	−24.0	75	1.6
Year	**−2.9**	**64**	**233.0**

WHY COME?

Mongolia has an enormous amount to offer visitors, from tumbling waterfalls to the wide open spaces of the fenceless steppe, not forgetting around 250 days of sunshine a year, while foreign investors may find more allure in Mongolia's mineral wealth – copper, gems, gold and oil. The country's major strengths are her unspoiled countryside, with natural beauty on a colossal scale, immeasurable steppes and unbelievable hospitality, such that the word takes on a new meaning. The generosity and kindness of ordinary Mongolians is overwhelming and ger hospitality is legendary.

Your eyes might scan the horizon and, sharpening focus, might see nestled together in the dip of a valley, or in some strategic place out of the wind, a tiny collection of ger (Mongol tents), set against an awe-inspiring background of mountains and river valleys. It is a land that invites exploration – a vast land of undisturbed beauty and wilderness areas, sparsely inhabited by some of the last nomadic people on earth.

Boundless space, like the ocean, encourages the visitor to relax – bumped around in the back seat of a Russian jeep on Mongolian roads you have no other choice! – or, if you ride on horseback or camel back for hours across country, relaxation becomes a matter of survival, otherwise you are liable to do some damage, or, more seriously, if pitched off, break bones. To experience the reality and to fully understand Mongolia's attractions, contradictions and surprises you must travel there and see for yourself. Mongolians are people of the moment, fun-loving as well as hospitable, and their outlook is 'come what may, let tomorrow look after itself'.

essential; otherwise, the thick felt boots worn by Mongolians are best and a Mongolian fleece-lined *deel* (the local winter attire) can be purchased on arrival. Several tour companies offer winter travel (see *Winter tours* under *Specialist tour operators*, page 152).

HIGHLIGHTS/SUGGESTED ITINERARIES

> The traveller must not count on the distance but on the nature of the ground when trying to estimate his marches.
>
> Douglas Carruthers, British explorer and surveyor in Central Asia
> (1910–11)

At a glance you will find the following activities in the different regions of Mongolia:

- **North** Around Lake Khövsgöl there is riding, fishing, *Tsaatan* (reindeer people), an ethnic minority living in wigwams, but difficult to reach, wildlife of the forest and steppe.
- **South** In the Gobi region are places where dinosaur fossils have been found, cliffs, camel rides, *ger* camps, cashmere goats and sand dunes.
- **East** In the grasslands are found Genghis Khan's memorial site, gazelles, camping areas, riding.
- **West** In Kazakh country are the Kazakh minority people, hunting for foxes and rodents with trained eagles, mountain peaks for climbers, *argali* sheep and other wildlife.

- **Central** Around Karakorum, ancient capital of the Mongol empire, are monasteries, good camping sites, rafting, waterfalls, ancient rock art.

Use the following as a broad indicator of what and how much can be done during visits of varying lengths:

- **A weekend** Visit Ulaanbaatar, with its restaurants, theatres, museums and temples.
- **Five days** Visit one countryside area near UB (eg: Terelj resort, eco-*gers*, or wild horses at Khüstain Nuruu National Park).
- **Ten days–two weeks** Visit countryside areas – fly/drive between provincial centres. Fly to Khovd, capital of Khovd Aimag, meet your horse and saddle up for a riding experience. Rest, hike and climb in the mountains, staying in tented camps or in local herders' *gers*, before returning to UB to explore the capital's museums, restaurants, bars and nightlife.
- **Three weeks** A good length of stay. Allows time to visit the countryside – to 'do' the Naadam festival and to travel the 'Golden Circuit' (Khövsgöl, the Orkhon valley and the South Gobi). After arriving and winding down in UB for a night, you could set out by jeep for Lake Khövsgöl, via Ambarayasgalant Monastery. Spend several days camping and exploring the country on horseback. Drive south to Kharkhorin and visit the famous monastery of Erdene Zuu, near by. If there is time, you might extend your journey to the South Gobi, by flying to Dalanzadgad (from Ulaanbaatar – its the only way) and visiting its major sites including the Flaming Cliff area, famous for dinosaur fossil finds. On your final return to Ulaanbaatar, allow a day to shop and see the city.
- **Two to three months** Time required to travel the country properly – you can do it in six weeks, but you should be aware of certain shortcomings regarding Mongolian roads (or lack of them) and the quality of transport and communication, especially in more remote areas, as they may have an impact on your plans.

Trans-Mongolian/Trans-Siberian rail journey

Might include tours of Beijing, Ulaanbaatar and Moscow. The great cities of Beijing and Moscow owe much of their importance to the Mongols. Beijing became the capital of the Mongol empire during the 14th century under Kublai Khan and his successors. Another of Genghis Khan's grandsons backed local princes, so that Moscow became the centre for Russian rule. A suggested route is to fly to Beijing and return by rail. Spend some days in Beijing visiting the wonders of the 'Forbidden City', home of the Chinese emperors for 500 years. If you have some days to spare, drive to a section of the Great Wall, passing through small towns and villages in Inner Mongolia before reaching the border with Mongolia where you may catch the train to UB. Otherwise take the train from Beijing (the Chinese terminus of the Trans-Siberian/Trans-Mongolian line) to Ulaanbaatar. You will pass other sections of the Great Wall and you will wake to see the Gobi Desert. Later that evening you will have time to go to your hotel and to visit parts of the city, like the Gandan Monastery. Spend a weekend at the Terelj National Park, which offers overnight stays with herders' families in traditional Mongolian *gers,* riding and other outdoor activities – fishing or hiking – before continuing the train jorney. Then you can settle down with a book, in the comfort of your compartment, or watch the countryside flash past, including Lake Baikal in southern Siberia, until, four days later you find yourself in Moscow – another fascinating capital to explore with its onion-domed churches and Kremlin treasures.

Tour operators such as Off the Map Tours, Regent Holidays, Genghis Expeditions and Mongolei Reisen GmbH can help to organise the above.

The 'Golden Circuit'

Mongolia's 'Golden Circuit' highlights the most-visited regions of the country: Lake Khövsgöl, the Orkhon Valley and the South Gobi. You may have time to visit one or two of the areas mentioned – all three, if you stay over three weeks. Lake Khövsgöl is the famous blue lake in northern Mongolia bordering Siberia, near many great fishing rivers. It is an area of outstanding natural beauty and offers good accommodation and many activities like riding, hiking and climbing. From Ulaanbaatar you may also travel to the Orkhon Valley, with its forested mountain landscape, waterfalls, spas and temple sites, to visit the site of Karakorum, the ancient capital of the Mongol empire and the monastery of Erdene Zuu. You may fly (via Ulaanbaatar – the hub of all transport) or drive to Dalanzadgad, the aimag centre of South Gobi Province, from where you may visit the golden dunes of the Gobi and the dinosaur area of the famous flaming cliffs at Bayanzag. From each of the areas mentioned above you will be able to visit national parks, spend time with nomadic families and ride across country camping out, or simply experience a day's riding in and around one of these areas. Mongolia's far western mountains and lakes and the eastern plains offer wonderful tours as well, although they are less visited.

TOUR OPERATORS

See *Responsible tourism* in *Chapter 4* for details of efforts to ensure that tour operators are environmentally responsible.

UK

Panoramic Journeys Gothic House, Church St, Charlbury, Oxon OX7 3PP; tel/fax: 01608 811690; email: info@panoramicjourneys.com; web: www.panoramicjourneys.com
Off the Map Tours UK agent: 20 The Meer, Fleckney, Leicester LE8 8UN; tel/fax: 0116 240 2625; email: info@mongolia.co.uk; web: www.mongolia.co.uk. Head office in Mongolia: Bayanzurkh District, 13th Microdistrict, Building 4, No148, Ulaanbaatar; tel: +976 11 458964; fax: +976 11 353353; email: offthemap@magicnet.mn. Active adventure tours, cultural experiences; specialists in train travel; mountain-bike tours.
4th World Adventure The Barn, Upper Goddards Farm, Skirmett, Oxon RG9 6TB; tel: 0845 1300448; fax: 01491 63959920; email: info@4thworldadventure.com; web: www.4thworldadventure.com. In Mongolia: Garage 24, Nature's Door, Khatgal, Khövsgöl (contact Bayandalai); tel: (mobile) 992 60919 or 961 69393; email and website as above.
Regent Holidays 15 John St, Bristol BS1 2HR; tel: 0117 921 1700; fax: 0117 925 4866; email: regent@regent-holidays.co.uk; web: www.regent-holidays.co.uk. Pioneers in travel to Mongolia for over 30 years. Experts in train travel and tailor-made tours.
Far Frontiers The Pound, Ampney Crucis, Glos GL7 5SA; tel: 01258 850962; fax: 01258 851575; email: info@farfrontiers.com; web: www.farfrontiers.com. Escorted journeys and tailor-made travel to lakes and mountains.
British Museum Traveller 46 Bloomsbury St, London WC1B 3QQ; tel: 020 7323 8895/1234; fax: 020 7520 8677; web: www.britishmuseum.org. 'Memories of Mongolia' tour, accompanied by a guest speaker.
Steppes East The Travel House, 51 Castle St, Cirencester GL7 1QD; tel: 01285 880920; fax: 01285 885888; email: sales@steppeseast.co.uk; web: www.steppeseast.co.uk. Classic Tours and Family Homestays; In the Steps of Genghis Khan; Riding with Eagles.
Discovery Initiatives The Travel House, 51 Castle St, Cirencester GL7 1QD; tel: 01285 643333; fax: 01285 885888; email: enquiry@discoveryinitiatives.com; web:

www.discoveryinitiatives.com. Specialist wildlife and conservation tours in different parts of the country – the Gobi Altai, the eastern plains, Lake Khövsgöl area.

Discover Adventure 5 Netherhampton Cottage, Netherhampton, Salisbury SP2 8PX; tel: 01722 741123; fax: 01722 741150; email: info@discoveradventure.com; web: www.discoveradventure.com. Mountain-biking, trekking and horse-riding holidays.

Himalayan Kingdoms Old Crown House, 18 Market St, Wotton-under-Edge, Glos GL12 7AE; tel: 01453 844400; fax: 01453 844422; email: info@himalayankingdoms.com; web: www.himalayankingdoms.com. Fully guided small-group treks.

The Oriental Caravan 36 Vanbrugh Court, Kennington, London SE11 4NS; tel/fax: 020 7582 0716; email: info@theorientalcaravan.com; web: www.theorientalcaravan.com

USA

Boojum Expeditions 14543 Kelly Canyon Rd, Bozeman, MT 59715; tel: +1 800 287 0125; email: info@boojum.com; web: www.boojum.com. Specialists in adventure travel.

Distant Horizons 350 Elm Av, Long Beach, CA 90802; tel: +1 562 983 8828, +1 800 3331240; fax: +1 562 983 8833. Cultural tours.

Mongol Caravan PO Box 191, Clifden, NJ 07011 0191; tel: +1 973 594 0655; fax: +1 209 729 4674; email: mc@mongolcaravan.com. Independent itineraries for travellers to Mongolia; 'The Mighty Mongolia' tour; 'The Naadam Festival' tour, with an optional add-on to the Great Wall of China.

Mongol Global Tour Company 4141 Ball Rd, 187 Cypress, CA 90630; tel/fax: +1 714 220 2579; email: MongolTour@aol.com; web: www.hometown.aol.com/mongoltour/index.html. Specialises in Indiana Jones-type adventures in Mongolia; customised tours.

Mongolian Travel USA 707 Alexander Rd, Suite 208, Princeton, NJ 08540; tel: +1 609 419 4416; fax: +1 609 275 3827; email: mongol@juno.com; web: www.mongoltravel.com

Nomadic Expeditions 1095 Cranbury-South River Rd, Suite 20A Jamesburg, NJ 08831; tel: +1 609 860 9008 or 1 800 998 6634; fax: +1 609 860 9608; email: info@nomadicexpeditions.com; web: www.nomadicexpeditions.com. Adventure and classic tours.

Australia

Karakorum Expeditions (Australian-run company based in Ulaanbaatar) Jiggur Grand Hotel, 13 Transport Street, (PO Box 542) Ulaanbaatar 46; tel/fax: +976 11 315655; mobile: 00 +976 99116729; email: info@GoMongolia.com; web: www.GoMongolia.com. Specialists in active adventure travel and ecotourism; Mongolian Getaways; cross-border itineraries to Inner Mongolia. Winners of the Pacific Asia Travel Association's (PATA) 2002 Gold Award for Ecotourism

Canada

Exotic Tours 1117 Ste Catherine, Suite 806 Montreal, Quebec H3B IH9; tel: +1 514 284 3324; fax: +1 514-843 5493; email: exotictours@exotictours.com

France

Air Sud 25 Bd Sebastopol, 75001 Paris; tel: +33-1-40416670; fax: +33 1 40 26 68 44

Terres d'Aventure 6 rue Saint-Victor, 75006 Paris; tel: +33 1 4825 847800; fax: +33 1 43 29 96 31; web: www.terdav.com

Terre Mongolie 17 rue de la Bucherie, 75005 Paris; tel: +33 1 44 321283; fax: +33 1 44 32 12 89; web: www.terre-mongolie.com

Germany

Mongolei Reisen Chausseestr 84, 10115 Berlin; tel: +49 30 44057646; fax: +49 30 44057645; email: juulchin@aol.com or info@mongoliajourneys.com; web: www.mongoliajourneys.com

Off the Map Tours German agent: Demminerstr 9b, 13059 Berlin; tel: + 49 30 9288344; email: enchsaichan@aol.com; web: www.mongolia.co.uk. See under *UK* for tours offered.

Marco Polo Reisen Dettweilerstr 15, 61476 Kronberg/Ts; tel: +49 61 73709716; fax: +49 61 737635; email: h-liebelt@marco-polo-reisen.com

Wikinger Reisen Koelnerstr 20, D-58135 Hagen; tel: +49 2331 904785; fax: +49 2331 904740; email: ovid.jakota@wikinger.de

Athena Weltweit Hohe Bleichen 21, 20354 Hamburg; tel: +49 40 351257; fax: +49 40 354362; email: info@athena-studienreisen.de

Italy

Focus World Services Corso C Colombo 10, 20144 Milano; tel: +39 2 89402052; fax: +39 2 89402433; email: focus.himalaya@virtualia.it

Japan

Mongol Juulchin Tours 3/Floor Dai-2 Kawana Building, 14-6, Shibuya 2-Chome, Shibuya-ku, Tokyo 150; tel: +81 3 34867351; fax: +81 3 34867740

Netherlands

Global Train Anne Kooistrahof 15, 1106 WG Amsterdam; tel: +31 20 6967585; fax: +31 20 6973587; email: goldentrains@pi.net

Life Unlimited Email: contact@life-unlimited.com; web: www.life-unlimited.com. Contact Annette Bolt. Sensational worldwide outdoor tours, including extraordinary horse-riding and fishing tours in Mongolia.

Specialist tour operators
Adventure

Run Wild 40 Miangat St, Building 68, Sükhbaatar District, Ulaanbaatar; tel/fax: +976 11 315374; email: info@outer-mongolia.com, runwild@magicnet.mn; websites: www.outer-mongolia.com and www.runwild.co.uk. Horse/camel riding, fishing, trekking and whitewater rafting. For further details, see *Bayan Olgii*, pages 340–5.

Mountaineering

Karakorum Expeditions See page 149 for contact details. 'Five Holy Peaks' of the Tavan Bogd tour; tailor-made climbing tours. 'Trekking with the Snow Leopard' offers trekking in the northwestern province of Uvs where snow leopards have been sighted.

Nomads PO Box 1008, Ulaanbaatar 13; tel/fax: 11 328146; email: nomads@magicnet.mn; web: www.mongoliadventure.com. 'The Five Kings of the Altai' and 'Pioneering through Western Mongolia' tours.

Riding (horses/camels)

The fence-free riding experience on the Mongolian steppes, the clear air, altitude and sunshine is a thrilling experience. Added to it is the exuberant company of Mongol horsemen, singing about the beauty of the countryside as they gallop along. Riding tours are generally unsupported by vehicles, people camp in tents and live outdoors, visiting nomadic herding families – often eating meals with them. Costs vary according to the number of people in a group. The season begins in June and goes on until late September. The most popular riding tours combine a ride before or after the Naadam Festival in mid-July. Approximate costs are £950

(US$1,425) for nine days, £1,300 (US$1,990) for two weeks, or £2,000 (US$3,065) for three weeks (excluding international flights). For further information on horseriding in Mongolia, see *Riding, biking and hiking*, pages 190–7.

Boojum Expeditions See page 149 for contact details.

Equitour Riding Holidays 15 Grangers Place, Bridge St, Witney, Oxon OX28 4BH; tel: 01993 849489; email: llequitour@aol.com; web: www.equitour.co.uk. Horse tours only. 'Riding with Eagles' and 'The Reindeer Herders of Khövsgöl' tours.

Genco Tour Bureau Bayangol Hotel B-201, 5 Genghis Khan Av, Ulaanbaatar 43; tel: 11 328960l; fax: 11 321705; email: genco@magicnet.mn; web: www.mol.mn/gtb. Horse- and camel-riding tours.

Gobiin Ogloo PO Box 1014, Ulaanbaatar 13; tel: 11 323394; email: gobinogloo@magnicnet.mn; web: www.mol.mn/gobinogloo. 'Galloping through the Empire of the Steppes', 'Riding & Fishing in the Khangai Mountains' and 'Camel Trekking & Yak Riding' tours.

In the Saddle Grove House, Lutchens Close, Chineham Court, Hants RG24 8AG; tel: 01256 851665; email: rides@inthesaddle.com; web: www.inthesaddle.com. Horse tours only. 'The Mongol Horse Trail' tour – run on six dates. Special itineraries include the Naadam Festival in July.

Mongolei Reisen/Juulchin German office: Schaussestr 84, 10115 Berlin; tel: 00 49 3044057646; email: info@mongoliajourneys.com; web: www.mongoliajourneys.com. 'Julia Roberts Horse Riding Holiday' tour.

Ride World Wide Staddon Farm, North Tawton, Devon EX20 2BX; tel: 01837 825544; email: RideWW@aol.com; web: www.rideworldwide.co.uk. Horse tours only. 'The Khenti Ride', 'Khövsgöl and the Reindeer People Ride' and 'Karakorum Ride' tours.

Ecotourism

To give credit to the tourist industry, nearly all travel companies offering tours in Mongolia are environmentally aware and eco-friendly. (See also *Responsible tourism*, pages 138–43.) The leading experts in the UK and Mongolia are listed below:

Boojum Expeditions See page 149 for contact details.

Discovery Initiatives See above, page 148, for contact details. Specialises in ecotourism linked to wildlife, nature and conservation, on foot or by horse; eco-tourists join wildlife experts and some tours support experts and researchers in national parks in the areas of the Gobi, Khövsgöl, Khentii and the Eastern Steppes. Other small groups on tailormade tours follow wildlife itineraries travelling by plane, jeep and on horseback across Mongolia.

Genghis Expeditions See page 225, for contact details.

Karakorum Expeditions See page 149, for contact details.

Off the Map Tours See page 148, for contact details.

Fishing

For further information on fishing in Mongolia, see *Sport and adventure*, pages 197–203.

Angling Travel Orchard House, Gunton Hall, Hanworth, Norfolk NR11 7HJ; tel/ fax: +44 01263 761602

Frontiers (US office) PO Box 959, Wexford PA 16090-0959; tel: +1 724 935 1577; fax: +1 724 935 5388; email: info@frontierstrvl.com; web: www.frontierstrvl.com

Frontiers London (European office) 18 Albemarle St, London W1S 4HR; tel: +44 020 7493 0798; fax: 020 7629 5569; email: london@frontierstrvl.com; web: www.frontierstrav.com

Roxton, Bailey Robertson Worldwide 25 High St, Hungerford, Berkshire RG17 ONF; tel: +44 01488 689701; fax: +44 01488 689730; email: fishing@roxtons.com; www.roxtons.com
Sweetwater Travel 411 South 3rd St, Livingston, Montana 59047; tel: +1 406 222 0624;

Local tour operators with fishing expertise
Juulchin (main headquarters) Genghis Khan Av 5B, Ulaanbaatar 210543; tel: 11 328428/328455; email: jlncorp@magicnet.mn; www.mol.mn/juulchin
Khövsgö Travel Company Ulaanbaatar; tel/fax: 11 687626/326478; mobile: 991 16227
Nature's Door Camp and Lakeside Lodges Lake Khövsgöl, Khatgal; email: andy@fishmongolia.co.uk; web: www.fishmongolia.co.uk. Andy Parkinson runs enjoyable guided fly-fishing and spinning trips for *taimen*, lenok, grayling and pike, including adventure-fishing expeditions to remote rivers in stunning locations; trips to fishing camps and lodges; tailormade itineraries.

Ox-cart adventure tours
This unusually slow method of touring allows you to relax completely and unwind as you travel at the pace of an ox cart in the Khentii mountains around Mount Asraltkhairkhan. For further information contact Mongol Khan Travel Company (email: mna-trg@magicnet.mn; www.mol.mn/mongolkhan).

Winter tours
Two UK travel companies specialise in winter travel in Mongolia:

4th World Adventure See page 148 for contact details. Some exciting winter itineraries around Lake Khövsgöl and can help to fit you out with Mongolian clothing. Their latest photo-brochure, entitled 'Welcome to the Freezer', says: 'This is a land that has to be seen: it is as though you have stepped back 100 years and are rediscovering another land, seemingly untouched even by the indigenous population. Nothing can compare to sitting in a wooden hut bathing in +40c hot springs while it is -30c outside. Living with the locals in such a harsh environment is both humbling and at the same time an exhilarating experience.'
Off the Map Tours See page 148 for contact details. Special winter weekend breaks to Terelj National Park on the edge of the Khentii mountains, near Ulaanbaatar. A typical weekend would include driving to Terelj and checking into a *ger* camp for three days, where you will have great opportunities to sit and chat with local people and taste some delicious Mongolian hot soups and stews. Return to Ulaanbaatar, visit the cashmere factory and the city's temples and museums.

TOURIST INFORMATION
Mongolian National Tourism Centre (MNTC)
The Mongolian National Tourism Centre (Genghis Khan Avenue 11, Ulaanbaatar 28, Mongolia 210628; tel: 11 318493/311102/318492; email: ntc@mongol.net; www.mongoliatourism.gov.mn) was established in 1999 to answer questions, provide information and support the development of Mongolian tourism, which is mainly based on the attraction of its rare wildlife and unspoiled natural landscapes. MNTC has an excellent website.

Mongolian Tourism Association (MTA)
The Mongolian Tourism Association (Sukhbaatar Square, Building of Mongolian Trade Unions Confederation, 3rd Floor, Rm 318, Ulaanbaatar 11; tel: 11 327820; email: info@travelmongolia.org; www.travelmongolia.org), a non-profit

founded in 1997, aims to help the development of the travel industry and tourism and improve the quality of tourism services. The association has a 68-strong membership.

RED TAPE
Entry and exit requirements
A valid passport and entry/exit visa are required prior to travel. Visitors to Mongolia should carry their passports with them at all times.

Visas
First check with the Mongolian embassy/consular department if you need a Mongolian visa, which depends on your nationality and length of stay. Citizens of the following countries are exempt for varying periods: Malaysia (one month), Singapore (two weeks), Philippines (three weeks), Kazakhstan (three months), Israel (one month), USA (one month). It is highly advisable to obtain your visa in advance from Mongolian embassies or consulates abroad (see list below, pages 154–5) rather than at points of entry, train stations and airports, as this facility once on offer has been withdrawn. You will be required to submit your passport, two passport photographs and to complete a visa form. Allow two weeks. A tourist visa for UK citizens for one month costs £30, and from three to six months costs £60. Check with the embassy for the current cost.

Extending visas
If you plan to stay in Mongolia for more than 30 days you will need to extend your visa at the Citizens' Information and Registration Centre. To extend a 30-day visa, go to the new office located on the left side of the Transport Ministry (Tevriin Yam), which stands on Chinggis Avenue, past the Bayangol Hotel; bear right to find the ministry building before Peace Bridge. (The location of this office changed in 2002 and again in 2003, which has caused great confusion.) The office is open in the mornings and closes at 17.00 sharp. Currently it is staffed by people who do not speak English, and forms are in Mongolian only. If you are a tourist, you will need a passport and official letter from your tour operator/company. If you are an independent traveller, you will need to submit your passport, one photo, and the fee, having completed the application form. If for work, you will need to submit your passport and an official letter from your employer.

If you arrive near to closing time, you may be told to leave your passport at the office for collection the following day. It is essential if you do not speak Mongolian to bring a translator with you. Both registration and de-registration (a stamp) are required, especially if you intend to travel immediately to the countryside or, for example, to China, within the period of your long-term stay in Mongolia. Heavy fines (up to US$1,000) have been made and some foreign travellers leaving the country without de-registering have had to return to Ulaanbaatar. The amount of these fines seems to vary considerably but the principle is the same – YOU MUST REMEMBER TO REGISTER AND DE-REGISTER (see below). Travellers arriving or departing from Mongolia through Russia or China should also be aware of Russian and Chinese visa regulations.

Police registration and de-registration
All visitors spending more than 30 days in Mongolia must register with the police department. Those visiting Mongolia for 30 days or less do not need to register. Visitors with a visa for more than 30 days or those who enter without passing through immigration must register within ten days of arrival in Mongolia. A

visitor's first registration must be made in Ulaanbaatar. Subsequent registrations can be made at the police departments in aimag (provincial) centres. Visitors staying over 30 days who travel and stay outside Ulaanbaatar for more than seven days in one place, should obtain permission before departing for the countryside. The required letter of permission available from the State Centre for Registration is free of charge. When a visitor stays in the countryside, they must register with the aimag police department on entry and exit from that location. Visitors who intend to visit several countryside locations, for more than seven days each, should obtain a letter of permission that can be used for all the aimags.

Police registrations are valid for as long as the visitor's visa is valid, up to a maximum of one year. The initial charge is T25,000. To de-register, it is important to remember to go to the same office and get a de-registration stamp on your registration paper. If you do not do this you may have to return to Ulaanbaatar from a border point, or an airport, to de-register.

Customs regulations

Tourists must complete a customs declaration form on entry, which should be kept until departure. This allows for the free import and re-export of articles intended for personal use for the duration of stay, like cameras and recorders, as well as personal jewellery. You may also have to register the amount of foreign currency you are carrying. Goods to the value of T20,000 are allowed to be exported from Mongolia. Prohibited items include: palaeontological and archaeological finds; uncertified antiques; collections of various plants and their seeds; raw skins, hides and furs without permission from the appropriate authorities.

Luggage

On international flights the luggage allowance is 20kg per passenger. Excess luggage is charged at US$1 dollar per kilo, subject to negotiation on the day.

Travel insurance

It is advisable to have a comprehensive policy in place and to let your insurance company know that you will be travelling in Mongolia. Make sure you will be covered if you have any health problems. There may be some additional charges.

MONGOLIAN EMBASSIES AND CONSULATES

Belgium 18 Av Besme, 1190 Bruxelles; tel: +2 344 6974; fax: +2 344 3215; email: Embassy.mongolia@skynet.be

Canada BCE Place Suite 1800, PO Box 754, 181 Bay St, Toronto, Ontario M5J 2T9; tel: +416 865 7779; fax: +416 863 1515; email: consulgen@mongolia.org

China 2 Xiushui Beijie, Jian Guo Men Wai Da Jie, Beijing; tel: +10 6532 1203; fax: +10 6532 5045; email: Monembbj@public3.bta.net.cn

Czech Republic Na Marne 5, Praha 6, 16000; tel: +243 11198; fax: +243 14827; email: mongemb@bohem-net.cz

France 5 Ave Robert Schumann, 92100 Boulogne-Billancourt, Paris; tel: +33 46 05 23 18; fax: +33 1 46 05 30 16; email: 106513.2672@compuserve.com

Germany Dietzgenstrasse 31, 13156 Berlin; tel: +49 3044 735122; fax: +49 3047480616; email: mongolbot@aol.com

India 34 Archbishop Makarios Marg, New Delhi 110003; tel: +11 463 1728; fax: +11 463 3240; email: embassy.mongolia@gems.vsni.net.in

Italy Via Giulia, 10-34126, Trieste; tel: +39 40 575422; fax: +39 40 575431

Japan Pine Crest Mansion, 21-4 Kamiyama-cho, Shibuya-ku, Tokyo 150; tel: +81 33 469 2088; fax: +81 33 469 2216; email: embmong@gol.com

Kazakhstan Almaty, ul. Aubakerova 1/1; tel: +3272 200865; fax: +3272 293259; email: monkazel@kazmail.asdc.kz
Korea, Republic 33-5 Hannam-Dong, Wongsan-ku, Seoul; tel: +2 794 1950; fax: +2 794 7605; email: monemb@uriel.net
Poland ul Rejtana 15 m 16, 00478 Warszaw; tel/fax: +22 849 9391; email: mongamb@ikp.atm.com.pl
Russian Federation ul Borisoglebovskaya 11, Moscow 121069; tel: +095 290 6792; fax: +095 291 6171; email: mongolia@glasnet.ru
Singapore 06-01 The Makena, 121 Meyer Rd, Singapore 437932; tel: +348 745; fax: +348 1753; email: sukhee@singnet.com.sg
UK 7 Kensington Court, London W8 5DL; tel: +44 020 7937 0150; fax: +44 020 7937 1117; email: embmong@aol.com. Open Mon–Fri 10.00–12.30.
United Nations 6 East 77th St, New York NY 10021; tel: +1 212 472 517; fax: +1 212 861 464; email: mngun@undp.org
USA 2833 M St NW, Washington DC20007; tel: +1 202 333 117, fax: +1 202 298 227; email monemb@aol.com

For overseas embassies in Mongolia, see page 235.

GETTING THERE AND AWAY
By air
The main connection to Mongolia from Europe is via Berlin with MIAT (Mongol Irgenii Agaaryn Teever – Mongolian Civil Air Transport). MIAT flies to international destinations such as Moscow, Beijing, Seoul, Irkutsk, Berlin, Huhhot (in Chinese Inner Mongolia) and Osaka. MIAT has branch offices in Korea, China, Taiwan, Japan, Germany, Italy, Holland, France, Russia, Canada and the United States. You may fly from most European capitals directly to Beijing in China and change planes (if on another carrier) to Air China in Beijing for the two-hour fight to Ulaanbaatar. There are direct flights from Moscow to Ulaanbaatar with Aeroflot. Costs vary, depending on when you travel – high or low season. Air fares normally increase by 4% to 5% annually.

Before departure remember the following three things:

• Reconfirm your return flight at least 24 hours prior to your departure.
• Check in two hours before your departure time for international flights.
• International departure tax is T17,500 (about US$16), payable in local currency.

Buyant-Ukhaa Airport is situated 18km southwest of the capital. Incoming flights arrive from all directions: Beijing in the south, Moscow in the west, Seoul in the east and Irkutsk in the north, and from many other places. Facilities at the airport include a restaurant, a café, bureau de change and several duty-free shops selling souvenirs, spirits and perfumes.

Airlines
MIAT (Mongolian Airlines) Head office in Mongolia: PO Box 45, Buyant-Ukhaa, Ulaanbaatar 34; tel: +976 11 325633, 379935, 379519; fax: +976 11 379973; web: www.miat.com.mn. Reservation and ticket office is newly located east of Sükhbaatar Square (opposite Puma Imperial Hotel); tel: +976 11 325633; fax: +976 11 313385. Office at Buyant-Ukhaa Airport: tel: +976 11 379935. Main European Branch Office, Germany: Chaussee Strasse 84, Berlin 10115; tel: +49 30 28498142; fax: +49 30 29498140. Route Berlin–Moscow. Flight: weekly flight on Sunday (winter); twice weekly, Thursday, Sunday (summer). Cost: £660 return. Travel time: 12 hours 40 minutes. To check international flights to and from Mongolia, and for further information, check the website.

British Airways 156 Regent St, London W1R 5TA; tel: +44 01914 907901 or +44 0845 7733377; web: www.britishairways.com. Route London–Beijing direct (transfer to Air China for Beijing–Ulaanbaatar flight). Flights: three times weekly – Monday, Wednesday, Saturday. Cost: London–Beijing economy return, including tax, £648 (winter), £573 (summer). Travel time: 10 hours.

Air China Main UK office: 41 Grosvenor Gardens, London SW1 W0BP; tel: +44 020 7630 0919/7678; fax: +44 020 7630 7792; web: www.air-china.com. Local offices: Room 201, Bayangol Hotel, Ulaanbaatar; Ikh Toiruu, 12 Khoroolol; tel: +976 11 328838. Route London–Beijing/Beijing–Ulaanbaatar. Flights: London–Beijing three times weekly in winter (more frequently in summer); Beijing–Ulaanbaatar three times weekly – Tuesday, Friday, Sunday. Cost: £784 (including tax) London–Ulaanbaatar direct via Beijing; London–Beijing costs £566 (including tax) in winter, £569 (including tax) in summer. Travel time: London–Beijing 10 hours; Beijing–Ulaanbaatar just over 2 hours.

Aeroflot (Russian airlines) UK Booking Office: 70 Piccadilly, London W1V 9HH; tel: 020 7355 2233; fax: 020 7493 1852; web: www.aeroflot.co.uk. Office in Mongolia: tel: +976 11 320720. IMS (Agents for Aeroflot in London) 9 Mandeville Place, London W1U 8AU; tel: 020 7224 4678; fax; 020 7224 2106; email: info@imstravel.co.uk; web: www.imstravel.co.uk. IMS will make bookings and you can pay by credit card. Route London–Moscow–Ulaanbaatar (changing planes in Moscow). Flights: once a week on Friday (winter); three times weekly Monday, Wednesday and Friday (summer). Cost: approximately £406 (including all taxes) low-season return, £450 (including all taxes) high-season return. Travel time: London–Moscow 3 hours, Moscow to Ulaanbaatar 8½ hours.

By rail

One of the most exciting railroads in the world – the Trans-Siberian Railway – runs from Moscow to Vladivostock. There are several branches on this line – one through Mongolia, another through Manchuria, while the main Siberian line continues to Vladivostock, the eastern terminus on the Pacific coast. The Trans-Mongolian (Ulaanbaatar) Railway is connected to the Trans-Siberian by a branch line from Ulan-Ude, providing a link between the Trans-Siberian and the Chinese railway system.

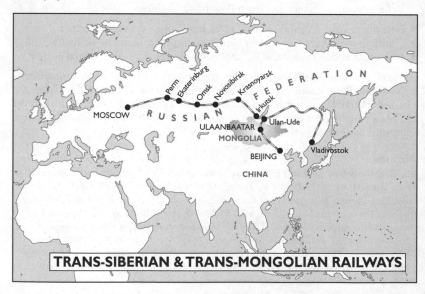

TRANS-SIBERIAN & TRANS-MONGOLIAN RAILWAYS

BY TRANS-SIBERIAN RAILWAY TO MONGOLIA
Neil McGowan

Many people are tempted by the chance to take one of the world's most renowned rail journeys on what is usually called the Trans-Siberian Railway. There is no train called 'The Trans-Siberian Express'. All trains which cross this central area of Russia are Trans-Siberian trains, whether their route is between Moscow and Beijing via Mongolia – sometimes called the Trans-Mongolian (although there is no train called that either) – or the non-Mongolian routes from Moscow to Beijing via Manchuria, and Moscow to Vladivostok on the Pacific coast.

From Moscow to Mongolia, there are two potential routes, of which only two are fully practicable. The less practicable one is unromantically named Train #4, informally known as 'The Chinese Train' (because it's the homeward run of a Chinese Railways train which came up to Moscow from Beijing the previous week – staff and rolling-stock are Chinese). It is also called The Trans-Mongolian. You board this train in Moscow for Beijing and intermediate stops are not permitted. So, you must buy a through-ticket to Beijing in order to leave the train at Ulaanbaatar. This train offers the highest level of on-board comfort of any train on the route – better than first class is deluxe class, which is unique to Chinese Railways. The two-berth (one up, one down) compartments have jet-air ventilation, an armchair and share a small WC/washroom with the neighbouring compartment. Byzantine but effective drop-lock systems guarantee your ablutions are not disturbed and ensure inter-compartmental security. Other carriages consist of four-berth compartments, called first and second class according to decor and comfort. Train #4 runs weekly from Moscow to Beijing so if you are going to jump off in Mongolia, then be ready to do so at around 08.00, UB time, five days later.

Train #6, sometimes called The UB Express, runs twice weekly between Moscow and UB. Train # 6 has first-class (two-berth) and second-class (four-berth) compartments. This train permits you to devise a multi-stop itinerary en route (joining or leaving the train at major stations along the way).

The traveller grapevine says that conditions on the Russian train are very much better than the Mongolian one. This is based on the fact that the Mongolian traders (who bring cheap Mongolian produce to sell in Moscow and return with hard-to-find consumer goods) can buy tickets much more cheaply on their own national railway than on a Russian train. You may find yourself sharing a compartment with several Mongolians, crammed into a small space with their latest purchases – a microwave, car tyres, a hot-water boiler and so on. Another option is to travel with the aim to stop en route in Siberia. Please note that you must have a pre-booked itinerary to do this before your Russian visa application will be processed.

Food on board is the same story for all the trains, including Train #4 (mentioned above). By international convention, the restaurant-car franchise on any international train goes to the country across whose territory you are travelling. This means that from Moscow to the Mongolian border, Russian Railways will be your hosts in the dining car, with a cafeteria-style menu at reasonable prices. In the past, caviar and champagne often featured, but they may no longer be on the menu at such fantastically low prices. Nevertheless, it is always a journey of a lifetime!

ROYAL MAIL TO ULAANBAATAR – THROUGH THE GOBI BY TRAIN
Nicolas Gardner

It was still daylight when the train reached Erlian on the Chinese Mongolian border. Another Queen's Messenger and myself had been travelling since 08.00 and memories were fading of the noisy chaos at Beijing railway station. It was more interesting to stay on board to watch the changing of the bogies for the larger gauge Mongolia track, and so I did. In an enormous shed, the carriages were swiftly separated and jacked up – the old bogies were lifted and new ones inserted in an operation directed by whistle blasts. These formalities complete, the train trundled gently into Mongolia at Zamyn-Üüd and we were met by smart-looking officials in uniforms, with polished knee-boots and high-peaked caps, who put their Chinese counterparts to shame. All passports were taken, and silence fell. Ages later they were returned, each with a neat entry stamp beside the Mongolian visa.

It was well after midnight when my fellow Queen's Messenger and I retired to our berths – soon to be tucked up in clean sheets and warm blankets for the night. Our adjoining compartments had an interconnecting bathroom where we stored our food bag. Past experience had taught us to self-cater rather than to risk the restaurant car. In the morning, hot water for morning tea was supplied by a Chinese attendant – who travels through to Moscow.

At last we entered the Gobi proper. It appeared absolutely huge and empty under a cloudless sky. There were distant hills (difficult to judge how far away they were) and very little vegetation other than a thin covering of dead-looking grass. No roads. Telephone poles and lines followed the railway track. Occasional groups of animals attended by herdsmen flashed by and isolated *gers* were glimpsed, looking to all the world like field mushrooms. I wished I had my binoculars as it was hard to tell if the animals were sheep, cattle or horses. We spotted small birds and, occasionally, larger hawk-like species; a single lorry motored alongside the train at a distance, trailing a plume of dust, until we came to a halt in a sad-looking village of tin-topped dwellings, with plaster peeling off the walls. A number of men wore traditional *deels* (tunics) with belts of brightly coloured cloth, topped by incongruous looking pork-pie hats. Energetic children looked inquisitively at us. Co-passengers descended to the platform for fresh air (but one of us remained behind to watch the bags). It was cooler here, being early September. Attendants shooed us on board and with a hoot of the horn we were off again. We lunched on corned beef, tinned sardines and excellent bread from the Beijing Hotel, which drew interested looks from passers-by in the corridor.

At last I spotted trees and we entered the grasslands. A herd of camels came into view and horsemen were seen galloping full pelt across the dry, flat steppe carrying long poles with lassos attached to the end, the Mongol method to ring animals. Finally, we saw the outskirts of Ulaanbaatar where modern construction is supplanting older Soviet-style buildings, but traditional *gers* remain in wooden-fenced compounds. After much blowing of the horn, the train halted. Swarms of flat, flushed Mongolian faces greeted us and we spotted the British Land Rovers and smiling embassy officers. The bacon had arrived!

Proposals to build a Trans-Siberian railway were put forward to the Russian government as early as 1857, by an American, Perry Collins, who proposed a steam railway to transit Siberia. His plan was rejected. A similar Russian proposal was also rejected, and so was the English proposal for a tramway driven by horses. In 1887, work began on the Western Siberian railway line, which was opened by the Tsar in May 1891. The mid-section, started in 1893, was completed in 1899. It took until 1904 to open the eastern sections around Lake Baikal. Finally, the railway line crossed a bridge over the Amur River to reach Vladivostok on the Pacific coast. The Mongolian sections were joined from the main line to Ulaanbaatar in 1949 and to China in1955. The Trans-Mongolian Railway from the Russian border to Ulaanbaatar opened in 1949, and was connected from Ulaanbaatar to the Chinese border in 1955. The total distance from Moscow to Ulaanbaatar is 6,304km, and from Moscow to Beijing (Peking) is 7,865km. The Trans-Mongolian covers 1,000km from the Russian border to the Chinese border passing through Ulaanbaatar and several other towns. The Trans-Mongolian railway line is of great economic importance to the country, since it handles most of Mongolia's export and import goods. The main line and its various branch lines in Mongolia carry internal freight, especially coal. It is also a transit route for goods traded between Russia and China.

There are three services a week between Beijing and Moscow that run throughout the year on the Trans-Mongolian and Trans-Manchurian routes. It takes six days to travel from Moscow to Beijing (a day from UB to Beijing). Train #3 leaves Beijing weekly at 19.40 on Wednesday and arrives in Moscow at 19.00 on Monday. China Train #4 leaves Moscow weekly at 19.50 on Tuesday and arrives in Beijing at 15.30 on Monday.

Since many student travellers arrive in China, travel up to Mongolia by train and return to China, or travel on to Moscow, it is important to understand the options offered by Trans-Siberian/Trans-Mongolian railways. There are Russian trains Moscow–UB–Beijing and Moscow–UB and return; there are Mongolian trains UB–Moscow and return; there are Chinese trains Beijing–UB–Moscow and return. The Russian, Chinese and Mongolian rail authorities decide on the annual schedules, so firm bookings may be taken, usually, after May. Although times may change, once you understand the routes, the basic information remains the same with small adjustments, and possible the inculsion of an additional train, so it is important to check the schedules when planning your travels.

International rail costs

Costs depend on the route you plan. A rough indication of costs in US dollars from UB to Moscow is from US$150 to US$220; from Ulaanbaatar to Beijing is US$75–120 (depending on the class). All trains have two classes, luxury or four-bed compartments. The Chinese trains offer an in-between class with softer beds. All classes are comfortable in terms of train travel. Boiling water is available from a large boiler at the end of each carriage for thermos flasks. Although most local travellers bring their own food, there is a restaurant car, which mainly serves Westerners and the better-off Chinese and Mongolian traders.

Organised tours make the journey run smoothly and all the ticketing is handled for you. The cost for a 16-day tour from Beijing via Ulaanbaatar to Moscow, for two–four people, is US$1,650 per person; for groups of ten and over, US$1,320 per person. This includes five nights on the train, three nights in Beijing, three nights in Ulaanbaatar, one night in a Mongolian *ger* (traditional tented accommodation) and three nights in Moscow.

Rail bookings in Mongolia
Railway bookings for international train fares only can be made at the Foreigner's Booking Office (Room 212, 2nd floor) in the International Railway Ticket Office, a yellow building beside the railway station in Ulaanbaatar. For reservations and information tel: 11 944868. Open Mon–Sat 09.00–18.00, Sun 10.00–14.00. It is essential to bring your passport if booking international rail tickets yourself. Mongolian tour companies will help you to make reservations for a small commission.

Tickets and itineraries based on the Trans-Siberian Railway
It is difficult to find your own way around the rail system (try it!) in order to book a fare from London to Ulaanbaatar. The simple shortcut is to contact Off the Map Tours who are experts on rail travel to Mongolia and offer some exciting itineraries, or Regent Holidays, who have pioneered this route for over 30 years (see *Tour operators*, pages 148–9). Regent organise the following itineraries for individual and group travel, book rail tickets and obtain visas:

The Trans-Siberian/Mongolian train journey from Moscow offers stopovers in Siberia and Mongolia, and continues to Beijing in China. Some Russian trains end the journey in Ulaanbaatar. At the start of the journey you will find yourself in Moscow tasting blini (meat-filled pancakes) and sipping ice-cold vodka, served outside the Kremlin. On the train journey you will travel in a first-class, two-berth compartment. The first stopover is Lake Baikal, giving you enough time to spend rambling along the lake's shore; next is a stopover in Mongolia, where you will spend several days camping in a traditional Mongolian *ger* – riding and joining in the lifestyle of the nomads. Some journeys continue south past the Great Wall and end with a kite-flying experience in Beijing's Tiananmen Square. There are a number of different itineraries to choose from in Mongolia. From Beijing you may wish to travel on to Hong Kong by train, or even further south to Vietnam.

By road
There are two main border crossings linking Mongolia by road to her big neighbours, Russia and China. They are at Sükhbaatar on the Russian-Mongol border in the north and at Zamyn-Üüd on the Chinese-Mongol border in the south. The border crossings in the far west are not used by foreigners and special permission is required if crossing into Russia or China on one of the 40 bilateral crossing points. All road border crossings are still limited to nationals of the border countries only – but this may change when a big border inspect station is completed at Altanbulag. There are no main border crossings in the east.

HEALTH
Vaccinations
No vaccinations are compulsory but the National Pharmaceutical Society of Great Britain recommends the following: hepatitis A, typhoid, tetanus, polio and meningitis A + C. You might want to add rabies, tuberculosis (BCG) and diphtheria if staying for some months and travelling in rural Mongolia.

Tetanus needs to be boosted ten-yearly and can be conveniently combined with diphtheria in a single vaccine (Diftavax). Both vaccines are also available separately if either one is currently in date. Likewise polio should be boosted if you haven't been immunised in the last ten years.

Hepatitis A vaccine (Havrix Monodose or Avaxim) consists of two injections taken about a year apart and costs around £100 in the UK. It is now felt that the vaccine can be used even close to the time of departure and has replaced the old-fashioned gamma globulin. The newer typhoid vaccines (eg: Typhim Vi) last for three years and are about 85% effective. They should be encouraged unless you are leaving within a few days for a trip of a week or less, when the vaccine would not be effective in time.

Meningitis A + C vaccine is recommended for all travellers but is essential if you are intending to visit the capital, Ulaanbaatar. A single dose of vaccine is effective for three years.

Vaccinations for rabies are advised for travellers visiting more remote areas when medical help could not be reached within 24 hours (see *Dog bites*, page 169).

Hepatitis B vaccination should be considered for longer trips (two months or more) or for those working with children or in situations where contact with blood is likely. Three injections are needed for the best protection and can be given over a four-week period if time is short. Longer schedules give more sustained protection and are therefore preferred if time allows.

A BCG vaccination against tuberculosis (TB) is also advised for trips of two months or more.

It is wise to go to your doctor or a travel clinic about eight weeks before departure to arrange your immunisations. For further information, see below.

Travel clinics and health information

A full list of current travel clinic websites worldwide is available on www.istm.org/. For other journey preparation information, consult www.tripprep.com. Information about various medications may be found on www.emedicine.com/wild/topiclist.htm.

UK

Berkeley Travel Clinic 32 Berkeley St, London W1J 8EL (near Green Park tube station); tel: 020 7629 6233

British Airways Travel Clinic and Immunisation Service There are two BA clinics in London, both on tel: 0845 600 2236; web: www.britishairways.com/travelclinics. Appointments only at 111 Cheapside; or walk-in service Mon–Sat at 156 Regent St. Apart from providing inoculations and malaria prevention, they sell a variety of health-related goods.

Fleet Street Travel Clinic 29 Fleet St, London EC4Y 1AA; tel: 020 7353 5678; web: www.fleetstreet.com. Injections, travel products and latest advice.

Hospital for Tropical Diseases Travel Clinic Mortimer Market Centre, 2nd Floor, Capper St (off Tottenham Ct Rd), London WC1E 6AU; tel: 020 7388 9600; web: www.thhtd.org. Offers consultations and advice, and is able to provide all necessary drugs and vaccines for travellers. Runs a healthline (09061 337733) for country-specific information and health hazards. Also stocks nets, water purification equipment and personal protection measures.

MASTA (Medical Advisory Service for Travellers Abroad), at the London School of Hygiene and Tropical Medicine, Keppel St, London WC1 7HT; tel: 09068 224100. This is a premium-line number, charged at 60p per minute. For a fee, they will provide an individually tailored health brief, with up-to-date information on how to stay healthy, inoculations and what to bring.

MASTA pre-travel clinics Tel: 01276 685040. Call for the nearest; there are currently 30 in Britain. Also sell malaria prophylaxis memory cards, treatment kits, bednets, net treatment kits.

NHS travel website, www.fitfortravel.scot.nhs.uk, provides country-by-country advice on immunisation and malaria, plus details of recent developments, and a list of relevant health organisations.

Nomad Travel Store 3–4 Wellington Terrace, Turnpike Lane, London N8 0PX; tel: 020 8889 7014; fax: 020 8889 9528; email: sales@nomadtravel.co.uk; web:

www.nomadtravel.co.uk. Also at 40 Bernard St, London WC1N 1LJ; tel: 020 7833 4114; fax: 020 7833 4470 and 43 Queens Rd, Bristol BS8 1QH; tel: 0117 922 6567; fax: 0117 922 7789. As well as dispensing health advice, Nomad stocks mosquito nets and other anti-bug devices, and an excellent range of adventure travel gear.

Thames Medical 157 Waterloo Rd, London SE1 8US; tel: 020 7902 9000. Competitively priced, one-stop travel health service. All profits go to their affiliated company, InterHealth, which provides health care for overseas workers on Christian projects.

Trailfinders Immunisation Centre 194 Kensington High St, London W8 7RG; tel: 020 7938 3999.

Travelpharm The Travelpharm website, www.travelpharm.com, offers up-to-date guidance on travel-related health and has a range of medications available through their online mini-pharmacy.

Irish Republic

Tropical Medical Bureau Grafton Street Medical Centre, Grafton Buildings, 34 Grafton St, Dublin 2; tel: 1 671 9200. Has a useful website specific to tropical destinations: www.tmb.ie.

USA

Centers for Disease Control 1600 Clifton Rd, Atlanta, GA 30333; tel: 877 FYI TRIP; 800 311 3435; web: www.cdc.gov/travel. The central source of travel information in the USA. Each summer they publish the invaluable *Health Information for International Travel*, available from the Division of Quarantine at the above address.

Connaught Laboratories PO Box 187, Swiftwater, PA 18370; tel: 800 822 2463. They will send a free list of specialist tropical-medicine physicians in your state.

IAMAT (International Association for Medical Assistance to Travelers) 417 Center St, Lewiston, NY 14092; tel: 716 754 4883; email: info@iamat.org; web: www.iamat.org. A non-profit organisation that provides lists of English-speaking doctors abroad.

Canada

IAMAT (International Association for Medical Assistance to Travellers) Suite 1, 1287 St Clair Av W, Toronto, Ontario M6E 1B8; tel: 416 652 0137; web: www.iamat.org

TMVC (Travel Doctors Group) Sulphur Springs Rd, Ancaster, Ontario; tel: 905 648 1112; web: www.tmvc.com.au

Australia, Thailand

TMVC Tel: 1300 65 88 44; web: www.tmvc.com.au. Twenty-two clinics in Australia, New Zealand and Thailand, including:

Auckland Canterbury Arcade, 170 Queen Street, Auckland City; tel: 373 3531

Brisbane Dr Deborah Mills, Qantas Domestic Building, 6th floor, 247 Adelaide St, Brisbane, QLD 4000; tel: 7 3221 9066; fax: 7 3321 7076

Melbourne Dr Sonny Lau, 393 Little Bourke St, 2nd floor, Melbourne, VIC 3000; tel: 3 9602 5788; fax: 3 9670 8394

Sydney Dr Mandy Hu, Dymocks Building, 7th Floor, 428 George St, Sydney, NSW2000; tel: 2 221 7133; fax: 2 221 8401

Europe

Pasteur Institute Centre for Vaccinations 209 Rue de Veaux Gerrard, Paris 15, France; tel: +33 1 45 68 80 00

IAMAT Europe This organisation provides health information and lists of English-speaking doctors abroad. 57 Voirets, 1212 Grand Lancy, Geneva; web: www.sentex.net/~iamat

New Zealand
TMVC See above
IAMAT PO Box 5049, Christchurch 5; web: www.iamat.org

South Africa
SAA-Netcare Travel Clinics PO Box 786692, Sandton 2146; fax: 011 883 6152; web: www.travelclinic.co.za or www.malaria.co.za. Clinics throughout South Africa.
TMVC 113 DF Malan Drive, Roosevelt Park, Johannesburg; tel: 011 888 7488; web: www.tmvc.com.au. Consult the website for details of clinics in South Africa.

Switzerland
IAMAT 57 Voirets, 1212 Grand Lancy, Geneva; web: www.iamat.org

Medical kit
When packing a basic medical kit, include good vitamin tablets (especially vitamin C), mineral tablets, water-purifying tablets, and charcoal (see box for explanation, page 165). One of the most vulnerable times for travellers is at the start of their journey. Echinacea (tincture) taken in water is said to reduce the risk of infection, especially during long-distance flights, and is an excellent preventative for colds.

You should consider including the following in your medical kit:

- throat lozenges, multivitamins and mineral tablets
- indigestion tablets (Alkaseltzer)
- analgesic pain relief (paracetamol, Ibuprofen)
- hydrocortisone cream (for bites, stings and allergic rashes)
- anti-diarrhoea capsules (Imodium); rehydration sachets (Dioralyte); Ciprofloxacin antibiotic 500mg x 6 (Norfloxacin, or nalidixic acid; for severe diarrhoea)
- laxative (for constipation)
- water-purifying tablets
- good drying antiseptic powder
- broad-spectrum antibiotic (eg: Amoxycillin) for respiratory, urinary or skin infections, if going to a remote area
- fine-pointed tweezers (to remove thorns and splinters)
- surgical spirit
- thermometer
- sunblock (factor 30 is recommended on biking trips)
- anti-mosquito and insect spray
- antihistamine tablets
- burn ointment (Hypericum or aloe vera)
- plasters (Band-aids) and Steristrips; cotton wool, scissors, bandages, medicated gauze
- syringe and needles
- support bandage (Tubigrip – an elastic tubular bandage for sprained ankles)

Pre-packed complete medical kits for travellers save you time and trouble in collecting the necessary first-aid kit. Lifesystems First Aid Kit for Travellers is excellent, part of the set ensures that travellers carry basic medical/dental single-use items which come into direct contact with the bloodstream and may not be available when they are needed. Knowing your blood group is a help. For Lifesystems kits contact tel: +44 020 8881 8283 or email explore@nomadtravel.co.uk.

ALTERNATIVE HEALTH SUPPLIES
Susie Penny

Important If you are taking medication please consult your doctor before making any dietary changes or supplementing with any of the herbal nutrient recommendations below.

Citricidal A natural all-in-one protection made from grapefruit seeds. A few drops in drinking water will help prevent infection. If you have diarrhoea, take ten drops in water three times a day. Always dilute when applying to the skin.

Lactogest The perfect travelling probiotic. The friendly bacteria in this formula are not sensitive to heat so there is no need for refrigeration. It will fight any foreign, unfriendly bacteria. Taken at mealtimes, it will boost your intestinal micro-flora and keep tummy upsets at bay. (Although Mongolian *airag* and yoghurt will more likely take care of that, they may also be the cause of it!)

Cat's claw (Peruvian rainforest bark) Packed with phyto-nutrients. It is a great immune booster and helps maintain optimum energy.

Supergar (garlic) and **B complex** A natural mosquito repellent (see box, *Age-old remedies*, opposite). Garlic has been used for centuries as a powerful protector against infection. Eat plenty of garlic supplemented with a B-vitamin complex. Starting at least one week before the holiday the combination can act as a skin deterrent to insects like mosquitoes.

MSM cream and **Aloe 300** MSM is a natural source of organic sulphur. Using MSM cream before and after sunbathing reduces UV damage and helps relieve sunburn. MSM cream and aloe vera gel can also be used to accelerate wound healing and prevent scarring in the event of any holiday accidents.

Vitamin C Nature's anti-histamine. If you suffer from prickly heat or heat rash then pack some vitamin C. This natural antihistamine helps to calm down the skin's inflammatory response to heat. True Food C (TM) is recommended. It is 11 times more powerful as an anti-oxidant than isolated vitamin C, and sustains vitamin C levels in the blood for well over eight hours.

The above products are available from many health stores. If in doubt, contact The Nutrition Centre, Burwash Common, East Sussex TN19 7LX, UK, tel: +44 01435 882880.

Alternative health supplies
Many people prefer to take some alternative health remedies. Many traditional herbal medicines are well accepted today. Alternative supplies do not replace the conventional medical kit. Talk to your GP before you travel if you are in any doubt about health matters, including alternative supplies.

In Mongolia
Advice for travellers
Thanks to the climate (although extreme) and its small population, Mongolia is a reasonably healthy place to travel. (See section on *Hazards*, page 168 – some of

the most likely hazards in Mongolia are from severe heat or cold.) There are several immediate things to watch out for, such as sore throats from the dry atmosphere – bring plenty of throat lozenges – and the possibility of stomach upsets due to a change of diet. One of the best tips is to keep your fingernails very short and wash your hands more often than usual. The maxim is peel it, boil it and cook it. Countryside cooking in Mongolia usually involves boiling or steaming. Vegetables and fruit are plentiful in the capital but not in the countryside, so you may need to travel with additional fibre in a pill form. Remember to drink plenty of water.

Drinking water

In Ulaanbaatar you can drink the tap water; however, as a general rule it is advisable to use iodine drops or water-purifying tablets, or to boil drinking water. In many parts of Mongolia, especially the mountain-forested regions, you will find springs of pure, crystal-clear water. In southern regions of the Gobi the water is often sandy and has a very high mineral content – as a result the local people suffer from stomach and tooth complaints. Wells installed in the Gobi during the socialist years have not been maintained, so water is now scarce and of dubious quality. When going there it is advisable to carry bottled water and/or to use purification tablets.

Altitude

Mongolia is located at altitude – the average is 1,580m above sea level – which affects people differently. Although Ulaanbaatar is only at 1,350m, some people are sensitive to this and will need several days to adjust, which means taking it easy on arrival and not rushing around immediately. This is usually sufficient to adjust. However, it is more likely that travellers will only experience problems over 2,000m. More adventurous trekkers may wish to visit the Khentii Nuruu, a popular and accessible mountain range to the northeast of the capital, where heights of up to 2,800m can be reached. Remember anyone, even the very fit, can suffer from altitude sickness (for symptoms, see below, page 167) if they try to ascend too fast. But if you have any heart or lung problems you should consult with your doctor to check that it is safe for you to go. Over 3,500m, about 50% of people will experience symptoms of altitude sickness. These may include

AGE-OLD REMEDIES

Charcoal Derives its medical value from its high absorbing capacity for all kinds of material, like toxins, poisons etc. It is a simple and highly effective treatment. It may also be taken as a remedy for upset stomachs. If you fall and graze yourself badly, make a paste using charcoal and water to put on the wound immediately to help to draw out any harmful matter. Available in capsule or biscuit form (traditional Braggs charcoal biscuits in the UK). A pharmacist can advise regarding powder form.

Garlic To cleanse the blood; also thought to keep fleas and insects at bay. Eat one clove of raw garlic a day. Do not chew and to avoid the smell, peel a clove, prick it with a sharp instrument (fork or tip of a knife) and swallow whole with water. Also available in capsule form.

Ginger An effective natural preventative for motion sickness and any type of nausea. Also helpful because of its warming and stimulating effects when suffering from cold injury. Available in root or capsule form.

LONG-HAUL FLIGHTS
Dr Felicity Nicholson

There is growing evidence, albeit circumstantial, that long-haul air travel increases the risk of developing deep vein thrombosis. This condition is potentially life threatening, but it should be stressed that the danger to the average traveller is slight. Certain risk factors specific to air travel have been identified. These include immobility, compression of the veins at the back of the knee by the edge of the seat, the decreased air pressure and slightly reduced oxygen in the cabin, and dehydration. Consuming alcohol may exacerbate the situation by increasing fluid loss and encouraging immobility.

In theory everyone is at risk, but those at highest risk are shown below:

- Passengers on journeys of longer than eight hours duration
- People over 40
- People with heart disease
- People with cancer
- People with clotting disorders
- People who have had recent surgery, especially on the legs
- Women on the pill or other oestrogen therapy
- Pregnancy
- People who are very tall (over 6ft/1.8m) or short (under 5ft/1.5m)

A deep vein thrombosis (DVT) is a clot of blood that forms in the leg veins. Symptoms include swelling and pain in the calf or thigh. The skin may feel hot to touch and becomes discoloured (light blue-red). A DVT is not dangerous in itself, but if a clot breaks down then it may travel to the lungs (pulmonary embolus). Symptoms of a pulmonary embolus (PE) include chest pain, shortness of breath and coughing up small amounts of blood.

Symptoms of a DVT rarely occur during the flight, and typically occur within three days of arrival, although symptoms of a DVT or PE have been reported up to two weeks later.

Anyone who suspects that they have these symptoms should see a doctor immediately as anticoagulation (blood thinning) treatment can be given.

Prevention of DVT
General measures to reduce the risk of thrombosis are shown below. This advice also applies to long train or bus journeys.

- While waiting to board the plane, walk around rather than sit.
- During the flight drink plenty of water (at least two small glasses every hour).
- Avoid excessive tea, coffee and alcohol.
- Perform leg-stretching exercises, such as pointing the toes up and down.
- Move around the cabin when practicable.

If you fit into the high-risk category (see above) ask your doctor if it is safe to travel. Additional protective measures such as graded compression stockings, aspirin or low molecular weight heparin can be given. No matter how tall you are, where possible request a seat with extra legroom.

headaches, nausea, anorexia and difficulty in sleeping. The best approach is to walk slowly and steadily and maintain a good fluid intake (at least three litres of water a day). However, if you do experience symptoms, however trivial they may seem, then you should alert someone (preferably your guide!). If the symptoms persist or you become breathless, lethargic, start to vomit, or suffer from vertigo, you should descend immediately. Even going down 500m is enough to start recovery.

If you are intending to reach heights in excess of 3,500m and a gradual ascent cannot be guaranteed (300m or less per day over 3,000m) then you may wish to use acetazolamide (Diamox). However, this drug should NEVER be used as an excuse to race up the mountain! It should only be taken after consultation with a (travel clinic) doctor and, although it may be beneficial in assisting adaptation to altitude, there may be some side effects. The current dose is 125–250mg twice a day for five days. Most doctors prefer that you try it for two days at least two weeks before travel to see if it suits you. For travellers aged 45 and above, pills containing glucose monohydrate (1.5g) and nicethamide (0.125g) prepared by Novartis, help in case of asthenia at high altitude. The late Dr Guido Pontecorvo, FRS, advised travellers to take 400mg of folic acid – combined with vitamin B complex – daily, for two weeks prior to your departure date. You will then acclimatise more easily when travelling to the mountains or areas above 1,500m.

One advantage of being in a 'higher' country is that there are fewer mosquitoes around and therefore no risk of malaria or Japanese encephalitis.

Medical help

If you need to see a doctor while you are in Ulaanbaatar, the Korean Friendship Hospital (tel: 11 310 945) is situated on Enkh Taivan (Peace Avenue), not far from the Foreign Ministry. There's a consultation fee (T5,000, roughly US$5) for any laboratory tests, and since few Mongolians can afford the fee, you will be seen quite quickly. Several staff speak English. Open Mon, Tue, Wed, working hours 09.00–17.00 (closed one hour for lunch), and mornings only Thu, Fri, Sat, 09.00–12.30. Closed Sun.

The new **SOS Medica Mongolia** off Chingis Avenue (not easy to find) has expatriate staff. Tel: 076 11 345526; mobile (24 hours): 99750967; email: sosmedicamongolia@mongolnet.com.

Emergency rescue service

In an emergency it is best to ask a Mongolian/English speaker to make the necessary calls to avoid language difficulties. In cases of medical emergency, you would be taken to the appropriate government hospital where a decision on the best action to take (treatment or repatriation) would be made by specialist staff. In the countryside some towns have a functioning hospital or health centre with qualified staff – usually a surgeon, an obstetrician and a paediatrician. However, treatment seems to follow the principle of the more the better and Mongolian health practitioners are particularly fond of injections. Sometimes medical staff are unavailable – so you may have a long wait to see a doctor in the countryside.

Pharmacies

In Ulaanbaatar and most larger towns there are pharmacies selling a variety of drugs. Counter assistants may not be qualified to give advice, so ask to speak to a doctor or pharmacist if you need medical help (bring a Mongolian friend or a translator with you in case of language problems). Travel with your own first-aid kit and definitely don't forget to bring an ample supply of any regularly prescribed medicines, because they may not be available in Mongolia. The Altai Pharmacy

TREATING TRAVELLERS' DIARRHOEA
Dr Felicity Nicholson

It is dehydration which makes you feel awful during a bout of diarrhoea and the most important part of treatment is drinking lots of clear fluids. Sachets of oral rehydration salts give the perfect biochemical mix to replace fluid loss but other recipes taste nicer. Any dilute mixture of sugar and salt in water will do you good: try Coke or orange squash with a three-finger pinch of salt added to each glass (if you are salt-depleted you won't taste the salt). Otherwise make a solution of a four-finger scoop of sugar with a three-finger pinch of salt in a glass of water. Or add eight level teaspoons of sugar (18g) and one level teaspoon of salt (3g) to one litre (five cups) of safe water. A squeeze of lemon or orange juice, if you can find the fruit in Mongolia, improves the taste and adds potassium, which is also lost in diarrhoea. Drink two large glasses after every bowel action, and more if you are thirsty. These solutions are still absorbed well if you are vomiting, but you will need to take sips at a time. If you are not eating you need to drink three litres a day. If you feel like eating, take a bland, high carbohydrate diet. Heavy greasy foods will probably give you cramps.

If the diarrhoea is severe and includes blood, or you have a fever, you will probably need antibiotics in addition to fluid replacement. A single dose of ciprofloxacin (500mg) repeated after 12 hours may be appropriate. If the diarrhoea is bulky and is accompanied by sulphurous (egg smell) burps, the likely cause is giardia. This is best treated with tinidazole (four x 500mg in one dose, repeated seven days later if symptoms persist).

(tel: 11 360 014 and 11 361 620) in the Bayangol District, Ulaanbaatar, has Western and Mongol medicine.

Health hazards

There are several health hazards worth mentioning, although they are, on the whole, rare. Drink raw (unpasteurised) milk with caution, since there is brucellosis in Mongolia. It is safer to drink boiled milk, which is what you are usually offered. There is a small chance that you might come across rabies and plague – treat both with great caution. The main risk here is if you are travelling alone in remote rural areas and see a dead animal in your path. If this happens, keep your distance and steer a very wide circle around it. Never approach to see what it is. It could be an animal dying of the plague – which can be caught from marmots in an infected area by inhaling air-borne bacteria, and by flea bites.

Illnesses
Travellers' diarrhoea

Travelling in Mongolia carries a fairly high risk of getting a dose of travellers' diarrhoea; perhaps 50% of visitors will suffer and the newer you are to exotic travel, the more likely you will be to suffer. By taking precautions against travellers' diarrhoea you will also avoid typhoid, cholera, hepatitis, dysentery, etc. Travellers' diarrhoea is passed from hand to mouth. The main precautions are care over what you eat and drink and washing hands after going to the lavatory, but even if the restaurant cook does not understand basic hygiene you will be safe if your food has been properly cooked and arrives piping hot. The maxim is:

PEEL IT, BOIL IT, COOK IT OR FORGET IT

This means that fruit you have washed and peeled yourself, and hot foods, should be safe but raw foods prepared by others, ice-cream and ice are all risky. Salads and fruit salads are rare in Mongolia. Foods kept lukewarm in hotel buffets are often dangerous. If you are struck, see box opposite for treatment.

Brucellosis
Mainly a disease of cattle, goats and sheep and humans catch it through infected milk, cheese or butter. It is prevented by making sure all milk is boiled. Symptoms are tiredness and aching joints. It is diagnosed by tests on blood serum.

Rabies
Caused by a bite or scratch from an infected animal. If you intend to travel widely in remote areas, a rabies vaccine might be advisable. Avoid dogs in the rural areas.

Treatment for dog bites
The wound must be thoroughly cleaned with plenty of soapy water (a ten-minute scrub), and free bleeding encouraged. Alcohol or tincture of iodine will help to destroy the virus. A charcoal paste may be applied. Medical attention should be sought immediately. Antibiotics and anti-tetanus immunisation should be given, along with protection against rabies. The vaccinations required depend on whether you have received pre-exposure vaccine. If you have, it will reduce the number of post-exposure doses needed and avoid having to track down the very expensive and scarce rabies immunoglobulin (RIG – about US$900 per dose!). A good reason for being well prepared for your trip.

Bubonic plague
Plague is still around in Mongolia, and causes a few deaths each summer. Outbreaks are reported to the authorities, who immediately quarantine the region. Bubonic plague is a contagious disease carried by fleas. However, these days it is easily curable by antibiotics, if you discover it in time. Towards the end of summer in certain remote areas in Mongolia there may be infection, where travel is banned, while in other places there is none. It is an extremely difficult disease to stamp out since it is carried by rodents, insects and fleas. Such animals, like the marmot, which disappear underground and hibernate in burrows, make its eradication virtually impossible. In the 1960s the reported incidences of human infection were practically nil, or went unreported, but since 1990 reported outbreaks have increased. Tourists should be aware of the risks, especially lone travellers. If you see a dying marmot, steer away. Do not even approach as this is an air-borne disease (like flu), transmitted within a short radius of an infected animal, and also transmitted by infected fleas. If you encounter any problems or need further advice get in touch with an institute for the prevention of infectious diseases in your home country, or the State Natural Nidus and Contagious Disease Fighting Board in Ulaanbaatar through the Ministry of Environment, Khudaldaany Street 5, Ulaanbaatar; tel: 11 326649; web: www.pmisgov.mn/menon.

Sexually transmitted diseases
Mongolia is not immune from sexually transmitted diseases, including AIDS. Preventative measures are essential, such as using condoms.

Injuries
Road accidents

Car/truck/jeep accidents happen so be aware and do what you can to reduce the risks – even if you have hired a vehicle and driver. Travel during daylight hours and listen to local advice concerning weather. Avoid high-risk situations where there is likely to be danger. When fording rivers, for example, use common sense. Check water levels with wading poles for safety. Be proactive; don't expect your driver to do all the thinking. If travelling at night, it is advisable for a passenger (or guide) to stay awake to help with navigation and to prevent him from falling asleep at the wheel.

Fractures

For arm fractures, remove the patient's watch and rings. Splints should be applied above and below the joint to give the maximum immobilisation. Never try to mend the fracture.

Heat injury
Sunburn

The intensity of UV radiation is increased by high altitudes. Watch out for the reflection of UV rays from snow, which may lead to severe sunburn. Dress to protect the skin and apply sunscreen frequently – not forgetting to apply lipsalve, which is essential for those with lip sores caused by herpes 1 (*Herpes labialis*).

Heat cramps

Occur in muscles after exercise has stopped; from loss of fluid through sweat; recent ingestion of alcohol; lack of sleep; inadequate diet; lack of acclimatisation. Relieve symptoms by stretching the cramped muscle. Treat fluid loss and rest in a cool environment. Salt tablets should be avoided.

Heat exhaustion

Weakness, fatigue, headache, dizziness, nausea, muscle cramps, confusion and irritability may occur. The cause is from dehydration following inadequate fluid intake especially during exercise in a hot climate. Treatment involves rest in a cool environment. Usually saline solutions are made to 0.9% saline solution because this is the same as body fluids. Instructions for making the correct rehydration fluid should be included with your medical kit; alternatively, it is available in sachet form (eg: Dioralyte).

Heat stroke

Can occur in young, healthy individuals on a sporting holiday, when unacclimatised. The onset is rapid. Treat by removing the patient to a cool place, taking off as much of their clothing as possible, and fanning and splashing water, if available, on the body. Apply cold packs to neck, groin and scalp.

Cold injury
Frostbite

Is associated with fatigue or accidents due to prolonged exposure to the cold. Signs of frostbite are intense pain at the site – cheeks, chin, ears, nose, hands and feet – followed by a hard whitening of the skin. The best advice is to be frequently checked by travelling companions because frostnip can quickly lead to frostbite. However, if you are travelling alone, check your fingers yourself for sensation by touching the little finger to the thumb, and check all parts of your face. If caught

SURVIVAL TACTICS

If your vehicle breaks down, the general advice is to stay by the vehicle. In Mongolia it is surprising to find how many people turn up in the middle of nowhere. For safety's sake let people know your route and try not to get lost! If caught out in the cold and snow, try to follow the following advice:

- Dig in, if the snow is deep enough.
- Build a windbreak.
- If there is any, use vegetation such as fir-tree branches to lie on.
- Make a fire (always carry a lighter or matches in your pocket).
- Put on the fire anything which will smoke to attract attention and signal for rescue. A properly prepared signal fire can be the difference between life and death.
- If you have an insulation (space) blanket, use it during the daylight to reflect light as an emergency signal.
- Drink. The body under stress produces more urine, and if you don't replace the fluids the body is in danger of dehydration. As a result, the danger of problems with circulation will increase.
- It is important to have a positive mental attitude. Do things to keep the spirits up, such as telling jokes or having sing songs.

in cold weather with frostbitten feet, it is advisable to continue walking in an attempt to reach safety.

Prevent by keeping dry, dressing sensibly, allowing for ventilation by wearing layers, wearing nothing too tight, covering your head and ears and watching out for each other. Treat frostnip by re-warming (eg: by blowing warm breath into a gloved hand). Do not rub the skin. Treat frostbite by protecting the affected part, and re-warming in water (not above 40°C).

Hypothermia

Occurs when the temperature of the body core falls below 35°C. Symptoms are exhaustion, numb skin – particularly the toes and fingers – shivering, slurred speech and muscle cramps. To treat this condition, remove the sufferer to a warm, dry place out of the wind. Insulate the patient's head, because up to 70% of the body's total heat production is lost via the head. Insulation should be provided between the patient's body and the ground. Remove wet clothing and put on layers of dry clothing. Do not rub the patient or put him or her near a fire. Encourage the patient to take liquids (not alcohol) and to eat. Surround the patient with human body heat, or place the patient in a warm tub of water, if available.

SAFETY
Women travellers

Many women travellers have survived alone in Mongolia without too many problems – they tell the usual funny stories about being chased around a *ger* by a friendly drunk. However, on a more cautionary note, women should be aware of heavy drinking and associated behaviour problems in Mongolia, as elsewhere. There is little to no danger from a cultural and social point of view. Use common sense, and when hitchhiking do not accept a lift if the driver's breath reeks of alcohol. Sometimes in isolated situations you have little choice but to accept the

WINTER TRANSPORT

You will need a reliable 4WD vehicle. Check your itinerary and travel preparations prior to departure with your guide and driver. Mongolians tend to set out and see what happens later .... Do not assume that you have sufficient petrol and emergency equipment on board. Check everything. In case your vehicle should be stuck in snow, bring a heavy ground sheet to put under tyres to help stop the wheels spinning; a shovel to dig out of snow drifts; a metal or wooden pole to probe the ground and measure the snow depth. Pack warm bedding, and food, water and a small fuel stove in case you get stuck.

In case of breakdown, Mongolian hospitality will most likely ensure that you will receive a warm welcome in the nearest *ger*. If you are more remote it is a question of waiting for help to arrive. Be sure that someone knows your route and is expecting your arrival. Unless you can get hold of some good 4WD transport in UB, you may have to hire old Russian jeeps used by many of the locals. If you are a party, it is best to take more vehicles than necessary, just in case there are problems.

You could find yourself in glorious isolation, marooned in a deserted, snow-covered *ger*, hunting for your dinner. Some of the best meals in Mongolia happen by chance – ones that might see you dining on wild meat and game such as partridge or duck.

first lift that comes along – that being the case, the consoling thought is that there is very little to hit in the wide expanse of the Mongolian steppe except, in order of seriousness, a large boulder, a deep rut or a dried-up river bed!

Advice if in trouble

If a foreign visitor is arrested and taken to a police station, the visitor is entitled to make a telephone call. The police must contact the visitor's representative embassy within 24 hours of the arrest.

Lost passport

Take extra passport-size photographs with you and a photocopy of the main pages of your passport, and a separate record of all details. An emergency one-way document can be issued by your embassy should there be insufficient time to replace a passport. Report the loss immediately to the local police.

Lost cash

Western Union (WU) are a quick and efficient way to have cash sent from home. A North American company founded in 1851, Western Union put the famous 'pony express' out of business. To send money from home to Mongolia can be done by telephone with a credit card. Authentication takes 1–2 hours, and the money transfer takes 15 minutes. Charges vary depending on the amount required: to transfer US$500 it costs around US$50. Western Union office in Ulaanbaatar: tel: +976 11 450444.

Lost travellers' cheques

Remember to note the numbers and carry a copy of the sales slip, which speeds up the process of replacing them.

Medical emergencies
Documentation – give the hospital photocopies and not the originals of your passport and other travel documents. If possible, take away any notes or x-rays when you are discharged. Keep all receipts.

Personal possessions
Don't bring valuables and keep jewellery to a minimum.

WHAT TO TAKE

> Pack courage in your suitcase – live as the local people do, if they have
> survived – most likely you will too!

> Ella Maillart, Swiss author, traveller and photographer

Packing advice
Mongolia is a country of extremes and what you take will depend on where, and when, you intend to travel, and the way in which you travel – with a backpack, on an expedition, on an organised tour, or on business. However, knowing what to pack is a great help, especially if packing in a hurry. Checklists are provided below for seasonal travel and special activities such as riding tours or expeditions.

There is one word you need to know when packing: reduce. Lay out everything you intend to bring and reduce it. Whatever way you travel basic packing principles are the same. When it is cold, put on layers: cotton, silk and cashmere . . . it sounds extravagant but it's not, as you will find plenty of cashmere jumpers, jackets and mittens at wonderful prices in Mongolia. In winter, hotels in Ulaanbaatar are overheated, so wear lightweight clothes and bring a down-filled coat. You can always buy leather gloves and a fur hat for outdoors locally. In summer, the lighter you pack the better, remembering a cashmere wrap or a fleece for the cool evenings. Select long jumpers and long jackets that cover your bottom as you may spend more time than you think sitting on the ground! If you are thinking of trekking it is

---

TRAVEL TIPS

Waist pouch Keep your passport, credit cards, cash and a list of emergency addresses, in your waist pouch.

Travel pack Put in your travel pack: airline tickets, 4–6 passport-sized photographs and a photocopy of the main pages of your passport, driving licence, insurance documents, travellers' cheques, bank account details, credit-card numbers (and expiry dates), a copy of all the relevant email addresses and telephone numbers, and a copy of medical and optical prescriptions.

Luggage Tag your bags. The essential thing is to travel light so don't pack too much. The final word in this section is to travel with an unencumbered mind – ie: leave your worries behind!

> Like the winds of the sea are the ways of fate,
> As we voyage along through life:
> 'Tis the set of a soul that decides its goal,
> And not the calm and the strife.

> E W Fox

essential to bring a backpack; otherwise travel with lightweight luggage and a day-sack. If on expedition, bring steel containers/boxes with locks for main supplies, which can withstand rough conditions and be left in storage with safety.

Clothing
For spring, summer and autumn
Tracksuit (to relax in), T-shirts, shirts (long- and short-sleeved), cotton polo-neck, cotton slacks, shorts (watch the backs of your legs for sunburn), fleece or cashmere jumper, dress or skirt (women), small scarves (cotton and silk), lightweight jacket and tie (men), cotton and light woollen socks, leather boots (tried and tested), trainers, lightweight shoes or sandals, sun hat (wide-brimmed), large cotton scarf or sarong (acts as towel, neck guard, sleeping wrap), 'long johns' (doubles for nightwear), small towel, lightweight poncho or alternative wet-weather gear (as below), waterproof suit (trousers and jacket).

For winter
You can buy Mongolian felt boots and a fleece-lined *deel* on arrival in addition to the warm clothes you bring. Wear layers of clothing: silk, wool and cotton under fleeces, furs and waterproofs. Bring thermal underwear, cotton shirts, polar jacket and trousers, fleece and fleece trousers, selection of cotton and woollen socks, leather boots (worn in and comfortable), gaiters (if skiing), ski gloves (with length of tape attached to each glove – pin on to coat to prevent losing), silk or cashmere under gloves, woollen hat with ear flaps, wet-weather gear (waterproof and windproof), good clothes for hotels. Otherwise the same as summer (see above).

Items for all seasons
- first-aid kit (see *Health*, page 163)
- money belt or neck pouch (for passport, documents and cash)
- washbag/personal kit (including some often-needed items such as eyedrops, throat lozenges, moisturising lotion, shampoo, insect repellent, sunblock, lipbalm, nail clippers, toothpicks)
- day bag (to carry water bottle, water-purification tablets, camera equipment, extra films)
- water bottle (one-litre size)
- high-protection sunglasses (2 pairs)
- extra prescription glasses (if worn)
- torch and extra batteries
- maps, magnifying sheet and map folder; compass, whistle
- notebook, pencils
- guidebook, phrasebook
- Swiss Army knife or equivalent (with blade, scissors, can opener, screw driver, corkscrew and file)
- reliable watch (with alarm)
- bio-friendly soap, toilet roll, sachet of clothes-washing powder, sealable plastic bags (for wet clothes)
- identification labels (to attach to items if travelling in a group)
- mini-sewing kit (scissors, needle and thread, safety pins)
- ear plugs, eye shades
- light binoculars
- snacks (eg: energy bars, energy powder that you add to water, glucose tablets, boiled sweets, chocolate)

- matches and lighter; candles (in case of power failure)
- insulation (space) blanket (for warmth and emergency use).

Extras

- song book (songs or poems you might like to recite)
- paints and sketch book
- Polaroid camera and films (many more rolls of film than you think you will use)
- inflatable travelling pillow (if camping)
- mobile phone or satellite phone (mobile phones do not work in remote areas)
- universal plug (if you bring a laptop)
- a car cigarette-lighter adaptor lead, useful on expedition for battery recharge
- world radio

Presents for your Mongolian hosts

You will, no doubt, be overwhelmed by the hospitality shown to you by Mongolian families. Giving money to show your appreciation can sometimes offend, but gifts are much appreciated. Bring a small bag of various useful and novel items as gifts for people of all ages. The ideal present in rural areas is a portrait photograph of your hosts, standing or sitting formally, wearing their best *deels* in front of their home. It is more effective if taken by a Polaroid camera. The delight on receiving the photograph, the marvelling looks as it develops, and the following peals of laughter definitely make it worth investing in this camera. Polaroid films are highly sensitive to heat and light so wrap them in foil. Watch out for batteries and camera equipment in the cold. Keep cameras well insulated, so the mechanisms do not freeze. Some other gift ideas are frisbees, balloons (children love them), small packs of crayons or felt markers (as a change from standard pens), tapes (folk music from home), postcards, chocolate, dried fruits, boiled sweets, ribbons and pretty clips for the girls' hair, pillow cases with brightly coloured embroidery, threads for the women, cotton handkerchiefs, small penknives or snuff for the men (buy in UB), sea shells.

Trips – and what to take

Camping and hiking

In addition to the clothes and essential items listed above, bring: backpack (with a waterproof liner – pack light and balance well), sleeping bag (three or four season), three-season mat for sleeping (alternatively use local felt or fleece), tent (sturdy and free-standing, three-person Terra Nova tents are recommended), camp stove and cooking pot, mug, dish, knife, fork and spoon set, tin foil (to protect films and for baking fish), thermal mountain blanket, waterproof cape (fleece lined in winter, lightweight in summer), talcum powder (invaluable to prevent blisters if hiking in summer), first-aid kit (including blister pack; see *Health*, page 163), one-litre water bottle (metal army-type, or Sigg water bottle), water-purifying tablets or system, night lights, kit bags for camping equipment and food supplies (see pages 176–7).

Biking

On a biking tour, a follow-up vehicle usually carries all the camping equipment and supplies. Bike specialists will provide bikes, although many experienced bikers choose to bring their own saddles and pedals. The following are the basic essentials: bum bag (waterproof and padded; avoid bum bags with water bottles, as they bounce around and may damage maps), front cycling bag (to attach to

EXPEDITION FOOD
Brought from home
Marmite – for the very British – perks up a fried egg no end!
Tabasco, chili sauce or mustard – if you find boiled mutton hard to swallow
Good-quality fruit or green tea
Vanilla pods – to take the edge off curdled milk
Good-quality coffee
Vitamin tablets
Mazola with dried fruit and nuts – to supplement bland porridge oats

To pick up in Mongolia
Porridge oats
Nuts, raisins
Rice
Stock cubes
Instant soup
Noodles – Mongolian spaghetti or packets of Chinese soup noodles
Garlic
Onions
Spices – chilies, bay leaves, small bottle of soy sauce
Black tea – comes in large blocks from China
Instant coffee – individual servings
Sugar and salt
Some tinned fish or meat
Boiled sweets
Chocolate
Supplemented by local meat and dairy products – buy along the way

bicycle; front bags usually have a plastic front cover for maps), water bottle, tools, wet-weather clothing (trousers and tops), padded cycling gloves (quick-dry material), long cycling trousers, helmet, helmet torch, cotton underwear, panty-liners (ladies), sun screen (high factor 30+ and total block for face), protective sunglasses (with plutonite lenses, for high-velocity impact). Bikers are recommended to pack the following in their first-aid kits: insect repellent, plasters, Vaseline (for saddle sores), arnica cream (for bruises), Ibuprofen (for pain relief), heat cream (for back ache and sore muscles), anti-fungal cream (for athlete's foot), antibiotics (a broad spectrum type such as Amoxycillin; Metronidazole is useful for anaerobic infections, including dental and vaginal infections and for acute amoebic dysentery and giardia, dehydration sachets (for diarrhoea), Imodium tablets (for diarrhoea; very strong, use only in emergencies), anti-bacterial gel (for washing hands – no water needed), wet wipes (they become your best friend!).

Horse-riding
Comfortable riding trousers, leather boots with leather or rubber soles (you may find yourself walking so it is vital to have comfortable footwear), low 'chaps' (to prevent chafing inner thighs), poncho (if it's one that rustles, beware when mounting your Mongolian pony – you may not reach the saddle before the animal bolts!), plastic bags (for wet clothes), extra mosquito repellent, hard hat, riding gloves, head torch, protective sunglasses (with a strong tie to prevent them flying off when galloping).

Fishing

Warm clothing (dress in layers), chest waders (experienced anglers only), windbreaker/fishing jacket, chamois flannel or fleece vests, hiking boots (waterproof), fishing hat with visor, woolly hat, fishing mitts, Polaroid sunglasses (2 pairs), a head net to protect against midges, camera and film (insulated and waterproof-packed), waterproof tackle bag. Pack the rods in tubes, and bring a wading rod, forceps or pliers to remove hooks from fishes' mouths, scales, a ruler and mousetraps!

Expedition supplies: food

If you are starting your travels from Ulaanbaatar provisions can be bought from numerous shops and markets (the State Department Store has a very good Western supermarket). The Black Market, also known as Ulaanbaatar Central Market, has everything you need from food to kitchen ware, clothes, boots, camping kit, saddles etc. There are certain items that are best brought from home – the little luxuries that make life kinder (see box opposite).

For expedition food supplies you will usually shop in Ulaanbaatar and supplement your provisions in country markets along the way. Mongolia's staple diet (whatever the season) is a rich mixture of meat and dairy products.

Clothing and equipment suppliers

Berghaus Tel: 01915 165600; web: www.berghaus.com. Polar wear, fleeces and rucksacks.
Coleman UK Tel: 01275 845024; web: www.coleman/eur.com. Camping equipment, stoves and lights.
Hunting World 16 East 53rd St New York City, NY 10022, USA; tel: +1 212 775 3310414; web: www.huntingworld.com. Clothes and camping equipment.
Karrimor Tel: 01254 893134; web: www.karrimor.com
Lillywhites Camping department, 24–36 Regent St, London SW1; tel: 08703 339600; website: www.sportssoccer.com
Travelling Light Tel: 01931 714488; web: www.travellinglight.co.uk. Shorts, skirts, and other useful items.

Best-buy tents

Eurohike's Wye the Wye In two- and three-person sizes. Low weight (3.3kg and 3.9kg) and low cost. Contact Millets (tel: 0800 214890).
Stormshield Xenon Durable and lightweight with a handy porch; sleeps two; weighs 3kg. Contact Blacks (tel: 0800 214890).
Macpac Microlite Excellent New Zealand-made tent; good in all weather; more expensive but spacious; sleeps one to two. Contact Snow and Rock (tel: 0845 100 1000).
Wild Country Zephyr Lightweight, 2.5kg, easy to pack and pitch; good in wind, at altitude, and also for general camping. Contact Terra Nova (tel: 01773 833300).
Moss Stardome Good four-season mountainering tent, 3.5kg. Contact Mountain Equipment Corp (MEC), Canada, or Recreational Equipment Inc (REI) in the USA; websites:www.mec.com, www.rei.com. They ship to anywhere in the world via DHL.

Maps

Under the Manchu empire areas of Mongol tribal pasture lands were recorded as early as 1686. Specific pasturelands were allocated to individual Mongol tribes to prevent territorial disputes and piles of stones marked the frontiers. The Western map-making process began in the second half of the 19th century, when explorers like Nikolai Przewalski made original maps and freehand drawings during their explorations in Mongolia.

Maps of Mongolia may be examined at the British Library and at the Royal Geographic Society in London. Stanfords Travel and Book Shop (12–14 Long Acre, London WC2E 9LP; tel: 020 7836 1321; web: www.stanfords.co.uk) provides the most up-to-date travel maps of Mongolia. Travel Map of Mongolia 1:1,200,000 by International Travel Maps and Books (2000) costs £7.95.

It was not easy to find good maps of Mongolia and until recently the only good, accurate maps were the Russian area maps for those who can read Cyrillic. There is now an excellent map shop in Ulaanbaatar, located on Ikh Toiruu (from Peace Avenue, turn towards Ganden Monastery; the map shop is on the apex of the right-hand turn between Ikh Toiruu and Peace Avenue; a smaller road continues to the monastery). The latest tourist travel maps can be bought in Ulaanbaatar at the major hotels and in bookstores in town. The University Library in Ulaanbaatar contains many early maps.

MONEY AND BUDGETING

The exchange rate at the time of writing (September 2003) is US$1 = T1,157. Make sure to change money at banks in Ulaanbaatar as it is impossible to change money in the Mongolian countryside. Most people carry US dollars cash and travellers' cheques. Shops accept new crisp dollar notes in small denominations as opposed to older notes dated before 1995. Mongolians are very fussy about damaged notes and may not accept them. Pounds sterling are not used locally and euros will take some getting used to! Credit cards are accepted by hotels and larger shops. American Express and Visa are the most-used credit cards, if you need to draw cash. It is advisable to have local currency in your wallet in shops and bazaars; otherwise you can settle your UB hotel bills and most major restaurant bills by credit card. Hotels will change US dollars cash. In the countryside even tourist *ger* camps will not accept travellers' cheques in place of cash. If you arrive in Mongolia at a weekend with travellers' cheques, you may find you have no time to exchange them for cash if setting out for the countryside immediately. So bring cash.

Banks

There are a few banks outside Ulaanbaatar, but don't rely on them. Banks open, in general, from 09.30–12.30 and 14.00–15.00 weekdays, and 09.30–11.30 on Saturday. Note that when changing money you should ensure that you give or receive crisp, undamaged dollar notes. For banks in Ulaanbaatar, see pages 233–4.

Tipping

On tour it is recommended to provide a generous tip (which supplements local wages and is in keeping with general expectations). Some suggestions (for two- to three-week trip):

- US$40 for the cook per group
- US$50 per group to each guide, interpreter or Mongolian staff member on the trek
- US$75 per group to each driver, a higher amount to the head driver

Use your discretion as to how to compensate helpers and trek leaders on a day-to-day basis. Tourists are advised not to pay their tip to tour staff in the form of a travellers' cheque.

It used to be the case that a barter arrangement was considered to be a fairer way to compensate herders for their kindness and hospitality. Nowadays people expect cash if they have gone to the trouble to provide horses, meals and other facilities that have overheads. This is not spoiling the market or ruining hospitality, it is simply being fair. Tipping in restaurants and hotels is up to the individual: 10% never goes wrong here, and would be fair in other circumstances as well.

Budgeting

The cost of living in Mongolia is lower than in Europe and the USA so your dollars will stretch further. Expect to pay the tourist price for services and transport. So, for example, internal airline tickets will cost about double for foreigners than for Mongolian nationals, and foreigners must pay in US dollars. Standard tourist costs for accommodation, food and drink, entertainment and transport are listed below:

Taxis T250 (roughly US$0.25) per kilometre
Airport transfer in Ulaanbaatar (by taxi) US$20 per vehicle (tourist price)
Hotels in Ulaanbaatar top hotel US$75 (single), US$95 (twin); good/medium hotel US$50 (single), US$80 (twin); guesthouse/small hotel US$10–15 (single) US$20–40 (twin)
Countryside hotel US$15 (standard single), US$20 (twin), US$30 (deluxe)
City restaurant US$5–25 (top). You can get a good two-course meal for US$10 in many Ulaanbaatar restaurants, hotel restaurants tend to charge more; credit cards are widely accepted in the city.
Museum entrance US$1–2 (T1,400/T2,300)
Theatre performance US$6 (T7,000)
Cinema T2,000 (Mongolian film); T2,000 (English-speaking video shown on large TV set)
Bars in UB beer prices T1,200–2,300 (US$1–2); whisky around US$8 (T9,000) per glass (10cl); vodka US$3 (T3,400) per glass
Night club/disco entrance average US$10 (T11,400; double in some places)
Food in UB T1,500 hamburger (US$1.3); roast chicken and chips T4,000 (US$3.5); pizza T2,000 (US$1.75); lasagne T2,500 (US$2.20)
Countryside canteen T600 (approx US$0.50) per plate, eg: mutton and rice
Buses in UB (flat rate) T200 per ticket; trolley bus T100
Buses (long-distance) T5,000 to Kharkhorin
Internal flights US$280 (return) Ulaanbaatar to Khovd; US$175 (return) to Mörön
Train fares Beijing to Ulaanbaatar (single) RMB600 (US$75) hard-sleeper; RMB800 (US$100) soft-sleeper. From Ulaanbaatar to Beijing (single) T60,000 (US$53) hard-sleeper; T95,000 (US$83) soft-sleeper ; Ulaanbaatar to Irkutsk (single) T45,000 US$40) hard sleeper, T63,000 (US$55) soft-sleeper; Ulaanbaatar to Moscow (single) T130,000 (US$114) hard-sleeper, T194,000 (US$170) soft-sleeper. Above prices are approximate and subject to change. At the time of writing, experience has shown it has been difficult to date for individuals to buy rail tickets, should a travel company purchase tickets on your behalf, add at least 50% to the above rail prices
Departure tax at the airport T17,500 (about US$16) paid in local currency

Student travellers can make it around Mongolia for US$20 a day making all their own arrangements, sharing transport, eating at local canteens, camping in the countryside and staying in guesthouses and local hotels in UB and provincial centres. Time is an important factor in these calculations. As one student traveller put it, unless you are on an organised tour, allow one month to do any major journey.

For those on **organised tours**, which include accommodation in good hotels/ger camps, itineraries, guides, interpreters, transport, meals, sightseeing, horses and so on, prices will vary depending on the size of the group. A typical tour for two people might cost US$150 per person, per day, whereas the same tour for a group of ten people would cost US$90 per day.

Day trips may be budgeted at US$75 per day, to include vehicle, driver and guide. *Ger* **camps**, including food, may be budgeted at US$50 per person per day (average price is US$35–45). The rate is reduced by the size of a group and the length of the stay. Organised **riding tours** cost around US$1,425 for 9 days, excluding international flights.

GETTING AROUND

Transport systems in Mongolia failed to develop in the same way as they have developed in the West for the simple reason that the horse and the camel are the most natural and effective means of transport in a land like Mongolia. This has resulted in an almost total lack of road and bridge building. Rivers were more easily forded on horseback and camels and horses could travel faster than any other means of transport in the 19th and early 20th centuries. But, with the arrival of the first American motor vehicles in the 1920s, followed by Soviet cars, jeeps and lorries from the 1930s and increasing numbers of Japanese motorbikes in the1990s, things are beginning to change and motorised transport is threatening to replace the nomads' four-legged friends.

By air

MIAT runs 95% of all internal flights. There are weekly flights to most provincial centres. Currently there are no scheduled services to district centres – other than to Bulgan, in Khovd Province, near the western border-crossing with China. MIAT offers chartered services to 25 domestic airports around the country. In addition to MIAT flights, there are some private local airlines – Tas (tel: 11 379657) and Hangard (tel: 11 311333) – flying on domestic routes. Note that on internal flights the luggage allowance is restricted to 5–10kg; it varies depending on the number of people on the flight. Tengeriin Ulaach runs air-transport operations; its helicopters are available for charter. For further information contact: tel: 11 379765 or email: skyhorsenew@yahoo.com.

By road

The red lines marked on many maps of Mongolia suggest that there is an established network of main roads, but few Mongolian roads have a hard surface, and most of those are in or between the main towns. What you drive on are simply sets of wheel ruts which criss-cross the countryside and following them can be hazardous, particularly after dark. In total, Mongolia has 5,406km of 'improved' roads, of which 1,640km are paved. Driving anywhere outside the towns takes a long time and is often rough and uncomfortable.

Most Mongolians leave the city by various modes of transport ranging from bus, train, mini bus, shared jeep or taxi. Hitching rides is considered a normal occurrence in Mongolia, especially in the countryside, when often there is no public transport. Travelling overland by jeep is the best option to reach the more remote areas, and a network of roads (mainly unpaved) connects the 21 aimags to the capital, and urban areas to smaller centres and remote settlements throughout the country. You may end up travelling with the help of a compass across virgin territory in the most remote regions – following no roads or tracks. Telegraph poles are often very useful route markers.

To experience the Mongolian spirit, take a journey by public transport (bus or jeep). You will be jostled and tossed together with your fellow passengers over many kilometres of bone-rattling roads and you'll find yourself clinging on to one another for mutual comfort and survival. It is somewhat disconcerting to see abandoned or broken-down trucks in remote areas. Do not be alarmed;

Mongolians are helpful, hospitable and resourceful and will always come to the rescue should your vehicle breakdown, although you may experience long hours of waiting by the roadside for a spare part to arrive. To cheer yourselves up on particularly monotonous sections of the journey, the tedium may be broken by singing traditional 'long songs', which provide great entertainment when everyone joins in. However, it can be unsettling to discover that your driver navigates according to his instinct and you may find that you are heading in the wrong direction, or about to strike a huge pot-hole. Somehow a sixth sense always seems to rescue Mongolian drivers, just in time to avert real disasters. In the summer months the rivers tend to flood and the search for a safe crossing point may divert you dozens of kilometres from your intended itinerary. For information on city transport, see *Chapter 6, Ulaanbaatar*, pages 220–5.

Car rental
Expect to pay T14,000 per day for a car and driver, and T10,000 per day (excluding petrol) for a motorbike (with a side-car).

Long-distance bus journeys
The long-distance bus terminal in Ulaanbaatar is located near the railway station, on the right-hand corner of Teeverchid Street and the outer ring road *Ikh Toiru*, which leads north to Gandan Monastery on Zanabazar Street. You will require local assistance and a translator to get to grips with the bus system. In the station, discover where and when your bus departs and buy your ticket. Always check the destination sign (name of the terminus) at the front of the bus before departure. When travelling by long-distance bus it is essential to realise that it is not the easiest way to travel, so you need time on your side and plenty of patience. Public transport in Mongolia is not well developed; buses run infrequently and not always

LAST WORD ON LONG-DISTANCE BUS TRAVEL
D Jargalsaikhan

Long-distance buses go to all aimag centres and to some of the smaller, less distant towns, such as Kharkhorin, that are frequently travelled to by road. Frequency depends on how popular the route is: buses to Tsetserleg, for example, go almost every day, while buses to the west perhaps go once a week. In any case these long-distance buses depart when full and not before.

Foreign travellers must ask at the information desk at the long-distance bus station for information on any particular route – though it is unlikely that anyone will speak English. The answer might be 'the bus to Khövsgöl leaves at 11.00 every day'. But that means it *usually* leaves at *about* 11.00. If it is already full at 09.00 it will depart earlier. If it doesn't get full that day it will wait until the next day, or if the bus has broken down you will have to wait until it's ready.

Regarding costs: the bus from Ulaanbaatar to Tsetserleg costs approximately T14,000 (US$12); UB to Mörön costs approximately T17,000 (US$15). Long-distance buses are often very crowded, hot and uncomfortable; paying the fare does not guarantee a seat. Sometimes the 'buses' are actually trucks with no windows. The bus will stop once in a while at a *guanz* (*ger* restaurant) for everyone to eat and occasionally for everyone to get out and relieve themselves.

TRAVELLING INDEPENDENTLY AS A SMALL GROUP
Marianne Herridge

For four women travelling together, I reckoned that the best way to get about would be to hire a couple of jeeps with drivers. We were all limited to three weeks' annual leave and had been warned about the problems of getting about by public transport in Mongolia. I had heard that the roads were difficult to use without someone with local knowledge, so it would not make sense for us to expect to hire a jeep and drive it ourselves. Emailing the list of travel agents in Ulaanbaatar nearly all of them responded with various ideas. Quite a few had packages that they could offer us, which they also provide to a number of foreign tourist companies. As we didn't want a package, one of the agents (MAT) stood out as seeming more flexible. Working out a circuit from UB to visit some of the places of interest in central Mongolia, we 'discussed', via email, routes and various options. The deal was two jeeps with drivers, an English-speaking guide and a cook for our three-week trip. Self-sufficient and camping most of the time, we used our own tents, as we were advised they would be more reliable. To illustrate this, for most of the trip the cook and guide were very lucky that it did not rain much, as whoever had packed their igloo tent had forgotten the flysheet. When visiting towns, we stayed in a variety of hotels or tourist gers for a few days along the way.

It was an excellent way to see the countryside and to meet local people in the towns, villages and tiny nomad settlements. Very conscious of how unspoilt the countryside is and how much we were a novelty as tourists, we were very keen to try to minimise our impact. On leaving our campsites, hopefully no one would have been able to detect much evidence of our stay. On visiting families in their gers, we were very careful to respect their customs and avoid abusing their hospitality.

The roads, if they can be called that, were mainly mud tracks that wriggled into the distance. It never ceased to amaze how our drivers never got lost. In any vehicle other than a jeep, many of the routes would have been inaccessible. Twice, the jeeps briefly took turns to sink in some mud, but after some mysterious adjustments to the wheels, we were off again without any problem. A few times we passed buses stopped by the roadside, with the passengers sitting nearby watching as huddles of men changed tyres or poked around underneath the stricken vehicles.

to a schedule, particularly to remote destinations (see box *The last word on long-distance bus travel*, previous page).

Timing
Long-distance bus journeys are difficult to arrange without the help of a Mongolian-speaking guide. The fare will cost slightly less if booked in advance, rather than on the day, but it does not mean the buses leave according to the time printed on a bus schedule.

Schedules
Buses travel at least once a week to all aimags with the exception of the three far western aimags – Khovd, Uvs and Bayan-Ölgii. Nearly all buses leave (not always punctually) at 08.30; you need to arrive one hour before departure.

Left Archer in the Khovd River valley

Below Mongolian wrestlers

Left Contortionist

Below Nomads preparing to race horses in trials for the Naadam competition, Lake Khövsgöl

Right Kazakh woman near Ölgii
Below Nomad's child, Lake Khövsgöl
Below right Young monk, Ulaanbaatar

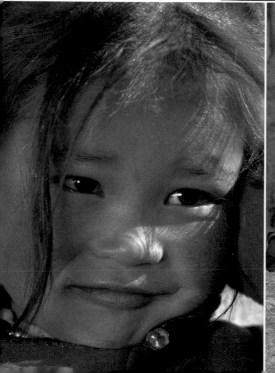

Shared jeeps and minibuses

Most tourists prefer to use shared jeeps or minibuses, which leave from the bus station when full. Minibuses are slightly more expensive, but much more comfortable to travel in than long-distance buses and you are guaranteed a seat. They depart in the afternoons and service the aimags surrounding the capital, although they also travel longer distances. The normal rate from Ulaanbaatar to Dalanzadgad in the South Gobi is around T15,000. Rates for Russian jeeps vary from T250 to T600 per kilometre. Japanese jeeps are more expensive and cost around T750 per kilometre.

Long-distance jeep journeys starting from the UB long-distance bus station located near the railway station are as follows:

Ulaanbaatar–Khövsgöl (671km)
Depart 08.30 Mon, Wed, Fri; transport company NIN TRANS
Depart:15.00 Tue, Wed, Thu, Sun; transport company Khövsgöl Teveriin Gazar; cost T18,000.

Ulaanbaatar–Tsetserleg (463km)
Depart 08.30 Mon, Wed, Thu, Fri; transport company PAO; cost: T10,600

It is important to arrive in plenty of time because jeeps may depart before the scheduled time if all seats are full. A person with a ticket is guaranteed a seat. Normally you pay the driver (not the ticket office); prices are the same for foreigners and locals. There is no guarantee as to reliability and safety of vehicle and driver.

Often the vehicle will be a UAZ 469 jeep (Mongolians call these vehicles, found throughout the country, *Jaran yus*, meaning '69'). Jeeps normally take four passengers, but if two people agree with the driver and pay for the extra two seats then the vehicle is theirs.

There are two contact telephone numbers, but be forewarned that no-one speaks English on either of these lines, so you may need the help of a translator.

Central bus/jeep transport information in Ulaanbaatar Tel: 11 321730.
Western destinations information Tel: 11 634902

Trucks

Passenger trucks (lorries with seating in the back for passengers) leave UB from the long-distance bus station from the southwest corner. They leave when the truck is full of passengers and not before. Costs vary and are best negotiated with the driver. The standard rate of T230 per kilometre applies and indicates the cost; hitchhikers usually negotiate costs with the truck driver; these amounts vary hugely depending on the journey.

Taxis

Taxis are limited to paved roads and well-worn rough tracks. They travel at speed around the city and can be hailed by raising a hand. You will be surprised at how many private cars turn into taxis at the wave of a hand. The fare is worked out at the end of the ride by the car's mileage or kilometre clock. Expect to pay T230 per kilometre. Tipping is optional. Taxi drivers are helpful and will often act as your local guide.

By water

Lake Khövsgöl and some of Mongolia's northern rivers are navigable during the summer but are rarely used as transport routes because the boating and leisure industry is undeveloped. You can hire a fishing boat on Lake Khövsgöl for US$5 an hour.

ACCOMMODATION

When planning your itineraries from base camp it is well to know that there are very few hotels of top/medium standard outside Ulaanbaatar. People rely on *ger* accommodation – which is excellent – or they camp. For hotels in Ulaanbaatar, see pages 227–30. Provincial hotels are listed in each province in Part Two.

Tourist ger camps

In the bigger towns and cities there are a few hotels, which may or may not have water, food and heating. Outside Ulaanbaatar by far the best option is to stay in *ger* camps. These have been set up in the most popular places to cater for travellers, both Mongolian and foreign. Most of the camps only run during the summer; the *gers* are taken down in October until the following spring. However, there are one or two near Ulaanbaatar which are open all year round and are used by hikers or cross-country skiers during the winter.

These traditional *gers* have brightly coloured furniture and a wood-burning stove in the centre (if it's cold they provide wood). Each *ger* has two, three or four beds. Most camps have a toilet and shower block nearby with hot water some or all of the time. Nearly all camps have a restaurant (often a large *ger*) where they serve Mongolian and European food. Vegetarians have to give the cook plenty of notice or they'll end up with the same as everyone else but minus the meat.

The cost of staying in a *ger* varies from US$35–50 per night and includes three meals. They'll often pack a picnic lunch for you if you ask, which is useful since you may be several hundred miles from the nearest shop. At some places you can make a deal just to pay for the bed (about US$16), and then you can bring your own food or just choose what you want from the restaurant menu and pay accordingly.

The *gers* are a really enjoyable and authentic form of accommodation; they are also warm in the winter and cool in summer. The main disadvantage is trying to book beforehand, and also you can't be sure of the standard of service until you get there. New *ger* camps are springing up all the time, and unprofitable ones closed down. At the height of the tourist season some camps are full, and at other times there may be no food or staff if they are not expecting you. The best way round this is to book through a local travel company, who would have the most up-to-date information on new camps and non-existent ones. It would be quite irritating to drive for several days on bad roads to reach a particular *ger* camp, only to arrive to find it gone!

The telephone numbers given in Part Two of this guide are often not the *ger* camps themselves, but the Ulaanbaatar offices of the companies operating the camps. Sometimes there are several *ger* camps owned by different companies situated in the same area (eg: Moltsog Els).

Countryside hotels

All the provincial centres provide hotel accommodation (listed in Part Two). The hotels are often pretty tatty and you cannot always rely on the services of food and water – often due to matters beyond the hoteliers' control – transport, the availability of items, delivery due to weather conditions and so forth. Standard country hotels cost approximately T15,000 (US$13).

Camping in the countryside

Most tour companies provide excellent camping gear – everything you are likely to need. Otherwise, as an individual traveller you will need to bring your own equipment. You can camp almost anywhere in Mongolia, the choice is vast – but you will need permission within national parks offices, locally, or in advance from the head office in Ulaanbaatar. If you want to use *ger*-camp or hotel facilities, it is polite to ask and possibly there will be a small fee.

Further information
Mongolian Hotel Association (MHA) (Mongolian Hotel Association, Mongolian Children's Palace, Genghis Khaan Avenue, Ulaanbaatar 210524; mail address: Central Post Office, PO Box 578, Ulaanbaatar; tel/fax: 11 311751) was founded in 1997 by the growing number of Mongolian hoteliers. Priorities are upgrading hotel facilities and services by officially licensed hotels and organising training schemes. The recently established Hotels Network Information and a Travel Service Centre is operated by MHA.

TRADITIONAL MONGOLIAN FOOD
Traditional Mongolian food has two main ingredients – meat and flour, in some shape or form. The most popular dishes are *buuz* (small, steamed meat dumplings) and *huushuur* (flat meat-filled fried pancakes). There are also soups, plain steamed buns (*mantuu*) and salads (usually either potato, cabbage or carrot, although increasingly, due to demand, green leaf salads are finding their way on to menus). Mongolia is becoming a nation of urban gardeners (at least in the capital), producing lettuce on 30,000 private vegetable plots, much to the surprise of foreign visitors who expect all Mongolians to be carnivores. In the past, Genghis Khan and his warriors survived on meat but many people forget that in ancient times, as well as today, Mongolians have supplemented their protein diet with local herbs and greens when they could find, or grow, them!

Out of necessity, Mongolians have found creative ways to use the milk of sheep, cattle, goats, camels and horses. *Öröm* is clotted cream; *aaruul* are the dried curds seen soaking up the sun on the *ger* tops in summer; and *tsötsgii* is cream. *Tarag* is a delicious sour-tasting yoghurt drink. *Shar tos* is made from melted butter and *tsagaan tos* is a mixture of boiled *öröm* with flour or fruit. Dried products are prepared during spring and summer to last over the long winter. One speciality is to cook the whole carcass of a goat, filling it with hot stones and roasting it on a spit over an open fire. Whole marmot is cooked in the same way.

Meat is usually mutton, boiled, fried in pancakes or served as dumplings. It can be fatty and taste strongly of sheep but it supplies the vitamins that are needed. A variation on this is *borts* – dried meat, usually beef and sometimes goat or sheep – similar to the South African *biltong*. It will keep for months and can jazz up otherwise dreary rice and noodles. The soldiers of the Mongol empire used to keep dried meat under their saddles and chew a piece of it as they rode along. The strips of meat are incredibly dry and brittle but will soften up if broken into manageable pieces and stewed in boiling water. Beware of toothache if a piece of meat is trapped between your teeth. Travel with a good supply of strong toothpicks. During the summer, most families in the countryside dry large quantities of meat in preparation for the winter and, if asked politely, will be happy to sell you some.

Summer in Mongolia is known as the 'white season' and herders and nomads work around the clock to process milk – turning it into cheese and a variety of other products to last them through the winter. Rock-hard curd, fermented mare's milk, distilled milk resembling vodka (*arkhi*), soured cream, milk skin, the list is endless. Fermented horses' or camels' milk, known as *koumiss* or *airag*, is, most definitely, the most popular – a slightly fizzy, cheesy beverage which is both refreshing and thirst quenching after a long day's ride. However, it is important not to overdo the intake of dairy products, as travellers are known to become ill.

IN DEFENCE OF MONGOL FOOD
Natalie Teich

People have maligned Mongolia with regard to food. I was very tempted to bring a lot of dried provisions with me in expectation of mutton, mutton and more mutton. But in fact, although there was a lot of mutton, there was also chicken and occasionally beef (particularly tongue), sometimes eggs, and rarely cheese or yoghurt (I am not sure why the latter two were not more frequently served). There was an abundance of coleslaw and gherkins, carrot salad and potatoes. Spaghetti was often served as an additional source of carbohydrate and arrived on all occasions with the ubiquitous rice. Desserts were prepared cakes, biscuits and canned fruit salad. Vegetarians will have no trouble surviving, especially if they eat fish. Some fresh fruit is available in the markets in Ulaanbaatar, but I found none outside the capital. When visiting nomadic families we were invited to share their hard cheeses, sour milk drinks, occasional yoghurt and rare fermented mare's milk (this last is usually much more readily available, but it had not been the best weather for the fermentation, so it was an exceptional offer – either that or the sensitive Mongolians were worried what it might do to our digestion).

Mongolians attribute the problem to foreigners' guts! Below are a few of the common foods and drinks:

- *Aarts* Dry white cakes made from the residue after straining whey. They are eaten with milk and sugar or coated in flour and boiled in water. Said to be very healthy for young children.
- *Buuz* Large dumplings made of dough, filled with meat, onion and garlic and steamed for 20 minutes. *Buuz* are served particularly in large quantities at *Tsagaan Sar*, the Mongolian New Year, when people may prepare as many as 1,000 dumplings for their guests.
- *Bansh* Smaller version of *buuz*, which are boiled in a soup.
- *Airag* Fermented mare's milk is the classic Mongolian drink. It is said to clean the system, but if you are not used to drinking it, make sure not to drink too much or your system will indeed be cleaned out!
- *Nermel* A home-distilled drink which is pretty lethal – a white spirit made from milk. It comes in many flavours and strengths and although it does not appear to be strong, be warned; a small amount may make you drunk very fast. *Nermel* means 'distilled' in Mongolian.

Country markets provide a variety of fresh and tinned food. Outdoor 'container' markets are found in every provincial centre, usually sited on or near the main central square. Local food stalls, usually located next to bus stations and in markets, provide take-away snacks and tea. The daily dish, mutton and noodles or boiled meat and dumplings, costs around T600. Supermarkets in Ulaanbaatar provide all sorts of fresh food, meat, vegetables and other products. See *Food shopping*, page 233. Restaurants in the capital are listed in *Chapter 6, Ulaanbaatar*, pages 230–2.

FESTIVALS
Naadam

Held annually in July, the great Naadam Festival is a thrilling three-day sporting event that has been happening for centuries. In Genghis Khan's time it happened at different times of the year, particularly in summer. Since 1922, when Sükhbaatar ordered a *naadam* to mark the first anniversary of the revolution on July 11 it has been held annually – from July 11 to 13. The festival highlights Mongolia's 'three manly sports' – horseracing, wrestling and archery. It continues to bring together Mongolian's sporting men and women from the remotest regions to compete at national level in Ulaanbaatar. It is also a celebration of the ordinary people – herders who ride into town and urbanites who leave their flats and offices to watch the games. The combination of people and events presents an unforgettable spectacle to the visitor: colourful silken tunics, fresh-faced nomads, thundering hooves, flying arrows, wrestling bouts, which thrill and entertain thousands of spectators. Mongolians like to show off centuries of tradition and celebrate the moment with plenty of *airag*. It is a time when people remember their glorious past and are proud of their equestrian skills, the stamina of their horses and the strength of their arms.

Although the main events are known as the 'three manly sports', women also compete (except in the wrestling contests) with just as much courage and daring as the men. These are the qualities that over the millennia produced the warrior nation of Genghis Khan. The root of the word *naadam* (game(s) festival) comes from *naadakh*, meaning to play or to have fun. Outside the capital, smaller games, or mini *naadams*, happen throughout the summer months. Visitors often come across them unannounced, which is a bonus, since you can get much closer to the action than you can during the national games held in Ulaanbaatar.

Mongolian festivals bring herders into the towns and their environs from isolated encampments to gatherings where they have the opportunity to participate in the events, to barter, flirt, mix, feast, sing and enjoy life to the full.

History of naadam

The history of the games began centuries ago at the time of the Hunnu or Hun empire (3rd century BC) when hunting and other events were wilder and more primitive. Later, during the Mongol empire (13th–15th centuries) the games lost some of their original glamour and impetus when the court of Kublai Khan moved to Peking and when the Mongol empire disintegrated. However, in the 17th century the tribes regrouped at Shireet Tsagaan Lake to celebrate the Danshig Naadam – a *naadam* of seven banners – accompanied by Buddhist religious ceremonies. The latter were stopped in 1921, making it a 'games only' festival.

In the 21st century there is a renewed interest in traditional folk activities. In the capital, towns and provincial centres, as well as in lonely *gers* in the remotest areas, you will, most likely, discover a lifestyle, arts and music that reflect the true national identity and culture of the Mongol people.

Order of events

The opening ceremony raising the horse-tail banners in the presence of the president begins at 11.00 at the Naadam Stadium. You need tickets to get into the stadium events, best booked in advance through a tour company. Tickets cost T15,000 (US$13) and are very difficult to get at the last minute. The horse races are held just outside the capital, at Yarmag, in a broad valley about 10km along the road to the airport – races begin at one end of the valley and contestants gallop the required distance towards the crowds who watch at the finishing post. There are plans in the future to hold the horse races at alternative locations. There is no cost. Buses or taxis are available from the city centre to take you there. If you are travelling outside an organised tour with your own car and driver, you will need a vehicle permit (obtained in advance from the traffic police in Ulaanbaatar). The driver should be able to arrange this. Wrestling competitions begin at noon in the central stadium and archery is held in another open stadium near by.

NAADAM – A TOURIST'S OBSERVATIONS
Natalie Teich

Naadam's opening ceremony is reminiscent of an Olympic Games opening, with traditional gala, pomp and circumstance. There is a covered grandstand area for which you need tickets. Parachutists float down to land in the sports arena (a rectangular field), swinging on brightly coloured parachutes, with Mongolian flags streamers and smoke trails flying behind them. The 'Mongolian standard', a series of stakes, nine poles topped by horse-tails and flags, are individually carried by mounted horsemen who thunder into the arena and circle the stadium with great fanfare before ceremoniously placing their standards on the podium. Then, the president officially declares the games open.

A succession of colourful and musical performances begins – marching bands, dancers with feathers and streamers, and ceremonial traditional dances reminiscent of warriors and hunters. These are accompanied by drummers situated around the field and by more traditional musicians playing horse-head fiddles and yatags, instruments like zithers (for details on musical instruments, see pages 94–6).

Next, the competitors arrive: archers clad in their traditional dress; jockeys, some as young as six or seven; wrestlers – 100 or so, wearing brief costumes – stomp across the field. (Mongolians come in all shapes and sizes, some incredibly tall, others small and slender.) The burly wrestlers circle the 'Standard', bow and touch their heads or caps to the standard poles and prance around waving their arms in a birdlike way. Then they bow to one another and the wrestling contests begin.

Archery takes place in the afternoon, both men and women competing simultaneously, although in separate groups. There are small brick-like targets, composed of leather and positioned in lines along the ground at distances of up to 25m. After each shot the adjudicators, near the targets, make hand signals and whistle to instruct the archer of the accuracy of his/her shot. Only three arrows are allowed per person. Everyone wears traditional costume.

While waiting for the horse racing to begin, the crowd is treated to some equestrian events. The police and military clear the area of stray horses and cows and the race is on! Excitement rises as a storm of dust in the distance heralds the approaching riders, then all too soon, the event is over. The winner receives a prize but it is the horse who is the hero of the day!

Tsagaan Sar

Tsagaan Sar is a family festival which is celebrated on the first day of the lunar new year to put some cheer in the endless winter months and mark the beginning of spring. This could be any date from late January to early March. Each year is named after one of the following 12 animals – mouse, cow, tiger, hare, dragon, snake, horse, ewe, monkey, chicken, dog or pig. The animals are alternately male and female. You need to plan well in advance if travelling to Mongolia in winter, as most Mongolians take this time off to be with their families. You also need special winter clothing to deal with temperatures as low as –30°C (see *What to take*, page 174).

Celebrations are not unlike Scottish hogmanay, when neighbourly visits take place home to home – or *ger* to *ger* – in the Mongolian countryside. The celebrations happen over several days, with feasting on the night of the new moon. Everyone dresses in their best clothes to visit family members. During the holiday, people are glued to their television sets to watch the national wrestling competitions. There are some horse races but the maximum distance is nine kilometres.

Throughout the ages the festival has been celebrated in the traditional way – family ties are renewed and in particular it is a time to honour the elderly. After the 1921 revolution many traditions, including Tsagaan Sar, were swept away but country people clung to their beliefs and fortunately for their culture the remoteness of the Mongolian hinterland protected such traditions. During the communist period, Tsagaan Sar was transformed into the 'Spring Festival of Herdsmen' to suit the authorities after collectivisation in 1957. Since 1990 it has reverted to its old name.

As a sign of respect, the younger adults greet their elders in a certain way, with a special arm-hold embrace (*zolgokh*), which symbolises both support and esteem. The elders' forearms are supported palm-to-elbow by the younger person and, in return, the elder places his or her forearms (palms down) on top of the younger person's forearms in a gentle, arm-locked embrace. The gesture is accompanied by the exchange of a ceremonial pale blue or white silk scarf (*khadag*). Gifts are usually given and received with both hands, or with the right hand supported at the elbow by the left. The *khadag* is folded in a special way to show trust, as part of the greeting, with the folded edge facing the elder.

A typical three- or four-day Tsaagan Sar programme would offer the following: wrestling matches at the National Wrestling Stadium; a New Year's eve dinner; horse racing in the countryside; and sightseeing in Ulaanbaatar, including evening performances of opera or ballet.

TSAAGAN SAR

If you receive an invitation from a Mongolian family to celebrate Tsaagan Sar with them, do not forget to buy a *khadag* (a blue silk scarf to present as a gift). Drape the *khadag* over your arms when greeting people, starting with the eldest. It is not necessary for men or women to remove their hats indoors when visiting a country *ger*. When offered a drink, always take a small sip or pass the cup to your mouth. Hot salty-milky tea is delicious and warming and so is Mongolian alcohol!

It is not a tradition to offer money or expensive gifts. Only children and other close relatives give money or special presents to their parents. Gifts between friends and relatives might be wine, cosmetic products, sweets and anything that is new and useful to the person.

Whole carcasses of lamb are cooked in advance, pans of *airag* and heated tea stand waiting, the table at the centre of the *ger* is decked with bread and dried cheese and piled high to symbolise prosperity. Steamed dumplings (*buuz*) filled with mutton appear as soon as you have drunk your welcome bowl of steaming salty-milky tea. Then the eating and drinking begins in earnest. The first piece of mutton is offered to the fire god and later choice pieces of mutton are served to the guests. Outside, cold weather and snow have long provided natural deep-freeze conditions to keep the meat fresh. Traditionally, after long bouts of feasting when alcohol flows freely, the Mongols settle down to hours of story-telling and, in this way, oral histories have been passed on from one generation to the next.

RIDING EXPERIENCE: MONGOLIA ON HORSEBACK
Antonia Tozer

In late summer 1992 I rode with a Mongolian companion for eight weeks through the Khentii Mountains to experience the grassroots of the country and its people. My main purpose was to reach Burkhan Khaldun, a mountain where Ghenghis Khan was reputedly buried. I soon discovered that since the departure of the Russians in 1990, practically all Mongolians had entered a period of 'Ghenghis Khan' mania and were clearly rejoicing in their heritage.

My visa extended, Tüvshin and I set off from the capital Ulaanbaatar to the one-street town of Batsümber. Tüvshin was a 22-year-old country boy who had taken part with me in an Operation Raleigh expedition and whom I felt I could trust to handle horses well. The first task was to buy our horses. By dusk, plied with plenty of *airag*, I succeeded in purchasing three pint-sized ponies for the princely sum of US$95. I am sure a decade from now travellers will have to spend more. The prices vary enormously, depending on whether or not the horses you buy are bred for racing.

I chose strong reliable ponies aged around nine years, all with relatively docile temperaments. Mongolian ponies are often unused to being handled and are ridden when only half broken-in. A peculiar trait (mainly due to a lack of training), is their dislike of being approached from their offside (right) – always approach from the left side or, in horsey language, the near side. This makes loading a pack animal difficult, although not impossible. Riding style is reminiscent of single-handed, cowboy neck-reining, or polo style. Certainly one is unwise to attempt to pick up any hoof without testing the water carefully!

Within 36 hours we had set out in a northeasterly direction along a wide track that led us through meadow after meadow of flowers, including entire

Other holidays
Other holidays include Mothers' and Children's Day, June 1, January 1, New Year's Day.

RIDING, HIKING AND BIKING
Horseriding
For information on tour operators offering horseriding trips, see *Specialist tour operators*, pages 150–1

If planning to organise your own riding trip, a thorough knowledge of horses is required. Such a journey should not be embarked upon by riders with little experience of either horses or the country itself unless on an arranged riding tour, or with friends who have riding experience. Mongolia offers the keen rider many different conditions – from desert-steppe to forested, mountain rides. For those with the will to endure a little hardship, the country is a dream come true. Mile upon mile of virgin pastureland and mountain ranges with no boundaries and often without tracks to follow open up in front of you.

The challenge for some people is to buy their own ponies and to have the excitement of planning a route. In doing this you will have a closer relationship with the nomads. If you stay in a family *ger*, you will be privileged to absorb their nomadic customs automatically. Others, through lack of time, or out of preference, leave all the planning and arrangements to a tour company. Numerous travel companies offer riding tours in Mongolia and take care of all the basic details. You will usually camp in tents or find *ger* accommodation, but rest assured, nothing is too tame or 'touristy' in Mongolia, so you will also experience the

fields of edelweiss. In eight weeks we travelled 1,000km, averaging 20km a day. Our routine was to rise early and journey during the cooler part of the day. After breakfast, we packed and loaded the ponies, which took around two hours. We rarely stopped for lunch and snacked instead in the saddle. By early afternoon we would look for a campsite where the grazing was good (most important), then hobble and turn the horses loose for a while, later tethering them to stop them from straying too far at night.

Despite their beauty, the cedar and larch forests of the Khentii are inhospitable. Fast-flowing rivers and tributaries cut between densely forested hills, which frequently made our way treacherous. We would find ourselves waist high in bog (hard to know whether to dismount or not) only to find the horses completely stuck and unable to move! River crossings were problematic – once I watched helplessly while our pack pony was swept half a mile downstream. Happily, in true Mongolian style, he recovered and seemed totally unaffected by his mishap! During less-stressful moments, Tüvshin would draw on his vast repertoire of Mongolian folk songs to lift our spirits as we rode along.

When we neared the holy mountain we passed through a small settlement where I was required to register with the somon head (Mongolia's equivalent of a local mayor). I was charged a tiny fee (US$0.15) for having a camera, then given a tourist souvenir depicting Ghenghis Khan and told that women were barred from climbing to the summit. I was mortified! I ended by sending my horses and my camera to the top with Tüvshin.

I spent the rest of the autumn with a local family who adopted me. Eventually I sold my horses to them at no profit but was happy they would be in good hands. After emotional farewells between me and my horses (which the Mongolians found hilarious!) and my hosts, I returned to UB aboard a passing jeep.

nomadic life. Generally you are so tired that by the end of the day you fall asleep immediately on the hard ground without even thinking.

Finding your horse

The Mongolian horse tends to be small, around 13 or 14hh (hands high), and to the Western eye may look bony and undernourished. These animals have tremendous stamina however and are well adapted to the harsh environment where they have survived over the centuries. You can ride a Mongolian horse for 100 miles a day but you must rest it for the following two days. On a long-distance ride, 20–30km a day is the normal pace, depending on the terrain.

When selecting a horse:

- Avoid wild, nervous horses as either riding or pack animals.
- Do not choose a horse that is too old, because it may not withstand hardships.
- Ask the owner to walk the horse around. It should move well with a free, springy action.
- Look at the horse's feet and mouth and judge for yourself whether it looks in good health.
- If possible, ride the horse you plan to buy before settling your price.
- Before saddling, brush the horse's back with your hand to ensure there are no sores and that the hair lies flat.

Some other useful tips on how to get the most out of your horses when on expedition are as follows:

BEGINNERS ON A RIDE IN MONGOLIA
Marianne Heredge

The idea of galloping across endless steppes made me decide that there was no way around it but to ignore my mistrust of horses and take some lessons. In the couple of months before leaving for Mongolia, I took eight one-hour-long riding lessons in a beginners' class at a local riding school until I knew how it felt to fall off! I had mastered getting the horse to trot. Another friend, also a complete beginner, managed to fit in a lesson before leaving. The other two in the group were quite experienced riders, so had no worries.

Touring around the Mongolian countryside, we were often approached by locals offering us their horses to ride. We were careful though (the thought of a broken leg bouncing along those dreadful roads....). The horses are small so aren't nearly as intimidating as some of the big horses encountered at the riding school, but they are often a bit wild. Mongolians alternate the horses that they ride so that they don't get too weak with being ridden all the time. When they need a fresh horse, they have to catch it and often have to almost break it in again.

On one occasion we hired some horses from a Mongolian and happily we were offered some quieter horses. Our guide took us riding down the valley one evening to get us used to our mounts, leading my horse and keeping a watchful eye on this nervous novice. As he and I rode along, the others fanned out behind. I hastily examined the ground for potential soft landings, as the horse had no saddle and I had no means of controlling the animal. Given the size of the horses, I was not too afraid, as if the horse wanted to throw me off, it wouldn't be very far to fall! I was very quickly won over by my little horse. It turned out that he was the fastest of the bunch.

Within half an hour of setting off, with sign language, the horseman had asked me if I wanted to go faster. Nodding my head, we charged off, galloping down the valley like wild things, leaving the others a long way behind. It was wonderful! My horse kept threatening to overtake the Mongolian's horse and I realised with some surprise that I wasn't at all worried at the speed. Rather than the hard, uncomfortable wooden saddles that most Mongolians use, we were treated to nice soft, comfortable Russian saddles. The stirrups were secure and gave solid support, giving the feeling of being glued to the horse's back. The friend who had had just the one lesson was also having a great time, although by the end of the ride she was having to urge her tired horse along!

The last couple of days were spent riding in the Terelj National Park, close to Ulaanbaatar. (This came as much as anything from nervousness at the idea of injury somewhere remote and far from a hospital.) We spent the rest of the afternoon galloping along the valleys near by, screaming 'yahoo', like mad things, to encourage the horses to go faster. Still nervous of riding at home, those few lessons before going were all that were needed to have a fantastic time.

- Decide how many animals you need and for what purposes – riding horses, and pack animals.
- It is a help to pack and load horses in pairs.
- Keep pack animals at a steady slow pace to prevent chafing.

- Allow more frequent rest periods if in hilly country.
- Veterinary care is 90% prevention. Bring iodine to pour on to wounds.
- Older, more experienced horses manage loads more easily.
- To stop a runaway horse, turn its head to the side
- Pull on the reins sideways to halt (not straight back, as in Western riding style)
- Shout 'chüü' to speed up your horse.

Tack and other equipment
A horse harness comprises a head collar and leading rope, which is rarely removed from the horse, a bridle with a simple steel bit, and a Russian steel-framed or European saddle. Tack is held together by leather straps and pieces of rope and no two Mongolian bridles look alike. Mongolian saddles, contrary to expectations, can be quite comfortable if well padded. You will find all this kit in Mongolia (there is no need to bring your own if on a riding tour), but if bound on an expedition – including very long journeys – you may prefer to arrive with your own saddle and other familiar tack.

Other items to remember to take on a riding expedition (not a riding tour) are a head collar, a crupper (to stop the riding saddle from sliding forwards when going steeply downhill), saddlebags (two identically sized bags, preferably leather, for packing equipment) and several good lengths of rope (can be bought in Mongolia). You should take basic veterinary drugs like worming tablets, saddle-sore ointments and a couple of bandages. For information on food and other supplies to take, see *What to take*, page 173.

Camel riding
with Ed Brown
For details of tour operators offering camel-riding trips, see *Specialist tour operators*, page 151.

An encounter with camels
When I arrived in Mongolia with the intention of buying camels I had no idea what I was looking for. One month, 800km and a desert later, I was no wiser. I had lived, breathed, contemplated eating and certainly smelt of camel and yet to call them curious beasts is an understatement. Their bitter whines of complaint drill through your head, a kick from their back legs can send a man flying three metres, and their acrid smell pervades all clothes, food and even toothpaste. However, as beasts of burden they are unsurpassable. Whether they are carrying you, your bags or pulling a 500kg cart, their strength is awesome, their long legs eat up the kilometres, and if properly fed and watered their stamina will most certainly outlast yours.

The indigenous camels of the vast areas of the Gobi Desert are wild and when on the move they can cover up to 70km a day. Wild male Bactrians have been known to infiltrate domestic herds to mate with the females. Herdsmen do not like this with the result that the wild camels are chased away from water holes.

The amateur's guide to buying a camel
Naturally it depends on what you intend your camel to do and how far you plan on taking it, but various pointers can be taken to insure that your camel will not fail its MOT (MOT = diagnostic check-up for those unfamiliar with the term!).

- Never completely trust the guy you are buying from.
- After discussions, bartering and vodka that will almost certainly go on for days, give in and trust him.

TOP CAMEL – BACTRIAN CAMELS ON TREK
Benedict Allen

Camels are not always the easiest of animals to handle, but even the most brutish, spitting beast can be transformed into a loyal friend – well, in theory at least. The key is to understand the camel's one little weakness. It has only this one, for, unlike a horse, or any other livestock animal, the camel does not need daily provision of water and grazing. The camel comes as a self-sufficient unit, and a Mongolian camel can last the entire, harsh, Gobi winter without water, obtaining its moisture from snow or grazing. If it comes to a battle of wills, the camel's flat feet, humps, nostrils and even eye-lashes ensure that it can survive in the desert a lot longer than any exasperated human. In short, the camel's loyalty cannot be bought; furthermore, the Bactrian is considerably taller and stronger than any Mongol horse, and has a formidable array of defences – it can bite (rare), box with its 'knees' (all too common), kick with all four feet (at the same time if necessary), and has a special weapon, the brisket or cartilaginous pad on its sternum. This it normally uses for resting its weight on when sitting - but it can also be usefully employed for crushing undesirables. So, if a camel is fed-up with its owner, it either battles, sits in protest or walks off in triumph – and the camel has an acute sense of direction. Furthermore, it has a photographic memory, so will have recorded the location of promising bushes it has passed. Jigjig, one treacherous camel of mine, abandoned me in the Gobi to amble 500km back home – arriving there three weeks later, and fatter than when it set off. So what can a human offer a camel? What is its one weakness? In a word, security. An animal adapted to the margins of existence, the camel has survival forever at the forefront of its mind. Its defence is its herd, and head of that herd is a leader, the 'top camel'. And essentially it is this formidable creature that a camel owner must become, if he is to be able to lead a camel train across the desert.

Becoming a top camel is a question of familiarising your potential camel team members with you – a stranger is outside the herd, and therefore another threat to a camel's security. This partly explains why tourists are always

- The best time for buying camels is late summer, when they have spent the summer months fattening up away from the homestead. The drawback is that they haven't seen humans for a while and might therefore be a little skittish.
- Buy them in good time before you depart on the trip to make sure they are in good condition and will not rapidly waste once on the road.
- Officially, a camel's age can be determined by its teeth and its feet. I have no idea of the technicalities, but if you are mad enough to brave the flying green cud and go near its mouth, then at least it looks as if you have a clue. Never let on about your ignorance.
- If you are in a large group, or intent on taking your camels through inhabited places, just check how the camel behaves when surrounded by people.
- The Bactrian camel possesses two humps and when fully watered these humps should be fully erect. If they are not then this is a possible sign of an aged camel that should therefore be left alone.
- Once the deal is sealed (usually over a barbecue and vodka), tie a piece of brightly coloured material round your camels' necks so as not to lose them in the crowd.

regarded with disdain by camels working the Egyptian pyramids. But, once your camel regards you as a familiar object, a companion, it will trust you to lead it away from familiar surroundings. Often the answer is to get the previous owner to walk with you for a couple of weeks, and effect a transfer of leadership (and other skills). Even then, a camel will be alert to any sign of nervousness on your part; once, I remember hesitating as I led my proud camel train up a dune, and the camels immediately anchored their feet in the sand, refusing to go on with me until I began humming contentedly again. The camels' natural neurosis is exacerbated in Mongolia, where nomads rarely go long-distances, and camels hardly ever leave the surroundings they know. Furthermore, bred for milk, fur and carrying gers, they have a close relationship with their owner's family, which has nurtured them since birth.

The potential of your camels – the distance they might go, the load they might carry – depends on day and night temperatures, and the strength and fitness of the animals. Prime time is the late summer, when camels are fat from grazing, and their fur is thickening again. Generally, if walking for months, camels should have a weekly rest day, grazing time at dawn and dusk, and be watered every other day – they can go for five, but their strength starts to be depleted. They can carry 100–200kg without too much strain. Mongolians load them with double this weight, but seldom walk for more than a day or two. Travel with castrated males if possible – they are anyway easier to obtain than females, which are wanted for breeding – and whatever happens, don't mix sexes. Do not ride camels if alone with them – it's a long way to fall, and not easy to regain control if a member of the train is having a panic, due to loosening baggage.

With time, a camel if treated kindly will do whatever you ask – and with what appears to be genuine affection. It's true that, even after a few weeks, a camel may still spit at you – actually it's vomiting – and demand to be top camel itself. However, if you can tolerate all this, and more besides, a camel is the best of all possible friends. If it has chosen to stay with you, you know you have been given the greatest accolade of all – that of the status of a fellow camel.

Watering your camels

Opinions differ as to how much water a camel needs and how often it needs to drink. Some say that a camel can go for seven days and often longer without water and when refuelling will drink up to 60 litres.

We were walking on average 26 miles a day and tried, whenever possible, to water our camels at least once during the day. The longest the two camels went without water was three days and they were beginning to complain seriously by the end of the third. It goes without saying that if a camel eats and drinks regularly and well, then the further it will walk and the less it will sit down and complain.

Camel saddles and other equipment

Try and get an all-inclusive package. Camels need saddles for both pack and people, they should have a good peg rammed through their nose and it is vital to have several strong leather hobbles. Camels have been known to move large distances when unhampered, so when camping for the night make sure the animals are properly hobbled. This allows them to move relatively freely but prevents an extra two-kilometre walk each morning to go and retrieve them.

Hiring a camel-helper and guide

Like many things, if you treat camels to the best of your abilities (easier said than done when trying to find good food and water every day in the desert), then you might almost become attached to them. However, the ultimate solution to all your camel worries is to rely on local knowledge and hire a Gobi guru. In any of the small desert towns you are guaranteed to find someone (however harebrained the trip might be) to come along and help with the camels. We found Baatar, gave him US$4 a day, food and an extra sleeping bag, endless cigarettes and his return train fare home. In return, he looked after the camels superbly, fetched them every morning, watered them and found them good grass. He was also able to tell the bemused herdsmen what we were doing and ask where the next well was. This is hugely important for, equipped with only an out-of-date Russian map and limited Mongolian, a wrong turn could have meant serious problems. Finding someone that you feel you can trust is obviously the hard part, but whoever you choose, they might ask to draw up a 'contract' of some sort in the presence of the local aimag or somon governor. This is no bad thing, for everyone knows where they stand and what's expected from them – a definite plus point considering Mongolian camel-helpers aren't renowned for their initiative.

BIKING EXPERIENCE IN MONGOLIA
Elizabeth Haynes

I travelled to Mongolia to participate in Macmillan Cancer Relief's 'Mongolia Cycling Challenge'. My challenge took me, and a group of 30 other like-minded people, to cycle off road for 385 gruelling kilometres (about 240 miles) in Mongolia. We started from the edge of the Gobi Desert, continued across the stunning Khangai Mountains, stopping at villages where we visited hot springs, which the Mongolians use for curing ailments. We climbed 2,600m and at the top was an *ovoo* – a pyramid of stones, sticks and silk scarves (usually blue in colour), a shamanistic offering to the gods. We then raced on to the ancient city of Karakorum.

We camped under the stars, scaled mountains and free-wheeled faster than the wild horses over the Mongolian steppes. The nomadic people we encountered were inquisitive. We had some fun together: we frequently exchanged our 21-gear mountain bikes for their horses and wooden saddles at our nightly camping grounds. We were invited into the nomads' *gers*, their round felt homes, which are extremely tidy and unlike the interior of our tents. Their diet is basic: in the summer they eat cheese and dairy foods, and in the winter meat. My personal memory will be the vast open spaces, a harsh environment – no shelter from the elements – few trees and nothing for miles. The country is a mixture of Russian industrialism and China's Buddhist lifestyle and temples, which I also found fascinating.

It was the experience of a lifetime, but one incident surprised me: in the market in Karakorum, a little girl just had to touch me – either to feel my Lycra cycling gear, or to see if I was human! I also found out that any amount of training in Richmond Park, in the gym and in spinning (fitness bike) classes over the winter months did not prepare me for the terrain, which was like cycling for miles over the pebbles on Brighton beach! Nor was I prepared for snow in early September.

Fitness

Personal fitness is one of the most important things to pack before setting out on a biking trip or any expedition that requires physical endurance. Run, walk or ride yourself into fitness for three months to a year by setting an easy-to-achieve daily fitness routine. Then when the going gets tough you are up to it. A healthy diet, gentle stretches and a simple practice routine does wonders over time. Strengthening the body does not happen overnight ... ease yourself into it.

Hiking

Mongolia is a paradise for hikers. The area of the Bogd Khan National Park and Terelj, near Ulaanbaatar, provides wonderful short-distance day-walks from the capital. To go further afield you will need a guide and transport. National parks around the country offer some of the best hiking routes and, depending on where you want to go, local tour companies, or the national park offices, will suggest or help to make the necessary arrangements. It is safest to hike in twos or threes. Essential gear includes a water bottle, good footwear and camping gear if travelling outside a guided tour. Don't forget to carry good maps, binoculars and a camera, and also some mosquito repellent during the summer season. For further information, see *What to take*, page 173.

Cycling/motorbiking

Make no mistake, the going is tough in Mongolia. At times you will be riding on pebbles and rough ground for mile after mile – it doesn't let up, especially if you are riding in a dry river bed over stony ground. Be realistic when estimating the distance you hope to achieve in a day, in training or on expedition. It is better to get there, bar accidents or breakdown, than to 'get lost' overnight. See special lists on what to bring on a biking tour in *What to take*, page 173. Specialist tour operators offering cycling include Off the Map Tours, Wildcat Bike Tours Ltd, Discover Adventure Ltd and Karakorum Expeditions. See page 151 for contact details. Juulchin Foreign Tourism Corporation (Genghis Khan Avenue 5B, Ulaanbaatar 210543; tel: 11 312095, 328428; fax: 11 320246; email: jlncorp@magicnet.mn) offers motor-biking tours in the Gobi with expert biking guides.

SPORT AND ADVENTURE
Polo

Polo has now become a booming success, for both local players and spectators. It is not considered an élitist sport in Mongolia, nor is it wildly expensive to keep horses to play polo, as it is elsewhere in the world.

The Genghis Khan Polo Club originated from an impromptu game played on a trip to Mongolia in 1997, when Jim Edwards (founder of World Elephant Polo) and his son Kristjan started the club with 12 founder members and a group of 'would-be' Mongolian players (see box, page 198). They discovered that Mongolian riders possess two great characteristics: remarkable co-ordination and extraordinary flexibility in the saddle. The Genghis Khan Polo Club is helping to rebuild an ancient Buddhist monastery. So far they have raised 40,000 pounds sterling towards the restoration costs. For further information contact Great Game Expeditions, Ulaanbaatar; tel: 11 324237; fax: +976 11 324777; email: Bizinfo@magicnet.mn.

Fishing

For information about tour operators offering fishing trips in Mongolia, see *Specialist tour operators*, pages 151–2.

THE GENGHIS KHAN POLO CLUB
Jim Edwards

Polo requires skill, balance and fearless riding – all of which the Mongol horseman has in abundance. They are polo naturals. What is more, Mongolia has all the essential resources – hard flat land and millions of free-roaming horses, so all that was needed were polo sticks and balls.

At first, we taught them how to make polo sticks using the branches of willow trees. Polo balls are also made of willow wood and are supposed to be roughly 3.5 inches in diameter and to weigh 4.5 ounces. Homemade balls are none the worse for three good coats of white paint. The club was formally registered with the authorities when Mongolia's first polo tournament took place as part of the 1997 Naadam Festival, featuring the 'three manly sports' to which polo was added – a possible fourth!

Our game (adapted to Mongolia) has two rules:

* no hitting the person or pony with a stick
* no hooking sticks above the waist

There was a third rule – no crossing – but it was abandoned. It also became obvious that Mongolian polo has no boundaries!

We were surprised by how much local spectators threw themselves into the game. To get started we presented the club members with 30 polo shirts and 50 balls (bought at Harrods in Knightsbridge!) and a number of Indian pith helmets, which we brought with us from Nepal.

In international polo the most dangerous thing is considered to be horse collisions; however, in Mongolia the horses swerve naturally to follow the ball and somehow also succeed in avoiding holes and rocks on the practice grounds. Their horse-herding instincts have replaced brakes. The polo ponies (ordinary Mongolian range ponies) are very agile and athletic, like the riders.

It is advisable to hold the polo stick close up to the heart and upright when not in play. Accuracy and command of the ball in forward play is extremely difficult. The idea is to hit a clean shot and follow up the ball to position it for a goal shot. The whole secret of direction lies in making the head of the stick travel along the line of the ball. Also, you want to aim to hit the ball before you get to it, so a player should try to foresee every stroke. It is best to hit the ball close beside one's leg, leaving room to swing the stick.

Although we don't know if Genghis Khan ever played polo, the sport certainly originated in the great Mongol warrior's empire. We are thrilled by the way polo has been received in Mongolia, and as a result we have developed a camp and training grounds for visitors. We are expecting to play a number of entertaining tournaments in the future.

For further information, contact Jim and Kristjan Edwards, The Genghis Khan Polo Club, PO Box 242, Lazimpat, Kathmandu, Nepal; tel: 977-11 411225; fax: 977-11 414075; email: info@tigermountain.com; web: www.tigermountain.com.

Mongolia is now among the top fly-fishing destinations in the world. The rivers are rugged and wild and offer a marvellous variety of fishing in landscapes of unrivalled scenic beauty. The dry-fly take of Mongolia's famous *taimen* fish is like nothing else in freshwater fishing. Where else in the world is it possible to cast dry flies to fish weighing over 22kg.

Mongolia's northern central rivers flow via Lake Baikal, the Angara and the Yenisey to the Arctic Ocean, whereas the rivers of the northeast and east flow to the Pacific via the Amur, another great Siberian river. The lake basin in the west has no outlet to the sea. Mongolia has a small organised fishing industry on the eastern border at Buir Lake, at Ögii Lake in central Mongolia and at the western lakes in the Darkhad basin. Some 300 tonnes of fish is exported. Little is consumed in the country since the Mongols have no taste for, or habit of, eating fish.

There are 60 species of fish in Mongolia, of which 30 are worth fishing. *Taimen*, the biggest, is related to the non-migratory huchen of the Danube and belongs to the salmon family. It has been described as prehistoric in appearance, with huge fins, the head of a conger eel and the teeth of a pike. Besides with flies, it is caught by using 'dummy' mice or, as the Mongolians do, by using dead mice, squirrel or marmot as bait. In late autumn, when migratory tundra mice cross the forming ice on the northern rivers and streams, giant *taimen* lie ready in wait below the frozen surfaces to snap them up for breakfast. In early spring *taimen* have even been seen catching young ducklings for dinner, such is their voracious appetite. Nobody knows where the land-locked *taimen* go in winter. It is thought they head for Lake Khövsgöl, the deepest freshwater lake in Central Asia, or lurk in the hollows of the deepest pools.

Lake-fish catches consist mostly of the Yenisei white fish, a species related to the famous omul fish of Lake Baikal in southern Siberia. Otherwise the catch usually consists of *taimen*, lenok and Arctic grayling. Two species of grayling are common in rivers of northern Mongolia: the Arctic grayling (*Thymallus arcticus*) and Mongolian grayling (*Thymallus brevirostris*). Roach, perch, pike and carp are also caught. Winter fishing produces burbot caught through holes in the ice. The Siberian sturgeon is a protected fish. One interesting and little-studied species of endemic fish is the Altai osman (*Oreoleuciscus potanini*).

Fishing, especially fly fishing, is a new leisure sport in Mongolia. Most Mongols rarely eat fish because of their Buddhist traditions, but despite this the rivers near Ulaanbaatar tend to be over-fished. Further afield the majority of Mongolian waters have never seen a fisherman. Equipment is difficult to rent anywhere in the country, so it is recommended to bring your own gear. Should you arrive unprepared all you need when fishing for the pot is a strong handline and a lure (see box *Fishing for the pot*, page 202).

What does it take? The swish of the line and the fly is freed from the water, on the forward movement it droops on the spot where in all likelihood a giant trout lies waiting below the surface. A sudden jerk and the fly is taken. You have caught your supper. It is that easy to land a fish in Mongolia, which sounds rather unsporting; on the other hand you will never experience better and more thrilling fishing conditions.

Seasons and weather

You can push the seasons at both ends in spring and autumn depending whether you get an early or late winter. Most fishing happens from late August until mid-October.

Spring fishing begins in May and June when the winter is over (one hopes) and rivers are at their lowest. Early spring is an idyllic time of year when the fishing is excellent and the hillsides are carpeted with alpine flowers

During the summer months of July and early August there is a low rainfall – not the ideal time for fishing. However, giant *taimen* may be fished throughout the season until early/mid-October. Thereafter temperatures plummet.

Autumn is also a beautiful time of year and the fishing is good.

THE FISH AND HOW TO CATCH THEM
Taimen (Hucho hucho taimen)

The *taimen* is among the largest, most ferocious, freshwater fish in the world. The species is only found in a few inaccessible parts of Siberia and Mongolia. It is the fastest-growing freshwater fish in the northern hemisphere. A standard *taimen* averages over a metre in length and weighs around nine kilograms. Lucky anglers have landed specimens up to 75 inches – over six feet (nearly 2m) long! (Mongolians record *taimen* by their length rather than their weight.) Because it is threatened with extinction the *taimen* is a highly valued trophy fish. It is described by experts as similar to fishing oversized Atlantic salmon. All catches are returned to the river.

Catching taimen

The favourite Mongolian method is to fish for *taimen* under a full moon using a stout line, a hook and a dead mouse as bait. Taimen are caught by anglers using all manner of spinners, spoons and plugs and can also be caught on dead fish and on fly in clear water. Large dry flies can take smaller fish at dusk. Bring a set of both dry and wet flies, dummy mice and other fish imitations plus sufficient backing of more than 150m.

Some *taimen* are very large – up to 30kg – so you will need powerful equipment. Fly fishermen are advised to bring a hefty 15ft fly rod (eight-, nine- or ten-weight). You may fish with either a two-handed or a single-handed rod (depending on your preference). Bring a leader, as heavy as practical, 14–20lb breaking strain. To date there are no nets large enough to land *taimen*. That is

During winter from November to April (and sometimes until June) Mongolian rivers are ice-covered, so that anyone fishing for food chops holes in the ice over deep pools to catch fish 'Greenland' style with a long line. Obviously not possible in shallow rivers which freeze through to the bottom in winter.

Conservation policy

Fishing camps recommend fishing with barbless hooks. It is common practice to release all trophy fish when caught.

Permission and licensing

Out-of-the way rivers are unpatrolled but that does not mean you don't need a licence. This means that tourists cannot pitch up and go fishing, although some 'pot' fishing is bound to happen with or without a licence. Permits are also available for a day's fishing from local national park administration offices. The price for a *taimen* permit is approximately US$10 per day. For anglers, a fishing licence may be obtained from the Mongolian Ministry of Nature and the Environment (Baga Toiruu 44, Ulaanbaatar; tel: 11 326617; fax: 11 328620).

Good fishing rivers and lakes

The best fishing rivers include the famous 'Five Rivers' area near Lake Khövsgöl – the Ider, Delgermörön, Bugsei, Selenge and Chuluut rivers. The Eg and Shishigt are also excellent fishing rivers.

Good lake fishing may be found at:

• Terkhiin Tsaagan Nuur (Great White Lake) in Arkhangai Province

a tricky business and one where you need a fishing guide on hand to help. Remember to pack a wading stick, forceps or pliers to remove hooks from fishes' mouths, scales, a ruler and mousetraps!

Lenok (Brachymystax lenok)
Lenok provides excellent dry-fly fishing for good-sized fish on light tackle. Like the *taimen* it belongs to the salmon family. The species is superficially like our rainbow brown trout, with a rich coral tinge. It's a wonderfully tasty fish. It reaches around 60cm (18–20 inches) and weighs approximately 3kg. Lenok can be caught with all kinds of bait and streamers. A lucky catch reaches 75cm (30 inches) and weighs 3.5–4.8kg (8–11lb)

Arctic grayling (Thymallus arcticus)
Known to some as the 'lady of the stream', grayling, like lenok, makes excellent eating if you picnic on the river for lunch. (*Taimen* consider them an 'arctic delicacy' and devour them in quantities.) Fish grayling using small dries and nymphs.

Catching lenok and grayling
This includes a light fly rod (four- to six-weight) with a leader of 3–5lb (1.3–2.2kg). Traditional river flies – the same flies you would use in the UK or Scandinavia. Czech nymphs and goldheads are good choices and have proved successful. Use a three- to five-weight rod and some hoppers to catch lenok, plus 4lb (1.7kg) leader material.

- Lake Khövsgöl in Khövsgöl Aimag. You may find omul, lenok, umber, roach, river perch, sturgeon and *taimen*. Fishing usually takes place from the shoreline or from bridges. The lakeshelf is very steep so don't attempt wading unless you have good local advice. Best spots include the bridge at Khatgal on the eastern shore.
- Lake Ögii in Arkhangai Aimag. The lake can be reached from the main road linking Tsetserleg with Ulaanbaatar and can also be reached on a day trip from Karakorum, in the Orkhon Valley.

Fishing camps
Most fishing camps are organised by top fly-fishing tour operators and are specifically set up for clients, often in very out-of-the-way sites on choice rivers. Some of these 'private' camps are located in river valleys four to five hours' journey southeast of Lake Khövsgöl; they are not geared to casual drop-in visitors who might turn up expecting to hire equipment for a day's fishing.

Helicopter transport is used to reach some of the more remote fishing camps, which provide a high standard of comfort (baths, showers, plenty of hot water and good meals, with freshly baked bread and, naturally, fish menus). Stoves warm the *gers* at night. Days are spent on the river. There are also marginally less-comfortable tented camps. It is possible to 'go it alone' and travel with tents in search of new waters, but this needs careful planning.

The camps listed below provide more spontaneous or casual fishing arrangements:

Tsaatan Camp Tel: 11 313 393. In Tsagaannuur Sum.

FISHING FOR THE POT
Anthony Wynn

A number of travel companies offer fishing tours to Mongolia, promising catches of giant *taimen* (*Hucho hucho taimen*) and other adventures, but all you need to catch fish on your own is a stout trout rod and a small box of flies. Once out of reach of Ulaanbaatar the rivers are full of Arctic char and grayling. The char go up to 1.7kg (4lb) and the black grayling in the west are very fine fighting fish up to 0.9kg (2lb). If fishing wet, a black pennel or grouse and claret will catch both fish. Grayling will also come spectacularly to a bushy, dry fly.

If you have forgotten to bring a rod, copy the Mongolians, who catch char with a hook and line attached to the end of a long pole. Scratch about under the stones to find caddis flies, attach them to the hook and go dapping. This requires some skill.

The rivers run cold and gin-clear for the most part, except during the brief summer rains, when they can colour up. Wading is not necessary. To cook your fish, take some foil with you. Find some wild spring onions to stuff them, wrap the fish in the foil and bake them over a fire of dried camel or yak dung. Nothing could be more delicious.

To catch *taimen* the Mongolian way, take a very stout line and tie a wooden 'mouse' wrapped in marmot fur and festooned with hooks to the end of it. Wait until dark and light a fire by the river bank over a deep pool. Throw the mouse out into the river and pull it back towards you. If you hook a fish, lash yourself to a friend, or a tree, and haul in. Some rural Mongolians regard fish as sacred (because they do not shut their eyes) and do not approve of fishing, but most of them have no objection. Be sensitive about this.

Toilogt Camp Tel: 11 328 428; fax: 11 320 246. To arrange bookings contact Juulchin's office in Ulaanbaatar (see *Tour operators*, page 148)
Huvsgul Travel Company Tel/fax: 11 687, 626, 11 326 478; mobile: Purevdorj on 99116227. In Ulaanbaatar.

For further information on tour operators offering fishing trips, see pages 151–2.

General equipment
Fishing is a new sport in Mongolia, so for those who are keen to fish the best advice at present is to come prepared and bring your own rod, although this situation should change in a few years' time. Fishing rods and equipment are difficult to buy or hire anywhere in the country, so bring what you need. Rods should have a 2½lb test curve. Bring lines of at least 18lb breaking strain, big fixed spool reels or multipliers, a good selection of spinners and spoons and plugs, including heavy sinking deep-diving plugs (10–12ft) and big splashy surface plugs with a good vivid action. High-quality reels such as Shimano's Aero GT or Stradic are recommended. Rods must be packed in travelling tubes for transport in the luggage compartment of the aircraft. For recommended tackle for specific species, see box on previous page.

What the ace anglers say
The rivers are classic trout rivers, teeming with fish, where the waters offer long dry fly glides. Deep pools and fast-flowing currents challenge the skills of any

angler. Not all Mongolian rivers are fly-fishing rivers by any means and it has taken experts like John and Joy Bailey of Angling Travel, the Vermillion brothers of Sweetwater Travel, and Will Bond of Frontiers to pioneer the way with Mongolian companies like Juulchin and Khövsgöl Travel.

Dan Vermillion, an American who pioneered Mongolian *taimen* fishing in the early 1990s, reported during the caddis and mayfly hatches, 'This is wild time for fish and fishermen alike, when grayling and lenok rise steadily and *taimen* cruise beneath them until they pick out their lunch.' According to Vermillion, this is when it is most difficult to decide whether to cast a mouse or a mayfly.

Cooking
Grilled fish makes a pleasant change from mutton for the evening meal. Proceed with caution and respect for local beliefs and customs. If you are not part of a fishing group, take charge of the cooking yourself. Mongolians tend to obliterate fish by boiling it like meat, so that all that remains is a thin white soup with a vaguely fishy taste. Bring tin foil to wrap your fish in, add herbs and cook in the campfire embers. You will not easily order fish in a restaurant again!

Mountaineering
There are many glaciers and permanently snow-capped mountains in Mongolia's western region, which attract climbers (see *Climbing* under *Bayan-Ölgii Aimag*, page 344). Mount Khüiten (Cold Mountain), Mongolia's highest peak (4,374m), was previously known as Mount Nairandal (Friendship Mountain); part of the Tavanbogd range located in Bayan-Ölgii Aimag, it lies on the borders of Mongolia, China and Russia. Other main peaks of the western region are:

- **Otgontenger Uul** (4,021m) in Zavkhan Aimag, also called Peace (Enkhtaivan) peak.
- **Türgen Uul** (3,978m) in Uvs Aimag, the highest peak in this range is Tsagaandelgi.
- **Kharkhiraa Uul** (4,037m) in Uvs Aimag (highest peak, Tsagaanshuvuut)
- **Sutai Uul** (4,234m) on the border between Gobi-Altai and Khovd aimags
- **Altan Tavan Uul** (4,150m) in Bayan-Ölgii Aimag; has a 19km glacier.
- **Tsast Uul** (4,204m) on the border between Bayan-Ölgii and Khovd aimags.
- **Tsambagarav Uul** (4,202m) in Khovd Aimag.
- **Mönkhkhairkhan Uul** (4,362m) on the border between Bayan-Ölgii and Khovd aimags. The main peak is Sükhbaatar or Tavankhumst (the name differs on various maps) at 4,204m.
- **Tavanbogd Uul** (4374m) in Bayan-Ölgii Aimag.

Note Heights of mountain peaks and ranges tend to differ on Mongolian maps, in statistical handbooks and encyclopaedias. Those given in this guide are the most recent.

The best time to climb is from the beginning of July until the end of August; you will need permits from the Ministry of Nature and Environment, Khudaldaany 5, Ulaanbaatar; tel: 11 326649; fax: 11 329968; email: env.pmis.gov.mn. The sport requires a high degree of professionalism: you must have the necessary experience, be fully equipped and hire local guides. Climbing trips are best arranged through your home climbing club with a specialist tour operator such as Graham Taylor of Karakorum Expeditions (see overleaf).

For serious mountaineering advice (not advice on hiking and mountain walks, mainly dealt with by the specialist tour operators listed below), climbers should write to the secretary of the Mongol Altai Club, PO Box 49-23, Ulaanbaatar.

'MONGOLIA SUNRISE TO SUNSET' – MONGOLIA'S ULTRA MARATHON

David Bernasconi

The 'Mongolia Sunrise to Sunset' Ultra Marathon allows one to explore Mongolia by taking part in the annual 42km marathon or 100km ultra marathon. Runners and supporters from around the world can join the group in Beijing, Seoul or Ulaanbaatar, from where travel is arranged by scheduled flights, and then chartered planes, to the remote lake region of Khövsgöl, situated on the northern borders of Mongolia with Russian Siberia. The lake, flanked by 3,000m mountains, is surrounded by forests of larch and spruce and is a spectacular setting for the race. Altitude at the basecamp is 1,650m, the optimum level for high-altitude training. Here, in the 'middle of nowhere', hot showers, good food and drink are all available, and visitors relish living in the unique ambience of traditional round-framed *gers*.

The race itself offers runners (and walkers) the opportunity to explore the picturesque lakeshore scenery and the mountain ranges above the lake. It begins at first light. The course follows a rough track through the woods and hugs the lakeshore for the first 12km. It then climbs above the treeline to the highest point, a 2,300m pass. There is a downhill stretch to marshy wetlands before the route ascends a second pass, a flower-covered meadow offering an opportunity to circle a ceremonial cairn, or *ovoo*, to honour an ancient religious tradition. From here the course descends back to the lakeshore for a final dash to the midway station to start a loop which takes the runners into new territory along unpaved roads and trails. The final 25km hugs the lakeshore path once more.

Water and first-aid stations mark every 12km of the course and a system is in place for contestants to write messages and relay them should they be in difficulty. Local horsemen gallop alongside ready to transport the messages, as they did in the days of Genghis Khan! Message pads, space blankets, a course map and a number of other items, like a whistle, are issued to each runner in case anyone should go off course.

Eco-tourism is part of the the race's ethos, an approach which respects this pristine wilderness area. Here the air is clear and sunshine is extremely strong with July temperatures around 18°C. For runners and non-runners alike, the days before the race can be spent soaking in the sun, horse riding, kayaking, mountain biking, hiking and, of course, running.

'Sunrise to Sunset' is a non-profitmaking event. Any proceeds are used to support projects that aid the sustainable development of Khövsgöl National Park, the park's nomadic communities and the villages that border the park. The race offers runners the opportunity to visit the land of 'Blue Skies' and to run beside one of the most beautiful lakes in the world.

For full information visit 'Mongolia Sunrise to Sunset's website: www.ultramongolia.com.

Specialist tour operators

Karakorum Expeditions (winners of the Pacific Asia Travel Association PATA's 2002 Gold Award for Ecotourism) Jiggur Grand Hotel, 13 Transport St, Ulaanbaatar; mobile: 99116729; tel/fax: 976 11 315655; email: info@GoMongolia.com; web: www.GoMongolia.com

Nomads PO Box 1008, Ulaanbaatar; tel/fax: 11 328146; email: nomads@magicnet.mn; web: www.mongoliadventure.com. Pioneering mountain tours in western Mongolia.

Skiing

Downhill skiing has not yet been developed as a winter sport in Mongolia but there is plenty of potential for cross-country skiing. Snow cover in the northern and central regions lasts throughout the long winters, some seven months of the year, although not in the warmer south where it falls periodically or not at all. The best months for skiing are January and February (when you may also participate in the family festival of Tsaagan Sar). The most accessible skiing areas are just outside Ulaanbaatar at the Terelj resort. You can hire skis and boots in Mongolia, but not the latest type of skis, so you may need to bring your own.

Ice-skating

Many Mongolians are keen ice-skaters. Although it is possible to buy ice skates in Mongolia, it would be more reliable to bring your own. For more details on skating contact Mr Darjaa on tel: 11 458964.

Adventure challenge

Mongolia is fast developing as a country for adventure tourism and offers challenges such as 'Sunset to Sunrise', Mongolia's annual ultra-distance marathon, a race internationally recognised for being a well-organised and an environmentally conscious event. It takes place annually in July in one of the most exotic settings in the world, beside Lake Khövsgöl in northern Mongolia (see box opposite). For full information, visit the 'Sunrise to Sunset' website: www.ultramongolia.com.

SHOPPING

Mongolia produces many specialist items based on natural products – from exotic cashmere garments to wooden toys, puzzles and games. Mongolian watercolour paintings are of exceptional quality. Other important items include jewellery and leather goods. The souvenir industry is developing – especially in the countryside, where it is worth supporting – so please save some shopping space for local traditional products when travelling outside the capital. Buy your cashmere in Ulaanbaatar. Mongolians tend not to barter so don't quibble over prices, even in the open markets. Finally, don't leave shopping until the last minute at the airport, or you may be disappointed.

What to look for

* **Cashmere jumpers**
* **Camel-hair waistcoats**
* **Wooden puzzles** – some of the best presents to bring home. There are also many kinds of traditional Mongolian board games – but you will need to play with Mongolians first in order to learn them.
* **Mongolian-style silk tunics (*deel*)** Made to measure at the State Department Store in the centre of Ulaanbaatar, where a dressmaker will finish your garment in less than a week. The usual cost is around T12,000.
* **Jewellery and silverware** Finely crafted in Altaic-knot designs (reminiscent of Celtic patterns).
* **Paintings** Mongolian landscapes in oil and watercolour, and Mongol *zurag* paintings (realistic, classical, nomadic lifestyle and landscape art are well worth buying.

• **Tapes, cassettes and CDs** Traditional Mongolian music – a must. This includes the extraordinary sound of overtone singing, unique to Mongolia (see page 95).

ARTS AND ENTERTAINMENT
Modern Mongolian art

The Art Gallery is located in the Palace of Culture on Sükhbaatar Square and exhibits contemporary Mongolian paintings and classical Mongol *zurag* works. The Exhibition Hall of the Union of Mongolian Artists exhibits the works of contemporary artists. Since 1990, many Mongolian artists have formed associations to help sell their art abroad, and to exhibit at different locations in Ulaanbaatar. One group is the *Oron Zai* (Space) Art Society. Its members – painters, sculptors, graphic artists and craftsmen – are mostly teachers at the UB Art College. Works in different styles, from traditional to modern, include portraits and landscape paintings by artists such as Ts Tsegmid, Kh Sodnomtseren, B Tömörbaatar, N Sergelen, S Dagvadorj, D Erdenebileg and Ch Boldbaatar. *Oron Zai* may be contacted via D Erdenebileg, Art College, Ulaanbaatar 210646. Prices range from US$200 to US$2,000.

The artworks of young modern artists (students of the above) are a mixture of different styles and mediums: abstract oils by D Bold and Ts Enkhjin; figurative and partially abstract works on Mongolian themes – horses, dreams, landscapes – by M Erdenebayar, Ts Enkhjargal, Ts Mönkhjin and Sh Chimeddorj; and colourful surrealistic works by S Sarantsatsralt. Prices overseas (on London's Cork Street) range from £350 to £2,000.

Theatre

Mongolian theatre has its roots in folklore and ceremonial events. In the 1920s plays centred around revolutionary ideology and propaganda. The State Central Theatre was founded in 1933 and put on a number of revolutionary plays and operas, such as the *Three Sad Hills* by D Natsagdorj, a founder of contemporary Mongolian literature. Apart from national plays, the Mongolian theatre has put on works by Shakespeare, Schiller and Gorky. In 2000, a production of *Carmen* – as a ballet, accompanied by the *morin khuur* (horse-head fiddle) orchestra – and *Porgy and Bess*, George Gershwin's opera, were both hits. Tickets cost US$6 each; your hotel receptionist will book them in advance and will advise you on how to get there. The dress code is casual/smart, similar to theatre dress around the world.

A number of musical and drama companies working in the capital also perform in rural Mongolia where every province has its own theatre. All these theatres have had to fight to survive the political changes – which has meant less money, since they used to be totally subsidised.

Film

Mongolia has its own film industry and has produced many films that are rarely seen by audiences outside Mongolia, such as *Argamshaa* and *Buyany* – not forgetting *Tsogt Taij*. Foreign-made films in Mongolia include *Taiga*, directed by Ulrike Ottinger – a documentary of a journey through parts of northern Mongolia. It was premiered in Berlin in 1992. The film portrays the unhurried pace of Mongolian life with opening shots of a rider approaching on horseback across seemingly endless steppe. Seen as a speck on the horizon, the horseman rides into a close-up frame to perform some pre-hunting rituals before sleeping. Events unfold during the production, which lasts over eight hours. The film is usually shown in three parts. If you choose to go to a Mongolian film you can usually understand the plot without knowing the language. The usual themes are love stories, sagas and eulogies about the Mongolian countryside. For information on cinemas, see *Chapter 6, Ulaanbaatar*, page 242.

PHOTOGRAPHY
Photographs - an instant to evaluate, a reminder to treasure.

The whole business of taking photographs often goes unmentioned although it has become a fundamental part of tourism. Incorporating photography and its art in our travels is an important thing to think about – both as a reminder of what we have experienced and a rediscovery and re-evaluation of where we find ourselves. In an indirect way, photographs 'belong' both to the photographer and to the subject being photographed. That is why when photographing people it is so important always to ask their permission. In general, Mongolians love to be photographed, but individuals are often disappointed when promises to send copies are broken. A simple solution is to have a few envelopes handy so people may write their addresses on them directly, or take a Polaroid. For technical suggestions, see overleaf.

Film
All kinds of film may be bought in Ulaanbaatar at the big tourist hotels and on Sükhbaatar Square in the Agfa Shop, which also develops films. It is advisable to come equipped with all the film you need as time sometimes runs out for shopping before you leave for the countryside. There are no places outside UB to get photographic equipment. The key advice is that while you can have your prints developed in Ulaanbaatar, it's best to take your slides home for processing.

MEDIA AND COMMUNICATIONS
Television, radio and newspapers
Television is available to all who have a TV set (and an electricity supply) – that is, essentially, the urban population. TV entertainment is a mix of Russian and American soap. Consumerist attitudes are everywhere in the new society in which collectivism has given way to individualism. Most standard hotels in Ulaanbaatar have a television in the bedroom, some connected to world programmes via satellite. Guesthouses and small hotels have televisions in the reception/lounge area. Mongolian Television broadcasts European (English, German, French, Russian) and American TV news.

Telegraph lines for commercial telegram traffic were operated between Russia and China in the 19th century – the main line running from Kyakhta via Urga (Ulaanbaatar) to Kalgan was built by a Dutch company, and a western line was built by the Russians from Kosh-Agach (Altai) to Khovd in 1913. Radio was first broadcast in 1934 through wired loudspeakers in urban housing and did not operate as 'wireless' until later.

Radios have played an important role in rural communications to help, for example, women in isolated situations by providing vital communication links and education programmes. The rural population, with battery-powered receivers, depends on radio broadcasts for home and foreign news. Topics of the 'lessons-by-radio' include making camel saddles, how to stitch a Mongol *deel* (traditional dress), various methods of collecting animal dung for making fuel, vegetable growing, family planning and small-business development. Given the vast land distances between nomadic families and the lack of opportunities provided by the government, women

MAKING THE BEST OF YOUR TRAVEL PHOTOGRAPHS
Subject, composition and lighting
If it doesn't look good through the viewfinder, it will never look good as a picture. Don't take photographs for the sake of taking them; film is far too expensive. Be patient and wait until the image looks right.

People
There's nothing like a wonderful face to stimulate interest. Travelling to remote corners of the world provides the opportunity for exotic photographs of colourful people and intriguing lifestyles which capture the very essence of a culture. A superb photograph should be capable of saying more than a thousand words.

Photographing people is never easy and more often than not it requires a fair share of luck plus sharp instinct, a conditioned photographic eye and the ability to handle light both aesthetically and technically.
- If you want to take a portrait shot, always ask first. Often the offer to send a copy of the photograph to the subject will break the ice – but do remember to send it!
- Focus on the eyes of your subject.
- The best portraits are obtained in early morning and late evening light. In harsh light, photograph without flash in the shadows.
- Respect people's wishes and customs. Remember that, in some countries, infringement can lead to serious trouble.
- Never photograph military subjects unless you have definite permission.
- Be prepared for the unexpected.

Wildlife
There is no mystique to good wildlife photography. The secret is getting into the right place at the right time and then knowing what to do when you are there. Look for striking poses, aspects of behaviour and distinctive features. Try to illustrate the species within the context of its environment. Alternatively, focus in close on a characteristic which can be emphasised.
- The eyes are all-important. Make sure they are sharp and try to ensure they contain a highlight.
- Get the surroundings right – there is nothing worse than a distracting twig or highlighted leaf lurking in the background.
- A powerful flashgun can transform a dreary picture by lifting the subject out of its surroundings and putting the all-important highlights into the eyes. Artificial light is no substitute for natural light, so use judiciously.
- Getting close to the subject correspondingly reduces the depth of field; for distances of less than a metre, apertures between f16 and f32 are necessary. This means using flash to provide enough light – build your own bracket and use one or two small flashguns to illuminate the subject from the side.

Landscapes
Landscapes are forever changing; good landscape photography is all about light and mood. Generally the first and last two hours of daylight are best, or when peculiar climatic conditions add drama or emphasise distinctive features.
- Never place the horizon in the centre – in your mind's eye divide the frame into thirds and exaggerate either the land or the sky.

Cameras
Keep things simple: light, reliable and simple cameras will reduce hassle. High humidity in tropical places can play havoc with electronics.
- For keen photographers, a single-lens reflex (SLR) camera should be at the heart of your outfit. Look for a model with the option of a range of different lenses and other accessories.
- Totally mechanical cameras which do not rely on batteries work even under extreme conditions. Combined with an exposure meter which doesn't require batteries, you have the perfect match. One of the best and most indestructible cameras available is the FM2 Nikon.

- Compact cameras are generally excellent, but because of restricted focal ranges they have severe limitations for wildlife.
- Automatic cameras are often noisy when winding on, and loading film.
- Flashy camera bags can draw unwelcome attention to your kit.

Lenses

The lens is the most important part of the camera, with the greatest influence on the final result. Choose the best you can afford – the type will be dictated by the subject and type of photograph you wish to take.

For people

- The lens should ideally should have a focal length of 90 or 105mm.
- If you are not intimidated by getting in close, buy one with a macro facility which will allow close focusing. For candid photographs, a 70–210 zoom lens is ideal.
- A fast lens (with a maximum aperture of around f2.8) will allow faster shutter speeds which will mean sharper photographs. Distracting backgrounds will be thrown out of focus, improving the images' aesthetic appeal.

For wildlife

- Choose a lens of at least 300mm for a reasonable image size.
- For birds, lenses of 400mm or 500mm may be needed. They should be held on a tripod, or a beanbag if shooting from a vehicle.
- Macro lenses of 55mm and 105mm cover most subjects, creating images up to half life size. To enlarge further, extension tubes are required.
- In low light, lenses with very fast apertures help.

For landscapes

- Wide-angle lenses (35mm or less) are ideal for tight habitat shots (eg: forests) and are an excellent alternative for close ups, as you can shoot the subject within the context of its environment.
- For other landscapes, use a medium telephoto lens (100–300mm) to pick out interesting aspects of a vista and compress the perspective.

Film

Two types of film are available: prints (negatives) and transparencies (colour reversal). Prints are instantly accessible, ideal for showing to friends and putting into albums. However, if you want to share your experiences with a wider audience, through lectures or in publication, then the extra quality offered by transparency film is necessary.

Film speed (ISO number) indicates the sensitivity of the film to light. The lower the number, the less sensitive the film, but the better quality the final image. For general print film and if you are using transparencies just for lectures, ISO 100 or 200 are ideal. However, if you want to get your work published, the superior quality of ISO 25 to 100 film is best.

- Film bought in developing countries may be outdated or badly stored.
- Try to keep your film cool. Never leave it in direct sunlight.
- Do not allow fast film (ISO 800 or more) to pass through X-ray machines.
- Under weak light conditions use a faster film (ISO 200 or 400).
- For accurate people shots use Kodachrome 64 for its warmth, mellowness and gentle gradation of contrast. Reliable skin tones can also be recorded with Fuji Astia 100.
- To jazz up your portraits, use Fuji Velvia (50 ISO) or Provia (100 ISO).
- If cost is your priority, use process-paid Fuji films such as Sensia 11.
- For black-and-white people shots take Kodax T Max or Fuji Neopan.
- For natural subjects, where greens are a feature, use Fujicolour Reala (prints) and Fujichrome Velvia and Provia (transparencies).

Nick Garbutt is a professional photographer, writer, artist and expedition leader, specialising in natural history. He is co-author of 'Madagascar Wildlife' (Bradt Publications), and a winner in the BBC Wildlife Photographer of the Year Competition. John R Jones is a professional travel photographer specialising in minority people, and author of the Bradt guides to 'Vietnam' and 'Laos and Cambodia'.

are encouraged to involve their families in putting traditional skills to good use. The women of the Gobi are versatile – survival is their way of life – but interaction and information flow are essential to bring them out of their isolation, and radio programmes act as a bridge towards using their traditional skills more broadly for commercial purposes and for entertainment – Mongolian 'Woman's Hour'.

The towns have plenty of Mongolian newspapers and magazines, but people living in the countryside have less money, and there are no regular deliveries of papers.

Newspapers/media (in English)

Among Mongolia's many local newspapers are two weekly papers published in English: *The Mongol Messenger* and the *UB Post*, both available in Ulaanbaatar at the Central Post Office, street vendors and leading hotels, cost T200. *The Mongol Messenger* costs US$78 annually for overseas subscribers (including postage and mailing), or US$52 for local subscribers (contact *The Mongol Messenger* c/o Montsame News Agency, PO Box 1514, Ulaanbaatar; tel: 916 1 327857; email: montsame@magicnet.mn or monmessenger@mongolnet.com; web: www.mol/montsame).

The *UB Post* also costs US$78 annually for overseas subscribers; contact *UB Post* at 20 Ikh Toiruu, Ulaanbaatar; tel: 976 11 313427; email argamag@magicnet.mn; web: www.mongoliaonline.mn/argamag/ub_post

For those with access to a computer the best way to follow Mongolian daily news (in English) is through Email Daily News (EDN), who provide an excellent service by email: edn@pop.magicnet.mn.

Telephone

Mongolians jumped straight on to mobile phones and have almost avoided land lines. However, the telecommunications system has recently been upgraded by the French company Alcatel. Until then a system of Dutch payphones operated in the cities of Ulaanbaatar, Erdenet and Darkhan. Three types of cards are in use: 150 units provide the possibility to make calls for 150 minutes within the city, 300 units provide long-distance calls and 3,000 units allow the user to make international calls. The cost of international calls is around T20,000 (US$18) for 3,000 units.

You can receive and make international calls from your hotel room at the larger hotels. Outside Ulaanbaatar it is difficult to connect telephone calls of any kind, and it is probably better to plan on that basis. There are telephone offices with satellite dishes but they are not reliable. Mongolian Telecom (PO Box 1166 Sükhbaatar Square 9, Ulaanbaatar; tel: +976 11 320597; email: contact@mtcome.net; web: www.mng.net) provides telecommunications services throughout the country.

Telephone codes

The international code for Mongolia is 976. Provincial codes within Mongolia are as follows:

Arkhangai	73	Dornogobi	63	Ömnögobi	53
Baganuur	31	Dundgobi	59	Övökhangai	55
Bayan-Ölgii	71	Erdenet	35	Selenge	49
Bayankhongor	69	Gobi-Altai	65	Sükhbaatar	51
Bulgan	67	Khentii	39	Töv	47
Choir	75	Khovd	43	Ulaanbaatar	11
Darkhan	37	Khövsgöl	41	Uvs	45
Dornod	61	Nalaikh	33	Zavkhan	57

Emergency and other useful numbers

The following numbers are for **Mongolian speakers**, unless you have a translator standing by!

Fire station 101
Police 102
Traffic police 321008
Ambulance 103
Central Railway Station enquiries 194
International telephone enquiries 106116 (operator speaks English)
Ulaanbaatar telephone directory enquiry 109

Satellite phone

For those wishing to communicate by using a satellite phone from the middle of the Gobi, or elsewhere on expedition in Mongolia, Inmarsat's mini M is recommended (see box *Online camel* overleaf). You will need to purchase a licence from the Ministry of Infrastructure (Government House ll, 12a United Nations Street, Ulaanbaatar 46; tel: 11 321713; fax: 11 310612) before bringing a satellite phone into Mongolia.

Post

The Central Post Office (CPO) in UB is fairly reliable, although letters take a long time to reach their destinations. Stamps cost as follows:

* letters abroad from T550
* postcards T400
* registered mail T2,000
* express mail T5,000

Stamps may also be purchased at large hotels.

The Mongol Post (Mongol Shuudan; PO Box 1106, Sukhbaatar Square 9, Ulaanbaatar; tel: 11 313421) handles all types of postal services and also handles the subscriptions of both local and foreign newspapers.

Mongolian stamps are particularly splashy and colourful, and well worth collecting. Genghis Khan features as well as well-known celebrities – even Princess Diana has a Mongolian stamp in her honour. The Mongolian Stamp Company (PO Box 794, Ulaanbaatar; tel: +976 11 360509; fax: +976 11 314124) was set up to cater for stamp collectors worldwide.

Internet

It is true to say that Mongolia leapt from a state of non-communication with the outside world to immediate global connections via the internet. Since 2000 internet cafés have sprung up in Ulaanbaatar (see page 235), connecting the city to the rest of the world. Internet connections cost around T2,500 per hour (T1,500 per hour for students). Outside UB, internet facilities are available in some towns, currently including Mörön, Khovd, Arvaikheer and Kharkhorin, and the list is growing.

Business centres in the larger hotels also provide full communications services including internet access.

BUSINESS

Business hours in Mongolia tend to vary and offices are frequently closed for lunch. Government offices operate 09.00–17.00 weekdays only, and most offices in general close on Sundays. Shops and private businesses tend to open around 10.00

ONLINE CAMEL – TRANSFER OF MONGOLIAN FIELD NOTES FROM THE GOBI TO HOME
Jane Blunden

I can't believe this. I am sitting on a camel in the middle of the Gobi Desert typing on my laptop with frozen fingers. We arrived here after a 15-hour journey on roads you shouldn't travel on at this time of year. On the way we passed abandoned vehicles and had to dig ourselves out of snowdrifts. We stayed last night with a herdsman's family where warmth, good food and drink revived our little band, including Gallchüü and Enkhbold, my guide and driver. This morning we set off at first light, and leaving the ice and snow behind we drove further south and into the Gobi proper.

It was perishing cold as we set off, around −20°C with a piercing wind, but as the sun climbed in the sky the day warmed up. Had we been marooned on the icy roadside in the pale light of the freezing dawn, I had faith enough in my protective clothing to know it would save me from freezing to death. But just to make doubly sure the cold stayed on the outside, our kind hosts of last night made me a special present of a pair of hand-knitted camel-wool socks.

As we moved into the Gobi there were sand dunes and forests of the hardy saxaul bush to left and right, as well as huge expanses of open land where nomads raise herds of domestic camel, horses and goats for their livelihood.

My base is a family *ger* (or yurt), one of a group of four white *gers*, mushroom-like and snuggled among the saxaul bushes in the middle of the dunes. Children have been buzzing around me, fascinated by my computer. My host is a nomadic herdsman, who is, I am told, also a champion wrestler and a friend of my guide. We met by chance on the road this morning. We had pulled off the track to photograph a saxaul outcrop and by happy coincidence he and another man rounded the corner riding on two magnificent camels. Had it not been for this lucky encounter we might have spent weeks trying to find them.

My host herds 100 camel and 30 horses and tends more than 50 goat and 70 sheep, in a herding operation which in this part of the world is considered small. He and his young wife married last year. I was brought to this wild place as part of my research for the guidebook you are now reading. When I set out, I realised immediately how useful it would be to download my notes straight on to my computer at home.

Another ambition was to send words and pictures to *The Times* newspaper from the back of a camel without having to get down, requiring only the photograph to be taken by a friend on the ground and handed back to me, in the form of a tiny camera card which implants into a receiver card slotted into the side of my laptop. The sequence is simple: take a photo, transfer the camera card and save it on the computer, create and address an email message, attach the photo to it, switch on the satellite phone, connect and send. I decided to wait for the evening light to make contact by satellite phone as there is no hurry here.

To ensure the link went as smoothly as possible I went for a practice ride to see how the camel and I bonded. My new herdsman-wrestler friend, whose name was Pürevbish, donned his padded overcoat and coaxed my camel on to its knees so I could mount; all the while he made a soft sound like 'sög sög' which he repeated several times while pulling on a rope attached to a peg in the camel's nose. The animal responded by swaying and gently dropping to the ground. On I climbed and the two of us rode off, out into the wide Gobi.

A disturbed brown eagle wheeled overhead with a low screech; perhaps it had been about to catch its prey, some exciting desert mouse. By now we were out of sight of the camp and with the Gobi Desert on all sides I was glad of Pürevbish's company.

Hot *buuz* – Mongolian dumplings – were waiting for us on our return. It was a special occasion. The herdsman's family had gathered and relatives arrived, as is the custom at Tsaagan Sar. The woman of the house greeted her guests outside the family *ger* and each person was received with a kiss and outstretched arms holding a blue scarf, which symbolises goodwill and eternity. The new arrivals have travelled from a nearby village to pay their respects to Pürevbish's father, Gelegraash. In the general commotion of arrivals and greetings, 15-month-old Saraa has knocked over a huge bowl of *airak*. But Mongolian people are so good-natured and friendly that little upsets them.

As the evening approached, I mounted the camel again, this time with my computer and satellite phone clutched between me and the first hump. I knew the plan. I handed Galkhuu the digital Olympus C900 zoom and he gallantly took the shot and returned the camera card to transfer the picture. As a precaution, Gelegraash stood alongside just in case the camel bolted. With a little more practice I could have typed the entire piece happily from this position and sent it whizzing across oceans and continents, photograph attached, without having to touch ground from the camel's back. But given the cold I finished the piece from the warmth of the *ger*.

Meantime the sun has set on a magnificent Gobi day. A sparkling, dark, deep velvet sky enfolds us sleepers in our isolated *gers* tonight. Tomorrow we drive north when we shall stay with another herder's family.

Equipment review

A few years ago the equipment to send pictures such as these would have been available only to professionals with the budget of a multinational corporation behind them. The equipment I used is all available off the peg: an Apple G3 Powerbook computer, an Inmarsat mini M satellite phone and an Olympus C-900 Zoom digital camera. Given the cold in the Gobi, my equipment worked well overall, but I learnt a few lessons:

- Spare batteries for the phone and camera were essential.
- The AppleMac gave excellent running for two hours on battery power.
- On the advice of Chris Bonington's report from his latest Everest expedition, I packed several yards of good-quality black cotton to keep sand away from the equipment or to shield the screen in bright light. He also urged thorough testing before departure.
- No amount of training matters, however, if equipment is damaged in transit. I managed to snap the mains connection to the Inmarsat socket in Ulaanbaatar. But thankfully a Mongolian computer engineer provided a car battery and connected the cigarette lighter lead to it, which did the trick, although the lead itself was damaged later and had to be 'bandaged' using my medical supplies.

and close in the evening some time between 17.00 and 20.00. Everything shuts down at Tsagaan Sar, the lunar New Year, three days around late January to late February depending on the moon, and at Naadam, July 11–13. Other holidays are Mothers' and Children's Day, June 1. However, holidays do not necessarily mean days off work for Mongolians.

ELECTRICITY
220 V, 50 HZ. Sockets take two round prongs of European style. Computer users should also bring a surge plug, as the current varies.

TIME
There are three time zones. Ulaanbaatar is eight hours on from GMT. Western Mongolia is one hour less and eastern Mongolia is one hour more than Ulaanbaatar time.

CULTURAL DOS AND DON'TS
The following customs are mostly observed by Mongolians. Tourists need not be inhibited or overwhelmed by any such rules, as visitors are always made to feel most welcome. Mongolians are naturally superstitious. Their traditions dictate ritual behaviour that is part of their folk culture and religious practices.

Do:

- keep your hat on when entering a *ger*, but lift it as a sign of greeting
- sit immediately – or the host may feel uneasy
- talk about where you come from and show photographs of home if you have any with you
- shake a person's hand if you accidentally tread on or kick his or her foot
- dip the ring finger in the vodka and flick it in the air as a blessing, when offered vodka
- receive food, a gift or anything similar from a Mongolian with both hands or with the right hand supported at the wrist or elbow by the left hand
- take at least a sip or nibble of the delicacies offered – hold the cup to your mouth if you don't want to drink
- ensure that your sleeves are rolled down
- move inside the *ger* in a clockwise direction
- have a song ready to sing
- give gifts on departure not on arrival – and place gifts on a table not on the floor, as a sign of respect

Do not:

- step on the threshold of the *ger* - since this insults the owner
- trip on the threshold – happiness is driven away; if you trip, return and place a piece of fuel on the fire
- enter the *ger* with a sigh – this is considered disrespectful
- cross the path of an elderly person – this shows a lack of respect
- step over a hat – this insults the owner
- step over a lasso – it brings bad luck
- take food from the plate with your left hand
- touch the rim of the cup with your fingers – that is a bad omen
- throw away tea leaves – they are otherwise used in animal feed
- sit in the back of the *ger* without being invited

- turn your back to the altar or sit in front of it
- whistle in a *ger* – it brings bad luck

Customs relating to fire
Do not:

- stamp out a fire with your feet – fire is sacred
- step on fire ashes – otherwise the spirit of the dead enters the ashes
- bring fire to people in another *ger* – unless closely related
- use an axe near a fire – it threatens the god of the fire
- lie with your feet pointing towards the fire – it drives out the household gods
- put anything into the fire

Bradt Travel Guides is a partner to the 'know before you go' campaign, masterminded by the UK Foreign and Commonwealth Office to promote the importance of finding out about a destination before you travel. By combining the up-to-date advice of the FCO with the in-depth knowledge of Bradt authors, you'll ensure that your trip will be as trouble-free as possible.

www.fco.gov.uk/knowbeforeyougo

small group exploration...

The Oriental Caravan

+44 (0)20 7582 0716

www.theorientalcaravan.com

Wanderlust

THE ULTIMATE TRAVEL MAGAZINE

Launched in 1993, *Wanderlust* is an inspirational magazine dedicated to free-spirited travel. It has become the essential companion for independent-minded travellers of all ages and interests, with readers in over 100 countries.

A one-year, 6-issue subscription carries a money-back guarantee – for further details:

Tel.+44 (0)1753 620426
Fax. +44 (0)1753 620474

or check the *Wanderlust* website, which has details of the latest issue, and where you can subscribe on-line:

www.wanderlust.co.uk

Part Two

The Guide

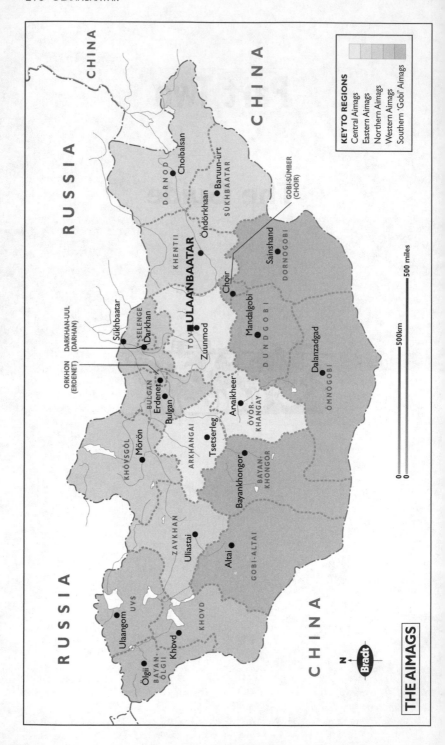

THE AIMAGS

KEY TO REGIONS
Central Aimags
Eastern Aimags
Northern Aimags
Western Aimags
Southern 'Gobi' Aimags

Ulaanbaatar

Ulaanbaatar is a thoroughly modern, concrete city, teeming with people and humming with taxis and buses, where only a hundred years ago men on horseback drove camel caravans and mule wagons along unpaved streets past hundreds of temple buildings, bells on the animal harnesses ringing loudly to attract attention to imported wares sold by Chinese, Russian and Mongol traders in the open-air markets. Today it is the general base for all business and development and it is the natural headquarters from which to plan all major travels to the countryside. Tourism operates essentially from the capital. Make the most of this opportunity and use the telephones to ring up and organise events in advance if travelling outside a tour group. You may also arrange concert tickets and so on for when you return to UB. International companies, UN and other development agencies are located in the capital, and political and government life is centred here.

Until recently, change happened slowly in Mongolia. Fifty years ago there were few buildings in the capital over five storeys high and the population was under 50,000. At the beginning of the 21st century, new hotels, restaurants and supermarkets have transformed the city from a fairly sleepy trading town into a thriving modern metropolis.

There is plenty of space. Soviet-style apartment blocks and government buildings line long, straight avenues, cut by ring roads and traversed by the main railway line between Moscow and Beijing (the Trans-Siberian/Trans-Mongolian Railway). The population has officially increased to over 800,000 people, and unofficially to almost a million, reflecting the drift of incoming herders who settle on the outskirts of town in makeshift *ger*-compounds. The city has all the conveniences of modern life and yet if you want to escape for a few hours the countryside is only a bus ride away.

The city is situated in a broad mountain valley near the River Tuul. Pine and fir forests cover the hillsides around the city, which is still fringed by *ger*. For much of its history Ulaanbaatar was known as Urga, a name that originated from the word *örgöö*, meaning a temple *ger*. In the mid-17th century, the monk Zanabazar, who became Mongolia's first religious leader (Öndör Gegeen), established a mobile capital. His residence moved from place to place along the Orkhon, Selenge and Tuul river valleys. In 1778, long after Zanabazar's death, the moving-capital of Mongolia finally settled on its present site. Thus Ulaanbaatar was once a felt-tented capital made up of thousands of *gers* and temples; indeed, it was known as *Ikh Khüree Khot*, the Great Monastery Town. Brick and stone temples were not constructed until 1837. In 1911 the city was renamed *Niislel Khüree* (Capital Monastery), when it became the political capital of autonomous Mongolia. In 1924, after further political upheaval, the city was renamed Ulaanbaatar after the

219

GREETINGS

The usual Mongolian greeting is *Sain bain uu?* (How are you?) and the expected answer is, *Sain, ta sain bain uu?* (Fine, how are you?), to which the response is, *Sain bainaa!* (fine!). This is usually followed by two key questions: *Ta khaanaas irsen be?* (Where have you come from?) and *Ta khaashaa yavakh ve?* (Where are you going?). When saying goodbye (*Bayartai*) Mongols may say *Sain yavaarai* (Have a good journey), to which the response is *Sain suuj baigaarai* (Stay well!). See *Appendix 1, Language*, page 373.

revolutionary leader, Sükhbaatar. During the 20th century most of the felt encampments gave way to high-rise apartment blocks and government buildings in the Soviet style. Most temple buildings were either destroyed or closed during the religious purges of the 1930s; one exception was Gandantegchinlen Monastery (see pages 235–6).

In this guide Ulaanbaatar is written as one word, the double vowels indicating long 'a's and stressed syllables. Although dubbed the 'coldest capital in the world', Ulaanbaatar gives the visitor a very warm welcome.

GETTING THERE

Transfers for groups from the airport to UB are usually pre-arranged involving a tour company and the transfer cost by minibus/taxi is US$20.

If you are not being met at the airport, transport into the centre of town (18km) is easily arranged. Taxis are available outside the airport; City Taxi tel:11 343433 or 11 344499; cost is approximately US$6 (roughly T7,000); locals pay less (around T5000). Yellow taxis are metered; taxis usually meet international flights; it is unlikely the Mongolian drivers speak any English but they understand hotel names and will get you there.

The airport bus into town costs US$4 (recommended for those who speak Mongolian or who are keen to pick up the language). Local public buses also travel to and from the airport but they are infrequent and often very crowded; cost T200.There are plenty of Mongolians keen to practise their language skills and eager to help new arrivals at the airport and in town, as those travelling on their own will find.

ORIENTATION

Ulaanbaatar is not an easy city to find your way around since street names and signposting is haphazard, but it is being improved. Signs are written in Cyrillic and addresses follow a local system that confuses even the Mongolians. Most people give directions not by street name and number but by saying that, for example, it's next to such-and-such a building with green walls. I recommend buying a large-scale city map of Ulaanbaatar on arrival to help find your way around and, if language fails, try the 'finger pointing' system with the map, used by travellers the world over. Maps of the city are now available in most tourist hotels, bookshops and at the Map Shop located on Ikh Toiruu 15 (outer ring road). See maps overleaf and on page 233, on how to get to the Map Shop.

Sükhbaatar Square lies at the heart of the city surrounded by government buildings and banks. The square is further surrounded by two ring roads: Baga Toiruu (the inner or smaller ring) and Ikh Toiruu (the outer or greater ring). The major avenue, Peace Avenue (Enkh Taivny Örgön Chölöö) borders the south section of the inner ring and runs east/west through the capital. Other avenues cross the smaller ring road on the west side to join the outer circle. Within the inner ring on the north side of the square you will find the Töriin Ordon (State Palace) buildings of the Mongolian Parliament, the Ikh Khural. A large equine monument to the revolutionary hero Sükhbaatar, who gave his name to the city, is the focus point of the square. The monument depicts Sükhbaatar as he sits astride his horse; at its base is the following statement: 'If we are able to unite our strength, then for us nothing will be impossible and we shall attain the heights of happiness for all.'

Finding your way around town

The city is divided into nine urban districts, including three outside the urban boundary, and many sub-districts.

North To the north of Sükhbaatar Square you will find Sükhbaatar district, with *ger* settlements sprawling to your left and right. The State Palace (Töriin Ordon), and the Sükhbaatar/Choibalsan mausoleum dominate the north side of the square. On the northwest side is the National History Museum and a block to the north is the Natural History Museum. Nearby you will find the police station.

South On the south side of Peace Avenue, below Sükhbaatar Square, stands the State Library and what is known as the 'Wedding Palace', where marriages take place. Below these buildings is the famous Children's Park, and near by is the Choyjin Lama Temple (five-minute walk from the square). The Bayangol and Edelweiss hotels are in this area; and a little further south (half-hour walk from the square, or a short taxi ride) is the Winter Palace of the Bogd Khan.

East On the eastern side of the square you will find the National Opera and Ballet Theatre, the Palace of Culture housing the Art Gallery and, nearby, the Institute of Technology. The Ulaanbaatar Hotel is in this area and a little further out is the Chinggis Khan Hotel. A number of embassies, including the British Embassy – on Peace Avenue – are located in this eastern quarter.

West Bordering the square on the west side is the main post office, banks, government buildings, MIAT airline offices and many small cafés and restaurants. A few blocks west along Peace Avenue is the State Department Store (Ikh Delger or 'Big Shop'), which is within walking distance from the square. The industrial part of town is across Peace Bridge, south of the railway line, a taxi ride away. The railway station is situated in the southwestern suburbs in Bayangol district and the long-distance bus station is next to it (see map overleaf). Beyond the outer ring road, to the northwest, you will find Gandan Monastery, Mongolia's largest Buddhist monastery, which is worth visiting (see pages 235–6).

Note The map of the city provided in this guide (see overleaf) lists the street names in transcribed Mongolian only. In the main text street names are referred to in English and transcribed Mongolian. For easy reference a transcription table (see page 377) is provided for those who want help to pronounce those signs written in Cyrillic (as many still are). Restaurant menus are often written in Mongolian, but more recently translated into English, especially in restaurants and bars frequented by tourists.

GETTING AROUND

Public transportation within the capital is extensive, cheap, and generally reliable.
    Mongolian trains service the route along the Trans-Mongolian line, the few stops include Darkhan and the border towns with Russia in the north and China in the south. Long-distance buses travel the country. Check timetables at the bus station.

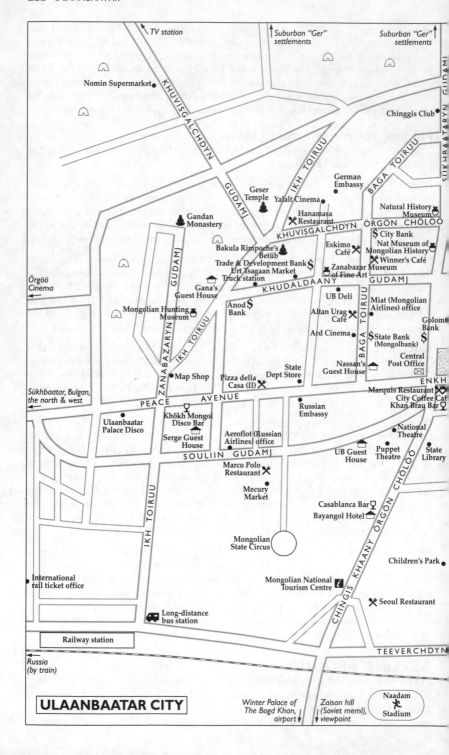

↑ TV station

↑ Suburban "Ger" settlements

↑ Suburban "Ger" settlements

Nomin Supermarket

Chinggis Club

KHUVISGALCHDYN

GUDAMI

IKH TOIRUU

BAGA TOIRUU

STIKHRAATARYN GUDAMI

Geser Temple

German Embassy

Yalalt Cinema

Gandan Monastery

Hanamasa Restaurant

Natural History Museum

ÖRGÖN CHOLOO

KHUVISGALCHDYN

$ City Bank

Bakula Rimpoche's Betüb

Eskimo Café

Nat Museum of Mongolian History

Trade & Development Bank $

Zanabazar Museum of Fine Art

Winner's Café

Örgöö Cinema

Urt Tsagaan Market
Truck station

KHUDALDAANY

GUDAMI

Gana's Guest House

UB Deli

Miat (Mongolian Airlines) office

Mongolian Hunting Museum

Anod $ Bank

Altan Urag Café

Golomt Bank

ZANABAZARYN

IKH TOIRUU

BAGA TOIRUU

Ard Cinema

$ State Bank (Mongolbank)

$

Central Post Office

Map Shop

Pizza della Casa (II)

State Dept Store

Nassan's Guest House

Sükhbaatar, Bulgan, the north & west ←

PEACE   AVENUE

Marquis Restaurant

ENKH

City Coffee Caf

Khan Brau Bar

Russian Embassy

Ulaanbaatar Palace Disco

Khökh Mongol Disco Bar

National Theatre

Serge Guest House

Aeroflot (Russian Airlines) office

UB Guest House

Puppet Theatre

State Library

SOULIIN GUDAMI

Marco Polo Restaurant

CHINGIS KHAANY ORGON CHOLOO

Mecury Market

Casablanca Bar

Bayangol Hotel

International rail ticket office

Mongolian State Circus

Children's Park

Mongolian National Tourism Centre

Seoul Restaurant

Long-distance bus station

Railway station

TEEVERCHDYN

← Russia (by train)

ULAANBAATAR CITY

Winter Palace of The Bogd Khan, airport ↓

Zaisan hill (Soviet meml), viewpoint ↓

Naadam Stadium

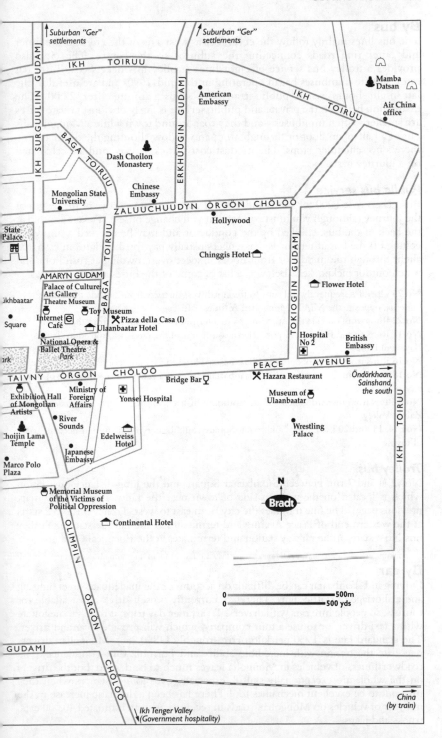

Suburban "Ger"
settlements

Suburban "Ger"
settlements

IKH TOIRUU

IKH TOIRUU

Mamba
Datsan

Air China
office

American
Embassy

IKH SURGUULIIN GUDAMJ

BAGA TOIRUU

ERKHUUGIIN GUDAMJ

Dash Choilon
Monastery

Chinese
Embassy

Mongolian State
University

ZALUUCHUUDYN ÖRGÖN CHÖLÖÖ

Hollywood

State
Palace

BAGA TOIRUU

Chinggis Hotel

TOKIOGIIN GUDAMJ

Flower Hotel

AMARYN GUDAMJ

Palace of Culture
Art Gallery
Theatre Museum

ikhbaatar

Toy Museum

Square

Internet
Café

Pizza della Casa (I)

Ulaanbaatar Hotel

National Opera &
Ballet Theatre
Park

Hospital
No 2

British
Embassy

ark

TAIVNY ÖRGÖN CHÖLÖÖ

PEACE AVENUE

Bridge Bar

Hazara Restaurant

Öndörkhaan,
Sainshand,
the south

Exhibition Hall
of Mongolian
Artists

Ministry of
Foreign
Affairs

Yonsei Hospital

Museum of
Ulaanbaatar

IKH TOIRUU

Choijin Lama
Temple

River
Sounds

Edelweiss
Hotel

Wrestling
Palace

Marco Polo
Plaza

Japanese
Embassy

Memorial Museum
of the Victims of
Political Oppression

N

Bradt

Continental Hotel

OLIMPIIN ÖRGÖN CHÖLÖÖ

0   500m
0   500 yds

GUDAMJ

CHÖLÖÖ

China
(by train)

Ikh Tenger Valley
(Government hospitality)

By bus

The bus lines mainly follow the central east–west axis of the city and the inner and outer ring roads connecting the suburbs to the centre. The city also provides a trolley bus service of eight lines (trolley bus tickets cost T100 flat rate). Private minibuses began operating in the mid-1990s and are useful in the late-night hours when public transport stops running after 22.00. The distinction between the private and public service is fairly obvious; private buses are smaller – often minibuses – and they roar around town while a Mongol leans out of a half-open door or through an open window shouting the destination – there's no scheduled stops. The modest cost of tickets vary, and are calculated on a journey basis.

Public bus service

Bus tickets cost T200 for adults and T50 for children, irrespective of the length of the journey (although you must pay again if you change buses). Tickets are sold at the back of the bus, checked by the conductor and may be checked again when getting off the bus at terminals. Passengers usually pay for their fares in cash and alight through the middle or front doors. Expect overcrowding at rush hour and watch out for pickpockets! Below is a list of some of the buses and their routes:

No 25 Operates frequently and runs to the northwest districts from outside the Ard Cinema, opposite the MIAT (Mongolian Airlines) offices.

No 22 Runs from outside the Ard Cinema to a terminus five minutes from the airport.

No 11 Runs to and from the airport (18km southwest of the city) and stops outside the Bayangol Hotel.

No 16 Runs from the park opposite Ulaanbaatar Hotel to a ger compound north of the city.

No 18 Runs from the park opposite Ulaanbaatar Hotel to a valley on the west side of the city.

No 7 Runs from the Ard Cinema to the southern districts of the city and terminates in the Zaisan Valley.

Nos 14, 15 and 20 leave from Sükhbaatar Square (Sükhbaataryn Talbai) to different parts of town.

Trolley bus

Nos 2, 4 and 7 run between Sükhbaatar Square and the long-distance bus station which is located on the western side of town near the railway station (see map, previous page). The line traverses the city from east to west. Trolley bus No 2 starts at the western end of Peace Avenue and terminates at the railway station. Trolley bus No 4 starts at the railway station and terminates at the Botanical Gardens.

By car

Driving in Ulaanbaatar can be difficult on account of the inadequate street lighting and a shortage of traffic signs. There are currently no self-drive cars available for tourists, so people hire cars with drivers. To arrange day trips, it is best to negotiate with a taxi driver, or to use a tour company, which will provide a car and driver. The standard rate is T250 per kilometre (roughly US$0.25c). Mongolian drivers negotiate the terrain with incredible ability and Formula-One confidence. The roadworthiness of vehicles in Mongolia leaves much to be desired, but the drivers on the whole are exceptionally skilful, especially over long distances when they turn out to be excellent mechanics too! There has been a dramatic increase in the number of vehicles on Mongolian roads in recent years – an estimated 40,000 cars, trucks and jeeps.

By taxi

Short taxi rides in and around UB, to and from your hotel to inner-city sights and restaurants will cost around T4,500 (US$4). Taxi ranks may be found outside the large hotels (eg: Ulaanbaatar Hotel), in front of museums such as the Zanabazar Museum, or outside the railway station during the main tourist season. When taxis are free they are readily hailed at any point. People tend to hail any passing car if they are stuck and negotiate a ride. This informal 'taxi service' operates at the moment. However, if you don't speak any Mongolian, this system presents difficulties and is not advisable. Some people ask the hotel receptionist or a Mongolian friend to write down travel details on a piece of paper to show the driver. Standard rates apply of T250 per kilometre (roughly US$0.25).

Taxi companies include City Taxi (24 hours, tel: 11 343433 and 11 344499). Han Gug (day time, tel: 11 451617 or 96111501); Taxi Ulaanbaatar(tel: 11 311385).

LOCAL TOUR OPERATORS

Many independent travellers deal directly with Mongolian tour companies; this is becoming more common year by year as people become more familiar with the use of the internet to get information and book holidays. Many travellers realise that behind all foreign tour operators is a Mongolian company doing the ground operations. The main difference between booking via a foreign travel company (ie: in your home country) and booking via the internet is the price; obviously foreign companies add a percentage to the price quoted by the ground operator. Things to consider when booking directly by internet are: ease of payment (most Mongolian tour companies do not yet accept credit card payments); insurance risks and reliability. Independent travellers use Mongolian companies on the spot and settle payments in cash (usually in US dollars or local currency), see list below.

In the following, the Classic tour (Mongolia's Golden Circuit) refers to a tour to one or more of the best known areas such as South Gobi, Lake Khövsgöl and the Orkhon Valley; often they include, among other things, sleeping in a *ger* and visiting nomadic families.

Ajnai Tours PO Box 49/1233, Ulaanbaatar; mobile: 99114890; fax: 11 312283; email: ajnai@magicnet.mn. Tours of the city, nomadic tours in the countryside.

Blue Wolf Expeditions PO Box 071, Bayan-Ölgii aimag; tel: 976 01 422; email: Canat_c@yahoo.com; web: www.mongoliaaltaiexpeditions.com. Travel experts in western Altai. Horse and camel treks, nature walks, cultural visits to Kazakh people.

Caravan Travel PO Box 46-268, Ulaanbaatar; tel/fax: 11 452486; email: caravan56@hotmail.com. Group tours, horseriding, birdwatching, botanic and photographic tours.

Chono Travel Room 27, Children's Palace, PO Box 825, Ulaanbaatar; tel: 11 369837, 11 311751; fax: 11 365158; email: chono@magicnet.mn. Mainly camping, horseriding.

Eden Tours PO Box 49/505, Ulaanbaatar; fax: 11 311273. Classic/group tours, trekking, birdwatching, horseriding.

Genco Tour Bureau Bayangol Hotel B-201, 5 Chinggis Khan Av, Ulaanbaatar; tel: 11 328960; fax: 11 321705; email: genco@magicnet.mn; web: www.mol.mn/gtb. Homestays with nomadic families, special-interest tours, fishing, trekking and cycling.

Genghis Expeditions PO Box 675, Ulaanbaatar; tel/fax: 11 310455; mobile: 11 992 98661; email: genghis-exp@magicnet.mn; web: www.genghisexpeditions.com. Cultural journeys, eco-tours, expeditions, adventure tours, short tours.

Gobiin Öglöö PO Box 1014, Ulaanbaatar; tel: 11 323394, 315552; fax: 11 459003; email: gobinogloo@magicnet.mn; web: www.mol.mn/gobinogloo. Classic cultural tours; horse-riding, trekking, camping, birdwatching, photo-safaris; Trans-Siberian and Trans-Chinese rail tours. 'Green Leaf Member' of PATA's code for Environmentally Responsible Tourism.

Huvsgul Travel PO Box 116, Ulaanbaatar; tel/fax: 11 326478; mobile: 11 991 16227. Outback adventures, nature tours, fishing, photography, riding, birdwatching.

Jules Vernes Mongolia Co Mongol Centre, Chingeltei District 2, Ulaanbaatar; tel/fax: 11 329854; mobile: 11 99195415; email: julesvernesmgl@mongol.net; web: www.tripmongolia.com. Tours to the desert and the steppes, yak-cart journeys and lake journeys.

Juulchin Foreign Tourism Corporation Genghis Khan Av 58, Ulaanbaatar; tel: 11 328428; email: juulchin@mongol.net or jlncorp@magicnet.mn; www.mol.mn/juulchin and www.mongoliaonline.mn/juulchin. Group/Classic tours, cultural and educational journeys, horseriding, trekking, kayaking, rafting, camel trekking, photo-safaris and big-game hunting.

Kara Korum Mongolian Youth Federation Bldg, PO Box 44/157, Ulaanbaatar; tel: 11 322188; email: karakorum@magicnet.mn. Classic/group tours, camping, horseriding.

Karakorum Expeditions PO Box 542, Ulaanbaatar; mobile: 99116729; email: info@GoMongolia.com; www.GoMongolia.com. Specialists in active adventure travel. Packages are all inclusive – transport, bikes, tents, accommodation. Tours include 'Magic of Mongolia' and 'Sands of the Gobi'; winners of the Pacific Asia Travel Association (PATA) 2002 Gold Award for Ecotourism.

Khovsgol Lodge Company Tel: 99115929; email: info@hovsgol.org; www.hovsgol.org. Amongest the oldest, most reliable tourism companies. Can make arrangements on short noice for custom travel throughout Mongolia; horseback riding, fishing, rafting, trekking.

MAT Bayangol Hotel Chinggis Khan Av, Ulaanbaatar; tel/fax: 11 310917. Classic/group tour, horseriding, birdwatching, hunting.

MAT D&G Mongolian Youth Federation Bldg, PO Box 46/937, Ulaanbaatar; tel: 11 327837; fax: 11 327837; email: mat@magicnet.mn. Camel riding, horseriding, camping, Classic tour.

Mat Outdoor Safaris Baga Toiruu 10, Mongolian Youth Federation Building, Room 414, Ulaanbaatar; tel/fax: 11 311008; mobile: 11 99114745; email: matos@magicnet.mn. Adventure tours, hunting.

Mon EcoTour Government Building 4, Room 36, Peace Avenue, Ulaanbaatar; tel: 11 451270; email: moneco@magicnet.mn. Rafting, fishing, birdwatching, camping.

MonAnd Company Government Building 4, Peace Av, Ulaanbaatar; tel: 11 452238, 310579; fax: 11 310579; email: MONAND@magicnet.mn or damost@magicnet.mn. Nature tours, camping, fishing, horseriding, cross-border travel to southern Siberia.

Mongol Altai Travel Company Chinggis Khan Hotel, Khükh Tenger St (recently changed to Tokyo St) 5, Ulaanbaatar; tel/fax: 11 325188. Classic/group tours, camping, trekking, horseriding and hunting.

Mongol Safari Baigal Ordon, Ulaanbaatar; tel: 11 360267, 363931; fax: 11 360067; email: monsafari@magicnet.mn. Hunting and trekking tours, eco-tours, horse journeys.

Mongol Tour OK PO Box 251, Ulaanbaatar; tel: 11 311447; email: mtour@magicnet.mn. Classic/group tours, horseriding, camping, photo-safaris, kayaking.

Mongol Tours PO Box 722, Ulaanbaatar; tel: 11 32330. Hunting and photo-safaris.

Mongolian Youth Development Centre/SSS Travel Mongolian Youth Federation Bldg, Room 207, Baga Toiruu 44, Ulaanbaatar; tel: 11 328410; email: sssmydc@magicnet mn; www.ssstravel.mn. Summer camps, educational and cultural tours, international exchanges.

Nature Tours Mongolian Youth Federation Building, Room 212, PO Box 49/53, Ulaanbaatar; tel: 11 311801; email: NATTOUR@magicnet.mn. Classic/group tours, camping, birdwatching, fishing.

Nature's Door and **Lakeside Lodges** (partners with 4th World Adventure, see page 148) Ulaanbaatar, Director Yadem Otgonbayar, mobile: 992 60919 or 961 69393; email:

info@4thworldadventure.com; web: www.4thworldadventure.com. Adventure holidays in the Khövsgöl area with own facilities including horses, mountain bikes, kayaks, trekking – all with experienced guides.

Nomadic Expeditions Building 76, Suite 28 (next to the State Department Store)1-40, Peace Av, Ulaanbaatar; tel: 11 313396, 11 325786; fax: 11 320311; email: mongolia@nomadicexpeditions.com; web: www.nomadicexpeditions.com. Horse tours, festival tours, Gobi tours.

Nomads Tours & Expeditions PO Box 1008, Ulaanbaatar; email: info@nomadstours.com; web: www.nomadstours.com. Arranges tours and expeditions, professional service and high standards, discreet, low key and highly efficient. Clients range from expedition tours to film crews and celebrities.

Nomin Tours State Department Store, 4th floor, 44 Peace Av, Ulaanbaatar; tel: 11 313232; fax: 11 314242; email: tour@nomin.net.mn; web: www.nomin.net.mn/tour. Classic tours to the Gobi, Terelj, Manzhsir Monastery, White Lake, the Tsaatan people of northern Mongolia, festivals and nature tours.

Nukht Ecological Travel PO Box 112, Nukht Hotel, Ulaanbaatar; tel: 11 310241; fax: 11 325630; email: nukht@magicnet.mn. Nature tours, Gobi tours, *ger* stays in Terelj resort, river rafting.

Off the Map Tours Bayanzurkh District, 13th Microdistrict, Building 4, No 148, Ulaanbaatar; tel: 11 458964; fax: 11 353353; email: offthemap@magicnet.mn. Adventure and cultural tours with friendly and experienced guides; flexible arrangements. Hiking, horse- and yak-riding. Specialists in mountain-biking and cross-country skiing. Trans-Siberian train journeys, including tours in Beijing and Moscow. Tours for individual travellers as well as large groups.

Run Wild 40 Miangat St, Building 68, Sükhbaatar District, Ulaanbaatar; tel/fax: 11 315374; email: info@outer-mongolia.com and runwild@magicnet.mn; web: www.outer-mongolia.com and www.runwild.co.uk. Experts in rafting and adventure travel; tailor-made holidays in Mongolia.

Samar Magic Tour Company PO Box 329, Ulaanbaatar; tel/fax: 11 327503; email: samartours@magicnet.mn. Horseriding, camping, Classic/group tours.

Shuren Sükhbaatar Square 11, Ulaanbaatar; tel: 11 323363; fax: 11 323363. Classic/group tours.

Tsolmon Travel Central State Library, Room 315, Chinggis Khan Av, Ulaanbaatar; tel: 11 322870; fax: 11 310323; email: tsolmon@magicnet.mn. Fishing, birdwatching, camping, horseriding.

Tulga Travel PO Box 482, Ulaanbaatar; tel: 11 312292; fax: 11 312292; email: tulgacom@magicnet.mn. Classic and camping tours.

Uvidast Tour Company PO Box 155, Ulaanbaatar; tel/fax: 11 312071; email: uvidasttour@magicnet.mn. Camping, classic/group tours, horseriding.

WHERE TO STAY

When travelling independently in Mongolia I usually stay at the Edelweiss or Bayangol. Another of my favourite hotels is Hotel Ulaanbaatar, the first place I stayed when visiting Mongolia in 1978. Back then it was known as Hotel A and foreign tourists had only one other choice, Hotel B, which no longer exists. Things have moved on considerably since those days and Ulaanbaatar offers new and exciting choices as more hotels open to accommodate the growing number of visitors. A selected number of hotels of differing prices are listed below. For visitors on business trips a number of these hotels – Ulaanbaatar, Bayangol, Continental, Flower and others – have good business centres with all the necessary communications facilities. The larger hotels all have restaurants and bars and many have shops too, so that you can buy presents and send postcards without a problem. The receptionists will take endless time and trouble to help travellers, book theatre tickets and generally help out in a hundred and one different ways.

Hotels

There are many hotels to choose from depending on what you want to pay. They range from US$15 for a single room at a hostel (less if you are prepared to share a dormitory at US$8), to a double room with bathroom at a top hotel for US$95 plus; de-luxe suites range from US$150 per night and presidential suites cost up to US$280. Credit-card payments are accepted in most hotels listed below, except in the hostels, where bills are normally settled in US dollars or local currency. The prices below are subject to change and quoted at high-season rates.

Upper range

Prices range from US$70 to US$150, deluxe US$200 plus.

Ulaanbaatar Hotel Sükhbaatar Square 14, Ulaanbaatar; tel: 11 320237; fax: 11 324485; email: ubHotel@magicnet.mn. Lots of comings and goings from this hotel, which is an excellent place to stay as it is centrally located. Rooms are large and airy, and there is something of an olde-worlde style to the décor. Good business centre; large dining-room; private rooms for entertaining and several bars and a dancing area. Private concerts and special parties are celebrated here. Rooms: 7 de luxe (US$185); 38 semi-de luxe (US$135); 50 first-class single (US$80); 24 first-class twin (US$110)

Bayangol Hotel Chinggis Khan Av 28, PO Box-43, Ulaanbaatar; tel: 11 312255, 3128869; fax: 11 326880; email: bayangol@magicnet.mn; web: www.mongoliaonline.mn/bayangol. This multi-storey building is one of the busiest and largest hotels in UB, frequented by tour groups and the business community. The hotel's Casablanca Bar is among the city's nightspots (see page 231); the foreigners' restaurant is usually full. Although fairly austere-looking in terms of architecture, Bayangol Hotel is a lively, fun place to stay. Rooms:19 de luxe (US$220); 157 twin (US$106); 22 single (US$81)

Chinggis Khaan Hotel Blue Sky, Khökh Tenger (now Tokyo) St 5, Ulaanbaatar; tel: 11 313380; fax: 11 312788; email: chinggis-hotel@magicnet.mn. This is a grand hotel of immense proportions and modern-style architecture, with lots of glass and chrome; it attracts tour groups and business people. The restaurants are fairly pricey – main courses cost T5–6,000, deserts T2,000, beer T1,800–2,300. The hotel has a swimming pool, gym and sauna and several restaurants and bars. The café in the entrance hall serves hot chocolate and other drinks. Rooms: 2 presidential suites (US$280); 36 de luxe (US$150); 105 twin (US$120); 35 single (US$80); breakfast included. The hotel has access to a large supermarket at the back of the building.

Continental Hotel Embassy St, Peace Av, Ulaanbaatar (just south of Sükhbaatar Square beside the Japanese Embassy); tel: 11 323829; fax: 11 329630; email: continental@magicnet.mn; web: www.ulaanbaatar.net/continentalHotel. A large modern hotel where diplomats and foreign groups stay. Facilities and services include a business and travel centre; banquet room; sauna and massage; swimming pool; comfortable rooms and prompt service. The Venus Restaurant and Bar serves European food. Rooms: 8 de luxe (US$170); 29 twin (US$135).

Edelweiss Hotel Peace Av, 15A/5, Ulaanbaatar; tel: 11 312186, 11 325091; fax: 11 325252; email: edelweiss@mongol.net. This is one of my favourites. Small and intimate, it has an easy-going atmosphere. A good place to hold quiet meetings and to entertain guests is in one the hotel's restaurants, serving European and Asian food. There is a sauna on the ground floor – open 15.00–21.00; massage, US$16 an hour; helpful reception. Rooms: 4 de luxe (US$95); 16 first-class twin (US$75).

Mid range

Prices US$70–100, suites US$155.

Bishrelt Hotel Khuvisgalchdyn Örgön Chölöö 3/1, Ulaanbaatar; tel: 11 313789, 310063; fax; 11 313792; email: bishrelt@magicnet.mn. This five-storey building left of the Chandmani Centre is a good, small hotel with comfortable rooms. Well located, it caters for tour groups and individual travellers. The restaurant serves Bulgarian food. Rooms: 1 presidential suite (US$132); 9 de luxe (US$99); 6 first-class twin (US$77).

Flower Hotel Blue Sky (Khökh Tenger) St 12, Ulaanbaatar; tel: 11 458330; fax: 11 455652; email: flower@magicnet.mn. Located near the British Embassy, the Flower caters for large groups. Prices are competitive, the food is good and receptionists are helpful. Rooms: 8 de luxe (US$154); 56 semi-de luxe (US$120); 88 twin (US$94); 32 standard single (US$70).

White House Hotel Amarsanaa St, Ulaanbaatar; tel: 11 367872; fax: 11 369973, 365158; email: chono@magicnet.mn; web: www.whitehouseHotel.mn. Rooms: double (US$94), single (US$70).

Less expensive hotels

Price range US$35–90.

Marco Polo Hotel Irkhüügyn St, Ulaanbaatar; tel: 11 310803; fax: 11 311273. Rooms: double (US$70); single (US$35).

Sarora Hotel Seoul St (Seüliin Gudamj) 12/b, Ulaanbaatar; tel: 11 327831; fax: 11 327239; email: sarora@magicnet.mn. Rooms: double (US$60); single (US$45).

Tuushin Hotel Amar St, Ulaanbaatar; tel: 11 323162; fax: 11 325903; email: tuushin@magicnet.mn. Rooms: double (US$90); single (US$40).

Undruul Hotel Peace Av, Ulaanbaatar ; tel: 11 455108; fax: 11 455016; email: undruul@magicnet.mn. Rooms: double (US$85); single (US$45).

Nuht Hotel Central PO Box 112, Ulaanbaatar; tel: 11 310025, 310241; fax: 11 325630; email: nuht@magicnet.mn. Rooms: double (US$60), single (US$40).

New Capital Hotel Friendship Av 39 (west of British Embassy), PO Box 1029/46, Ulaanbaatar; tel: 11 458235; fax: 11 458281. Rooms: double (US$50); single (US$30).

Guesthouses/hostels

Prices range from US$8 to US$20.

Backpackers' Hostel Seoul (Seüliin) Av, near the State Department Store, Peace Av; tel:11 313380, 11 315398, 11 328 410. Will pick up at the airport; located near the Mercury market for food shopping. Fax and email service, laundry and travel service; café food.

Gana's Guest House Tel: 11 321078; email: ganasger@magicnet.mn. Near the Ganden Monastery in the suburbs of a ger compound. Slightly run down but cheap and cheerful.

Nassan's Hostel Near Sükhbaatar Square; tel: 11 321078; email: nassan2037@yahoo.com. Helpful and friendly; will arrange travel and help organise onward journeys, provide guides and transport. Guests can use the kitchen to prepare their own food.

Serge Guest House Off Peace Av near the railway and long-distance bus station; tel 11 320267, mobile: 99198204; email: sergtour@hotmail.com. Provides cheap accommodation and an information service for independent travellers (ie: backpackers).

Ger accommodation

Many ger compounds surround the city. They are seen but generally not visited by tourists who are itching to leave UB and get out into the countryside to experience the life of the nomads and stay in a ger!

Family gers and ger camps provide warm hospitality and comfortable, rudimentary accommodation; prices range from around US$35 per night to US$50, including three meals. They top the list for the unique experience they offer. Private *gers* and *ger* camps welcome visitors during the tourist season from June to late September. Some camps remain open in winter, while others close. Please check the *ger* camp list (see Appendix 2, pages 278–80).

WHERE TO EAT AND DRINK

The majority of Mongolians eat meat with lots of fat, which sustains them through the long cold winters, especially if they live in the countryside where people kill their own food. However, there are a number of newly opened international restaurants in the capital, including French, Italian, Indian, Chinese and Korean. There are also several 'foreign' cafés but they open and close quite frequently.

Cafés

Millie's Café has moved to a new building in the Marco Polo Plaza next to the Choijin Lama Temple; tel: 11 328721. One of the long-time favourites of foreign residents in UB, with a relaxed atmosphere and friendly service. Serves cheeseburgers, sandwiches and milkshakes; famous for creamy coffee, homemade pies and ice-cream. Open Mon–Sat 10.00–19.00, Sun 11.00–15.00.

Winner's Café Centre of town off Sükhbaatar Square; mobile tel: 99118822. Serves European cuisine, wine and soft drinks. Open daily 07.00–23.00.

Altan Urag Café Located off the small ring road (Baga Toiruu); tel: 11 328900. Serves European food, a variety of steaks, beers, wine and soft drinks. Open daily 10.00–01.00.

City Coffee Café Off Chinggis Av, a few minutes' walk south of Sükhbaatar Square; tel: 11 328077. Serves Japanese and Korean hotpot, grilled meat, sweet cakes and fresh bread; beer and soft drinks; coffee. Open Mon–Fri 08.00–24.00, Sat–Sun 10.00–24.00.

Backerei Conditorei Café On the small ring road (Baga Toiruu) west of Sükhbaatar Square within walking distance; tel: 11 324734. Serves Austrian-style cakes, coffee, hot chocolate and soft drinks. Open daily 08.00–20.30.

Eskimo Café Outer ring road (Ikh Toiruu) near Ganden Monastery, west of Sükhbaatar Square; tel: 11 316651. Serves Ukrainian food, soft drinks and beer. Open 10.00–24.00 daily.

California Café Souliin Gudamj (Seoul Av) opposite Aeroflot. Very popular café with the best loos in UB. Open daily 10.00–24.00.

Selected restaurants

In addition to the following, see the list of *Bars* below, many of which serve meals.

Marquis Restaurant Corner of Chinggis Av (Chinggis Khaany Örgön Chölöö) and Peace Av, immediately south of Sükhbaatar Square; tel: 11 318285. Serves French and international cuisine, free aperitifs. Cost US$25 per meal. Open daily 12.00–24.00.

Seoul Restaurant Children's (Nairamdal) Park; tel: 11 329709, 315394. Has its own bakery on the ground floor, a restaurant on the first floor and a popular buffet on the second floor. Serves Asian (Korean) and international cuisine. Average cost: US$10 (buffet) US$25 (restaurant) per meal. Open 12.00–2400 daily.

Hanamasa Restaurant Corner of Khövsgöl Av and Peace Av. Serves Japanese and Chinese food. Pleasant surroundings with wooden tables, high-backed chairs. Diners cook their own choice of raw meat and vegetables on hotplates centred on each table, creating their own special dish. Also serves bowls of raw vegetables, nuts, garlic, tofu and salads (for vegetarians). Paul Klee posters decorate the walls. There is a bar in the entrance area. The average price for a meal is US$10. Drinks are additional. Whisky costs US$3.40 a glass; Mongolian vodka US$3 a glass. Open 12.00–24.00 daily.

Hazara Restaurant Peace Av 6, Bayanzürkh District; tel: 11 455071. Northern Indian cuisine, with a popular lunchtime menu. An excellent place to eat for vegetarians. Special dishes include vegetable curries, Tandoori chicken and kebabs. Cost US$10–20 a meal. Open 12.00–14.30, 18.00–22.00 daily.

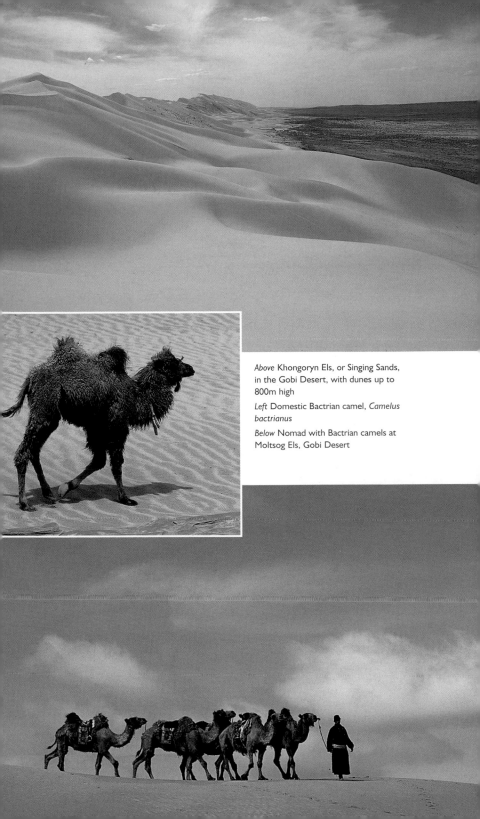

Above Khongoryn Els, or Singing Sands, in the Gobi Desert, with dunes up to 800m high

Left Domestic Bactrian camel, *Camelus bactrianus*

Below Nomad with Bactrian camels at Moltsog Els, Gobi Desert

Above Nomads moving livestock to summer grazing in northern Mongolia

Right Yak, *Bos mutus*, with traditional saddle near Lake Khövsgöl

Below Przewalski's horse or *takhi, Equus przewalskii*, the only wild horse to survive in modern times

Below right Long-eared Asiatic hedgehog, *Erinaceus auritus*, Gobi Desert

Marco Polo Restaurant In a white five-storey building off Eldev-Ochirin Gudamj, near the United Nations building; tel:11 310783. Serves a large variety of dishes; international-style food. Cost US$10–20. Open 12.00–21.00 daily.

Khandorjiin Urguu Ger Restaurant Seoul St near the Bayangol Hotel; tel:11 320763. Mongolian and European food, plus beer, wine and soft drinks. Interesting architecture and great ambience. Cost US$15–20. Open 10.00–24.00 daily.

Avtai Khan Urguu Ger Restaurant Ulaanbaatar 12, north east of Sukhbaatar Square (you may need a taxi to get there), near the Chinggis Khan Hotel; tel: 11 888090. Serves traditional Mongolian food in a *ger* setting, with wine, beer and soft drinks available. Cost US$15–20. Open 11.00–23.00 daily.

Khan Kalbi Restaurant Ider Centre, Bayangol District; tel:11 300828. Good quality, reasonably priced Korean food at an average price of US$10. Open 12.00–21.00 daily.

Pizza de la Casa On Peace Av, left of the State Department Store; tel: 11 324114, 323991; also on the outer side of the small ring road (Baga Toiruu) opposite Ulaanbaatar Hotel; tel: 11 312072. Good place to meet friends but make sure you arrange which of the two locations to meet. Serves many different kinds of pizza, pasta, burgers and fresh bread – convenient and fast. Average price US$8. Open Mon–Fri 08.00–21.00, Sat and Sun 10.00–19.00.

Los Bandidos Restaurant Behind the small post office situated opposite the Peace and Friendship Palace. Both Mexican dishes with hot sauces and Indian cusine. Tequila (super-strong Mexican alcohol), *lassie* (yoghurt drink), draught beer, wine and soft drinks; tel: 11 194618. Cost US$10–20. Open 12.00–23.00 daily.

Silk Road Bar & Grill North of Marco Polo Plaza opposite Choijin Monastery; mobile: 919 14455; web: www.silkroad.com. Excellent Sunday lunch buffet; good steaks. Open daily 12.00–24.00.

Bars and discos

Nightlife centres on the bars and discos where food as well as drink is often also available and live music predominates. Many places listed below stay open to

MODERN MUSIC – POP AND ROCK
Gunjiimaa Ganbat

Soyol Erdene was the first professional rock band in Mongolia in the 1970s. B Naranbaatar, a founding member of the group, went on to work in Siberia with the well-known Ensemble Baikal in Buryatia – one of the most popular folk-song ensembles. Örgöö, a popular rock band of the 1980s, is back in fashion after some time in oblivion. I Bolooj is still the leader of the eight-man group. The group has recently launched the Örgöö, a club in downtown Ulaanbaatar at the Bogdkhangai Restaurant. Other rock groups include Haranga, Kamerton and Freezone.

B Sarantuyaa (known as Saraa) was the top pop idol of the 20th century, with 71.3% of votes in the opinion poll conducted by a Mongolian newspaper. The all-female group Lipstick are famous for their hit song *Uchralyn Blues (Rendezvous Blues)*. Lipstick were contracted to perform as part of the 2000 election campaign by the present government. The group Chinggis Khan made sensational news when they gave a free performance in Khentii Aimag to promote the MPRP (Mongolian People's Revolutionary Party) during the election campaign.

The singer D Oyuuntülkhüür introduced Mongolian music to Japan and has been recognised for her charity work. Concerts in Ulaanbaatar can attract audiences of up to 3,000 people.

midnight and later. Until 1990 there were very few bars in Ulaanbaatar, but nowadays a huge number have opened and it is difficult to keep track of them. Beer is the most popular drink and costs T1,200–2,000, with vodka at T1,200–2,000; food is also served. Prices may vary slightly from place to place. The discos have all the latest chart music and, yes, Mongolians have their own Spice Girls – a band called Lipstick, the Spice Girls of the steppes. Mongolian youth are keen to look good and take a great interest in trendy gear. Most teenagers just want to hang out in the bars and discos, chatting with friends and listening to music. Traditional circle dancing is when everyone stands in a circle and one person dances in the centre, similar to Celtic dances, except in UB people just sway to the music – no steps. Nightclubs charge an entrance fee, and tourists should expect to pay around US$10–20 (Mongolians pay less).

Bridge Bar Peace Av (Enkh Taivny Örgön Chölöö), a two-storey building east of the Selbe River bridge; tel: 11 450784. Live music, jazz, and a variety of performances. Open daily 09.00–0400.
Casablanca Bar Bayangol Hotel; reservations tel: 11 312255 ext 6102. Romantic and a good place for 'oldies' – that is, anyone over 35! You may sit and listen to light Mongolian music and drink an ice-cold beer or vodka. The menu provides both Western and Asian cusine: T-bone steak, lamb and pork chops; fish and chips; Thai and Malay dishes. Open daily 12.00–03.00.
Chinggis Club 5–10-minute walk north of Sükhbaatar Square; tel: 99191163. Live traditional and pop music. Serves European cuisine at reasonable prices and home-brewed Mongolian beer. Open 10.00–22.00 daily.
Dave's Place East of Sükhbaatar Square near the Opera House (Sükhbaatar's statue gestures towards the pub so it's unmissable!). Great Cornish pasties. Popular quiz night Thu. Open daily 09.00–24.00.
Face Club Midway between Khovsgol Av and Peace Av, west of Sükhbaatar Square, near the small ring road (Baga Toiruu); tel: 11 311976. Live music, pop and jazz. Serves cocktails, wine and soft drinks. Open daily 20.00–04.00.
Hollywood Disco Bar Across the River Selbe opposite the Chinngis Khan Hotel; tel: 11 188888. Long-time favourite restaurant and bar with billiard table, serving wine, beer, hot drinks and food. Restaurant open Mon–Sat 10.00–24.00; bar open daily 19.00–02.00.
Khan Bräu Bar Chinggis Khan Av; tel: 11 324064. Serves beer-garden style food with beer; disco dancing. Open 10.00–22.00 daily.
Khökh Mongol Disco Bar Peace Av near the Map Shop; tel: 99121005. Popular nightclub, with disco dancing and bar, serving beer and soft drinks. Open 20.00–03.00.
River Sounds Olympic (formerly Marx) Av, within walking distance south of Sükhbaatar Square; tel: 11 320497. New and popular, has live music and disco dancing. Beer and soft drinks available. Open daily 13.00–02.00.
Tuushin Bar Amar St; tel: 11 323162, 325850. Chilled beer and other drinks. Open 15.00–24.00 (closed Sun).
Ulaanbaatar Palace Disco Bar Peace Av, south side, near the outer ring road. Provides a sauna and massage; karaoke and dancing; tel: 11 682892. Open daily 11.00–04.00.

SHOPPING
In general, shops open 9.00–18.00 weekdays and Saturdays. Most are closed on Sunday. Markets open later (10.00) and stay open in the evenings to 20.00.

Where to go
Gobi Factory shop Beside the Gobi Factory, Khan-Uul District, Ulaanbaatar; tel: 11 342713, fax: 11 343081. For cashmere. Go there by taxi, as it is difficult to find.
Buyan Cashmere Shop Zanabazar St (which leads to Ganden Monastery); tel: 11 325423

Gobi Cashmere House
Revolutionaries' Av (Khuvisgalchdyn
Örgön Chölöö), in the same building as
the Hanamasa Restaurant.
Khan's Ger Right side of the Youth
Federation Building, behind the
Ulaanbaatar Hotel, near the small ring
road (Baga Toiruu); tel: 11 328410.
Souvenirs, traditional arts and crafts.
Map Shop Ikh Toiruu 15, Ulaanbaatar
44; mobile: 91156023, 91148698; fax: 11
322164; email: caen@mongol.net. See
opposite.
Xanadu Marco Polo Plaza; tel: 11
319748; web: www.xanadu.mn.
Bookshop and provider of fine wines.

MAP SHOP, ULAANBAATAR

For **art**, those galleries exhibiting paintings for sale are found beside Gandan
Monastery, near the State Department Store, at the Exhibition Hall of the Union
of Mongolian Artists, located near the Central Post Office on Chinngis Avenue,
south of Sükhbaatar Square (tel: 11 327474), and in the Marco Polo Plaza Gallery
(tel: 11 330269). Hotel lobbies are now a favourite place to find small works –
prices vary from around US$20–200 for the work of unknown artists.

Food and general supplies

Western and Asian goods and foodstuffs are available in the main markets and
supermarkets, including the famous outdoor Black Market (Ulaanbaatar Central
Market). Also known as Narantuul Market, it is the biggest in town. Recently more
than T5 billion was spent on constructing the stalls which sell food, clothing,
shoes, household items and DIY building and decorating items, antiques and
souvenirs. Some 70–140,000 people visit the market daily. Watch your handbag
and wallets as pickpockets operate in the crowds. For tourists the best way to get
there is by taxi – a ten-minute drive from Sükhbaatar Square.

Another open market is Urt Tsagaan Market, located within walking distance
west of Sükhbaatar Square; closed on Tuesday. It provides clothing and travel
necessities. Indoor markets and supermarkets include Nomin Supermarket, the
fastest-growing supermarket in UB, located in the western district above Gandan
Monastery. It provides fresh food and vegetables. The UB Deli in the Aero Voyage
Building (2nd floor) on Khudaldaany Avenue (tel: 325240; email:
cashell@netvigator.com; web: www.apipcorp.com) offers a delivery service. The
State Department Store is one of the older more traditional stores, located on Peace
Avenue. Easy to get to, it offers food, leather goods, clothes and souvenirs. Open
weekdays 09.00–20.00 and Sunday 10.00–18.00. Despite modern designer clothes
the Mongolian traditional dress outshines them all – the elegant, long-sleeved,
wrap-around robe, tied at the waist by a colourful sash. However, American-style
clothes are common and there are two Wrangler jeans stores in UB.

PRACTICALITIES
Banks

Anod Bank Khudaldaany St, Ulaanbaatar; tel: 11 312412; fax: 11 313070;
email:anod@magicnet.mn; web:www.anod.mn. Open Mon–Fri 09.00–13.00, 14.00–17.00.
On Barilgachdyn Square, near the Trade and Development Bank.

FOOD SHOPPING IN ULAANBAATAR
Nicolle Webb

There are numerous places in UB to buy food, clothes and other essentials. They range from little kiosks and small shops to larger shopping centres and markets. The huge, open-air central market is commonly called the 'Black Market' (not an illegal market) where you can find almost anything you need. It is always very crowded (watch your handbags and wallets!). In the centre of the city there is a large food market called the Mercury Market (also known as the New Circus Market) located off Seoul Avenue, which offers a wide range of fruit, vegetables, meat and imported foodstuffs. It is also where most foreigners shop, so prices are higher. The State Department Store (Ikh Delgüür) has undergone a major renovation in recent years. Its first floor offers much the same products as the Mercury Market. For those who don't want to pay top prices for everything there are alternatives. Beside the circus building, in the centre of town, is a small wholesale store that has low prices. For bulk value, the Container Market near the Yalalt cinema offers the best deal on almost all the foodstuffs you need. Household necessities, toys and beauty products are available there as well. Small food markets in the various city districts offer competitive pricing and a good variety of products. Finally, there is the new Sky Market behind the Chinggis Khan Hotel that has everything from frozen smoked salmon to leopard-skin steering-wheel covers and fish bowls of tropical fish!

Bank of Mongolia Khudaldaany St 6, Ulaanbaatar; tel: 11 322166; fax: 11 311471; email:adm@mglbank.com.mn; web:www.mglbank.mn. Open Mon–Fri 09.00–13.00, 14.00–18.00. Behind the MIAT ticket office.

Bank of Ulaanbaatar Baga Toiruu 15, Ulaanbaatar; tel: 11 312155; fax: 11 325017. Open Mon–Fri 09.00–13.00, 14.00–16.00.

Golomt Bank Sükhbaatar Square 3, Ulaanbaatar; tel: 11 311530, 327812, 311971, 326535; fax: 11 312307; email: Mail@golomtbank.com; web:www.golomtbank.com. Open Mon–Fri 09.00–16.00. Travellers' cheques: cashes Amex, Visa, Mastercard, City Cooperation.

Innovation Bank Khuvisgalchdyn St 5-1, Ulaanbaatar; tel: 11 312531; fax: 11 310833; email: innbk@magicnet.mn. Open 09.00–13.00, 14.00–16.00.

Mongolian Post Office Bank Central Post Office, Ulaanbaatar; tel: 11 310993, 310603; fax: 11 312351. Open 09.00–13.00, 14.00–18.00.

Savings Bank Khudaldaany Street 6, Ulaanbaatar; tel: 11 327467, 311966, 327329, 320057, 310621; fax: 11 310621, 320057; email:savbank@mongol.net. Open Mon–Fri 09.00–13.00, 14.00–18.00.

Trade and Development Bank, corner of Khudaldaany Street and Baga Toiruu, Ulaanbaatar; tel: 11 312362; fax: 11 325449; email:tdbmts@magicnet.mn; web:www.mol.mn/TDBM. Open Mon–Fri 09.00–12.30, 14.00–15.30. Accepts AMEX, Visa, Mastercard, credit-card cash advances. Multi-storey modern building with a new room on one side (outside) that caters especially for foreigners. Do not go upstairs to the second floor (old information).

Communications
Post
The Central Post Office (CPO) in UB is fairly reliable, although letters take a long time to reach their destinations. It is open at different times for different services:

parcel and stamps: Mon–Fri 08.00–17.00; Sat 08.00–14.00, closed Sun. Telephone services are open 24 hours.

Internet
Internet cafés in Ulaanbaatar have sprung up between new dance clubs and bars:

Icafé In the Building of Science and Education, *Baga Toiruu* (small ring road); email: icafe@magicnet.mn. Open weekdays 08.30–21.00, weekends 10.00–16.00.
Internet Café Solongo Restaurant building; email: bodicom@mongolnet.mn. Open: weekdays 10.00–19.00, Sat 11.00–18.00, closed Sun.
Internet and Information The Central Library; email: ubpic@magicnet.mn. Open 09.00–17.00 Mon–Sat, closed Sun.
Internet House Café Youth Federation Building, *Baga Toiruu* (small ring road) behind the Ulaanbaatar Hotel; email: byambaa@mongol.net. Open 09.00–17.00 Mon-Sat, closed Sun.

Most of the larger hotels have full business centres, including internet access.

Foreign embassies and consulates
France Apartment 48, Diplomatic Corps Building, Ulaanbaaatar; tel: 324519; fax: 329633
Germany Negdsen ündesnii gudamj 5, Ulaanbaaatar; tel: 323325, fax: 323905
India Zaluuchuudyn örgön chölöö 10, Ulaanbaatar, tel: 329522, fax: 329532
Japan Zaluuchuudyn örgön chölöö 12, Ulaanbaaatar; tel: 320777, fax: 313332
Kazakhstan Apartment 11, Diplomatic Corps Building, Ulaanbaatar; tel: 312240, fax: 312204
Korea Republic Olimpiin gudamj 10, Ulaanbaatar; tel: 321548, fax: 311157
Russia Enkhtaivny gudamj A-6, Ulaanbaatar; tel: 326037, fax: 324425
Turkey Enkhtaivny gudamj 5, Ulaanbaatar; tel: 311200, fax: 313992
UK Enkhtaivny gudamj 30, Ulaanbaatar; tel: 458133, fax: 458036
USA Ikh toiruu 59/1, Ulaanbaatar; tel: 329606, fax: 320776

WHAT TO SEE AND DO
Main Buddhist monasteries and temples
The three main temples are Gandan Monastery (the major monastery of the city, and the only working monastery during the entire communist period), Bogd Khan Palace Museum (where there are several temples in the grounds) and the Choijin Lama Temple/Museum. Ulaanbaatar is also the home of several important religious institutions, including the *ger*-shaped Dashchoilon Monastery, whose abbot is the country's second-most-senior religious leader. Mongolian and Tibetan traditional medicine is taught and practised and there is a Buddhist centre of astronomy and astrology. Nuns have their own monastery called the Tögsbayasgalant Süm (temple). Buddhism in Mongolia follows the Yellow Hat school, although a Red Hat monastery may be found at Namdoldenchinlin Monastery in Bayanhoshuu district (see *Religion*, page 79).

Gandantegchinlen Monastery
Tel: 11 360023. Open Mon-Sat 09.00–11.00, Sun 09.00–13.00.
This is the centre of Mongolian Buddhism, known as 'Gandan' monastery for short. The abbot of Gandan monastery, the senior Buddhist in Mongolia today, studied at the Dalai Lama's religious academy in India and has the title of *Gavj*. Gandan's Sanskrit name means 'Paradise of Mahayana'. The monastery comprises a complex of buildings on the hillside northwest of the city centre, near the television tower. It is easily recognised from a distance by its multi-

storey temple, housing a 23m statue. Before the 1921 revolution, Mongol herders traditionally sent one of their sons to study Buddhism. Most of the monasteries were destroyed in the 1930s, but Gandan escaped. As a teaching monastery, Gandan houses the Mongolian Buddhist University. It has a large library of rare books and manuscripts in Mongol and Tibetan on Buddhist philosophy, astrology and medicine. Visitors can attend services. No photography is allowed inside the temples.

There are five temple buildings in the complex:

The Temple of Vajradara (Ochirdar) Built between 1840 and 1841 in stone and brick, with a tiled roof. Most important religious ceremonies are held in this temple. The statue of Vajradara, sculpted in 1683 by Zanabazar, is to be found here.

The Temple of Zuu (The Jewel Temple) Built in 1869 to house the remains of the young seventh Bogd Gegeen, who died in his teens. 'Zuu' means Buddha.

The Temple of Didan-Lavran The former library of the 5th Bogd Gegeen. The 13th Dalai Lama stayed here when fleeing Tibet in 1904. Another temple was built in 1924 to house the library of the monastery, which contains a collection of over 50,000 rare books and manuscripts and can be visited only by special permission from the head monk of the library temple, which can be arranged in advance, ie: by special request through a tour operator; tel: 11 360023.

The Temple of Megjid Janraiseg (Avalokiteshvara) Built in 1911–12 to commemorate the end of Manchu rule in Mongolia, and perhaps as a plea for the healing of the Bogd Gegeen's blindness. It contained an immense statue of Avalokiteshvara-Janraiseg, which was destroyed and taken in pieces to the Soviet Union in the 1930s. The statue was rebuilt in the 1990s.

School of Advanced Religious Studies Housed in a fifth temple building, monks from Mongolia and now from all parts of the globe gather here to study.

The Bogd Khan's Green Palace (or Winter Palace)
Zaisan Street (Zaisany Gudamj), south of Peace Bridge; tel: 11 342195. Open 10.00–17.00, closed Thu in summer, and Wed and Thu in winter.
The European-style Winter Palace was built in 1905 by Tsar Nicholas ll of Russia for the eighth and last Öndör Gegeen, Mongolia's last religious and political leader, who died in 1924. It stands next to a large temple complex with a very elaborate entrance gate within a wooden-fenced compound on the south side of Ulaanbaatar, not far from the River Tuul and Bogd Uul Mountain. In 1961 it became a museum and it now contains many treasures including works by Zanabazar, magnificent furs such as the Öndör Geegen's *ger* covered by snow-leopard skins, jewels and many gifts which were received by the Bogd Khan. There is a collection of stuffed animals (from his private zoo) and some erotic drawings.

The temples
The temples of the Winter Palace are known as the 'temples of the monastery that spreads wisdom'. Visitors enter the complex of buildings via the visitors' entrance (see map). It is found on the left-hand side of the formal entrance, the stone screen (yampai) an ornate triple gate which is closed.

The temples include the Temple of Maharajas, where Mongolian musical instruments are housed, along with pictures, jewellery and precious stones; the Temple of the Apostles (Naidan), where prayers were said for the happiness and long life of the Bogd Gegeen, with two smaller temples to the east and west (with displays

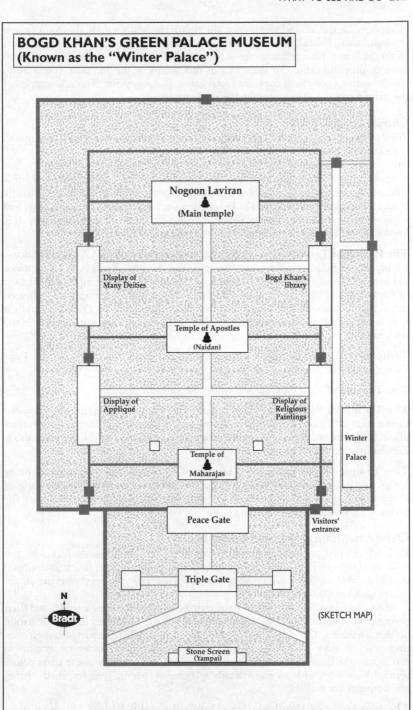

BOGD KHAN'S GREEN PALACE MUSEUM
(Known as the "Winter Palace")

Nogoon Laviran
(Main temple)

Display of
Many Deities

Bogd Khan's
library

Temple of Apostles
(Naidan)

Display of
Appliqué

Display of
Religious
Paintings

Winter
Palace

Temple of
Maharajas

Peace Gate

Visitors'
entrance

Triple Gate

N

Bradt

(SKETCH MAP)

Stone Screen
(Yampai)

of appliqué on the left and painting on the right); the Main temple (Nogoon Lavran or High Lama's Palace), where sculptures by Mongolian, Tibetan and Chinese artists of the 18th and 19th centuries are exhibited, and where the eighth Bogd Gegeen came to pray in private. To the south of this temple is the Jüdkhan Tantra Süm, which houses a portrait of the third Dalai Lama, Sodnomjamts. The side temples of the main temple used to house the Bogd Khan's library.

Choijin Lama Temple

Tel: 11 324788. Open 10.00–18.00 daily in summer. Check opening times if visiting out of the tourist season.
Built in the first decade of the 20th century for the younger brother of the last religious ruler of Mongolia who was also the state oracle. The temple/museum is situated in the centre of Ulaanbaatar not far from the Wedding Palace, directly below Sükhbaatar Square, south of Peace Avenue. It has a fine collection of art and religious relics, including *tsam* masks and costumes used in religious dances. It is known as one of the most beautiful monasteries in Mongolia.

The Principal Temple (the 'temple that spreads compassion') At the entrance is a sculpture of Buddha and his two disciples and the embalmed body of the tutor to the seventh and eighth Bogd Gegeens. In the middle of the temple is the throne of the Bogd Gegeen. Also to be found in this temple are some important religious texts: 108 volumes of the Ganjur and the 226 volumes of the Danjur (Buddhist holy texts) as well as many paintings depicting the horrors awaiting sinners in the underworld.

Temple of the Makharaji Consecrated to the Four Guardians of the Four Directions of the World.

The Temple of Zuu Consecrated to the Sakyamuni Buddha.

The Temple of Yadam Forbidden to ordinary believers, this temple was devoted to the gods of Yadam (a protective deity) and it was where Tantric rituals took place. Sculptures in bronze depict the doctrine of Tantric Buddhism. Here too is Zanabazar's statue of Sitasamvara.

The Temple of Amgalan (or **Temple of Öndör Gegeen**) Contains many sculptures, bas-reliefs of the Sixteen Arhad (enlightened ones) and many works of Zanabazar, including a self-portrait. Of particular significance is the statue of the goddess Tara, beloved by the nomads.

Other monasteries and temples

Full addresses are not currently available for all the temples monasteries below, but with a taxi driver's help, the help of a Mongolian guide, and persistent asking, you should be able to find the following temples. Generally visiting hours are in the mornings from 09.00 to 12.00.

Mongolia is piecing together its past heritage because so many temples and their contents were destroyed in the religious purges of the 1930s and little information on them remains. The elderly are counted on to remember the past – though even they are few now – and the process of interviewing the older generation to restructure the history of temple life is happening, but it will be some years before printed brochures with accurate details relating to specific temples, their history and contents are available.

The monastery of Dambadarjaa (Dambadarjaalin Khiid) This used to be known as the 'temple that spreads religion' and was built in 1795 on the northern outskirts of Ulaanbaatar by the Manchu emperor to house the remains of the second Bogd Gegeen (which were later transferred to Bogdyn Khüree at Dambadarjaa).

The Temple of Vajrayogini The temple was inaugurated in 1995 and replaces an earlier temple built at the beginning of the 20th century. It is consecrated to Padmasambhava, the Indian Grand Master from Kashmir, who introduced Tantric Buddhism to Tibet in the 8th century. The doctrine of Red Hat Lamaism is based on the teachings of Padmasambhava). Part of the temple is Narokhajid, a school for nuns, which opened in 1995.

Dashchoilon Monastery Located between the outer and the inner ring roads in the north of the city, the monastery was built in 1991 in the style of a *ger*. This temple is also dedicated to Padmasambhava and follows the doctrine of 'Red Hat' Buddhism. Open daily 10.00–12.00.

Mamba Datsan Located northeast of the city, outside the outer ring road (Ikh Toiruu) in Batanzurkh district; specialises in teaching Buddhist medicine; tel: 11 358489. Open 09.00–12.00 daily.

Baku Rimpoche's Betüb Monastery Founded by Bakula Rimpoche, the former Indian ambassador to Mongolia and a high-ranking Buddhist. Inaugurated in 1999, this monastery is a symbol of Indian/Mongolian co-operation. Located on the corner of Ikh Toiruu (outer ring road) and Revolutionaries' Avenue, near the Geser Temple. The old form of Mongolian writing in cursive script is taught here.

Geser Temple Northwest of the city on the outer ring road (Ikh Toiruu). This temple, named after the Tibetan hero Geser Khan, is part of Gandan. The building is in Chinese style and is much frequented by local people. Medicinal herbs are sold on stalls there. Open: 09.00–12.00 daily

Namdoldechinlin Monastery Located in Bayanhoshuu district. Open 09.00–11.00 daily.

Museums

There are a number of museums in the capital which are interesting, informative and well worth taking the time to visit. Most museums charge entrance fees. The standard rate for foreign tourists is currently around US$2 (T2,300) though this varies slightly.

National Museum of Mongolian History

Tel: 11 325656. Open during the tourist season Sun, Mon 10.00–16.00, Tue 10.00–14.30, Wed closed, Thu–Sat 10.00–16.00. Check opening times out of season.
This museum on Commerce Street (Khudaldaany Gudamj) 2, opposite the Golomt Bank, presents Mongolian history and culture from prehistoric times to the present day. It features the costumes and accessories of Mongolia's many ethnic groups, a collection of Mongol saddles and a replica of a traditionally furnished nomadic *ger*. Gift shop.

Museum of Natural History

Tel: 11 315679. Open Mon 10.00–15.00, Tue–Sun 10.00–16.30 in summer. Check opening times out of season.
This museum, on Khuvisgalchdyn Örgön Chölöö, covers geology, zoology, botany, anthropology and palaeontology. Exhibits include the famous fighting dinosaurs,

dinosaur nests, bone and fossil fragments of other ancient creatures, expedition material from anthropological digs and the American palaeontologist Roy Chapman Andrews' fossil finds in the 1920s. Don't forget to see the Golden Camel Museum on the second floor which exhibits camel paraphernalia. Gift shop.

Zanabazar Museum of Fine Art

Tel: 11 323986. Open 09.00–18.00 daily (summer and autumn), 10.00–17.00 (winter and spring).

On the east side of Builders' Square (Barilgachdyn Talbai) along from the Trade and Development Bank on Commerce Street, the museum is named after the religious leader Zanabazar (1635–1723). Its collection shows art from Neolithic times through to the Turkic period (6th–7th centuries AD), masks and paintings of the 13th-century Mongol khans to early-20th-century art. Highlights include: figures of Buddha sculpted in bronze by Zanabazar; a silver, gold and pearl mandala; traditional Mongol *zurag* paintings by famous Mongolian artists; a section on appliqué wall hangings and items of Mongolian ritual dances. Gift shop.

Theatre Museum

Tel: 11 326820. Open 10.00–18.00 daily; closed Thursday.

Located within the Palace of Culture building (3rd floor), Sükhbaatar Square. The collection shows the history of Mongolian theatre from 1921 through a series of photographs and film. Theatrical costumes are also modelled and there are sections on puppets, the circus, folk music and dance as well as a good exhibit of *tsam* (Buddhist dance) masks.

Memorial Museum of the Victims of Political Oppression

Open 10.00–16.30 daily (summer), Sat 13.00–14.30, Sun closed.

Located in Genden Street (Gendengiin Gudamj) between the Ministry of Foreign Affairs and the Wedding Palace, Sükhbaatar District. Designed by German-Swiss architects in the 1930s, the wooden building with its sloping roofs was once the home of the late Prime Minister Genden, a victim of the purges, shot in 1937 in Moscow at the order of Joseph Stalin. He was replaced by Prime Minister Anandyn Amar, who was also executed in the USSR, in 1941. It became a museum in 1996 and is dedicated to the Mongolians who lost their lives in the 1930 purges. Around 30,000 Mongolians died and records of personal belongings and political reports bring this tragic story to life. Genden's daughter was the curator.

Ulaanbaatar City Museum

Open Mon–Fri 09.00–18.00, closed weekends.

On Blue Sky Street (Khökh Tengeriin Gudamj), in an old-style Russian house. The history of Ulaanbaatar, from its founding in 1639 to the present day, is shown through the collections, photographs, paintings and tapestries. Special items of interest include a panoramic view of the city carved on an elephant tusk and a famous series of wood block prints by the artist Natsagdorj.

Military History Museum

Tel: 11 451640. Open Thursday– Monday 10.00–17.00 (summer season), closed Tuesday, Wednesday.

On Lkhagvasürengiin Gudamj. The east wing shows Mongolian history from the Stone Age to the 19th-century Manchu period, while the west wing houses post-1921 military history; paintings in Mongol *zurag* style depict the Battle of Kyakhta, fought in 1921. Various tanks and artillery are displayed outside the museum.

Mongolian Hunting Museum
Tel: 11 360248, 11 360879. Open daily 09.00–18.00 except Sun.
This museum is found in a two-storey yellow building on the right side of the road leading to Gandan Monastery, Bayangol district. The museum exhibits many stuffed animals shown in their 'natural environment' depicted by artists. They include wild horses, wild camel and several different types of deer. There is a model of an ancient hunter's camp and many other interesting items and equipment to do with hunting.

Mongolian Toy Museum
Open Mon–Sat 10.00–17.00, closed Sun.
Housed in a four-storey building behind the Ulaanbaatar Hotel off the small ring road (Baga Toiruu). Exhibits over 500 Mongolian and international puzzles and games.

Museum of Geology and Mineral Resources
Open 09.00–12.00.
Second floor of the Mongolian Technical University. This museum has a collection showing Mongolia's diverse minerals including interesting exhibit items of agate and jade. It is divided into three areas: geology, mineral resources and mineral description.

Galleries
Art exhibitions are held at the Hall of Mongolian Artists, located immediately south of Sükhbaatar Square on Peace Avenue. Paintings are usually for sale. For current exhibitions look in the *Mongol Messenger* (English-language Mongolian weekly) or ask the hotel receptionist to find out what is on and how to get there.

The Art Gallery
Tel: 11 328486. Open daily in summer, 09.00–13.00, 14.00–18.00. Prices vary depending on the fame of the artist and the works on show. (See also *Arts and entertainment* in *Chapter 5*, page 206).
Located in the Palace of Culture on Sükhbaatar Square, off Peace Avenue, this is the largest art gallery in Mongolia and features 20th-century paintings. Important works include the *Black Camel* by Sengetsokhio, *Fighting Stallions* by Tsevegjav and the *Tale of the Great Horse* by Tengisbold. One room is devoted to traditional Mongol *zurag* painting. Paintings and photographic works are for sale. Contemporary works are accessible as they tend to fuse Eastern and Western traditions, combining the characteristics and the techniques of both.

Music and theatre
Music, poetry and folk tales play a large role in Mongolian cultural life and are woven into opera and ballet productions. To arrange theatre, folk dance or opera tickets you may do this yourself at the box office or book through a local tour agent. Of course if you make your own arrangements the cost is slightly cheaper (T5,000 – roughly US$4); otherwise, expect to pay US$6 standard tourist price for performances (Mongolians pay T3,500).

The National Opera and Ballet Theatre
For bookings tel: 11 322854 or 323339. Tickets cost US$6 (T7,000).
Found in the southeast corner of Sükhbaatar Square, the theatre stages Mongolian and classical opera and concerts. Operas performed there include Tchaikovsky's

Eugene Onegin. Performances begin around 18.00 – best booked by a tour company who can also help to arrange transport. Otherwise take a taxi or walk following the map of the city.

The National Theatre
For information or bookings, tel: 11 323402. Tickets cost US$6 (T7,000).
Large, orange-walled building on Chinngis Avenue, next to the Bayangol Hotel. The National Folk Song and Dance ensemble is based here and puts on classical Mongolian and international theatre productions, traditional *khöömii* (overtone or throat-singing) accompanied by the *morin-khuur* (horse-head fiddle). Performances daily except Tuesdays.

Puppet Theatre
For bookings, tel: 11 321669. Tickets cost US$6 (T7,00).
Located on the left side of the National Theatre. Open during peak season July–September; performances by special arrangement (eg: by a tour group manager).

Mongolian Song and Dance Ensemble Tümen Ekh
Tel: 11 322238 or 327916. The entertainment starts at 18.00 on Tuesdays in spring and summer. Tickets cost US$6 (T7,000).
Tumen Ekh Dance Ensemble consists of 35 artists who perform traditional folk dances, accompanied by Mongolian musical instruments, and overtone singing (*khöömii*). Performances take place in the exhibition centre in the Children's Park.

Cinemas
Not many tourists want to go to the cinema in Ulaanbaatar as the theatre performances of traditional music and folk dance are more popular. However, it is worth experiencing a Mongolian film – with the themes of romantic love and traditional life centred around Genghis Khan. Look at the back page for 'What's on' in the *Mongol Messenger*, or ask the receptionist at your hotel to check the film listings. The main cinemas are shown on the UB map on pages 222–3.

Yalalt Cinema Revolutionaries' Avenue (Khuvisgalchdyn Örgön Chölöö) and the inner ring road; tel: 11 312178. Shows Mongolian films. Tickets cost T1,500 (US$1.30).
Ard Cinema Opposite MIAT offices in the town centre; tel: 11 327193. Inside the building there is a bingo hall and a place to change money upstairs. Shows Mongolian films and, occasionally, translated or dubbed foreign films. Tickets cost T1,500 (US$1.30)
Örgöö Cinema In the third district beside the Nomin Supermarket and the Moscow Restaurant; tel: 11 367445 or 324187. This cinema shows English films. Tickets cost T1,500.
Café Cinema Shows video films in English in a room attached to the Ristorante della Casa Pizza, located between the Centrepoint Shopping Centre and Peace and Friendship House on Peace Avenue. Open evenings after 20.00. There is a wide selection of recent videos to choose from. You are left alone with the remote controls to view the video, seated on a large, leather sofa – where you may also eat your pizza. Showings are on weekdays after 20.00. Cost: T2,000 (roughly US$2) per person.

Other attractions
Nairamdal Park (Children's Park)
Cost US$6 (T7,000).
This large park near the city centre has amusement rides for children, a real maze, a pond and boat rides. Every evening at 18.00 during the summer tourist season there is a performance of traditional song and dance held in the theatre here.

Zaisan Memorial
This tall memorial is dedicated to Mongol-Soviet comradeship-in-arms. It is situated on a small hill directly south of UB, the high ground providing wonderful views of the city.

Wrestling Palace
On the east side of the city, south of Peace Avenue, near the British Embassy, the new Wrestling Palace, completed in 1998, is an imposing circular, domed stadium which seats 2,500 people. Viewing is exceptionally good. During competitions several hundred wrestlers wrestle in pairs, simultaneously, in the 770m^2 arena, until one pair remains to compete for the victory title. Tickets cost US$4 (T4,500) tourist price. National tournaments are held during Tsagaan Sar (New Year) and Naadam festivals (in early July), although during Naadam the main wrestling tournaments are held in the Central Stadium, or Naadam Stadium, south of the city. (For information on these, see pages 186–90.)

Mongolian State Circus
Performances begin at 17.00. For bookings, tel: 11 320795. Tickets cost US$6 (T7,000).
Found in a blue-domed building on Seoul Street (Seüliin Gudamj), Bayangol district near the railway station. The programme includes acrobatic displays, high-wire balancing acts by trapeze artists, along with animal performances. Provides tremendous fun and entertainment. Acts include Daggy the Camel, water juggling, clowns, Bungle and Fumble, and the Ace Contortionists Duo Sükhbaatar. Unfortunately, since the circus performers are frequently on a world tour, the number of performances has dropped. A recent grant of T30 million should help to remedy this.

ONE- OR TWO-DAY TRIPS FROM ULAANBAATAR
Terelj *Ger* Resort (80km from UB) Overnight stay in a *ger* or small wooden cabin within the national park is easily arranged via any number of tour companies based in UB (see list, pages 225–7). On the way you can stop at a dinosaur amusement park.

Manzshir Monastery (45km from UB; 5km northeast of Zuunmod, Töv Aimag centre) Many of the temples of this 18th-century monastery are currently being restored; up-to-date tourist brochures are being published; further information should be available at the monastery.

Khustain Nuruu National Park (100km from UB) See the famous Mongolian wild horses the *takhi*. Accommodation for overnight visitors is in a *ger* camp. For full details on Khustain Nuruu National Park and how to get there see pages 129 and 254.

Nükht National Park In the Khan-Uul district, Ulaanbaatar; tel: 11 325417; fax: 11 325630. 16km from UB, a nature resort with elk, antelope and other wildlife in a natural valley setting, with a hotel and restaurant of the same name, on the outskirts of the capital.

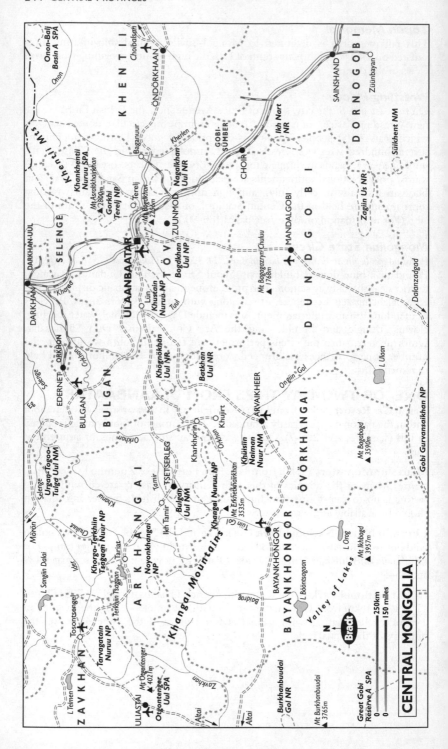

CENTRAL MONGOLIA

Central Provinces

7

The more possessions you have the more you are robbed of your freedom.

Wilfred Thesiger, writer and explorer

The central provinces offer some of the most exciting Mongolian landscape and are the obvious choice for less-mobile travellers, or those with not much time on their hands. There is plenty to see, from Erdene Zuu Monastery in the Orkhon Valley to lesser-known temples and ruins. The valleys of Terelj, so close to the capital, are as wild and beautiful as the more distant parts of the country. The ranges of the Khentii in the northeast and the Khangai in the west give rise to many rivers, including the Orkhon River, with its magnificent waterfall. The provinces' national parks and game reserves are full of wildlife and the vast steppe itself offers both cultural tours and exciting places to explore.

TÖV AIMAG

BRIEF FACTS
Population 111,900
Population density 1.51 per km²
Area 77,400km²
Aimag centre Zuunmod
Districts 27
Elevation of Zuunmod 1,529m
Livestock and crops Horses, cattle, sheep/potatoes
Ethnic groups Khalkh, Kazakh and Barga
Distance from Zuunmod to Ulaanbaatar 40km
Average temperatures July 15.6°C, January –20.4°C

Töv literally means 'central', and although Ulaanbaatar (an autonomous municipality) lies within its boundaries, the aimag capital is the small town of Zuunmod. Due to its proximity to Ulaanbaatar and the good local transport system to and from the capital, this aimag is an excellent place to start exploring the country through a series of day trips. If you are waiting for a visa extension or planning an expedition further afield, Zuunmod offers you a good day trip and is a conveniently short distance away from the noise and hassle of the capital. The landscape is predominantly forested mountain/steppe, where wild berries, mushrooms and medicinal herbs grow in abundance. In the central province there are over 30 clear-water rivers (good for fishing), among them the Kherlen and Tuul. A number of mineral spas and hot springs are found at Janchivlin, Bööröljüüt and Elstei. Towns include the aimag centre Zuunmod, the former coal-mining town of Nalaikh, and the peaceful settlements of Gachuurt and Khandgait. Resorts, besides the most popular resort of Terelj, include Nairamdal Zuslan (the Children's Centre), sometimes known as Bayangol, where a new ski resort is currently being developed, and the Nükht Hotel Resort, both of which offer accommodation and are close to Ulaanbaatar.

Highlights
• Terelj Resort
• National parks and cultural sites within them: Manzshir Monastery in the Bogd Khan Strictly Protected Area and Günjiin Süm (temple) in Terelj National Park (although the temple is derelict, the walk to get there is worth it!).
• Wild horses at Khustain Nuruu National Park
• Eco-*gers* in Khankhentii Strictly Protected Area

Zuunmod
Located 40km south of Ulaanbaatar, Zuunmod is a relaxed town of around 17,000 people. It makes sense to stay a night here when hiking in the mountains or visiting Manzshir Monastery nearby. The town is laid out around the central park with a post office, theatre, cinema and administrative building. The main tourist attractions are two museums (described overleaf) and the small monastery (*khiid*) of Dashichoinkhorlin, located southeast of the town. It is not of the same standard as the Manzshir Monastery but it is still worth a visit.

Getting there from Ulaanbaatar
By car Accessible without 4WD. From Ulaanbaatar take the airport road and drive 40km to Zuunmod.

By minibus Operates from the bus station between 08.00 and 18.00. Cost T500; buses run every half hour.

By local bus From Ulaanbaatar long-distance bus station to Zuumod bus station, west of the main street.

By shared taxi Shared taxis can be picked up in the tourist season on the main street in Zuunmod or from the bus station in Ulaanbaatar. They are more comfortable and cost around US$12 (T14,000) one way with an additional waiting fee of US$2–3, if requested to wait at Manzshir Monastery.

Where to stay
Hotel Zuunmod A minute's walk northeast of the town square and central park; provides ordinary rooms at standard/cheap rates; cost US$15 (T17,100).
Government Hotel Located northeast of the town square and central park (opposite Zuumod Hotel): refurbished de-luxe rooms cost US$20 (T22,800).
Öndör Dov Ger Camp Tel: 11 455108; fax: 11 455016; email: undtour@magicnet.mn. Located 8km west of Zuumond. It has a large concrete restaurant and a large number of *gers*; cost: US$45 per night including meals, sauna, hot shower. If camping in and around the monastery, it is polite to ask for permission first at the monastery office.

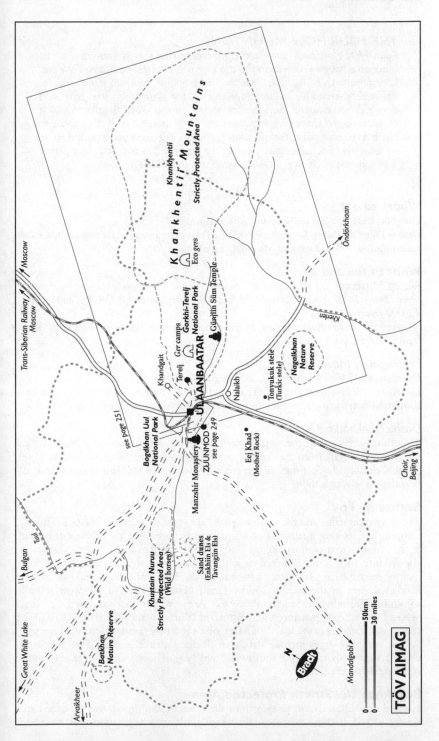

TÖV AIMAG

Trans-Siberian Railway → Moscow
Moscow

Khankhentii

Khankhentii Mountains
Strictly Protected Area

Eco gers

Öndörkhaan

Gorkhi-Terelj
National Park

Günjiin Süm Temple

Kheree

Khandgait
Ger camps
Terelj
ULAANBAATAR
Nalaikh

Nagalkhan
Nature
Reserve

Tonyukuk stele
(Turkic stele)

see page 251

**Bogdkhan Uul
National Park**

Manzshir Monastery
ZUUNMOD
see page 249

Eej Khad
(Mother Rock)

Choir,
Beijing

Bulgan

Tuul

Khustain Nuruu
Strictly Protected Area
(Wild horses)

Sand dunes
(Enkhiin Els &
Tavangiin Els)

Great White Lake

Batkhan
Nature Reserve

Arvaikheer

Mandalgobi

N

Bradt

50km
30 miles

THE FOUR HOLY MOUNTAINS
Four 'Holy Mountains' surround Ulaanbaatar (*Uul* means 'mountain'). The mountains roughly correspond to the four points of the compass. They are: Chingeltei Uul in the north; Bogdkhan Uul in the south; Bayanzürkhkhairkhan Uul (Bayanzürkh for short) in the east and Songinokhairkhan Uul (Songino for short), in the west. Bogdkhan Uul is considered the most magnificent of the holy mountains. It is possible to climb its highest peak, Tsetsee Gün (2,265m), but you need a permit to do so from the park authorities; contact the Parks' office at Commerce Street 5 (Khudaldaany Gudamj), Ulaanbaatar; tel: 11 312656.

Where to eat
Dölgöön Café East side of the central park in Zuunmod.
Öndör Dov Ger Camp See above for details. The restaurant opens for tour groups; meals include grilled or boiled meat, noodles and vegetables.

What to see and do
Aimag Museum
Open 09.00–16.00 (closed 13.00–14.00 for lunch) every day except Tuesday; entrance fee T1,000 (roughly US$1).
Situated in the southwest corner of the central park. Exhibits local geology, flora, fauna, historic photographs.

Ethnography Museum
Open 10.00–17.00; entrance fee T1,000 (roughly US$1).
Down a small lane southwest of the central park (5-minute walk); exhibits include some traditional artefacts with a fully furnished *ger* as the main showpiece.

Dashichoinkhorlin Khiid
This monastery lies on the southeastern outskirts of town across a small creek a 10–15-minute walk from the central park. Religious ceremonies are held at 11.00, though double-check times of ceremonies with the resident monks and ask permission to watch them.

Sights in Töv
The holy mountains and the national parks are great recreational places for hiking, camping and looking at nature, besides many other activities like riding, rafting and, in the winter, cross-country skiing. The forests are full of birds (over 250 species), and wildlife, such as musk deer, ibex, and roe deer. Such areas of natural interest are mainly contained in Töv's five national parks. They include: Bogdkhan Strictly Protected Area in the south; Gorkhi-Terelj National Park in the west and the adjoining Khankhentii Strictly Protected Area, which extends northwest into Selenge and Khentii provinces; and Khustain Nuruu National Park, 100km to the southeast – famous as the home of Mongolia's recently reintroduced wild horses.

The nature reserves include Batkhaan (located on the border of neighbouring Övörkhangai Province in the southwest) and Nagalkhaan mountain reserve in the southern Khentii mountains.

Bogdkhan Uul Strictly Protected Area
Located near Ulaanbaatar, just north of the town of Zuunmod, this protected area covers 41,651 hectares of mountain range with taiga vegetation and bare rock

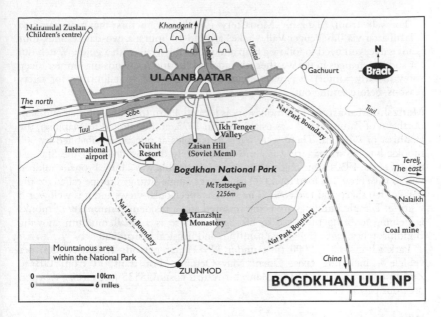

Map labels:
Nairamdal Zuslan (Children's centre)
Khandgait
Uliastai
Selbe
ULAANBAATAR
Gachuurt
N
Bradt
The north
Selbe
Tuul
Tuul
Nat Park Boundary
Ikh Tenger Valley
International airport
Nükht Resort
Zaisan Hill (Soviet Meml)
Bogdkhan National Park
Mt Tsetseegün 2256m
Terelj, The east
Nalaikh
Manzshir Monastery
Nat Park Boundary
Coal mine
Mountainous area within the National Park
China
0 ——— 10km
0 ——— 6 miles
ZUUNMOD
Nat Park Boundary
BOGDKHAN UUL NP

peaks; it encompasses forests of Siberian larch, birch, cedar, pine, poplar and fir trees. The forested area extends to grasslands which form the major part of the reserve situated on the borderline of the forest/steppe zones. There is a buffer area of 13,433 hectares and a transition zone of some 12,216 hectares between the strictly protected areas and areas lived in by local people and visited by the public. Bogdkhan Uul became an officially protected area in 1778, and is Mongolia's earliest protected area, but it was first recognised as a sacred mountain as long ago as the 12th century when logging and hunting were prohibited.

Special attractions include: Manzshir Monastery, near Zuunmod; a winter camp of nomads; and the peak, Tsetsee Gün (2,256m). Seventy families, including rangers, live in this quiet reserve and many tourists visit it. Wildlife includes 47 mammal species, 116 bird species, four species of reptile and over 500 vascular plants. The park has been nominated as a biosphere reserve by UNESCO (United Nations Scientific and Cultural Organisation). For hiking permits and further information contact the administration of Bogdkhan Uul Strictly Protected Area, Commerce Street 5 (Khudaldaany Gudamj), Ulaanbaatar; tel: 11 312656.

Getting there
Bogdkhan Uul is easily accessible from Ulaanbaatar by bus, or by taxi to Zuunmod; cost T500 (bus); US$15 (T17,000) taxi one way. You can hike across the mountains (camping en route) from the Nükht Hotel Resort (see overleaf), situated in a mountain valley 16km outside the capital.

Hiking to Tsetsee Gün Uul
Tsetsee Gün is the highest point (2,256m) in the Bogdkhan Strictly Protected Area. A hiking permit is required (see above). The park entrance fee costs T1,000 (just under US$1) per person and T3,000 (US$3) per vehicle; tickets are available at the park gate and are also obtainable at Manzshir Khiid.

There are many different approaches to the summit though note that there are no marked routes.

To walk from Manzshir Monastery (see below) across the mountains to Ulaanbaatar via Ikh Tenger Valley takes around 10 hours; a two-day walking tour is advisable; you need to follow a map and preferably walk with a guide. Watch out for sudden changes in the weather (thunderstorms and icy winds in summer, deep snow in early winter). It is wise to inform someone of your journey, for safety reasons, before setting out.

Manzshir Monastery This monastery is located 45km from Ulaanbaatar and 5km northeast of Zuunmod. It was established in 1773, and dedicated to Manjusri, the Bodhisat of Wisdom. There were over 20 temples at one time, inhabited by 300 monks, but the monastery was almost completely destroyed during the Stalinist purges of the 1930s. One object that was indestructible was a huge bronze cauldron said to have provided food for 1,000 monks at a single sitting; a recipe called for the meat of ten sheep and two cows. The site has spectacular views and it is well worth visiting. Temple buildings are being restored and a resident community of monks is helping to bring the place to life again. There is a small museum showing Buddhist relics, *tanka* (religious) paintings and musical instruments.

Park admission: T1,000 (just under US$1) per person; T3,000 (US$3) per vehicle – including taxis. Open: May–October. For transport from UB to Zuunmod; a taxi from UB to Manzshir return costs US$35 (see *Getting there*, on previous page).

Where to stay
Nükht Resort Contact Nükht Hotel (director Mr Gankhuyag), tel: 11 325417, 310421; fax: 11 325630. The hotel and other facilities are located 16km southwest of Ulaanbaatar off the main airport road, at the head of a secluded mountain valley. The resort provides accommodation for large groups at the hotel; also *ger* accommodation, with hot running water, showers and restaurant facilities. It is a convenient place to stay for local sightseeing and during the *Naadam* (national games), as the horse races take place nearby. Overnight hiking arrangements can be can be organised by the resort. Accommodation cost per person: US$45 *ger* camp; US$60–95 hotel.

Chinggis Khan Khüree Ger Camp and Restaurant tel: 11 379923, 311783. This camp lies at the western entrance of the Bogdkhan Strictly Protected Area, along the main Ulaanbaatar/Zuunmod road; beside the *ger* camp there is a small museum which houses the costumes, weapons and armoury formerly used when making an epic film on Genghis Khan; the camp's restaurant is well known and decorated in the same theme. To stay at the *ger* camp costs US$35 per day; three meals in the restaurant cost around US$15 per person.

Gorkhi-Terelj National Park
Northeast of Ulaanbaatar, Terelj has long been a holiday resort for people from the capital. The entrance to the park is 16km from Terelj village on the main UB/Terelj road. Established as a national park in 1993, the area covers 293,168 hectares; precious stones have been mined there for over a hundred years and continue to be mined. Parts of the park are permanently inhabited by local herders who keep livestock in the buffer zones. The entrance fee is T1,000 (just under US$1) per person and T3,000 (US$3) per vehicle. Pay at the park gate.

Terelj Resort
Lying in the valley of the Terelj river 80km northeast of Ulaanbaatar, this resort is part of the Gorkhi-Terelj National Park. It is one of the most visited areas in Mongolia due to its magnificent scenery and its proximity to Ulaanbaatar. During

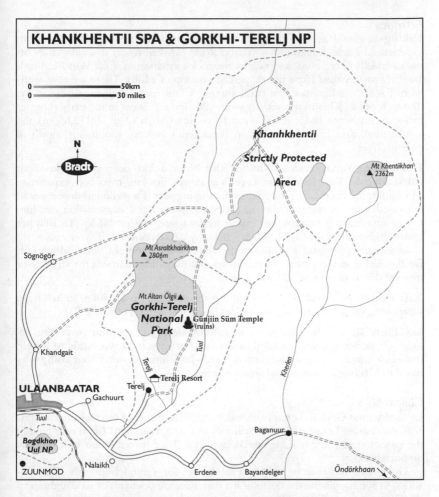

KHANKHENTII SPA & GORKHI-TERELJ NP

0 ▬▬▬▬ 50km
0 ▬▬▬▬ 30 miles

N
Bradt

Khanhkhentii

Strictly Protected

Area

Mt Khentiikhan
▲ 2362m

Sögnögör

Mt Asraltkhairkhan
▲ 2806m

Mt Altan Ölgii ▲
Gorkhi-Terelj
National Günjiin Süm Temple
Park (ruins)

Tuul

Khandgait

Terelj

Kherlen

Terelj Resort

ULAANBAATAR Terelj
Gachuurt

Tuul

Baganuur

Bogdkhan
Uul NP

Nalaikh
ZUUNMOD Erdene Bayandelger Öndörkhaan

the summer season there are great opportunities for hiking, rock climbing, swimming, rafting, riding and birdwatching. In winter frozen rivers provide skating and the snow-covered valleys are ideal for cross-country skiing. The resort provides good accommodation with the hotels and *ger* camps mainly clustered around Terelj village. It is a friendly and interesting place to visit, and one of the 'show *gers*' is romantically lit by a candelabrum, dropped from the *ger*'s roof ring! Eco-*gers* are situated further afield in the visitors' zone of the quieter, more remote Khankhentii Strictly Protected Area, a far cry from candelabra but equally inviting. Local people are enormously generous and entertaining; the warm bowls of tea and the friendly welcomes just 'do it' for most visitors.

To get to Terelj, the bus departs from UB long-distance bus station daily at 15.00 and returns to UB, from a stop beside the UB2 Camp, at around 20.00. Otherwise take a taxi (the road is paved so a jeep is unnecessary) and pay US$25/30 (T28,500–34,200) one way. You might be charged more if the return journey is empty. If you are on a day trip, pre-arrange waiting time (US$2–3) and return cost at the long-distance bus station in UB (many taxis leave from there on Sundays in summer).

Activities

Hiking You will need a compass and good maps or arrange to go with an experienced guide. Look out for 'Turtle Rock' (*Melkhii Khad*) in a side valley off the main UB/Terelj road, and nearby the rock formation of 'Old Man Reading a Book' (a rock shaped like a figure, perched on top of a hill). There are easy, well-worn flat paths where you can stroll along the Tuul and Terelj riverbanks in the direction of the Khentii mountains with wild alpine flowers in the early summer including edelweiss and irises. You can also walk to Altan-Ölgii Uul (2,656m), the source of Akhain River, and walk in Bagakhentii Nuruu (mountains) north of Akhain River.

Horseriding You can ride to Khagiin Khar Nuur, a 20m-deep glacial lake about 80km along the Tuul River from Terelj's *ger* camps. For long treks both experience and a guide are necessary, plus your own camping gear if travelling independently; organised tours provide all the necessary equipment and horses. You can hire horses from most *ger* camps, but expect to pay tourist prices: US$5 (T5,700) per hour; and from US$12 (T14,000) per day. Alternatively, if you make no arrangements and want to ride on the spur of the moment, local Mongolian families living in the area also have horses and may hire them out for an hour or more at the standard rate (US$5 per hour).

Raft Tuul River provides excellent rafting; the best section is a 40km stretch from Dörgöntiin Gatsaa (north of Terelj Ger Camp) to Gachuurt (near UB).

Ski There are no set trails for cross-country skiing; bring your own skis; ask locals/*ger* camps to recommended safe areas. For organised weekends to Terelj, including winter skiing tours, contact Terelj-Juulchin and other tour companies based in UB (see *Mongolian tour operators*, pages 225–7).

Günjiin Süm

Located within Gorkhi-Terelj National Park, 30km north of the main resort area, at Baruunbayar. To get there, hike directly over the mountains (with tour guide); the easier/longer route is along the Baruunbayar River (two days for trek, one day on horseback).

The temple was built in 1740 by Efu Dondovdorj (grandchild of the Tüsheet-Khan) to commemorate the death of his first wife, the youngest of six daughters of the Qing emperor, Kangxi. The princess, a great beauty, died tragically following a long illness brought on by the discovery that her new-born son had been secretly murdered and replaced (for reasons of state) by another child (son of her husband's Mongol concubine). The princess's child was supposed to succeed the Bogd Geegen to become the country's spiritual leader and ruler, but this was not to be. The deception broke the Manchu princess's health and heart. The temple was not destroyed during the religious purges of the 1930s, although it has been neglected over the years. Some original monastery walls remain around the small main temple. The site is under-developed at present with no signs and no facilities.

Khankhentii Strictly Protected Area

Located in Töv, Selenge and Khentii aimags, this protected area covers over 1.2 million hectares of the desolate and wild Khentii Mountains, stretching northeast from just outside Ulaanbaatar to the Russian border. Perennially snow-covered mountains and dense forests at the core of this remote wilderness area are uninhabited and accessible only by foot or on horseback. Several peaks rise above 2,500m. The highest is Asraltkhairkhan (peak), rising to 2,800m. The headwaters of three major river systems spring from the protected area: the Tuul, which flows into the Orkhon and Selenge to Russia's Lake Baikal and continues to the Arctic Ocean and the Onon and Kherlen rivers which flow east to join the River Amur before entering the Pacific Ocean. The reserve contains 10% of Mongolia's forests and defines the southern edge of Siberia's taiga. Hot springs used for medicinal purposes lie along the Onon River, and elsewhere, in the protected area. Eco-*gers* developed for tourism by the park and the local people provide limited but very select accommodation.

Eco-*gers* in the Khankhentii An eco-*ger* project is run by the Khan Khentii Strictly Protected Area's administration; three secluded *gers* are situated about 10km apart in the park; one at Sain Ovoo (junction of Tuul and Baruunbayan rivers), one at Buutin Khoshuu in Baruunbayan Valley; and one at Khalzangiin Adag (further up the Tuul River). The cost is US$20 (T23,000) per person, excluding food; horse hire costs from US$12 (T14,000) a day, including guide. A small percentage of the money received is kept by the park for administration purposes otherwise it benefits the local people. For bookings and further details contact T Selenge; tel: 11 329323; email:gtznaturecom@magicnet.mn.

Ger camps in the Gorkhi-Terelj and Khankhentii areas

Some *ger* accommodation is difficult to book due to a lack of telephones; where possible book ahead in the summer season. In winter check with local people and with the park authorities whether the camps are open. Note that some open for individuals, while others cater only for organised tours.

Dinosaur Camp Tel: 11 313031, 458623; mobile: 99150876; email: dinosaur@mol.mn; web: www.dinosaur.mn. A *ger* camp surrounded by concrete dinosaurs, located on the way to Terelj village beside the main UB/Terelj road.

Bolor Gers 10km along the road from the main Gorkhi-Terelj park. Provides food, or you may bring your own food and cook it there. No telephone. Rates: T3,500 (US$3) per person.

Tsolom Ger Camp 13km along the main road from the Gorkhi-Terelj park entrance, in a secluded valley 3km east of the main road (tel: 11 322870). *Gers* cost US$12–20 per person (T14,000–23,000) depending on the number of people. Cabins sleep 3; costs vary from US$14–24 (T16,000–T27,000). Food costs US$18 (T20,500) per person for three meals.

Miraj Gers 14km along main road from park entrance (tel: 11 325188). Good place for hiking. Hot showers are available. Horse for hire at standard rates of US$5 (T5,700) an hour or US$12 (T14,000) a day. Rates of accommodation around US$17/10 (T19,000/11,400) per person with/without three meals.

Buuveit Camp Web: www.tsolomtravel.com. 65km northeast of the capital; open year round. Offers local countryside tours.

Gorkhi Gers 15km along main road from park entrance in a secluded valley 5km west of main road, past Turtle Rock; no telephone. Rates US$22/12 (T25,000/14,000) with/without three meals.

Temüjinii Otog Gers 15.5km along main road from park entrance, near the concrete dinosaurs; tel: 11 456087. *Gers* with hot showers. Children welcome. Rates US$35 (T40,000) per person including three meals, US$20 (T23,000) without meals.

San Gers 18.5km along main UB/Terelj road, frequented by Mongolian visitors. *Gers* cost US$5 (T5,700) per person (no showers); hotel rooms cost US$10 (T11,400); three meals cost US$12 (T14,000).

Terelj-Juulchin On the main road 25.5km from main entrance; tel: 11 324978. Complex of buildings with good facilities including hot showers, sauna, restaurant. *Gers* cost US$14 (T16,000) per person; cabins cost US$10 (T11,400) per person, hotel rooms are US$14 (T16,000) per person.

UB2 27km from the park entrance next to Terelj village; tel: 11 309016. Large hotel complex. Rates are US$5 (T5,600) per person in a *ger*, US$10 (T11,400) per person for a room. De-luxe rooms cost US$20–30 (T23,000–34,200) for a single/double room. Good restaurant serves Mongolian food.

Other reserves in Töv Aimag
Khustain Nuruu National Park
Located about 100km west of Ulaanbaatar this 50,620ha reserve is home to the Mongolian wild horse, *takhi* (for more details, see pages 75 and 113). It is run by the Mongolian Association for the Conservation of Nature and the Environment (MACNE) in co-operation with a Dutch foundation, Foundation Reserves for the Prezewalski Horse (FRPH). The steppe and forest-steppe environment is inhabited by maral, steppe gazelle, deer, boar, wildcat, wolf, and lynx.

There is no scheduled public transport to the park. You can take a local bus to the turn off for Khustain Nuruu along the main UB to Kharkhorin road, signposted 10km south of the park's entrance. It is best to have your own transport (jeep); cost US$80 round trip.

Note that it is worth spending a night at Khustain Nuruu, if possible, as wildlife is best seen at dusk and dawn.

The **Takhi Information Centre** inside the park has poster displays which tell the story of the wild horses' return to Mongolia. Moilt Ger Camp on the border of the park provides accommodation; cost: US$15 (T17,100) per person; a room in the main *ger* camp building costs US$20 (T23,000) per person. To book accomodation contact MACNE in Ulaanbaatar; tel/fax: 11 321 426; email: macne@magicnet.mn; camping is not allowed inside the park. Park entry costs US$5 (T5,700) one-time fee (T500 for locals). To see the wild horses in their enclosures you must be accompanied by a park guide; keep to existing tracks. There is plenty to do from hiking to horseriding; horse hire costs US$10 (T11,400) per day; there are Turkic graves southeast of the park which you can ride or drive to see; a day's outing. To go fishing, you will need your own transport to drive 30km (half-hour's drive) to the River Tuul. A fishing permit, obtainable from the park's office, costs US$8. Eco-volunteer programmes (of three weeks) helps to fund research projects like that of the *takhi* and other current programmes; if interested see web: www.ecovolunteer.org

Nagalkhan Nature Reserve
Located approximately 110km southeast of Ulaanbaatar, this area of some 3,076 hectares is designated to protect the southernmost limit of the Khangai and Khentii mountain ranges. It is not a particularly well-visited area, nor is it developed for tourism.

Batkhan Uul Nature Reserve
This reserve, located on the western border extending into Övörkhangai Aimag, is described in *Övörkhangai Aimag*, pages 257–64, and in *Natural History and Conservation*, page 126.

Towns and other attractions in Töv
Khandgait
Khandgait lies 40km north of Ulaanbaatar in an area of cow pastures, hills and pine forests, with meadows of wildflowers surrounding the small village. Less touristy (and cheaper) than Terelj, and lacking in facilities, it is not in the national park so camping is permitted. There's plenty to do: activities include hiking, walking, rock climbing, fishing, and ice-skating and skiing in winter.

There's a lack of scheduled transport to Khandgait. The first half of the road from UB is paved, the second half is pretty rough. It continues north from Khandgait to smaller valleys, where there are wooden huts, once used as summerhouses, but now abandoned. To get there, take a taxi or share a minibus; a taxi is easiest and costs around US$25 (T28,500) return, plus US$2–3 waiting time. There is no tourist accommodation so you will need to bring a tent if staying overnight.

Gachuurt

Located 21km from Ulaanbaatar Gachuurt is a pretty village in quiet surroundings. It offers no hotel or restaurant facilities but there are plenty of sporting opportunities like horseriding, fishing, hiking and rafting in the area.

You can camp outside the village or stay with local people – private *ger* accommodation may be arranged on the spot.

There's also a *ger* camp 3km up the Tuul River from town. It costs US$5 per person a day, with meals an extra US$5–10. Horse hire costs US$12 (T14,000) per day. Contact Gana's Guest House in Ulaanbaatar for bookings; tel: 11 321078; email: ganasger@magnicnet.mn.

To get there, buses leave every hour from the long-distance bus station in UB (unreliable) or you can take a taxi. The paved road continues beyond Gachuurt to Sansar, but there is no public transport out there.

Nairamdal Zuslan, or Bayangol (Children's Centre)

Located in the foothills 30km northwest of Ulaanbaatar, Nairamdal Zuslan (tel: 11 332776) is situated at a lower altitude than Terelj's resort and has milder weather during the winter. The scenery is spectacular and it is a good place to go if you are travelling with children. There is a small hotel where you can stay with your family; prices are reasonable and services are good. It is advisable, however, to book in advance.

Activities include cultural displays, archery competitions, horseriding in summer; cross-country skiing in winter; furthermore, a skiing area with lifts is currently being developed.

There's an admission charge of US$15–30 (T17,100–34,200) for children, US$40–80 (T45,600–91,120) adults, including accommodation, meals, guides and transport from the city. It's open all year, though it might be full in summer.

Nalaikh

Located 35km southeast of Ulaanbaatar, Nalaikh is a coal-mining town which supplied Ulaanbaatar in the early 1900s. In 1950, the Kazakh minority people from Bayan-Ölgii were brought here to work in the mines and stayed on after mining stopped in 1990. There is a small mosque which may be visited off the main road on the outskirts of town.

Buses depart to Nalaikh from UB long-distance bus station every half hour (daytime only) and cost T250. It is safer and more reliable to take a taxi (US$30 return). Jeeps are approximately T500 per kilometre; Japanese jeeps can be more expensive at T750 per kilometre.

Tonyukuk – Turkic stele

Around 16km southeast of Nalaikh there's a massive block of stone showing runic characters dedicated to the Turkic sage Tonyukuk. Discovered in 1897, the stele dates back to the 2nd khanate of the Eastern Turks and is thought to have been erected in AD725. Tonyukuk, born in China around AD645, was adviser to three

Turkic rulers, the last being Bilge Khan. Tonyukuk married Bilge's daughter, a brilliant young woman. The advice Tonyukuk gave to his son-in-law (who intended to build a town in the Orkhon Valley) was to remain a nomad. He warned of the attendant dangers of the settled life, when compared to the advantages of mobility and flexibility of nomadic existence. Many centuries later the same advice was given by Genghis Khan to his sons. There are stone figures and grave slabs nearby.

To get there you'll need to have your own transport; drive southeast from Nalaikh on an unpaved road where you'll find the site in a small enclosure. The cost of a return trip by jeep from UB is US$33.

Eej Khad – Mother Rock

Eej Khad stands near the village of Khöshigiin Ar, 15km south of Zuunmod near Mount Avdarkhangai. According to the local people this rock is said to have special spiritual powers and a popular cult has sprung up around it. The story is that a virtuous young girl and her flock of sheep were transformed into rock. Rumours are that the rock can heal the broken-hearted. Visitors place silk scarves on the rock along with other offerings. There is nowhere to stay nearby but you can camp, although it is not recommended due to the litter which surrounds the rock, and the stray dogs which it attracts. Apparently since the ground is sacred nothing can be removed. Cost by jeep return to UB, US$35/40.

Enkhiin Els and Tavangiin Els

These belts of sculptured sand dunes lie in the area of Ikh Khairkhan Mountain (1,668m), and are described as old beaches in an ancient landscape

To get there, hire your own vehicle and drive 102km on a paved road from Ulaanbaatar to Enkhiin Els (Moltsog), and from there on unpaved tracks 30km south to the dune area. A return trip by jeep from UB costs US$80.

Suggested itinerary
Horse trek in Gorkhi-Terelj National Park

To experience the openness and hospitality of Mongolian people and to see some magnificent landscape it is possible to ride and hike in mountains that lie just 80km from the capital in Gorkhi-Terelj National Park. This ten-day itinerary is organised by Off the Map Tours (see page 227).

To climb Khürel Togoot (Bronze Pot) and to hike and ride in the Altan Ölgii mountains, you start from Ar Khurakh Ger Camp and ride through wooded grasslands to Khalazan Bürged. Having camped there, you then continue on horseback for a day to Tögöl Mod, from where an early morning start on foot (leaving the horses at the camp) gets you to the top of the 500m 'pot'. The climb is on loose shale, so bring good boots. The alpine scenery is breathtaking. Returning to camp, the next day you ride on to the Zaan (Elephant) River and up and over Khavirgan Davaa (a mountain pass). This brings you to the far side of the Altan Ölgii Mountains. Tether the horses and leave them with a guardian, then climb the west flank on foot, to the flat summit from where there are marvellous views over the surrounding countryside. The return ride brings you to Günjiin Temple ruins, from where you ride downhill to Baruun Bayan River, the winter quarters of several nomadic families. Having paid a visit to them, you then return by jeep to Ulaanbaatar.

Karakoram Expeditions (see page 226) offer biking and hiking tours to Terelj. Indeed, most tour companies based in Ulaanbaatar (see page 225) will provide itineraries to Terelj and the environs.

ÖVÖRKHANGAI AIMAG

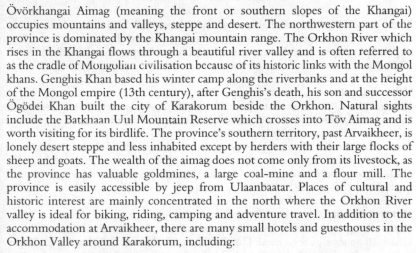

BRIEF FACTS
Population density 1.88 per km²
Area 62,900km²
Aimag centre Arvaikheer
Districts 19
Elevation of Arvaikheer 1,913m
Livestock and crops Horses, cattle, goats, sheep/wheat
Ethnic groups Khalkha
Distance from Arvaikheer to Ulaanbaatar 430km
Average temperatures July +15.3°C, January –14.7°C

Övörkhangai Aimag (meaning the front or southern slopes of the Khangai) occupies mountains and valleys, steppe and desert. The northwestern part of the province is dominated by the Khangai mountain range. The Orkhon River which rises in the Khangai flows through a beautiful river valley and is often referred to as the cradle of Mongolian civilisation because of its historic links with the Mongol khans. Genghis Khan based his winter camp along the riverbanks and at the height of the Mongol empire (13th century), after Genghis's death, his son and successor Ögödei Khan built the city of Karakorum beside the Orkhon. Natural sights include the Batkhaan Uul Mountain Reserve which crosses into Töv Aimag and is worth visiting for its birdlife. The province's southern territory, past Arvaikheer, is lonely desert steppe and less inhabited except by herders with their large flocks of sheep and goats. The wealth of the aimag does not come only from its livestock, as the province has valuable goldmines, a large coal-mine and a flour mill. The province is easily accessible by jeep from Ulaanbaatar. Places of cultural and historic interest are mainly concentrated in the north where the Orkhon River valley is ideal for biking, riding, camping and adventure travel. In addition to the accommodation at Arvaikheer, there are many small hotels and guesthouses in the Orkhon Valley around Karakorum, including:

Bayan Bürd Hotel Tel: 55 2315
Möngön Mod Hotel Tel: 55 2777
Hotel Zon Tel: 55 2945
Orkhon Hotel

Private *gers* and *ger* camps provide traditional accommodation at US$35–45 (including meals) per day. A typical dinner would be barbecued mutton; beer costs T1,200. *Ger* camps in the region include **Kublai Khan Ger Camp**, **Chandmani Ger Camp**, **Möngön Mod Ger Camp** and **Anar Ger Camp**. Camping is popular along the Orkhon River.

Highlights
• Erdene Zuu Monastery
• Hot springs at Khujirt
• Orkhon waterfall and river valley

Arvaikheer
Located in the southern part of the Khangai mountain range, Arvaikheer means 'barley fields'. It is a friendly service town with limited tourist facilities, though this

doesn't stop some travellers from stopping over to eat, sleep and prepare for their onward journey. Arvaikheer has a number of bars, a post office, cinema and a theatre. There is a good, daily market for food supplies. Local visitor sites include two museums and a large monastery (listed below).

Getting there from Ulaanbaatar
By road
There is a paved road from Ulaanbaatar to Arvaikheer (via Kharkhorin) which finishes west of Arvaikheer; a 200km rough road continues west to Bayankhongor (centre of Bayankhongor Aimag). The bus for Bayankhongor leaves Arvaikheer petrol station between 15.00–16.00 daily. Ulaanbaatar to Arvaikheer costs T9,000 by bus; T10,000 by minibus, otherwise hire a jeep and driver in Ulaanbaatar and expect to pay T500 per kilometre, approximately US$190 in total; limited jeep transport is available locally.

By air
There's a MIAT scheduled flight from Ulaanbaatar on Tuesdays (one-hour flight), with some direct flights to Kharkhorin landing strip in the summer only. The airport is 1km south of the town; for MIAT's local representative office, tel: 55 2237.

Where to stay
Khangai Hotel West of the town square; tel: 55 2676. Rooms start at US$13 (T14,800).
Bayan Bulag Hotel A block south of the square. Has a restaurant and bar, serving local food and beer. Rooms cost US$15 (T17,100).
Altan Ovoo Hotel A block south of the square next to Bayan Bulag Hotel; tel: 55 2360. Has de-luxe rooms with showers. Cost US$30 (T34,170).
Orkhon Hotel On the outskirts of town; tel: 55 2434. A good hotel with en-suite rooms and bathrooms. Cost: US$15 (T17,100) per room.

Where to eat
Bayan Bulag and Altan Ovoo hotel restaurants (see locations above charge US$8–10 on average for a meal. Hotels will also pack picnic lunches for US$5 per person; order ahead of time. Otherwise, food supplies can be bought at the shop in the Khangai Hotel or at the local market on the town square.

Local canteens (*guanz*) and noodle stalls near the square supply fast food such as meat and noodle soup for T600/700.

What to see and do
Gandan Muntsaglan Khiid
North of the town square, this monastery was built in 1991. It has a collection of *tanka* (religious scroll paintings) and a shop which sells religious items. The entrance fee is currently T1,000 (just under US$1).

Aimag Museum
A five–ten-minute walk south of the square, the Aimag Museum's exhibits include stuffed mountain/desert animals, fossils and local artwork. It's open weekdays 09.00–12.00/15.00–18.00; entrance fee T1,000 (just under US$1).

Zanabazar Memorial Museum
Near the Aimag Museum, south of the square beside the park, this museum displays works by Zanabazar (1635–1723), the first religious leader of Mongolia

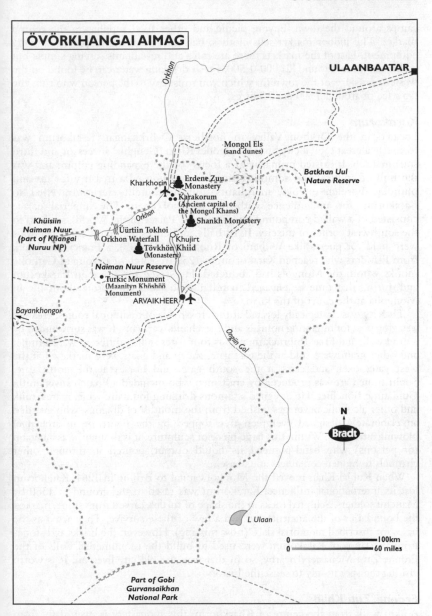

ÖVÖRKHANGAI AIMAG

ULAANBAATAR

Orkhon

Mongol Els
(sand dunes)

Kharkhorin
Erdene Zuu
Monastery

Batkhan Uul
Nature Reserve

Karakorum
(Ancient capital of
the Mongol Khans)

Orkhon

Shankh Monastery

Khüisiin
Naiman Nuur
(part of Khangai
Nuruu NP)

Üürtiin Tokhoi
Orkhon Waterfall

Khujirt

Tövkhön Khiid
(Monastery)

Naiman Nuur Reserve

Turkic Monument
(Maanityn Khöshöö
Monument)

ARVAIKHEER

Bayankhongor

Orgiin Gol

N

Bradt

L Ulaan

0 ———— 100km
0 ———— 60 miles

Part of Gobi
Gurvansaikhan
National Park

and an extremely accomplished Buddhist artist and sculptor. The entrance fee is just T1,000 (just under US$1).

Sights in Övörkhangai Aimag
Kharkhorin
Located 373km southwest of Ulaanbaatar, this modern, agricultural service town is built near the site of ancient Karakorum, the great Mongolian capital, established in 1235. Kharkhorin offers limited tourist facilities and most groups stay in *ger*

camps around the town, buying picnic and other food supplies in the central market. The indoor market sells clothes, hats and a limited supply of camping equipment. East of the markets there are cafés and restaurants serving simple but edible dishes for around T1,000–1,500. Fresh drinking water can be found on the western outskirts of the town for which you must pay to the person who runs the tap a fee of around T500 per 2.5 litres.

Karakorum

Located in the Orkhon Valley in northern Övörkhangai, Karakorum was formerly a great capital city built by Ögödei Khan (Genghis' successor and third son) in 1235. It existed primarily as a focus for the expanding empire and was the hub of political and administrative life and housed a treasury for tax and plunder. Foreign envoys, merchants and prominent clerics travelled to Karakorum for an audience with the Mongol khan. The imperial palace consisted of a walled compound known as the 'Palace of the World', situated in the southwest corner of the city. In its halls, audiences, banquets and receptions were held for guests like William of Rubruck (1215–95), a Franciscan monk from Flanders who reached Karakorum in 1253 in search of a group of Catholic monks whom the Mongols had abducted. He stayed for a year in Karakorum and during that time he engaged in religious debates and wrote about life in Mongolia at the court of the khan.

The city was strategically located at the crossroads of traditional routes, creating a staging post for migrating nomads and merchants' caravans. It was surrounded by a mud wall, and Friar Rubruck mentions four gates selling different wares: millet and other grain were sold at the east gate, sheep and goats were marketed at the west gate, oxen and carts at the south gate, and horses at the north gate. Sophisticated art was produced by craftsmen who included a French silversmith, Guillaume Bouchier. He designed a famous drinking fountain: wine, mares' milk and other alcoholic beverages gushed from the mouths' of dragons, who guarded an elaborately designed evergreen tree topped by the figure of an archangel blowing a trumpet. Within this large piece of sculpture, it is thought, was a person (or persons) who hand-pumped its liquid output, poured in through other channels to hidden containers at its base.

When Kublai Khan moved the Mongol capital to Beijing in 1264, Karakorum lost its international influence. Karakorum was rased to the ground in 1380 by Manchu soldiers. Sculpted rocks in the shape of turtles, carved from stone, marked the boundaries of the ancient city, and a few of these survive. They acted as the bases for inscribed memorial slabs (now missing). However, the bricks and stones from the ruins of Karakorum were used to build the monumental walls of the Erdene Zuu Monastery nearby, so in that way the old city lives on. It is worth visiting the spot if only to sense the history.

Erdene Zuu Khiid

A 2km walk from the centre of Kharkhorin, this monastery is open daily from 09.00–21.00, though the museum closes at 17.00. Entrance to the monastery grounds·is free, but to enter the temples you must buy a ticket (US$3 or T3,000) which includes a guided tour. The shop located inside the compound (see map) is well-stocked with souvenirs, and there are computers, with email access and a telephone line that travellers can use.

Erdene Zuu probably means 'Precious Buddha', since the main object of veneration at Erdene Zuu is the Zandan Zuu (Sandalwood Buddha). It is Mongolia's oldest Buddhist monastery, founded in 1586 by Abtai Khan, and was one of the few

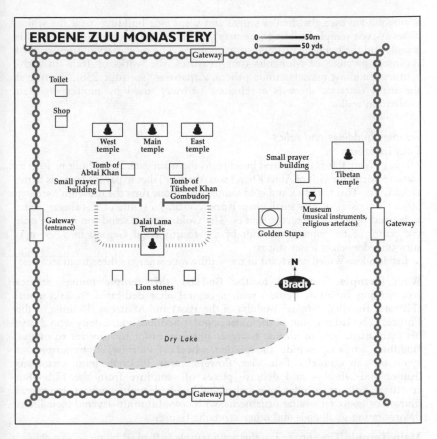

ERDENE ZUU MONASTERY

0 ▬▬▬▬ 50m
0 ▬▬▬▬ 50 yds

Gateway

Toilet

Shop

West temple

Main temple

East temple

Small prayer building

Tibetan temple

Tomb of Abtai Khan

Small prayer building

Tomb of Tüsheet Khan Gombudorj

Gateway (entrance)

Dalai Lama Temple

Museum (musical instruments, religious artefacts)

Golden Stupa

Gateway

Lion stones

N

Bradt

Dry Lake

Gateway

monasteries to survive, partly intact, the destruction of religious establishments in the 1930s. The colossal grey brick walls (400m x 400m) that enclose the monastery compound were constructed using the stones and bricks from the ruined capital of Karakorum city. The defensive walls are extremely thick and every hundred yards or so they bear huge stupas, funeral monuments or relic holders of Buddhist saints. Each wall has a gateway at midpoint. In total there are 108 similarly sized, white-painted stupas which tower above the stout, outer walls (108 being a symbolic, sacred Buddhist number). They are placed at slightly irregular intervals (see map). Heavy damage was inflicted on the temple buildings in 1731 by Manchu forces but they were later repaired. From 1941–90 the religious life of the monastery was virtually shut down, and Erdene Zuu became a national museum with no monks in residence. A few special visitors were shown around. Religious life began again during the 1990s. In 1997, the government decided to restore the monastery.

At its height Erdene Zuu had around a hundred temples as part of the monastery complex, with a thousand resident monks, who lived in nearby *gers*. Five temples, stupas, some small buildings used for prayer and some tombs remain (described overleaf). A surprising number of statues, masks and Buddhist scroll paintings (*tankas*) somehow survived the religious purges in the 20th century – hidden or buried in the nearby mountains or stored in local homes at great risk to the owners. An important building which survived is the large golden-topped stupa, which stands almost opposite the main entrance and is surrounded by eight smaller stupas and some side buildings near the white, Tibetan-style temple building (see map). Religious ceremonies are held in this temple and the public can attend some of them. The monastery houses some of the most precious of Mongolia's art treasures, the works of 16th- to 19th-century Buddhist masters, among them, Zanabazar (see page 258). Starting at the main entrance there is a religious pathway, used by monks on their meditation walks.

Temples buildings and relics
Dalai Lama Süm
All on its own, this is the nearest building to the main gate. It was built in 1675 to commemorate the visit of Abtai Khan's son Altan to Tibet to pay his respects to the Dalai Lama. This red brick and gold temple was at one time the museum's archive office. It consists of two small chapels and contains a statue of Zanabazar, some *tankas* and figures of protective deities. The Golden Stupa stands on its own near the centre of the monastery; built by the fourth Bogd Gegeen in 1799, it is surrounded by eight lesser stupas.

Inside a low-walled courtyard in the southwest corner are three main temples:

West Temple Dedicated to the Buddha, this temple houses statues representing Buddhist deities, with a central altar dedicated to Sakyamuni (Historic Buddha), Sanjaa (Buddha of the Past) and Maitreya (Buddha of the Future). The latter is one of the most popular bodhisattvas, a deity who delays his own attainment of *nirvana* (state of bliss) in order to minister to others. Buddhist artefacts include the golden wheel of eternity, eight auspicious symbols – an umbrella, fish, vase, flowers, cards, lucky diagram, victorious banner and wheel – and delicate pieces of sculpture from the 17th–18th centuries. Folk art includes *balin*, baked and highly decorated, wheat-dough and mutton or goose fat as altar ornaments, with colouful multi-layered medallions incorporating small gods and other symbolic figures.

Main Temple The entrance to the main temple is flanked by protective deities: on the left is Gongor, known as Sita Mahakala, while on the right is Baldan Lkham, known as Sridevi. Inside the temple the central statue is of the child Buddha. To his right is the Buddha of medicine, Otoch or Manla in Tibetan and, to his left, Amida, also called Amitabha, the Buddha of Infinite Light. There are statues to the sun and the moon gods and other works of art including guardian figures and *tsam* (religious dance) masks dating from the 16th–17th century, including works by Zanabazar.

East Temple In this temple the central statue is of the adolescent Buddha. On his right is a statue of Tsongkhapa who founded the Yellow Hat sect of Buddhism, while on his left is a statue of Janraisig, the Buddha of Compassion.

In front of the three temples are the gravestones of Abtai Khan (1554–88) and his grandson Tüsheet Khan Gombodorj (the father of Zanabazar). The side building (see map) located next to the Golden Stupa is the oldest building in the complex. It has a mandala, a mystical diagram used for meditation purposes, on the ceiling.

Lavrin Süm
Located in the northwest corner (see map) is a large, white-walled, Tibetan-style temple building where daily ceremonies are held – usually at 11.00; times may vary so ask at the visitor centre.

Other relics

There are two **stone turtles** (symbols of eternity and protection) located northwest of the monastery as a reminder of the past. Originally they numbered four, and marked the boundaries of the city of Karakorum.

Square of Happiness and Prosperity, an open area, is located in front of a small temple dedicated to the Dalai Lama; to its northeast are the foundation stones on top of which a gigantic *ger* was constructed. The *ger* is thought to have accommodated up to 300 people during the assemblies of local khans in the heyday of the Mongol empire.

The **Phallic Rock** stands a half-hour's walk from the monastery and can be seen from the main Ulaanbaatar road, a kilometre from Kharkhorin. As the name suggests, it is a large rock in the shape of a phallus. It was meant to warn monks to keep away from women: one story has it that the stone represents the phallus of a womanising monk who was castrated. Many visitors take the opportunity to go for a walk and see it, particularly women who want children; you can't get lost as the path is clearly worn.

Khujirt Hot Springs

Located on the banks of the River Khüjirt, this is a health spa, opened in 1941, that grew up around the hot water springs. The spa is frequented by local people, and now welcomes foreign visitors. Water temperatures can reach 55°C. If you visit you may see a local doctor who will take your pulse and blood pressure and advise you to keep warm and to avoid alcohol for at least two weeks! A new hotel is under construction as part of tourist development in the region. There is a *ger* camp nearby which offers accommodation and meals for around US$35–40; you will need your own transport to get there.

Orkhon Khürkhree

You'll need your own transport to get to these waterfalls, 80km west of Khujirt. Formed by volcanic eruptions about 20,000 years ago, the waterfall cascades from a height of 20m. It is a scenic, tranquil spot and the surrounding nature is undisturbed, since so few people live here. As such, there are opportunities for good walking or riding in the area. Downstream there is a deep gorge and 10km away are the cold springs of Uurtiin Tokhoi, where there is a second, smaller waterfall (with a 4.5m drop).

Shankhyn Khiid

You'll find this monastery in Shankh village, on the main road halfway between Kharkhorin to Khüjirt and about 20km south of Erdene Zuu Monastery in the Sarnai River valley. The main temple (of three) has been restored and houses a small community of monks. Ceremonies take place in the main temple at 09.00; visitors are welcome, though there's an entrance fee of US$2 (T2,300).

Historically the monastery was known as the Western Monastery. Its full name is Shankhyn Baruun Khüree or Ribogandanshaduulin Khiid, one of several monasteries built in the early to mid-1700s, during the lifetime of Zanabazar. It was a monastery of importance and once housed Genghis Khan's black, military banner. Previously home to 1,500 monks and surrounded by wooden buildings, it was closed in 1937, the buildings and their contents destroyed and the monks dispersed. There is a story that five monks continued their religious practices in secret for many years, meeting in a local *ger*. When the monastery re-opened in 1990, one of them returned; local people are fund-raising to build a stupa in his honour.

These remote temples and monasteries are best reached on foot and are often incorporated in riding or hiking tours as somewhere interesting to stop and see on a day's journey. One monastery worth mentioning is Dövkhön (or Tövkhön) Khiid, located in the forested hills of Bat-Ölzii district, 68km from Erdene Zuu. It is famous for its cave and a smaller meditation rock chamber used by Zanabazar.

Mongol Els
Lying on the eastern border of Övörkhangai Aimag on the Ulaanbaatar road (270km west of the capital) in Bürd district, Mongol Els is a belt of sand dunes covering an area of around 2,800km². Many people stop there on their way to Arvaikheer, and the magnificent dunes, surrounded by hills with willow trees, streams and bushes are worth stopping for. The dunes liven up a stretch of otherwise uninteresting road and give the visitor a taste of the desert. You can hire horses and camels to ride in the region and around the dunes.

Bayangobi Ger Camp offers accommodation, charging US$40 (T45,600) per person, including meals. For reservations contact Juulchin Foreign Tourism Corporation, Genghis Khan Avenue 5B, Ulaanbaatar tel: 976 11 328428; fax: 11 320246; email: juulchin@mongol.net; web: www.mol.mn/juulchin.

Batkhaan Uul Nature Reserve
Located on the northwest border of the aimag extending into Töv Aimag, this mountainous area is part of the Khangai and Khentii mountain ranges. Visitors driving west from Ulaanbaatar often stop to camp and enjoy and scenery, as the area is conveniently near the main road from Ulaanbaatar to Arvaikheer. Bayangobi Ger Camp (see above) is nearby.

Khankhentii National Park
This remote mountainous forest region, in the northwest corner of the aimag, extends into Bayankhongor Aimag and is described there. Apart from the Eight Lakes area (described below), the park is not well visited due to transport difficulties.

Eight Lakes (Naiman Nuur)
Formed by volcanic eruptions centuries ago and lying 70km southwest of Orkhon waterfall, the Eight Lakes are part of the Khangai Nuruu National Park and lie in a long and broad valley which divides the Gobi Altai from the Khangai mountain range. Access is difficult as earth roads are often impassable due to marshy ground and weather conditions.

Activities
Mountain biking in the Orkhon River valley
This ten-day biking holiday is offered by Off the Map Tours (see page 227). The itinerary takes you from Kharkhorin along the Orkhon River valley and back again. You will bike along typical dirt roads and tracks across rolling hilly countryside and camp by rivers and mountain streams, where you can to experience the vastness of the steppe scenery and the beauty and silence of the mountains. You will also eat outdoors around campfires and in local restaurants and spend some well-earned rest in a hot, open-air spring bath. Furthermore, you will also have the chance to meet with nomadic families, drink fermented mare's or cow's milk vodka and salty-milky-tea with yak-herding families and see their yaks grazing on the high pastures above Khayasaan Gorge. The itinerary also offers the chance, when biking along the River Orkhon, to stop at a magnificent waterfall where you can rest your weary muscles, before continuing along the valley to Khujirt, where you will find more hot spring baths to recuperate in and where you can relax and totally let go.

ARKHANGAI AIMAG

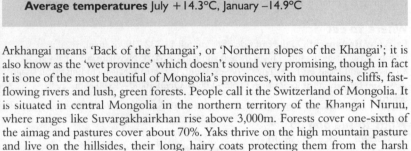

BRIEF FACTS
Population 104,300
Area 55,300km²
Aimag centre Tsetserleg
Districts 19
Elevation of Tsetserleg 1,631m
Livestock/crops horses, yaks/potatoes, hay
Ethnic groups Khalkha, Ööld
Distance from Tsetserleg to Ulaanbaatar 463km
Average temperatures July +14.3°C, January –14.9°C

Arkhangai means 'Back of the Khangai', or 'Northern slopes of the Khangai'; it is also know as the 'wet province' which doesn't sound very promising, though in fact it is one of the most beautiful of Mongolia's provinces, with mountains, cliffs, fast-flowing rivers and lush, green forests. People call it the Switzerland of Mongolia. It is situated in central Mongolia in the northern territory of the Khangai Nuruu, where ranges like Suvargakhairkhan rise above 3,000m. Forests cover one-sixth of the aimag and pastures cover about 70%. Yaks thrive on the high mountain pasture and live on the hillsides, their long, hairy coats protecting them from the harsh winter weather. The nature, along with the opportunity for adventure travel to lakes and rivers, are the main attractions of this province.

Highlights
* Ögii Nuur – lake
* Chuluut river fishing
* Terkhiin Tsagaan Nuur (Great White Lake) – sightseeing, hiking and camping
* Tsenkher and Shivert – hot springs
* Turkic (6th–8th century), Uighur (8th–10th century) – archaeological sites

Tsetserleg
Tsetserleg (meaning 'garden') is situated at the southern foot of the Bulgan Mountain, the site of Zayayn Khüree Lamasery. The town is laid out with spacious streets and has more charm than most other aimag centres. Peaks of the Khangai range are seen in the south and Bulgan rises sharply to the north. Behind the museum, a path leads to a small unoccupied temple in the hills which is worth visiting for the view. Tsetserleg is an excellent place to use as a base if you are touring the Mongolian lakes – Ögii and Terkhiin Tsagaan Nuur (Great White Lake). It is a busy market town where you can pick up supplies at the daily market for your journeys.

Getting there from Ulaanbaatar
By air
There are currently no scheduled flights from Ulaanbaatar to Tsetserleg but this situation may change in the future. The airport is located 1km south of town.
By road
Most tourists travel to Tsetserleg by public bus/minibus or private jeep. Buses run between UB and Tsetserleg daily (except Tues) leaving around 08.00 (or later, sometimes waiting until the bus is full). The fare is T14,000 (roughly US$12),

with a travel time of approximately 9 hours. To hire a jeep with a driver costs from T250–500 per km depending on the sort of jeep (which works out at between US$100–200 from UB, cheaper if travelling in a shared jeep).

Where to stay

Hotel Bulgan East of the town square; tel: 73 2233. This is one of the better hotels. Rooms with bathrooms cost US$18 (T20,500).

Hotel Sasa 2–3 minutes' walk east of the town square; no telephone. Has a friendly atmosphere and good service. Rooms cost from US$10 (T11,400).

Hotel Sundur South of the town beside the market on the UB road; tel: 73 2359. Simple, cheap rooms and a restaurant. Rates US$10 (T11,400).

Camping is possible several kilometres south of the town along the riverbank.

Where to eat

Fairview Restaurant On the east side of town; tel: 11 332 21096; email: twonomads@magicnet.mn. This is owned and run by Mark Newham, and many foreigners and locals eat here. They serve excellent, low-cost meals including pizza, lasagne, stews and burgers, all at local prices (T600–1,000). Open 10.00—15.00 Monday to Saturday.

What to see and do

Arkhangai Palace Museum

This museum is housed in the temple buildings of the former Zayayn Khüree Monastery, founded in 1631. In the 17th century the monastery was one of the most active in Mongolia. It had five temples and housed 1,000 monks, and on ceremonial occasions over 4,000 monks were known to have participated in events there. Two of its main temples were destroyed in the religious purges of the 1930s; it survived destruction to be used as a storehouse. Three temples remain: Gandan, Niser and Lavran; their architecture is a mixture of Mongolian and Tibetan styles.

The museum exhibits Buddhist ritual objects and features a collection of traditional Mongolian costumes, traditional tools, a *ger*, musical instruments, saddles and weapons; and a collection of 20th-century paintings by local artists. It's open weekdays 09.00–16.00, and there's an entry fee of US$2–3 (T2,380–3,420).

Buyandelgerüülekh Khiid

This is the main active monastery, located just north of the town square. Regular services are held in the mornings in the main hall or in a neighbouring *ger*; if you want to attend, ask the monks.

Sights in Arkhangai Aimag

Terkhiin Tsaagan Nuur

In the northwest part of the province, Terkhiin Tsaagan Nuur ('White Lake of River Terleh') is a beautiful body of water surrounded by extinct volcanoes. The lake covers 16km x 20km, and is 10m deep. Some parts of its shoreline are sandy and in summer the water is warm enough to swim. The area offers excellent opportunities for fishing (pike and perch). It is also possible to hike from the northeastern shore to Khorgo Uul volcano (2,965m). A local guide will help you to find the best route. On the way there are caves worth exploring. You may also spot deer, *argali* (wild sheep) and wild boar. The lake, the surrounding volcanoes, and the animal and birdlife are now protected within the 73,000-hectare Khorgo/Terkhiin Tsaagan Nuur National Park.

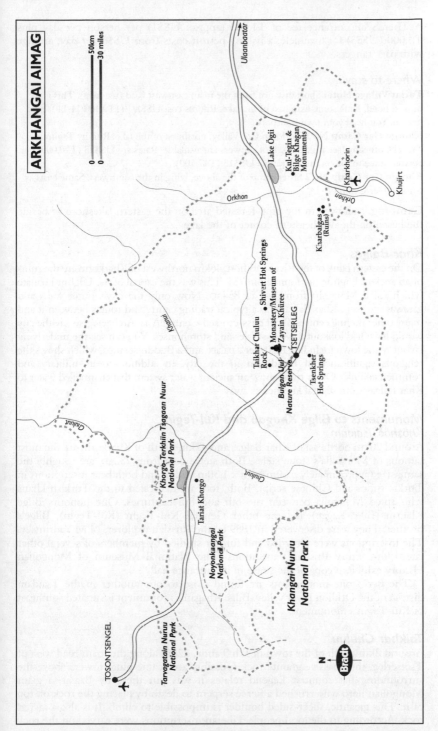

There's an entrance fee of T1,000 (approx US$1) per person per day plus T3,000 (US$3) for a vehicle; a fishing permit costs from US$8 per day; arrange with park rangers.

Where to stay

Tariat Village Hotel Short distance from the main east/west road (see map). This is the nearest hotel, lying some 6km east of the lake. Rooms cost US$8/10 (T9,100/11,140) per person. You need your own transport.

Khorgo Ger Camp No 1 Zürkhiin Gol Valley, northeast of the lake. Run by Tsolmon Travel Company (see page 227). Hot showers are available. Rates are US$25 (T28,000) per person; three meals cost an additional US$15 (T17,100).

Khorgo Ger Camp No 2 Sister camp of the above, lying in the southwest. Same costs as Khorgo Ger Camp No l.

Camping is allowed in the pine-forested area on the eastern lakeshore or beside the beach on the northeastern corner of the lake.

Khar Balgas

On the eastern bank of the River Orkhon, 46km northwest of Kharkorin are the ruins of an ancient Uighur city founded in 751. This was the capital of the Uighur khanate which ruled Mongolia from 745 to 854AD. Now only the city's outer walls and gateways remain. Khar Balgas was a typical trading centre and routes between it and many other trading centres like it criss-crossed Central Asia. Archaelogists say the city would have had lookout towers, stables and storehouses. You can see the underlying layout of the town including the ruler's palace and a Buddhist stupa, which shows the religious significance of Buddhism in the city, in addition to its military and commercial links. Other ruins show an ancient water system that channelled water to Khar Balgas from several kilometres away.

Monuments to Bilge Khagan and Kul-Tegin
Khöshöö Tsaidam

Around 20km northeast of Khar Balgas and 47km north of Kharkorin are the most famous of Mongolia's stone steles. Both stelae date from 732AD, are roughly the same size (approximately 3.30m high x 1.30m wide), and both bear inscriptions in Turkic runes and Chinese script. Both, too, are dedicated to the Turkish khans who ruled Mongolia between the 6th and 8th centuries. One honours Bilge Khagan (Bilgä-Kagan) and the other General Kul-Tegin (Köl-Tegin), Bilge's brother. They were discovered in 1889 by the Russian explorer, N M Yadrintsev. The inscriptions were recorded and further studied by members of several other late 19th-century Russian expeditions. The National Museum of Mongolian History exhibits a copy of the stelae in its entrance hall.

The two stone monuments are found close to one another in the Tsaidam district of the Orkhon River valley. Bilge Khagan's monument is situated southeast of Kul-Tegin's monument.

Taikhar Chuluu

Around 2km north of the town of Ikh Tamir, 22km along the main road west of Tsetserleg, this massive granite rock (possibly a volcanic plug) towers above the surrounding flat country. Legend relates it was put there by Baatar, a giant Mongolian hero who crushed a fierce serpent to death by placing the rock on top of it. This gigantic, sheer-sided boulder is impossible to climb. It is also a sacred rock. According to the local people Tibetan inscriptions were carved on the rock but sadly they are covered by graffiti markings (of the recent past), which have destroyed them.

Close to the rock there is an excellent *ger* camp run by Mongolian Outdoor Safaris. Rates are US$45 including meals; tel: 11 311008.

Tsenkher hot springs

These springs lie south of Tsetserleg in Tsenkher district, a ten-hour drive or two-hour flight plus a four-hour jeep ride from UB. The springs and streams are well-developed and jointly owned by a Japanese company. The waters are supposed to have curative properties for joints and other ailments. Outdoor pools are attended by staff who can cool or heat the water via a water-gate system; there are also indoor pools. Men and women bathe separately. Electricity is generated using sunlight and the temperature difference between the hot springs and the river water. It is an excellent place to relax.

Nearby Tsenkher Hot Springs Ger Camp (tel/fax: 11 358005) sleeps up to 60 people and costs US$35 per day including meals such as stone-grilled mutton, greenhouse vegetables, eggs (when available) boiled in the hot springs, and fermented mares' milk or cows' milk vodka.

Shivert hot springs

Located in a valley some 50km northwest of Tsetserleg (see map), you will need to ride or hike to get to these springs, and you'll need a 4WD. Allow plenty of travel time. The hot springs are natural chlorine- and potassium-compound springs and are currently very undeveloped. Apart from the springs the region has interesting deer stones and is an attractive place to camp, ride and hike.

Lake Ögii

Lake Ögii lies off the main Ulaanbaatar/Tsetserleg road as you enter the province, about 150km from Tsetserleg. This is a wonderful area for fishing and camping, birdwatching and generally chilling out to enjoy the freedom of the countryside. See itinerary section for further details.

National parks and protected areas
Khorgo Terkhiin Tsagaan Nuur National Park
See page 128.

Noyonkhangai National Park
Located on the western boundary of the province (see map) in a very remote mountain area, this park has been a national park since 1998, largely thanks to its curative mineral waters and wildlife. Access is difficult, due to poor road conditions in Khangai sum (district). To get there by jeep, drive to Noyonkhangai village, which lies outside the park's boundaries on the north side. This area is not frequented by tourists and there are no tourist facilities. The entrance fee is US$2; pay a ranger, if and when you meet one. There is no fencing; there are no park gates and no offices *in situ*.

Bulgan Uul Nature Reserve
Covering an 18km² area of mountain range immediately north of Tsetserleg, this has been a natural reserve since 1985 due to the diversity of its birdlife. The mountains, whose northern slopes are larch covered, reach almost 2,000m. Pictographs and carvings of deer and other animals are found on rocks in the area dating from the Bronze Age. The entrance fee is US$2, paid to a ranger.

Tarvagatain Nuruu National Park
Located on the western border of the aimag with Zavkhan Aimag, the national park extends into Zavkhan and is described on pages 129–30.

Khangai Nuruu National Park
Covering a remote mountainous area in the southwest part of the aimag, extending into Bayankhongor Aimag (see page 129).

Activities
Some of the best fishing takes place in this aimag. The rivers Tamir and Chuluut rise in the Khangai Mountains and flow north with the Orkhon River (which runs through the western part of the province) to join the great Selenge River which flows into Lake Baikal in Southern Siberia and from there to the Arctic Ocean.

Fishing outfitters
There's a new shop in Ulaanbaatar that provides a good standard of fishing gear and other camping equipment:

Ayanchin Outfitters Seoul Av, near State Department Store at Seoul Street Building 21; tel: 11 319211; email: avanchin@magicnet.com; web: www.avanchin.com. Open Mon–Fri 10.00–19.00; Sat–Sun 11.00–18.00.

Suggested itinerary
A riding/driving holiday
For this itinerary you will need to work out timing and logistics with a Mongolian travel company in advance, or with a guide/translator and driver on the spot. Allow 10–14 days for this tour, which begins with a drive by jeep from Ulaanbaatar to the Great White Lake stopping en route for the night at Khustain Nuruu, the wild horse reserve 100km west of UB. From there, continue the next day by jeep to the Orkhon Valley, paying a visit to the famous Buddhist monastery of Erdene Zuu. From here you can arrange horses to ride north into Arkhangai Aimag, where you'll find yourself galloping across unfenced pastureland under the craggy granite mountains of the Khangai range. Ride and camp for a few days before handing the horses back. Stop in Tsetserleg to sightsee and camp overnight beside the sacred rock, Taikhar Chuluu, then continue by jeep to the Great White Lake in the northwest, spending a day hiking around the lake. To ease stiff and aching joints take an open-air bath in the hot mineral springs at Tsenkher, before finally returning to Ulaanbaatar via the sand dunes at Mongol Els, where you may hire a horse or camel to experience riding in desert conditions.

Fishing and sightseeing in the Chuluut area
As with the above, costs and logistics for this trip can be worked out in advance with a tour company or on the spot with a guide/translator and jeep driver. This itinerary begins with a jeep ride to Arkhangai (150km west of Tsetserleg) where you can make camp beside the Chuluut River. Visit the Chuulut River gorge with its dramatic scenery and camp there, spending a few days fishing or birdwatching. From there, drive (45km) to Tariat village and trek to the volcanic crater above the Great White Lake, where you can pitch your tent by the lakeside. Next morning relax on the sandy beach by the lake, allowing plenty of time to take in the scenery before driving back to Ulaanbaatar via the sand dune area at Elsentasarkhai, where you may ride a camel or hire a horse for the day.

Southern Region: Gobi Aimags

Gobi is defined as 'treeless terrain without marmots and with very little surface water'. It encompasses the world's most northern desert (the sand dunes in Uvs Aimag), and it shelters frozen snow melt throughout the summer in a canyon in the South Gobi. The topography of this vast territory is predominately a closed drainage depression. The landscape includes mountain ranges, springs, forests, sand dunes and steppes. Towards the west the Altai peaks rise to over 4,000m. Subsoil is rich in copper, molybdenum, gold, tin, iron ore and coal; forests of poplar, elm, willow and aspen grow in the mountains and near oases, feather grass and leek cover the plains. Few plants grow in the bare soils of the semi-desert and sand dunes are almost devoid of plant life though a bushy shrub called *zag* thrives in places where there is enough ground water. The Gobi may be described as land waiting to be watered, with the slightest amount of precipitation shrubs and wild flowers bloom and flourish. Fierce sand and wind storms are common and nearly all the region's soil has been removed by prevailing northwesterly winds and deposited in North Central China as loess. There are many types of Gobi – 33 in all and they differ from one another, usually based on location, minerals and water supply.

The landscape commonly known as 'Gobi' stretches 3,000 miles along Mongolia's southern border and extends to parts of the far northwest, running between the Altai and the Khangai mountain ranges, as well as south into northern China. Principally the Gobi spans five Mongolian provinces (aimags) which include: Ömnögobi, Dornogobi, Dundgobi, Bayankhongor and Gobi Altai. It is a wide-open place of huge extremes: mostly it is one huge gravel plain quite unlike any other desert on earth. Of the total Gobi area only 3% is the sandy desert type. Despite these arid conditions, wildlife abounds.

Two hundred million years ago the Gobi desert was an inland sea. During this period, western Siberia and the Jungarian plains formed one vast sheet of water. Warm, damp conditions prevailed with abundant vegetation. The site of this ancient inland sea was discovered to be a treasure trove of fossilised dinosaur bones. In the 1920s the American palaeontologist, Roy Chapman Andrews, made some exciting dinosaur discoveries including fossilised dinosaur eggs and later expeditions have discovered giant prehistoric animals. (See box *Dragon bones – Bayankhongor Aimag*, page 296.)

Overall, the entire Gobi region is very sparsely populated but the modest and plain life of the people living there inspires respect. There are few roads and most places are entirely undeveloped but that is part of their charm. Behind the romance of the desert is the harsh reality of an inhospitable land. A mixture of foolhardiness and bravery is needed to travel long-distance in the Gobi, as explorer Benedict

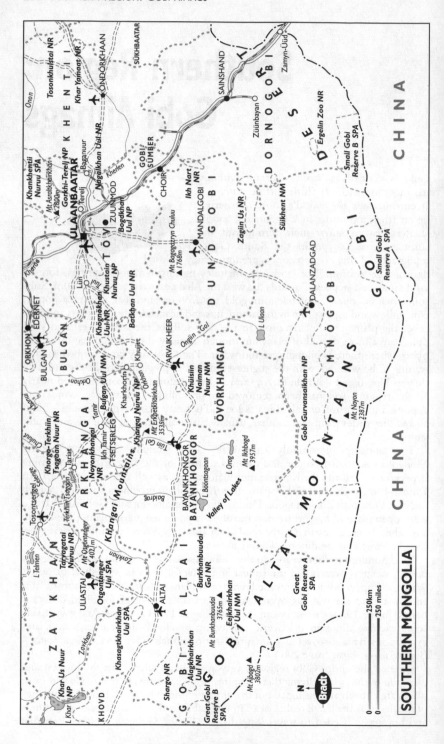

Allen discovered on his recent thousand-mile trek from the northwestern border of Mongolia, to where the Trans-Mongolian Railway cuts through the south eastern end of the Gobi.

Travel risks

Do not go into this country unprepared or underestimate the hazards of getting lost, even in broad daylight. When the sun goes down and the distant mountain profiles disappear into darkness, you very easily become disoriented, especially on a moonless night. Individual travellers should take good maps, a torch, a compass, plenty of water and some food if travelling by jeep. In the Gobi vegetation clings to the slightest root and precipitation is truly a matter of life and death. Desert terrain is a mixture of great fragility and extraordinary toughness, like the people who inhabit it.

Another thing to watch out for is estimated distance. In a desert such as the Gobi, mountain ranges appear to be much closer than they actually are. Mirages, too, tantalise and look so real that you might even start preparing your water bottle for a refill. This terrain is deceptive. Ancient travellers have long bemoaned the strangeness of the Gobi with its whispering sands and unaccountable, shrill, eerie noises. Desert caravans along the old trade routes frequently complained they lost people who wandered off following the hum of human voices that were completely imaginary.

Sudden desert storms are also a real hazard. These freak meteorological incidents last from moments to hours and can literally destroy a campsite. Dust storms, flash floods, and sudden cold snaps are unpredictable and happen mostly during the winter and spring months, but can happen at other times of year including summer.

ÖMNÖGOBI AIMAG

BRIEF FACTS
Population 46,300
Population density 0.28 per km²
Area 165,400km²
Aimag centre Dalanzadgad
Districts 15
Elevation of Dalanzadgad 1,465m
Livestock Goats, sheep, camels
Ethnic groups Khalkha
Distance from Dalanzadgad to Ulaanbaatar 553km
Average temperatures July +21.2°C, January –15.4°C

Ömnögobi is more commonly known to foreigners as the South Gobi. It is part of Mongolia's Golden Circuit, referred to in this guide as one of the classic routes. The aimag has many visitors, despite being the hottest and driest region of Mongolia: summer temperatures reach 38°C and annual precipitation is 130mm. Mountains capture what little surface moisture there is as snow which melts into streams supplying much-needed water for wildlife, livestock and the human population. Apart from the extensive Gurvansaikhan Nuruu range, known as the 'Three Beauties', the aimag is predominately flat. The desert supports thousands of black-tailed gazelles, but it is too dry to graze large domestic herds of cattle and

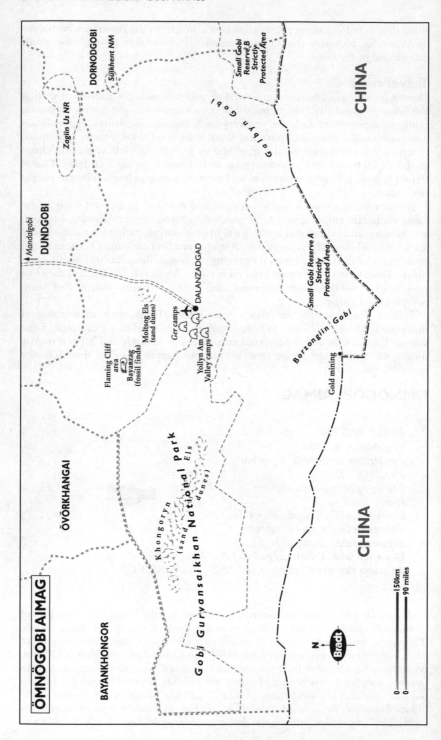

sheep which thrive on the province's steppe land further north. The Gobi is home to a quarter of Mongolia's domestic camels; they include Gobi red and Gobi brown camels, both native stock, prized for their high productivity and endurance, though their numbers are now in decline. Sadly, the wild camel appears to be endangered. The Gobi is famous for its cashmere goats: there are three species: the Gobi gurvansaikhan (brown goat), the Gurvantes (blue goat) and the Buur Nomgon (red goat). South Gobi's goats yield tonnes of soft, raw cashmere wool annually. Apart from the livestock industry, the South Gobi has a flour mill and factories for wool-scouring and candle-making, set up recently with the help of foreign investment. The aimag has mining interests in the extreme south near the border with China. Small farms produce potatoes and vegetables. Future plans for the province include upgrading the airport, possibly enabling direct flights to China and elsewhere, as part of tourism development.

Highlights
* Gurvansaikhan National Park
* Yolyn Am valley – country museum, gorge and glacier
* Bayanzag – dinosaur bones
* Khongoryn Els – sand dunes

Dalanzadgad
Dalanzadgad is located roughly 600km from Ulaanbaatar at the eastern extremity of the Altai mountain range. The town is Mongolia's most southerly aimag centre, with a population of around 13,000. It is typical of many centres with Soviet-style white, stone administrative buildings with green roofs; the town is surrounded by *ger* compounds. There is more to this isolated Gobi centre than meets the eye – a real sense of community exists and the local government has made a big effort to make the town attractive by planting trees. Beyond the town, on three sides, is endless flat steppe, while to the west are the Gurvansaikhan mountains (the 'Three Beauties').

Amongst the facilities are shops with a good supply of Western foods; a well-stocked pharmacy; a telephone exchange where international calls, faxes and emails can be sent; two reasonable hotels and two bars (one of which doubles as a nightclub); a sauna; a bank (which changes dollars) and a local airport outside the town. Entertainment includes traditional throat singing (*khöömii*) and folk dancing, which take place during festival times when the town comes alive. Dalanzadgad has a theatre and supports a group of local singers.

Getting there from Ulaanbaatar
By air
MIAT airlines fly from Ulaanbaatar to Dalandzagad (direct on Tuesdays; and via Mandalgobi on Fridays); there are also some tourist flights to Turbaaz, Juulchin Gobi camp site; it is advisable to book in advance and **confirm your flight** since double bookings in the past have caused problems. There's a luggage allowance of 15kg per person; the flight time is 90 minutes. Airport tel: 53 2657. Local MIAT office, tel: 53 2237.

By road
It is 553km from Ulaanbaatar to Dalanzadgad and it is possible to cover the distance in one day if you start very early. Two buses leave Ulaanbaatar for the South Gobi each week (Mon, Fri), stopping en route at Mandalgobi in Dundgobi Aimag. The journey time is 24 hours or more return to UB. The bus leaves from

beside the hospital on the main UB road out of town in Dalanzadgad on Wed and Sun; tickets cost around T9,000 (US$8) and can be purchased at the bus office (tel: 53 3708) beside the hospital, or in Ulaanbaatar at the long-distance bus station in the centre of town.

If hiring a car, try not to complete the trip in one go since the road conditions are bad. Instead, it is preferable to break the journey either by camping, or staying overnight in a local family ger, or at a hotel in Mandalgobi (see page 289). Petrol is available at Mandalgobi, though it is advisable to bring a supply with you.

Facilities
Changing money
ITI Bank (tel: 53-2330) is at the eastern end of town and changes US dollars; open: 9.00–18.00 (closed 13.00–14.00 for lunch).

Telephone (or Communications Centre)
This is on the main street opposite the Trade Centre. It's open 24 hours a day. You can dial direct to Ulaanbaatar and send e-mails and faxes worldwide. International calls are expensive, costing around US$8 for a 2–3 minute call.

Post office
The post office (tel: 53 2232) is at the eastern end of town and is open every day (closed 13.00–14.00) except Sunday. It is also closed when a flight arrives bringing post. It is a reliable and friendly service. Stamps for local mail (to UB) cost T200, (postcards) around T300 (letters), letters abroad cost from T550 and postcards T400.

Medical services
The hospital is situated on the main road to UB; there are English-speaking doctors and a range of Western medicine is available.

Electricity
Supplies are generally adequate in Dalanzadgad and there are in addition small generator for emergencies. In remoter areas of the Gobi power gets switched off between 11.00–18.00.

Interpreters
There are a number of young people in Dalanzadgad who are willing to act as interpreters if you need their help; the local rate is US$7 per day.

Where to stay
There are three tourist hotels in Dalanzadgad. Two are of the same standard, situated opposite each other in the town centre. Hot water comes from solar heating. Both have restaurants. The third hotel is smaller and open in winter only. Most organised tours stay outside the town in ger camps (see list below).

Gurvansaikhan Hotel (tel: 53-3830). Rates: suite (sitting room, TV and bathroom) US$20 (T22,800); a basic room (without bathroom) US$10 (T11,400).
Devshil Hotel (tel: 53-3786). De-luxe room US$20 (T22,800), simple room US$15 (T17,100).
Palace Hotel (open in winter only) Provides double rooms with twin beds, toilet and shower. The rooms are spacious and clean with bright duvet covers and colourful towels

arranged in fan shapes on the pillows. The dining-room walls are painted ice-cream pink, with grand white mouldings around an archway which leads to the bar. The hotel has only four rooms and it is difficult to book in advance. Rates are US$15 (T17,100).

Where to eat

There is no shortage of places to eat in Dalanzadgad, including the simple lunchtime road-side eating houses with fixed meals near the Trade Centre. Lunch at the **Gurvansaikhan Hotel** costs around US$2 (T2,300). The **Devshil**'s restaurant is comfortable and lunch costs around US$1–2 (T1,139–2,300). The **Simbo Bar** (tel: 053 3207) is a converted village hall to the southwest which has occasional disco dancing; open:12.00–24.00. The **Mazzala Bar** (tel: 053 3040) is cosier and more conveniently located at the centre of town, open 12.00–24.00. Both bars are quiet places. Beer costs T900 a bottle; tax (T500) is charged to male guests at the bars.

A word of warning: it is best to book meals in advance.

Typical hotel food consists of well-flavoured noodles with meat and vegetables, with a breakfast of cold meats, scrambled eggs, tea and toast. Picnic packages typically include cold noodle salad, meatballs and a litre bottle of spring water per person. The cost is roughly US$15 per day for 3 meals.

Ger camps in Ömnögobi Aimag

Tüvshin Ger Camp 42km west of Dalanzadgad(tel: 11 326419). Sleeps 110 in 42 *gers*. Has good showers, a restaurant and bar. The site was chosen for practical reasons rather than aesthetic ones. The cost of US$45 (T51,300) per person includes meals and is discounted to US$25 (T28,500) for a party of five or more.

Turbaaz, Juulchin Gobi Ger Camp 35km from Dalanzadgad; tel: 11 312769; fax: 11 311744. There are some direct local flights in summer from Ulaanbaatar to the landing strip at this camp, which sleeps 100 and is popular with organised tours, though the site itself is uninspiring. Cost: US$40 (T45,500) per person including meals.

Khavtsgait Ger Camp Near Yol valley, 40km west of Dalanzadgad; tel: 11 311521; fax:11 384097. Sleeps 100; well-situated with good activities including camel rides in the vicinity. Rates are US$40 (T45,500) per person including meals.

Duutmankhan Ger Camp Near the Khongor Els (sand dunes). Rates are $35–40 (T34,000–45,500) per person with all meals.

Mongol Baigal Ger Camp 22km from Dalanzadgad. 25 *gers*, basic arrangements with food on request. Rates are US$30 (T34,200) excluding meals; three meals cost US$18 (T20,500).

New *ger* camps are springing up in two places at Borzongiin Gobi, 700km from Ulaanbaatar. At the time of writing there are plans to fly direct to Borzongiin Gobi but it has not yet happened; to reach the camps you must fly to Dalanzadgad and travel the 70–110km from there by jeep.

Sights in Ömnögobi Aimag
Yolyn Am

Around 45km west of Dalanzadgad in the Gurvansaikhan Mountains is Yolyn Am gorge. Yol in Mongolian means 'bearded vulture' and Yolyn Am means Vulture's Gorge. This magnificent mountain valley has a 40km-long canyon containing a small area of frozen snow melt at the far end. You enter the valley on a winding mountain road which takes you to the start of the gorge. Here there is a car park and a WC – a simple pit latrine which is clearly visible as it is situated in a prominent position above the car park! Over the winter months the river water builds up a thick layer of ice which thaws slowly. In addition, the cliffs of the canyon rise so steeply that they block the sunlight from the river below, so that

SAXAUL

Saxaul (*Haloxylon ammodendron*) is the perfect plant for the Gobi: it burns like coal, it tolerates saltwater and droughts and it provides fodder. The Gobi's terrain supports 4.5 million hectares of this woody desert shrub which grows, very slowly, up to a height of 4m and is dependent on underground water sources. Known as *zag* in Mongolian, saxaul is crucial to the desert ecology. Mature saxaul (ie: 25 years and over) is a natural desert stabiliser, preventing wind erosion and the expansion of desert sands. Under favourable conditions saxaul survives for several hundred years. However, there is concern about its recent decrease. Diminishing rainfall, intensive use as camel pasture and overuse as a source of fuel are the main reasons for its decline. Old *arats* (herdsmen) can remember times when it was difficult to ride a camel through *zag* country and when it was difficult to spot free-ranging camels between the branches. Saxaul depends on underground water supplies. Another bush which thrives in the Gobi is *Reamuria songorica* which is abundant in low-lying areas and plains.

parts of it remain frozen throughout the year, although on particularly hot years it melts completely. This sunless canyon, although cold and dark, has a particular beauty as you'll find when you follow the narrow path that hugs the river, broadening in places between the rocks, while buzzards and eagles wheel and glide in the blue skies above.

Yolyn Am Valley Museum

West of Dalanzadgad, within the Gurvansaikhan National Park at the entrance to Yolyn Am is a museum containing a small but excellent collection of stuffed

DINOSAURS

That Mongolia is one of the world's greatest fossil fields is thoroughly confirmed. It will require 100 years of work by many expeditions to exhaust these huge deposits.

Roy Chapman Andrews, American palaeontologist

The Mongolian Gobi is a paradise for palaeontologists. One of the major attractions has been the accessibility of fossils near the surface in areas like the famous Flaming Cliffs where, in the 1920s, American paleontologist Roy Chapman Andrews discovered huge fossil finds including the first ever nest of fossilised dinosaur eggs.

Nine years after a communist government came to power in Mongolia in 1921, Andrews' expeditions were stopped. This signalled the end of all Western exploration from 1930 until 1990. In the early 1990s, at the invitation of the Mongolian government, American scientists Malcolm McKenna, Mark Norell and Michael Novacek of the American Museum of Natural History gained access to remote regions in the Gobi where they found numerous new fossils which included a complete protoceratops skeleton, oviraptor eggs, velociraptor claws and a collection of ancient mammals. One significant discovery was the skull of a juvenile hadrosaur, possibly the first hadrosaur found at the Flaming Cliffs area in the South Gobi.

Above Khovd River valley
Below left Dandelions brighten up Lake Khövsgöl
Below right Siberian columbine, *Aquilegia sibirica*

Above Kazakh hunter and eagle
Right Detail of Kazakh belt
Below Kazakh *gers* near Mt Tsengelkhairkhan
in western Mongolia

animals and birds, the handiwork of the museum's director and owner. The hall features a spectacular eagle with its huge wings outstretched hanging over a collection of various mountain/steppe species including ibex, steppe fox (*korak*), wild goat and different types of rodents such as the hairless mouse, the principal protein in the eagles' diet. The museum also houses a small collection of dinosaur remains, eggs and bones, while antelope antlers and *argali* horns line the corridor walls. A hunter's tent and camping equipment from the 1920s is exhibited with traps and an ancient musket, along with an assortment of wolf, fox and antelope skins. In the final room is a model of the Gobi landscape in which displays of Mongolian gazelle and wild ass feature. You can also shop here for postcards and there's a small collection of books and watercolour paintings that can all be purchased at a desk near the exit. The museum is free, though there is an entrance fee of T1,500 (US$1.30) for the park.

Khongoryn Els

Lying around 180km from Dalanzadgad, the dunes of Khongoryn Els are also known as the 'singing sands'. You will need to hire a jeep (around US$80 round trip) or join an organised tour to reach the dunes which are well worth a day's outing. Swept into constantly varying shapes by the wind, part of their attraction is the impressive colours that the yellow-white sands take on with the changing light of day. When the wind blows over the dunes it makes strange sounds like the high-pitched tone of an aeroplane engine about to take off or land. These dunes are the largest accumulation of sand in the Gobi Gurvansaikhan National Park, covering 965km^2. They rise abruptly from the plain, reaching a height of 800m and extend over an area 6–12km wide by 150km long. The dunes are bordered by lush green vegetation supported by a small river, the Khongoryn Gol, which is fed by underground sources from surrounding mountains. Nomads graze their camels and horses in this area at the northern limit of the dunes.

Man and dinosaurs never walked the earth together. To give this statement some perspective palaeontologists take as an example the hands of a clock. If the history of dinosaurs is measured from 12 to 5 o'clock, when they became extinct, human history is recorded in the last three seconds of the hour. (See box, *Dragon bones*, page 296.) As such, almost our entire knowledge of these creatures and the violent world they inhabited comes from these fossils. Bone by bone a new picture is emerging to describe what prehistoric life was like in the Mongolian Gobi.

There is a widely accepted theory that today's birds may well be the descendants of small meat-eating dinosaurs. Scientists now think that oviraptor, velociraptor and other theropod dinosaurs are the relatives of modern birds. In other words, birds are living dinosaurs. Apart from key skeletal features, it is thought that behaviour like brooding and nesting first arose in dinosaurs. The presence of protofeathers in these primitive animals indicates that they and birds all descend from a common ancestor.

The excavations in the Gobi so far have confirmed that flightless creatures the size of small turkeys wandered the Mongolian steppe 80 million years ago. What we as yet do not know is when they first took off and flew, or evolved beaks instead of jaws and wings instead of claws. Further excavations will be necessary before we have the answer to these questions.

Bayanzag – the Flaming Cliffs

The red sandstone cliffs and canyons of Bayanzag ('Rich in Saxaul'), 65km northwest of Dalanzadgad, are where the American palaeontologist, Roy Chapman Andrews, first discovered fossil beds of dinosaur bones and the first ever recorded dinosaur eggs in 1922 – discoveries which made world headlines. Subsequent expeditions by the American Natural History Museum followed and, though they were discontinued during the communist period, they have now been resumed. Scientists say that the dinosaurs were buried under the soil by sudden landslides. The barren cliffs look strikingly flame-like, especially at sunset.

Nearby there are two areas worth exploring: the dunes at Moltsog Els (22km northeast of Bayanzag) where, alongside, there's a stand of saxaul; and a site called Tögrögiin Shiree, northwest of Bayanzag, where the dinosaur protoceratops was discovered. These areas can only be reached by jeep, a day's outing with jeep and driver costing around US$80 (T91,000).

National parks and protected areas
Gobi Gurvansaikhan National Park

This park covers over 2 million hectares and lies within a few kilometres of Dalanzadgad. It extends 380km from east to west and some 80km north to south. The Gobi Gurvansaikhan National Park is the largest of Mongolia's national parks and the second largest protected area in Mongolia. The park comprises gravel and rubble plains, salt wetlands, dry valleys, springs and oases. Surprisingly, despite the barren landscape and hostile climate, the Gobi Gurvansaikhan provides a home to a wealth of wildlife. Fifty-two mammal species have been recorded in the park including wild ass, pikas, hamsters, gerbils, jerboas, Gobi bear, wolf, snow leopard, wildcat, *argali*, ibex and gazelles. There have also been 246 kinds of birds recorded: the majority are resident breeding birds. Part of the park is a strictly protected area, although it welcomes visitors in non-restricted areas and eco-tourism is one of its strengths. In the mountains you might find snow leopard trails although it is virtually impossible to spot them. Their haunts are known and it's easy to see their droppings. Keep a look out for ibex and *argali* (wild sheep) on mountain climbs. Views to the distant horizons from the summits are stunning. The foothills of the mountains consist of red cretaceous sandstone which has eroded into gorges. The shortage of water limits the living conditions for people and animals. Drinking water comes from wells and domestic animals are watered in the Gobi by means of hand-drawn water, bucketed into wooden troughs.

One thousand families (around 5,000 people) live within the national park, either as nomads or in small settlements. Their livelihood depends on their camel and goat herds, totalling over 250,000 animals. A number of herders supplement their income by undertaking park activities such as monitoring, research, or collecting park entrance fees.

The peak tourist season tends to be between mid-June and September when the climate is more favourable – a slightly longer season than other parts of Mongolia. The park welcomes between 3,000 and 5,000 foreign visitors each year, the majority from East Asia, Australia and Western Europe and most arriving through Mongolian tour operators. There remains a lack of tourist infrastructure.

Where to stay

For accommodation, you can base yourself in one of the *ger* camps around the park or in the hotels in Dalanzadgad. Entrance fees are T1,500 (US$1.30) per person per day and T3,000 (US$3) per vehicle per day. It is expected that these fees will increase.

MINERALS, GEMS AND MINING
There are some 160 deposits of more than 30 kinds of minerals in the aimag, including gold and coal; there are a growing number of goldmines and 12 coalfields. Other mineral resources include platinum, lead and iron ore. Precious stones are used for decorative purposes and jewellery is designed and created from the Gobi's semi-precious stones. Small craft-based industries are developing to meet tourist demands.

The park's staff welcome all visitors and are happy to help, where possible, with transport and accommodation. They also welcome enquiries from foreign tour operators, travel agents, tourism organisations and the media to help facilitate interesting programmes. For further information contact: South Gobi Areas' National Parks Administration; tel: 53 3973; fax: 53 1227; email: gtzgobi@magicnetnet.mn.

Other protected areas in Ömnögobi
Zagiin Us Nature Reserve
In the far northwest corner of the province extending north into Dundgobi (described in *Dundgobi Aimag*, page 290).

Small Gobi Strictly Protected Area (parts A and B)
Located along the southern border with China, this strictly protected area is designated to preserve the main habitat for rare and very rare wildlife such as *khulan* (wild ass), black-tailed gazelle, *argali* (mountain sheep), and ibex. About 50% of the *khulan* population of Mongolia inhabits this area. It is not open to tourism.

Activities
Camel trekking
One of the best ways to experience the Gobi is from the back of a camel. They are surprisingly easy to ride, so don't be put off: it may even turn out to be the highlight of your journey. Do take care when mounting: too many accidents have happened this way, including falling over the other side in the excitement of it all – nothing to do with the camel. One of the best places to go is to climb Khongoryn Els, the huge sand dunes. You don't have to gallop like Lawrence of Arabia; a quiet stroll will give you the same feeling of floating along. Camels have a rocking motion and after a while when you know the temperament of your camel, you may be able to control the direction you want to go in. They are quite obstinate with definite minds of their own. But fear not, for there are usually people alongside to help you. The standard cost of camel rides is US$5 per hour (tourist price).

Camel trekking is easily arranged. Day rides can be organised through a guide or directly with the camel owners if you speak some Mongolian. The price of a 15-day camel riding holiday is roughly US$1,450 per person, reduced to US$1,250 if you are a party of six or more.

Horseriding
Tour companies offer horseback tours complete with both your mount, pack animals, tents and food. Guides, cooks and translators will make all the necessary arrangements and travel with you. However, local herdsman are taking advantage of the growing market by offering individuals horse rides. You may even try out their traditional wooden saddles, though most visitors find them too

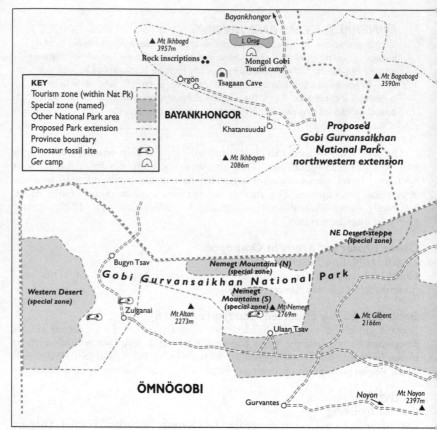

uncomfortable. To hire a horse costs US$5 per hour (same as a camel); or it's
US$12 per day with a guide.

Dinosaur hunting

Mongolia is second in importance to the USA for its dinosaur records, listing 40
species to the US's 64. China comes next with 36 species and the UK with 26. You
need a permit to dig for dinosaur remains and it is strictly forbidden to take them out
of the country. Twelve to fifteen fossil egg types have been found in the Gobi. Some
belong to dinosaurs, others to crocodiles and others possibly to birds. Dinosaurs and
their eggs have been excavated in Bayanzag, Tost, Nemegt and Khermentsav.

Among the seven large sub-orders of dinosaur, five are represented in
Mongolia, and range in age from 100 million to 65 million years ago. One unique
find consisted of the skeletons of two dinosaurs, protoceratops and velociraptor,
locked in combat. Prior to that time Mongolia was part of a warm inland sea and
marine life dominated. This stage ended about 200 million years ago with the
shrinking of the seas, although the Gobi remained a lake area surrounded by lush
vegetation. Segnosaurus is exclusively a Mongolian predatory dinosaur. Another
species, saichania, the armoured dinosaur, is named after the Gobi's
Gurvansaikan Mountains.

Amateur enthusiasts are welcome to contribute to this fascinating search, but
most amateurs are sensible enough to leave a find where it is and seek expert help.

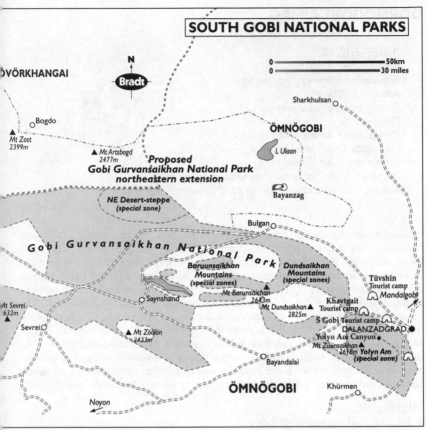

SOUTH GOBI NATIONAL PARKS

N

0 ━━━━━━ 50km
0 ━━━━━━ 30 miles

ÖVÖRKHANGAI

Sharkhulsan

ÖMNÖGOBI

Bogdo

Mt Zost
2399m

L Ulaan

Mt Artsbogd
2477m   Proposed
Gobi Gurvansaikhan National Park
northeastern extension

NE Desert-steppe
(special zone)

Bayanzag

Bulgan

Gobi Gurvansaikhan National Park

Baruunsaikhan
Mountains
(special zones)

Dundsaikhan
Mountains
(special zones)

Tüvshin
Tourist camp

Mt Barunsaikhan
2613m

Saynshand

Mt Sevrei
632m

Mandalgobi

Mt Dundsaikhan
2825m

Khavtgait
Tourist camp

Sevrei

S Gobi Tourist camp

Mt Zöölön
2433m

DALANZADGAD

Yolyn Am Canyon

Mt Züünsaikhan
2618m Yolyn Am
(special zone)

Bayandalai

ÖMNÖGOBI

Khürmen

Noyon

Do not pocket any fossils, even the tiniest ones, as souvenirs. It is hard to stop
people doing this ... though the customs do try.

Suggested itineraries

A typical Gobi itinerary might begin with a flight to the Gobi to check into a *ger*
camp (see page 379), from where you can drive by jeep to Yolyn Am and its
museum. On the return journey you can stop to visit a camel-herding family and
picnic with them, enjoying the experience of sitting around a campfire or *ger* stove
eating with local nomads. Early the next day you can drive through the Gobi
Gurvansaikhan National Park to the sand dunes of Khongoryn Els, returning via
Dalanzadgad and the Bayanzag Flaming Cliffs at sunset.

Gobi tour experts include

Mongolei Reisen (German office) Chausseestr 84, 10115 Berlin, Germany; tel: 00 49 30
44057646; fax: 44057645; email: juulchin@aol.com or info@mongoliajourneys.com; web:
www.mongoliajourneys.com
Juulchin Foreign Tourism Corporation Genghis Khan Avenue 5B, Ulaanbaatar; tel: 11
328428; fax: 11 320246; email: juulchin@mongol.net; web: www.mol.mn/juulchin
Nomadic Expeditions Building 76, Suite 28 (next to the State Department Store)1 40
000, Peace Avenue, Ulaanbaatar; tel: 11 313 396 or 325-786; fax: 11 320 311; email:
Mongolia@NomadicExpeditions.com; web: www.NomadicExpeditions.com

DORNOGOBI AIMAG

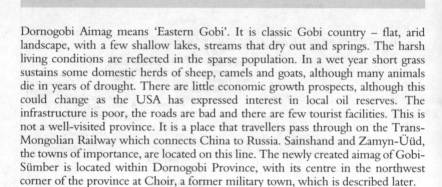

BRIEF FACTS
Population 50,000
Population density 0.46 per km²
Area 115,000km²
Aimag centre Sainshand
Districts 14
Elevation of Sainshand 938m
Livestock Goats, sheep, cattle, horses
Ethnic groups Khalkha
Distance from Sainshand to Ulaanbaatar 463km
Average temperatures July +23.2°C, January −18.4°C

Dornogobi Aimag means 'Eastern Gobi'. It is classic Gobi country – flat, arid landscape, with a few shallow lakes, streams that dry out and springs. The harsh living conditions are reflected in the sparse population. In a wet year short grass sustains some domestic herds of sheep, camels and goats, although many animals die in years of drought. There are little economic growth prospects, although this could change as the USA has expressed interest in local oil reserves. The infrastructure is poor, the roads are bad and there are few tourist facilities. This is not a well-visited province. It is a place that travellers pass through on the Trans-Mongolian Railway which connects China to Russia. Sainshand and Zamyn-Üüd, the towns of importance, are located on this line. The newly created aimag of Gobi-Sümber is located within Dornogobi Province, with its centre in the northwest corner of the province at Choir, a former military town, which is described later.

Highlights
- Khalzan Uul – curative springs
- Senjit Khad – rock formation
- Tsonjiin Chuluu – volcanic rocks
- Burdene Bulag – dunes and mineral springs
- Petrified trees – at Tsagaan Tsav and Süikhent

Sainshand
Sainshand sits on the main railway line to China not far from the Chinese border. The name means 'Good Spring' and it is a good place to stop and stock up with fuel, water and food supplies before heading into the Gobi. The population is 20,000.

Getting there from Ulaanbaatar
By train
Local trains connect Sainshand with Choir and Zamyn-Üüd, the border in the south. The Trans-Mongolian express train also stops at Sainshand. It is by far the best way to travel here. A train ticket from Ulaanbaatar to Sainshand costs around US$7 (T8,000) one way, although the local schedules are often at awkward hours such as 02.00 in the morning and it is also difficult to buy tickets for Sainshand on the Trans-Mongolian express. Sainshand railway station tel: 63 3899.

By road
Private jeeps and minibuses ply this route. For bus schedules, check at the long-distance bus station in Ulaanbaatar.

What to see and do
Aimag Museum
In the town centre beside the post office, this museums' exhibits include stuffed Gobi animals, seashells and marine fossils and some dinosaur fossils. It's worth a visit and is open 09.00–17.00; entry US$1.

Museum of Danzanravjaa
In the town centre opposite the post office, this museum is dedicated to Noyon Khutagt Danzanravjaa (1803–56), Mongolian writer, composer, painter and physician who was revered as a sage by local people. Exhibits include gifts given to Danzanravjaa by Chinese and Tibetan leaders, costumes from his plays and some of his paintings. In addition, there is a wild herb collection as he was interested in traditional medicine. An urn containing his ashes stands in front of his statue. The museum is open weekdays 10.00–17.00 (closed for lunch) and entry costs US$1.

Sainshand Theatre Group
Just off the main through-road in the town centre, this is considered to be the best theatre outside Ulaanbaatar. The theatre puts on plays featuring local history and

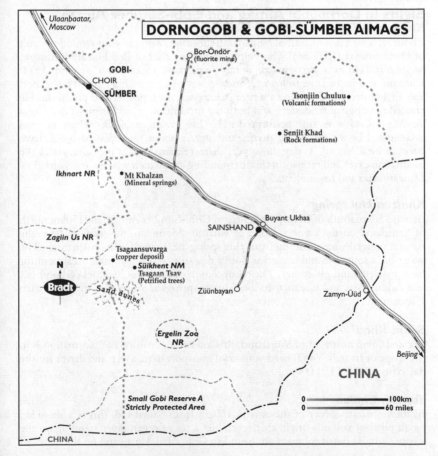

DORNOGOBI & GOBI-SÜMBER AIMAGS

folklore, and is well worth enquiring about if you spend a night in town. Ask at the hotel or find a local guide who will be able to advise you of performances. The cost is US$5 (T5,700) for tourists.

Monastery of Dashchoilon Khural

On the airport road at the entry to the north of the town, this monastery was re-opened in 1991 and today friendly young monks welcome visitors. Services are held in the mornings.

Where to stay

Ikh Goviin Naran Hotel Just off the main through-road at the centre of town. Provides rooms and food at reasonable rates, charging around US$10 (T11,400).

Od Hotel Centre of town. Provides dormitory rooms at low prices (US$3/4); otherwise there is plenty of space to camp outside the town if you bring a tent.

Where to eat

Ergeliin Zuu Restaurant Beside the Ikh Goviin Naran Hotel (above). Provides good local dishes including dumplings, grilled meat and stews, with prices starting at T2,000 .

Sights in Dornogobi Aimag and Gobi-Sümber Aimag

Khamaryn Khiid

About an hour's drive south of Sainshand, this monastery grew up around the cult of Danzanravjaa (1803–56), who belonged to the order of Red Hat Buddhism in Mongolia. He was recognised as an important incarnation around 1811. Danzanravjaa had a large following, and he was also a writer, a martial arts expert and an architect besides being a writer, composer, poet, painter and physician. He created the original monastery and built the local theatre, and his play *Life Story of the Moon Cuckoo* is still performed. His life ended tragically when he was assassinated by a rival. Many myths and stories about this talented monk have become local legend. Today, however, there remains only a monastery and the meditation caves and retreats in the surrounding area which were formerly used by Danzanravjaa and his students.

Khalzan Uul spring

Around 50km south of Choir, the centre of Gobi-Sümber Aimag, and150km north of Sainshand on the western slope of Khalzan Mountain, the locals believe the natural mineral waters issuing from this spring are a cure for many diseases. The water has a sour taste and is used as both a digestive and as a popular treatment for liver problems and gall stones. The composition of the water includes carbonic gas and radioactivity and is similar to the famous springs at Yessentuki in the Russian Caucasus.

Senjit Khad

Located 95km northeast of Sainshand, this interesting, natural rock formation is in the shape of an arch. You'll need your own transport here; a jeep and driver for the day costs US$80 (T91,000).

Tsonjiin Chuluu

In the northeast corner of the aimag, 160km from Sainshand, this is a six-sided basalt pillar of volcanic origin that resembles a set of organ pipes standing on the steppe. Similar basalt columns are found in Gobi Altai Aimag and on the banks of the Tamir River in Arkhangai. As with the above, you must have your own transport; the jeep costs are similar to the above too.

Burdene Bulag mineral springs
Located about 30km southwest of Erdene (railway station); some of the largest sand dunes in the Gobi; the dunes are easily accessible but a guide is needed to find the cold-water springs; jeep cost as above.

Cliffs of archaeological interest
Located in the area around Khatanbulag near the ruins of Demchigiin Khiid; ancient archaeological artefacts and rock drawings showing Gobi animals can be found here; own jeep transport necessary and a guide who knows the area; jeep cost as above.

Petrified trees at Süikhent
The petrified trees at Süikhent, 130km west of Sainshand, are worth visiting. Tsagaan Tsav in Mandakh district, around 40km north of Suikhent, is a particularly good area to see these rare trees and is often visited by tourists. The petrified trees lie on the desert surface and many more exist beneath the sands. The petrified tree area at Süikhent is 500m long by 80m wide and the logs can measure up to 20m long by 1.5m in diameter. You will need your own jeep transport as well as a guide; jeep costs are as above.

Nature reserves
Ikh Nart
The reserve of 43,740 hectares is situated in the mid-western part of the province close to the boundary with Dundgobi Aimag. It protects the northeastern limit of the *argali* (wild sheep) habitat and was designated to extend their territory and to protect the natural environment. It is an off-road area not frequented by tourists.

Ergeliin Zoo Nature Reserve
This area of 60,910 hectares is situated on the southwest border of Dornogobi with Dundgobi Aimag. Many famous dinosaur-fossil finds have been discovered here. People refer to the region as 'Altan Uul' (Golden Mountain). Tourists visit the area with their own transport and guides; they are cautioned not to keep any fossil finds and to leave bones and other objects where they are.

Small Gobi Strictly Protected Area, part B
This occupies the southern border area of the aimag and affords protection to some of Mongolia's rare species such as wild ass and *argali* sheep. It extends west into Ömnögobi Aimag and is described there.

Towns
Zamyn-Üüd
Located on the border with China, Zamyn-Üüd is the town with the highest temperatures in Mongolia. Zamyn-Üüd is prospering thanks to cross-border trade and the railway line which runs through the town connecting it with Ulaanbaatar, Beijing and Moscow. There are several hotels: Jintin Hotel; Tsagaan Shonkhor Hotel and Bayangol Hotel providing standard rooms at US$15 per room; restaurants in the town serve mainly Asian food at reasonable prices of around T600–700 (under US$1 per dish) with rice; hotel restaurants serve European meals and charge roughly US$10.

GOBI-SÜMBER AIMAG

(see map)
This aimag was created in 1994 from the northern part of Dorngobi Aimag. The former Soviet army camp no 10 at Sümber was handed over to the Mongolian authorities in 1991. Sümber has a station on the Trans-Mongolian Railway. Local resources include coal, tin and florspar, mineral pigments and ornamental stones.

Choir, the aimag centre and main town is also on the railway line in the northwest corner of the province, halfway between Ulaanbaatar and Sainshand. It is a good fuelling stop. You can explore the nearby springs at Khalzan Uul. Choir Mountain, nearby, is part of a granite belt which offers good hiking.

Getting there from Ulaanbaatar

By train
Choir is a local stop from UB on the Trans-Mongolian line. It costs approximately US$7 per ticket; whereas by jeep you can expect to pay roughly US$100 (different rates if you are touring and sharing a jeep).

Where to stay
Altan Gobi Hotel Near the station. Rooms cost roughly US$8 (T9,000). The hotel restaurant provides local dishes and will pack picnics (cost US$3–4) if asked ahead of time.

Activities and itineraries
Genco Tour Bureau (Bayangol Hotel B-201, 5 Chinggis Khan Avenue, Ulaanbaatar; tel:11 328960, fax:11 321705; email: genco@magicnet.mn; web: www.mol.mn/gtb) can organise the following 3- to 4-day itinerary, which begins with a drive by jeep from Sainshand to Bürden Bulag to visit the dunes and drink from the springs there. Camping overnight, the next day you can look at the fossil remains in the rocks at Ergeliin Zoo Nature Reserve, located 30km northwest of Khatanbulag district centre and from there drive to the petrified forest area and camp. En route back to Sainshand, stop to look at the saxaul groves southwest of the town; if you're lucky, you may spot some black-tailed gazelles.

DUNDGOBI AIMAG

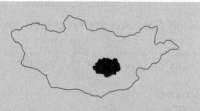

BRIEF FACTS
Population 52,000
Population density 0.73 per km²
Area: 74,700km²
Aimag centre Mandalgobi
Districts 16
Elevation of Mandalgobi 1,393m
Livestock Camels, goats
Ethnic groups Khalkha
Distance from Mandalgobi to Ulaanbaatar 260km
Average temperatures July +18.8°C, January -18°C

Dundgobi means 'Middle Gobi' and consists mainly of steppe, dry plains and unusual rock formations. The north is relatively green, but going south the land gradually turns into the semi-desert of the arid Gobi. Throughout the province there are hundreds of graves of ancient warriors, easily spotted as they are usually under small piles of rocks. These rock mounds are sacred, respected and left untouched, even though the graves may contain bronze or gold objects. Many are thought to pre-date Genghis Khan's era. The area is little visited as most tourists fly straight from Ulaanbaatar to more developed tourist areas.

Highlights
- Bagadgazryn Chuluu – sacred rock
- Ikhgazryn Chuluu – sacred rock
- Tsogt Taijiin Chuluu – rock inscriptions
- Birdwatching

Mandalgobi
Mandalgobi sits in the centre of the province with a population of around 11,000 people. It is a useful stopover where you can refuel and buy supplies. Climb to the top of a nearby hill for a view of the town. A monument there is dedicated to the 'everlasting friendship' between Mongolia and the former Soviet Union.

Getting there from Ulaanbaatar
By road
Mandalgobi is on the main Ulaanbaatar/South Gobi route, so many cars, trucks and buses pass through. It is a desolate, unattractive, dusty and dry-looking town of concrete buildings and nearby *ger* compounds.

By air
Scheduled MIAT 45-minute flight once weekly on Fridays, continuing to Dalanzadgad in the South Gobi. Local MIAT representative's office, tel: 59 2269, 59 2200.

Where to stay
Both hotels have adequate rooms and charge US$7–8 per room.

Mandalgobi Hotel On the park in the centre of town.
Builders' Hotel On the south side of town.

Where to eat
Delgerkhangai Restaurant, within walking distance south of the central park, serves Mongolian dishes from T1,000; local canteens (*guanz*) serve fast food and salty-milky tea for T500–600.

What to see and do
Aimag Museum
In the town centre, this museum has a natural history section that displays stuffed animals, as well as an ethnography and history section with a bronze Buddha by Zanabazar and some Buddhist scroll paintings.

Dashgimpeliin Khiid
Northeast of the town centre off the road to Ulaanbaatar, this monastery was re-built in 1991. The temple consists of one small building and the monks' *ger* but it is still an active place of worship and the monks welcome visitors. Services are held in the mornings.

Sights in Dundgobi Aimag
Zagiin Us
The reserve of 273,606 hectares extends south into Ömnögobi Aimag. It's a valley area composed of saline soil with dry, circular salt marshes and sand dunes, a mixed landscape of special ecological interest. Saxaul, or *zag* as its known in Mongolian, grows in this semi-desert, and it is also the northern limit of the black-tailed gazelle's distribution range and the western extension of the white-tailed gazelle's range. It is an area popular for viewing wild animals and for its sand dunes which are visited by tourists. You will need your own transport. The usual entry fees of US$1 per person and US$3 per vehicle apply.

Bagagazryn Uul
Situated about 60km northwest of Mandalgobi in a remote area of desert plain, the rocks here are worshipped by local people. Genghis Khan is said to have camped in the area too. The highest peak is Bagagazaryn Uul (1768m), which takes about 5 hours to climb. This mountain also contains a cave with an underground lake. There are plenty of mineral springs in the area as well as rocky hills topped with *ovoos* (rock shrines). You need your own transport. Hiring a jeep and driver for the day costs US$80 (T91,000), cheaper if organised for several days.

Ikhgazryn Chuluu
Seventy kilometres northeast of Mandalgobi, this granite rock formation is sacred and has long been worshipped by local people as a place of pilgrimage. In the 19th

centuries two monks who lived here made rock drawings which have become a tourist attraction in their own right, although it is a very remote place. There are no facilities here and you will need your own transport.

Tsagaan Suvraga

This is an eroded landscape that was once beneath the sea. It lies 115km southwest of Mandalgobi near the aimag border with Ömnögobi Aimag. Rich in marine fossils and clam shells, some of the chalk mounds are up to 30m in height. Rock paintings dating from 3000BC exist in the area, though they're very difficult to find without an expert guide and you'll need your own transport.

Birdlife at Sangiin Dalai Nuur

Located west of Mandalgobi near the settlement of Sangiin Dalai Khiid, this isolated area is remarkable for the birdlife that lives around the lake and its small island in the middle. You will need a jeep and an experienced driver as it is difficult to find. Travelling in this aimag involves going off-the-beaten track and usually off-road. Transport costs by private jeep are as above.

Khökh Bürd Süm

Lying 120km west of Mandalgobi, on the island in the middle of Sangiin Dalai Lake, are the remains of the Khökh Bürd Süm. Built in the 10th century, this temple is on the same site as the ruins of a later palace, built around 300 years ago. The poet, writer, composer, painter and physician Danzanravjaa (1803–56), supporter of Red Hat Buddhism, constructed a stage on top of the palace ruins for open-air performances. The place is now abandoned but there are good camping spots around the lake. A health spa/sanatorium on the south side of the lake provides accommodation. Once again, you'll need your own transport; the cost of jeep hire is as above.

Gimpildarjaalan Khiid

Located 115km northwest of Mandalgobi near the camel-herding centre of Erdenedalai, this monastery was built in the 18th century to commemorate the first visit by a Dalai Lama to Mongolia in the 16th century. The monastery survived the destruction of the 1930s by becoming a warehouse and shop, re-opening as a monastery in 1990. There is a spacious temple with a statue of Tsongkhapa, some large parasols and huge drums. The caretaker will open up for visitors if there are no monks around.

Ongiin Khiid

Nestling in a bend of the Ongiin Gol (river) in the extreme west of the aimag, about 240km from Mandalgobi and near the settlement of Saikhan Ovoo, this site comprises the remains of two monasteries: Barlim Khiid and Khutagt Khiid. Although there is little left, it is interesting to go there to explore the ruins.

You'll need your own jeep or minibus and driver as there's no public transport to here.

Nearby there's accomodation at two *ger* camps: Saikhan Ovoo Ger Camp and Mongol Khaan Ger Camp. Eleven kilometres further away there's Saikhan Gobi Ger Camp.

Suggested itineraries

Travel in this province mostly involves a through journey from Ulaanbaatar to the South Gobi, with a stopover in Mandalgobi to refuel or to stay overnight.

GOBI SURVIVAL BAR

Christine Sapiepha Freemantle

We were eight 'tourists' with a BBC film crew doing the 'adventure tourism' segment for a series called *The Tourist*, made in the mid 1990s during two visits to Mongolia. Once we had crossed the Mongol Altai mountains we joined up with the camels and the real adventure began. I think it was probably the first time that I had been in an environment where nothing passed through the human mind: no roads, no overhead wires, no villages, no petrol stations, no aeroplanes. No sound but the wind. Nothing but the endless plain, with rose, yellow and silver tufty bushes, high cloud, bright sun and rain in the distance. Nature alone rules, unobstructed by man's intervention. Our objective was the Mother Mountain about 40km away. There was a swampy area that we had to ride around and the directions were, 'when you get to the dead camel, turn right'. It was so exhilarating that I started to sing and one of the camel drivers dropped back and rode beside me so that he could whistle and sing too. It's a morning I shall never forget.

We camped for three days at the base of Mother Mountain, Eej Khairkhan, near a cave where a Buddhist lama had spent 11 years hiding from the communists, following the anti-religious purges of the 1930s. One afternoon we rode further into the ravines on the other side of our campsite where we saw a fairly recent pug mark of a snow leopard and some tiny hoof marks, probably gazelle. No sign of a kill, but... We then came to a particularly

There are other routes which take you to desert oases, sand dunes and rock formations chiselled and sculpted by the wind and sand. You might also care to take a side trip to see the cliffs at Tsaagan Suvraga or visit the sacred mountain of Kharaat Uul in the south east of the province where people come every year to celebrate the autumn moon. A good tour company for this area is MonAnd Company, Government Building 4, Peace Avenue, Ulaanbaatar; tel: 11 452238, 310579; fax: 11 310579; email: monand@magicnet.mn or damost@magicnet.mn).

BAYANKHONGOR AIMAG

BRIEF FACTS

Population 90,000
Population density 0.80 per km²
Area 116,000km²
Aimag centre Bayankhongor
Districts 20
Elevation of Bayankhongor 1859m
Livestock Sheep, goats, horses
Ethnic groups Khalkha
Distance from Bayankhongor to Ulaanbaatar 630km
Average temperatures July +15°C January –18.4°C

Bayankhongor is a province of hot springs, dinosaur fossils and contrasting landscapes. Khongor in Mongolian means 'Light Chestnut' (as in the colour of a

beautiful valley with small trees with silver bark and golden leaves, and tall, pale, gold tufts of grass, greenish at the root. There was a wonderful sweet smell and dark cliffs on both sides. I wondered if the perfume came from the sand jujube (*Eloeagnus latifolia*) as described by Cable and French in their book *The Gobi Desert*.

Our journey home was quite rough: we were caught by the first blizzards of winter as we struggled to drive back across the Gobi-Altai. One of the trucks did not have 4WD and had to be dug out over and over again, hard work at 9,000ft in a driving cross wind. And when we finally took off for Moscow three days later, we had landing problems at Novosibirsk.

Lessons from the trip: learn some songs, like old ballads that tell a tale, to sing around the campfire in the evenings. Make your own survival rations, ie: my Gobi Bars (see below). One other piece of advice: try to travel with those of a like mind and with a well-grounded leader who speaks Mongolian and keeps a firm grip on the consumption of alcohol. Learn some Mongolian and familiarise yourself with the Cyrillic alphabet.

Christine's recipe for Gobi Survival Bars: dark chocolate, some instant coffee granules, some sultanas soaked in brandy or whiskey, chopped hazelnuts and almonds. Melt the chocolate, stir in the ingredients, spread about 2" thick on foil to harden. Before its gets brittle, cut into Mars-bar size lengths and wrap individually. This really will take you through a blizzard and many hours marooned on airport tarmac.

chestnut horse). The north is dominated by the Khangai mountain range, where fast-flowing rivers water the valleys and plains. Herding – camels, goats, sheep and horses – is the principal occupation of the nomadic and semi-nomadic population. The south is part of the Gobi Desert, where arid conditions make life hard. This region includes the mountains of the Mongol Altai range, the habitat of wild sheep and ibex. The Great Gobi Strictly Protected Area A (off-limits to tourists) extends across the extreme southern border with China and is home to the native wild camel and the rare Gobi bear. The province is rich in precious metals and famous for its natural mineral springs. Medicinal plants grow wild. This remote province is not well-visited, but that is part of its attraction.

Highlights
- Shargaljuut rashaan – hot springs
- Birdwatching at Bööntsaagan Nuur
- Oasis life at Ekhiin Gol

Bayankhongor
The town is located where the Khangai Nuruu meets the northern part of the Gobi and provides a good starting point for exploring the more fertile northern region and the remote, dry, southern regions. It has a population of 23,000. A stupa stands on the hill to the west of the town; there are a few tourist attractions (see overleaf).

Getting there from Ulaanbaatar
By air
There's a MIAT scheduled flight to Bayankhongor on Tuesdays; local MIAT representative office tel: 69 2294.

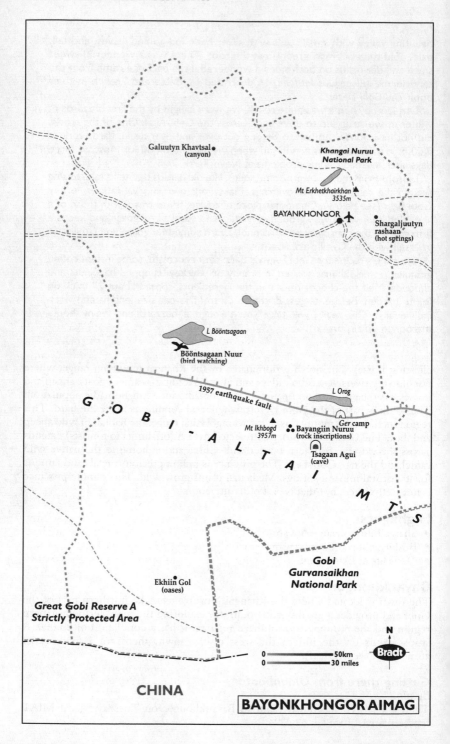

Galuutyn Khavtsal
(canyon)

Khangai Nuruu
National Park

Mt Erkhetkhairkhan
3535m

BAYANKHONGOR

Shargaljuutyn
rashaan
(hot springs)

L Bööntsagaan

Bööntsagaan Nuur
(bird watching)

1957 earthquake fault

L Orog

G O B I - A L T A I   M T S

Ger camp

Mt Ikhbogd
3957m

Bayangiin Nuruu
(rock inscriptions)

Tsagaan Agui
(cave)

Gobi
Gurvansaikhan
National Park

Ekhiin Gol
(oases)

Great Gobi Reserve A
Strictly Protected Area

N

Bradt

0 ────── 50km
0 ────── 30 miles

CHINA

BAYONKHONGOR AIMAG

By road
Private jeep or minibus; by public bus, check the current schedules at the long-distance bus station in Ulaanbaatar (see page 224).

Where to stay and eat
Hotel Negdelchin On the airport road on the right side as you enter town, opposite the truck station. Provides simple rooms and serves food. Rates are US$10 a room, while food prices are from T1,000 per dish of meat or stew.

What to see and do
Aimag Museum
This museum exhibits Buddhist art, including two statues of the popular goddess, Tara, *tanka* paintings, and *tsam* masks and costumes. Open 09.00–17.00 weekdays, the entrance is US$1 (tourist rate) or T350 (US$0.30) for locals.

Natural History Museum
Southeast of the central park this museum has exhibits of dinosaur fossils and has a replica of a tarbosaurus dinosaur skeleton. Open 10.00–17.00 (closed for lunch). The entry cost is T1,000.

Lamyn Gegeenii Dedlen Khiid
On the main street in the centre of town, this is a new monastery that has replaced the original of the same name that stood 20km east of Bayankhongor. The original once housed up to 10,000 monks but was completely destroyed in the 1930s. Today, the new monastery, established in 1991, has a new community of monks. The principal brick-built temple is in the shape of a *ger* and the central hall contains a statue of Sakyamuni (Historical Buddha).

Sights in Bayankhongor Aimag
There are two protected areas in this aimag; Khangai Nuruu National Park in the extreme north and part of the Great Gobi Strictly Protected Area in the far south. The southern area is not frequented by tourists since it is a strictly protected area on the border with China and is set up to protect wild animals such as the *mazaalai* (Gobi bear), *khulan* (wild ass) and *argali* (wild sheep). (See box *Ekhiin Gol* on pages 298–9.)

Khankhentii Nuruu National Park
Set in a remote mountainous region in the far north, parts of the Khankhentii mountains are possible to explore if you are equipped with transport and supplies. These forested mountains are sandwiched between the Eurasian forest taiga and the Central Asian steppe. Three major river systems spring from the protected area: the Tuul, which flows into the Orkhon, then the Selenge then on to Russia's Lake Baikal and, eventually, into the Arctic Ocean; while the Onon and Kherlen rivers flow east to join the Amur which flows into the Pacific Ocean. The area represents taiga landscape, which comprises frozen landscape of poor vegetation when topsoil is frozen for up to nine months of the year; mosses, lichens and trees such as pine and spruce. It is also the home of Genghis Khan.

Shargaljuut Rashaan
Located northeast of Bayankhongor town, between the peaks of Myangan Ugalzat Uul (3,483m) and Shargaljuut (3,137m), this well-known health spa consists of over 300 springs that vary in temperature from very hot to icy cold. The waters are diverted to pools and baths (indoor and outdoor) and, for the sake of privacy, to

DRAGON BONES

Ancient cartographers filled in unknown areas of their maps with the words: 'Here be Dragons'. In the 1920s this notice appeared across maps of the Gobi. From 1921 until 1930 five expeditions were launched by the American paleontologist Roy Chapman Andrews. One of the expedition's aims was to search for the origins of man. What he discovered was a treasure trove of fossils or 'dragon bones' as the Mongols and Chinese called them. This surprisingly rich discovery yielded the first nest of dinosaur eggs, which made front-page headlines worldwide.

Until then the Gobi had held little interest for scientists. In the early 20th century, travellers avoided this harsh, upland desert area. Furthermore, the political situation between Mongolia and China was turbulent, if not dangerous at the time. The Mongols were trying to defend themselves against the territorial ambitions of the Chinese; indeed, a driver on the 1921 expedition was shot by Chinese soldiers. That year, the Bolsheviks helped the Mongolian Revolutionaries to power. Afterwards the civil war between the Bolsheviks and the Tsarists continued in Russian but not in Mongolia.

All this was far from the minds of 'dragon collectors', whose finds surpassed all expectations. Even the expedition drivers helped on the dig as excitement mounted over the finding of teeth, skulls and claws, many of which were revealed just beneath the surface of the sands. Chapman Andrews' Asiatic Expeditions were initially budgeted, a total of US$250,000, though they ended by costing the American Natural History Museum and its sponsors way over that amount – costing US$10 million.

American paleontologists had to wait until the communist period ended in1990 before returning. A team under Professor Malcolm McKenna, his wife Priscilla and two colleagues from the American Museum of Natural History, Dr Mark Norell and Dr Michael Novacek, returned to the Gobi, and in 1991 they retraced some of the steps of the earlier Chapman Andrews route. As McKenna said, 'We spent hours on our hands and knees finding thousands of "little chaps" that would not make the headlines.'

Fighting dinosaurs

One of the world's most famous fossil finds are two dinosaurs interlocked in mortal combat. It is likely the plant-eating protoceratops was stalked by the meat eating velociraptor, a dinosaur with savage jaws and a long pointed tail. It is thought they were preserved in their dying moment by a collapsing sand dune which buried them alive.

In an exhibit in New York at the Natural History Museum, artists have created the appearance of what these dinosaurs looked like from their fossil remains. No details have escaped their recreation: even the skin patterns of the pebbly skinned protoceratops are accurately portrayed as far as we can tell from the fossil remains, which were etched on the surface of sandstone rocks in the Gobi. Virtual reality takes a further step in showing us (in terrifying reality) video footage of a *Jurassic Park*-style battle between the fighting dinosaurs in a superbly reconstructed landscape of the late Cretaceous Period. For further information go to web: www.amnh.org, and see the *Dinosaur* section on pages 278–9.

individual *gers*. The hot water is thought to cure all kinds of ailments, especially rheumatic complaints and skin disorders. Many Mongolians come for treatments and stay at the nearby sanatorium, a Soviet-style concrete block of a building. As well as the hotel at the sanatorium there is a *ger* camp ; the cost for either is around US$35 (tourist price). Otherwise camp along the valley.

Galuutyn Khavtsal
Around 38km northwest of Galuut village and 85km from Bayankhongor, this is a 25m-deep canyon that is only a metre wide in places. Nearby are many deer stones and rock inscriptions. To reach here your own transport is essential, while a jeep and driver for the day costs US$80 (T91,000); it's cheaper if organised for several days.

Tsagaan Agui
This cave is supposed to have sheltered Stone-Age people around 700,000 years ago. It is found around 150km south of Bayankhongor in the Bogd Uul area of Orog Nuur. A fee of T500 is charged to enter it. Transport costs are as above.

Bayangiin Nuruu
This is a canyon with rock engravings and petroglyphs, some of which are 5,000 years old, around 150km south of Bayankhongor town near Tsaagan Agui. As above, you can get here only by private jeep.

Orog Nuur
Set in the foothills of Ikhbogd Uul (3,957m),110km south of Bayankhongor, this saltwater lake is good for birdwatching. The summit of Ikh Bogd Uul is accessible by jeep (take a guide) and provides stunning views.

You can stay here at both the Orog Ger Camp and the Mongol Gobi Resort, which provide standard *ger* camp accommodation. The rates are around US$35 per night excluding food, while meals are US$18. Once again you'll need your own transport; for the cost of hiring a jeep and driver, see above.

Nogoon Tsav
These small hills (*tsav* means 'hillocks') lie in the extreme southeast of the aimag, around 145km from Bayankhongor as the crow flies (see map). Be warned that it may take much longer than you think to travel across this type of country, either off-track or on dry, rutted routes. At the end your reward is a valley 2m wide by 10km long which is renowned as an area of dinosaur fossil finds. Unsurprisingly there is no public transport here so you will need your own; the costs of hiring are as above.

Birdwatching at Bööntsaagan Nuur
Located 90km southwest of Bayankhongor town, this large saltwater lake is home to many rare species of birds including the relic gull, whooper swan and geese. There are also interesting volcanic formations, canyons with streams and ancient cave paintings in the area. Own transport needed: costs are given above.

Rock paintings
Tsagaanbulag is a white rock that features drawings of a helmeted figure, believed by the locals to have been made by aliens. It is the only one of its kind among other rock paintings in the area. To get there you will need a jeep and driver; standard costs to hire a jeep are given above.

EKHIIN GOL
Lucia Scalisi
This little Eden in South Gobi is marked as a 'look out' on most maps of Bayankhongar Aimag. The tiny oasis, developed in the 1970s, was actually originally a successful 'greening of the desert' project that was abandoned 20 years later for economic reasons – though not by the families living there. Those that had moved to work there remained and with little effort everything continues to grow in abundance. Harvest time sees bumper crops of melon, marrow, peppers, tomatoes and even grapes flourishing amidst marigolds, sunflowers, anemones and *Amaranthus caudatus*.

Country idyll though this may seem, the village remains virtually cut off from the rest of the country. It is a good six hours' drive from the dusty town of Shinejinst – where simple accommodation is available in the administration building if the wind and dust get too much for tents – travelling south towards Segs Tsagaanbogd, the highest peak in the province on the border with China.

Remarkable though Ekhiin Gol is, the main reason for heading there is that the region is home to the dwindling population of *mazaalai*, the Gobi bear. In this Strictly Protected Area access must be undertaken with your own vehicle accompanied by the ranger, Mr Davaadorj, who has lived at Ekhiin Gol for the last 20 years. Driving is made complicated as rarely used routes disappear under the desert dust; even the experienced ranger sometimes loses the way.

You are unlikely to spot *mazaalai*. Rarely seen, numbers for this small bear verge on extinction at around 35–45 bears. It is possible, though, to see the

Petrified forest
Ulaan Shand, 66km southwest of Bayangobi, is interesting for its fossil finds, though you are not allowed to pick up one – even the smallest – to take home as a souvenir.

Oases
Ekhiin Gol lies at the eastern side of the Tsuvliur Mountains and covers an area 17km long by 5km wide. It is said to be the hottest place in Mongolia, with a maximum air temperature of 42.2°C. Annual precipitation is 13.4mm. Travelling south towards the Gobi there are many oases such as Jartyn Khöv (*khöv* means 'pool'), Daltyn Khöv, Burkhant and Zuunmod. As usual your own transport is essential, with private jeep costs as above.

Finding fossils
Dinosaur fossils are found in Bugiin Khöndii (Demon's Valley) – many of the fossils found here are exhibited at Ulaanbaatar's Natural History Museum – Yasnee Tsav and Khermen Tsav (which neighbours Ömnögobi).

Suggested itineraries
Gobi Camels' Ger Camp is a good base, located in a sheltered valley in the heart of the Gobi about 200km south of Bayankhongor. This remote *ger* camp is owned and run by Genghis Expeditions (see page 225). To the north of it, Ikh Bogd Mountain towers above the camp while to the south endless desert plains stretch to the horizon. Your accommodation is in traditional *gers* and a large dining *ger* is set up where staff serve meals including barbecued meat and other Mongolian dishes. The camp provides all the things you need for both a comfortable stay and

small, grassy oases in which it makes its home. The ranger is tuned in to spotting pawprints and recently used nests. With several oases in this region, it would be impossible to locate them without an experienced guide.

Interestingly, a feeding project is currently underway. Feeding stations (high-sided steel containers) are positioned at two sites. The idea is not that the bears and their buddies get to rely on a regular dinner service but that when they come out of hibernation they have an immediate one-off food supply. This, it is hoped, will support and encourage breeding.

It is a sparse landscape, also inhabited by *argali*, wild ass and gazelle. Tiny finches flit through the tall grasses, desert grouse flushed from hiding fly up the cliffs to scold from on high. Evidence of wolf can be found and camel, both wild, and those of the border guards who trek 20km through the mountains to the watering holes. When this happens the area gets trampled and the bears hide out in the surrounding hills. Once the soldiers have left the animals return to scavenge detritus: it is a great service to gather up the tins and plastic left behind in this otherwise pristine area.

Visiting Ekhiin Gol is not a day trip; camping gear is required as is taking your own water. Ekhiin Gol has no accommodation but with permission you should be able to camp. If you haven't made a prior arrangement, it could be difficult to turn up on spec. There are no stores and, as in most remote regions, radio is the only method of communication in Elkin Gol. Surprisingly there is a sports hall with a sprung wooden floor, so if you fancy a game of badminton be sure to take your rackets! To find out more about the project contact email: ecobund@magicnet.mn.

to explore the area: the tour guides and camp staff are professional and experienced pioneers of adventure and cultural travel in this area, and hot showers are available when you arrive back tired and dusty after a day spent looking at rock drawings or visiting a local camel herder. The *ger* charges US$45 a day per person including meals.

GOBI-ALTAI AIMAG

BRIEF FACTS
Population 74,000
Population density 0.52 per km²
Area 141,500km²
Aimag centre Altai
Districts 18
Elevation of Altai 2,181m
Livestock goats, camels, horses
Ethnic groups Khalkha
Distance from Altai to Ulaanbaatar 1,001km
Average temperatures July +14°C, January −18.9°C

Gobi-Altai is the second-largest aimag in Mongolia and is a land where the parched steppe grasslands of the Gobi meet the rocky landscape of the foothills and mountains of the Altai range. There is great natural beauty but it is a hard place to

CROSS-BORDER CONSERVATION

Wild Bactrian camels know no frontiers. They wander south from a protected area in the Great Gobi in Mongolia across the border area into China where, currently, they are completely unprotected. It is interesting to note that the narrow paths of age-old migratory routes are etched into the hard desert ground. It is one of the most exciting things to sense from the narrow, hard worn trails that this wild species continues to survive in these deserted desert hills and plains. But at this stage, both the wild camel and the Gobi bear need help if they are to continue to survive (see box *Conservation of the Wild Camel*, pages 302–3). Food for the Gobi bear is running out due to climate changes which have raised the ground temperatures by 2°C.

live both for people and livestock. The most settled part is the northeast corner, where melting snow from the Khangai Nuruu feeds provides irrigation and water supplies. Many plants and animals of this region are listed in the *Red Book* of Mongolia's rare and endangered wildlife species, among them Przewalski's horse, the Mongolian wild horse or *takhi*.

Highlights
- Climbing the Altai peaks
- Visiting the national parks – eco-tourism
- Sighting rare wild animals such as *argali*

Altai
Altai is an attractive, off-the-beaten-track town with a population of 17,500. It's an exciting place to visit, and serves as a stopover to and from Khovd for those on their way to the national parks and the wild horse reserve at Takhiin Tal, which is not often visited due to its remote location and lack of facilities of any kind. You will find a delicious cheap sherry wine in Altai hotels. *Ger* settlements – fenced compounds – surround the town, where local people, especially the children, are excited to see foreign visitors.

Getting there
By air
MIAT scheduled flights (just over 2 hours' flying time) on Tuesdays, Thursdays and Saturdays; local MIAT representative office tel: 65 3544, 65 4044.

By road
Private jeep or minibus – on bumpy, dusty tracks – cost T250–500 per kilometre, up to T750 if it is a new/top-range vehicle. For public transport, by bus, check current schedules at the long-distance bus station in Ulaanbaatar.

Where to stay
Both of the following hotels serve food at local prices, with meat dishes around T1,000, and rates are US$10–15 per room.

Altai Hotel Main street on the west side of town; provides simple comforts and adequate meals.
Birj Hotel Centre of town. Standard countryside hotel.

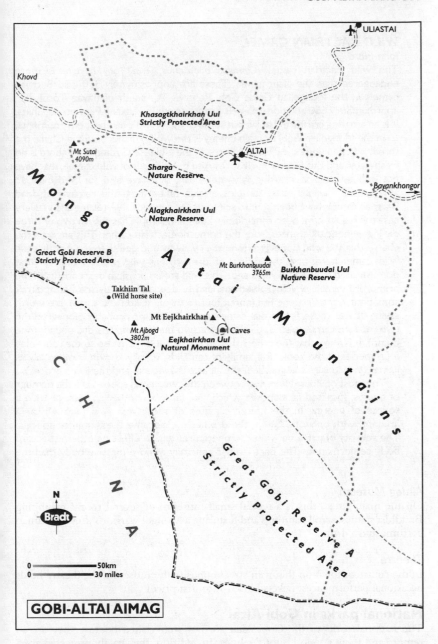

ULIASTAI

Khovd

**Khasagtkhairkhan Uul
Strictly Protected Area**

Mt Sutai
4090m

ALTAI

**Sharga
Nature Reserve**

Bayankhongor

**Alagkhairkhan Uul
Nature Reserve**

**Great Gobi Reserve B
Strictly Protected Area**

Mt Burkhanbuudai
3765m

**Burkhanbuudai Uul
Nature Reserve**

Takhiin Tal
(Wild horse site)

Mt Eejkhairkhan

Mt Ajbogd
3802m

Caves

**Eejkhairkhan Uul
Natural Monument**

N

Bradt

0 ——— 50km
0 ——— 30 miles

GOBI-ALTAI AIMAG

Mongol Altai Mountains

CHINA

**Great Gobi Reserve A
Strictly Protected Area**

What to see and do
Dashpeljeelen Khiid
On the outskirts of town off the airport road, this is a new monastery, founded in 1990. It has a small community of monks and visitors are welcomed to attend their morning ceremonies.

WILD BACTRIAN CAMEL
John Hare

The wild Bactrian camel (*Camelus bactrianus ferus*) or *khavtgai* is more endangered than the giant panda. There are approximately 350 wild Bactrian camels in the Mongolian Great Gobi Reserve 'A', south of Bayan Toroi, and approximately 650 additional camels further south in Xinjiang Province in China. It is amazing creature that lives in some of the world's harshest environments.

In the Mongolian Gobi its main enemy is the wolf. Further south in China, the threat is from hunters and illegal miners. In the Chinese Gashun Gobi there is no freshwater and this former nuclear test site holds herds of wild camels that have not only adapted to drinking saltwater slush, but have also survived over 43 atmospheric nuclear tests. Samples of skin taken from the remains of dead Bactrian camels have been sent to scientists for genetic DNA testing and in every case the results have been remarkable. Each skin sample has shown two or three distinct genetic differences from the domestic Bactrian camel. This answers the charge that the wild camel is a domestic runaway and points to the fact that the wild camel herds are the relics of the original wild stock that man first domesticated over 4,000 years ago. This wild stock, possible descendants of the primordial camels which crossed the land bridge replaced by the Bering Strait sometime in the Pliocene Era (about four to three million years ago), are worth saving. It was those primordial camels going west that probably pioneered the two modern camel species, the Bactrian (two humps) and the dromedary (one hump). It is likely that the others that ventured south gave rise to the remaining four species of the zoological family of camelids, usually known communally as llamas (individually: the guanaco, the alpaca, the vicuna, and the llama proper).

The most obvious difference between the two camel species are the number of humps, localised fat deposits which, like fat in any other species, provide a source of energy. In the hotter climates of southwest Asia (and Africa) a 'mutant' with only one hump, the dromedary, became the dominant species. The severity of extreme winter temperatures has an effect on other aspects of body conformation. The Bactrian has generally a more massive body than the

Aimag Museum
On the main street, this is a typical small museum of several rooms exhibiting Buddhist statues, scroll paintings and featuring a Mongol warrior's dress, a shaman costume and a drum.

Theatre
In the centre of town on the main street opposite the museum, the theatre holds occasional performances; tickets US$3–4 (tourist price).

National parks in Gobi Altai
The national parks of the Gobi Altai are not well visited because they are so remote and there are no visitor facilities. In addition, the strictly protected areas are off limits to tourists except those with permission to help with research programmes.

Great Gobi Strictly Protected Area
Great Gobi is actually a mistranslation; 'Large Gobi' is the more correct translation, but the name Great Gobi has stuck and it sounds better!

dromedary, is set on shorter legs and clad in longer, darker hair – all useful attributes in conserving heat. Both species have a long gestation period (the dromedary with 12–13 months, the Bactrian 13–14 months) and at most one calf is born every other year. With puberty late at 4–5 years and low calving rates, it is incredibly time-consuming to build up a declining camel population, domestic or wild. Compared to its domestic cousins, the wild Bactrian is greyer, slimmer and with smaller-sized humps. But the fact that the dromedary foetus commences development with two humps but is born with only one points to a long-term development from the Bactrian and makes these remaining wild Bactrians exceptionally important.

Back in 1877, it was Przewalski, the distinguished Polish explorer, who took three skins and a skull of a "wild" Bactrian to St. Petersburg and introduced the wild camel to the outside world. But the Petersburg zoologists could not determine whether Przewalski's specimens were original wild stock. Today there are more sophisticated methods to draw on. It is estimated that probably no more than 660 wild Bactrian camels and possibly as few as 500 survive in China. In Mongolia there are thought to be between 300 and 400. What is quite clear is that they are all under ever-increasing threat from hunting, illegal mining and, in the Trans Altai Gobi in Mongolia, wolf predation. Only the wild camels in the Gashun Gobi in Xinjiang are completely isolated from domestic camels. This lack of an opportunity to hybridise is what makes their survival so vital. It is these remaining herds that the Wild Camel Protection Foundation is striving to save by establishing the Lop Nuur Nature Sanctuary in China. Another new reserve is planned close to the Mongolian border in the non-protected area of Gansu. It will also embrace the wild camel population in Mongolia, thereby becoming a two-country project and a future example of cross-border conservation. Should you wish to make a donation or to help in any other way please contact the Wild Camel Protection Foundation, School Farm, Benenden, Kent, TN17 4EU, England; tel: +44 01580 241132; fax: +44 01580 240960; web: www.wildcamels.com.

The area covers 4.4 million hectares and is divided into two sections, A and B. It is a UNESCO Biosphere Reserve, nominated by the United Nations. Part A, in the southeast, lies along the national border with China and extends into Bayankhongor Aimag. You need special permission to enter its territory. The protection of the area contributes greatly to the survival of the Gobi bear and the wild camel.

Part B (sometimes referred to as Jungarian Gobi B, Jungaria being on the Chinese side of the border), the smaller part at 881,000 hectares, lies in the southwest part of the aimag along the national border with China and extends into Khovd Aimag. It is not possible to visit without special permission. Both parts form the fourth largest biosphere reserve in the world, protecting wild horses (*takhi*), Gobi bears (*mazaali*), wild Bactrian camels, saiga antelopes, wild asses (*khulan*) and many small, unusual rodent species. The area is not visited by tourists.

Eejkhairkhan Nature Reserve
Located 150km south of Altai, this nature reserve of 22,475 hectares is designated to protect the local environment. There are some interesting rock pools and caves

SACRED MOTHER MOUNTAIN – EEJKHAIRKHAN
John Man

This is a sacred area to Buddhists and was worshipped long before Buddhism. It is Mongolia's equivalent to Australia's Ayer's Rock, rising abruptly from a sea of sand. Situated northwest of the Edren Ridge and south of the foothills of the Mongol Altai range, its southwestern reaches are gravel plains. The Sacred Mother Mountain was declared a national monument in 1992. The area of the site is 216km². It takes 58km to circumnavigate it completely; there are no paths and the sand makes hard going at times.

As a sacred place of pilgrimage Mother Rock is visited by Mongolians seeking solace and wisdom. The peace and quiet of the place allow the traveller to rest. The rounded shape of this huge granite mountain is surprisingly beautiful. The mountain appears to be alive with colour and movement; its lower slopes are covered, in places, with rose bushes.

The tracks of a snow leopard have been seen on the ground at Mother Rock. The leopard must have crossed the desert to reach the mountain and its water sources. Gazelles, goats and lynx have been recorded at the two known oases. Climbing the mountain, from a height you can see streams flowing between boulders on the pilgrimage trail, known as the 'Nine Pots'.

John Man is author of 'Gobi – Tracking the Desert', published by Weidenfeld & Nicolson (1997)

with well-preserved rock paintings of ibex, horsemen and archers near the base of Eejkhairkhan Uul. A guide is needed to help locate them.

Khasagtkhairkhan Strictly Protected Area
Situated in the northern part of Gobi-Altai, this is an area of 27,448 hectares designated to protect *argali* (wild sheep) and the Mongol Altai mountain environment.

Sharga Nature Reserve
Located in the eastern part of Gobi-Altai this reserve is designated to protect the habitat of the highly endangered saiga antelope. These small, snub-nosed antelopes have short legs and light-coloured coats and survive in remote, semi-arid desert conditions. Since it is located just south of the Altai to Khovd road it is possible to visit the reserve. There are limited tourist facilities and the usual entrance charges apply.

Takhiin Tal – the takhi release site
Beside the Takhiin Shar Nuruu range near the border with China, this is the home of a number of recently released wild horses (*takhi*) from European and American zoos. The last sighting of wild horses in the wild was in this area in 1968, thereafter the species became extinct outside of captivity. Captive-bred *takhi* were re-introduced from reserves and zoos worldwide in an effort to save the species. The first shipments reached Takhiin Tal in 1992 and later shipments came in 1996 and 2002. It is hoped that the released horses will survive the tough Gobi climate. Rarely visited by tourists, there are no facilities here.

Activities in Gobi-Altai Aimag
Climbing

Adventurous and experienced climbers are tempted here to climb the Altai and peaks such as the Khüren Tovon Uul (3,802m) and Burkhanbuudai Uul (3,765m). The Burkhanbuudai Mountain area (521km²) was placed under special state protection in 1996 along with the snow-capped Sutai Uul (4,090m).

Sutai Uul Located on the boundary with Khovd Aimag, this is the highest peak in Gobi-Altai and provides excellent climbing – most climbers approach from the Khovd side.

Eejkhairkhan Uul (2,275m) This stands just north of Gobi A Strictly Protected Area. Since 1992 the mountain has been under special state protection. You will need a permit to climb there (see box opposite).

Itineraries

For interesting local environmental tours contact the experts, Gobiin Ogloo (see page 151). Escorted journeys and tailor-made travel to out-of-the-way places in this area are possible through Far Frontiers (see page 148).

Mountain Biking and Adventure Vacations in Mongolia

Off The Map Tours

Visit: www.mongolia.co.uk   Contact: info@mongolia.co.uk

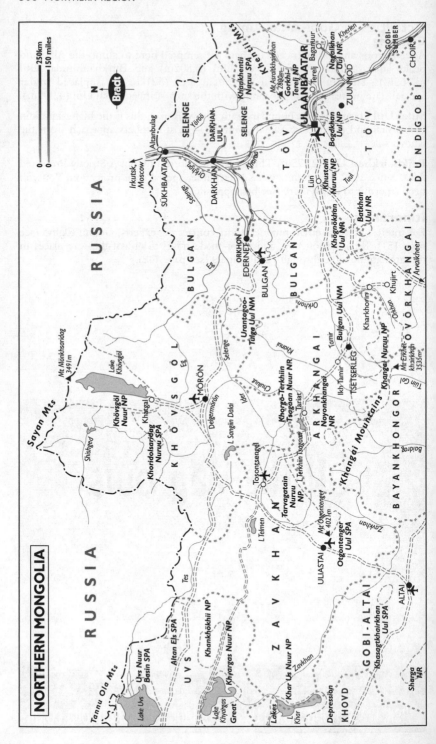

Northern Region

It surprises many would-be visitors to learn that Mongolia is not one huge desert but a country of lakes, rivers, mountains and heavily forested regions, where hillsides and valley meadows are spangled with alpine flowers. Despite the long cold winters northern Mongolia basks in summer sunshine (with a few showers as opposed to long-lasting, gloomy weather). Opportunities for tourism are endless, and new *ger* camps in well-located sites provide comfortable facilities, good food and hot showers, which make all the difference at the end of a travelling day.

Mongolia's northern aimags are: Khövsgöl, Zavkhan, Bulgan and Selenge. Within the Selenge and Bulgan aimags are the smaller aimags of Orkhon and Darkhan-Uul.

The northern region's taiga (forest) zone is adjacent to and part of the vast forested region of southern Siberia. In the taiga of northern Khövsgöl you will find coniferous forests of Siberian larch and pine, as well as rocks covered with mosses and lichens of brown, green and amber colours. Animals of the forest are hunted for their hides and skins. To combat this, Mongolia's conservation movement efforts to protect rare species (among them snow leopard and musk deer) have included engaging the help of ex-hunters to train the national parks' staff. They in turn ensure that campers leave their camping sites with no trace of having being there and 'tread lightly', as the green slogans say, in this wonderful, wild part of the world.

The economy of this region is based on timber and agriculture; the country's timber industry is centred in Bulgan Aimag. The northern provinces of Selenge and Bulgan are relatively prosperous and well connected by rail links to the capital, via the Trans-Mongolian Railway.

KHÖVSGÖL AIMAG

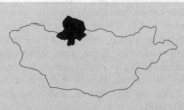

BRIEF FACTS
Population 124,500
Population density 1.24 per km²
Area 100,600km²
Aimag centre Mörön
Districts 23
Elevation of Mörön 1,283m
Livestock and crops Sheep, goats, cattle, horses/hay
Ethnic groups Khalkha, Buryat, Tsaatan, Uriankhai, Darkhad, Khotgoid
Distance from Mörön to Ulaanbaatar 671km
Average temperatures July +16.9°C January –23.8°C

Khövsgöl Aimag is named after Lake Khövsgöl, one of Mongolia's largest lakes. The lake and its surroundings are spectacular and the area is a natural draw for tourists. Mongolia's northernmost province is situated on the border with the Tuvan and Buryat republics of the Russian Federation. Local minorities include Tannu Uriankhai (Tuvans), Darkhad, Khotgoid and Tsaatan (reindeer people). The western and eastern parts of the aimag are mountainous with an intricate system of wetlands and lakes in the northwest Darkhad Basin, which includes Lake Tsagaan. Rivers such as the Ider and Selenge cross the southern part of the province, joined by the Delgermörön, which flows from the northwest through Mörön, the aimag centre. The Sayan Mountains lie along the northern border with Russia; the highest peak, Mönkh Saridag (3,491m), stands between the northern tip of the lake and the Russian border. Another mountain range, the Khoridolsaridag, extends west from Lake Khövsgöl. The mountain regions are forested throughout and are rich in animal and birdlife. The wet meadows and lagoons are important for waterfowl. Tsaatan people, who have domesticated reindeer for generations, live in birch-bark wigwams in the remote, forested areas northwest of Lake Khövsgöl.

The road into Russia is for local traffic only, since no tourist vehicles can enter or exit this way. The main east–west road in the northern regions from Ulaanbaatar is mostly unpaved and crosses the country via Bulgan Aimag, to Mörön and on to the far west. New *ger* camps have sprung up along the lakeshores; their facilities are excellent and in keeping with the natural environment. Lake Khövsgöl and the national park are part of Mongolia's 'Golden Circuit', a popular triangle of the most visited places which includes the Orkhon Valley and South Gobi, and the local economy is being rebuilt around tourism. The lake freezes in winter and there are opportunities for skating and also for cross-country skiing (see suggested itineraries for winter tourism at the end of this section).

Highlights

* Lake Khövsgöl
* Tsaagan Nuur (lake) – waterfowl and Tsaatan (reindeer people)
* Five Rivers – fishing
* Mineral springs and hot springs
* Camping and riding (suggested itineraries)

Mörön

Located 100km south of Lake Khövsgöl; Mörön means 'river' in Mongolian. The Delgermörön River, a great fishing river, passes south of the town. The climate in this mountainous part of Mongolia is cooler. Local people tend to build wooden houses rather than live in tents, so you will see fewer traditional *gers*. Mörön is not a tourist town; foreigners usually arrive at the airport and drive through to Lake Khövsgöl stopping, perhaps, at the market to shop on their way. You can buy meat, potatoes, onions, garlic, and some other vegetables. The market, the jeep and minibus stand and petrol station are situated 1.5km northwest of the town centre. There are several hotels in town. Daatgal Bank is located in a grey building, northeast of the square, and changes US dollar notes. It's open weekdays: 09.00–1600.

Getting there from Ulaanbaatar
By air
MIAT has a direct flight from UB to Mörön on Wednesdays (one-and-a-half-hour flight time). The airport is situated 5km from the centre of town; jeeps, taxis or

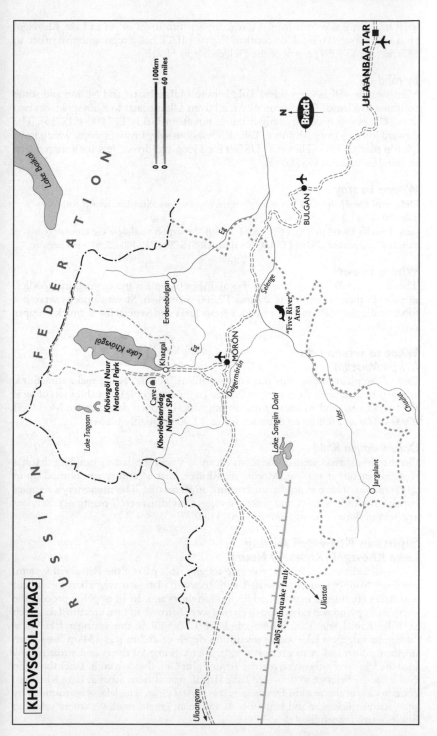

KHÖVSGÖL AIMAG

local buses will take you from Mörön airport into town or on to Lake Khövsgöl (and vice versa). To book or confirm flights MIAT has a representative office in Mörön (tel: 43 3297) north of the Delgermörön Hotel.

By road

Mini-vans as well as jeeps travel daily between Ulaanbaatar and Mörön and some continue to Khatgal. The journey by road from Ulaanbaatar to Khövsgöl takes two days. The one-way cost by long-distance bus from UB is T17,000 (US$15). The onward journey from Mörön to Lake Khövsgöl usually involves jeeps, which leave Mörön market daily. They cost US$60 for a jeep and driver, less for a shared jeep or minibus (around US$12/15).

Where to stay

Delgermörön Hotel One block north of the main square. Standard rooms cost from T20,000 (US$18).

Gov Tourist Hotel (tel: 41 3479; fax 41 21020)The airport road near the monastery. Standard rooms cost US$30 (T34,000), cabins US$15–20 (T17,100–22,800) per person.

Where to eat

The above hotels have restaurants. Local dishes include mutton, yoghurt, noodles, meat and onion soup; cost is around T2,500 main dish. Street canteens serve hot food, while the daily market provides fresh food and vegetables at much cheaper rates (T600).

What to see and do
Mörön Museum

East of the main square, this museum's exhibits include, as the main attractions, artefacts belonging to the minority Tsataan (reindeer people), an exhibition of local flora and fauna, and an ancient mammoth tusk. It's open daily (except Mondays) 09.00–18.00 and there's an entrance fee of T1,000 (roughly US$1).

Danzandarjaa Khiid

On the airport road west of the town centre is a new monastery building that has replaced an earlier version, Möröngiin Khüree, that a century ago housed up to 2,000 monks. There is now a community of 30 monks. The monastery's temples contain Buddhist statues and *tanka* paintings (Buddhist scroll paintings). Services are held in the mornings around 10.30–11.00.

Sights in Khövsgöl Aimag
Lake Khövsgöl (Khövsgöl Nuur)

Khövsgöl Lake was created by volcanic activity. It is part of the Baikal rift system, resulting from pressures associated with tectonic plate activity, when the Indian and Asian continents met around 55 million years ago. In an ongoing process the surrounding land was raised and deep rifts were formed, in turn creating lakes such as Lake Baikal and Lake Khövsgöl; Lake Khövsgöl is the younger lake. It is Mongolia's deepest lake with a maximum depth of 262m; it is 134km long from north to south and at its greatest width, 39km. Some 90 rivers and streams flow into the lake, and only one river, the River Egiin Gol, flows from it. Later the Egiin Gol joins the Selenge to flow into Lake Baikal, in southern Siberia. Lake Khövsgöl contains 2% of the world's freshwater; it is crystal clear. The lake is surrounded by mountains, thick pine and larch forests and lush, green meadows where yaks and horses graze peacefully.

LAKE KHÖVSGÖL'S LEGEND – THE MOUNTAIN TOP AND THE PLUG

Years ago an old hag was wandering in the northern regions in a particularly remote part covered by volcanic rocks, surrounded on all sides by mountains. She was surprised to meet a tiny child the size of an elf, who decided to accompany her on her desolate journey. They travelled for three days without food and rest until they came to a large rock, under which was a trickle of water; they stayed in its shade and dug around the spring to make a well. Life became possible and they settled there. The boy grew to normal size, he hunted and sang and the pair looked after each other. Everyday they drank spring water from their well at the base of the large boulder, but they were always careful to place a stone over the well to stop it flowing over. One day the boy's singing attracted a beautiful girl who was passing and in time it became clear that they would marry.

All went well and the old woman accepted the girl. Unfortunately, one inauspicious day the young couple forgot to replace the stone on top of the well and a huge quantity of water poured out and flooded the area. A monster arrived to have a drink and the boy, who was now strong and bold, killed it and buried it under a mountain top. Water was still pouring from the well, so the old lady, seeing the predicament, dived into the lake and placed a stone on the spring to plug it. Sadly, she drowned in the process.

To this day, the small island in the middle of Lake Khövsgöl is known as the plug, and the larger island is said to be the mountain top under which the monster is buried. If you climb Mount Urandösh (2,793m) to the west of the lake you will notice it has a flat summit ... the young couple named the lake 'mother lake' in honour of the old lady.

The western shore offers the best hiking and camping possibilities. You may pitch your tent there if you are on your own, or book into one of the *ger* camps situated near the shore (see pages 312–3). The lake and its rivers offer some wonderful fishing. Among the nine species in the lake are the Baikal omul, lenok, umber, Siberian roach and a kind of grayling endemic to Khövsgöl. The main attractions of the region are the scenery, hiking, fishing, camping and the lifestyle of the local people, including the reindeer herders. Some of the best views are seen from the hills and mountain summits, so they are well worth the climb, but it is advisable to take a guide. It takes two days to climb Mount Urandösh (near the *ger* camps west of the lake) and some routes are extremely dangerous. People may chose to ride across the mountains over passes to the Darkhad Basin.

Khövsgöl Nuur National Park

Located on the shores of Lake Khövsgöl, the park was established in 1992 to preserve the lake and its watershed. It comprises thousands of square kilometres of mountains, forests, pastures and meadowland, which includes the lake, the basin of the River Üür (to the east of the lake), part of the Sayan mountain range, as well as the villages of Khankh and Khatgal, towns to the north and south of Lake Khövsgöl.

The taiga surrounding the lake are inhabited by moose, reindeer, *argali*, Siberian ibex, lynx, snow leopard, red deer, Siberian roe deer and wild boar, while birds such as capercaillie and hazel grouse live in the upland regions. Eurasian otter hunt for fish in the rivers and black stork, osprey cranes and water fowl inhabit the lowlands, lakes and marshes. Wild flowers such as orchids, anemones, saxifrages,

rock jasmine, and gentians are found on the mountain ridges between the rocks, while meadow flowers include edelweiss and many herbs which are used for medicinal purposes.

Entrance fees costs T1,000 (roughly US$1) per person; T3,000 (US$3) per vehicle. This is collected at the park gates on the main road several kilometres before Khatgal; if the gate is unattended you can buy your permit at the park's headquarters, or from a ranger.

Ger camps on the shores of Lake Khövsgöl

There are many camps along the lake, and some excellent ones at Toilogt. Costs vary between US$30/35 (T34,200/40,000) per person depending on the area and what is offered. Self-catering camps cost from US$10 (T11,400), while camping near a *ger* camp and using their facilities costs US$3 (T3,400) per person. You can hire a fishing boat to fish or go for a quiet row; cost US$5 (T5,700) an hour.

Juulchin's Camp Located in Toilogt (see map), at a marvellous site near the lakeshore, this is a comfortable, long-established *ger* camp with good facilities. Costs are US$35/45 (T40,000/51,300) per night including meals. Contact Juulchin Foreign Tourism Corporation, Genghis Khan Avenue 58, Ulaanbaatar; tel: 11

328428; fax: 11 320246; email: juulchin@mongol.net or jlncorp@magicnet.mn; web: www.mol.mn/juulchin and www.mongoliaonline.mn/juulchin.

Toilogt Ger Camp On the isthmus at Toilogt, this camp is run by Huvsgul Travel Company (based in Mörön). It has hot showers, good food and excellent service; unsurprisingly, the camp is often totally booked in the summer months by tour groups. Costs are US$45 (T51,300) per night with meals. Contact Huvsgul Travel PO Box 116, Ulaanbaatar; tel/fax: 11 326478; mobile: 11 99116227.

4th World Adventure/Nature's Door Expedition Centre and Ger Camp Located a half-hour's boat trip from Khatgal, these attractive wooden lodges and traditional *gers* are situated in a lakeside meadow carpeted with edelweiss and wild thyme. Facilities include hot showers and a glass-fronted restaurant overlooking the lake. They serve excellent food and the cost is US$35 (T40,000) per person per day in shared *ger* accommodation (3–4 sharing). They also offer an 'Adventure Lodge Package' which includes luxury lodge accommodation (twin or double) with facilities and food, plus all other outdoor activities and excursions from US$150 per day. No telephone. For bookings: email: info@4thworldadventure.com or naturesdoor@magicnet.mn; or telephone Ben on 00976 91916722.

Khantaiga and Khangard *ger* camps 5km north of Khatgal in the Jankhai area, these camps cater for large tour groups and cost US$30/35 (T34,200/40,000) including meals. No telephone.

Jankhai and Erdene Uul *ger* camps Situated where the road meets the lake in the Jankhai area, these cabins and *gers* charge reasonable rates – with hot showers and saunas included. Erdeen Uul is self-catering. Prices start from US$20 (T22,800) per person. No telephone.

Khatgal Town
Located on the southern tip of Lake Khövsgöl is a collection of log cabins known as Khatgal. Originally founded as a camp for Manchu soldiers (1727), it later became a Russian trading town. In the early 20th century the first steamboat operated on the lake between Khatgal and Khankh, the town on its northern shores closest to Russia. Mongolia's first wool-washing mill was built here in the 1930s. Khatgal became the aimag centre until the airport brought more prosperity to Mörön. Gradually the town declined in importance but, since 1990 and the opening of the national park headquarters, Khatgal has gradually been redeveloped as a centre for tourism with new *ger* camps and shops. The Craft Store is located at the Blue Pearl Hotel on the main street where you can buy locally knitted. hand-spun camel-hair socks, gloves and mitts, as well as traditional carvings, games, such as *daam* (draughts), and other souvenirs – all of which help to support the local economy and sustain jobs associated with tourism in the area.

Where to stay
Blue Pearl Hotel On Khatgal's main street. Provides comfortable and clean rooms; hot showers; room service, meals are brought to your room; costs from US$25 (T28,500).
Khövsgöl Lake Hotel (also called the **National Park Hotel** as it is run by the national park) On the main street, 100m from the Blue Pearl Hotel. Caters for the park staff but also has some rooms for guests; costs from US$15 (T17,100) per person.
Garage 24 (hostel and *gers*) Garages (belonging to the former Soviet Union) converted into a friendly, low-budget hostel run by Nature's Door in association with 4th World Adventure (who organise expeditions and tours). Offers well-designed accommodation in bunk-room dormitories (costing US$5 per night) and provides traditional *ger*

ENVIRONMENTALLY CONSCIOUS DEVELOPMENT

4th World Adventure/Nature's Door has invested in two camps in the Khövsgöl area and is helping to develop small businesses in the region, linked to tourism and sustainable development. The company, like others, believes that tourism should respect the environment and benefit the local community.

At the campsites the aim is to leave no trace. 4th World Adventure tour company installed a mobile sawmill at Khatgal, where wood was cut for the camp buildings using timber from outside the national park and old, dry timber from derelict log cabins in Khatgal. Furniture is also locally made, and the company has undertaken a tree-planting programme to replace the trees. Pürevdorj, the owner of another Toilgot *ger* camp, has added an innovative element to the camp's activities by bringing a Swiss-cheese-maker to Khövsgöl. Environmental awareness is helping to ensure proper sewage treatment, whereby camps have installed composting toilets, and some (including Nature's Door camps) are powered using solar energy, while special solar-powered water filtration systems help to ensure that no pollution reaches the lake water. Nature's Door also grow their own vegetables and keep hens which helps them to be self-sufficient. These practical steps are encouraging others to do likewise and to ensure that the lake remains unpolluted.

accommodation, hot showers and a restaurant/bar with a south-facing veranda for morning coffee. Cost is US$25 (T28,500) per person per day. Nature's Door/4th World Adventure also jointly run an **expedition centre and** *ger* **camp** on the lakeshore (see page 313).

Offices

Khövsgöl Nuur National Park Headquarters (completed in 2000) are based in the centre of Khatgal village, the gateway to Lake Khövsgöl. You will see displays of the park's wildlife and receive information on where to go and what to do. If you want to understand the park in some detail, the chief ranger and his staff give introductory talks on the flora and fauna of the region – well worth attending. Lecture times are posted on a noticeboard; if not, ask when the next talk will take place.

Khövsgöl Guide Association (based at the Blue Pearl Hotel in Khatgal) will help to organise hiking or horse treks with English-speaking guides trained by the national park staff – experts in low-impact camping. Horse trails follow the western shore and some cross to the Darkhad Basin; the eastern lakeshore is not as well visited nor as attractive.

Khöridolsaridag Nuruu Strictly Protected Area borders Lake Khövsgöl National Park on the western side and was designated to protect a unique combination of landscape and wildlife habitat comprising a steep-sided mountain range which combines tundra, taiga, forested steppe and mountains – all at close proximity. Wildlife species such as *argali*, ibex, Siberian moose, snowcock and sable inhabit these areas. It is not an area that is open for visitors.

Other attractions around Lake Khövsgöl
Mineral springs and hot springs

Multiple mineral springs rise and flow from the sides of mountain valleys around Lake Khövsgöl; these waters are known throughout Mongolia for their medicinal properties. In Mongolia it is thought that if you eat the fish from the streams, they too are said to have curative properties.

Khar Us (Black Water) spring
Just 65km along the western shore of Lake Khövsgöl, where the trail turns west via the Jigleg Pass (Jiglegiin Davaa) to Tsaagan Nuur, spring water gushes from beneath a large rock and from many smaller springs nearby. Each spring is marked with a sign to say which part of the body they are thought to cure.

Bolnain Rashaan
Situated 60km east of the lake from Mörön, these springs flow into pools of varying temperatures where you can bathe. The water is said to have curative properties and it is also an excellent place to relax. Plan a two-day return trip if travelling from one of the western shore *ger* camps. You will thus need to camp overnight or stay with a herding family, and this can be arranged with tour companies and local guides. There are several other springs in the area but this is the most popular one.

Cave at Dayan Derkh
This cave lies on the west shore of the lake. Inside there are some cave paintings of interest and it's worth exploring. At the time of writing full descriptions are being compiled by local tour operators.

Tsagaan Nuur and the Darkhad Basin
Lying 50km west of Khövsgöl Lake, this low-lying area has more than 200 lakes, the largest being Tsagaan Nuur (64 km^2). Tsagaan Nuur village is located near the lake in a district of the same name. It is surrounded by the extensive marshland, mountains and forested hills, the natural home of the Tsaatan minority reindeer people. The Tsaatan are difficult to find and usually avoid contact with strangers, though sometimes visitors will come across their camps. Other than the Tsaatan, the main attraction of the area is its waterfowl. There are also great possibilities for fishing and birdwatching, though remember to bring plenty of repellent and mosquito nets. Transport and access to inland, off-road places in the area is difficult.

There is also a standard visitor fee to the area of T5,000 (US$4.40) per person per day; in addition a permit is required when visiting Tsagaan Nuur district (obtainable from the local administration via your guide). Boojum Expeditions (see page 149, USA) arrange tours in the Khövsgöl region, with their own *ger* camps at Renchinlkhümbe (www.hovsgol.org/camp.html), and Jigleg (on the pass to Darkhad Basin). For Bulgan Fault see *Zavkhan Aimag*, pages 318–21.

Activities
Birdwatching
Khövsgöl area offers a variety of birdlife, so don't forget your binoculars. Here you will find birds of the forest such as red-throated thrush, blue woodpecker, three-toed woodpecker, yellow-crested bunting and pine bunting, while in the meadows there are wagtails, Ortolan bunting, demoiselle crane, sandpiper, lapwings and ringed-plovers, and in the lagoons birds such as tufted duck, ruddy shell duck, golden-eye duck, shoveller, teal, Slavonian grebe and whooper swans are all present.

Fishing
The **Five Rivers area**, approximately 50km south of Mörön, on the border with the Arkhangai Aimag, is where five rivers (the Ider, Delgermörön, Bügsei, Selenge

THE TSAATAN

Tsaatan (reindeer people) comprise 80 families of a small but growing population. They are now making efforts to marry Mongolians in a bid to increase their community. They live in the high mountains of northern Khövsgöl Aimag. Originally they are Tannu Uriankhai or Tuvan, related to the Turkic people of the neighbouring Republic of Tuva. In the early 1980s the government grouped them around Lake Tsagaan in an attempt to settle them, though they would not be 'settled' easily.

Like Mongolia, Tuva was part of the Qing Empire but became separated from Mongolia at the beginning of the twentieth century as a result of Russian interference. Tuvans wrote in the old Mongolian classical script until they received the Latin, then the Cyrillic alphabet in the 1930s. Subsequently, when Mongols were forced into collectives by socialist reformers, these shy Tsaatan herders disappeared into the woods and mountains with their reindeer.

Nature is on the side of the Tsaatan and not the tourist as they inhabit one of the harshest and most inaccessible regions of the world. The northern fringes of Mongolia are on the edge of civilisation. Their encampments are usually found after riding long distances through larch and silver-birch forests, and tend to be more easily accessible in spring and summer. (If you are going to undertake such a journey, bring a fishing rod as there are many excellent opportunities to fish in the streams and rivers.) Tsaatan, who possess few ways of communication, travel with the seasons journeying in summer by canoe on rivers and in winter, when the cold weather comes and the river water freezes, crossing these rivers while riding on their reindeer. They barter goods in exchange for wool hide and furs. In spring, unsettled weather breaks the ice while strong winds and sudden storms buffet the land. In the hot, short summers, marigolds, forget-me-nots, primroses and anemones bloom, as if by magic, and in the skies the winds carry thousands of migratory birds. Forests are predominately made up of larch but there are also pine, birch, poplar and some spruce. Pine thrives on the south-facing slopes, while trees like poplar, aspen and birch grow on the less sunny, northern slopes.

Tsaatan construct birch-bark, teepee-style dwellings and hunt using horns made of larch wood to imitate animal calls. They catch fish by spearing them with long poles; reindeer milk is part of their staple food from which they make cheese, butter and yoghurt. Occasionally, they eat reindeer meat but overall they prefer not to kill their deer. They have become a focus of attention for tourists who now flock to see them. One wonders if this is a good thing: having admirably survived the 20th-century political changes, are they now to end up dependent upon handouts from one 'chopper' visit to the next? If so, and should they choose, don't be surprised if they employ their disappearing tactics again.

and Chuluut) converge. The area offers excellent fishing, and specialised companies have set up their own fishing camps here. On pages 197–203 you'll find all the information you need on what to bring, the choice of fish and equipment, the best season to go and so forth, as well as a list of expert international fishing tour companies and UK suppliers of fishing tackle.

Suggested itinerary

In the Saddle (see page 151) offers a Mongolian riding holiday including some fishing. The itinerary begins with a flight from Ulaanbaatar to Mörön, Khövsgöl's provincial centre, from where you travel north 140km by jeep to a fishing camp on the River Ider. There you spend a week camping and fishing for lenok, taimen and greyling, and you should also have time to explore the nearby hills and mountains, pick wild berries, drink plenty of vodka and generally chill out.

Eco-tourism

Discovery Initiatives (see page 148), a UK company founded by Julian Matthews who runs the business with a team of scientific helpers, arrange programmes involving eco-tourist projects and run them in association with national parks' staff. Previous successful programmes were based around Lake Khövsgöl and have involved participants joining with park staff to learn surveying techniques and standard field biology methods to investigate mammals, birds and plants in the area. The results of the research are designed to help future monitoring programmes, with particular attention given to wildlife under threat from (illegal) hunting, notably the snow leopard, *argali*, brown bear and musk deer. The team is joined by ex-hunters and park rangers: it is a great way to get to know the country and the lives of local people; for further details contact: Discovery Initiatives, Travel House, 51 Castle Street, Cirencester GL7 1QD; tel: 01285 643333; fax: 01285 885888; email: enquiry@discoveryinitiatives.com; web: www.discoveryinitiatives.com.

In addition, Discovery Initiatives recently published a booklet called *Lake Khövsgöl National Park, Visitors Guide* which is on sale in Ulaanbaatar at US$7 or available directly from the above address. It has a good chapter on nomadic life and also some excellent pictures of flora and fauna (some of which appear in this guide).

Khövsgöl under snow

4th World Adventure (see page 148) arrange this tour which begins by flying from Ulaanbaatar to Mörön, were you base yourself at the Expedition Lodge (owned by 4th World Adventure/Nature's Door). From there you can arrange with the tour company's guides to cross the Jiglig Pass to Renchinlkhümbe and stay with a herder's family in *gers*. You can also spend time with a Tsaatan family in the village, drive to Tsagaan Lake, visit taiga and witness the splendour of taiga under snow. If you are lucky you may also come across some reindeer herders. The trip offers plenty of opportunities to ski and to warm up later beside wood-burning stoves, when no doubt you will be offered a bowl of home-brewed vodka. If time allows and road conditions are favourable, visit the hot springs

---

REINDEER

At the end of the 20th century Mongolian reindeer were on the verge of extinction and their numbers had decreased drastically from 2,280 to 616. Life was becoming more difficult as a result for the Tsaatan reindeer herders, whose name literally means 'those who have reindeer' (*tsaa buga*). To try to counteract this, the Mongolian Reindeer Herders Society and the Mongolian Red Cross Society, together with Italian researchers, have helped to deliver food and aid to the herders over the recent hard winters of 1999 to 2001. Thanks to their support, reindeer slaughtering and trading was reduced and the herds have begun to increase once more.

near Lake Khövsgöl, returning by plane to Ulaanbaatar before flying back to London via Moscow. The price of the above 12-day itinerary is approximately £1,950, US$3,014 (ex international flights). This includes a donation to the Reindeer Foundation.

The **Reindeer Foundation**, a voluntary organisation, was recently established by tour operators and local people with the aim of introducing new reindeer stock from Russia to help a local minority living in Tsaagan Nuur, the Darkhad. The secondary school was built in Tsaagan Nuur village to help the children there.

One other company worth mentioning for outback adventures, nature tours, fishing, photography, riding and birdwatching tours in the Khövsgöl area is Huvsgul Travel (Khövsgöl) PO Box 116, Ulaanbaatar; mobile: 99116227; tel/fax: 11 326478.

ZAVKHAN AIMAG

> ### BRIEF FACTS
> **Population** 106,000
> **Population density** 1.26 per km²
> **Area** 82,500km²
> **Aimag centre** Uliastai
> **Districts** 24
> **Elevation of Zavkhan** 1760m
> **Livestock and crops** sheep, goats, cattle, horses/ potatoes
> **Ethnic groups** Khalkha
> **Distance from Uliastai to Ulaanbaatar** 984km
> **Average temperatures** July +15.4°C January –23.1°C

Zavkhan Province has some wonderful and varied scenery, dominated by the high, snow-capped mountains of the Khangai range, with many rivers (Ider, Tes, Zavkhan and Buyant), lakes and springs. In contrast are the low, rolling dunes of Altan Els and Borkhyn Els which continue into neighbouring Uvs Province in the west. While the southern and western parts are dominated by deserts and salt lakes, mountains and rivers dominate the rest – the Zavkhan River sets a natural border to Gobi-Altai Aimag before it enters Lake Airag in Uvs Aimag. Zavkhan shares a boundary with many provinces: Khovd and Uvs (in the west), Gobi-Altai and Bayankhongor (in the south), Arkhangai (in the southeast). It also borders the Russian Federation in the north and shares its northeastern boundary with Khövsgöl Aimag. As might be expected, Uliastai is a convenient place to stop when travelling around the country, although most people prefer the better southern roads when driving west from Ulaanbaatar.

Zavkhan's economy is based largely on livestock, particularly sheep raising. Zavkhan has an important lumber business, based at Tosontsengel. Minority people include the Khotgoid and Khoshuud. Views from some mountain passes, like the Zagastain Davaa at 2,500m on the road from Tosontsengel to Uliastai, are alone worth the journey.

Highlights
• Otgontenger Mountain
• Otgontenger hot spring
• Bulgan fault

ZAVKHAN AIMAG

RUSSIAN FEDERATION

Ulaangom

MÖRÖN

1905 earthquake fault — Lake Oigon
L Sangiin
Dalai

Lake Kholboo
Lake Telmen

Lake Bayan
Tosontsengel

Lake Khar

Tarvagatain Nuruu
National Park

Lake Khar

Borkhyn Els
(sand dunes)

Zagastai Pass
2500m

Solongot Pass
2000m

Lake Dögön

Sand dunes

ULIASTAI

Tsetserleg

N

Sand dunes

Mt Otgontenger
4021m

Otgontenger Uul
Strictly Protected Area

Bradt

Gants Pass
2000m

ALTAI

0 ——— 50km
0 ——— 30 miles

Uliastai

This town is quiet and pleasant, with a central area consisting of hotels, restaurants and markets and an industrial part of town taken up with offices and stockyards for the timber and livestock businesses. A climb to a pavilion on a hill near the town will give you some good views. At the top you will find some pieces of animal sculpture of elk, *argali* and ibex.

Getting there from Ulaanbaatar
By air
MIAT scheduled flights on Mondays and Wednesdays (just over two hours' flight time); MIAT's local representative office can be reached on tel: 57 2384.

By road
Private jeep or minibus. For public transport, check on current schedules and costs at the long-distance bus station in Ulaanbaatar.

Where to stay and eat
The **Uliastai Hotel** and **Tegsh Hotel** both serve food and charge similar rates: single rooms cost US$5 (T5,700) per person, double rooms US$10–15 (T11,400–17,100) per person.

The **Chigistei Restaurant** in the centre of town provides Mongolian dishes, charging around T1,500 for a main dish.

What to see and do
History Museum
Also known as the Museum of Famous People, this is in the centre of town on the main street south of the square. It exhibits the works of well-known local people such as the writer Yavuukhulan and the first democratically elected president, P Ochirbat. The entry charge is T500.

Dechindarjaa Khiid
This is located in a *ger* district 3.5km north of the town (look out for a shiny tin roof). Opened in 1990, the monastery has a friendly community of monks who allow visitors to attend their ceremonies.

Sights in Zavkhan Aimag
Otgontenger Uul
Standing about 40km east of Uliastai, Otgontenger Mountain (4,021m) is Mongolia's second-highest mountain and remains snow covered throughout the year. The mountain is part of the Otgontenger Strictly Protected Area, which protects many rare species of animals, such as red deer, Siberian ibex and musk deer, and rare plants. As one of the country's sacred mountains Otgontenger is worshipped by local people.

Otgontenger hot springs
Located 20km south of the Otgontenger peak in the Rashaan River valley, this is part of the Baga Mountains, a spur of Otgontenger. There are 30 springs and the water temperature reaches 50°C here. A spa resort has developed around these hot springs at an altitude of 2,500m. The resort is mainly used by Mongolians for specific medical purposes, although tourists are now welcome. The tourist price is US$35 (T40,000).

Sand dunes
You will need your own transport to see these dunes which are found mainly in the western part of the province at Altan Els, Mongol Els and Borkhyn Els. In the southwest the Mongol Els dunes stretch 330km along the Zavkhan River, a scenic route to Lake Erdene. Borkhyn Els dunes are easily accessible from the road when driving south from Uliastai to Altai, the centre of Gobi-Altai. The main attraction is the changing light on the dunes seen when driving in the area.

Earthquake Fault
This fault lies in Zavkhan Province near Lake Oigon running from the Khangiltsag River west to Sangiin Dalai Lake in Khövsgöl Aimag. The fault, the world's longest active volcanic land-fault, was created by an earthquake in 1905, measuring 8.2 on the Richter scale. The quakes opened fissures 60m deep and 10m wide. The fault line can be traced for 400km by a trail of broken ground and streams, including a land slippage (ie: a ledge) of 11m where the land fell or was raised along the fault.

Suggested itineraries
Otgontenger hot springs
From Uliastai drive east to Otgontenger and the spa resort, 20km south of the peak. Base yourself in the mountains, take walks and daily hot baths and have a

restful time. You can find accommodation at *ger* camps along the Rashaan River valley for around US$35 per day. For transport, to hire a jeep costs US$80 per day, less if touring – negotiable with the driver.

Southern route by jeep (a 3–4 day camping journey)
From Uliastai drive south (44km) to the Gaata Pass in Tsagaankhairkhan district and continue southeast to Otgon district (86km), from where you should turn north along the River Buyant, a mountain/lake area. Return via the sand dunes at Altan Els and Borkhyn Els (100km) before arriving back in Uliastai. The timing and logistics should be worked out with a Mongolian tour company, and/or local guide/translator.

For further information on these itineraries contact Nomin Tours or Gobiin Ogloo (see pages 227 and 151).

BULGAN AIMAG

> **BRIEF FACTS**
> **Population** 67,300
> **Population density** 1.38 per km²
> **Area** 48,700km²
> **Aimag centre** Bulgan
> **Districts** 16
> **Elevation of Bulgan** 1,208m
> **Livestock and crops** Sheep, camels, goats, horses/potatoes, hay, wheat
> **Ethnic groups** Khalkha, Buryat and Russian
> **Distance from Bulgan to Ulaanbaatar** 318km
> **Average temperatures** July +16°C, January –20.5°C

Bulgan Aimag is a mixture of dry grasslands in the south and forests in the north, bordering Siberia. The territory has huge resources of wild fruit, berries and medicinal herbs and grows around 50,000 hectares of wheat and vegetables. There are coal deposits, and rich gold, copper and molybdenum mines. Orkhon Aimag was created in 1994 around the city of Erdenet where the copper deposits are mined. Other industries are connected with animal products, namely hides and meat, fur and wool. The province has good roads and a railway line connecting Erdenet to the Trans-Mongolian Railway. The Orkhon River crosses the province in the south and in the north it is crossed by the Selenge River. Ethnic minorities include the Buryat.

Highlights
- Uran Uul and Togoo Uul extinct volcanos
- Eg Tarvagtain Bilcheer – scenic area (bilcheer means pasture)
- Deer stones and Turkic *balbal* (stone figures)

Bulgan
The town is centred around a long, narrow park which runs parallel to the Achuut River. The city hall, stadium and Aimag Museum stand together on the main street. Bulgan Hotel is opposite on the other side of the park near the river; there is a bank on the main street; the daily market is on a parallel street on the north side of town.

Getting there from Ulaanbaatar
By air
MIAT flies between Ulaanbaatar and Bulgan on Tuesdays and Fridays; for MIAT's local representative office, tel: 67 2379, 67 2252.

By road
There are a few direct buses between Ulaanbaatar and Bulgan but it is more common to take a minibus from Ulaanbaatar to Erdenet (around US$7 or T8,000) or an overnight train (US$5, T5,700). On arrival, hire a jeep (cost from T250–500 per kilometre).

Where to stay
Bulgan Hotel South side of the park in the town centre (west end). Has de-luxe rooms with bathrooms. Rates are US$25/30 (T28,500/34,200), while standard rooms with bathroom cost around US$10/15 (T11,400/17,100).

Artsat Mogoi Hotel (Snake Hotel) Northeast corner of the central park; standard rooms cost US$10 (T11,400) per person.

Where to eat
There is a restaurant at the Bulgan Hotel (see above) that serves Mongolian food, with dishes costing T1,500–2,500. Canteens in town serve hot food and cold drinks at cheaper prices; expect to pay around T650 for meat dumplings.

What to see and do
Aimag Museum
This museum stands on the main street beside the Ethnographic Museum. Exhibits include displays on local history and culture, as well as one on Mongolia's first astronaut, J Gürragchaa.

Ethnographic Museum
Located on the main street beside the Aimag Museum, this museum exhibits items of rural use such as hide bags for fermented mare's milk and saddles.

Dashchoinkhorlon Khiid
Situated 3km west of the city, this is a modern monastery, built in 1992 to replace the older one which was destroyed in the 1930s. It houses a statue of Tsongkhapa, the great reformer of Tibetan Buddhism and founder of the Gelugpa order, who lived from 1357 to 1419. A small community of monks still lives here.

Sights in Bulgan Aimag
Uran Uul and Togoo Uul volcanoes
Located 60/70km west of Bulgan city; the extinct volcano Uran Uul is part of the 1,600-hectare Urantogoo Tulga Mountain Natural Reserve. Uran Uul crater is around 600m wide and 50m deep, and at the bottom of it is a small lake 20m in diameter. In the centre of the lake on some high ground are some green trees. Other extinct volcanoes are Tulga, Togoo and Jalavch Uul; they stand 12km south of Uran Uul and also enjoy protection in the reserve. Tulga Mountain looks like a brazier which is the Mongolian meaning of its name.

Eg Tarvagtain Bilcheer
Located in Teshig district, this is a scenic area of forests, rivers and mountains, ideal for hiking and camping. Unfortunately, access is not easy due to poor road conditions.

Deer stones

Around 20km southeast of Bulgan are seven ancient grave stones, decorated with images of deer and thought to date from the 7th to the 3rd centuries BC. In the extreme south of the province, approximately 75km south of Bulgan, is the Tsakhiurt stele, an ancient standing stone that is also decorated with deer images. To get there you will need a jeep and driver and travel by off-road routes.

Stone statues

Standing stones are found throughout the country and date from different periods. (See box on *Deer stones*, page 324 of the Turkic period, such as the ones found 25km north of Bulgan, are referred to as *balbal*, and mark the graves of warriors and chieftains.

STANDING STONES

Tall standing stones may have been placed in the landscape to commemorate a dead chieftain or warrior. Over the centuries some have been destroyed but many have been left untouched because they are said to be sacred. A number are known as 'deer stones', as images of deer are engraved on them. Some depict deer in a flying gallop, while others are engraved with deer images particularly notable for their large, curved antlers, executed in a highly stylised manner. The standing stones measure from 3–5m high and are usually 50–60cm thick; these monuments bear a silent record, since so little is known of their history.

DEER STONES

Deer stones are standing stones – cultural monuments dating from the Bronze Age (4th to 3rd centuries BC). They are usually located at burial sites and erected to mark the grave or commemorate a local person of high rank. Mongolian people are proud of their forebears and regard these ancestral burial stones as sacred. Often small piles of rocks are found beside them. These, too, are considered sacred. They may date from another period or perhaps they represent the number of enemies that a particular person killed and are in some way related to a particular deer stone.

The deer is significant in that it reflects a belief that the Mongol nation sprang from the union of a male and a female, represented by a wolf and a doe. This is the opening passage in *The Secret History of the Mongols* – the 13th-century chronicle of the life and times of Genghis Khan and the birth of the Mongol nation. The deer are very often stylised in form with elongated bodies and large curved antlers. Good examples are found in many provinces, particularly in the western, northern and eastern regions. Deer stones are widespread in Western Eurasia and Central Asia and are known as the Scytho-Siberian type. Hundreds of deer stones found in the northwestern part of Mongolia belong to the Mongol-Transbaikal type.

ORKHON AIMAG
Erdenet

Orkhon Aimag was created in 1994 and is surrounded on all sides by Bulgan Aimag. Erdenet, the centre of Orkhon Aimag, is a very modern city, built in 1974. Its existence is due to the big copper mine nearby. Some 350km northwest of Ulaanbaatar, Erdenet is Mongolia's third-largest city. It was built with Soviet aid following the Soviet model and has a population of 74,000 (2000). Copper-ore mining, the main industry, employs about 8,000 people who work in shifts as the factory is open 24 hours a day throughout the year. It is possible to visit only with special permission. Erdenet is linked by a spur railway line to Darkhan and the Trans-Mongolian Railway.

Getting there from Ulaanbaatar
By train
Ulaanbaatar to Erdenet via Darkhan takes around 14 hours and costs T3,000 (hard seat) and T7,200 (soft seat). The station is 10km east of Erdenet town centre.

By bus
Long-distance buses travel to and from other aimags. The station lies on the road to the train station on the east side of town. Mini buses and jeeps are found south of the square beside the market. The standard rate is T250–500 per kilometre, depending on the type of vehicle and the deal you strike with the driver.

Where to stay and eat
Hotel Selenge Opposite the post office on Sükhbaatar St, west of the park. A modern hotel building, with a good standard of rooms with bathroom for US$20 (T22,800) each.
Aladdin Hotel Beside the square on Sükhbaatar St, the Aladdin is better known for its restaurant. Rooms cost US$15–20 (T17,100–22,800).
Togos Hotel Sükhbaatar St east of the park. De-luxe rooms (with cable TV) US$15–25 (T17,100–28,500) per person.

STONE STATUES (ALSO KNOWN AS 'STONE MEN')

Stone men, like deer stones, are thought to commemorate local chieftains, dignitaries and military leaders. The earliest standing stones date from the Bronze Age (Hun period), while others are associated with the Turkic and Uighur periods of the sixth–tenth centuries. Turkic funerary stones, known as balbal, appear to commemorate military leaders. Some good examples are found in the Shine-ider district. Fourteen deer stones are found in the Delgermörön River valley, around the Delgersaikhan River west of Mörön in Khövsgöl Aimag.

Many of these stone men in Mongolia are found headless; nobody is sure when they were decapitated. It is most likely the work of a new tribe taking over the territory of a previous one – like the Uighurs taking over from the Turks. Typical examples show stone men wearing tunics and holding drinking cups in their hands. Such examples are found in Bulgan Aimag, for example the statue at Züünturuu north of the village of Bulgan in Bugat district, the anthropomorphic figures in Saikhan district which probably dates from the Turkic period, and the famous Enkh-Tolgoi statue in Selenge Aimag, which was 'fed' by local people as may be seen from the state of its mouth.

The hotels serve food, usually beef steak, burgers and Chinese beer. Otherwise try the local market canteens and bars in town.

Shopping
Carpets and rugs can be bought from the carpet factory (2km west of town) or from the department store on Sükhbaatar Street.

What to see and do
Mining Museum
On the second floor of the Cultural Palace, on the square off Sükhbaatar Street.

Cultural Palace
On the square off Sükhbaatar Street. Puts on films and song and traditional dance performances as well as pop concerts and classical music recitals.

Sports Palace
South of Sükhbaatar Street, opposite the square, the Sports Palace holds wrestling competitions, and ice skating in winter.

Sights in Orkhon Aimag
Khöngnökhan Uul Nature Reserve is situated in the extreme south of the province. It was designated to protect taiga and steppe plants in an area that comprises several different natural vegetation and climatic zones from mountain forest to grassland steppe. It is a sacred mountain worshipped by local people. The area is visited by tourists although access to the mountain requires a 4WD vehicle.

Itineraries
Camping and exploring the past
Much of Mongolia's charm lies in the fact that you have the freedom to camp and wander at will through some magnificent countryside. You might choose to follow

a line of discovery leading through some exciting countryside in quest of ancient burial monuments such as deer stones and *balbal*. A Mongolian tour company can help to arrange a local guide with knowledge of where the stones are and how to plan an itinerary based around horseriding, fishing, and/or camping. Contact Nukht Ecological Travel (see page 227).

SELENGE AIMAG

BRIEF FACTS
Population 103,000
Population density 2.64 per km²
Area 41,200km²
Aimag centre Sükhbaatar
Districts 17
Elevation of Selenge 626m (lowest administrative centre in Mongolia)
Livestock and crops Sheep, goats, cattle, horses/potatoes, hay, wheat, fruit
Ethnic groups Khalkha, Buryat, Dörvöd, Ööld, Russian
Distance from Sükhbaatar to Ulaanbaatar 311km
Average temperatures July +19.1°C, January –1.9°C

Selenge Province borders on Töv (south), Bulgan (west), Khentii (east) and the Russian Federation in the north. If you look for Selenge Province on a large-scale map, you'll see that it lies around 250km south of Lake Baikal, a well-known landmark in Southern Siberia. There are mountain ranges such as the Bürengiin Nuruu in the west and the Khankhentii mountains in the east, and two major river valleys bring Mongolia's great rivers, the Selenge and the Orkhon (which enters the province from the southwest), to a point where they converge just south of Sükhbaatar, the aimag centre. The river flows north to enter Lake Baikal. Selenge is a prosperous and interesting province with livestock and large-scale agriculture, producing 40% of the nation's grain. The transport system is good; the Trans-Mongolian railway bisects the province in a north–south direction, and express trains pass through between China and Russia, though there are also local services. Altanbulag is Mongolia's northern border town on the main road to Ulan-Ude in Russia, which at present is closed to foreign tourist traffic. Kyakhta is the Russian border town. The main city of importance within the province is Darkhan, an industrial town, surrounded by its own administrative aimag, Darkhan-Uul, created in 1994 (described at the end of this section). The key cultural site of Selenge Aimag is Amarbayasgalant Monastery.

Highlights
• Amarbayasgalant Khiid
• Selenge Gol
• Yöröö Bayan Golyn Rashaan – spa
• Honey bees

Sükhbaatar
Located in the extreme north near the Russian border, this is a quiet agricultural frontier town. The daily market behind the Selenge Hotel is a thriving one. Money can be changed at the bank during normal opening hours or with moneychangers who frequent the market when the trains arrive. The station is in the centre of

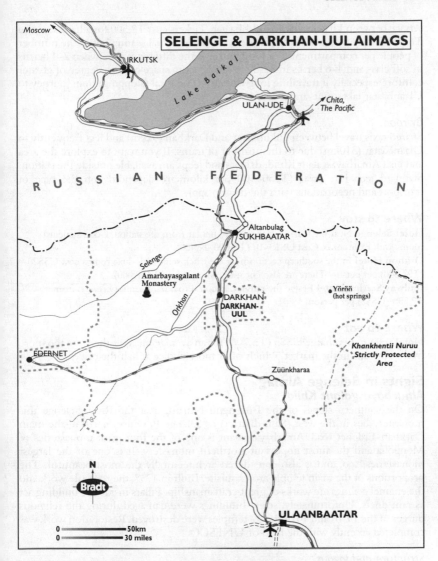

SELENGE & DARKHAN-UUL AIMAGS

Moscow
IRKUTSK
Lake Baikal
ULAN-UDE
Chita,
The Pacific

R U S S I A N   F E D E R A T I O N

Altanbulag
SÜKHBAATAR
Selenge
Amarbayasgalant
Monastery
Orkhon
DARKHAN-
DARKHAN-
UUL
Yöröö
(hot springs)
EDERNET
Khankhentii Nuruu
Strictly Protected
Area
Züünkharaa
N
Bradt
ULAANBAATAR
0   50km
0   30 miles

town and plays a dominant role in its life and structure. Sükhbaatar is a long, narrow town that follows the railway track. The market and town square are in the northern part, while the truck station and one of the main hotels, the Orkhon Hotel, are found south of the town, on the road to Ulaanbaatar.

Getting there from Ulaanbaatar
There is no local airport since the train takes most of the passenger traffic and cargo.

By train
International trains to and from Beijing and Moscow usually stop late at night or early in the morning at the border crossing for about two hours. There is a local

service between Ulaanbaatar to Sükhbaatar. Tickets cost T2,500 for a hard seat and T6,500 for a soft seat. The difference is not in the actual seating but in the number of people per compartment. For long journeys the difference is between 2–4 berths in soft class and 4–6 berths in hard class. The extra space offers a degree of greater comfort, especially if travelling long distance. The local (stopping) train journey to Ulaanbaatar takes nine-and-a-half hours.

By road
Shared taxis travel between Sükhbaatar and Darkhan (92km) and less frequently to Ulaanbaatar (310km) due to the number of trains. If you want to explore the area and visit Amarbayasgalant Khiid, drivers and jeeps are available outside the station. Standard jeep hire costs (T250–500 per kilometre depending on the type of transport and negotiations with the driver) apply.

Where to stay
Hotel Selenge Near the market in the north, not far from the station. Good standard rooms with bathrooms. Cost US$8–10 (T9,000–11,400).
Orkhon Hotel In the southern section near the truck station; de-luxe rooms cost US$20 (T22,800) per person. There are also cheaper rooms at US$8 (T9,000).
Railway Station Hotel Beside the railway station. Provides dormitory rooms from T2,500 (US$2) per person.

Where to eat
Hotel restaurants charge US$5 (T5,700) for an average meal, or there are the more lively canteens in the market, which offer more choice at half the price.

Sights in Selenge Aimag
Amarbayasgalant Khiid
On the southern slopes of the Bürengiin Nuruu, near the River Selenge this monastery lies in the west (Sant district) of Selenge Province, north of the main Darkhan–Erdenet road. Amarbayasgalant is one of the four great monasteries of Mongolia and the most important northern monastery. It is one of the largest monasteries, too, and is also considered architecturally the most beautiful. The proportions of the main temple are exquisite. Built in 1737, the roof-tile work and the enamel ceilings are works of great craftsmanship. Pillars inside the building act as rain ducts. Unfortunately, some buildings were damaged during the religious purges of the 1930s and 10 of the 37 temples were destroyed. Restoration work was completed recently with the help of UNESCO.

Structure and layout
The style of the monastery is predominantly Chinese and it has a more unified composition than Erdene Zuu Monastery in the Orkhon River valley. A wall surrounds the temple buildings with the main gate facing south. The symmetric layout can best be seen from a diagram showing the ground plan of Amarbayasgalant Khiid. Principal buildings are situated along the north–south axis with secondary temples alongside. The main two-storey temple (Tsogchin Dugan) and Labrang (the Bogd Gegeens' living quarters) are central to the whole on the north–south axis. East and west of the entrance are identical temples, the Bell and the Drum temples. Two pavilions stand to the east and west of the main temple, while behind it are to the north are temples of guardian figures and other divinities. The tomb of Zanabazar, the 16th-century religious and state leader, is situated among these temples. At the beginning of the 20th century the

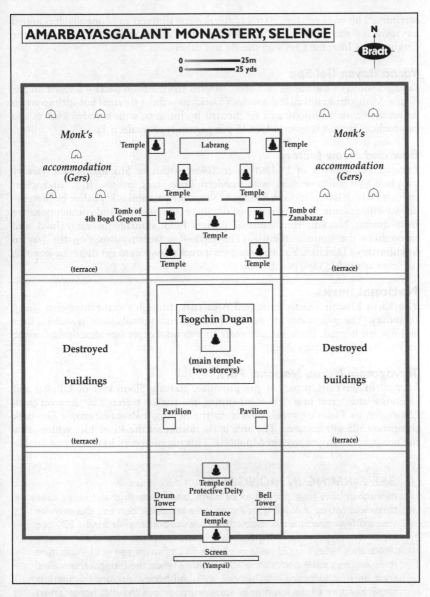

AMARBAYASGALANT MONASTERY, SELENGE

N

Bradt

0 ▬▬▬▬ 25m
0 ▬▬▬▬ 25 yds

Monk's
accommodation
(Gers)

Temple

Labrang

Temple

Monk's
accommodation
(Gers)

Temple   Temple

Tomb of
4th Bogd Gegeen

Tomb of
Zanabazar

Temple

(terrace)   Temple   Temple   (terrace)

Tsogchin Dugan

(main temple-
two storeys)

Destroyed

buildings

Destroyed

buildings

Pavilion   Pavilion

(terrace)   (terrace)

Temple of
Protective Deity

Drum
Tower

Bell
Tower

Entrance
temple

Screen

(Yampai)

monastery housed around 8,000 monks, who each had his own special place of worship and lived in *ger* compounds which once surrounded the temples on the east and west side.

Selenge Gol

The largest river of Mongolia, the Selenge rises in the Khangai Mountains to flow northeast through southern Khövsgöl, Bulgan and Selenge provinces, before entering Lake Baikal which is linked to the Arctic Ocean via the Angara and Yenisey rivers. It is 992km long, most of which (593km) flows through Mongolian territory. This river receives 30.6% of the flow of all rivers in Mongolia. It is joined by some of the greatest fishing rivers in the country: the Möröndelger, the Orkhon, the Ider, the Chuluut, the Eg and others.

Yöröö Bayan Gol Spa

Located south of the village of Yöröö, 100km from Züünkharaa – a town on the Trans-Mongolian railway line south of Darkhan – these thermal hot springs are in an attractive mountainous area frequented by hunters, with wooden chalets and hot baths. The cost is around US$15 per person (cabins sleep 4).

Bow and arrow factory

Located at the town of Dulaankhaan, 60km south of Sükhbaatar; the factory supplies Mongolian archers with modern bows and arrows. It is an ancient industry which has its roots in Mongolia's warrior past and is kept alive by present-day sporting events. Archery is one of the three manly sports and competitions are held during Naadam (the national games, held annually in early July) and throughout the summer months. The factory is worth visiting on the way to Sükhbaatar or Darkhan. You will need your own transport to get there; by jeep this will cost around US$80 per day trip.

National parks

The Khan Khentii Strictly Protected Area cuts through the northwestern aimag boundary. The mountains are densely forested and animals such as wolves, deer and elk are hunted. Birds include owls and woodpeckers (see description of the park in Töv Aimag, page 252).

Tarvagatain Nuruu National Park

Located in the eastern part of the province, starting 50km east of Uliastai and extending north east into Arkhangai Aimag, the park is bisected by the road from Ulaangom to Tseterleg which travels via the Solongot Pass (see map). The park comprises 525,440 hectares. The area is the source of the River Ider which joins the Selenge, the largest river in Mongolia. This national park has great potential to

---

BEE FARMING IN MONGOLIA

Mongolian bees have proved to be hardy and industrious and range over three kilometres. Ask for honey with your breakfast bun and discover for yourself how delicious the honey these bees produce is! Around 1,500 bee swarms are registered. Mongolians would like to invest more in this industry which they believe could be as profitable as cashmere and gold. Apiculture (bee-keeping) dates back to the 13th century when the Mongol khans filled their drinking fountains with alcohol, milk and honey. Ancient manuscripts show a picture of the fountain in Karakorum, where mead (a honey drink) poured from one of the branches of a silver tree/fountain. Mongolian folklore and folk songs extol the quality of its honey. Beekeeping has been developed in several aimags including Selenge. In 1959, 20 swarms were imported to the province from Buryatia and put into hives in Shaamar Research Centre, Shaamar district. Nearly 5,000 swarms were raised in Selenge, in the Bilgüün Sudar bee-keeping farm in Darkhan, and elsewhere. Övörkhangai Aimag produces up to 30 tonnes of honey a year but recently the production has fallen due to financial problems.

develop its mineral water springs as health spas for tourism, but these areas are not yet developed.

DARKHAN-UUL AIMAG

The small aimag Darkhan-Uul is one of the youngest of Mongolia's provinces. The aimag centre is Darkhan, located 219km from Ulaanbaatar. It is one of three new aimags created in 1994; the others are Orkhon Aimag, with its centre of Erdenet, next to Bulgan Aimag (northwest); and Gobi-Sümber Aimag, with Choir as its centre, next to Dornogobi Aimag (south).

Darkhan

Mongolia's second town is situated some 100km south of the border with Russia and is connected to Ulaanbaatar by a surfaced road. Originally a small settlement, the town grew to become an important town with a population of around 72,600 (2,000). It is surrounded by agricultural land and the Trans-Mongolian Railway passes through it. Darkhan is divided into four parts: the older town near the railway station with the new town south of it, and two industrial estates to the north and south. Businesses include the production of building materials, textiles (processing raw hides to produce leather and sheepskin coats), agricultural produce (centred around meat processing for export), fruit and vegetable canning and flour milling. Coal is mined at Sharyn Gol, 63km from Darkhan. There are also a large number of schools and colleges. Although not highly geared for tourism the city has good shopping and is a popular stop for tourists on their way to Amarbayasgalant Monastery.

Getting there from Ulaanbaatar
By train
There are five trains a day from Ulaanbaatar to Darkhan, a journey of seven-and-a-half hours. Trains between Ulaanbaatar and Erdenet stop at Darkhan. The ticket office at Darkhan train station is open daily from 08.00–12.00, 16.00–18.00 and 22.00–02.00, and a ticket (one way) from Ulaanbaatar to Darkhan costs US$5 (local price). An international office deals with tickets to Irkutsk and Moscow.

By road
There is a good paved road from Ulaanbaatar to Darkhan and the journey takes five-plus hours, depending on the form of transport. Shared taxis and mini-vans depart frequently to Ulaanbaatar (south), less often (north) to Sükhbaatar; they leave from the main square in the new town.

Jeeps for hire (with drivers) are found at the market and at the railway station; the average cost is T500 per kilometre.

Where to stay
The Kiwi Hotel Darkhan. This is one of the top hotels outside Ulaanbaatar. Rooms are comfortable and well decorated, the service is excellent and bars and restaurants also are highly rated. Rooms cost from US$65 (T74,000) per night.

Darkhan Hotel New town on the east side of the park. Standard double rooms with bathrooms cost US$20 (T22,800).

Woods Hotel New town just south of the park. Modern and comfortable rooms cost US$20 (T22,800).

Nomin Hotel New town on the east side of the park. Standard single rooms with bathrooms cost US$8 (T9,000).

Where to eat
Darkhan and Woods hotel restaurants charge around T6,000 for a main meal. Cafés and bars in the old town serve cheaper food at around T1,000 per dish. You will find beef as well as mutton dishes and more vegetables on the menu than in other parts of the country.

What to see and do
Kharaagiin Khiid
In the old town of Darkhan, the temple is in an interesting wooden building. There is an active community of monks and religious items are on sale.

Aimag Museum
(Darkhan Uul) Located in the new town, southeast of the park near the post office, this museum has exhibits of traditional costumes, religious artefacts and archaeological finds. It's open daily 10.00–17.00 (closed Sunday). The cost is T500.

Suggested itineraries
Travel from Ulaanbaatar by train to Darkhan and stay overnight in the town. Set out by jeep with a guide the following day to visit Amarbayasgalant Monastery, including picnicking in the hills nearby so you can look down on the rooftops and the general layout of this splendid temple complex. Return to Darkhan and have dinner there. Using the same jeep and driver, visit the hot springs at Yöröö Bayan Gol, east of Darkhan, then relax and/or go hiking and enjoy the outdoor life. It is a very out-of-the-way place and roads are not paved so allow five days for the journey. Plan with a tour company, in advance, or a guide/translator and jeep driver on the spot.

For more information contact Juulchin Foreign Tourism Corporation, Mongolei Reisen GmbH (in association with Juulchin).

Western Mongolia

The western aimags – Bayan-Ölgii, Khovd, Uvs – are very attractive and well worth a visit for the hardier traveller. They are remote and transport is not easy, with very few public bus services. Despite the fact that villages are run down and there is little tourist infrastructure, those with a pioneering spirit and good stamina will much enjoy the region, which is quite unlike other parts of Mongolia. Just bear in mind that the roads are appalling and be prepared to rough it.

In recent years students on their long summer break, hunters and a few tourists have ventured out west. The overland trip from Ulaanbaatar to Ulaangom (Uvs Aimag) takes a minimum of two days' hard driving. The journey from Ulaanbaatar to Khovd can be achieved in two days, or in a day if you are prepared to drive almost non-stop from 04.00 in the morning onwards...

The many ethnic minorities of the western region include, besides the Khalcha majority, Khoton, Kazakh, Uriankhai, Zakhchin, Myangad, Ööld and Torgut.

KHOVD AIMAG

> **BRIEF FACTS**
> **Population** 90,000
> **Population density** 1.24 per km²
> **Area** 76,100km²
> **Aimag centre** Khovd
> **Districts** 17
> **Elevation of Khovd** 1,405m
> **Livestock and crops** Goat, sheep, cattle, horse, camel/potatoes, wheat, melons
> **Ethnic groups** Khalkha, Kazakh, Uriankhai, Zakhchin, Myangad, Torgut, Ööld and Khoton
> **Distance from Khovd to Ulaanbaatar** 1,425km
> **Average temperatures** July +18.9°C, January –25.4°C

Khovd (also known as Khobdo) is the most visited of the western aimags. The province is divided by the Mongol Altai range. Melting snow from the mountains replenishes the water table every spring, providing Khovd with more than 200 fast-flowing rivers as well as many lakes and streams. The rivers run into the sands and disappear. This subterranean ground water comes to the surface in springs, creating green oases in the desert, and provides water for livestock, and wild

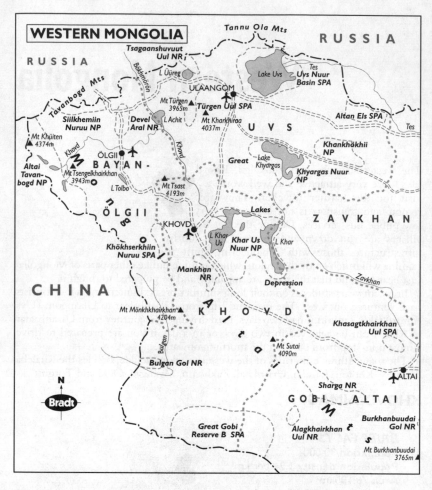

WESTERN MONGOLIA

animals in remote places. Semi-desert and saltwater marshes characterise the aimag where the southern and northern sections are barren and dotted with salt lakes. The Great Gobi Strictly Protected Area B extends from Gobi-Altai Aimag in the south into Khovd, along the border with China.

Highlights
- Cave paintings at Tsenkheriin Agui
- National parks' mountains and lakes
- Birdwatching, climbing, hiking and riding
- Deer stones and rock carvings

Khovd
Khovd was founded in 1731 as a Manchu outpost. The city is situated on the River Buyant, a tributary of the Khovd River, northern Mongolia's biggest river, after which it is named; at one time it was called Jargalant, which means 'happy'. With its attractive, tree-lined streets – poplars, planted when the Manchus occupied the place – it is a busy, bustling city. From a farming community,

producing livestock products (hides and wool), it has emerged as western Mongolia's major industrial city with a population of 35,000 people. The main college in the west is centred here. Of special historical interest is the Manchu fort, and the ruins of a walled compound at the northern side of the city, built during the Manchu (Qing) dynasty in the late 1700s; its walls were surrounded by a moat, now filled in. The compound included temples, a Chinese graveyard and the homes of the ruling Chinese families, mostly destroyed when the Manchus were forced to leave the region some 200 years later, in 1912 following a fierce two-day battle after a ten-day siege. There is a thriving market south of the town near the truck station, where you can buy carrots, cabbage, turnips, beetroot, radishes and watermelons – for which the province is famous. Like most markets it is surrounded by a container market selling tinned foods, tea and dumplings at low prices – T500–600.

Getting there from Ulaanbaatar
By air
MIAT offers direct flights to Khovd from UB on Tuesdays, Thursdays and Saturdays (almost four hours' flight time) and to Khovd via Bulgan on Mondays. The local representative office can be reached on tel: 43 2518. From Khovd to UB by plane (tourist price) costs approximately US$150; return fares (UB–Khovd) are cheaper at around US$280 (all prices are subject to change).

By road
Roads are appalling, so be forewarned. For short distances riding a horse or a camel is a lot easier and more comfortable. Shared jeeps are the best way to get around if travelling in a small group; to hire a jeep and driver will cost in the region of US$70–80 per day; touring costs less and is negotiable with the driver. Buses also travel to and from Khovd via Arvaikheer, Bayankhongor and Altai; the cost is around T17,000 (US$15) one way (a very bumpy two–three-day journey).

Where to stay
There are a number of hotels in the city centre but there are also excellent opportunities to camp along the Buyant River – that is, until the weather turns cold. In summer many local families choose to move out of the city and enjoy camping along the riverbanks where the water is fresh and cool.

Buyant Hotel Southeast of the main square. The best hotel in town. Provides excellent food and drink and is a comfortable place to stay. Rooms US$20–45 (T22,800–51,255). The hotel shop sells chocolate, coffee, fizzy drinks and beer.
Khovd Hotel East of the main square. Provides cheap accommodation. Rooms from US$10 (T11,400); recently it has been closed for repairs.

Where to eat
Both hotels (above) have restaurants. Otherwise local food is to be found at market stalls and in street canteens at the going rate: currently around T600–700 per dish. You will find many more vegetables here, including root crops like radishes and beetroot; rice is popular and noodles are also served.

What to see and do
Aimag Museum
One block north of the main square, the museum features a facsimile of the cave paintings at Tsenkheriin Agui (see overleaf).

Türeemel Amarjuulagai Khiid

Just two minutes' walk north of the main square, this monastery replaced the original Shar Süm (Yellow Temple), which was built in the 1770s on the outskirts of the city. It was completely destroyed in the religious purges of 1937.

Magsarjav Theatre

In the centre of town off the main square (east side), the theatre offers traditional local song and dance entertainment. Tickets cost US$5 (tourist price).

Yamaat Ulaan Uul ('Red Mountain of Goats')

To the northeast of the town, this bright red granite hill rises abruptly and offers a fairly tough day's hike to the summit. Ibex may be spotted on the mountain sides.

Sights in Khovd Aimag

Tsenkheriin Agui (caves)

Some 90km southeast of Khovd city, these caves are famous for their remarkable paintings that date from the Palaeolithic Age (20,000–15,000 years ago). The paintings are an outstanding example of the cave art of Stone Age man depicting bulls, ibex, wild sheep (*argali*), camels and gazelles and, interestingly, showing mammoths and ostriches which lived in Mongolia at that time. The animals, birds, snakes and trees are painted on a yellow and white background in deep red and brown pigments, but unfortunately they have been defaced by graffiti.

Two caves were excavated in 1967 by a joint Soviet-Mongol team. Research confirms that Stone Age hunters populated the whole of the mountainous region of western Mongolia along the Altai and the Great Lakes, also proving that cave paintings were not just executed in Europe. The largest cave is 15m high with a floor measurement of 12m x 18m. Bring a good torch, warm clothes and watch out for bird droppings underfoot.

National parks and nature reserves

Bulgan Gol Nature Reserve

Located near the southwestern national border over 250km from Khovd, the reserve was originally established to preserve sable, beaver and stone marten. It is very difficult to reach, with no proper roads, and is not visited by tourists.

Great Gobi Strictly Protected Areas – A and B

On the southern border with China, 300km from Khovd, the protected area is designated in two sections: A and B. The areas protect wild ass, wild camels and rare antelopes; also many small rodent species including rare pikas and jerboas. Again, they are not visited by tourists. For further details on protected areas see *Chapter 4, Natural history and conservation.*

Khar Us Nuur National Park

In the northwest part of the province, around 60km east of Khovd city, this national park was set up in the basin of the Great Lakes of western Mongolia to protect water- and marsh birds. It comprises three large lakes: Khar Us, Khar and Dörgön – the home of rare migrant pelicans. The steppe area around them protects the habitat of steppe antelope. Birds of prey like falcons, steppe eagles and buzzards inhabit the region, living on many small rodent kills, as well as larger kills of marmot and desert fox. The bird sanctuary on the western shore of the lake is open to tourists; visitor fee T1,000 and US$3 per vehicle.

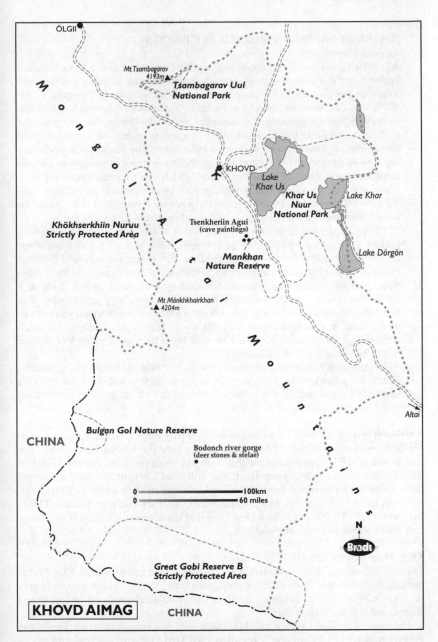

ÖLGII

Mt Tsambagarav
4193m
Tsambagarav Uul
National Park

Mongol

KHOVD

Lake
Khar Us

Khar Us
Nuur
National Park

Lake Khar

Altai

Lake Dörgön

Khökhserkhiin Nuruu
Strictly Protected Area

Tsenkheriin Agui
(cave paintings)

Mankhan
Nature Reserve

Mt Mönkhkhairkhan
4204m

Mountains

Altai

CHINA

Bulgan Gol Nature Reserve

Bodonch river gorge
(deer stones & stelae)

0 ————————— 100km
0 ————————— 60 miles

N

Bradt

Great Gobi Reserve B
Strictly Protected Area

KHOVD AIMAG   CHINA

Khar Us Nuur ('Black Water Lake')

Mongolia's second-largest freshwater lake (72km x 27km) is in the eponymous national park. It is relatively shallow with an average depth of 4m. Many rare species of birds inhabit the lake shores, including some lesser-known gulls; it is the perfect habitat for waterfowl, wild ducks, geese and other birds. The best times to visit to see the birds is in May and in late August. Since the lake is huge and access

JOURNEY HOME – FINDING MY ROOTS
Azjargal Ulziitogtokh

All my life I grew up hearing about and imagining my grandfather's birthplace, but I never went there until I was old enough and the political situation had changed. This was the case for most people who grew up in cities in Mongolia in the 1970s/80s. Our summer holidays were spent in *dachas* (small, wooden, Russian-style cabins) on the outskirts of Ulaanbaatar. As a child, I remember my granddad told me stories about the province where he came from. He was a very educated and intelligent person and he was also a lama (monk); he studied in a monastery until the revolution of 1921. Later during the anti-religious campaigns to destroy Buddhism my granddad left the monastery. He became an accountant and a part-time herdsman; somehow he managed to look after his four small children since my grandmother died when the youngest was only a year old. How pleased he would have been to see the successful lives of my uncles and aunts today.

My grandparents came from Khovd Aimag. They are Uriankhai people – known as the Altai Mongols, an ethnic population in Khovd and Bayan-Ölgii provinces. Uriankhai follow strict customs which in fact are followed by most Mongols. We were taught as children to respect older people and learn from them. We were taught by example and through traditional sayings. Even as a child, this advice always sounded better than preaching or nagging. For example, if a child was lazy and didn't finish a job, they would say: if you put salt in the food, it should dissolve; meaning if you start a job, finish it. To teach respect they would say: you have a brother like a coat has a collar. We learned not to be spoiled, but to be tough.

It is the local Uriankhai custom to arrange marriages between young people. There is a ceremony to introduce the bride to each member of the groom's family. It is important for the bride to respect her in-laws, and in turn for them

is difficult it is advisable to be accompanied by a park ranger, who can bring you to the best birdwatching spots. The marsh delta where the Khovd River enters the lake is one of the best places for birdlife, but watch out for mosquitoes – they like the place too, so bring insect repellent. You will need a permit to visit the national park; these can be obtained from the Khar Us National Park office in Khovd, tel: 43 2334; fax: 43 1231; email: kharus@magicnet.mn. Park entrance fees are TI,000 per person and T3,000 per vehicle, but note that these prices are subject to change and are expected to be raised soon.

Khar Nuur (Black Lake)
On the northeastern aimag boundary with Zavhan, 100km east of Khovd, Khar Nuur, the lake receives water from Khar Us and drains into Dörgön Lake. It covers an area of 37km x 24km with a maximum depth of 7m. Birdlife abounds on its low desert shores, and it is also rich in fish.

Between the Khar and Khar Us lakes are the twin peaks of **Jargalant Khairkhan Uul** (3,796m) and **Yargaitin Ekh Uul** (3,464m) – wonderful places to hike.

Dörgön Nuur
To the south of Khar Lake, Dörgön Nuur is 145km southeast of Khovd city, on the boundary with Zavhan and Gobi-Altai aimags. Although it receives freshwater from Khar Nuur, it is a saltwater lake, covering an area of 305km².

to respect her. It is believed that family blood is cleared after nine generations, therefore it is important to marry 'out of the family'. People say that this is one reason why there are so many talented and intelligent people among the Uriankhai!

Having heard my granddad's tales in my youth I finally got to see the western region and learn more about their hospitality and local customs. People in Khovd region are so friendly, you almost feel uncomfortable to take so much pleasure, and they will insist on providing meals and giving gifts. Most people eat dairy products and meat, especially boiled mutton and steamed dumplings. As half the population grow watermelons, there are always plenty of melons to offer guests.

First journey to Khovd

I flew to Khovd Aimag in a small Russian plane, normally used for domestic flights. It took three hours and it was an amazing experience for me as I felt I could almost reach out and touch the mountain tops. My second visit was by jeep – the usual way to travel. We do not have paved roads like those in Western countries, so much of the time you travel on unpaved or dirt tracks. If you know the route, you can get to Khovd within two days. However, that depends on the quality of the roads, the weather, and on the type of vehicle.

Second journey to Mönkhkhairkhan district

We left Ulaanbaatar at dawn (06.00) on Tuesday and arrived at our destination, Mönkhkhairkhan district, on Thursday evening at seven o'clock. On our way we passed through Töv, Övörkhangai, Bayankhongor and Gobi-Altai aimags. It is best to take food with you. The road is difficult and we needed an experienced driver to negotiate the high mountain passes. There is a Mongolian saying: 'To see it once is better than to hear it a thousand times.'

Khökhserkhiin Nuruu Strictly Protected Area

Located on the northwest border with Bayan-Ölgii, 50km west of Khovd, this protected area of 65,920 hectares is designated to protect the habitat of *argali* sheep, ibex and snow leopard. Access is difficult and as a strictly protected area it may not be visited by tourists.

Mankhan Nature Reserve

A protected area for endangered species of antelopes, Mankhan is located 95km southeast of Khovd city. The park, also a bird sanctuary (so bring binoculars) is often visited due to its proximity to the cave paintings at Tsenkheriin Agui. Entry fee T1,000 per person, T3,000 per vehicle (US$3); limited tourist facilities.

Tsambagarav Uul National Park

On the northwestern boundary of Khovd with Bayan-Ölgii Aimag, 80km north of Khovd, the 110,960-hectare national park was set up to protect the habitat of rare species like the snow leopard. It offers possibilities for climbing and hiking. Despite its height of 4,202m, Tsambagarav Bogd, Mongolia's third-highest mountain, is fairly accessible. Any mountain tour requires good planning and competent, experienced guides. For climbing you will need crampons, an ice axe and ropes, and climbing experience to reach the summit.

For more casual visitors, there is a jeep route to the mountain base from the main Khovd-Ölgii road, leading through Kazakh villages along the Namarjin

Valley to a turquoise lake. Another place to visit is the Bayangol Valley, which has remarkable views of Khar Us Nuur. Driving is difficult due to poor road conditions, so it is advisable to find a driver who knows the area. If you want to hike and climb there are several tour companies specialising in mountaineering or hiking in the area (see *Specialist tour operators*, page 150).

Activities
Whitewater rafting
Mongolia has many rivers offering every different grade of rafting during the season from May to October. Besides rafting, you will have an opportunity to fish and birdwatch and to visit some of Mongolia's minority nationalities. Run Wild tour company (see page 150) offers rafting tours in western Mongolia with international experts.

BAYAN-ÖLGII AIMAG

> ### BRIEF FACTS
> **Population** 90,000
> **Population density** 2.14 per km²
> **Area** 45.700km²
> **Aimag centre** Ölgii
> **Districts** 14
> **Elevation of Ölgii** 1710m
> **Livestock and crops** Goats, sheep, cattle
> **Ethnic groups** Kazakh, Khalkha, Dörvöd, Uriankhai, Tuva
> **Distance from Ölgii to Ulaanbaatar** 1,636km
> **Average temperatures July** 15.5°C, January –17.8°C

Bayan-Ölgii Aimag nestles among the towering snow-capped peaks of the Altai range, with steep ravines falling to dry, arid steppe. The province borders on China's Xinjiang Autonomous region in the southwest and the Altai Republic (part of the Russian Federation) in the northwest. In the far north of Bayan-Ölgii there is a short length of border with the Tuva Republic (also part of the Russian Federation). Mongolia's highest mountain, Mount Khüiten (4,374m), in the Tavan Bogd Mountains belongs to this area, located in the northwest where the borders of three countries, Mongolia, China and Russia meet. Mount Khüiten is surrounded by glaciers and permanent snow; its lower reaches are covered by pine and larch forests while willow trees grow by mountain streams. Much of the aimag is treeless and vegetation is sparse. Camels are well-adapted to the harsh, arid conditions; they give wool and milk and provide much-needed transport but unfortunately herd sizes are in decline. Hunting and subsistence agriculture are the main occupations. This westernmost aimag of Mongolia is unlike Mongolia's other provinces. The population consists primarily of Turkic Kazakhs – the largest minority in Mongolia. Kazakhs have their own language and customs. Around 90% of the population are Muslims. Many emigrated to Kazakhstan in the 1990s but found that life was no easier there and some have returned.

The alpine lakes and mountains are protected by a number of national parks (see national parks section). Besides natural beauty, the aimag offers many archaeological sites including balbal (Turkic stone figures), deer stones, *kurgan* (burial mounds) and 10,000 petroglyphs at Tsagaan Salaa (Baga Oigor River).

RUSSIAN FEDERATION

Tavanbogd Mts

Mt Khüiten ▲
4374m

Siilkhemiin Nuruu
Nature Reserve

Potanin Glacier

Ulaangom

Tsagaannuur

Lake Achit

Khovd

Devel Aral
Nature Reserve

Altai Tavanbogd
National Park

Tsengel Village:
Tsagaan Denjiin
Ulaan Khus
(deer stones nearby)

ÖLGII

▲ Mt Tsengelkhairkhan
3943m

Tsagaan Salaa petroglyphs
(Bronze Age stone drawings)

Lake Tolbo &
nearby springs

Tolbo

Mt Tsambagarav
4202m

▲

Tsambagarav Uul
National Park

C H I N A

Lake Döröö

Ulaangom

Khökhserkhiin
Strictly Protected
Area

KHOVD

N

Bradt

Altai

0 ━━━━━ 50km
0 ━━━━━ 30 miles

Mt Mönkhkhairkhan
▲ 4204m

BAYAN-ÖLGII AIMAG

Highlights
- Hot springs
- National parks, with their mountains and lakes
- Minority people
- Adventure tourism – climbing, hiking, rafting

Ölgii
Located in the valley of the Khovd River, Bayan-Ölgii means rich cradle or birthplace. The town square is surrounded by local government buildings, shops and a museum. Four main streets run in parallel pairs from the main square. There is a post office, the bus station, a department store, a cinema and a number of restaurants. The flat-roofed buildings, made from twigs and mud, give the town a Middle Eastern look; other obvious Islamic-style buildings include a mosque and *madrasah* (Muslim place of learning). The earth-oven flat bread is typically Kazakh and is baked in much the same way throughout Central Asia. Kazakh can be written in Arabic script, as you will notice on street signs, but mostly they're Cyrillic.

Getting there from Ulaanbaatar
By air
There are scheduled four-hour flights from Ulaanbaatar on Tuesdays, Thursdays and Saturdays; it is also possible to fly out of Bayan-Ölgii to Kazakhstan or elsewhere in Central Asia, with a tour group. Local airline office, tel: 71 3018; MIAT airline office, tel: 11 310917.

By road
Jeep (hired or shared) is the usual means of long-distance transport; from UB to the far west costs around US$400 per jeep and driver.

Where to stay and eat
Hotel Tavan Bogd A short distance from the main square (west side). The best hotel in town. The hotel restaurant serves local spicy dishes for around T2,000–3,000 (US$2–3). Rooms cost from US$15.

Good local food is served at the Tavan Bogd Hotel, and at Kazakh teahouses and restaurants; the market-bazaar sells kebabs at T250–300.

What to see and do
Kazakh National Theatre
A few minutes' walk south of the main square, the theatre puts on local cultural performances in the tourist season; cost US$4 (tourist price)

Aimag Museum
In the centre of town, the exhibits here give an overview of Kazakh culture and history. The entrance fee is T1,000 (roughly US$1) and it's open 10.00–17.00 daily (closes for lunch) except Sunday.

Sights in Bayan-Ölgii Aimag
Hot springs
High above the tree line at 2,480m, 50km west of Delüün district centre and around 100km southwest of Bayan-Ölgii, to visit the hot springs you will need your own transport. It is a beautiful area, undeveloped at present, but has potential for tourism.

Lake Tolbo
Meaning spot or stain, Lake Tolbo is on the road from Khovd to Ölgii (140km northwest of the former, 70km south of the latter); a high-altitude freshwater lake, Tolbo was the venue of a major battle fought between Bolshevik and White Russians. The shoreline is tree-less and the water is clean but it is ice-cold and only the bravest swimmers dip in there; Chikhertiin Rashaan (springs) are east of the lake (see above entry).

CAMELS OF THE WEST
Mongolia has the third largest camel population in the world. Camels of the west have thick, russet or red-brown wool and are very handsome creatures; fine camel hair is one of Mongolia's exotic exports. Camels are the two-humped Bactrian variety which, unlike the single-humped dromedary, can survive exceedingly cold temperatures; milking is a special skill and females have to be coaxed by whistles and songs to let milk down. The milk is rather salty and, like Guinness, is an acquired taste.

KAZAKH HUNTERS

Kazakhs have a tradition of hunting on horseback with trained steppe eagles. The trainer wears a heavily padded glove on the right arm on which a hooded eagle perches, until its little leather hood (*tomega*) is removed and it sees its quarry, a fox or squirrel, and within moments it plummets and seizes it. A well-trained eagle flies back to his masters saddle when other horses approach. Following the hunt there is entertainment in Kazakh *gers*, which differ from the usual Mongol *gers* in that they are highly decorated with woven carpets and textiles. Rock-hard camel cheese is served, followed by the boiled head of a sheep and often a local delicacy which turns out to be horse sausages. Kazakhs drink very strong tea; despite the ban on alcohol, there is plenty of goats milk, *airag*, which is offered to visitors.

Kazakh greetings and useful phrases

The Kazakh greeting is *Salyametsiz be*, and the response is the same.

The toast is *densaulik üshin* rather than the usual Mongol toast *erüül mendiin tölöö* (both meaning 'To your health'); 'goodbye' in Kazakh is *sau boliniz* (literally 'be well'); 'thank you' is *rakhmet*.

Lake Döröö

Located in a remote part of Tolbo district on the main road to Khovd, 45km from Tolbo town and 75km south of Ölgii, this is a superb mountain lake. The area around the lake seems to have been an important burial site as there are many tombs there. It's an ideal place for camping and hiking, though you'll need your own transport.

Petroglyphs and deer stones

These can be found at Tsagaan Salaa, some 50km south of Ölgii, where petroglyphs of the Stone and Bronze ages are located near the Bayan-Ölgii/Khovd road. Deer stones are also found near Tsagaan village, around 100km west of Ölgii at Tsagaan Denji, and Ulaan Khus beside the River Khovd in the northwest part of the province (see map). Your own transport is essential to visit these sites, as is a driver who know the region.

National parks

Khökhserkhiin Nuruu (mountain range) is a strictly protected area shared with neighbouring Khovd Aimag. It lies roughly 130km south of Ölgii. The Khökhserkhiin Mountains extend over 50km southeast to the mountains of the Mongol Altai range. Here you may see snowcock and rare fauna such as lynx, ibex, Siberian deer and *argali* (wild sheep). The park is not frequented by tourists.

Altai Tavanbogd National Park

This park of some 636,161 hectares is the largest Mongolian national park. It lies some 150km west of the aimag centre, Ölgii, and within its boundaries are Mongolia's highest mountain, Mount Khüiten, and some stunning mountain lakes, among them Khoton, Khorgon and Dayan. Rare species of wildlife found here include *argali*, ibex, Asiatic red deer (maral deer) and elk, while Altai snowcock and eagles are among the bird species. Besides natural attractions the area also has archaeological sites including burial mounds near the main road towards the southern end of Khorgon Lake. There is also a wooden mosque in the area which serves the local Kazakh community. Entry is T1,000, T3,000 for vehicles. Activities include hiking, fishing and rafting. Accommodation is confined to camping; bring your own gear if travelling independently; alternatively, tour operators provide tents.

There are two ways to approach the park: via the main road from Tsengel, which might require being pulled through a 200m-wide stream by a local truck, or the longer scenic route from Sagsai to Dayan Lake.

Siilkhemiin Nuruu National Park

Designated to protect Mongolia's wild sheep, this park lies along the province's international border with the Russian Federation and on the aimag's eastern boundary is Devel Aral Nature Reserve, home of the ring-necked pheasant, wild boar and beaver. The reserve extends into neighbouring Uvs Aimag. These remote areas are not frequented by tourists and going there involves expedition-type travel, bringing with you all the necessary equipment and supplies.

On the border with Khovd Aimag are two protected areas: **Tsambagarav Uul National Park** (110, 960 hectares) and **Khökhserkhiin Strictly Protected Area** (14,080 hectares). The first was established to protect its glaciers, habitat of snow leopards, while the latter was designated to protect *argali* and ibex.

Permits to enter and information about the parks can be obtained at the Mongol Altai Nuruu Special Protected Area office in Ölgii; tel: 71 2122 for further information. This office can also help with mountaineering queries. A visit to the Tavanbogd National Park requires a special permit from the local office of the Border Guards Department (in Mongolian: Khiliin Tsergiin Gazar). This may involve permission from the local Tagnuulyn Gazar (Office of Intelligence) and would require you to visit the barracks northwest of the town. Altai Tours, a local travel agency, can help organise permits; tel: 71 2309.

Climbing

For information on climbing and the addresses of specialist tour operators, see page 150.

The massif of Tavanbogd (Five Holy Peaks) comprises five peaks; the highest is Khüiten (4,374m) which means cold peak. It was first climbed in 1955 and was given the name Mount Nairamdal (Friendship Mountain). All the high peaks are snow capped and the mountains around them contain large glaciers; the largest is the Potanin Glacier at 19km long. The mountain peak marking the meeting point of the Chinese, Russian and Mongolian borders is 4,082m high but is not named.

Mountaineering

The mountaineering season runs from June to September. Mongolia has over 100 glaciers and 30–40 permanently snow-capped mountains, mostly located in the western region. To climb any mountain you must have the necessary experience, be fully equipped, and hire local guides. You must have permission too; a climbing permit is required before climbing any mountain in a Mongolian national park; permits are available from the Ministry of Nature and Environment in Ulaanbaatar (Khudaldaany 5, Ulaanbaatar; tel: 11 326649; fax: 11 329968; email: env.pmis@gov.mn). The Mongol Altai Club (contactable by writing to PO Box 49-23, Ulaanbaatar) are the undisputed experts in mountain climbing in Mongolia and should be consulted before undertaking any serious climbing activities.

Mountaineering tours to the 'Five Holy Peaks' of the Tavanbogd, tailor-made climbing tours and mountain treks in areas where snow leopards have been sighted are offered by Karakorum Expeditions (see page 149). Nomads (see page 150) offer pioneering mountain tours in western Mongolia; journey on horseback, by camel and in jeeps to visit the high mountains and lakes of Bayan-Ölgii and Uvs aimags.

Suggested itineraries in the western region

Tours around the western region may be arranged by Nomads, Karakorum Expeditions or Blue Wolf Expeditions (see pages 148, 149 and 150). One itinerary could begin with a flight to Bayan-Ölgii, where you can camp with nomad families near the city and visit the Kazakh eagle hunters. Driving north to Lake Achit, which borders both provinces, continue to Lake Üüreg (Uvs Aimag) and camp in the Türgen Mountains. Ride to the edge of the snow and glaciers, then drive the next day to the sand dunes near Uvs Lake, camping at Lake Bayan. You can return to Ulaanbaatar from Ulaangom, or you may continue into Zavkhan Aimag, flying to Bayan-Ölgii, riding, climbing and exploring the glaciers and foothills of the Tavanbogd Mountains.

River rafting

For the following itinerary contact Run Wild (see page 150). Don't forget travel insurance; waterproofs; mosquito repellent and sleeping bag. The itinerary begins with a flight to Ölgii, from where you drive to Khoton Lake, a beautiful place with snow-capped mountains and fast-flowing rivers. Rafting 25km from Khorgan Lake (also called Khurgon Lake) to Mogoit River on 2–3 class rapids, you continue to Tsengel district and visit Kazakh and Tuvan families. You then raft through high mountain cliffs areas on 3–4 class rapids surrounded by towering mountain ranges where you may spot *argali* and ibex. Overnighting in Ulaan Khus district, you then drive to Ölgii town and on to Tsagaan Aral (150km). This trip travels through the Gobi. From Tsagaan Aral you raft to Bayan Lake (1–2 class rapids) through a mixed landscape of desert, forest and mountains, passing Tsambagarav Mountain (4,202m) on the way. Camp and continue rafting from Bayan Lake to Ulaan Tag (2–4 class rapids), surrounded by high, rocky cliffs; then on from Ulaan Tag to Erdenebüren in Khovd Aimag (1–5 class rapids, where you camp overnight and drive by car in the direction of Khovd town (106km). The next night you camp near the beautiful Khar Us Lake, where you can go fishing or hiking, before flying back to Ulaanbaatar.

Many tour operators will make special arrangements for you. Explore the general list on pages 148–52 and devise your own itineraries with their help – but if climbing or rafting make sure you go with specialist tour operators.

UVS AIMAG

BRIEF FACTS
Population 102,000
Population density 1.41 per km²
Area 69,600km²
Aimag centre Ulaangom
Districts 20
Elevation of Ulaangom 939m
Livestock and crops sheep, goat, cattle, horse/hay, millet
Ethnic groups Dörvöd, Khalkha, Bayad, Khoton
Distance from Ulaangom to Ulaanbaatar 1,336m
Average temperatures July +19.2°C, January –33.6°C

Uvs Aimag is dominated by the Great Lakes Basin, a chain of lakes, wetlands, sand dunes and marshes sitting beside mountains and forests which stretch across the province from the aimag's southwestern boundary with Bayan-Ölgii and Khovd to its eastern boundary with Zavkhan, around the enormous Uvs Lake. The avifauna is diverse: geese, swans and rare pink pelicans inhabit the lakes and wetlands, while pheasants are found in the highlands. The economy of the province is dominated by livestock breeding. Recently some light industry has developed. Uvs supplies the western region with fuel from its coal and lignite mines. Ethnically the area is dominated by the Dörvöd (almost 50%), from which the aimag received its original name 'Dörvöd'. Historical monuments include the Oirat Altan Khan's Palace. The main attractions of the province are its natural sites – lakes, mountains and birdlife. Volcanic ruptures and faulting can be seen on the journey between Öndörkhangai and Züünkhangai.

Highlights

- Adventure tourism, camping
- Natural sites – mountains and lakes
- Uvs Nuur – lake
- Kharkhiraa Valley
- Achit Nuur – lake

Ulaangom

Located around 25km southwest of Uvs Lake in the Great Lakes Basin area, Ulaangom is a relaxed, tree-lined town with a good range of shops, hotels and a rapidly growing market which sells clothes, household goods and other items including furs and hides. The main square at the town's centre is surrounded by public buildings including the city hall, post office, cinema and the bath house; Hotel Kharkhiraa, the main hotel, is also on the square. There is a public park to the west side. Uvs Strictly Protected Area office, which provides information on the national parks, is located beside the public park on the main road leading west to Bayan-Ölgii Aimag. The airport is situated on the southeast side, 1km from the town centre on the road to Khovd. The jeep/truck station and market are located northeast of the main square.

Getting there from Ulaanbaatar
By air
Scheduled flights from Ulaanbaatar leave on Mondays, Wednesdays and Fridays (almost 4 hours in flight time); MIAT airlines local representative's office tel: 45 2600.

By road
Expect exciting and bumpy drives over high mountain passes; this is one area where it is well worthwhile hiring a jeep and driver who knows the country. The area offers an amazing variety of scenery in a single day's journey, from sand dunes to alpine lakes. Jeeps are available for hire at the jeep station (northeast of the main square); standard costs range from T250–500 and up to T750 if hiring a top range vehicle, which you are more likely to find in UB.

Where to stay and eat
Both the following hotels have restaurants serving local food, meat and rice.

Kharkhiraa Hotel In the town centre on the main square. Standard rooms cost US$10 (T11,400); de-luxe rooms cost US$15 (T17,100).

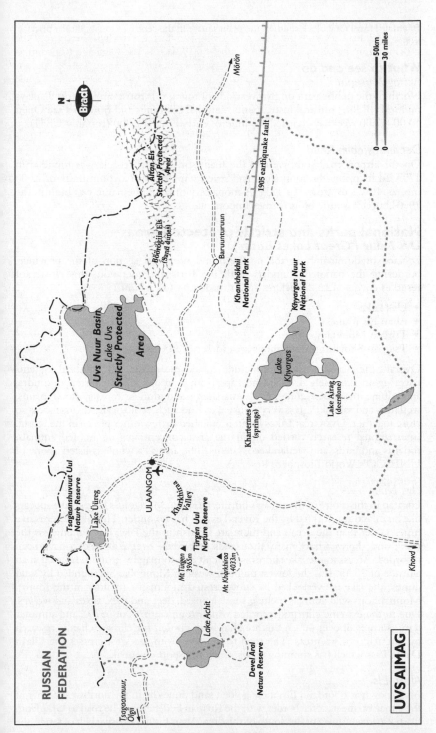

Bayalag Hotel One block south of the main square in the centre of town. Similar prices to the above.

What to see and do
Aimag Museum
North of the public park on the west side of town, this museum features displays on local wildlife, musical instruments, national costumes and Buddhist art. Open 10.00–17.00 weekdays (closed for lunch); entry costs T1,000 (roughly US$1).

Dechinravjaalin Khiid
On the airport road southwest of the main square, this temple was founded in 1757. In its prime the monastery had seven temples with a community of 2,000 monks. It was destroyed in 1937. A monastery of the same name was built in the 1990s but it has little of its former importance.

National parks and strictly protected areas
Uvs Nuur ('Great Lakes Basin')
Located predominately in the northern and northeast section of the province, bordering the national boundary with the Russian Federation, this cluster of reserves covers 712,545 hectares and is made up of four units:

- Uvs Lake
- Altan Els (dunes)
- Türgen Mountain
- Tsagaan Shuvuut mountainous area (described below)

Overall, the major ecosystems include mixed mountain and highland systems covering an extremely diverse landscape from cold desert, desert-steppe, tundra, and alpine mountain zones, with marshes, sand dunes, forests, flood plains, wetlands and salt lakes. It is very unusual to find such ecologically diverse areas so close together; Uvs Great Lakes Basin is matched by few other places in the world. International research carried on in the area concentrates on hoofed animals, rodents and birds, and wetland ecosystems. The area as a whole is listed as one of UNESCO's World Biosphere Reserves.

Uvs Nuur
Located in the centre of the aimag's northern region, Mongolia's largest lake appears like an inland sea. It is fed by the River Tes and has no outlet. The lake water is five times saltier than the ocean and there are no fish in the lake, but nonetheless the water and shores attract many thousands of birds – over 200 species have been recorded. Access to the lake shores is difficult due to marshy ground. Located at an altitude of 759m, it is the lowest point in western Mongolia. Surrounded by sand dunes, the lake is overlooked by snow-crested mountains (mainly in the south). Mountainous wild animals include snow leopard, deer and ibex, foxes and wolves. Due to the extreme climate (recorded winter temperatures of –57°C and summer temperatures of over 40°C) this area has been chosen for climate change research by international scientists. The road to the lake from the west crosses the Ulaan Davaa Pass which has stunning views. Own transport essential.

Altan Els
Also known as Böörögiin Els, these golden sand dunes lie in the northwest corner of the aimag on the national border with the Russian Federation. The road to Ulaangom from Zavkhan Aimag passes south of this area. Altan Els is a massive belt of sands, the

most northern sand dunes in the world, extending from the eastern part of Uvs Lake across many hundreds of kilometres to Altan Els Strictly Protected Area. The park offers a place of natural beauty with plenty of wildlife. Plan to be completely self-sufficient as there are few facilities in the region, ie: bring plenty of petrol, food, water and camping gear.

Türgen Uul Nature Reserve
Located around 40km southwest of Ulaangom, the way into the reserve is via Kharkhiraa River valley, about 30km from Ulaangom. Türgen Mountain (3,965m) and Kharkhiraa Mountain are both part of the Türgen Uul Nature Reserve, often visited by campers and hikers because of the area's beautiful scenery.

Kharkhiraa Valley
Kharkhiraa River valley is an excellent camping spot and a good base from which to see the surrounding countryside. You'll find it 30km southwest of Ulaangom. This beautiful river valley is surrounded by pine forests and meadows carpeted with wild flowers in early summer. The twin peaks of Kharkhiraa Uul (4,037m) and Türgen Uul (3,978m) dominate the area. Khoton people, known for their shamanistic practices, inhabit the region.

To get there it is necessary to hire a jeep and driver; make arrangements to be collected if you are staying overnight and bring plenty of food as you will need to be self-sufficient. Local families are very hospitable and often provide food and lodging in family *gers*; log cabins and huts provide lodging if you are not camping but it is difficult to book them in advance as there are no telephones.

Tsagaan Shuvuut Uul
Located on the northwestern border near Lake Üüreg, Tsagaan Shuvuut rises 3,496m and is easiest to appreciate at a distance for its stunning mountain peaks. There are few visitor facilities and you will need your own transport, camping equipment and supplies.

Achit Nuur
On the western border, over 150km from Ulaangom and extending into Bayan-Ölgii Aimag, this is the largest freshwater lake in the province and provides stunning views at sunset when reflections are mirrored in its waters. It's a scenic place to camp; there is fishing and birdlife, but watch out for millions of mosquitoes. Achit Lake is home to around 20 breeding pairs of Dalmatian pelicans, though their number has declined dramatically in recent years due to hunting. Again you will need your own transport to reach here.

Devel Aral Nature Reserve
The reserve (extending into Bayan-Ölgii Aimag) is situated in the basin of the Usan Khooloi and Khovd rivers that feed from Achit Lake, between Bayan-Ölgii and Uvs aimags. This protected area, comprising 10,300 hectares, is home to ring-necked pheasant, wild boar and beaver; the latter two species are becoming increasingly rare in Mongolia. It is a main distribution area of sea buckthorn. There are no tourist facilities and again you will need your own transport.

Ölgii Nuur
Ölgii Nuur lies in the southwest near a small town of the same name, just off the main road from Ulaangom (100km south) to Khovd (120km north), not far from Khar Us Lake. Access is easy. The lake is fed by the Orlogo River and offers fishing

(grayling) but the lake waters are brackish. It is not an area for camping due to the exposed conditions and lack of shelter from the wind.

Üüreg Nuur

This lake lies in the northwest part of Uvs, 95km from Ulaangom above the road from Ulaangom to Ölgii (250km) between two mountain passes, Ulaan Davaa (southwest) and Ogotor Khamar Davaa (southeast). Üüreg nuur is a saltwater lake containing unidentified minerals. It is surrounded by 3,000m-plus peaks such as the Tsagaan Shuvuut Uul (3,496m) and is a great place for swimming, fishing and hiking. A great advantage is its accessibility, just off the main road. The lake shores offer the best camping ground in this area, though you'll need your own transport and there are no tourist facilities.

Khyargas Nuur National Park

Nestling in the southern mountains of Uvs Aimag, 130km southeast of Ulaangom, this protected area was established as a national park in 2000. It comprises some 332,800 hectares. The saltwater lake receives less attention than Uvs Nuur and although it is smaller (84km x 32km) and less spectacular, it still has abundant fish. The range of birdlife alone makes it worth a stopover. There are some hot springs at the northwestern side of the lake. Park entrance costs T1,500 payable to a ranger when you see one; vehicles are charged T3,000.

Lake Airag

South of Khyargas Nuur (above), this is part of the Khyargas Nuur National Park and is connected to the larger lake by a water channel. Deer stones are found in the vicinity, though little is known about them. These monuments should be better signposted in future years as Mongolian tourism develops.

Khankhökhii-Khyargas National Park

This national park, established in 2000, lies in the southeastern section of Uvs Aimag and covers an area of 220,550 hectares of forested mountains. The highest peak is Altanduulga Uul (2,928m). Entry costs are as above; there are few visitor facilities here.

Suggested itineraries
Four-lakes tour

This tour begins with a four-hour flight from Ulaanbaatar to Ulaangom followed by a 75km drive by jeep to the northwest point of Khyargas Lake to visit the mineral springs at Khartermesiin Rashaan, before heading southwest, following the lake shores, to birdwatch. Next you drive west to Ölgii Lake (just over 100km by road), camping along the way, and continue a further 100km west to Lake Achit, crossing mountain passes and fording rivers on the way.

As you'd expect, this leg of the itinerary needs an experienced driver and guide as some of it is off road. Take enough food to be completely self-sufficient, although you may find that you can buy food from the Dörvöd, a minority people who live in this region. From Achit Lake drive 89km via the Khamar Pass to Lake Üüreg, where you can explore the Tsagaan River gorge on the west side of the lake. Keep a look out for ancient rock paintings of animals. You then return to Ulaangom (95km) via the Ulaan Davaa with its magnificent views.

Logistics and timing need to be carefully worked out with a tour operator, using local transport, equipment and guides. A three-week tour would cost around US$2,250.

Western mountains and lakes riding tour

The following itinerary can be arranged by Run Wild Tours (see page 150). You begin your tour by flying from Ulaanbaatar to Ulaangom, where you stay overnight, then drive 95km to Üüreg Lake and from there on to Tsagaan Nuur (a small lake not marked on tourist maps). Camp overnight then drive to Khöshööt to meet up with the guides and horses, to begin a six-day ride to Tsengel Uul, south along the Khargant River, enjoying wonderful mountain lake scenery before returning to Buyant settlement (not marked on tourist maps). The total distance is around 160km and is covered over 5–6 days.

Dune and mountain/desert tour

This camping/riding/walking tour is also arranged by Run Wild (see page 150). The itinerary begins with a flight to Ulaangom, where the trek begins in the desert-steppe. The first day is spent hiking around the sand dunes of Böörögiin Els looking at desert herbs. The next day you can hike to visit nomadic families, see their horses and yak carts in action and meet up with herders who provide horses which you can hire for the day (cost: US$10); alternatively, you may prefer to hike and experience some magnificent mountain views. There are caves to explore in the area.

Panoramic Journeys (see page 148) are specialists in tailor-made travel and adventure tours to remote western regions. Cultural, riding and fishing expeditions are accompanied by expert Mongolian drivers, translators and guides.

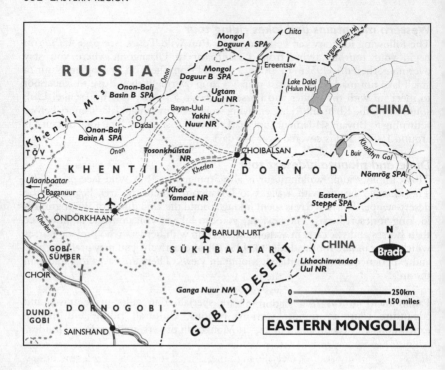

Eastern Region

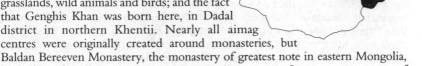

The eastern region of Mongolia consists of Khentii, Sükhbaatar and Dornod provinces. The main attractions of this region are the grasslands, wild animals and birds; and the fact that Genghis Khan was born here, in Dadal district in northern Khentii. Nearly all aimag centres were originally created around monasteries, but Baldan Bereeven Monastery, the monastery of greatest note in eastern Mongolia, located in Khentii Province, was never an aimag centre. It was a great centre of Buddhism prior to its destruction in the communist government's anti-religious purges of the 1930s; the temples are currently being restored.

Extensive grasslands, or steppe, stretch across eastern Mongolia from the Khentii Mountains to the eastern border with China and Russia. There are some areas of mixed landscape, especially in the southeast, which has golden sand dunes, lakes and mineral springs. The grasslands, which predominate, provide important grazing lands for livestock, although most of Mongolia's eastern steppe is uninhabited and underdeveloped. This may not last because oil has been discovered in the region and although difficult to drill and transport this sort of development would mean economic growth. But it would also cause great disturbance to the wildlife. The steppes of eastern Mongolia are the world's last unfragmented natural grasslands; they are considered to be of global importance because they have remained so undisturbed, whereas the grasslands of neighbouring Russia and China have been slowly modified by agriculture and industrial development. Traditional herding practices are still used in Mongolia, and livestock densities are relatively low, particularly in the easternmost province of Dornod.

Apart from its unique grasslands, eastern Mongolia is home to rare species of cranes and vast herds of migratory gazelles. Gazelles were once widespread in Mongolia and neighbouring areas of Russia and China but are now limited largely to the eastern steppes of Mongolia because of habitat destruction and hunting in China and Russia, and the disruption of their migration routes. Mongolian gazelle population, too, has declined in range and population size over the last few decades; its continued survival is threatened if present trends continue. There are estimated to be over two million gazelles, but migrating species always pose a conservation challenge as they cannot be confined to protected areas and they often cross international borders. Cross-border conservation projects are now in place.

KHENTII AIMAG

The aimag is named after the Khentii Mountains which dominates the north-western part of the province. Mountains in the region are under 2,000m and are thickly forested and well-watered. The watershed of three huge drainage basins –

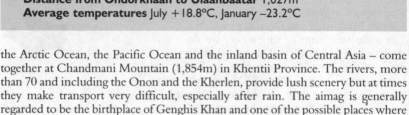

BRIEF FACTS
Population 75,200
Population density 0.98 per km²
Area 80,300km²
Aimag centre Öndörkhaan
Districts 19
Elevation of Öndörkhaan 1,027m
Main livestock and crops sheep, cattle, horses
Ethnic groups Khalkha, Buryat
Distance from Öndörkhaan to Ulaanbaatar 1,027m
Average temperatures July + 18.8°C, January –23.2°C

the Arctic Ocean, the Pacific Ocean and the inland basin of Central Asia – come together at Chandmani Mountain (1,854m) in Khentii Province. The rivers, more than 70 and including the Onon and the Kherlen, provide lush scenery but at times they make transport very difficult, especially after rain. The aimag is generally regarded to be the birthplace of Genghis Khan and one of the possible places where he is buried.

Highlights
- Dadal district – birthplace of Genghis Khan
- Galtai cave
- Baldan Bereeven Monastery

Öndörkhaan
The aimag centre is located on the northern bank of the Kherlenn River. The main public buildings are centred around a central park and include a theatre, museums, a town hall and shops. The bus station is on the west side of town on the road to Ulaanbaatar, while the sports stadium, post office and monastery are on the southeast side; the town is surrounded by flat steppe land.

Getting there from Ulaanbaatar
By air
Local scheduled 50-minute flight from Ulaanbaatar with MIAT on Thursdays (tel: 11 310917).

By road
Shared jeeps and mini-vans make the journey regularly from Ulaanbaatar; allow a day's drive. Jeep and driver costs are around US$70/80 per day or T250–500 per kilometre (long-distance rates are negotiable).

Where to stay
Kherlenn Hotel Town centre, south of the park on the main road to the airport. Standard rooms US$5 (T5,500) per person.
Bayan Bulag Hotel On the edge of town on the airport road; rooms from US$10 (T11,400) per person.

Where to eat
The best food in town is found at the local market and at street canteens where you can eat well and cheaply for T500–600.

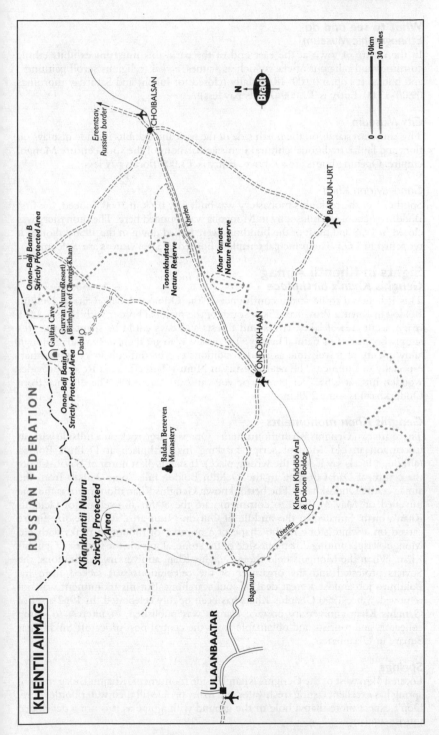

What to see and do
Ethnographic Museum
In the centre of town at the east end of the park, this museum exhibits ethnic costumes and religious artefacts such as statues, *tankas* (religious scroll paintings) and books. It's open 09.00–18.00 daily (closed for lunch) and Saturday mornings 09.00–13.00. Entry is T1,000 (locals pay less).

City Museum
This museum stands on the north side of the park and exhibits include displays on flora and fauna, traditional cultural items and armour of the 13th-century Mongol empire. Opening hours are as above. Entry is T1,000 (locals pay less).

Gundgavirlan Khiid
Southeast of the park, this monastery was built way back in 1660. Indeed, the first Buddhist School of Philosophy in Mongolia was founded here. The monastery was closed in 1938 and most of the buildings were pulled down in the 1950s, though it reopened in 1992. The principal temple is housed in a *ger*; visitors are welcome.

Sights in Khentii Aimag
Genghis Khan's birthplace
This is believed to lie at the confluence of the Onon and Balj rivers at Delüün Boldog in Khentii Province, 25km south of the national border with Russia. It's a magnificent area of lakes, rivers and forests and days could be spent in the area simply because of its natural beauty. The best way to get there is by road, although allow plenty of travel time as road conditions can be difficult in rainy weather, especially in summer. The nearby Gurvan Nuur ('Three Lakes') Resort provides wooden huts at US$5 per person or you can camp close by. The distance from Öndörkhaan is some 250km.

Genghis Khan monuments
There are two Genghis Khan monuments. One is a large rock on a hillside with an inscription in old Mongol script marking his birthplace at Delüün Boldog (although locals say it is in the wrong place). It stands 3km north of Bayan-Övoo, the centre of Dadal district, in the Delüün Boldog hills some 250km from the aimag centre Öndörkhaan. The better known Genghis Khan monument is the one unveiled on May 31 1962 to commemorate the 800th anniversary of Genghis Khan's birth. Situated in the middle of Gurvan Nuur area, it's a life-size figure carved on a white stone in the shape of a number of mountain peaks with old Mongol script running down one side of the stone, alongside the figure of Genghis Khan. When the Mongols held their Genghis Khan anniversary celebrations, the Soviets protested and the organiser of the celebrations was sacked from his Politburo job amidst a great deal of soul searching. But his monument was not removed. Since 1990 Genghis Khan has been openly celebrated. In 1962 a set of Genghis Khan anniversary postage stamps was published, of interest to stamp collectors and tourists and obtainable from the central post office off Sükhbaatar Square in Ulaanbaatar.

Springs
Located 1km west of the Genghis Khan hillside monument, Khajuu Bulag mineral spring has excellent tasting freshwater and many people fill their water bottles here. Don't expect more than a hole in the ground with a pipe as it is not a developed tourist site (yet).

'Wall' of Genghis Khan

Situated in the northeast part of Khentii the wall or ancient rampart extends through Dornod Province to China and Russia. Most likely, it has nothing to do with Genghis Khan but locals like to think it has and have named it after their hero. The wall itself is mostly in ruins. It can be seen along the main road from Öndörkhaan towards Bayan-Uul town (in Dornod).

Galtai Agui

At 80m depth, Galtai Agui is the deepest cave in Mongolia. It lies 70km northwest of Bayan-Övoo, Dadal district centre, and practically on the national border with Russia. Since the caves are so near the Russian border you need permission from the local police to visit the area. If you want to go there a local guide/translator will help to arrange the permit; otherwise contact the police directly, which is best done in Öndörkhaan, tel: 39 2109.

Archaeological sites

Many Bronze Age graves and tombstones (though not 'tombstones' as we would know them) are located at different sites on the south bank of the Kherlenn River in Jargaltkhaan district. Some sites are listed below. To find them you will definitely need a guide who knows the area well, as well as your own transport. Many of these ancient tombs were found and identified by archaeologists searching for the tomb of Genghis Khan. In 1993 a media announcement stated that during the search in Delgerkhaan district by a joint Japanese/Mongolian team more than 3,500 tombs were identified dating from the Hun period to the Mongol Middle Ages. In the summer of 1993 several large tombs were discovered, thought to be the tombs of high-ranking officials from the court of Genghis Khan, although this has not been confirmed. Mongolian people found the whole idea of disturbing ancestral tombs upsetting, but despite this archaeological research continues.

Bronze Age graves are found in Batshireet district at Barkha and at upper Onon; in Ölziit district at Deed Ölziit; in Delgerkhaan district at Doloon Uul and on the south bank of the Kherlenn River at Kherlenn Bayan-Ulaan; in Tsenkhermandal district at Melzelei Uul. They are also found in groups (memorial stones/graveyards) in the mid-Kherlenn region; in Bayanmönkh district on the north bank of the Kherlenn River at Bayan Tsögts; and finally, there's a group of tombstones in Dadal district that include those known as the Onon group at Sügtein Adag.

Stone Age petroglyphs

Discoveries of ancient rock drawings and figures sculpted in stone (know locally as Stone Men) were made in 1974 by a Soviet/Mongol team in the Binder district in the northeastern part of the province. Designs on the rocks consist of circles and geometric figures and even prints in the shape of feet (as opposed to the hand prints found at Lascaux caves in France). Many of the drawings resemble those of the same period found in western Mongolia that depict rhinoceroses, bulls and boars, like those discovered at Tsenkheriin Agui in Khovd Aimag.

Sacred mountain ovoos at Arshaan Khad

Mesolithic to early Neolithic petroglyphs have been discovered at Mount Arshaan Khad (meaning 'Cliff with Springs'), a sacred site located in the Binder district in the northeastern part of the province. It is worshipped by local people who continue the tradition of worshipping here by placing a stone or some precious object on a cairn-like pile of rocks, called ovoos; they are sacred and offerings placed on them are consecrated to mountain spirits, the most important

LUCY'S JOURNEY ON HORSEBACK

In summer 1997 Lucy rode 500km alone in eastern Mongolia, simply by following a river course. She took with her a stray dog called 'Wolfie', who followed her all the way.

> Mongolians watched me play with Wolfie in the early mornings, gadding about in the grasslands, warming up and letting Wolfie chew my gloves. I always felt ridiculous when they revealed themselves from the undergrowth ... they were more fascinated in watching me and the dog play, than in who I was or where I came from.

Lucy found Mongolia was one of the safest places to travel for a woman on her own. She organised her ride in a haphazard and charming way (not always recommended, but in this case, it worked).

> I didn't think it through, I just made friends with a Mongolian I felt I could trust on arrival at the train station and the journey opened up from there.

She adopted the dog in Ulaanbaatar. He terrified most Mongolians who treat their dogs as guard dogs, not pets. The first night she camped alone he scared her to death:

> I thought he was a wolf when he appeared out of the darkness. I upset my dinner and jumped over the campfire. That's how he got his name.

She admitted she was scared at times:

> My two anxieties were that my horse Trigger would disappear, or, that I would be kicked and injured, miles from anywhere. But I was lucky. I hobbled the horse each

ones are at the mountain's summit. Over the centuries many offerings have been made here, although such worship was frowned upon during the communist period in the 20th century. To get here you'll need your own transport, camping equipment and supplies.

Stone statues

It is not clear whether or not these stone figures are grave markers, as there are not always graves nearby. Some carry inscriptions in several languages including Tibetan, Chinese, Mongolian and Arabic. You need time, a good map and a local guide/translator to find the following sites, although some are quite easily found, including the stone figure (1.8m high) west of the town of Öndörkhaan near the airport, and the five stone statues located in Batshireet district on the northern arm of the river Egiin Gol at the far end of Givkhistei Valley. Furthermore, to the north of the statues in Batshireet district there is a row of Turkic stone men and in front of them is a burial site marked by stones placed in a square.

Turkic inscriptions on stones are found in Burgalt Valley, Tsenkhermandal district, in Binderiin Rashaan and in Batshireet district. This is a short list to work from if you have an experienced guide. Without one it's almost impossible to locate the sites, because there is no signposting and none of the sites is developed for tourism. They simply stand on their own, symbols of an ancient past.

Qidan ruins (947–1125)

Ruins of the town of Züünkherem (meaning eastern fortress) are associated with the Qidan period, whose Chinese dynasty, the Liao, reigned from the mid-10th to early 12th centuries. They lie 25km west of Öndörkhaan in Mörön district, the northern

evening and slept out under the stars ... guarded by my faithful dog. Occasionally I heard wolves howling in the distance but they kept away.

Lucy travelled with food for two weeks: rations were limited to a hunk of yak meat, rice, potatoes and the delicacy of muesli. The cooker she bought proved useless. She recommends a small Russian-made pump-up paraffin stove, (bought in China) for cooking; otherwise she made fires, something the Mongolians are wary of encouraging, since steppe fire devastate the countryside each year.

Eventually, it was the cold – the perishing September evenings – that forced Lucy to turn back.

Although I wore thousands of layers, it still wasn't enough to keep out the biting chill. My toes were frostbitten and there was little I could do about it. I spent most of my time walking alongside Trigger to warm up.

Back in Ulaanbaatar Lucy renewed her visa for a further month. At a ger hostel on the outskirts of town, she was introduced to the delights of a Mongolian foot-pump shower and was further surprised by technology to find that the music in local discos was more up-to-date than in the UK. 'People wore the latest gear and I had to pinch myself to realise where I was.'
She also said a sad farewell to Wolfie.

I never had to say goodbye, I just brought him to the part of town where I found him and ducked away as a crowd of dogs chased him in the other direction. I felt bad but there was little else I could do ... I was moving on.

frontier of the Qidan (also spelled Kitan) empire. Ruins of the fortress of Öglögchiin Kherem are on the slopes of Mount Binder. The remains include parts of the fortress walls (7–12m high x 1.5–3m thick), a double rampart of granite and the ruins of the town of Baruunkherem (western fortress) with its seven gates (now destroyed).

National parks and protected areas
Khankhentii Strictly Protected Area
This protected area enters the province in the northwest corner. It is predominately based in neighbouring Töv Aimag and is described there. Specially zoned areas allow visitors.

Onon-Balj Basin Strictly Protected Area
Divided into two areas (A and B), this park is located on the northern international border with the Russian Federation. It is designated to protect a unique geographical zone of northern taiga forest surrounded by arid-desert steppe valleys.

Toson Khustai Nature Reserve
This area of 469,928 hectares is located on the eastern border and extends into the neighbouring Dornod aimags. Toson Khustai Nuur and Salbarn valleys are the main habitats of the white-tailed gazelle. The reserve was designated to extend its habitat from the Kherlenn River northwards.

Khar Yamaat Nature Reserve
Located on the eastern border of Khentii Aimag and extending into Dornod Aimag, the reserve protects Khar Yamaat and Turuu Öndör Mountains, a

continuation of the Khankhentii mountain range. Natural vegetation includes pine and aspen groves, and many unusual medicinal plants rarely found in steppe areas. It is a relatively unvisited area with few tourist facilities. To visit the reserve you will need your own transport.

Baldan Bereeven Monastery (also known as Palden Drepung)

Baldan Bereeven Monastery is situated in beautiful countryside in the Khankhentii Mountains, 300km northeast of Ulaanbaatar (UB) in Ömnödelger district in Khentii Province. It takes nine hours to drive there from UB. It is advisable to check the route in advance, if possible, as muddy conditions may hamper your journey, especially after heavy rain, which can fall in summer.

The monastery's history begins in the late 1700s, when the Öndör Gegeen, Mongolia's 'Living Buddha', sent a group of monks to find an auspicious site on which to build a monastery in the east, as the three other directions (north, south and west) had already established monasteries. The monks chose this eastern site because of its extraordinary geographical position, and the auspicious omens, such as rocks shaped in the form of animals and birds by the searing power of wind and extreme weather, of it. In their search the monks discovered a landscape which included the shapes of a lion, a tiger, a Garuda bird and a serpent. They also noticed at the time an old couple boiling tea. This was interpreted as a welcoming sign to build on that particular site. Three Tibetan-style temples and a number of other smaller buildings were constructed and the building was completed in the 1780s. Gers surrounded the monastery to house several thousand monks, and a nunnery was built on the far side of the mountain valley. Unfortunately, the main temples and many of the adjacent buildings were destroyed in 1937, in accordance with the communist government's anti-religious policy. This kind of destruction was systematic and country-wide. In 1991 restoration work began when one of the side twin-temples was rebuilt by the local community.

Statues of several Buddhas, regarded as living spirits, continue to be worshipped there, including deities such as Maitreya Buddha, who symbolises the continuity of the Buddhist teachings, and Tsongkhapa, a master of 14th-century Buddhist teaching and founder of 'Gelugpa' Tibetan Buddhism. In the grounds, all that remains of the past is a circular path of stone that was used for meditation walks, two old stoves and a cave, Eej or Mother Cave. It is believed that when you enter and then emerge from this cave you will be regarded as a newly created being, having left the 'mother's' womb. The only surviving painting in the monastery is of a soyombo, the Mongolian state symbol, painted by an anonymous Buddhist artist. The artist predicted that it would survive through periods of great difficulty, which has proved true as it was shot through by three bullets during the anti-religious campaigns of the 1930s, but was not destroyed.

Although local people believe that Baldan Bereeven is the holiest place in the world, two harmful spirits are said to live there, causing the monks to become distracted from their studies. The most harmful is a giant devil. In order to subdue it, a small statue stands on its head (in the side temple which has been restored) with a large stone on its toe so it will never stand upright again; the other malevolent spirit, Mara, is said to live on the northern side of the monastery in a mountain gap. In order to subdue it and to restore harmony, a Buddha statue is placed there among the rocks.

Volunteers required
Tourist-volunteers are needed to help with the restoration work at Baldan Bereeven and an American-run organisation has helped to make this a reality. For more details contact Mark A Hintzke, Director of Baldan Bereeven's Cultural Restoration Tourism Project; 410 Paloma Avenue, Pacifica, CA 94044, USA; tel: +1 415 563 7221; email: info@crtp.net; web: www.crtp.net.

SÜKHBAATAR AIMAG

BRIEF FACTS
Population 59,700
Population density 0.73 per km²
Area 82,300 km²
Aimag centre Baruun-Urt
Districts 13
Elevation of Baruun-Urt 981m
Livestock and crops Sheep, goat, cattle
Ethnic groups Khalkha, Dariganga, Üzemchin
Distance from Baruun-Urt to Ulaanbaatar 560km
Average temperatures July 19.9°C, January –23.3°C

Sükhbaatar Aimag is situated at the eastern edge of the Gobi Desert and consists of the open steppes of eastern Mongolia – a landscape of interminable grasslands stretching for as far as the eye can see – broken only by a few hills surrounded by colourful wild flowers. There are many small lakes and some extinct volcanoes. The province is sparsely populated by Khalkha and two minorities, Dariganga and Üzemchin, who live mostly in the south. Sükhbaatar, after whom the province is named, was one of the leaders of the revolution of 1921; his father came from the region. The southeastern Dariganga region and the mountains of Shiliin Bogd Uul are of interest for the local culture and natural landscape but they are remote and transport must be arranged privately. You also need a permit since it is close to the border with China.

Highlights
- Shiliin Bogd Uul – holy mountain
- Taliin Agui – cave
- Altan Ovoo – volcano
- Archaeological sites

Baruun-Urt
Located in the centre of Sükhbaatar Aimag, the town is mainly populated by mine workers who work at the nearby zinc and coal mines. The levels of sulphur in the area mean that it is better to drink bottled water only. This is an undeveloped area and few tourists come here. There are several hotels and the Aimag Museum is worth visiting.

Getting there from Ulaanbaatar
By air
Scheduled flights take just over two hours from Ulaanbaatar to Baruun-Urt (via Öndörkhaan) on Thursdays. For MIAT's local office, tel: 51 259; MIAT's UB head office, tel: 11 379935.

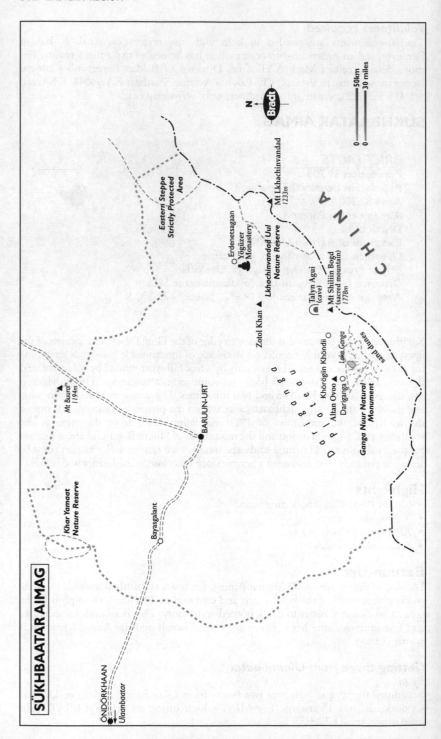

By road

You have the option of long-distance buses from the capital; private jeeps and minibuses (hire in UB or locally). A jeep and driver cost around US$245 from UB; touring costs are negotiable and local jeep-hire rates are less than in UB at around T250 per kilometre.

Where to stay

All of the following are comfortable, with good service. Rates are around US$15 (T17,100) for a standard room.

Hotel Delger East of the main square in the centre of town.
Sharga Hotel West of the main square in the centre of town.
Ganga Hotel A short walk from the centre of town in the northeast suburbs.

Where to eat

You could try the hotel restaurants (above), or there are a number of bars and restaurants in town serving Mongolian and Chinese food. Simple noodles and meat dishes cost T750.

What to see and do
Aimag Museum

In the centre of town, this museum exhibits costumes representing the region's three ethnic groups. The silversmiths and blacksmiths of Dariganga were once famous. Entrance fee is T1,000 (locals pay less).

Erdenemandal Khiid

The original monastery, 20km outside Baruun-Urt, was destroyed in the 1930s. It is gradually emerging as a new site just west of the town square. Statues of Gombo and Sendem, Buddhist deities, hidden during the communist years of the 20th century when Buddhism was persecuted, are now on display in this new temple. Visitors are welcome.

Sights in Sükhbaatar Aimag
Shiliin Bogd Uul

Located 60km southeast of Dariganga district centre, this is the highest peak in Sükhbaatar at 1,778m. The mountain is sacred to Mongols and is surrounded by stories that tell of renewed strength for those who climb it. Shiliin Uul is one of around 180 extinct volcanoes in the area. Its crater is 2km wide and over 300m deep. From the crater rim there are excellent views across Inner Mongolia to the south; sunrise and sunset are the best times to be there. Because it is in a border area, a permit is required to visit Shiliin Bogd, obtainable at the police station (tel: 51 751) in Baruun-Urt, which is on the west side of town.

Altan Ovoo

Standing in Dariganga district, 60km northeast of Shiliin Bogd (above), this is a sacred, extinct volcano worshipped by the local people and offers wonderful views and a good half-day's hiking, though you'll need your own transport to get there.

Taliin Agui

Fourteen kilometres northwest of Shiliin Bogd Uul, Taliin Agui is a 200m-long basalt cave with stalagmites. The cave walls are naturally multi-coloured and very beautiful. You'll need to bring a torch and beware of the slippery ground; you'll need your own transport to get here too.

Dariganga Plateau

Dariganga Plateau lies in the southern part of the province and is where the sand dunes of the Gobi and the grassy plains of the northern steppe converge to create what looks like thousands of hectares of perfectly natural golf courses.

Around 10km east of Ganga Nuur, the tour company Juulchin has built a new *ger* camp and charges US$40 per person including meals. Once again, you'll need your own transport to get here if you're not on an organised tour.

Archaeological sites

Stone men found in Khentii Aimag differ from those of other provinces by the cut of the stone and other small details. Four stone men statues measuring more than a metre tall are located in Darigango district. The figures are shown in a kneeling position with their left hands resting on one knee. Three of them, carved in marble, are found at Altan Ovoo (Dariganga district). As usual, you'll need your own transport and a good local guide to find these sites.

Khörögiin Khöndii stone men

Located 35km north of Shiliin Bogd Uul in Khörögiin Khöndii, Khörög Valley, there's a famous statue of a seated figure wearing boots and a conical hat with a drinking bowl in his right hand, his left hand resting on one knee. There are more than 50 such statues in the region which is well worth exploring if you have your own transport and guide.

Erdenetsagaan stone men and tombstones

There are several stone figures in this area, located in Naran. Some have beards and others earrings and they may be seen as individual characters. Numerous interesting stone figures are found in the same district several kilometres east of Naran. One has a large nose, an earring in one ear and holds a drinking bowl in his right hand, while his left hand rests on his belt. Another stone statue close to him is easily recognised by a pot belly. Bronze Age graves are found at Zunkhovd in Erdenetsagaan district as well as at Zalaa and Shar Khad in Mönkhkhaan district.

National parks and protected areas

Part of the Eastern Steppe Strictly Protected Area is located on the southeastern border. It extends east into Dornod Aimag and is described there (page 370). The area protects the natural steppe and is not designed for tourist development.

Lkhachinvandad Uul Nature Reserve

Located 200km southeast of Baruun-Urt near the border with China. The purpose of the reserve is to preserve and protect the elk habitat in the mountain steppe. This area is gradually opening up for eco-tourism, though there are few tourist facilities at present. To reach it you'll need your own transport. Juulchin's new *ger* camp at Ganga Nuur provides accommodation and charges US$40 per person including meals.

Ganga Nuur Protected area

This lake lies some 200km due south of Baruun-Urt, close to the border with China. The area surrounding the lake grew as a result of a sand block formed by wind movement. It is a beautiful freshwater lake located between the mountain steppe and Gobi with its own special micro-climate.

The Mongolian tour company Juulchin provides a new *ger* camp 10km east of the lake. It charges US$40 per person including meals, though you'll need your own transport if you're not on an organised tour. Permits will be checked if travelling independently and you'll need to arrange this in advance; Baruun-Urt police station (tel: 51 751), on the west side of town, provides permits.

Suggested itinerary

Juulchin Foreign Tourism Corporation arrange this tour which begins by flying from Ulaanbaatar to Baruun-Urt, from where you can drive 190km south over the grasslands to visit the dunes at Ganga Nuur. Staying at the *ger* camp near the lake for several days, you can explore the sacred volcanic mountains at Altan Ovoo and Shiliin Bogd (a permit is required to visit this border area and visit the cave at Taliin Agui). You can also explore the local archaeological sites and Lkhachinvandad Uul Nature Reserve. where you may be lucky enough to see elk in the mountains, though you will be more likely to see antelopes on the surrounding steppe.

DORNOD AIMAG

BRIEF FACTS
Population 84,500
Population density 0.66 per km²
Area 123,600km²
Aimag centre Choibalsan
Districts 14
Elevation of Choibalsan 747m
Livestock and crops Sheep, cattle, goat, horse/ hay
Ethnic groups Khalkha, Buryat, Barga, Üzemchin
Distance from Choibalsan to Ulaanbaatar 655km
Average temperatures July +19.9°C, January –21.3°C

Dornod Aimag is the easternmost aimag of Mongolia, a land of remote grassy steppes where Mongolia meets both of its big neighbours, sharing the border with China to the southeast and Russia to the northeast. Far from Ulaanbaatar, the province is probably the least visited in Mongolia. The territory is made up of the Great Dornod Steppe and the well-known Menengiin Tal plain, famous for the huge population of white-tailed gazelles that graze there and the rare crane species that breed in this area. The River Kherlenn cuts through the province. Choibalsan, the aimag centre, was named after Choibalsan, Mongolia's prime minister from 1939–52 (see box, page 367). There are several national parks and new cross-border programmes are now operating to help to preserve the natural habitats and breeding grounds of rare wild species. The battle fought in 1939 by Mongolian and Russian forces against the Japanese (see box, page 28) took place on Khalkhyn Gol, on the eastern border with China. There are two ethnic groups: Buryats living in Bayandun, Bayan-Uul and Dashbalbar districts; and the Üzemchin who live in Sergelen district.

Highlights

- National parks and protected areas
- Menengiin Tal – grassland plain
- Buir Nuur and Khökh Nuur
- Kherlenn Bars Khot – ruins of the Qidan period

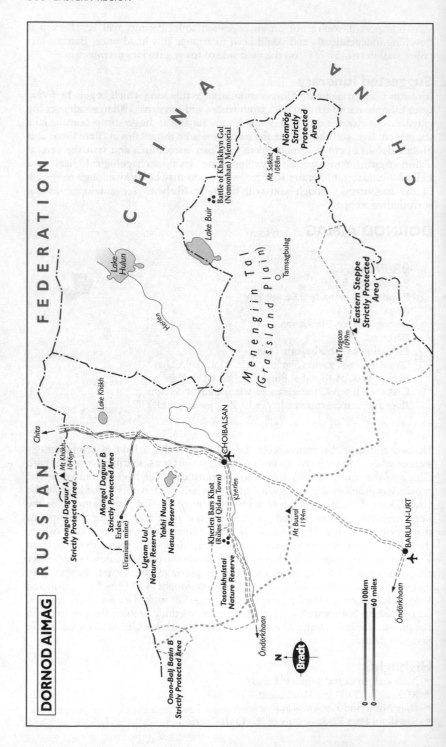

DORNOD AIMAG

RUSSIAN FEDERATION

CHINA

Chita

Mongol Daguur A
Strictly Protected Area
▲ Mt Khökh-
1046m

Mongol Daguur B
Strictly Protected Area

Lake Khökh

Hailen

Lake Hulun

Lake Buir

Battle of Khalkhyn Gol
(Nomonhan) Memorial

Mt Salkhit
1088m

Nömrög
Strictly
Protected
Area

Tamsagbulag

M e n e n g i i n   T a l
(G r a s s l a n d   P l a i n)

Mt Tsagaan
1099m

Eastern Steppe
Strictly Protected
Area

Erdes
(Uranium mine)

Ugtam Uul
Nature Reserve

Yakhi Nuur
Nature Reserve

Kherlen Bars Khot
(Ruins of Qidan Town)

Kherlen

CHOIBALSAN

Tosonkhulstai
Nature Reserve

Mt Buural
1194m

BARUUN-URT

Onon-Balj Basin B
Strictly Protected Area

Öndörkhaan

Öndörkhaan

0   100km
0   60 miles

N

Bradt

CHOIBALSAN (1895–1952)

Choibalsan worked his way from being a night-watchman to becoming Mongolian prime minister. He was a member of a revolutionary group in 1918 and was a founder member of the Mongolian People's Party. Along with Sükhbaatar he was elected a member of the provisional revolutionary government. In 1922 he was appointed minister for eastern border affairs. He left that position a year later to train in the military academy in Moscow. He was elected a member of the MPRP, the ruling Mongolian People's Revolutionary Party's central committee and became commander-in-chief of the People's Revolutionary Troops. His political/military life enabled him to become foreign minister from 1930–31. He was awarded the rank of marshal in 1936 and became prime minister in 1939. People privately called him Mongolia's Stalin, because he was utterly ruthless, and it's true that Choibalsan was close to Stalin and he used his power to create a system of dictatorship by ruthlessly suppressing any opposition. From the time he became minister of the interior in 1936, horrific purges took place, including the destruction of the monasteries and the death of many Mongolian monks and ordinary citizens, as well as the death of two prime ministers, Genden and Amar.

Choibalsan

Located in a central position on the Kherlenn River, centuries ago this was a trading centre on the caravan route. As Bayantümen, it became a town in the 19th century and is now the centre of economic development in eastern Mongolia. Following the departure of the Soviet Russians in 1990, buildings were looted in the old town on the west side. The buildings still look rundown and the town is looking forward to a burst of economic activity associated with oil drilling. The population includes minority people, Khalkha Mongols and Chinese residents/workers. The new buildings in the eastern sector include the National Parks Office, the market, the Business Development Centre, and an internet café in the Library building.

Getting there from Ulaanbaatar
By air
There are scheduled flight (one-and-a-half hours) from Ulaanbaatar on Fridays (MIAT's UB head office, tel: 11 379935).

By road
Limited through traffic, with few roads, mostly unpaved. You'll need to organise private transport to visit the countryside, best done through a tour company in Ulaanbaatar. Or you can hire a jeep and driver: the journey from UB costs around US$330 (touring rates negotiable).

Where to stay and eat
Kherlenn Hotel New hotel in town centre. Rooms cost from US$10 (T11,400).
Scorpion Corporation Hotel Business Development Centre of Eastern Mongolia. Rooms cost US$15 (T17,100).

For food, you can try the hotel restaurants, street canteens, and the market located on the east side of town, where local dishes of meat, rice and noodles go for around T700.

What to see and do
Natural History Museum
In the old town on the square, this museum has exhibits on the flora and fauna of the steppe region. Open weekdays 09.00–17.00; entry T1,000.

City Museum
Housed in the former Government House in the old town, this museum has memorabilia from the former communist period. It's open weekdays 09.00–17.00; entry T1,000.

Sights in Dornod Aimag
Menengiin Tal
This dry, unspoiled steppeland was declared a strictly protected area in 1992. Herds of up to 40,000 Mongolian gazelle migrate across the plain, reminiscent of the great East African migrations of wildebeest and antelope. It is an example of the last large undisturbed steppe ecosystem in the world. Within it, Sangiin Dalai Nuur is a salt lake covering 7.5km². It's rarely visited and you'll need your own transport.

Buir Nuur
Located on the eastern border with China, this is the largest freshwater lake in Eastern Mongolia, covering 615km². Part of the lake (the northwest shore) belongs to China. It is a beautiful area in terms of wildlife, and the lake itself has many different species of fish including mirror carp, golden carp, silver carp, grayling, amur catfish, burbot and whitefish. But unfortunately this leads to poaching and fishing disputes with fishermen from Inner Mongolia (part of China). The lake is rarely visited by tourists and there are few facilities for those that do. You'll also need your own transport to get here.

Khökh Nuur
The 'Blue Lake' is a shallow salt lake in an area where the elevation of the land is just 552m – the lowest point in Mongolia. It lies in the northeast corner of the province, 180km from Choibalsan off the main road to the Russian border, 50km south of the border town of Ereentsav. The lake covers an area of 95km². It is possible to visit the lake on the way to Mongol Daguur Nature Reserve which is situated along the border with Russia, 50km northwest of the lake. You'll need to bring your own transport, camping equipment and supplies.

Ruins of the Qidan towns of Kherlenn Bars Khot
In the River Kherlen valley on the north side of the road, 90km west of Choibalsan in Tsagaan-ovoo district, are the ruins of three fortress towns, settlements of the Qidan period (947–1125). They have been grouped under the general name Bars Khot. They were built by the Qidan (also called Kitan) and used into the Mongol empire period. In the area there are some Turkic *balbals* (stone figures) and a rock known as Genghis Khan's bed, as he was supposed to have stayed there.

Within the **first town** are the remains of four temples with tiled roofs, the pedestals of three statues and, not far from the ruined temples, some stupas and, nearby, two towers in a very bad condition.

The **second town** lies one kilometre from the first settlement and is known as Baruun Düüregiin Kherem. Here are found some relics of the ancient period of the Xiongnu, suggesting a settlement was here that predates these ruins.

Fifteen kilometres north of the first town, the fortified **third town** is thought to be the encampment of a Yuan dynasty khan called Togoon Tömör who reigned from 1333 to 1370. He may have fled in defeat to this area from China although records say he died in Inner Mongolia.

Tombstones and stone statues

Tombstones can be found in Gurvanzagal district west of Choibalsan. The tombs, dating from the end of the Bronze Age, are surrounded by large stones placed in the ground to form a square wall. There's a large square tomb at a place called Gotsogiin Bulag in the same area. West of it are some inscribed stones figures. Stone men statues are located at Gotsogiin Bulag. You need local help to find these sites and your own transport.

Battle of Khalkhyn Gol (Nomonhan) memorial

On the battle ground on the eastern border with China; for background information on the battle see box page 28.

National parks
Nömrög Strictly Protected Area

Located in the most eastern part of Mongolia, over 350km east of Choibalsan and surrounded on three sides by Inner Mongolia (China), this protected area of 311,000 hectares includes the foothill region of the Hingan Mountains. Originally it was a deciduous forest area which over time has become a region of predominantly herbaceous meadow steppe. Numerous small streams rise in the mountains and are thickly lined with willow, aspen and birch. The climate of the Hingan mountain area is moist, in contrast to the surrounding dry steppeland to the west. Adjacent arid plains are characterised by small freshwater lakes, thin pine forests and poplar trees.

The park's flora and fauna are influenced by neighbouring Manchuria. As a result, many of the plant and animal species living here cannot be found elsewhere in Mongolia, such as the Ussuri Moose. The area is important because it protects a naturally structured transition zone from the Manchurian mountains to the eastern Mongolian steppelands. In contrast to much of Mongolia, Nömrög is virtually unpopulated and untouched with less than 1% of the land used for agriculture. Such isolation and remoteness has

THE DECLINE OF THE MONGOLIAN GAZELLE

Following the construction of the Trans-Mongolian Railway, gazelle numbers drastically declined and their range became almost entirely restricted to eastern Mongolia. Continued livestock grazing, hunting and poaching have also taken their toll. The eastern steppe has particular importance as a feeding ground and as a rest site for the remaining herds of Mongolian gazelle before they migrate. It is still possible to see more than 20,000 gazelles gather in one herd for the autumn migration; as many as 50,000 antelopes have been observed in one day within the protected area.

The Mongolian government plans to expand the territory to the northwest in the form of a migration corridor, with particular emphasis on the antelopes' calving grounds. Hunting is prohibited, but moderate livestock grazing should still be possible.

CRANES OF MONGOLIA
George Archibald

Six of the world's 15 species of cranes are found in Mongolia, although two species, the Siberian and the red-crowned, are only occasionally observed in a few areas of the Far East. Of the remaining species, the Demoiselle crane is abundant and widespread throughout much of the country while the Eurasian, hooded and white-naped are found only in the northeast. Although hooded cranes do not breed in Mongolia, Eurasian cranes occasionally breed here and white-naped cranes are regular breeding residents on wetlands of the northeast.

The **Demoiselle crane** is the smallest of cranes. Unlike most other cranes that build platform nests in shallow wetlands, Demoiselle cranes often nest in grasslands and agricultural fields. Two dark speckled eggs are laid on dry ground. Mongolian people admire and protect Demoiselles. Sometimes the cranes are found near *gers* and they appear to benefit from the herds of domestic animals maintained by Mongolian nomads. The name of the Demoiselle in Mongolian means 'lovely bird'.

In autumn the Demoiselle cranes migrate across the Gobi Desert, the Tibetan Plateau and the Himalayas before reaching their wintering grounds on the plains of India. The **Eurasian cranes** that summer in Mongolia migrate either to India or to southeast China. **Hooded cranes** migrate to Japan and southern China.

The Daurian Steppe of eastern Mongolia and adjacent Russia has the world's largest number of breeding **white-naped cranes**. In autumn, white-naped cranes gather in large numbers on open land. They fly across northeast China

protected the area so far. The government is working with the WWF and other organisations to expand this protected area to the west in order to secure the future of this exceptional natural ecosystem. For further details visit www.panda.org/resources.

Flora and fauna
At least 47 mammal and 255 bird species have been documented in the park, including numerous rare and endangered species, among them the blue-rock thrush, the yellow-bellied flycatcher and the great black water snake. There's also the Chinese parrotbill, which is known to nest on two small steppe lakes near the Hingan mountains.

Eastern Steppe Strictly Protected Area
Located in southeast Mongolia on the border with Inner Mongolia (China), some 250km from Choibalsan and extending west into Sükhbaatar Aimag, this is eastern Mongolia's largest protected area (570,374 hectares). It was established in 1992 to protect the country's last intact steppe community from overpopulation and overgrazing. The territory extends in a wide strip for 200km along the Chinese–Mongolian border and belongs to the highest category of protected area: No visitors, unless with special permission for research purposes, are allowed in the area.

Flora and fauna
The dominant feature of the land is the feather grass steppe consisting of various stipa species. In the western section of the region, this becomes sandy desert steppe

to the mouth of the Yellow River and from there, southwest to the middle regions of the Yangtze River.

The **Siberian crane** is the most threatened of crane species. There are less than 2,000 birds alive and their survival is based on vast expanses of shallow wetlands. Unfortunately, many critical wetlands where these cranes spend the winter in China are being heavily impacted by the activities of humans. Occasionally sub-adult Siberian cranes spend the summer in northeast Mongolia.

The **red-crowned crane** is the second rarest of the crane species. Numbering just over 2,000 birds, about 700 cranes are non-migratory residents of Japan's most northern island, Hokkaido. The remaining birds are migratory and breed in northern China and southeastern Siberia and winter on the Korean peninsula and coastal China just north of the mouth of the Yangtze River. A few pairs are sometimes reported on wetlands in summer in eastern Mongolia.

During the past decade, considerable research has been done on white-naped cranes in northeast Mongolia. Over one hundred thousand hectares of wetlands and grasslands along the Ulz River and adjacent areas have been protected as Mongol Daguur Nature Reserve.

Russia, China and Mongolia have signed an agreement to protect important crane habitat on the Daurian Steppes, by joining separately managed nature reserves in the three countries into a single international protected area. These rolling steppes, with many lakes and wetlands, are among Asia's most important and most beautiful regions for breeding cranes, ducks and other water birds.

For more information about cranes and other water birds, please contact the International Crane Foundation, PO Box 447, Baraboo, WI 53913-0047, USA; tel: 00 1 608 356-9462; email: cranes@savingcranes.org.

covered with caragana bush. Trees, such as willow and poplar, grow near springs and marshes. Twenty-five species of mammals and 154 species of bird (including 88 breeding species), two amphibians and five reptile species have been recorded living within the park boundaries. Mongolian gazelle, a species of antelope which a few decades ago was found in the steppe regions throughout the country, is now limited to the eastern steppes, as well as neighbouring regions in Russia and China.

Mongol Daguur Strictly Protected Areas

This area lies on the northern boundary with the Russian Federation, over 200km from Choibalsan. Founded in 1992, the protected area consists of around 103,000 hectares and is divided into two distinct zones: area A consists of hilly steppes south of the Tari Lakes basin (in Russia), while area B, 30km away, is a 20km corridor of wetland on the River Ulz. The Daurian Mountain steppes and system of wetlands and forested hills has some important natural features. Visitors may see Siberian plants and animals as well as desert/steppe species in this region.

Flora and fauna

Over 300 plant species have been found here including several endemic to the region. Over 100 medicinally important plants species are, as yet, unstudied.

Mongol Daguur is an important breeding and resting site for countless numbers of endangered bird species. These include six species of crane, including the rare Siberian crane, Manchurian crane and hooded crane, unique in Central Asia. Three of these crane species, the white-naped crane, common crane and

SPECIES CONSERVATION
White-naped crane (Grus vipio)
A project involving the white-naped crane is part of an overall project known as Project Dornod 2000, in which Mongolian and German scientists worked side by side to study the conservation of this threatened crane species. Local Mongolian rangers were trained by German ornithologists, camping by the lakes and rivers of Mongol Daguur in eastern Mongolia. This training was done in co-operation with the Eastern Steppe Biodiversity Project (ESBP) to give the Mongolian rangers a greater responsibility by identifying the birds and assessing the importance of their breeding and feeding areas. The team found that livestock, agriculture and steppe fires had destroyed large parts of the cranes' breeding grounds. It is an example of ongoing conservation work in the area.

Demoiselle crane, breed in the protected area. Some of the 260 documented bird species in the region are listed as globally endangered including the relict gull, the Manchurian duck and the great bustard.

There are also 29 mammal species inhabiting the Daurian Strictly Protected Areas, including the Daurian hedgehog, which occurs exclusively in northeastern Mongolia, and Pallas' cat, which reaches its northernmost range here.

In 1995, the Government of Mongolia, with support from WWF, founded Mongolia's first cross-boundary protected area. The establishment of the International Daurian Protected Area, in the boundary region between Russia, China and Mongolia, is a milestone in conservation history. This initiative is largely due to Dr George Archibald, who kindly wrote the specialist box on *Cranes* on pages 370–1.

Yakhi Nuur Nature Reserve
Located in the northwest part of the province around 70km northwest of Choibalsan, this reserve was established in 1998. It is an area of 251,388 hectares and protects the lake and its surroundings.

Ugtam Uul Nature Reserve
This area of 46,160 hectares on the River Ulz, 175km northwest of Choibalsan, protects two holy mountains, Mount Ugtam and Mount Khairkhan, as well as the ruins of a Buddhist monastery. The area is the frontier between the forest steppe and the steppe zones. Little is known about the monastery and research is being done on its history at the time of writing. To visit you will need your own transport, camping equipment and supplies.

Suggested itineraries
For research trips (currently being planned) to Mongolia's eastern steppe contact Discovery Initiatives (see page 148).

Appendix 1

LANGUAGE

For general information about the Mongolian language, see *Chapter 2, Language*, pages 78–9.
The following is just a brief introduction to the Mongolian language. If you'd like to learn Mongolian, there is a self-study course for beginners, *Colloquial Mongolian* by Alan J K Sanders and Jantsangiin Bat-Ireedüi, published by Routledge in 1999 and reprinted in 2002, ISBN 0-415-16714-0, price £16.99, or as a pack with two one-hour audio cassettes £32.00.

Pronunciation
Consonants

Mongolian consonants generally are pronounced pretty much as in English, as are pairs like ch, sh and ts , but there are a few points to note:

j is like the j in 'jam'
kh is like the ch in 'loch'
z is like the dz in 'adze'
final n is nasalised as 'ng'

The consonants f, k and p are found only in loan-words, and f and p are pronounced rather similarly. The Cyrillic letter 'shch' is found only in Russian words.

Vowels

Back vowels (from the back of the mouth) and front vowels (from the front) do not appear in the same word, but neutral vowels (i and ii) may appear with either. Vowels may be short, long, and glided:

Back vowels

short: a as a in cat
long: aa as a in bath
o as in hot
oo as au in haunt
u as u in Yorkshire us
uu as oo in ooze
i as short i in ill

y as long i
short ya as yu in yumyum
long: yaa as ya in yarn
yo as ya in yacht
yoo as in yore
yu as you in you
yuu as long you

Front vowels

short: e as e in den
long: ee as a in Dane
ö as in earn
öö as long ea in earn

ü as u in put
üü as long ü
short: ye as ye in yes
long: yüü as in Yusuf

Neutral vowels

short: i as i in tin

long: ii as ea in team

373

Diphthongs

The diphthongs in Mongolian include ai (as in 'eye'), ei (as in 'pay'), oi (as in 'boy') and üi (as in 'Louis')

Stress

In words with short (single) vowels, the stress falls on the first short vowel. In words containing a long (double) vowel or diphthong, the stress falls on the long vowel or diphthong. In words with more than one long vowel the stress falls on the penultimate long vowel.

Useful words and expressions
Greetings and basic communication

hello (good		bad	_muu_
morning, etc)	_sainbaimuu_	good	_sain_
goodbye	_bayartai_	how far?	_ali khir kholve_
yes	_tiim_	how long?	_khir udaanve_
no	_ügüi_	how much?	_yamar ünteive_
please give me	_ögönüü_	when?	_khezee_
please tell me	_khelenüü_	where?	_khaan_
thank you	_bayarlaa_	excuse me!	_uuchlaarai_
less	_bag khemjee_	help me, please	_tuslaarai_
more	_dakhiad_	go away!	_yav yav!_
enough	_khangalttai_	it doesn't matter	_khamaagüi_
now	_odoo_	don't mention it	_zügeer_
later	_daraa_		

Some useful sentences

I do not understand.	_bi oilgokhgüi baina_
Speak more slowly, please.	_ta jaal udaan yarinuu_
Repeat that, please.	_ta dakhiad neg khelj ögönüü_
Write it down for me, please.	_ta nadad bichij ögööch_
I want (need).	_nadad kheregtei_
I do not want (need).	_nadad khereggüi_
Please wait for me!	_namaig khüleej üzeerei_

Travelling

passport	_pasport_	hand luggage	_gar teesh_
valid	_khüchintei_	customs	_gaali_
entry/exit visa	_orokh/garakh viz_	customs duty	_gaaliin tatvar_
transit visa	_dairan öngörökh viz_	bus stop	_avtobusny zogsool_
travel on official		railway station	_galt teregnii buudal_
business	_alban ajlaar yavakh_	street	_gudamj_
travel on a		square	_talbai_
tourist trip	_juulchilakh_	policeman	_tsagdaa_
airport	_nisekh ongotsny buudal_	northwards	_khoid züg rüü_
ticket	_tasalbar_	southwards	_ömön züg rüü_
boarding pass	_ongotsond suukh tasalbar_	to the east/left	_züün tiish_
baggage	_achaa_	to the west/right	_baruun tiish_
excess baggage	_ilüü achaa_	straight ahead	_chigeeree_

Some useful sentences relating to travel

I have lost my luggage	_bi achaagaa geechikhlee_
I have lost my way	_bi törchikhlöö_

How do I get to the town centre? *khotyn töv khürtel yaaj yavakhve*
Call a taxi, please *taksi duudaarai*

Accommodation

hotel	*zochid buudal*	WC (lavatory)	*jorlong, biye zasakh gazar*
vacant room	*sul öröö*	toilet paper	*jorlongiin tsaas*
single room	*neg khünii öröö*	hot water	*khaluun us*
double room	*khoyor khünii öröö*	cold water	*khüiten us*
with bath/shower	*vaantai/shürshiüürtei*	there isn't (any)	*baikhgüi*

Useful sentences relating to accommodation

Can I have this clothing cleaned? *en khuvtsasyg tseverlüülj bolokhuu*
Can I have this clothing laundered? *en khuvtsasyg ugaalgaj bolokhuu*

Health

doctor	*emch*	arm/hand	*gar*
pharmacy	*emiin sang*	leg/foot	*khöl*
hospital	*emneleg*	heart	*zürkh*
blood	*tsus*	stomach	*gedes*
chest	*tseej*	throat	*khooloi*
ear	*chikh*	tooth	*shüd*
eye	*nüd*		

Some useful sentences relating to health

I'm not feeling well. *minii biye muu bain*
It hurts here. *end övdöj bain*
Send for a doctor! *emchid khüng duudaarai*
Call an ambulance! *türgen tuslamj duudaarai*

Money

bank	*bank*	traveller's cheque	*zamyn chek*
money exchange		commission	*khuuramj*
desk	*möngö solikh gazar*	money order	*möngönii guivuulag*
currency exchange		credit card	*zeeliin/kredit kart*
rate	*valyutyn khansh*		

Shopping

shop	*delgüür*	gold	*alt*
department store	*ihh delgüür*	silver	*möngö*
grocer's	*khünsnii delgüür*	jewellery	*alt möngön edlel*
market	*zakh*	musical instruments	*khögjmiin zemseg*
books	*nom*	paintings	*uran zurag*
carpets	*khivs*	souvenirs	*beleg dursgal*
embroidery	*khatgamal*		

Please show me that. *ta üüniig nadad üzüülenüü*
I'd like to buy. *bi avmaar bain*
How much does it cost? *en yamar ünteive*
Can you do it cheaper? *ta ün buulgakhuu*
I'll give you (insert appropriate number) *bi tand ... tögrög ögyi*
... togrogs

Restaurants and meals
Drink

beer	*shar airag*	vodka	*arkhi*
milk	*süü*	red wine	*ulaan dars*
coffee	*kofe*	white wine	*tsagaan dars*
drinking water	*uukh us*	koumiss	*airag*
juice	*shüüs*	tea (black)	*khar tsai*
tea-based milky drink	*süütei tsai*		
mineral water	*rashaan us* (or *gaztai us* - from Russian 'gas' = 'sparkling')		

Food

meat	*makh*	potatoes	*tömös*
beef	*ükhriin makh*	green salad	*nogoon zuush*
pork	*gakhain makh*	vegetables	*nogoo*
mutton	*khoniny makh*	cabbage	*baitsaa*
chicken	*takhia*	bread	*talkh*
fish	*zagas*	salt	*davs*
boiled	*chanasan*	sugar	*chikher*
fried	*sharsan*	soup	*shöl*
baked	*khuursan*	vegetarian (person)	*nogoon khoolton*
rice	*tsagaan budaa*		

Numbers

1	*neg*	40	*döch*
2	*khoyor*	41	*döchin neg*
3	*gurav*	50	*tavi*
4	*döröv*	51	*tavin neg*
5	*tav*	60	*jar*
6	*zurgaa*	61	*jaran neg*
7	*doloo*	70	*dal*
8	*naim*	71	*dalan neg*
9	*yös*	80	*naya*
10	*arav*	81	*nayan neg*
11	*arvan neg*	90	*yör*
12	*arvan khoyor*	91	*yören neg*
20	*khori*	100	*zuu*
21	*khorin neg*	101	*zuun neg*
30	*guch*	200	*khoyor zuun*
31	*guchin neg*	1,000	*myang*

In the table above, note that the numerals adopt an '-n' form when objects are counted — eg: 40 is *döch* but 41 is *döchin neg*. Similarly 'three' is *gurav* but 'three books' is *gurvan nom* (literally 'three book'). The plural suffix of nouns is not used when the number of objects is specified: *olon nom* = 'many books'.

When used, the plural suffixes include uu/üü, eg: *nomuud* 'books'; or s is added, eg: *ügs* from *üg* 'word', etc.

Time

day	*ödör*	this month/year	*en sar/jil*
night	*shön*	this morning/	
today	*önöödör*	evening	*önöö öglöö/üdesh*
tomorrow	*margaash*	What time is it?	*kheden tsag bolj bain*

| yesterday | öchigdör | At what time? | kheden tsagt |
| this week | en doloo khonog | At half past four. | döröv khagast |

Days

Monday	davaa or negdekh ödör
Tuesday	myagmar or khoyordokh ödör
Wednesday	lkhavag or guravdakh ödör
Thursday	pürev or dövövdekh ödör
Friday	baasan or tardakgh ödör
Saturday	byamb or khagas sain ödör
Sunday	nyam or büten sain ödör

THE MONGOL CYRILLIC ALPHABETIC

Mongol Cyrillic	Transliteration	Mongol Cyrillic	Transliteration
Аа	Aa	Рр	Rr
Бб	Bb	Сс	Ss
Вв	Vv	Тт	Tt
Гг	Gg	Уу	Uu
Дд	Dd	Үү	Üü
Ее	Yö/yö	Фф	Ff
Ёё	Yo/yo	Хх	Kh/kh
Жж	Jj	Цц	Ts/ts
Зз	Zz	Чч	Ch/ch
Ии/Йй	Ii	Шш	Sh/sh
Кк	Kk	Щщ	Shch/shch
Лл	Ll	ъ	(nil)
Мм	Mm	ы	y
Нн	Nn	ь	i
Оо	Oo	Ээ	Ee
Өө	Öö	Юю	Yu/yu or Yü/yü
Пп	Pp	Яя	ya

Note: The Cyrillic letters ъ, ы and ь do not appear as the first letter in Mongolian words. The hard sign ъ is not transcribed. The letter ю is transcribed as yu at the beginning of back-vowel words and yü at the beginning of front-vowel words.

Appendix 2

TOURIST *GER* CAMPS

This is a comprehensive list of all the tourist *ger* camps in Mongolia grouped by aimag (district). New *ger* camps are springing up all the time, and unprofitable ones closed down. At the height of the tourist season some camps are full, and at other times there may be no food or staff if they are not expecting you. Therefore, it is advisable to pre-book rather than to turn up hoping for the best.

Where a telephone number is listed, it is often not the *ger* camp itself, but the Ulaanbaatar office of the company operating that camp. Sometimes there are several *ger* camps owned by different companies situated in the same area.

In the bigger towns and cities there are a few hotels, which may or may not have water, food and heating. Outside Ulaanbaatar by far the best option is to stay in *ger* camps. These have been set up in the most popular places to cater for travellers, both Mongolian and foreign. Most of the camps only run during the summer; the *gers* are taken down in October until the following spring. However, there are one or two near Ulaanbaatar which are open all year round and are used by hikers or cross-country skiers during the winter.

These traditional *gers* have brightly coloured furniture and a wood-burning stove in the centre (if it's cold they provide wood). Each *ger* has two, three or four beds. Most camps have a toilet and shower block nearby with hot water some or all of the time. Nearly all camps have a restaurant (often a large *ger*) where they serve Mongolian and European food. Vegetarians have to give the cook plenty of notice, otherwise they'll end up with the same as everyone else but minus the meat.

The cost to stay in a *ger* varies from US$30 to US$50 per night and includes three meals. They'll often pack a picnic lunch for you if you ask, which is useful since you may be several hundred miles from the nearest shop. At some places you can make a deal just to pay for the bed (about US$20), and then you can bring your own food or just choose what you want from the restaurant menu and pay accordingly.

The *gers* are a really enjoyable and authentic form of accommodation; warm in the winter and cool in summer. The main disadvantage is trying to book beforehand, and also you can't be sure of the standard of service until you get there. The best way round this is to book through a local travel company, who would have the most up-to-date information on new camps and non-existent ones. It would be quite irritating to drive for several days on bad roads to reach a particular *ger* camp, only to arrive to find it gone!

Central Mongolia

Name of camp	Place	Telephone
Karakorum	Kharkhorin sum, Övörkhangai Aimag	322188
Khanbayan	Kharkhorin sum, Övörkhangai Aimag	
Chandman	Kharkhorin sum, Övörkhangai Aimag	360768
Ogoodei	Kharkhorin sum, Övörkhangai Aimag	
Nomiin	Kharkhorin sum, Övörkhangai Aimag	452238
Kharkhorin	Kharkhorin	99113185

Name of camp	Place	Telephone
Anar	Kharkhorin	055422662
Bayangobi	Övörkhangai	322118, 312393
Chinghis Khaan Huree	Bogdkhan Mountain	322079
Terelj	Terelj	324978
Riverside	Öndörshireet sum	312309
Manzshir	Zuunmod	
Khan Khentii	Gorkhi Terelj	313393
Moltsog Els	Argalant sum, Tov Aimag	313393/312480
Gorkhit	Gorkhi Terelj	328737/321489
Temujin's Tribe	Erdene sum	311375
Bayankhangai	Bayanchandman sum	362264
Mirage	Erdene sum	313380
Under Dov	Öndör dov	329471
Forest Lind	Bogdkhan Mountain	310539
Bombat	Bogdkhan Mountain	
Khustain Nuruu	National Park	367345
Buuveit	UB	
Bayangobi	Burd sum, Övörkhangai Aimag	327982
Khogno Khan	Rashaant sum, Bulgan Aimag	312392
Batkhaan	Rashaant sum, Bulgan Aimag	362909/367243
Khogno Gobi	Rashaant sum, Bulgan Aimag	
Burd	Khashaat sum, Arkhangai Aimag	
Mongol Els	Gurvanbulag sum, Bulgan Aimag	313393

Gobi

Name of camp	Place	Telephone
Juulchin Gobi	Khankhongor sum	99117399
Tuvshin	Khankhongor sum	326419
Khavtsgait	Khankhongor sum	
Bag Khongor	Khankhongor sum	311874
Doot Mankhan	Sevrei som	321150

Northern Mongolia

Name of camp	Place	Telephone
Toilogt	Khövsgöl	
Dood Modot Bolan	Khatgal village	311333
Ulaan Khad	Erdenebulgan sum	324844
Jankhai	Khatgal village	
Zalaat	Renchinlkhümbe sum	2398/3724
Tsaatan	Tsagaan Nuur sum	313393

Eastern Mongolia

Name of camp	Place	Telephone
Bayangol	Ömnödelger sum	320127
Khodoo Aral	Delgerkhaan sum	2280
Onon	Gurvan Nuur, Dadal sum	310334

Other districts

Name of camp	Place	Telephone
Jargalant	Jargalant Mountain, Bulgan sum	342443/51032
Amarbayasgalant	Selenge Aimag	383025
Dondgov	Erdenedalai sum, Dondgob Aimag	
Shiliin Bogd	Dariganga sum, Sükhbaatar Aimag	328428
Juulchin Altai	Bayantokhoi, Gobi Altai Aimag	358658/365471
Tsenkher Jiguur	Tsenkher sum, Arkhangai Aimag	450941
Khuren Dokh	Bayanjargalan sum, Dundgob Aimag	321958
Gurvan Tsenkher	Mankhan sum, Khovd Aimag	2348
Altai Tour	Olgii sum, Bayan Ölgii Aimag	2829/2179
Khurkheree	Batö Olzii sum, Övörkhangai	2796
Altain Gov	Bogd sum, Bayankhongor Aimag	2445
Takhir Choloo	Ikh Tamir sum, Arkhangai Aimag	99 11 4745/682256
Khorgo	Tariat sum, Arkhangai Aimag	322870

Appendix 3

SPRINGS AND MINERAL SPAS

Mongolia has thousands of springs which provide water for survival in desert and semi-desert places; besides drinking water there are hot and cold mineral springs which have special uses and properties. There is evidence from the rocks and stones left around hot springs to suggest that ancient proto-Mongol tribes knew the benefits of taking a hot bath in these waters. Health resorts have been built on about 20 thermal springs and there is great potential for further development The spas welcome visitors.

The important or developed springs numbered below are listed at the beginning of each aimag chapter. Others are listed below. Note that *sum* means 'district'.

Central aimags
Töv
Janchivlin cold spring spa (70km from Ulaanbaatar): cold spring spa: calcium and magnesium carbonate and carbon dioxide, treatment of liver and stomach disorders
Bööröljüüt spring (Arkhust sum): calcium and sodium carbonates, hydrocarbonates and sulphates, treatment of nervous disorders and skin conditions
Baidlag spring (Möngönmorit sum): calcium hydrocarbonate and hydrogen sulphide
Devsenbulag spring (Khangai mountains area): potassium hydrocarbonate

Övörkhangai
Khujirt radioactive hot spring spa (Khujirt sum centre): alkalines, hydrogen sulphide, mud treatment of injuries, disabilities and disorders of the joints, heart and nervous system
Mogoit hot spring (Bat-Ölzii sum): sodium hydrocarbonate and sulphate and hydrogen sulphide, treatment of joint and nervous disorders and gynaecological conditions
Khüremt hot spring (Taragt sum): sodium hydrocarbonate and sulphate, treatment of joint and nervous disorders
Üürtiin Tokhoi (Bat-Ölzii sum): spring in the river Orkhon valley; calcium and sodium hydrocarbonates
Emt hot spring (Taragt sum): hydrogen sulphide
Saikhanbulag spring (Khujirt sum): spring in the River Orkhon valley
Gyatruun spring (Bat-Ölzii sum): sodium hydrocarbonate
Taats spring (Dalantarüü) (Uyanga sum): carbon dioxide and hydrogen sulphide

Arkhangai
Shivert hot spring spa (northeast of Tsetserleg): chlorine and potassium compounds
Tsenkher curative spring (Tsenkher sum): sodium carbonate, hydrocarbonate and sulphate, fluorine compounds and hydrogen sulphide, treatment of damaged joints and nervous disorders
Bilgekh curative spring (Öndör-Ulaan sum): waters drunk for internal disorders
Tsagaan Süm spring (Khoton and Tsenkher sums): sodium carbonate, hydrocarbonate and sulphate, hydrogen sulphide and silicic acid, treatment of damaged joints and nervous disorders

Ulaan Ereg spring (Chuluut sum): calcium, magnesium and sodium hydrocarbonates, treatment of digestive disorders
Bortal spring (Tsenkher sum): sodium hydrocarbonate and sulphate
Khadat spring (Tariat sum): calcium hydrocarbonate
Khökhsüm spring (Tsenkher sum): calcium, magnesium and sodium hydrocarbonates
Mukharkhujirt spring (Tsetserleg sum): calcium and sodium hydrocarbonates
Noyonkhangai spring (Khangai mountains): sodium hydrocarbonate
Tsats spring (Battsengel sum): calcium and magnesium hydrocarbonates
Tsats Tsagaantolgoi spring (Ögiinuur sum): calcium and sodium hydrocarbonates

Gobi aimags
Ömnögobi
Khadat cold spring (Bulgan sum): calcium and magnesium hydrocarbonates
Talkh spring (Mandal-Ovoo sum): calcium and magnesium hydrocarbonates and chlorides
Zöölön spring (Gobi-Altai mountains): sodium chloride and hydrocarbonate

Dornogobi
Khalzan uul radioactive cold spring (Dalanjargalan sum): calcium and chlorine hydrocarbonates and carbon dioxide, waters drunk for treatment of digestive disorders
Toli Bulag cold spring (Mandakh sum): sodium chloride and hydrocarbonate

Dundgobi
Olgoi spring (Saintsagaan sum): treatment of joint disabilities and skin disorders
Togoo cold spring (34km from Mandalgobi town): calcium and sodium chlorides, hydrocarbonates and sulphates
Düüren Khargan well (Delgerkhangai mountains): calcium and sodium hydrocarbonates

Bayankhongor
Shargaljuut (east of Bayankhongor town) hot spring: sodium hydrocarbonate and sulphate, treatment of disabilities of the joints and kidney and nervous disorders
Örgööt hot spring (Mandal sum): sodium hydrocarbonate
Ükheg hot spring (Galuut sum): calcium and sodium hydrocarbonates and sulphates, treatment of joint disabilities and nervous disorders
Khaliut spring (Zag sum): calcium, magnesium and sodium hydrocarbonates

Gobi-Altai
Ulaankhairkhan spring (Jargalant sum): carbon and iron, waters drunk for treatment of internal disorders
Khünkher Zuslan spring (Jargalant sum): calcium and magnesium hydrocarbonates, treatment of digestive disorders
Argalant spring (Khökhmorit sum): calcium and sodium hydrocarbonates and sulphates

Northern aimags
Khövsgöl
Bulnai hot springs (Khalkhan Gol) (Chandmani-Öndör sum) radioactive hot spring: hydrocarbonates and sulphates
Asgat spring (Bürentogtokh sum): calcium hydrocarbonate
Khönjil spring (Jargalan sum): sodium sulphate and chloride
Tsagaantolgoi spring (Tosontsengel sum): calcium hydrocarbonate

Zavkhan

Otgontenger hot spring spa (Baga Otgontenger Mountain) hot spring spa: calcium, potassium and sodium carbonates, hydrocarbonates and sulphates, hydrogen sulphide, treatment of disorders of the joints, skin, nervous system and stomach and gynaecological conditions

Bayanzürkh spring (Nömrög sum): calcium and magnesium hydrocarbonates and sulphates, waters drunk for treatment of stomach, liver and kidney disorders

Tsatsyn Bulag spring (Aldarkhaan sum): water drunk for internal disorders

Ulaankhaalga hot spring (Aldarkhaan sum) hot spring: hydrocarbonates, hydrogen sulphide and silicic acid, treatment of disorders of the joints and nerves

Tsetsüükh spring (Ikh-Uul sum): sodium hydrocarbonate and sulphate, treatment of internal and nervous disorders

Zart (Zartyn Gol valley) hot spring: sodium hydrocarbonate and sulphate, treatment of conditions of the joints, kidneys and skin and nervous disorders

Khojuul Gol spring (Tarvagatai mountains): sodium hydrocarbonate

Mukharmod spring (Ikh-Uul sum): calcium and sodium hydrocarbonates and sulphates

Bulgan

Khunt Nuur (Saikhan sum) cold spring: mud treatment for disabilities of the joints, waters for digestive disorders

Khulj hot spring (Mogod sum): sodium sulphate

Asgat (Saikhan sum) spring: magnesium and sodium hydrocarbonates

Chuluut (Khangal sum) spring: calcium and sodium hydrocarbonates

Dalaibulag (Bayan-agt sum) spring: calcium, magnesium and sodium hydrocarbonates

Khanui (Bayan-agt sum) spring: potassium and sodium hydrocarbonates and chlorides

Orkhon (Orkhon sum) spring: calcium and magnesium hydrocarbonates

Orkhon

Erdenet spring (Erdenet Mountain) spring: calcium hydrocarbonate and sulphate

Selenge

Khondyn Rashaan cold spring spa (near Altanbulag): calcium and sodium hydrocarbonates

Yestiin Gol hot spring (near Yöröö): sodium hydrocarbonate, treatment of joint and skin conditions and nervous disorders

Yöröö hot spring (Khentii mountains): sodium carbonate and sulphate, treatment of disorders of joints and nervous system

Yöröö Bayan Gol spring (Yöröö sum): calcium and magnesium hydrocarbonates, carbon dioxide

Western aimags
Khovd

Nevt hot spring (Duut sum): calcium and magnesium hydrocarbonates, treatment of digestive disorders

Bulgan hot spring (Inder) (Bulgan sum) hot spring: calcium and sodium chlorides, hydrocarbonates and sulphates

Bayan-Ölgii

Chikhert (Chigirt) (Delüün sum) warm spring: sodium carbonate and hydrocarbonate, hydrogen sulphide, silicic acid, treatment of disorders of the joints and nervous system

Gantsmod hot spring (Delüün sum): calcium and sodium hydrocarbonates and sulphates

Uvs

Khartermes spring (near Lake Khyargas): calcium and sodium hydrocarbonates, treatment of digestive disorders
Burgastai spring (Türgen sum, near Lake Üüreg): calcium and magnesium hydrocarbonates
Khavtsal Boom spring (Türgen sum): calcium and magnesium hydrocarbonates

Eastern aimags
Khentii

Onongiin Ikh Rashaan hot spring (Onon river): sodium hydrocarbonate, treatment of disorders of the joints and nervous system and gynaecological conditions
Avarga spring (Delgerkhaan sum, 11km from Toson Nuur) spring: sodium hydrocarbonate, treatment of digestive disorders
Arangat spring (Batshiree sum) spring: potassium hydrocarbonate
Toson Nuur cold spring (Delgerkhaan sum): calcium, chlorine and sodium hydrocarbonates, waters and mud treatment of heart and skin disorders and nervous conditions
Gurvan Nuur spring (Dadal sum) spa: calcium, potassium and sodium hydrocarbonates and chlorides, treatment of joint disabilities
Urtyn Rashaan spring (Jargaltkhaan sum): calcium and magnesium hydrocarbonates

Sükhbaatar

Ereentolgoi radioactive spring (Dariganga sum): magnesium and sodium hydrocarbonates, treatment of digestive disorders
Talbulag curative spring (36km from Baruun-Urt): calcium, magnesium and sodium hydrocarbonates, treatment of stomach, liver and gallbladder disorders
Tsatsir Gurvanbulag cold spring (Tüvshinshiree sum): calcium, magnesium and sodium hydrocarbonates, waters drunk for treatment of stomach and digestive disorders
Dalai Bulag spring (Erdenetsagaan sum): sodium sulphate and chloride

Dornod

Utaatminchüür hot steam spring (Choibalsan sum): ammonium chloride, treatment of kidney and nervous disorders
Tsagaankhöndii (Dashbalbar sum) cold spring: calcium and sodium hydrocarbonates, treatment of digestive system
Tsagaanchuluut (Gurvanzagal sum): calcium and magnesium hydrocarbonates and rare-earth elements
Baruun Emt (Dashbalbar sum) spring: calcium and magnesium hydrocarbonates
Bayankhutag (Choibalsan sum) spring: hydrogen sulphide
Ereen (Bayan-Uul sum) spring: hydrocarbonates

Appendix 4

FURTHER READING
Books
Travel

Allen, Benedict *Edge of Blue Heaven* BBC Publications, 2000. Exciting adventure travel by horse and camel.

Becker, J *The Lost Country: Mongolia Revealed* Hodder & Stoughton, London & Sydney, 1992. Mixture of Mongolian fact and fiction.

De Botton, Alain *The Art of Travel* Hamish Hamilton, 2002. Perfect antidote to guidebooks that tell us what to do when we get there.

Hare, J *The Lost Camels of Tartary* Little Brown, 1998. A courageous journey to search for wild camels and ways to ensure their survival.

Kemp, H. *Step by Step*, Interserve, 2000. The indigenous Christian church in Mongolia.

Man, J *Gobi: Tracking the Desert* Weidenfeld & Nicolson, London, 1997. An interesting and sensitive account of the life of Gobi people.

Middleton, N *The Last Disco in Outer Mongolia* Sinclair-Stevenson, London, 1992. Upbeat view of the first impact of democracy on young Mongolians.

Novacek, M *Dinosaurs of the Flaming Cliffs* Anchor Books, Doubleday, New York and London, 1996. Exploring for dinosaurs in the Gobi.

Severin, T *In Search of Genghis Khan* Hutchinson, London and Sydney, 1992. Well-known traveller's account of life among Mongolian horsemen.

Stewart, S *In the Empire of Genghis Khan: A Journey among Nomads* Harper Collins, 2000. An epic journey by horseback across Mongolia.

Golden oldies

Andrews, R *Across Mongolian Plains* Appleton, New York and London, 1921 (reprint by Lightning Source, 2001). The famous naturalist's account of his first visit in 1919.

Andrews, R *The New Conquest of Central Asia* American Museum of Natural History, 1932. Reports on the expeditions of 1921–30.

Carruthers, D *Unknown Mongolia* Hutchinson, London, 1913 (reprint by Asian Education Services, New Delhi, 1994). Travels in Tuva and Mongolia in 1910-11; a great book on early exploration and travel in Mongolia.

Haslund-Christensen, H *Men and Gods in Mongolia* Dutton, New York, 1935 (reprint by Adventures Unlimited, USA, 1992). Travels amongst the Torgut Mongols, translated from Swedish.

Haslund-Christensen, H *Tents in Mongolia* reprint by Paul Kegan, 2002. Travels from Beijing to Khövsgöl in 1923, translated from Swedish.

Ossendowski, F *Beasts, Men and Gods* Dutton, New York, 1922. Disturbing picture of the revolutionary war in Mongolia.

General

Jeffries, Ian *Economics in Transition, a guide to China, Mongolia, North Korea and Vietnam at the turn of 21st century* Routledge, 2001. International case studies of countries in a state of economic flux.

Goldstein, M, & Beall, C *The Changing World of Mongolia's Nomads* The Guidebook Company, Hong Kong, 1994. Anthropologists' colourful picture of nomadic life and the impact of change.

Grubov, V I *Plants of Central Asia - plant collections from China and Mongolia* Science Publishers, 2003. Authoritative work on plants, costly.

Lattimore, O *The Desert Road to Turkestan* Kodansha America, 1995. Travels in Mongolia in the 1930s by Owen and Eleanor Lattimore

Lawless J *Wild East: the New Mongolia* Summersdale, 2002. A portrait of Mongolia; an account of social change.

MPR Academy of Sciences *Information Mongolia* Pergamon, Oxford, 1990. Sound articles and good illustrations compensate for the communist politics of this encyclopaedia.

Nordby, J *Mongolia* World Bibliographical Series Vol.156, Clio Press, Oxford, 1993. Invaluable guide to English-language books about Mongolia.

Sanders, A *Historical Dictionary of Mongolia* Scarecrow Press, Lanham and London, 2003. Alphabetical listing of people and places mostly from the modern period, with bibliography and appendices.

Sneath, D *Changing Inner Mongolia* Oxford University Press, 2000.

Sokolov, V E Lobatchev, V S *Mammals of Mongolia*, Academia Press, 1998. Authoritative work on mammals.

Waugh, Louisa *Hearing Birds Fly* Little, Brown, 2003; an account of nomadic life dominated by the seasons.

History

Bawden, C R *The Modern History of Mongolia* Kegan Paul, 2002. Insight into Mongolian life from the 17th century to the 1960s.

Man, J *Genghis Khan* Bantham Press, 2004. A gripping account of Genghis's rise and conquests.

Morgan, D *The Mongols* Blackwell, Oxford, 1990. Popular account with a touch of humour of the birth and growth of the Mongol empire.

Onon, U *The Secret History of the Mongols* Curzon Press, 2001. A modern translation of the oldest known Mongolian account of the life and times of Genghis Khan.

Tucker, Jonathan. *The Silk Road: Art and History* Philip Wilson, 2003. A celebration of the cultural heritage of countries along the Silk Route, exploring trade links between Europe and the Far East.

Language

Sanders, A and Bat-Ireedui, J *Colloquial Mongolian* Routledge, London, 1999 (cassettes). Up-to-date self-study grammar with cultural insights.

Bawden, C *Mongolian-English Dictionary* Kegan Paul International, London, 1997. The best and most up-to-date dictionary, based on modern Mongolian usage.

Guides available in Mongolia (or direct from the author)

Shagdar, Sh *Fifty Routes through Mongolia* MBDA and TACIS,1997. Available in Mongolian book shops.

D Myagmarsuren (ed)*Special Protected Areas of Mongolia* Munkhyn Useg, 2000. Available in Mongolia from the National Parks Office Ministry of Nature and the Environment, Baga Toiruu 44, Ulaanbaatar 11; tel: +976 11 326617; fax: +976 11 328620.

Lake Khövsgöl National Park - A Visitor's Guide published by Discovery Initiatives, 1997. Available from The Travel House, 51 Castle St, Cirencester GL7 1QD, UK; tel: 01285

643333; fax: 01285 885888; email: julian@discoveryinitiatives.com; cost: £7.50 if
ordered in the UK including postage; US$12 for international orders including postage.
Steinhauer-Burkart, Bernd *The Gobi Gurvansaikhan National Park* published in Mongolia,
2000. Available from the author, Elisabeth-Walterstrasse 24, D-69151 Neckargemuend,
Germany; tel: +49 6223 74482; email: Steinhauer-Burkart@t-online.de.
Mongolia's Wild Heritage joint publication by the Mongolian Ministry of Nature and
Environment and the World Wildlife Fund for Nature, Mongolia, 2001. Hard copies in
English or Mongolian can be ordered for US$15 from the United Nations
Development Programme (UNDP), 7 Rehuu Street, PO Box 49/207, Ulaanbaatar.
Scott, P and R Fitter *The Penitent Butchers* Collins, 1978.

Health

Lankester, Ted *The Travellers' Good Health Guide* Sheldon Press, 1999.
Juel-Jensen, B (ed) *Expedition Medicine* available at the Expedition Advisory Centre, Royal
Geographical Society, 1 Kensington Gore, London SW7 2AR.
Wilson-Howarth, Dr Jane *Bugs, Bites and Bowels* Cadogan, 2001.

Specialist bookshops
UK

The Travel Bookshop 13/15 Blenheim Crescent, London W11 2EE; tel: +44 020 7229 5260; web:
www.the travel bookshop.co.uk
Daunt Books for Travellers 83 Marylebone High St, London W1; tel: +44 020 7224 2295
John Sandoe (Books) Ltd 10 Blacklands Terrace, Chelsea, London SW3 2SR; tel: +44 20 7589 9474

Websites
General

www.infomongol.com
www.mongolnet.com
www.mongolmedia.com
www.mgl-uk.com
www.un-mongolia.mn

Government

Ministry of Education, Culture and Science www.mef.pmis.gov.mn
Ministry of Finance and Economy www.mof.pmis.gov.mn

Other

Mongolian Airlines (MIAT) www.miat.com
Mongolian Business Development Agency (MBDA) www.mol.mn/mbda
Mongolian Chamber of Commerce and Industry (MCCI) www.mol.mn/mcci
Mongolian Tourism Board www.mongoliatourism.gov.mn

Index